SABRA AN

MW00626646

SABRA AND SHATILA

September 1982

Bayan Nuwayhed al-Hout

Pluto Press

LONDON • ANN ARBOR, MI

First published 2004 by Pluto Press
345 Archway Road, London N6 5AA
and 839 Greene Street, Ann Arbor, MI 48106

www.plutobooks.com

© Bayan Nuwayhed al-Hout 2004

The right of Bayan Nuwayhed al-Hout to be identified as the author of this work has been asserted
by her in accordance with the Copyright, Designs and Patents Act 1988.

British Library Cataloguing in Publication Data
A catalogue record for this book is available from the British Library

ISBN 0 7453 2303 0 hardback
ISBN 0 7453 2302 2 paperback

Library of Congress Cataloging in Publication Data applied for

10 9 8 7 6 5 4 3 2 1

Designed and produced for Pluto Press by
Chase Publishing Services, Fortescue, Sidmouth, EX10 9QG, England
Typeset from disk by Newgen Imaging Systems, India
Printed and bound in Canada by
Transcontinental Printing

*In Remembrance of the victims of
Sabra and Shatila*

Contents

Acknowledgements

If I were to mention every person whose efforts I feel merit acknowledgement, the number would be literally in the hundreds.

First and foremost, I must thank all those, victims' relatives or witnesses, with whom I conducted lengthy interviews, and all those who provided whatever information they had to members of the field study team. My gratitude is further due to those who assisted me in recording testimonies or filling out questionnaires. Without the help of all these, the present book would have been quite simply impossible.

Then there are the friends: those who opened their doors to allow me to conduct interviews with victims' relatives in their homes; and those who, by concealing the initial tapes and documents, not only aided the project but, still more, made me feel I was not alone.

I thank all the friends who, through later 1982 and 1983, provided support from abroad – from Washington, London, Bonn or Rome – sending whatever press cuttings, books or videotapes they could find. This, needless to say, was material I could have found at local bookshops had the security situation been otherwise.

Who, I ask myself, has remained by my side through those 20 years? Who did I turn to? And who made a point of providing me with encouragement and support?

I must begin with those who have accompanied me through the various periods of the project, from the very beginning.

First, my husband Shafiq al-Hout, who, from the time we were married in the early 1960s, never ceased to encourage me to go on with my writing; while I concluded my university studies, then, afterwards, through every piece of scholarly work. Yet with the Sabra and Shatila project his role went beyond simple encouragement. He had to bear the whole burden with me, including the review of each and every chapter as I completed it at the turn of the new century. His comments and remarks were always highly significant, and I never failed to give them the most thorough consideration. He has in fact, from the time he was appointed as representative of the Palestine Liberation Organization in 1964, been a leading expert in Palestinian–Lebanese relations, and he is also an astute critic – one of the few who has been able, in daily and intellectual life, to manage that difficult trio: struggle, politics and writing.

There were times, occasionally, when I wondered if it was possible to go on. However, Shafiq would countenance no doubt. His friends are right when they describe him as exceptionally courageous, and I would add that his courage is not simply a matter of outlook but also a way of life.

Then there were those friends and scholars who provided more than moral support; who also supplied concrete ideas and suggestions. Let me here mention a number of these, in the order in which they made their respective contributions to the project.

Dr Edward Said, a close friend, followed the progress of my work without once asking me the conventional question as to 'how it was going'. His subsequent contribution, though, was a special one no other person could have made.

Whenever I visited the United States to attend a conference, the phone would ring where I was staying, and there would be Edward at the other end, telling me (for example) that I might find it useful to meet with the Director of the Oral History Research Office at Columbia University. And the visit would be arranged.

Columbia University, in New York, was the first university anywhere in the world to establish, in 1948, a specific department for the study of oral history, and I derived great profit from my meeting, in October 1985, with Dr Ronald G. Grele.

On one visit, Edward's voice came over once more, energetic and firm. This time, he told me, it would be outside New York. Was I, he asked, familiar with the foundation of the Holocaust Archive at Yale University? He thought probably not, as it had been set up only recently. Could I go to Yale? He would request the necessary permit for me.

And so I went to New Haven, where I spent five hours in the room of the newly established Video Archive for Holocaust Testimonies at Yale. I watched some videos. I listened to an account of the pain and suffering, narrated at first hand by a woman who had been a little girl at Auschwitz but still recalled everything that had happened to her family. I listened to others too, and learned a great deal in those few short hours.

Dr Walid al-Khalidi I had met several times in the 1970s, in connection with documentary projects at the Institute for Palestine Studies. When, though, I met him at his office in Boston in the winter of 1989, I had, as I told him, no direct request to make. I simply felt that, if a book were to be published about Sabra and Shatila, he should be aware of it.

Up to then I had not known Dr al-Khalidi well. From that day, though, dated an enduring collaboration and friendship. Whenever he came to Beirut he never failed to meet with me to discuss *Sabra and Shatila*. He would read a few pages and comment on some aspect and, time and again, I would put to him questions I had posed to myself and others; then, after a few moments' silent reflection, he would be the one person to provide a sure and thoughtful answer – remaining, indeed, deeply reflective even when the conversation was over. He was always seeking some improvement, and our discussions are implicitly reflected in the pages of this book.

Dr Salma Khadra Jayyusi I have known since my childhood. She was one of the first people to impress us children in Jerusalem, when, before 1948, she returned from the American University in Beirut with a degree in Arabic literature. Fifty years passed between that time and my first discussion with her about the Sabra and Shatila book, when she was visiting Beirut in 1996 to supervise one of her scholarly projects.

Whether it sprang from the humane motives that make her appear to be reporting a personal tragedy when discussing Sabra and Shatila, or from her evident boundless love for Palestine, or from her superior scholarly spirit, or perhaps from a combination of all these, one thing I know. If I were to be asked who showed the greatest general and particular interest in the book, who stood foremost in making heartfelt enquiries about its progress, I would answer: Salma.

Dr Iqbal Ahmad, an international scholar, Pakistani by birth, was a close friend of my husband's, and, from our first talk together, a friend of my own too.

He saw nothing wrong in wearing the simplest of shirts (made, he would proudly point out, in Pakistan), yet his talk on the podium, shirt and all, was that of a philosopher prince. For all his popular and spontaneous air, Iqbal would captivate the hearer with the calm aptness of his words. He had known of the project for some time and was waiting for me to approach him about it. When we talked together during his last visit to Beirut in 1997, the questions he asked outnumbered the suggestions he made. This was the essence of Iqbal Ahmad; the initiative, he implied, was with me. From then on I asked no more questions. Iqbal Ahmad, may God bless his soul, passed away the following year.

Dr Khair el-Din Haseeb, Director-General of the Centre for Arab Unity Studies, I had begun to know well from the late 1970s on, when I spent a year in charge of the Centre's Documentation Department before becoming a professor at the Lebanese University. One of his most significant qualities, as I soon discovered, was his ability to combine two strengths that rarely exist in the same person: minute accuracy and outstanding general efficiency. His personal example made sure deadlines were always met.

Our encounters continued through the national and Islamic meetings held from the early 1990s; meetings that testified alike to his precise organizational skills and his firm principles. He was, I once told him, the only friend to enquire into small details of the project – something he had never done with any of my other works. It was as though he had, in some strange way, been familiar with everything beforehand. He replied with his usual decisive air. This, he said, was in the nature of the Sabra and Shatila massacre. Along with a few other friends of similar calibre, Khair el-Din Haseeb remained a sure refuge in the most difficult times.

Mahmoud Soueid is an old college friend, and his position as Director of the Institute for Palestine Studies meant that we met countless times to talk about this book. Its publication in Arabic, though, only became a major preoccupation at the final stage. Through all the stages Mahmoud Soueid supplied unfailing encouragement, concerned equally with the detail and the main subject matter. I understood now why many in Lebanon supposed him to be Palestinian rather than Lebanese; even his Lebanese accent, when he appeared on television, did nothing to change this, so fully was he (like other, similar people) mentally and emotionally engaged with Palestine. Indeed, he and others of his kind are Arabs rather than specifically Lebanese or Palestinian.

Ma'an Bachour is a committed nationalist, always ready with courageous views and rational analysis about the contemporary Arab world; to be found at scholarly and national conventions, surrounded by people waiting to hear what he has to say. My acquaintance with him is a long one, and we have often met at such conventions. The new generation has, though, come to know him only since the early 1990s, as the founder of Al-Muntada al-Qawmi al-Arabi, whose members now number in the hundreds throughout Lebanon.

There was no way a book like this could come out without long dialogues with Ma'an Bachour. I must thank him most profoundly for what he has said to me, and also for what he has not said.

Counsellor Michel Eddé was the first Minister of Culture and Higher Education in Lebanon, and an insightful writer on the Arab-Israeli conflict and the history of Zionism. I first came to know him through my interest in his writings and through watching his interviews on television. Later we became connected in more concrete fashion through the Al-Quds Institution, founded in 2001, of which he became a Vice-President of the Board of Trustees, chaired by Shaykh Dr Yousef al-Qaradawi. I was myself a member of the Directory Board and we would attend the same sessions. It is difficult here to do justice to a man of such principle and outstanding courage, and to such a scholar, whose speech is like a surging sea. He is of the kind whose faith deepens with time, and who never retreats no matter how fierce the hardships grow.

I can think of no person who has addressed me with such a depth of enthusiasm, such acuteness of mind and such firmness of opinion as Michel Eddé. Such an impact did his guidance have on the project, in its final stages, that I was left wondering what the effect would have been had we met at the beginning.

There were other friends I approached with the request to review specific chapters or, in some cases, the whole typescript. Any author can benefit from a second opinion, all the more so when the one providing it is endowed with special gifts: of balanced viewpoint, cultural refinement, breadth of vision or profound human insight. Each of those involved contributed, beyond all doubt, a major improvement, not merely by the particular ideas or modifications proposed, but above all through a dedicated participation without which I could hardly have continued.

All I can do to the friends and prominent writers in question is to express my most heartfelt thanks. These people are, in order of my connection with them, the novelist Elias Khoury, the diplomat Bernd Erbel, the writer and scholar Mohammad Sammak and Counsellor Dr Salah Dabbagh.

There are others, too, whose writings lightened the darkness of lonely nights. I cannot recall any time of my life when I did not read poetry, but at no time was it such a source of inspiration as in the years when I lived day and night with Sabra and Shatila.

The poems of the great Mahmoud Darwish, so very familiar from the past, I now felt as though I was reading for the first time.

For many long years now I have been hearing the voices of afflicted people, telling of quite horrific experiences, whether sitting there in front of me or played to me from tapes, and night after night I have read what has been written about Sabra and Shatila by writers from all parts of the world, but never in all truth have I heard or read anything more utterly compelling than the words of Mahmoud Darwish. The reader indeed may judge, for him- or herself simply from the four lines of 'Praising the High Shadow', which introduce Part I of this book, and the four further lines that open Part II.

Finally, I should like wholeheartedly to acknowledge the efforts of a group of photographers. With some of these I was already acquainted; others I came to know through Sabra and Shatila.

All showed immediate enthusiasm to take part in this book, swiftly sending me their collections of photos with the assurance that these represented a contribution on their part. For me, and for all my colleagues involved in the editing and production of the book, the most joyful moments would be when we received a package from some country containing photographs. We received collections from the United States, Germany, Japan and, of course, Lebanon itself.

As it happened, the first collection I saw, early in 1983, was that of the highly professional American photographer Mya Shone, who was in Beirut with her husband Ralph Schoenman during the days of the massacre. They were in fact among the first to enter the site. They left Lebanon subsequently, and, when they returned a few months later, I had the opportunity to look at Mya's precious collection of slides, which she projected on the wall of our living room. She was the first photographer I was in touch with, and also the first contributor.

As for Günther Altenburg, Chargé d'Affaires at the German Embassy in Beirut, he was already a family friend, and I was well enough aware of his intellectual and human qualities, and of his thorough analysis of contemporary concerns. We talked, I recall, about Sabra and Shatila, but he did not tell me then how he had shot pictures there. He justified this later by saying he had had no wish to add to our anguish by having us see the photos in question. Only when I told him on the telephone, 20 years after the massacre, that I was finalizing the typescript and arranging the appendix of photographs did he tell me, to my surprise, that he would like to make his contribution. A few days later, I received by mail a large package containing an amazing collection of photos, unparalleled by any I had seen in any exhibition or book linked to the 1982 invasion. The gift was utterly invaluable, not just because it was unexpected, but as an indication that new evidence, new details and photos, would continue to emerge in years to come.

As for the Japanese photographer Ryuichi Hirokawa, the first time I met him was in Bonn in the spring of 1985 while we were both attending the convention held by the International Commission of Inquiry into Israeli Crimes Against the Lebanese and Palestinian Peoples. Hirokawa then held an exhibition of his photos and talked to me of what he had observed, but I came to know him better through his famous illustrated book, issued in English under the title *Beirut 1982: From the Israeli Invasion to the Massacre of Sabra and Shatila Camps*. It can have occurred to no one that Hirokawa would come in due course to Beirut, in September 2002, in the company of the Italian, Spanish, Belgian, French, German and Canadian delegation there to commemorate the twentieth anniversary of Sabra and Shatila. He sent me a collection of photos, with exemplary promptness, the moment he set foot back in Japan.

The photographer of *Al-Safir* newspaper, Ali Hasan Salman, was one of those Lebanese photographers whose photos of the massacre had been published without their names appearing; consequently the search for such 'unknowns' was difficult. I had in fact seen Ali Salman's quite awe-inspiring book (*Beirut: Memories of the Difficult Times*) when it appeared in the mid-1990s, with its scenes of the destruction of Beirut through the bloody years as portrayed through his insightful lens. What I did not know then was that he was one of those who had penetrated all obstacles to enter Sabra and Shatila.

Ramzi Haydar, another Lebanese photographer, was one of the first to enter the bloody zone of Sabra and Shatila and kept dozens of highly professional photos on CD. Many of these became widely published. Ramzi Haydar later became a prominent photographer at the Agence France Presse in Beirut, and one of the first Lebanese photographers to achieve world-wide recognition.

In addition to all those above, let me simply say, without going into details, that a number of friends stood by me in the darkest times in a way I shall never forget. Let me, without titles or introductions, express my grateful love to the following: Mona Nsouli, Mona Sukkarieh, Jacqueline Inglessis, Elaine Hagopian, Salwa al-Hout, Adela Labban, Fatima Makhzoum, Claudia Altenburg, Grace Said, Ellen Siegel and Rihab Mukahal.

Nevertheless, the man to whom I feel my thanks and appreciation should be directed first and last is the professor and historian who taught me the basics of scholarly research, leading me to seek the truth, through the mazes, without fear: and that is Dr Anis Sayigh, who, over six years or so in the 1970s, supervised my PhD thesis at the Lebanese University. It was no coincidence that the thesis should have dealt with political leaderships and institutions in Palestine during the Mandate period, and that Dr Anis Sayigh, as Director-General of the Research Centre of the Palestine Liberation Organization, should have been the supervising professor, for he is among the few who have devoted their lives to research for the Palestinian cause, reading, training, supervising and producing.

To Dr Sayigh, my heartfelt thanks once more. His unforgettable guidelines were like lighthouses near and far, guiding me through the seas for a full six years of my life.

*   *   *

Although both the Arabic- and English-language typescripts were completed in 2002, it was the former that first appeared (in 2003). Publishing the latter necessitated substantial sponsorship, and since the events of Sabra and Shatila had not been in the headlines for more than two decades, the 'mission' was anything but easy.

After several early failures, I decided to consult Shaykh Faisal Mawlawi, head of the Management Council of the Al-Quds Institution and a man widely respected for his good works both inside and outside his native Lebanon. I came to know him through his highly enlightening writings and through our meetings at the Al-Quds Institution, whose members represent a variety of Arab countries, several faiths and numerous political persuasions – all united by a love for Jerusalem. Shaykh Mawlawi spared me further worries when he said at the very beginning of our first talk on the subject that the book should have come out in English first, 'so all the world could know what really happened. Our organization works for justice, too. I'll bring up the subsidizing issue, and how we can help you obtain it, at our very next meeting.'

Finally it was time for the most delicate part: coming to an agreement with an English-language publisher.

At this point I was lucky to have as a friend Professor Elaine Hagopian, for it was she who advised me to entrust my work to Pluto Press and put me in contact with the head of the publishing house, Dr Roger van Zwanenberg.

Arriving at an agreement with someone I had never met was a completely next experience for me. Roger's informative and thoughtful e-mails paved the way for a balanced understanding, though, proving that for Pluto Press being progressive is not just a slogan but also a practised reality. I extend my deepest thanks, therefore, to Roger and to all of his colleagues.

As the twentieth century neared its end, and after I had completed a few chapters, I reached an impasse. Having made the decision to begin translating the typescript into English, according to a timetable for publication almost parallel with the Arabic original, I realized sponsorship would be necessary. The problem was solved: I received welcome and encouragement from three principled and honourable senior figures who provided sufficient funds to cover the whole translation project. None of these, I am well aware, expects to be thanked, but the people of Sabra and Shatila would certainly wish to thank them in any case. On these people's behalf, I express my gratitude.

* * *

Finally, there are three anonymous 'soldiers' whose contribution to this book, through the days and nights, cannot be overlooked. Each played a direct part in modifying a word or a paragraph here, proposing omission of a sentence there, each making painstaking comment on the other's work. These three, personally unknown to one another, are the editor of the Arabic text, the translator into English and the editor of the English text. Our experience together (mostly electronic due to the distances involved) was governed by a marvellous co-operative spirit. I have been happy indeed to act as co-ordinator among them, not in the role of author but rather as reader and arbiter. This provided my first reading of the book before it was published, and I thank each one of them from the bottom of my heart.

Bayan Nuwayhed al-Hout
Beirut, March 2004

Introduction

For 40 continuous hours between sunset on Thursday 16 September and midday on Saturday 18 September 1982, the massacre of Sabra and Shatila took place, one of the most barbaric of the twentieth century.

Sabra Street and Shatila Camp lie in a popular residential area of Beirut, where there are in fact several small quarters set together. However, because of the presence of Shatila Camp in its midst, the whole district came to be known as the Sabra and Shatila Camps. It was this district's destiny to become the arena of the massacre.

Shatila Camp was one of the first camps to be founded in Beirut. Most of its residents came originally from the Palestine coast and Upper Galilee, being among those forced to seek refuge in Lebanon, either by sea to the nearest harbours or by land over the Palestine–Lebanon border, in the wake of the 1948 war. This war is referred to by Arabs as the War of *al-Nakba* (Disaster), and by the Israelis as the War of Independence.

Shatila is also among the smallest of the Palestinian camps and, with numbers of residents increasing by the year, the time came when it could no longer accommodate new arrivals. It was possible, however, for very humble refugee homes to extend beyond the camp borders fixed by the Lebanese government in the middle of the twentieth century.

One result of this expansion of Palestinian refugees, and of mutual interaction (especially from the 1970s on, with Lebanese living nearby) was the transformation of the Sabra and Shatila Camps district into a place attracting labourers and families from many countries – the common factor being poverty, which unites peoples and nations. So it was that residents were no longer simply Palestinian or Lebanese but also began to include Syrians, Egyptians, Jordanians, Pakistanis, Bangladeshis, Iranians and Algerians. Victims of the massacre represented all these nationalities.

On 6 June 1982, about three months before the massacre, the Israeli Army invaded Lebanon, moving northward towards the capital. The siege of Beirut lasted longer than any previously experienced by an Arab city over the whole sequence of Arab-Israeli wars. For the Arabs this invasion was known as the Sixth Israeli-Arab War, or the Treacherous Israeli Invasion of Lebanon, while the Israelis referred to it as Peace for the Galilee.

The war was finally ended after a famous agreement brokered primarily by the American envoy Philip Habib, who was of Lebanese descent, and as such the agreement came to be known as the Habib Agreement. Its main purpose was the permanent evacuation of Palestinian fighters from Beirut, carried out, in the interests of their safety, under the supervision of the United States and other Western nations. The agreement also guaranteed the protection of civilian residents or refugees in the camps thereafter. This was the understanding at the time.

Following the signing of this agreement, in whose contents the Palestinian leadership trusted, Palestinian fighters began to depart in groups, one by one, from 21 August on, supposing their families' safety had been entrusted to the United States. They left wearing their uniforms and carrying their personal arms and essential belongings, giving a victory sign as they did so.

Thousands of West Beirut residents, Lebanese and Palestinian, would go out each day to bid them farewell, gathering in the

Mal'ab al-Baladi, the central meeting place, or standing on balconies and public roads; or else they would insist on going to the port of Beirut itself, where ships waited at anchor to take aboard the fighters leaving for new exiles.

As Palestinian troops were thus leaving Beirut daily, as French troops from the multinational forces deployed in the centre of the port were monitoring departure operations, and as the Israeli Army also vigilantly monitored departures – especially with regard to the number of fighters leaving – while simultaneously reinforcing its positions in several parts of Lebanon, Bashir al-Gemayel, leader of the Lebanese Forces and head of one of the two combatant sides in the sequence of civil wars fought from the mid-1970s on, was elected President of the Lebanese Republic on 23 August.

Beirut was in a state of shock. If cities had characters like human beings, the Lebanese capital might, in those days, have been said to be suffering from a severely split personality. Few capitals in history had undergone such an experience; for one half of Beirut the election day was one of glorious victory, while the other half viewed it as a day of mourning. Joy at the new presidency of the 34-year-old son of the Chairman of the Lebanese Phalangist Party, Shaykh Pierre al-Gemayel, was celebrated throughout East Beirut. West Beirut, in contrast, was in a state of fury.

By the first day of September, Palestinian and Syrian fighters had left Beirut, either by sea or land, and soon afterwards, regarding their mission as over, the multinational forces, American, Italian and French, began making preparations for their own departure. The French troops were the last to leave, on 11 September.

The Palestinian fighters had left, the Israeli siege went on, and Beirut remained without water or electricity. The astonishing thing was that, over this crucial period, no one from any side voiced concern over who was responsible for safety in the Palestinian camps.

The residents of West Beirut – apart, that is, from those who never left at all during the siege (except to move from one street to another, looking, over crucial days and nights, for some degree of safety from concentrated Israeli shelling or crazy, random shelling by air, sea and land) – quickly returned to Beirut when the war was over. Soon they were all busy repairing their homes, shops or other properties. Virtually every apartment and house needed new glass put in or repairs to cracked walls. As for those directly hit by bombs or rockets, they were mostly in need of major restoration or rebuilding.

The common topic among those hurriedly meeting in the street – after greetings and personal enquiries made without waiting for an answer – was the immediate future. What, people asked, would be the aftermath of the occupation nightmare? How would Beirut pick up the pieces?

As for those Palestinians living in the camps, to which many had returned to start building and repair work like everyone else in Beirut, their deepest thoughts and concerns were still far away with their departed loved ones, from whom no letters had yet been received. How had they settled in their new exiles?

Many refugees did not even know where their loved ones had been headed. Considerations of security had been pre-eminent, and these dictated that, for some of the departing fighters, the final destination should remain secret for a time – many of the fighters themselves knew nothing of their destination on the day they left. The hardest thing for a Palestinian refugee is not refugee life itself but continuation of that life from one emigration to another, and from one exile to the next.

Residents of East Beirut, whose quarters and homes had been spared Israeli bombs and rockets through the invasion months, were still holding festivals to celebrate Bashir al-Gemayel's victory in the presidential elections. As for the President-elect himself, he had already begun delivering speeches; he meant, he said, to be not a militia leader, not the leader of one group to the exclusion of others, but President of the whole of Lebanon. Then came Tuesday 14 September. At half past four that afternoon there was a horrific explosion at the

Lebanese Forces centre in the Ashrafieh district of East Beirut, killing the President-elect and leaving 21 others dead and 59 wounded.

At dawn next day, the Israeli Army marched into Beirut from several sides. Their first concern was the encirclement of the Sabra and Shatila Camps; then, over the rest of the day, they succeeded in occupying the whole city.

The occupation was preceded by a number of Israeli claims centred on the (alleged) continued presence of 2,500 Palestinian fighters in Beirut. The initial pretext for occupying Beirut and besieging Sabra and Shatila was the need to deal with these.

According to Israeli claims made directly after the assassination and published by the Israeli media, a bloodbath was expected in West Beirut between supporters of the President-elect and members of the Lebanese National Movement; or – to use the civil war language of the 1970s – between Christians and Muslims. These claims provided the second pretext for an Israeli occupation of West Beirut.

The two pretexts were quickly discovered to be false. There was no fighting between Lebanese Muslims and Christians, nor did the Israeli Army find, in Sabra and Shatila or anywhere else in West Beirut, the 2,500 fighters who had, it was claimed, remained behind in Beirut in contravention of the Habib Agreement.

The true bloodbath was not a matter of fighting between Lebanese Muslims and Christians, it was the bloody massacre in the Sabra and Shatila district, masterminded by Israeli Minister of Defence Ariel Sharon and Chief of Staff Lieutenant General Rafael Eitan, and carried out by militias of the Lebanese Forces and other militias and individuals supporting them.

Straight after the massacre, press and television, both Western and Lebanese, entered the district to which entry had been forbidden over the past three bloody days. Footage and photographs taken by the first correspondents, along with the reports and articles of the first reporters and journalists, showed no evidence of any battle, or of the presence of 2,500 or even a few hundred fighters. There had merely, it turned out, been small groups of young men carrying Kalashnikovs, with the air more of angry patriots than of professional fighters. Everything at the site of the massacre confirmed this, and such was the message accordingly conveyed by members of the foreign media, on television screens and on the front pages of newspapers, throughout the world. In less than 24 hours, the Sabra and Shatila massacre had become the most significant piece of world news, and broadcasters were urging that children should be spared the sight of the pictures shown.

International human rights organizations, along with decent people everywhere, were actively digesting what had happened and considering what crimes against humanity had been committed during the Israeli invasion of Lebanon and in the Sabra and Shatila massacre. Before the end of 1982 the Lebanese (secret) official report, known as the Jermanos Report after the military examining judge Ass'ad Jermanos, had been published. Then in the wake of this came the Israeli (public) official report, known as the Kahan Report after the judge Yitzak Kahan, who had presided over a three-member court and heard evidence from large numbers of witnesses. The testimonies of these latter were made public – in contrast to those heard by the Lebanese investigators, which remained secret.

A common factor between the two reports was (it subsequently emerged) a reliance on 'justifying claims' based on the presence of '2,500 fighters'. On the other hand, there was a remarkable difference, if not contradiction, between the two reports over the identity of the armed militias carrying out the massacre. The public Kahan Report specified the Lebanese Forces, whereas the preceding secret Lebanese report denied this.

* * *

I am writing this Introduction in the summer of 2002, 20 years after the massacre of Sabra and Shatila.

In light of the common factor, referred to above, between the Lebanese and Israeli reports, and in light of points on which they agree and disagree, there is no difficulty in laying out the major objectives of this book, which are as follows:

1. To show conclusively that what took place in Sabra and Shatila between 16 and 18 September 1982 was a massacre, not a battle.
2. To show conclusively that the Palestine Liberation Organization did not break its promises, since there were definitely not 2,500 Palestinian fighters either in Sabra and Shatila or in West Beirut as a whole.
3. To show conclusively the incorrectness of the victim count in the two reports, and to provide evidence for estimated figures closer to reality.
4. To document victims' names as far as possible, based on various primary sources.
5. To specify the identity of the militias and members carrying out the massacre.

The above objectives developed over two and a half years during the documentation phase. At the outset of the Oral History Project in November 1982, the aim was simply the documentation and preservation of testimonies, carried out under circumstances of such stringent security that even ongoing meetings with witnesses could not be guaranteed. As work continued, however, the research plan became subject to constant review, maturer consideration leading to new plans and projects not previously envisaged. This reflects an essential difference between the historiography of massacres and that of other historical events.

Why should such a difference exist? Because the researcher, in each fresh phase, discovers certain facts or encounters particular obstacles which result in a completely fresh start. Because massacres are, with rare exceptions, characterized by secrecy. Because massacres normally involve no documents or records, except when (in a few cases in the distant past) perpetrators have preferred to describe massacres as 'glorious victories' – in which case the facts were trumpeted complete with exaggeration.

Because massacres have known beginnings but no endings. It may seem to contemporaries and researchers that they have distinct endings, but time invariably proves the opposite. Those who survive do not live on like people truly alive: their lives are, in every case, influenced, modified or developed in ways they do not wish, as painful memories pull them back, consciously or unconsciously, to their tragic experience.

Because the researcher of massacres constantly uncovers things previously unknown, even in the single story of a single family. Witnesses constantly remember more, telling, in later meetings, things they had not revealed at the start.

Because, in sum, it is the historiography of massacres that leads the researcher, and not vice versa.

Why, then, should the facts not be simply stated? There was not, at the outset, any comprehensive plan for this book, involving the methodologies of oral history, field research and historical research. When I first started recording the testimonies of victims' relatives towards the end of 1982, my sole aim was to document these for their own sake. Even the idea of having them published did not occur to me – this was simply not my concern. My focus was frankly humanitarian, leading me just to record those testimonies over the first difficult months.

I was not initially aware of the significance of collecting victims' names. The massacre was deafening and heart-breaking, a cause for tears. A single photograph would obviate the need for dozens of pages. What I was seeking was the depth of the tragic event.

As for the figures – what real difference was there between one figure and another? Suppose we were to say the number of victims was 1,000 rather than 3,000, or just 300 rather than 1,000? Would that reduce or minimize the hateful nature of the crimes, of the torture and killing of unarmed, innocent people?

I had no thought, either, of collecting all that had been published, and was still being published, about the meetings, conferences and investigations related to the massacre. By the spring of 1985, though, I was doing precisely that, and what I have done has sprung, primarily and quite simply, from reaction to the challenges and obstacles I faced.

And so I had no choice, in the summer of 1985, but to begin writing the text. It proved, however, to be a remarkably difficult job at an exhausting time; and I decided in consequence to postpone the task for a year or two – which stretched out, for various reasons, into a much longer period, until the twentieth century was almost at an end. Such was the background to the main introduction below.

*   *   *

At noon on Saturday 18 September 1982, I was at home alone, waiting to hear the news on the Monte Carlo radio station. Apart from myself there were, in the whole building of 20 apartments, just three families, returned to repair their damaged homes.

I live in a street called Jabal al-Arab, off Corniche al-Mazra'a and Unesco Street. Although small, no more than 7 metres wide and 300 metres long, it contained the residences of several national leaders, not to mention the centres of some Lebanese political parties, the most important of these being the Lebanese National Movement, half-way down. On the corner, on the Corniche al-Mazra'a side, was the office of the Palestine Liberation Organization.

Since Thursday, two days before, the Israeli Army had established a command headquarters at the PLO office. The Mirkava tanks were rolling back and forth in our small street, sometimes slowly, sometimes angrily and nervously. It was apparent that most of those who had managed to return to the district had quickly left again on the approach of the tanks come to prevent the supposed bloodbath in West Beirut.

During my long wait for the news, I pondered on the vast difference between this day and the previous one. I was alone now. The day before, though, again right at noon, the apartment had been filled with four Israeli soldiers. It was an unforgettable moment. A neighbour had come by and frantically rung the doorbell, telling me, the moment I opened the door, how the Israelis

had been asking him where Shafiq al-Hout lived. They'd been carrying maps, he went on, showing all the houses in which they were interested, and they were bound to come. The news, I assured him, was not unexpected. It was hardly likely the Israelis would occupy the PLO office without also looking for the home of its director.

My first thought, as I closed the door, was to protect the three small children playing in one of the rooms: my brother-in-law's children, whose mother was preparing food for them in the kitchen. Fearing for their safety, I called them and told them to go back at once to their home on the sixth floor. To my surprise I heard a voice saying, calmly and firmly: 'The children are staying here. There's no way I'm leaving you alone.'

It was the children's mother, who'd come from the kitchen without my noticing. It was clear she'd overheard what the neighbour said and that she'd made the decision to stay with me. This moment was among the most difficult of my life. Suppose they started hitting the children in front of us? Only the day before, the two of us had heard how an Israeli officer threatened the wife of a Palestinian leader, saying he would take her baby daughter as a hostage until the father returned and gave himself up. Could she have forgotten that?

Hana' al-Hout, the mother of the three children, was a close friend of mine, as well as a relative and neighbour. I knew her firmness and strength of character well enough. How could I dissuade her? And was there time in any case? I told her, quickly and emphatically, that I appreciated her stand but didn't want her there, and I asked her to leave at once with the children. Then I ran to fetch the children, but she took hold of me, refusing to budge.

The situation was resolved by a sharp knocking on the door, and for some reason the knocking took all my fear away, leaving me quite calm. I went to the door and opened it, to find four Israeli soldiers armed to the teeth with a variety of dangerous-looking weapons. Wariness was etched on their faces, except for that of their leader, who asked me loudly, in English: 'Is Shafiq al-Hout at home?' 'No,' I answered. 'He's not.'

There was silence for a few seconds. Then, without waiting to be asked, he walked in, followed by the other three with their weapons.

Wariness and extreme caution were still written all over the other three soldiers' faces. As for the fourth, the leader, he immediately raised his voice. 'Are your husbands', he asked, his tone deliberately arrogant, 'in the habit of running off and leaving the women behind?' I answered him, clearly and calmly, in the same language. 'You ought to know', I said, 'from the newspapers if nowhere else, that my husband hasn't left Beirut all this summer. You should also know a discussion of the Palestine issue's due at the United Nations. He's been attending all the sessions, by virtue of his PLO position, twice a year since the mid-1970s. He's now on his way to New York.'

I paid no attention to the secret gesture he made to those with him. But I certainly noticed what happened next. The leader's voice became more normal, the arrogant tone gone, while the others removed all their weapons apart from their pistols, leaving one of their number to guard them at the entrance.

The search lasted half an hour. They looked over shelves and examined book titles and old files, and they scrutinized the pictures and paintings on the walls. One of them made sure to look through the attic above the bathroom, but naturally – and as he had expected – found no one there!

The leader's name, as I subsequently learned from his picture and news of him in the papers, after he became assistant to the Israeli commander in the South, was Roberto Barak. As they were leaving the house, he asked me in a tone to which some arrogance had returned: 'Will you testify that we treated you in a civilized manner?'

It was hardly a question I had been expecting. Only then did I feel some confusion. What kind of 'civilization' was this? What was I to say in the face of thick wire wound for more than ten loops, almost to the height of the table? Wasn't that enough to blow the place up if they decided to do it? At the same time I remembered the three small children. I remembered how their

mother had asked the soldier at the door, the one guarding the weapons, to let them go down and play. He'd stepped aside at once, threatening and harming no one. A few seconds went by. Then I found myself saying: 'You were more civilized with me than I expected. But I haven't been with you in other homes, to know how you behaved there.'

We shut the door behind them.

And here I was now, 24 hours later, sitting alone and waiting for some news: of the blowing up of an Israeli tank, perhaps, or of one powerful state at least protesting against the unjustified occupation. As I waited, each minute seemed like an hour.

Then the broadcaster's voice came. I don't recall how he introduced the news, but I do remember how he started telling what had happened in the Sabra and Shatila massacre. His voice trembled more and more, till finally it broke completely. I no longer knew where I was or what the broadcaster had actually been saying. I recall some words about bodies being flung onto roads and into corners, about old men and women and children. I recall words about the mutilation of corpses, about the marks of bulldozers on sand drenched with blood, about the screaming of traumatized survivors, about the Red Cross cars stopping at the entrance to the camps and asking to enter. I recall that the broadcaster was talking and the whole world listening, while I was weeping alone with no one to hear me.

Throughout the Israeli invasion, death was continually close to us, to our loved ones, to our friends, to our children and to our neighbours' children. We often wept, both for those we had known and those we had not.

And yet, on that Saturday, death wasn't the same. It was more mortal. It was death of the soul rather than the body, of the nation's soul, which died before that of the children and women and old people.

All that blood. All that torture and death. And where? Just a few minutes by car from my home. How was it we didn't know – I and my neighbours and all the other people living in Beirut? How could we have failed to sense something?

Never in my life have I felt such pain and impotence as I did that Saturday and in the weeks that followed. I would hear, each day, about victims buried in mass graves, about others still being searched for, and about others whose remains even their families were unable to recognize.

Those dead were the living dead, in the time of the dead living. Those dead people were falling right at noon on Friday, while the Israeli officer was asking me: 'Will you testify that we treated you in a civilized manner?' He, the officer in charge, could never have asked that particular question after news of the massacre had broken, after it became clear the Israeli Army, which had surrounded the Sabra and Shatila district, knew what was going on in its squares and alleys.

Days went by. Even hours passed slowly in West Beirut, a city in which destruction was still not lifted, where remains were still not buried, while its people were in open revolt around the alleys, shooting at the occupying soldiers and, every so often, damaging a Mirkava tank. My sense of impotence became complete because I couldn't even get near Sabra and Shatila. The roads were controlled by the Israeli occupation army which had come to Beirut to stop the 'imminent bloodbath'.

As soon as the occupation army left West Beirut at the end of September, and as soon as we could make contact with one another, a few friends and myself expended all our efforts to offer love and support to the victims' families.

I had never worked in the social field, but I found it to be the most effective one in those harsh times. I did indeed return to my teaching post when the Lebanese University reopened, but, my lectures apart, I devoted myself to social work.

Plunged in all this, I quite forgot how, since the previous winter, I had been waiting for summer to start work on an oral history project, involving meetings with Palestinians who had sought refuge in Lebanon in 1948. The aim was to discover what had really happened. Had it been emigration or displacement? The Israeli invasion stopped all that. During one very hot and humid night of unbroken Israeli shelling, while we in the shelter were praying to God for dawn to break and the shelling to stop, I decided to replace that project just as soon as the war ended. Palestinian refugees would hardly feel like talking about the 1948 war, more than 30 years before, when they were just emerging from a war still more savage and brutal.

I had already agreed the 1948 Emigration project with the Institute of Arab Studies in the United States. The head of the board of directors was Professor Edward Said, an international scholar and innovative Arab-American writer in a number of fields. What was not known about him, though, was his keen interest in oral history. I was sure Edward Said would understand the situation and give his blessing to the new project. It never occurred to me that the invasion itself would become so quickly part of the past, as if days were years or decades even, vis-à-vis Sabra and Shatila.

And yet the enormous tragedy of the event paralysed my ability to write; I could not even envisage it. The prime concern of my friends and myself was to maintain contact with the victims' families. What could we do for them? The noblest thing was to secure a room or two to house a family whose home had been wrecked, or provide medication for someone injured. Scope for initiative was limited and co-ordination with others in the field extraordinarily difficult, but the chief thing was to try as hard as possible.

The steadfast, weeping women told us of more than one case. Some talked about their own personal tragedy in Sabra and Shatila, or that of their neighbours or relatives. We listened, and the sense of anguish deepened. We quickly became part of the tragedy, with full knowledge of its details. We would enquire about the victims; asking, for example, whether Abu Rabi''s body had been found, or whether Ass'ad had returned after being abducted near the Kuwaiti Embassy on the Friday morning.

At the same time I would follow, as far as I could, everything being published and broadcast about the massacre by the Western media. Those of us living in Beirut itself would read and learn from what was being published in New York, London and Paris. In the weeks immediately after the incident it seemed to us that everything was written that could be written. But once the stage of shock was past, I began to focus on three crucial issues.

The first issue concerned my discovery that the events and tragedies of the massacre were more profound than anything published or whispered. According to my evidence, every woman with a personal experience was relating new things.

The second issue concerned the astonishing transformation of Beirut, as the wailing and weeping and front-page pictures of the massacre gave way to total silence. The policy of the Lebanese authorities was no longer a secret: it was complete suppression of what had happened.

The third issue concerned the four Israeli soldiers who had searched my home. Their leader's question – 'Will you testify that we treated you in a civilized manner?' – was still in need of an answer.

In the light of these three issues, I decided to embark on extensive interviews with the victims' families and with other witnesses before it was too late, and irrespective of the obstacles.

The first phase: the Oral History Project

News coverage at the time of the incident was highly significant. But, like the event itself, it was soon over. It is the nature of the daily media to seek the new, while historical writing aims at reviving the past in the interest of the future. Peoples' memories are a spring that never dries up; the scream of pain at the instant of the event is merely the first chapter, and the story never finishes with that first chapter alone. This was what prompted me to launch the Oral History Project.

I began this project on 10 November 1982. In the initial interviews I limited myself to taking notes while explaining the importance of the project to the men and women I spoke to. Only when I was sure people were accepting the project, and even

welcoming it, did I start, with the permission of the person concerned, to record conversations on tape. I assured everyone I spoke to that their family names need not be published; that I would limit references to initial letters or first names unless they chose otherwise. But even this promise did not stop some speakers being extremely cautious and preferring not to have anything recorded on tape, while in a few other cases objective circumstances precluded recording. Clear indication is given, both in the list of interview sources in the bibliography and in the notes, of the nature of the interview: whether it is recorded or one during which notes were taken.

As said above, my sole aim for the whole Oral History Project at this stage was to document and preserve testimonies in any way possible, for fear they should be lost, or else face the negative impact of proscription. I was fortunate enough to gain the help of some of the men in the district, whom I knew very well, and who facilitated interviews, arranged appointments and escorted victims' relatives. After the initial interviews, the victims' relatives themselves began to introduce me to friends or neighbours of theirs. Interviews were normally carried out at my home, but later I did a few in some of my friends' homes, and also in Sabra and Shatila. I would not, I need hardly say, have hesitated to conduct all the interviews in the homes of these anguished and steadfast people had that been possible. However, this was ruled out for security reasons: the scene of the disaster was under constant surveillance. After Western media coverage of the first difficult days had subsided, the slightest mention of the massacre was forbidden.

This proscription lasted for many long years, compelling me not only to avoid interviews at the scene of the massacre but also to avoid continuous interviews anywhere else in West Beirut, so as to evade detectives' surveillance and reports.

Most of the interviews, then, took place at my home. Even this, in fact, would not have been feasible but for my personal position as wife of the PLO representative in Lebanon. The Lebanese authorities had forbidden the reopening of the PLO office after the Israeli occupation had died down (though the ban was de facto rather than legitimate), and as such it was normal for anyone finding the office closed to come to the representative's home. This, in turn, made it seem natural to the detectives and their superiors that large numbers of camp residents should visit this particular apartment. For all that, I had to limit my use of the situation, out of concern for the project itself and because of the secrecy I had promised to the horror-struck, honest interviewees – whose mere offer of testimony was an act of considerable courage during times that, far from soothing the pain and misery of Palestinians, had witnessed their further subjugation.

If I note the specific place of interview rather than noting 'Beirut' generally (as is commonly done), it is to emphasize the overall atmosphere of the period. As for myself, my memories of each interview remained inseparable from the place where it was conducted, as if the place itself were inseparable from the interview, or, come to that, from the whole tragic event. In the homes of victims' families, talk would be in whispers, as if the very walls had ears, and the talk itself was always supplemented by pointing to pictures hanging on the wall (these at least had been spared by public or secret proscription orders). When interviews were being held in their homes, my friends would nervously check the time, fearing their children would arrive home from school before the interview ended.

Eventually I suggested to some enthusiastic men and women from the camp, who were thoroughly familiar with the camp and its residents, that they should start recording their own interviews with witnesses and victims' families there. Three men and one woman contrived to conduct 21 interviews whose impact was significant, indeed exceptional, in the overall context of the testimonies. What mainly made these interviews special was that they were conducted with men and women who for various reasons had found it difficult to leave the camp and its vicinity.

Interviews went on spontaneously, without any need for pre-planning or pre-selection: the people we sought to talk to were victims' families, witnesses, nurses and rescue workers who all lived in the one city, mostly even in the one district. The experience we were striving to recapture was a very recent one. It was also a common one involving all the residents of the district, adults and children alike.

I expected the Oral History phase to end within one year. In fact it went on for more than twice that, and here I must mention the first major obstacle. This came from a source hardly supposed to be an obstacle at all: the Kahan Report issued in February 1983. I went through it as soon as it was published, translated into Arabic, in the daily newspaper *Al-Safir*, and what I read made me furiously angry. Why I became so angry, and how I reacted to this, is dealt with below in my description of the second phase, that of the collection of names.

The experience of the interviews dealing with the Sabra and Shatila massacre was quite unique, something I had never been through in any previous oral history project. If I were asked what remained most significantly in my memory, I should have to say it was the abnormally secret, even impossible, atmosphere surrounding the whole affair. Let me give just two examples.

The first example concerns the production of a second copy of the tapes. This procedure is not a basic requirement of oral history; it may, under normal circumstances, be carried out just in case one or more tapes should be damaged for some reason. In a project like that of Sabra and Shatila, however, and given the worsening security situation, retention of a second copy was essential; keeping just the one would have been an unforgivable lapse. And so, to avoid tampering or confiscation, the tapes had to be duplicated and copies kept elsewhere.

I made a point of copying the tape or tapes on the day of the interview or very shortly afterwards. Then, every ten tapes, I would place the copies in their small cardboard box and wrap this in coloured paper used for gifts. This would then be put with a friend for safe-keeping – and second copies were spread in more than one place. Frequently the tapes moved from one place to another; if the householder travelled, for instance.

The second example concerns the typed transcription of the interviews. Under normal circumstances such a task might simply be carried out by a typist working in an office. The situation here was not normal, and I ruled out the idea.

I thought of delegating the job to a typist for extra work at home, but three I knew and trusted turned me down, very apologetically, through fear of and for family members. One was even afraid of the neighbours. 'Why are you so scared of the neighbours?' I asked, astonished. 'Does your neighbour drop by suddenly? If so, why don't you type in a locked room?' 'The noise is the problem,' she answered. 'She'd hear it even at home, because her apartment's right next to ours.' (The computer age had barely dawned in Beirut in the early 1980s.) 'Our neighbour', she went on, 'is pretty shrewd, and she's very curious. She'd notice the breaks in typing from the tape – as opposed to constant typing from a written text. She'd ask me what I was typing – and you know there aren't any conferences or recorded lectures now. So, do I tell her what the tapes are for? How can I?'

Finally, the only solution in that first phase was to transcribe the contents of the tapes by hand. A courageous young woman undertook this task, waiting till her mother and brother were asleep to avoid their questions about what she was doing. She would lock herself in her room and silently carry out her task. In this way, she managed to finish more than 90 tapes.

When I returned to the Sabra and Shatila project in 1998, I recorded a number of new interviews so as to tie up some loose ends, while others went ahead and recorded further interviews. The main difference between transcribing tapes in the first phase and the last was that the latter could be done directly on computer in a research organization, without fear or precaution, exactly as would happen with a regular project under normal circumstances.

One further remark should be made on the nature and significance of the Oral History Project. It reflects the side of the victim exclusively, even though knowledge exists on two other sides: the Israeli side and that of the militias committing the massacre. It was impossible for any Arab researcher in my situation, alone in the Beirut of the first half of the mid-1980s, to carry out interviews with the three parties or explore the three sides of the triangle. It was ruled out not only by the political and security contexts, but by the national and psychological ones as well.

The project limits itself, then, to testimonies from the victims' side. This does not, even so, make it any less necessary, throughout the book, to return to newspaper and television interviews involving the other two sides, and to Western and Israeli investigations and writings, for quotation and reference.

There were, it must be said, a number of similar interviews with victims' families and with witnesses, appearing in various Western and Arab media in the first days and afterwards. However, the significance of the Oral History Project I undertook between November 1982 and January 1985, and returned to complete in the last two years of the twentieth century, lies above all in its comprehensive nature.

The significance springs, too, from the project's timing. In the days and weeks immediately after the massacre, people spoke in tones of horror and shock. Later they spoke with profound pain, but this was accompanied by deep awareness and by memory still fresh and untainted. They were in desperate need of someone to listen to them – and this is why they spoke out in the first phase, despite the military surveillance imposed on the whole district which extended to proscription of the mere word 'massacre'.

The importance of the timing will become clearer if I say this: had I not launched the Sabra and Shatila project when I did – had I, let us say, initiated a similar project now – various problematic factors would have arisen, notably demographic and psychological ones.

In conclusion, the importance of this work springs basically from its timing; history is established direct through people's collected memories and awareness.

The second phase: the collection of names

The Israeli Commission of Inquiry into events at the refugee camps led, on 7 February 1983, to the issuing of the famous Kahan Report. The report was not, it must be said, without its democratic elements; yet this does not excuse the absence of conclusions that might have been drawn from data available in the report itself, or the presence of errors of information and misleading figures. We might, as one example, note the statement (taken from the secret report mentioned earlier) concerning the number of women and children victims, where the number of females was put at 15, the number of children at just 20!

What human mind, or humane conscience, can believe such a thing, when a single photograph or a single piece of television footage has revealed a larger number? Equally, a single witness will speak of more victims than this.

Until I read the Kahan Report, I believed in the philosophical statement made by the British historian Arnold Toynbee: 'Every increase in numbers produces an increase in suffering. But it is impossible to be wicked or criminal more than one hundred per cent.' He was responding to Yaacov Hertzog, the then Israeli ambassador to Canada, in a famous debate that took place in 1961. Toynbee had drawn an analogy between what happened to the Palestinians at Deir Yassin in 1948 and what happened to the Jews in Europe at the hands of the Nazis. Hertzog had become furious at this, shouting that a few hundred Palestinians at Deir Yassin should not be mentioned in the same breath as the millions of Jewish victims of the Nazis. Toynbee's meaning was that it is enough to kill once to become a killer.

After reading the Kahan Report, I became convinced we were living in the time of Kahan and Hertzog rather than the time of Toynbee. I see no need, now, to express just how much anger and grief I felt whenever I laid down the report during those bitter days. But I do see a need to point out what I learned from it: namely, the extent to which facts can be distorted through incorrect figures.

Prior to the publication of the Kahan Report, I was, as I said above, gazing into the depths of human tragedy. I would hardly, for example, interrupt a weeping mother to say: 'What's your daughter's name? You've been talking about her for a full hour, and you haven't mentioned her name yet.' There was no way I felt I could ask such a question before the Kahan Report was issued. What difference did it make whether her daughter's name was Leila or Mariam? Besides, the very mention of the name might deepen the mother's anguish – in contrast to another woman who never stopped repeating the name of her daughter, Zainab, whom she had sought for a full week before finding her. When she did find her, she began weeping all over again, and went through with the burial thanking God her daughter's beautiful face had been only slightly marred.

After the Kahan Report, I made up my mind to seek out names and numbers. I also decided to publish the interviews in a subsequent book, and to publish the list of names in a special appendix out of respect for the victims' memory.

The starting point for the collection of names was a new tendency in the questions asked. It became mandatory to ask families the names of their victims, along with any they knew among neighbours and relatives and friends. I naturally had to explain to victims' families the reasons for my interest in the names and how important their help would be in providing accurate information, in the event of my managing to produce a book about the massacre.

It must be said that they co-operated overwhelmingly. It must also be said that, for all this co-operation, interviews with victims' families alone could not lead me to all the names needed. The scope of oral history is, after all, never such as to cover everyone involved in a common experience. What, then, was I to do?

My next step was to approach workers in various humanitarian institutions, with a view to collecting their testimonies and lists of names. These were the people who had entered Sabra and Shatila, working for two weeks without respite: collecting victims' bodies from the roads, alleys and houses;

digging out bodies buried by the bulldozers; facilitating the identification of victims by their families, and recording the victims' names.

However, because the Sabra and Shatila massacre was totally suppressed at the time, I could not tell civil defence workers of our aim to document events. I needed press cover, which would provide legitimacy, not to mention ease in moving from the subject of the Israeli invasion as a whole to the massacre as a specific event.

I applied to a young woman journalist, Muna Sukkarieh, who was a friend of mine and an up-and-coming figure in the Lebanese press of the time. She threw herself into the task with enormous courage and enthusiasm, and recorded a number of interviews to the enrichment of the Oral History Project, especially in the phase involving the search for victims.

When Muna tried to ask rescue workers or the civil defence, at humanitarian government or international institutions, about a list of names, she met with a blank wall: the lists were classified. Some workers did in fact tell her their (non-governmental) institutions had listed victims' names, and they asked for time to submit a case to their superiors and prepare the lists. However, when she returned to make enquiries a few weeks later, she failed to get a single list. Everyone backed out, with various excuses. Perhaps the excuses were justified.

Faced by this retreat, I had to find another way. It was evident that fear was killing the will even of patriots and those willing to help. It was evident, too, that lists of victims' names were one of the red lines everyone feared to cross. I felt constantly frustrated. Nevertheless, I had to go on, and tried a third means.

It was 1983, under the regime of President Amin al-Gemayel, who had been elected by the Lebanese Parliament following the assassination of his younger brother Bashir. In contrast to the latter, Amin was favourably regarded in West Beirut circles, having from the first given the impression of being more moderate and more considerate of the feelings of all Lebanese, and even of Palestinians. His period was, nonetheless, still marked by subjugation to Israeli hegemony, and the Lebanese Forces, from which the two President brothers had come, were still effectively dominant in the various government cadres. There was widespread frustration at the 17 May agreement between Lebanon and Israel, for this, if implemented, would place Lebanon under Israeli hegemony even in times of peace.

The same Lebanese Parliament that approved this 1983 agreement annulled it the following year. Indeed, growing national resistance to the Israeli occupation was the major factor spurring the deputies on to effect the annulment.

Thus, between 1983 and 1984, between the approval of the agreement and its annulment, I saw a ray of hope, nourished by the continuing growth of the Resistance. In the meantime, though, my only access to Lebanese officials I knew and trusted was to Dr Abdul Rahman al-Labban, a psychiatrist and a true human being in every sense. He was also Minister of Social Affairs in the government of Prime Minister Shafiq al-Wazzan. I submitted the problem to him and requested his assistance in retrieving at least the lists adopted by the Lebanese government from the government and international humanitarian organizations. His response came faster than I had expected: after just 24 hours there were, on my desk, copies of the lists of the International Red Cross and the Lebanese Civil Defence, along with a number of further documents.

I was thus on a sure footing with the names – though it should be noted that the two lists in question have never been published, at least up to the time of writing this Introduction.

My chief discovery on analysing these authorized lists and comparing them with the list I had derived from the Oral History was that the number of individual names significantly exceeded all those I already had. It was imperative, therefore, to go on searching for further, unofficial and unauthorized lists. Since the civil defence workers had backed off from their promises, the only course was to launch a personal private project with a view to listing the names and collecting all possible information about the victims themselves. In other words, it was back to square one.

And so a fourth stage became necessary: the collection of victims' names. This involved, initially, the launch of a statistical field research project, with the distribution of uniform questionnaires among victims' families and witnesses of the massacre. Such a project could not, however, go ahead without major changes on the political and security front. This will be touched on below.

There was, it should be noted, a positive correlation between the later field research (in 1984) and the retrieval of lists of names at that time. The main reason for this, perhaps, was the calibre of the team I had assembled to enter the massacre district and distribute the questionnaires, for this lessened the embarrassment of a number of institutions that had earlier refused to provide copies of their own lists. With field research being carried out in any case, they relented, handing over whatever they had.

A few further lists of names were released in recent years, before the massacre was 20 years old. Finally, the sources of reference for the names of victims, comprising victims and those abducted or missing, numbered 17.

On the basis of these sources, the total number of victims reached 906; the number of those abducted or missing, 484. Thus the total number of names available to us, for victim/martyrs, abducted and missing combined, was 1,390; none of the abducted ever returned, nor were any of the missing ever found. This figure is almost double the estimated figure of 700–800 victims adopted by the Kahan Report on the basis of Israeli Defence Forces information. The real figure, even after all the individual efforts made to supply names, can only be guessed at.

I would conclude this section by admitting, frankly, that the collection of names was the most difficult operation in the entire documentary work. Shortcomings still remained up to the time the field study was completed.

The third phase: the Field Study Project

Convinced, finally, that the documentation of victims' names through the collection of

as many lists as possible could not even approach the minimum estimated figure, I decided to prepare for a field study.

Such a study became a clear possibility following the events of 6 February 1984 which had a major impact on the contemporary history of Beirut. Up to then West Beirut had been, in principle, under the control of the Lebanese Army as a whole; in reality it had been subject to control by particular members of the Lebanese Forces serving in the army. 6 February saw a radical change in the balance of power within the army, as the 6th brigade forced its way into West Beirut and succeeded in driving out the 2nd brigade that had held effective control to that point. In appearance power had simply been transferred from one brigade to another within the same army; in fact power had passed from one set of influential officers and soldiers of the Lebanese Forces to another influential group belonging to the National Groups (as they were then called).

This transfer of power had major implications for the Sabra and Shatila district. It meant, quite simply, that the Lebanese Forces, accused of carrying out the massacre and in control of security by virtue of their presence in army positions in the camps, no longer had their soldiers and officers in the district. In their place, members of the Amal Movement took de facto charge of the camps' security. This movement had been founded and launched by Imam Moussa al-Sadr as a movement for all deprived people, and it was a national movement with Arab principles.

The country was, at this time, impatiently awaiting the formation of a new government. In the meantime, men and women went on distributing the questionnaires, one for each victim, including the information set out below.

First the particular category of victim was specified: whether martyr, abducted or missing. Next came, most importantly, gender, age, nationality, place of residence, profession, economic situation and fate. Details of victims included identification of the body, exact place where killed (where possible), and the exact date of the killing to the day and hour (where possible). As for the abducted and missing, details chiefly covered the exact place, the date and the availability of witnesses.

The second kind of information related to Palestinian families, chiefly covering place of residence prior to 1948, movements since 1948, loss of family members in the course of these, and the exodus following the massacre.

The district where the massacre took place was divided into sections, and volunteers were similarly divided into evenly numbered groups. They began by questioning the closest relatives and neighbours, then moved on to more distant sources.

The questionnaires finally totalled 530: 430 for martyrs and 100 for abducted. We knew from our estimates that the number of abducted and missing was actually far greater, but we had to stop at 100 for purely humane reasons: the families of those abducted and missing had insisted on discussing sons and relatives abducted from the mid-1970s on, since the Tall al-Za'tar siege and the time of the famous 'Forces' checkpoints just outside Beirut. They would insist, when filling out the questionnaires, on including these names of people previously abducted. Intially we felt unable to refuse. As we went on, however, we found we were raising families' hopes for the return of their loved ones abducted and missing. Finally I decided to stop at 100 to avoid reviving pain and dashing hopes.

The really difficult part of all this was the conversion of human experience into numbers and percentages. Yet someone had to do it, in response to the misleading figures provided before. Attempts to launch a similar field study now would not, certainly, be without significance, but it would be extremely hard to arrive at results as accurate as those we contrived to obtain less than two years after the massacre.

When all phases of the project were finalized in the summer of 1984, computer systems were still limited to certain institutions and not widespread in homes. Moreover, computer analysts were few. I had to hunt round to find one, and, by the spring of 1985, had finally succeeded. The expert did an excellent job and, after two weeks of unremitting toil, she handed over the completed charts for the field research, including all the required figures and percentages.

* * *

The oral history venture was, then, accompanied by the collection of names, and followed by a field study, the latter, by its nature, leading to the retrieval of lists of names unavailable before. Other outcomes of the field study were that I became acquainted with new families and conducted new interviews in Sabra and Shatila. As such, the Oral History Project could effectively only end when developing research had led to the finalization of the other two projects. In many cases overlapping among all these projects led to an expansion of their framework.

If I could return today to the atmosphere of that period, on the psychological level at least, the present summer of 2002 would seem a different world. Research of this kind was then hampered, primarily, by the refusal of the Lebanese authorities to reveal the facts, and not only by hiding away the official Lebanese report concerning the massacre.

This negative situation imposed absolute secrecy. We had more to fear, too, than break-ins leading to confiscation of tapes and papers, or project workers being prevented from operating. There was, over and above this, the unrelenting anxiety from the general atmosphere, which frequently forced us to prolong the project time in a way that would have been unjustified in other, similar projects.

Outside the country things were remarkably different. A number of testimonies, articles and photographs about Sabra and Shatila appeared abroad, such as the articles of Robert Fisk and others, the investigations of Sean MacBride and others, the testimony of Jean Genet and others. There were also conferences held in many capitals and cities throughout the world, especially in the three years following the massacre; the most important being held in Cyprus, Oslo, Athens, Tokyo and Bonn.

In the 1990s, we began to read newspaper testimonies that used full names for the first time, without any fear – whereas proscription of the publishing of names had been a basic condition for witnesses of the massacre immediately following the event.

Parts of the book

As noted above, this book entails more than one research methodology. It is in fact in two basic parts, plus a conclusion and appendices.

Part I comprises six chapters and is based primarily on oral history as recounted by the victims' families and by witnesses. Chapter 1 deals with historical time and place. Chapter 2 covers the encirclement of the district by the Israeli Army. Chapters 3–5 treat the events of the massacre according to the time schedule, each of the three days being accorded a separate chapter. Chapter 6 contains the testimonies of survivors and of workers in the humanitarian organizations during the search for the victims following the massacre.

I have selected 46 personal accounts of the tragedies of particular families or individuals, distributed within the chapters according to the time schedule: each chapter – each day in other words – has its own accounts, given separate headings and also serial numbers to separate them from the others. Where events were not concluded in a single day, we return to finish the account later; the 'main actor' in accounts of the massacre is not the person but rather the hour, or even the minute.

Part II comprises two comprehensive chapters, with two main subjects.

Chapter 7 provides analysis of the results of the field study I undertook in spring 1984. The relevant charts, figures and percentages provide answers to a number of questions raised at the beginning of this Introduction. Chapter 8 is analysis of the number of victims emerging from the lists of names provided by the various original sources, and from the estimated numbers based on the reports of commissions and on a number of authorized sources.

The Conclusion discusses the question of who was responsible.

The book contains four appendices. Appendix 1 contains 28 tables related to Chapter 7. Appendix 2 lists victims' names, based on 17 sources as stated above. Out of respect for the victims' memories, the source or sources from which the name has been derived is given, together with what basic information we had available. This appendix is followed by an appendix of photographs and a further one of maps. It is not inconceivable that others will be able to add to these appendices in the future, based on other witnesses and documents.

Last word

This is not a definitive piece of research about Sabra and Shatila; everything so far released about the massacre, this book included, remains deficient. The full horrifying picture of the massacre will not be supplied till the diaries of victims' families witnessing the events are published, including the diaries of people who were still adolescents during those three bloody days.

By the same token the picture will not be complete until the witnessing Israeli soldiers and officers, along with the attackers themselves, have matured appreciably. Those large numbers of people who watched or took part in the massacre were mostly in their twenties or thirties then. Some of these, inevitably, will recount their memories after they retire.

Research into massacres can only be said to end, finally, with the death of all the witnesses and killers. This implies the passage of two, even three generations.

Part I

Testimonies and Accounts

Oh slow dawn of Beirut
Quicken your pace a little.
Quicken your pace so I may truly know
If I am dead or alive.

Mahmoud Darwish
'Praising the High Shadow'

1

The Place and the Residents: Between the Emigrations of 1948 and 1982

On 29 November 1947, the General Assembly of the United Nations issued the celebrated Resolution 181, known as the Partition Resolution. This proposed the termination of the British Mandate in Palestine at the earliest opportunity, along with the subsequent partition of Palestine into three parts: one for the establishment of an Arab state; one for the establishment of a Jewish state; and a third comprising the city of Jerusalem with its surrounding villages and territories, to be subject to a separate international order administered by the United Nations.[1]

The Resolution was enthusiastically received – regarded indeed as a significant victory – by Jews both in Palestine and throughout the world. The Arab Palestinian people, in contrast, met the proposed partition with a declaration of mourning, strikes and revolt. They, after all, were the people who had resisted the British Mandate over three decades, striving to create a single democratic Palestinian state based on their own historical, political and natural rights, and on their continuous presence in the country since the seventh century AD. Iraq, Jordan, Lebanon and Syria had all achieved their independence. Why should Palestine not do the same?

On its side, the Jewish/Zionist Movement, established since the tail end of the nineteenth century (1897), had agreed on what subsequently became known as the Basle Programme. This embodied four objectives, of which the most important was that 'Zionism strives to create for the Jewish people a home in Palestine secured by public law.'[2] Zionist endeavours to establish this homeland/state for Jews were based on an Old Testament claim – to the effect, briefly, that Palestine was the Promised Land – and on a historical claim involving, among other things, the establishment of the Kingdom of David and Solomon 3,000 years before. As for the endeavours of Zionist leaders to obtain some kind of promise or support on the international level, beginning with Theodor Herzl, on through Chaim Weizmann, and ending with David Ben-Gurion, these were founded primarily on common interests with the colonialist centres of power: with London during the First World War and with the United States, correspondingly, in the Second World War. Just as London issued the Balfour Declaration in 1917, so the US-sponsored United Nations issued the Partition Resolution 30 years later.

The issuing of the Partition Resolution led to ceaseless turmoil, which resulted finally in the Jewish side gaining control over a large part of Palestine. With the end of the British Mandate and the declaration of the state of Israel on 15 May 1948, Arab armies marched under the aegis of the Arab League and the banner of saving Palestine. However, the First Arab-Israeli War swiftly ended in an initial truce, soon to be followed by other, secondary truce agreements between Israel and each of the neighbouring Arab states. These truces subsequently became permanent.

By the end of the 1940s, Palestine, whose area was 27,009 square kilometres, had for practical purposes been divided into four parts, none of these comprising an Arab Palestinian state. The Jewish/Zionist state was established in the largest part, which covered approximately three-quarters of Palestine, while the remaining land west of the River Jordan was joined to the Jordanian state, the Gaza Strip was placed under Egyptian administration, and the Himmeh region was annexed to Syria. Lebanon made repeated demands in the course of the 1949 Lausanne Conference for Western Galilee to be placed under its administration and control, but these met with no success.[3]

The partition of the country was not, however, the worst the people of Palestine had to face; far graver was the displacement and dispersion of the people itself and the transformation of very large numbers of them into refugees.

Over the two years 1947–48, which witnessed bloody strikes and war in the country, some Palestinians emigrated, exactly as happens in the course of wars anywhere on earth. A great many, though, were specifically driven out, through the use of every kind of force, by the Haganah and other armed Jewish organizations. Then, following the emergence of the State of Israel and the formation of the Israeli Army, officers of the latter completed the expulsion operations. Official Israeli accounts repeatedly denied Israeli involvement in any violent and forcible expulsion of Palestinians. Nevertheless, the revelation of official documents a quarter of a century after the state's creation made it clear to numerous researchers (including Zionists) that these claims were false.

Throughout the second half of the twentieth century, the case of the Palestinian refugees took precedence over all other refugee cases throughout the world. It was, moreover, marked out by one significant factor. In the normal run of things, refugees fleeing unjust rule in their homelands refuse to return even if the state in question offers them immunity. In this case, in contrast, it is the Palestinian refugees themselves who have always insisted on returning home, regardless of the cost. The Israeli and imperialist powers have nonetheless kept them under surveillance; and these too are the force behind the naturalization projects – the alternatives to return – continually faced, and refused, by the refugees.

On 11 December 1948, near the end of the year of the *Nakba*, or Disaster, the General Assembly of the United Nations issued Resolution 194, famously known as the Return Resolution. This declared that 'refugees wishing to return to their homes and live at peace with their neighbours should be permitted to do so at the earliest practicable date';[4] and over the years a further series of international decisions expressed support for the full and inalienable rights of the Palestinian people. Nevertheless, while the United States approved Resolution 194 at the time, it never exerted any practical pressure on Israel, which persistently refused to permit the return of refugees, maintaining this position even after the convening of the Madrid Middle East Peace Conference in 1991.

Lebanon's proximity to Palestine meant that the country was involved with the refugees from the beginning, and this involvement constitutes the general subject matter of the present chapter. More specifically, the chapter deals on a detailed personal basis with the residents of Sabra and Shatila, focusing on the nature of life in this small part of Beirut, whose narrow alleys were destined to be the arena for the three bloody days of massacre.

Palestinian emigration to Lebanon

The harsh circumstances under which the Palestinians were forced to leave their land allowed them no choice of the country in which they would seek refuge. However, quite apart from the common land border with Palestine, Lebanon's ports of Tyre, Sidon and Beirut were among the nearest to those of Haifa and Jaffa, and it was only natural that Lebanon should receive large numbers of refugees.

In addition to those refugees – the majority – who left as a result of coercion and force, a number of Palestinians came to Lebanon of their own free will and choice. These latter were either from well-to-do families in the habit of spending the summer in Lebanon or from families whose original roots had been Lebanese: that is to say, those whose fathers or grandfathers had moved from Lebanon to Palestine towards the end of the Ottoman era, when the Ottoman state was single and unified and a degree of mobility was normal among its peoples. Even when rule in the Arab East, geographically known as the *Sham* Land, was transferred from the Ottomans to the British and French Mandates, many Lebanese continued to move to Palestine for work and residence – mostly to the mixed coastal cities, such as Haifa, with its projects and labour needs, and Jaffa, surrounded by its orange groves and arable land.

Such Lebanese families never, throughout the first half of the twentieth century, lost the family links with their relatives in Lebanon. Visits were regularly exchanged and, in view of this, a number of these families supposed they were coming to spend just a few months in Lebanon until things in Palestine had cooled down. This time, though, there was to be no return.

During the first few months, a number of international institutions offered help to the refugees. Later, on 8 December 1949, the United Nations issued Resolution 302, calling for 'the establishment of the UN Relief and Works Agency for Palestine Refugees', or UNRWA.[5] This began work on 1 May 1950, its initial mission being to strive to effect an improvement in the situation of the refugees, in collaboration with the local governments, and to supply work opportunities for them, with the proviso that such relief efforts should cease after one year. However, for various reasons, mostly economic and political, the agency failed to achieve this, continuing, instead, with its basic programmes for offering nutritional, medical, social and educational aid.[6]

The UNRWA is regarded in law as an international agency, insofar as it acquires its legitimacy from the General Assembly of the United Nations. It operates on behalf of the international community, while remaining nevertheless subject, in its operations, to the approval of the host state.[7]

Within Lebanon itself, various monasteries made donations of land to accommodate refugees, while individual citizens leased lands to the UNRWA for a period of 99 years. It was on these territories that the Palestinian camps, as they were subsequently called, were established under state supervision.

The number of Palestinian refugees leaving the country between 1947 and 1949 has been estimated at around three-quarters of a million, these being spread, proportionately, through the following countries and regions: Jordan, to which the largest number emigrated, then the Gaza Strip, the West Bank, Lebanon and Syria; and the UNRWA accordingly concentrated its services and responsibilities in these. As for the refugees who left for other Arab and foreign countries, these were scattered and small in number. As such they never appeared in UNRWA records and never received its benefits.

In 1951 the UNRWA carried out an official census of Palestinian refugees. The number in Lebanon in that year was assessed at 106,800.[8] This figure excluded Palestinians who had not registered with the UNRWA in the Lebanese territories, either because they supposed their emigration to be temporary or because they had no need of UNRWA services, or because they were simply too embarrassed at the thought of acquaintances seeing them in the welfare queues. In Parliament and among the people, the number of refugees, registered and non-registered combined, was generally believed to be around 120,000.

Such a number was undoubtedly high, given Lebanon's particular circumstances: the indigenous population, in the early 1950s, was still below 1 million; the area of the country was quite small; the country lacked employment opportunities even for its own people; and there was an unusual demographic distribution among the population – there were in fact no fewer than 16 sectarian groups in 1950s Lebanon. Touching this last, Lebanon was notably disinclined to tamper with sectarian distribution for fear of influencing the political role of one group or another; and, since 90 per cent of Palestinian refugees were Sunni Muslims, there was a powerful incentive to isolate refugees within camps for years on end.

This policy of containing refugees in camps was general throughout the 1950s and 1960s, and it was accompanied by a degree of painfully felt oppression and persecution, exercised under the pretext of a policy barring Palestinian integration into Lebanese society. Yet for all the bitterness springing from this, refugees retained positive experiences of the love and the humane fraternal feelings received from Lebanese on all sides. President Bishara al-Khoury made a point of going to Tyre to receive refugees, telling them: 'Enter your country.'[9] As for Prime Minister Riad al-Solh, who had visited Palestine a number of times and taken part in many of the country's national conventions, he took a special stand when, in its session of 4 September 1945, the Lebanese Parliament discussed the United Nations charter and unanimously recognized it. Prime Minister al-Solh (who was also a deputy) expressed a reservation vis-à-vis the charter, fearing that the United States might, at some future date, promulgate a decision on Palestine that would not be welcomed by the Arabs.[10] It was clear that the fate of Palestine had become subject to the will of the international powers that had founded the new world organization, and the United States was pre-eminent among these.

On the popular level, various women's committees, parties and popular organizations vied in offering sympathy and aid to the refugees, and individual citizens did the same everywhere and without exception. Even Christian Lebanese employers normally had no hesitation in hiring Palestinian labourers for their sites or factories. Dib, a mason from among the Shatila residents, says the following about his employment situation during this early phase:

In the beginning our relations with the Christians were good. We used to work alongside them ... Even the Christians used to like us, and we used to like them, and we went on working with them more ... They'd never cheat us or pay us late, they were straight.

We used to feel we were inferior even so, not isolated, no, but inferior. I didn't belong with them, I had no nationality, no social status, a refugee, the least word they'd tell us: 'Refugee, or ... so-and-so Palestinian.' A rung lower, I mean, and that meant degradation.

During the 1970s war, there wasn't a single one of us who didn't lose a child, or two, from the war with the Phalangists and from the shelling. My son died from a shell from the Phalangists, and so did plenty of others ... we used to get big shells from the East side ...

Everything changed ...[11]

Hana' Ahmad, a Palestinian teacher of Lebanese origin, tells of a similar experience of the way people would classify refugees. She was a small girl when her parents arrived in Lebanon to stay with relatives before moving to a private residence in the town of Shuwaifat, near Beirut. There she attended a missionary school. She says:

When we first came to Lebanon, I was very excited about meeting our relatives, it was my first visit to Lebanon ... In Palestine we had no relatives at all, and so it was very nice to meet my cousins whose photos I'd seen and names I'd known. And I think maybe that was why I didn't feel the same way as the others did about what it meant to be refugees. And my mother would always tell me we'd be going back to Palestine for sure when things cooled down.

But ... things never did cool down.

My parents got me into a school in Shuwaifat, which was known as the Miss Malek school. My girlfriends from Jaffa and Haifa, who were living on bare necessities, were the first to tell me about what had been going on in the camps. Even if they hadn't been living in the camps themselves, many of their relatives were. One of them, her father was an employee at the UNRWA, she'd tell us everything her father used to tell them about the suffering of the people living in the camps.

I had a friend from Jaffa, we were in the same class. Her name was Rose, and her sister was a teacher at the same school. Through her I found out that the salaries of all the Palestinian teachers were low, a lot less than those of the Lebanese teachers ... Maybe that was the first injustice I suffered from in my life.

I had a Lebanese friend too, her name was Salwa. She was a very close friend of mine, and she used to ask me about Palestine and I used to tell her. Not once did I feel she was different, until one day when we were walking in the school yard and another Lebanese friend of hers, from a different school, came by. She gave her friend so much attention I thought she'd forgotten to introduce me to her, out of excitement. But her friend herself asked her: 'How come you haven't introduced me to this friend of yours? Who is she?' To my surprise Salwa became embarrassed. She hesitated, then she pulled her aside and she whispered in her ear: 'Those are refugees.'

The word struck me, and I don't know what happened next. I ran right off ... and I cried ... and I cried ...

Even Salwa didn't speak out my name, but said: 'Those are refugees.'[12]

Palestinian refugees very commonly recall at least one incident where they were insulted, whether intentionally or not, on the mere grounds of being a refugee. Eventually the very tragedy of refugee status became the prime common denominator among the people of Palestine.

As time passed, the UNRWA's role developed till finally it had assumed responsibility for establishing primary, intermediate and then secondary schools, as well as ensuring sanitary and social services for all those refugees whose names were registered with them. These latter primarily comprised camp residents, since the UNRWA welfare services did not make direct contact elsewhere. Even those refugees living in groups on their own initiative, some of them in dire straits, lacked the right to full benefits. The number of these groups actually exceeded the number of camps: there were thirteen such groups in Lebanon, compared to twelve camps.[13]

The UNRWA was not, then, in a position to provide benefits for all refugees; and, even for those receiving such benefits, what was supplied was not sufficient to lead proper lives. Since their prospects of employment in Lebanon were poor at that time, Palestinians inevitably set off for other Arab countries in search of work. In the 1950s and 1960s it was the Gulf states that were readiest to receive Palestinians. Indeed, but for the hundreds of young men and women absorbed into the economies of those countries, the economic and psychological plight of Palestinian families, especially in Lebanon, would have been scarcely imaginable.

In 1982, the year of the invasion and massacre, there were, as said, twelve camps on Lebanese territory: Rashidiyyeh, Bass and Burj al-Shamali in the Tyre region; Ain al-Hilweh and Miyyeh wa Miyyeh in the Sidon region; Wiefel in Baalbek; Shatila, Mar Elias, Burj al-Barajneh and Dbayyeh in the Beirut region, and Nahr al-Bared and Beddawi in the Tripoli region. In terms of geographical area, the Ain al-Hilweh and Nahr al-Bared camps were viewed as being among the largest. Shatila was the smallest.

In addition to these, there was the Nabatiyyeh Camp, which was totally razed by Israeli shelling in 1975. The Tyre and Sidon camps were partially destroyed on a number of occasions, and those of Jisr al-Basha and Tall al-Za'tar were completely destroyed in 1976 as a result of the various civil wars within Lebanon, the second suffering prolonged siege. The Dbayyeh Camp was also partially destroyed.[14]

Whether such destruction resulted from Israeli shelling or internal war, it was always the refugees who paid the price, the main consequence being a growth in transfer between camps. Countless families moved from Nabatiyyeh to Tall al-Za'tar, from Tall al-Za'tar to Shatila or Damour, and finally from Damour to Shatila.

Legal status and security status

The legal status of Palestinian refugees differed from one Arab country to another. In some, such as Jordan and Syria, they legally enjoyed the same social and civil rights as the citizens of the host country. In most others, entitlement to stay and to work was subject to varying conditions. One Arab country alone (for all its initially warm welcome to refugees) deprived them of the most basic human rights with regard to mobility and work. That country was Lebanon.

The Lebanese state's persistence in disregarding the legal status of refugees reached scarcely imaginable proportions. The legal file contained just two documents – or rather one, since the second was actually an annex to the first.

The first document was a legislative decree issued on 30 March 1959, a full twelve years after the influx of refugees had begun; this called for 'administration of the affairs of Palestinian refugees by the Ministry of the Interior'. A second, presidential, decree, No. 927, issued on the same date, defined the jurisdictions of this administration. These two decrees might have been satisfactory had they dealt with relations between refugees and the host state: on refugees' rights as residents in the Lebanese territories and on their duties towards the host state. Instead they were limited to control of the Palestinian presence throughout the Lebanese territories, leaving actual implementation of this control to the military cadres.[15]

As such, there was no specific legal reference to serve as a basis for appeal or arbitration. Moreover, since they were not citizens of a member country of the United Nations or Arab League, Palestinian refugees did not benefit from the legal principle of reciprocity applied widely through the world.

State policy at this time was based broadly on an assumption that the Palestinian presence was merely an emergency and temporary one. As a result, conflicts arose over who actually had authority for decisions related to refugees: some decisions would be made by the General Security Department, others by the Ministry of the Interior, still others by the Deuxième Bureau (Military Intelligence) of the Lebanese Army. For all these, the primary concern was surveillance and control of refugees' movements and political association, with no regard for or interest in their socio-economic situation.[16]

The tribulations of those first 20 years of refugee life in Lebanon will be fixed for ever in the Palestinian memory: haphazard detentions without trial, mass punishments, fines on the most ludicrous grounds, prevention of movement between camps except by permission of the security authorities. This last was not easily gained. In many cases a refugee would be unable to attend the funeral or wedding of a relative who happened to be living in a different camp!

Detention and torture were applied mostly to young men who were members of political parties. Much detention was based on unjustified accusation: the moment a demonstration began in the streets of Beirut, Tripoli or Sidon, led by Lebanese parties with Lebanese citizens taking part carrying their flags and placards, security men would rush to arrest this or that person from the camp, even though they were well enough aware that a Palestinian from, say, Shatila Camp in the heart of Beirut could not possibly have been taking part in a demonstration in Tripoli more that an hour's drive away – he would, indeed, be at home in Shatila when arrested! Such detention was routine nevertheless, and was routinely accompanied by torture and interrogation. It might last for days, weeks or months.[17]

No less important was the intrusive surveillance in effect over these 20 years, involving as it did the constant humiliation of family members who had to report in advance any visit by a guest or relative. Women's charity committees had, like everyone else, to request prior approval for any visit in connection with their work. If not their members would be subject to interrogation and arrest.

Khaled Abadi, a Palestinian born in Tall al-Za'tar in the 1960s, grew up hearing of his family's security problems. He has never forgotten the scenes of oppression he witnessed as a young schoolboy:

It was the Deuxième Bureau that was responsible for the situation in the camps ... Security and social status ... anything civil wasn't really a civil matter at all. The relation of Palestinians with the Deuxième Bureau was military. I mean, the camps, from the time they started up till 1969, had relations with the Deuxième Bureau. So it was officers who were dealing with people. There was no civil collaboration, no ministry, the Ministry of the Interior was barely in evidence ... Even when they operated the Department of [Refugees'] Affairs, the last word was with the security authorities. The least you heard was 'Remove people ... and place others' – and then there was questioning.

After he was taken away, the detainee wouldn't be held with the judicial police or the gendarmerie. Rather, he might be taken from Tall al-Za'tar and sent to the Riyaq Caserne, the air force base. They used to take people and imprison them there. They used to keep people for a month, two, or six, with no one knowing what they were accused of, no one, no lawyer, and no one saying why they were imprisoned ... no one ...

I recall the gendarmerie station at Tall al-Za'tar. We used to pass by it every day on the way to school. We never spoke as we got close. Abu Abboud, the man in charge of the station, was more famous for us than Charles Hélou, the President of the Republic. One day I'll never forget, they came suddenly to our house looking for weapons, and they didn't find anything, but they still dragged my father out forcibly, in front of our eyes, and he disappeared ...

More than once they arrested my father ...

People suffered a lot ... until the Revolution came.[18]

As for Dib, the mason, he laughingly tells of the time in the 1950s – and Palestinians rarely laugh when describing events of the 1950s and 1960s – when a microphone was lost at a police station at the Wiefel Camp in Baalbek:

Once, at Baalbek Camp, at Wiefel Camp, the microphone they used to give out orders at the police station was stolen. They started coming and screaming: 'Muhammad, you, you, you ... come here. Seven, eight, ten, come here ... you're going to Beirut.' In Beirut they'd get them to the Deux-ième Bureau Centre, and they'd flog them really hard, they hit them hard, kept on hitting, hitting, for no reason. They kept on whipping them for two hours, three, from morning till evening. In the evening they'd tell them: 'All right, you can go ... '

Next day, same story: 'You come here, you, and you ...' Every day they'd take around seven or eight, the whole camp went from Baalbek to Beirut, to the Intelligence Centre ...

I mean ... [Mu'allem Dib started laughing all over again] as if everyone, on his own expense, had to go from Beka'a to Beirut, get hit, and come back.[19]

Refugees had no complaints about lack of employment during the three years following the Disaster: they worked in the vocational, agrarian and other sectors. As for the well-to-do ones, these had brought enough money to be able to open shops or make their contribution to economic institutions. Moreover, the UNRWA institutions absorbed numbers of teachers and employees, quite apart from supplying monthly welfare benefits during this initial phase, including most of the basic stocks of food.

However, when the truce was signed between Lebanon and Israel on 23 March 1949, it became clear the refugee problem might be a lasting one, and the government of Abdallah al-Yafi began, in consequence, to cut down on work opportunities for refugees, disregarding agreements concluded by the UN organization with earlier governments calling for the employment of refugees in the various development sectors. In addition, it would be unjust to consider any financial crisis caused by the refugees' presence and the work opportunities provided for them without also considering the revenues Lebanon gained from the Palestinian presence at that time. The most important of these were: capital imported and invested by well-to-do refugees, donations reaching refugees from various Arab and Islamic peoples and nations, the very considerable proportion of the UNRWA budget devoted to Lebanon, and the sums remitted monthly by those able to work abroad.

Nevertheless, the government decided it had no alternative but to restrict work opportunities, even render them impossible in many cases. By the end of 1951 it had issued a law forbidding any Palestinian to go on working without a work permit, while all new job applicants had to obtain a work permit in advance. In other words, Palestinian refugees were now subject to the same law applicable to foreigners. Such a permit had not previously been required; now it was a legal requisite and obtaining one was not easy in practice.[20]

The law was the subject of vigorous controversy in the Parliament. Political, economic, ideological and sentimental considerations all overlapped. Some 50,000 Lebanese were unemployed, and these, it was claimed, should have priority. The fact that refugee labourers earned far less than their Lebanese counterparts was also raised. However, those bringing up the issues had to be content with words. The most realistic solution was, it was decided, that put forward by Deputy Pierre Eddé, who said in Parliament that the refugee issue was a matter for all Lebanese. Everybody (he went on) agreed the Palestinians should be helped, Lebanon being a refuge for all oppressed people. Nevertheless, the Lebanese government was incapable of handling this problem alone, and he suggested participation by the Arab League and the UN.[21]

Deputy Emile al-Bustani's speech at the session of 13 December 1951 was characterized by the humane and Arab commitment, and the courage, for which he was celebrated throughout his economic and political career. Addressing the Prime Minister, he said:

I have asked you what you intend to do about the matter of the refugees, whose only guilt was that they happened to believe in the Arab leaders' deception. You answered that the government would take care of them. What has this care amounted to? ...

The refugees, sir, did not come as strangers when they received the fatal blow, and we are responsible, along with the other Arab governments, for the disaster that has been inflicted upon them ...

Does the government take satisfaction in controlling and persecuting these Arab refugees, while the Jews in this country go back and forth as they please? What has the government done against the Jews of Syria and Iraq, who came to this country and settled here? ...

I know an Iraqi Jew who came to this country and settled here, and who issues orders and prohibitions just as he likes. I was present once at a party on a yacht, and this Jew, speaking of Palestine, said publicly that the Lebanese government should make up with Israel. This Jew and others like him do whatever they please, and we take no action. Yet we persecute the wretched refugees and prevent them from earning their daily livelihood.[22]

When Prime Minister Abdallah al-Yafi gave his response to the deputies who had raised objections against this law, he expressed still more sympathy and concern for the refugees, without, however, seeking to amend the legal text under attack. As for the Minister for Social Affairs, Emile Lahoud, his response was purely legal. It invoked, in brief, the need to adhere to rules internationally acknowledged: the Ministry normally accorded permission only to those carrying out specialist work that the Lebanese were unable to do; or, alternatively, it accorded permission to foreigners from countries that allowed Lebanese to work there. Under all circumstances, the decision to issue or refuse work permits remained with the Ministry. He concluded by saying that the refugee matter was an emergency, and that the Ministry was still being lenient with them and according them preferential treatment so long as their interest did not conflict with that of the Lebanese. In the latter case, however, Lebanese were more entitled and deserving.[23]

The general government position might have been logical and convincing had the Palestinian refugees come to Lebanon in search of work of their own free will, as was the case, for example, with Lebanese or Syrians who left their home country and travelled overseas to earn a living. The refugees, however, had come to Lebanon under duress, not in any attempt to improve their standard of living. There were two further considerations. First, the Arab states retained a special responsibility for the fate of the refugees, given the 'Palestine decision' freely made under the auspices of the Arab League. Second, appeal to the notion of reciprocity necessarily ruled out any possibility of work for Palestinian refugees, since the latter possessed no country and belonged to no nation. When they had possessed a homeland, they had, as a matter of fact, offered optimum work opportunities for Lebanese coming to live in their country; the Palestinian nation had never treated them as foreigners. It was paradoxes such as these that led a number of Lebanese institutions to stand against the labour law vis-à-vis the refugees.

As time passed, problems sprang more from misapplication of the law than from the law itself. In many cases where the law should have made it possible and permissible for a Palestinian to obtain a work permit, the permit was not in fact granted and the Palestinian remained without work. Approval or rejection of a permit was invariably subject to tortuous political processes, and also to bribery, and the socio-economic situation of the camps went from bad to worse as a result. The flagrant injustice suffered by refugees had all the potential for explosion.

In 1964 the Palestine Liberation Organization (PLO) was founded, and in the same year Lebanon became the first country in which a PLO office was opened and recognized. By so doing Lebanon achieved a diplomatic coup in the Arab arena. Yet the action produced no practical change to the internal situation of the camps, for the same oppressive policy was maintained. As for the subsequently established Administration of Refugees' Affairs, the most significant service it had to offer was the issuing of passports for Palestinians. It played no part in civil supervision of the refugee camps, and the oppressive operations of the Deuxième Bureau and the various other security authorities went on as before; they alone made the decisions in the camps, in large and small matters alike.

Lebanon now experienced a series of bloody civil and local wars, continuing over 17 years. This subject is beyond our present scope, all the more so in view of the various causes and various involved parties, both internal and external, which inevitably underlie a continuous civil war of this nature. On the one hand, the conflict involved a natural and fundamental tension between the rationale of the revolution – not just that of the Palestinians but of the Lebanese too – and the rationale of the state. On the other hand, there existed a cluster of internal contradictions within Lebanese society itself in connection with sectarianism, class struggle, nationalist ideologies and national identity, and the position vis-à-vis Israel and consequently vis-à-vis the Palestine question. This resulted in a very sharp split

over the Cairo Agreement, which was reached in 1969 during the time of President Charles Hélou, and was designed to regulate relations between Lebanon and the Organization. In practice the agreement widened the split over the Palestine question.

When the Palestinian Command, together with the various armed factions, moved from Jordan to Lebanon in the wake of the bloody events in Amman in September 1970, the Lebanese National Movement stood by it. Just a few years later it was the Lebanese National Movement itself that needed support, and the Palestinian Command then took the initiative and provided it. Such mutual support was natural in view of the common national and political principles involved. However, given the prevailing state of affairs within Lebanon, it effectively meant standing with one half of the country against the other.

The question remains, why did the Palestinian Revolution move on to Lebanon after quitting Jordan? Had this been planned in advance? Or was the choice rather one based on immediate practical considerations? Shafiq al-Hout, a member of the Palestine National Council, indicated the prime factor in his speech during the 16th session in Algiers in February 1983:

The Palestine Revolution did not move to Lebanon in response to official or even popular invitation. Nor did the Revolution select Lebanon in preference to other Arab nations, on the grounds that it held the strongest belief in Arabism or revolution. The Revolution landed in Lebanon because it [Lebanon] was a garden without a fence.[24]

Herein lies the essence of the Lebanese tragedy: that the country was a 'garden without a fence', and the hidden underlying cause for the escalation and spread of the tragedy in question, to yet more painful and terrifying levels, was that Lebanon, in the course of a series of bloody wars, had tended to become a number of gardens without a fence – embodying, too, the 'garden' of Sabra and Shatila. The latter prospered during the Revolution period: its houses grew wider and taller; Lebanese came to live there, along with Arab and Muslim peoples of all nationalities, till there was no room left; and finally the security authorities that had controlled the camps no longer wielded any authority over them (this point is developed at some length below). Nevertheless, this 'freedom' and 'prosperity' proved to be 'without a fence' indeed during the three-month Israeli invasion and the bloody three-day massacre.

From tents to compact houses

The Abdul Halim family, which had emigrated to Lebanon from Safad in northern Palestine, was, in 1949, among the first families to settle in Shatila Camp. Abdul Halim was then a young man, and he remembered the fig and prickly pear trees that once lined the main street known today as Shatila Street, which lies outside the borders of the camp. He confirmed that a large, shady fig tree once rose on the spot of the Ali Hamdar Café, whose name has become far more widely known since the days of the massacre, making it a familiar landmark.

The number of residents began to swell. A typical family would bring in relatives who had emigrated, say, to Tyre in the South or Tripoli in the North; and so the camp population grew within a few years from the initial 20 families to 100 families. The place came to be known as Shatila Camp, after Pasha Shatila, who had, in time past, rented the land to the UNRWA.[25]

Hajj Abu Ahmad relates how the UNRWA came to rent the land from the Pasha. In the beginning, he says, people sought refuge in the rural districts; his own family first moved to Ya'tur, a town in Bint Jbeil province, where they pitched their tents and settled. When it became obvious that going back to Palestine was still a far-fetched dream he came to Beirut and opened a bicycle shop in Ras al-Nab'eh. There was as yet no Shatila Camp, and he describes the place where the refugees gathered:

There were Palestinian families sitting in the Horsh. You know where they put up the children's swings during the Eid [feast]? You know Qasqas? There.

He goes on to describe Hajj Amin al-Husseini's attempts to secure the land:

Abed Bishr was a friend of, and believer in, Hajj Amin al-Husseini. He told him, 'We want to stay in al-Horsh, things are dragging on.' Hajj Amin told him: 'Check out a piece of land and we'll set up a camp in it.' Abed Bishr went off, and he was a friend of Pasha Shatila, and his authorized agent. Abed Bishr saw the Pasha and asked him about the land. He got this answer: 'You want it, you go and take it.' ... The land was all hills. This land used to belong to the French arsenal.

Hajj Amin phoned the UNRWA and told them about the land. They came and saw it, and they rented it from Pasha Shatila.[26]

Hajj Abu Ahmad then moved and settled in the western part of the camp.

Many other families moved in similar circumstances, including that of Mahmoud Yafawi ('Yafawi' is a pseudonym used for the purposes of this volume), which had emigrated from al-Kabri in northern Palestine. His family had lived for two years in the Qar'oun before moving on to Shatila Camp. Mahmoud likewise confirmed that the whole district had been planted with prickly pears and was full of thorns. In the early years the refugees relied to a great extent on UNRWA welfare. As for work, most men were labourers hired by the day, the majority working on construction sites throughout Beirut or as porters at the port. Within the camp itself the commonest profession was patching and repairing tents. Only a very few camp residents were traders, and this amounted to nothing more than selling vegetables from carts, or necessary items for the camp's women, or cigarettes for adults and sweets for children.[27]

In the early 1950s there were some single-storey houses occupied by Lebanese. As for the Palestinians, the UNRWA would provide them with tents: in Shatila Camp there were 18 tents, large and small. A large tent would provide accommodation for five families. The first UNRWA school was composed of three large tents.

The 'erection of the tents' developed only slowly, with the UNRWA, it must be said, playing its part. A typical family man would begin to build two or three *midmaks*, with tinplate on top (a *midmak* is a stone layer approximately 20 cm in height – a lucky refugee would build up to four such layers and then use cloth provided by UNRWA to finish the walls and ceiling of the shelter). The most superior kind of development involved building with bricks – but casting concrete was forbidden. Even the striking of nails was forbidden, according to Abu Qassem. Anyone striking a nail would be dragged off for questioning by the Deux-ième Bureau. And should anyone ask why, the answer would always be ready. Ceilings could only be made from zinc sheets because a cast ceiling implied continuity, over a prolonged period; and this was not appropriate to refugee life, which was a temporary matter pending return to Palestine.[28]

Hasan Abu Ali, one of the prominent inhabitants at the 'time of the Revolution', as people then called it, described Shatila Camp as it was in 1959, the year he arrived there:

Shatila was made up of tents. Inside there were six or seven bonds covered on top by wooden boards with stones over them. The Shatila residents who couldn't put stones inside the tent used to put zinc boards or tinplate – tinplate, that is, wrapped in cloth and reinforced with stones. Whenever it got windy, the tent would swell out like a balloon, and people would start running. Those who'd anchored the tent would hold on to the anchor; and those who'd gone beyond the required limits would reinforce the ceiling with wood or go up and sit on the ceiling. The typical family man would stand up against the wind with his chest, just so the ceiling wouldn't fly away.

The zinc ceilings were no easier. That's because the strong wind would tear away the boards, however well strengthened they'd been, and that was serious. Time after time people got injured as they chased the zinc boards that were flying around.[29]

Hajj Abu Khodr talked with equal eagerness about the erection development, complementing the two testimonies above despite a 17-year time difference between them and him – so united is the collective Palestinian memory over this bitter experience that it has overridden personal memory. He said:

At the start the tents were down to the ground. Later people started to develop, they'd build four

bonds, less than a metre. In the bottom there were four stones and the rest was a tent of canvas. Then people would reach the ceiling using zinc. When did it start being zinc? When people had reached the moon.

We were using zinc right up to 1970.

When the men came and the Revolution took off, you could get concrete. But from 1970 back to 1950, it was all zinc and tents.

And before that, I swear no one could bang a nail. During the time of the gendarmerie, I wanted to put up some stones in place of the zinc barrier, I paid 25 lira so they'd give me a licence … I paid a bribe in other words … and you had to finish building in one day … it was forbidden to bang a nail. Anyone banging a nail, of course, would be heard right through the place, and everybody would ask: Who's that? Why's he nailing? What's he nailing? And you had to say you were nailing the zinc: that was the only thing allowed.[30]

The beginnings of Sabra were little different from those of Shatila. In the words of Hajj Abu Ahmad:

Most of Sabra belongs to the Sabra family, you know the Dana petrol station, and that big building of the Sabras near it, they called the street Sabra after it.

At the start people settled in the al-Da'ouk cemetery, Muhammad al-Da'ouk, he had it made as a cemetery. When the Palestinians came, he told them they could stay in it. So we lived in Shatila, they and us, together. In the beginning it was all tents … Most of the people living in the al-Da'ouk cemetery were from Safad and Jaffa.[31]

Mu'allem Dib's memories confirm Abu Ahmad's account:

When we first came, there was no Sabra, from Dana onwards there wasn't a single house. When the airport was here, there wasn't a single house. The Palestinians came, al-Da'ouk let them live in the cemetery. None of these buildings were around either. They got built later. There were tents instead … [32]

In the early, lean years between the end of the 1940s and the end of the 1950s, Sabra, the district between Shatila and Tariq al-Jadida, was poorer, sandier and emptier than Shatila. It had only some alleys and old buildings, each of them merely a room and a kitchen, with nothing more. Palestinians began to live in Sabra from the late 1950s on.[33]

In the early 1960s, the state decided to dig a major street connecting Sabra with the Bir Hasan and Ouza'i quarters, the street now known as Shatila Main Street. Since it had to be around eight metres wide, the state, as people tell, had forcibly to demolish many of the houses standing there. As compensation, the state granted landlords the right to build new houses on a piece of land adjacent to Shatila Camp and Hayy Farhat.

This right to build did not, however, imply the right to build a ceiling, and so construction for Palestinians simply meant the erection of walls, without a concrete ceiling. This last remained forbidden till the start of the PLO period in the 1970s, and even then those too poor to erect the reinforced ceiling, or lacking direct connections with the military factions, were excluded. Such people simply had to wait. So it was that the Abdul Halim family had to wait till after the 1982 Israeli invasion, in which their small house was destroyed; they had no alternative, subsequently, but to build two rooms and a kitchen to replace the old house. The family was thrilled beyond measure when the new ceiling was cast in concrete.[34]

Initially Shatila Main Street was neither asphalted nor paved. For all its ample width, it remained a sandy street, not properly surfaced for cars. Little by little, small houses began to spread along its right-hand side, north to south, from Sabra to Bir Hasan. Building on this side had been forbidden. Indeed, it had been forbidden over the whole district formed at the time of President Camille Chamoun, whose borders extended to Shatila Street – this district belonged to the state. To prevent buildings being put up there it had been used as a site for refuse tips and as a sewer for the Sports City, so that it was filled with intolerable smells. Yet for all that, some people had no choice, in the absence of other opportunities, but to initiate construction. Largely due to special connections with the gendarmes, a blind eye was turned to illegal buildings which began to spring up from 1968 on. However, after the departure of the Deuxième Bureau and the gendarmerie from the camps, people focused construction on this relatively empty district, till finally buildings extended as far as the Kuwaiti Embassy and the Golf Court.[35]

Initially a large number of Syrians built and lived in this particular district, but many left after the civil war – the two-year war of the mid-1970s, that is – and returned home due to shortage of work. Southern Lebanese families settled in their place, especially following the Israeli invasion of southern Lebanon in 1978.[36]

Demolition of some buildings alongside Shatila Main Street once more became necessary so the street could be asphalted. This time, though, demolition occurred in the time of the Palestine Revolution and under its jurisdiction of camps and refugees. In fact, these new buildings, which had been erected on the sides of the road, encroaching on the sandy street itself, were simply torn down. Having no specific indication where Shatila Street began or ended, the surveyors in charge adopted arbitrary points starting from the Ali Hamdar Café, which had been built on the site of the celebrated fig tree, and on this basis worked to a straight line up to the end of the street intersecting with that of the Kuwaiti Embassy.

Many houses were demolished, as one resident recalls: 'They demolished Qassem Mukahhal's house, they demolished Dib al-Shafi's house; they demolished their houses and promised to build for them on the inside, when the street was finished.' The word 'inside' denoted the 'interior', that is, the district between Shatila Street and Shatila Camp. Generally speaking, sites in this spot were either rented out to the UNRWA or owned by Lebanese families. They were not, like the land opposite, between Shatila Street and the Sports City, the property of the state.

One of the anecdotes about Shatila Main Street, never forgotten by residents of the district, concerned the depth of the street vis-à-vis the sidewalk parallel to the camp, which involved a discrepancy of between five and seven metres. This had led one of the early shop owners to erect a 'bridge' between his shop and the street, to allow cars to pass over. With every road construction, asphalting or sewer installation, the level of the street would rise due to the added backfill.[37]

Such sloping is a particular characteristic of the land lying behind the Sports City as far as Shatila Camp, including the district very close by and known as the Horsh (lying between Kuwaiti Embassy Street and the camp, originally the Pine district). The land at the Sports City starts relatively high, then sinks to its lowest point at al-Horsh, large parts of this becoming near permanent swamp in winter, as if all the rainwater in Beirut had found its way there. Because of this it was infested with mosquitoes and flies.

The camp inhabitants have never forgotten the day a Lebanese minister first came to visit these 'swamps' in 1972, at the time of the so-called Youth Government led by Saeb Salam. The visitor in question was Henri Eddé, Minister for Public Works.

The Minister had been surprised, initially, to hear the request of these Palestinians who had ventured to knock on his office door, asking him to visit the camp. 'I,' he had said, 'visit the camp?' They had managed, eventually, to convince him that Lebanon was a single country and Shatila Camp part of it. The Minister agreed to come.

One of the men in question, Hasan Abu Ali, who later became one of those in charge of building in Shatila, recalls this visit, which took place in March 1972. He says:

Minister Henri Eddé saw the swamp and al-Horsh. At that time, people in al-Horsh hadn't started building yet, al-Horsh was empty. It was a beautiful pine forest. In the past, people had called it Horsh al-Nawar ['Gypsies' Horsh'], because of all the tents of the gypsies, who hadn't found anywhere else to go in the early 1960s. But even the gypsies had left al-Horsh, hadn't stayed there. We used to call it Horsh Tabet too, after its owner, so they say. And sometimes we'd call it Horsh al-Qatil ['Horsh of the Murdered'] – we were scared to go through it at night. There were dense 'forests' there, but it was clean. Where did we go in summer? Either we went to the seashore or to al-Horsh. We'd take a blanket, play cards; we had fun, we'd talk, and we'd gossip about people.

When Minister Eddé came and saw the lake (the swamp, that is), he said: 'This is unbelievable.

Unbelievable! I'll undertake to backfill it. How can human beings live in a swamp like this?'

And the Minister kept his word. In due course he had the swamp filled at Ministry expense. He kept his word over planting trees too, sending trees so we could plant the camp.

Don't forget there was a campaign then, by some officials and politicians, to have the camp removed, because it lowered the tone of the Sports City. Kamal Junblatt, who was Minister and Head of the Progressive Socialist Party, made a witty suggestion to the officials. 'To save you seeing Beirut in tinplate,' he said, 'we'll encourage the Palestinians to plant cinchona trees, one to each house. When the whole district's a cinchona forest, you won't see the tinplate houses any more.'[38]

Kamal Junblatt's chief source of fame, given Lebanon's sectarian nature, was that he had been leader of the Druze sect, despite founding his Progressive Socialist Party on the grounds of conviction and principle. He was well known, too, for his deep humanity, profound culture, and his wide-ranging philosophical, religious and economic studies. Less well known, except in private circles, was his rare and exquisite sarcasm, as illustrated in his proposal to cover the tinplate refugee houses with cinchona trees, so as to spare the eyes of those who hated the refugees.

The trees sent by Minister Henri Eddé were of the tall cypress kind, which would help mark borders for the street. These were in fact planted, but not all survived. Only two tall ones remained, in front of Abu Lutfi's house, to witness the days of the massacre.

As for building in the Horsh district (or Horsh Tabet, or 'Horsh of the Murdered' – Horsh was deserted at this time, and therefore a favoured location for acts of violence or even murder), not a single house appeared there before 1973, due to a total ban on construction. However, in the wake of the skirmish, in May of that year, between forces from the Lebanese Army and Palestinian Forces, 'Horsh of the Murdered' was turned into a refuge and shelter for needy Palestinians and Lebanese, equally divided. It became filled with small houses; each person in need of a home would uproot a couple of trees and build a small two-room dwelling. The Revolution Command would accord priority to build to the Lebanese, coming from the South or wherever, especially following the Israeli invasion of the South in 1978 and the immigration into Beirut that followed.

No one could have imagined that this particular district, Horsh Tabet, would become the first exposed to the massacre of the early hours, with the killers' knives or silent guns making no distinction between Lebanese and Palestinian.

The history of the district includes a further violation preceding the building at Horsh Tabet: the piping in of water from the airport district. The Minister of Water and Electrical Resources, at that time, was attorney Anwar al-Khatib, and he was visited by a camp delegation headed by the lawbreakers, supplemented by a committee of old men in their *kufiyyehs* (square pieces of cloth of 'pied de poule' design, folded and worn as headdresses – especially by freedom fighters, for whom it symbolised the Revolution) and headbands. The aim was that these 'elders', in their venerable popular dress, should enter the office first, so emphasizing to the Minister the heritage and authenticity of their people.

In fact a learned and prominent law professor like Mr Anwar al-Khatib, under whose tutelage hundreds of Lebanese University lawyers had graduated, needed no guidance to discern the thin line that sometimes separates strict application of the law from the most basic and natural human rights. He smiled calmly as the men made halting attempts to explain the situation:

Your Excellency, Your Excellency, we have come to tell Your Excellency that the camp now has water.

And we request the State, Your Excellency, to send us employees, on her behalf, to meter the water, so that we can pay for it. We don't want water for free, Your Excellency.

Minister Anwar al-Khatib replied, still smiling:

Go, may God be with you. So long as it's a matter of common interest. If we find the time, we'll send some people to meter the water in your homes. Go, may God be with you.[39]

The problem was not simply with water; the people also had to solve the other subsistence problems, all the more so as the directives of the Palestine National Movement and local factions were insufficient to meet all the Shatila residents' needs – either because these bodies had been too immersed in political matters, or because their administration of affairs involving local subsistence had been confined to a few committees or individuals. It was this that led some people to take the initiative and carry out their duty under the auspices of Fatah or other bodies; for example, the paving of the main street inside Shatila Camp and the installation of sewer lines.

Money was, of course, initially needed for such things, and it was decided to sell off the residents' shares of a six-month supply of kerosene, with which the UNRWA supplied refugees free of charge. Those acting on behalf of Fatah confiscated it without the organization's knowledge, distributing part of it, before the sale, only to camp residents in exceptional need. With the money so obtained they bought around 30 truckloads of gravel, dumping this on the road in question and obstructing the traffic, particularly where refugees passed to receive the bags of flour and other food supplies made available in the UNRWA warehouses. The men then suggested that the only way for flour and other supplies to reach the warehouses in the first place, for subsequent distribution to families, was for everyone to co-operate in paving the street, each in front of his own house. And so it happened. A building site sprang up, with men, women and children taking up hammers and shaping the stones. Students from the American University who had been sympathetic towards the Revolution, especially among Arabists, Communists and Syrian National Social Party members, also came along, and stone-breaking made swift progress. This was in the early 1970s.[40]

Just as the street-paving problem was solved, so was that of the sewage system within the camp. The latter problem could not, though, have been resolved before a solution had been found to the problem of overall sewer lines outside the camp; that is, in the large main street known as Shatila Street. This was clearly a matter for the Lebanese state, but the crisis was resolved, by accident or error, during the execution of a trench project. The original idea was not to install sewer lines at all, but rather to excavate a large trench, two metres deep by two metres wide, suitable for use as a mass shelter for people during shelling. It would, equally, help ordinary individuals move, during difficult times, between the Ali Hamdar Café and the end of the street at the meeting point with Kuwaiti Embassy Street.

Excavation works began, with compensation payments made, particularly to those whose homes were right above the trench. However, insufficient study of the project, especially regarding the difference in street levels, led to technical errors and to the withdrawal of the contractor in charge. Consequently the project was not, as planned, completed in terms of shelters or a transportation tunnel. The optimum solution was instead to use the trench to establish a sewage system through which all the waste of Sabra and Shatila could be discharged.[41]

The commercial market was developed in Shatila Main Street in the early 1970s. Before the advent of the Palestine National Movement and the various factions from Jordan in the aftermath of Black September – that is, in the autumn of 1970 – there had been no stores or even small shops on the right-hand side of the street coming from the Kuwaiti Embassy, or from the south heading north. There had just been a few residential buildings. From that date, though, the situation began to change year on year: shops started to spring up on the two sides, in ever greater numbers, till the street finally became a vital lifeline, a place where every item could be found. Everything was transformed. Indeed, the end of the street now became its beginning. Before Shatila Main Street was opened up, those coming from Sabra had regarded the Sabra–Shatila intersection as the beginning of Shatila, with the end at the intersection with Kuwaiti Embassy Street. Now, however, people coming from the airport or the sea were equally likely to enter from the latter end.

Abu Jamal, owner of a car repair garage, was among the first to build a large shop on the right-hand side of the street. He described, as follows, how some things appeared on the two sides of Shatila Street, before the June 1982 Israeli invasion:

The first things you saw when you came into Shatila Street from the embassy were the freedom fighters, on the right and left. Beyond that there was the house of Abu Ali al-Miqdad. Inside, his son owned a shop for casting iron. On the left there were offices, beyond that there was a sawmill, a sawmill belonging to the Shahrour, and next to that was a big garage belonging to Fatah. Opposite that there was a restaurant and a steel casting shop. There was a textile shop too, it belonged to someone from the al-Itani family.

If you walked a bit further, there were big shops rented out as warehouses, facing that there was a car body shop on the right, and beyond that there was a mechanic's shop of the Abu Khalaf family. They had mechanics' storehouses on the other side of the road as well. A bit further on was the shop of a Lebanese man, and another of a man called Abu Mahmoud, a store for big sawmill machines, saws and other large equipment. He used to work and do repairs there. Those were on the left, and opposite to them there was an office where the freedom fighters used to sleep. Next to that was a double-door car body shop, belonging to Palestinians. Next to that was another double-door car body shop, belonging to Palestinians again. Opposite to it on the left was the al-Miqdad family, further down there was a double-door garage that belonged to Ali al-Miqdad. That wasn't Abu Ali al-Miqdad's son. It was the son of Abu Suhail, he was a relative of theirs. On the right-hand side there was my garage – I had a big sawmill along with lodging for Jordanian labourers behind the garage. Opposite the garage on the left was a big sawmill, which used to produce oriental carpentry, couches and furniture. Opposite that sawmill there were some Palestinians' shops, and on the left of those was a restaurant and a tyre shop belonging to some people from the South, and there was an oil change shop, and a second-hand clothes shop – all the owners came from the South. Close to them there was a big blacksmith's owned by a Palestinian, who used to do general steel work along with spraying buildings and installing windows and doors. Opposite him there was a grocery store, next to a big restaurant and facing a Lebanese blacksmith's. There was a greengrocer's too, of a southern Lebanese.

Further down was a shop selling chicken and eggs, owned by some southern Lebanese people. There was a mechanic's shop too, owned by a Beiruti Lebanese. On top of it there was the factory of a Lebanese man for producing biscuits, Turkish delight and other things – it used to export abroad. Opposite that, a bit further down, there was a bicycle shop, a welder, and an Arab blacksmith who used to make hammers and chisels for construction workers, that shop belonged to a Beiruti ...[42]

Abu Jamal continued with his description of shops and their owners, repeating the same professions on Shatila Main Street heading north, and adding pharmacies, shops for repairing appliances, shops for repairing windows, shops selling home tools, new and second-hand clothes and home appliances, along with wholesale and retail shops for food and beverages. Even home furniture was available – not of the luxury kind, he said jokingly, but of the popular sort. As for the owners of these shops, they were Lebanese, Palestinians and Syrians.[43]

Shatila Street, so vibrantly described by Abu Jamal as it was in the early summer of 1982, was returned to by its residents after the departure of the Palestinian fighters. Nor did these residents find the enormous destruction they had anticipated. Some houses, certainly, had been damaged far more than others, while others still, inside the camp, had been demolished; yet for all that the destruction was unexpectedly small, especially as West Beirut had been subjected to thousands of rockets and shells over 90 days during the Israeli invasion and siege.

It was clear to the city's inhabitants that some districts had been targeted more than others, and others not even targeted at all. It was, though, contrary to all expectations that Shatila should not have been a prime target on the list. Why, people asked, should this have been? What was the underlying reason?

If the houses destroyed were few in number, this did not, nevertheless, eliminate the need for replacement of all the broken glass or the restoration of walls pierced by rockets, in addition to the cleaning up of the entire district. The OGER institution (a private contractor) had in fact come and cleaned up all the main streets, raised all the barricades, removed all dust and rubble, and searched out all mines with a view to removing them. So it was that this popular district, almost deserted during the summer of the invasion, was transformed into a fresh locale welcoming not only original but new residents – this because numbers of displaced Lebanese, unable to return to their destroyed southern villages, came to Shatila in search of empty offices and apartments after the fighters had left.

Yet during the three bloody days of the massacre, Shatila Street, this vibrant street, became the principal arena of the massacre. Every living organism and every stone in it was violated. This is attested to by Abu Jamal himself, who, as we shall read later, was actually standing on the rubble of the destroyed shops, which had reached the level of the street – had in fact become history. Abu Jamal speaks of the 'tragedy', that of stone as well as human.

Just as the Sabra district had been different from Shatila before the massacre, so it was afterwards: it did not meet with destruction and bulldozing in the same way that Shatila did. Development and construction had also been greater in Sabra, a large, organized fruit and vegetable market having been built there in the 1960s. This, commonly known as the Sabra market, was flocked to by housewives from all over Beirut, causing the district to flourish before it was assailed by civil war in the mid-1970s.[44]

Sabra further witnessed the establishment of the Ma'wa al-Ajaza Hospital (which translates as the 'old people's refuge') to the west of Sabra Main Street, on a side road between the Sports City and Sabra Street, known as Ghana Street, and the Gaza Hospital was established to the east of the same street, next to the al-Da'ouk cemetery. The former was owned by Lebanese, while the latter belonged to the Palestinian Red Crescent (PRC). Shatila itself had no hospital as such, but the residents of the camp and the neighbourhood were able to utilize the three hospitals, which lay not so very far from the heart of the camp. Shatila Camp lay at a focal point between the northern borders of Gaza Hospital, the southern borders of the Akka (Acre) Hospital, on Kuwaiti Embassy Street, and the Ma'wa al-Ajaza Hospital, which was on the west side, ten minutes' walk from the camp.

The general prosperity witnessed by Shatila in the 1970s, particularly after the asphalting of the road and installation of sewer lines in the middle of the decade, was paralleled by a doubling in the number of schools. Likewise, many public clubs and nursery homes were established, some as a result of local effort, others deriving from foreign help, such as the two centres receiving Norwegian and Danish funds respectively. As a result of further institutions providing classes in tailoring and needlework, local committees and labour and women's unions began to make active contributions to the improvement of families' standard of living and to the preservation of the popular heritage.

The Israeli invasion of the South in 1978 aroused anxiety over a further possible invasion, and this led various Palestinian organizations and factions to embark on the construction of shelters. When the 1982 Israeli invasion was launched, many shelters were in fact ready and prepared against the dangers of war. During the massacres, however, these shelters became, effectively, a kind of counter-weaponry. There, in the shelters, people would be buried alive, or their shattered bodies interred; or else they would be forcibly hauled out to be killed facing a wall, in an open space or in some district where the signs could easily be erased by the bulldozers.

Departure of the Palestinian fighters

The main Israeli pretext for the siege of Sabra and Shatila was the claim that 2,500 Palestinian fighters had stayed on there after the departure of the troops.

Israeli sources had in fact begun to talk of these before the troops even left. The number cited was not always the same.

I shall examine this claim, critically and in detail, in later chapters of this work, especially in the conclusion dealing with responsibility.

Here I shall confine myself to accounts of the departure from Beirut, together with the state of weaponry there. A fighter without weapons has no more significance, than inaccessible stores of weapons.

Every Palestinian fighter not classified as a 1948 refugee was given the order to leave. Among such refugees, however – that is, among those whose families had come to Lebanon as a result of the Disaster – there were people who had actually joined the Palestine Liberation Army or were among the senior fighters. In these cases, some involving people who had undoubtedly taken part in the fighting, the option, or the decision, depended on individual circumstances. There was, nevertheless, a recommendation that those regarded as 'wanted' people by the Lebanese state should leave; the Council of the Palestine Revolutionary Judiciary had in fact delivered all files and details of cases to the state.

Those fighters who received direct orders were ready enough to comply, believing as they did that the fate of the Palestinian Revolution depended on surviving these difficult times and picking up the pieces in new places of exile. The hard choices were those faced by the men to whom an individual and personal option was given. It was a fateful question for each one. Should he leave or should he stay? Those placed in this dilemma belonged ideologically to various organizations, just as they held a variety of jobs: fighters, nurses, teachers, administrative workers, and so on.

A Palestinian man from Fatah gave an account of these difficult days. When, he said, the talks with Philip Habib were in their final stage, a letter arrived from the General Commander to all cadres. A very short memo, it included a general circular on departure and about the ships, emphasizing that there should be no panic. New places of exile were not a matter of choice; rather, men should go where they were ordered to go. This man also said that, two days prior to the dispatch of the circular, around mid-August, Commander Abu Jihad had held an unofficial meeting with a group of his aides, at which he himself had been present. According to him, one of those at the meeting, Abu Mazen, had asked the Commander: 'Brother Abu Jihad ... How about us?' What, he meant, should those original refugees in Lebanon do, fighters and non-fighters? The speaker gave an account of Abu Jihad's reply:

Abu Jihad answered him as follows, word for word, and I remember this session was a restricted one, it wasn't a more general meeting ... among us, of course, were Palestinians and also Lebanese, of course we were all Fatah. It looked as though, up to that day, they hadn't taken a final decision in the Fatah Central Committee about the people of 1948, whether or not they should leave. Abu Jihad said:

'Personally, speaking as Abu Jihad, I'd say anyone who isn't Lebanese should leave – we're subject to commitments, as you know, that Lebanese people should stay, as the legal system in the country protects them ... I'd like to make one more thing clear: we're leaving the country on the assumption none of us will be coming back, and that's a crucial point. Everyone's leaving his people and his family behind, we don't know how circumstances will change. In other words, the Palestinian who's leaving shouldn't forget his people are here, and he shouldn't forget the camps are still here ...'

I remember what he said, word for word: 'You should know we're talking of an authority that won't come to build homes or lay carpets for you.'

The people there got scared, they were afraid whoever left wouldn't come back, while his relatives would still be there in the country – they'd be standing alone in other words. There was panic at the meeting. Each one had to make his own decision.

The problem was how to leave our people ... where should we go, we were taking ship for the unknown. That was the overall picture, and it wasn't being presented by just anybody but by Abu Jihad ... the person we trusted the most. He was sole commander as far as we were concerned.

And frankly ... we lived in a state of horror, horror, horror.[45]

At the same time, another Palestinian man from Fatah, who worked for the Palestinian Red Crescent, attended another meeting at the Collège Protestant, which had been converted into a field hospital during the invasion. Dr Fathi Arafat, President of the Palestinian Red Crescent Committee, was presiding, and he was asked the same question as Abu Jihad by one of those there:

'Dr Fathi, what if the [Lebanese] army were to come and take us?'

Fathi Arafat answered him exactly as follows: 'If I were to be walking with Bashir al-Gemayel, hand in hand, and I saw the Lebanese Army taking one of you, you there, or you there, or any one of you, I wouldn't intervene.'

Fathi Arafat gave the guy that answer. I mean, we felt lost like that. I went to tell it to the guys who hadn't been at the meeting, and then we all felt lost. We felt lost, because why would Fathi Arafat say that? We were expecting to be open to insults, but that they'd give us up like that? ...

How can I describe the situation we were in?

We were at a loss ... we didn't know what to do. What might happen?[46]

Between fear and loss, the crisis was born. On the basis of Abu Jihad's words, they felt that their personal safety and that of their people, and the preservation of their civil institutions, were a priority for the great revolutionary leader. He never asked them to stay as fighters, yet as a man in charge and as a human being he sensed the various aspects of the situation. He recognized that those who had originally sought refuge in Lebanon, had been born there, had lived there, were in no position to emigrate once more with their people. Even if they left, alone, there was no way for them to return.

The men requested a meeting with the Chairman, Abu Ammar (Yasser Arafat). He sent his apologies, dispatching instead the man in charge of the district, Fayez Freiji, to talk to them. Fayez Freiji was not, deep down, convinced of what he was saying. What he said was naturally similar to what the other superiors had said, to the extent that men began to envisage some kind of protest, or move. But what exactly?

The main questions facing those known as the 1948 refugees were 'What are we going to do tomorrow? Who will employ us? Where will we find jobs?' There were many other issues before them.

Other military commanders were no less confused than the young members. One of the latter told of what a Palestinian military leader had said to three troubled young men:

I swear, honestly, I can still hear his words in my ears. A million times we'd repeat his words and laugh. 'True,' he said, 'what can anyone say? OK, I'll go, I honestly don't know where, brothers, I'm not sure where I'm going. I'm boarding the ship without knowing where for.' Instead of him calming us down, we got tenser. Then he made the joke he became famous for: 'So, where do you want to go? Yemen? You can't find even an orange there.'[47]

After the first ship, loaded with the wounded, had left, the men requested a meeting with Abu Jihad, and he agreed to see them. The meeting was held at a centre of the Syrian National Social Party in the Raouché district. As the discussion grew ever more tense and vehement, Abu Jihad spoke as follows:

'I can't tell anyone to stay or leave … Our people are here, our children, our camps, our hospitals and our schools; but I say to the one who stays that the Lebanese state isn't about to come and build him a house and offer him a salary. The state may imprison him, just like all the Arab regimes, we have to face that fact.' Suddenly we saw him get angry and say: 'For myself, I don't want to leave you alone, I'd like to stay with you, but this is what's happened, and those are our circumstances.'[48]

Abu Jihad did not specify the names of those who were leaving or those who were staying, from among men who had been with their people since 1948. Viewing the matter not as a simple political one but rather as a human one, he left it to every man to make his own judgement according to his particular circumstances.

The men grew still more perplexed and the inner turmoil became worse. One of them suggested that they go with one final question to the PLO representative in Lebanon, Shafiq al-Hout, who, having been himself among the 1948 refugees, might perhaps be able to shed some light. 'He's not a military man,' they reflected, 'but he's a leader, and a Palestinian, and from '48', and they knew he was there in the country. They sent their query through one of the guards at the PLO office. The question was: 'What shall we do?' The answer came back the same day. 'Anyone who wants to stay must pay the price, and a couple of slaps are inevitable.'[49]

What these two men reported above was repeated among other organizations, for they had been in contact with their friends there and the situation was no better in those places.

However, that was not the end of the story.

Many men had made up their minds to stay then suddenly insisted on leaving. Many others had made their decision to leave then changed their minds at the last moment. These memories at least they could recall with laughter.

Khaled Abadi told what happened to him and two of his friends:

I had these two friends who were bent on staying. We'd reached the last days, then these two guys came suddenly while I was asleep, in the middle of the night. They opened the door as if they wanted to kill me, and one of them screamed in my face: 'Get up! Is this a joke for you, wise guy, preaching to us how we'll just be slapped a couple of times? Only a couple of times? We just heard on Israel radio that they want the Murabitoun to leave the country. If the Murabitoun left, who were born in this country, where would we live?'

Next morning the two guys left on a motorcycle, which they threw down on the road afterwards, and boarded the ship for Latakia.

One of them was a relative of mine, and his name was Khaled like mine. I saw his mother come next day with a pot of bamyia [okra]. She knew her son had stayed overnight with me several times, and she told me: 'Khaled likes bamyia, son.' So I had to tell her her son was in Latakia now.[50]

Khaled Abadi experienced the reverse of that of his relative who was so fond of bamyia. Day by day he'd take satisfaction from making his farewells; then, one day, he decided to leave. He got his suitcase ready and resolved to leave on the ship that had taken Abu Maher al-Yamani to Latakia. He was due to depart along with other comrades who had suddenly decided to leave. They numbered around 20 men, all from Abu Jihad's group, and they had been wearing the khaki uniforms required for departure, which they normally wore on a daily basis. As they approached the ship, they saw their leader, Abu Jihad, standing ready to bid them farewell, and alongside him was a friend of his they all knew, Ahmad Hassoun. As soon as he saw them, Ahmad drew Abu Jihad's attention, telling him: 'There's a group of men.'

Abu Jihad gazed at them intently. Then, as some of them came closer, he said: 'Are you men travelling? May God be with you. May He be with you.' They all said at once: 'No. We've come to say goodbye. We always come to say goodbye to our comrades.' 'But,' Abu Jihad answered with a laugh, 'you have *kufiyyehs* on your heads.' At this one of them, unable to bear the situation any longer, said:

I swear, to be honest, we don't know whether we're leaving or not. We're talking just the way we did when we were kids. 'We'll count to ten, from here up to the gangplank. If we reach ten, we go up, if not we'll come back.'[51]

Abu Jihad laughed again, and the men went back from the port, without counting to ten.

There is a third story, about another Khaled (this is a common name among Palestinians), Khaled Hamad, who intended to travel, but, having qualms about what he was doing, told no one he was about to leave. He covered his face with a red *kufiyyeh*, so that only his eyes were visible, and took pains to change his voice; and no one, in fact, recognized him until the last moments. There in the port, just a few steps from the gangplank, stood a woman, a neighbour of his, who would go down every day to say goodbye to those leaving, whether she knew them or not. He had seen her there a number of times. This time, though, to his surprise, he heard her say: 'What's going on, Khaled? What's going on? Nobody told us you were leaving.' 'No,' Khaled answered. 'I just came to say goodbye.' And he did not leave.[52]

Ibrahim Iraqi, the senior nurse at the Crescent, left to board the first ship carrying the wounded. He had registered his name for the journey and received all his friends the night before, so as to say goodbye. Then, at the very moment he was boarding the ship, he remembered his mother and his brothers and sisters. How could he leave them all behind? How could he? In a flash he had called on a friend of his to take over, and he left the ship in a car belonging to one of his superiors at the Lebanese Red Cross.[53]

Abu Muhammad Ali, one of Abu Jihad's men, packed his suitcase and left the rest of his things there in the room, so that the person coming to live in the place could make use of them. Telling his elderly landlady Um Said (al-Mughrabi) that he was leaving, he said goodbye to her, and she tearfully returned his farewell. When he reached the port, in the midst of the crowd he began to hesitate. At that moment he saw a friend of his on a motorcycle; and, giving him the suitcase, he asked him to take it back to his lodgings as he would not need it on his trip – in point of fact, he had not yet really decided whether to leave or not. He reached the point where those travelling had to board a truck belonging to the Lebanese Army, and indeed he took two steps up. Then he came back down, claiming to have forgotten something. The same day he went back to his room – only to find that Um Said, the old lady who had wept at his departure, had already rented it out to someone else.[54]

This phase of affairs was more problematic than the invasion itself. Those in command had no more answers to give, while the members began to be afraid of asking questions, all the more so as they had no confidence they would receive firm answers. The whole matter was one of outright despair.

A number of details remained pending: the fact, for instance, that half the camps had been wiped out, and the fact that half the refugees were now displaced once more, with no obvious present means of protection. The refugees' return to their camps, and the construction of camps for the purposes of protection, should have been ensured. One of the men explained the situation:

When Bashir came to power, it was a shock. Our people's main concern was whether Bashir had secured and approved the agreement, the arrival of multinational forces for protection. Bashir used to talk about electricity and water bills, he didn't address anything else, what about the security of the camps? The multinational forces, in the first place, take instructions from the State, so did Bashir al-Gemayel intend to ask them to protect the camps? What did he intend to do?

At that time we weren't able to locate Abu Ammar to ask him. At the beginning, during the invasion, anyone could see Abu Ammar, any day. You could ask for an appointment any time, or even drop by without appointment. It was different now, and there were a number of superiors we couldn't see any more. I was one of those who wanted an answer regarding Bashir al-Gemayel's position. Was he in favour of the multinational forces or not? As fighters in Fatah, we didn't normally pose questions to Abu Ammar direct, but through the man in charge of the organization we were part of. Now even he couldn't get to see Abu Ammar. Our overall military head and area supervisor was Nabil Ma'arouf [at present Palestinian Ambassador in Madrid]. We knew him by his pseudonym 'Abdul Mohsen al-Za'tar'; he was in charge of the *Iqlim* [district] committee, and a close companion of Abu Ammar's. Abdul Mohsen didn't answer us. Once, in front of me, and in the presence of several of the brothers, he said in so many words: 'Military – civilian – it doesn't matter – protect yourselves.' He came back and said: 'I've been trying to see him for two days, without any success.'[55]

The fact of the matter is that Abu Ammar stated his outright opinion in a final meeting of the *Iqlim* Command. The superior Fayez Freiji, who was naturally present, reported the details of the meeting, including Abu Ammar's answers to his comrades, as one of these recalls:

Abu Ammar was faced with two questions: Where are we going? If we do go, how about the others? These were two important questions for Abu Ammar to answer. This was according to Fayez, because he told us what happened in the meeting, as he was bound to do – he was living alongside us, after all, and at any minute we could tell him, that's what you said. Fayez used to tell us how, more than once, he asked Abu Ammar about the guarantees, and he'd say: 'I'm the guarantees, I have the guarantees', and he'd strike his forehead, point to his pocket, 'The guarantees are all present here [meaning that they were written down and in his pocket], and no one [meaning civilians] is going to interfere with them.' These words were said and

repeated in the meeting held after the election of Bashir al-Gemayel, of course.[56]

When a man of Fayez Freiji's stamp was persuaded, convincing others became easier, not least because, as he described it, Abu Ammar's 'words were firm'. Other organizations held similar meetings, and the men would talk among themselves and exchange their fears and news.

A good many of the commanders shaved and made ready for departure, especially those among the command units that had come in the 1970s. Their behaviour irritated some. Such irritation was in fact unjustified, since these men had been required to depart without delay. However, this did not prevent those living with their own people from venturing some hard words with them. 'You came and messed everything up for us,' one said, 'and now, apparently, you're going off as if nothing had happened.' Panic ensued, till, finally, there was almost a split among Fatah members, between the so-called '48 and '67 groups; but reason prevailed and the matter was settled. In addition, the situation made it necessary to hold a number of meetings for all the cadres, the largest of these being the one held in one of the Raouché buildings, with various union representatives present.

Weapons in and around Shatila Camp

How much weaponry was contained in and around Shatila Camp, the district surrounded by the Israeli Army from dawn on Wednesday 15 September? We need, initially, to examine the general matter of weapons held by the Palestinian factions following the fighters' departure from Beirut.

The PLO had possessed large stores of weapons, distributed through several parts of West Beirut. Before the departure of PLO Chairman Yasser Arafat in early September, these stores were handed over to Lebanese nationalist parties and forces; particularly to those forming part of the 'common forces', which had included both Lebanese and Palestinian fighters.

The quality of available weapons varied. They included the Czecha, anti-aircraft artillery positioned over tanks. There was also the quadruple Czecha 23 calibre, one of the most effective anti-aircraft devices, recently arrived from the Soviet Union. Large numbers of Katiocha and Grad rockets, together with handguns, were also handed over.[57]

As for guns held privately by the men, these were a problem, since orders issued before the departure had not made it clear to the remaining members what they should do with such weapons. As a result, each group made its own judgement according to the particular situation.

A group of these men agreed among themselves on a plan aimed at keeping hold of these weapons. The men in question had two things in common: membership of Fatah and the Tall al-Za'tar experience – they had been among those forced into a new emigration following the camp's fall at the hands of the Lebanese Christian militias in the summer of 1976. Their fate had led them to Damour, a town on the coast between Sidon and Beirut, but they had been forced to emigrate yet again after the Israeli Army, from June on, had stationed their tanks on the coastal road from the South up to Beirut. As a result they had had to be lodged in temporary homes and rooms through several districts of West Beirut, pending the end of the war and resolution of the conflicts.

The members of this group agreed to retain their personal arms for the purposes of self-defence, and in view of possible unforeseen circumstances, as long as the Israeli Defence Forces were still in this or that district on the outskirts of Beirut.

Abu Muhammad Ali was a member of this group, and one of those responsible during the invasion for supervising a large Fatah weapons store and subsequently distributing its contents to the Lebanese parties. As for those weapons still remaining in the store, he had, as he reported, agreed with five of his comrades to leave these in place. Should one of them travel or be killed, the rest of the group knew the place.[58]

Abu Khalil Mahmoud was another member of this particular Fatah group, and he described a further aspect of the group's experience regarding the personal weapons

they continued to hold during the war. He elected, in conjunction with the others, to transfer the weapons to the interior of Shatila, even though none of them was resident there. He said:

After the fighters had left, we started collecting our personal weapons, and we decided to hide them because we didn't know what was going to happen. There were no men in charge we could refer to. We made the decision among ourselves. I mean, before the fighters left, there were no discussions at all about what to do with individual weapons.

We thought of hiding them in Shatila, because we felt the camps were the safest possible place. None of us was from Shatila, but we knew a Palestinian guy who was a relative of a member of our group. He was from al-Horsh, his name was Muhammad, and people called him Shaykh Muhammad. He was ready to hide the weapons under the tiles in his house, which was inside al-Horsh, where they started the massacre later, and in front of the house was a big yard. This guy wasn't from Fatah, but we trusted him even so.

We started collecting and greasing and packing the weapons. I mean, we wrapped them so they wouldn't rust, because we were going to bury them in the ground, and we did, in front of Shaykh Muhammad's house. We'd smear them with grease, wrap them in nylon, put them inside a car wheel and close it up from both sides, they used to call it 'the wheel of the sea'. We'd pierce it on one side and push the greased weapons in, then close it up from the two sides and put it down in the ground. There was a good quantity. I mean, about the quantity, we were a bunch of friends, and each of us had one or two Kalashnikovs. Each one of us would get them ready and transfer them, and there were B7 grenades, and there was a new Diktaryov. The organization had new guns too, which had come in from China, Chinese Kalashnikovs, that is. That's what they handed over to us from the stores. No one had used them before.

We buried the weapons in the outer yard, then poured a thin layer of concrete over them.

I could tell you just how many weapons we buried. I had two machine guns and one handgun, and each of my friends, there were around five or six of us, had the same. But we also buried, with our weapons, the new Chinese Kalashnikovs, and we buried a B7 launcher and a B2 launcher, that's for the tanks, for the vehicles, but it isn't as powerful as the B7.

We buried them in a day, it takes a full day to cast concrete. And it was the last Sunday before Bashir al-Gemayel's death.[59]

That Sunday night, 11 September, these men went to sleep feeling reasonably safe; their weapons, they thought, were secure and ready for use at any time. All they had to do was pierce the thin layer of concrete then remove and clean the weapons – an operation that would, they estimated, take half an hour at the most.

The question, however, was this: were they in fact able to get to the weapons on the massacre days? Where were they themselves during those days? And did others succeed in getting hold of these arms? A still more important question concerned the availability of weapons in Shatila Camp generally and within the Shatila district as a whole.

The district of the Palestinian camps was far from being the safest during the summer of the invasion; as such, stored weapons needed to be taken out rather than the reverse. And Shatila Camp in particular was almost deserted in the wake of the constant shelling to which it had been subjected. There were, indeed, fears that the camp would be totally destroyed, and this led to the removal, at the start of the invasion, of most of the weapons hidden in the stores.

As a result, there were, when the massacre began, no more than two weapons stores in the whole of Greater Shatila (and these, as will be noted below, were blown up by those in charge of them). As for individual guns, the residents really had no idea what to do with them, since – as pointed out above – the departed commanders had issued no orders in respect of them. Even the local commanders had given no orders or recommendations. They were content to retain some of the weapons inside their offices for self-defence should the need arise.

Abu Muhammad Ali told how people would fling weapons anywhere, thinking this spelled security:

People in the camp got frightened after the fighters had left. They started throwing the weapons away. The camp became a target. They got frightened

because the camp was liable to inspections and raids now, and so people started junking the weapons, especially after Israel got in. And it was a really painful sight to find a gun or a rifle, wrapped up in 20 layers of newspapers and nylon paper, in the dunghills or piles of rubble, here and there in the streets of Beirut. The people in Sabra and Shatila threw away their weapons too, for fear of Israel and its microphones which had been bellowing out: 'Bring your guns to the Sports City' and 'Surrender and you won't be harmed.'

Let's remember, though, there weren't so very many weapons in the camp in the first place, because the camp was completely deserted, or nearly deserted.

I can tell you, during the invasion no one stored weapons in the camp or took them in there. Quite the reverse. The idea was to get the weapons out of the camp, because it was going to be a special target, so let's keep our distance, people thought.

After the commands had left, it was obvious the camp was the prime target for the Lebanese Army. People thought, for sure, they'd soon start looking for weapons.

I mean, there were no weapons in Shatila, except what were there in the offices, and they were for guarding.[60]

Entries in the diaries of Comrade Hussein, the superior at the Popular Front, regarding the situation in Shatila, confirm the statements of Abu Muhammad Ali and Abu Khalil Mahmoud (who were both from the Fatah organization):

The camp was not disarmed, but the Lebanese Army launched raids on residential quarters. There were many and various weapons on the 'dunghills', and remarkably … No doubt some members had hidden and buried weaponry that spelled danger for the family. But the general scenario was to get rid of the weapons … As for the weapons stores, those were handed over to the Lebanese National Movement, Murabitoun, Communist Party, etc.[61]

Abu Jamal, the shop owner on Shatila Main Street and not linked to any organization, provided a vivid description of the situation with regard to weapons and armed men:

When the invasion was over, we went back, we repaired the shops, I went on repairing for two weeks. Not one guy from anywhere dared enter the camp, and the camp residents didn't want to have him in the district. The residents themselves said they wanted no armed people there, while Israel was close by – we were no match for anyone, and we had women and children, so, please, we want no armed people in with us …

The camp residents started telling those who wanted to hold on to their weapons: 'For God's sake, if you want to have weapons, hide them and get out of here, we're peaceful people and we've no fighters left, and we don't want a single shot out of the camp.' And that's what happened – not a single shot was fired out of the camp after the people got back, and we didn't see gunmen like before, not at all. All of this, before any Lebanese army had arrived, no army, no nobody.

The actual people living in the camp, those who'd stayed and those who'd come back, wouldn't stand for gunmen there any more – we've kids, they'd say, our houses are destroyed and need repairing, our houses can't take any more shelling.

One thing I can tell you, I heard it from several people. Being dispersed for so long, in Hamra or Raouché or wherever, had taught them that their houses, however small they were or however much repair they needed, meant security because they'd all be together. What I'm trying to say is, there were a lot of people living in their houses while there was still no water, no electricity, the windows were hanging, and they were in the middle of repairs when all these things happened.[62]

Nawal Husari, a nurse at the Red Crescent, said:

I can confirm there were no weapons, that's because, when the freedom fighters left, they disarmed the camp. The fighters themselves collected the weapons when they left. I saw my neighbours with my own eyes, going from one house to another and asking around. If we'd had weapons, we would have resisted, but we're no fighters, the fighters had left.[63]

Um Akram, a freedom fighter's wife, said:

I used to wander around in Sabra and Shatila, and there wasn't a single fighter. I know the people, I was raised in the camp, and my husband's a fighter from the '48 group, I mean, he wasn't young any more, he was one of those who stayed and gave up their weapons. My God. If there'd been fighters, all those things, which wouldn't happen even in the jungle, wouldn't have happened.[64]

The above extracts demonstrate that the Greater Shatila district was not a secure place for the storage of weapons from the beginning of the Israeli invasion of Beirut on 6 June 1982. No new weapons were stored there right through the summer. On the contrary, weapons had become liable to removal to keep them safe while the war lasted. After the war was over and the Palestinian fighters had left, what few weapons remained were removed to ensure the safety of the civilian population.

In other words, the removal of weapons was a voluntary affair carried out on an individual basis. The Shatila district had not yet been subject to disarmament by the appropriate Lebanese authorities, perhaps because events overtook it before search operations could take place (these did in fact take place later, after the massacre). All this does not, indeed, obscure the fact that some organizations and senior individuals from Sabra and Shatila contrived to keep their personal guns. We shall demonstrate that guns used by their owners, in addition to the limited number of weapons hurriedly brought in from outside the district on the first day, particularly in the Horsh district, did have their effect on the confrontation. This will be discussed in due course.

The residents

How many residents were there? And what were their nationalities – the nationalities, that is to say, of those who were among the witnesses or victims of the massacre?

The number is not easy to determine, but an assessment can be made on two initial bases: first, by taking the known figure prior to the Israeli invasion of that summer; and second, by following the events that took place thereafter.

Between the early 1970s and the early 1980s, the number of residents multiplied in the camp – or rather, in the camp district, that is, in Shatila and all the adjacent or nearby quarters that were an arena for the massacre. The number had escalated from 6,000 or 7,000 to more than 20,000 people by the beginning of the Israeli invasion.

As for residents' nationalities, not all were Palestinian as has been assumed. As noted earlier, residents of the Horsh district, Horsh Tabet, were a mixture of Lebanese and Palestinian, and so, apart from the small Shatila camp itself, were those of most of the bordering quarters contributing to form Greater Shatila.

The residents of Shatila Main Street were of various Arab nationalities: in addition to Lebanese and Palestinians, there were Syrians, Egyptians and Jordanians. Homes in the district lining the street between the Sports City and Shatila Street belonged mostly to Palestinians. Behind the Sports City, on the other hand, homes were mostly those of Lebanese. There were, equally, the homes of Syrians, Egyptians, and others only recognized by the Lebanese state as resident on Lebanese soil, without nationality. These last were identified in the official files as people whose nationalities were 'under examination'.[65]

As for construction outside the smaller Shatila district, or camp proper, this developed more swiftly than inside. If it had started off with stones and zinc, concrete ceilings came, in time, to replace zinc ones, and some structures in fact became two-storey units.

It was natural that a targeted district like Sabra and Shatila should be evacuated by many of its residents throughout the summer months of the Israeli invasion. However, many returned, following the signing of the agreements and the departure of the fighters, and began to repair their houses, till it eventually became normal to see the streets crowded with people. Some estimate that 70 per cent of the residents returned, others give a somewhat higher or lower figure. The overall consensus suggests 60–70 per cent.

Location and 'borders' of the massacre

The commonly given location for the massacre – that of the Sabra and Shatila Camps – does not conform to the massacre's true location or identify the full geographical area it encompassed. The designation has become confused between reality and generalization.

We should note, first of all, five flaws regarding the common expression 'Sabra and Shatila Camps'. (It should also be said that using a plural form, without noting that there are simply two districts in reality, introduces an extra element of dread and significance that is at odds with reality.)

What are the five flaws? What is the reality of the matter? And what were the 'borders' of the massacre?

The first flaw is to say that there are even two camps, let alone many camps, in this part of Beirut. There is, in point of fact, just the one camp: that of Shatila. The term 'Sabra Camp' is inaccurate, for there is, strictly speaking, no such thing. The residential district known as Sabra is a Lebanese popular area cut through by a long commercial street, and it extends from Tariq al-Jadida in the north to Shatila in the south. Sabra is inhabited by Lebanese, Palestinians and others; it is certainly not a Palestinian camp or a Palestinian district.

The second flaw is the simplistic habit of mentioning Shatila Camp in isolation while ignoring the various adjacent Lebanese quarters that were an arena of the massacre. Shatila Camp itself occupies an area of 15,000 square metres, no more. Moreover, the camp proper forms no more than one-tenth of the larger district of which it is part, and which became known as the Shatila district – a case of a whole being named after a part. The district bordering Shatila includes various popular quarters that sprung up around it as years went by: Hayy Farhat, Hayy al-Miqdad and Horsh Tabet to the south; Shatila Main Street, along with the area behind the Sports City, to the west; and Hayy Ersal and Hayy al-Gharbi to the south-west. To say, therefore, that the massacre focused only on Shatila Camp is at odds with events. It was indeed aimed at the Palestinian camp, but it also extended through the neighbouring quarters.

The third flaw is to imply that the residents of the 'massacre district' were all Palestinian – with the added insinuation that they were no doubt 'terrorists', as refugees in camp areas are so often assumed to be, or that they at least had 'terrorists' hidden among them. This flaw may be refuted by reference to the nationalities of the residents, whose poverty served to bring them together in such popular districts. The residents of the Shatila district (or Greater Shatila for that matter) and those of the Sabra district are reckoned to have comprised Palestinians and Lebanese in equal proportions, along with Syrians, Egyptians, Jordanians, Bengalis, Pakistanis and others.

The fourth flaw is to imply that the Sabra and Shatila districts were, in their entirety, an arena for the massacre. The main objective, of violating the area as a whole, was achieved, but in reality the massacre in the Shatila district extended only as far as Shatila Main Street outside the borders of the camp, along with neighbouring quarters that become collectively included within the Shatila district: Hayy al-Horsh, Hayy al-Farhat, Hayy al-Miqdad and Hayy Ersal. However, the massacre never reached the heart of Shatila Camp, nor did it extend beyond the camp's border on the west side. As for the Sabra district, the massacre reached there only on the morning of the third day. Indeed, it only extended to the Gaza Hospital, the main square of Sabra, and the street of Ma'wa al-Ajaza, that is, the southern part of the Sabra district. Sabra Main Street, and the part north of the Square – the most significant part of Sabra – remained isolated from the massacre.

The fifth flaw is to ignore a residential district that was among the first to be exposed to the massacre: namely that of Bir Hasan, where the Kuwaiti Embassy and the Akka Hospital area are located. Bir Hasan faces Shatila from the south side, and the two are separated by a main street connecting the airport roundabout to the east and that of the Kuwaiti Embassy to the west.

To conclude: the massacre covered all quarters of the Shatila district except Shatila Camp, the southern part of Sabra adjacent to the Shatila district and part of the Bir Hasan district.

Yet for all this, the designation of the massacre as that of 'Sabra and Shatila' remains dominant; similarly, the designation of the place as the 'Sabra and Shatila Camps' remains common, since the main objective was to kill Palestinians and gain access to the heart of the camp. While this objective was not achieved in strict geographical terms, it was achieved in practice through the killing of Palestinians living in the neighbouring quarters, of those camp residents who had sought refuge in the shelters, and of those who were forced out on to the roads (see Appendix 4, Map 3).

Conclusion

- The 1969 Cairo Agreement may be regarded as a watershed for the life of Palestinian refugees in Lebanon. Random detentions, mass punishments and unjustified fines were characteristic of the first 20 years of refugee life. From the end of the 1960s, however, the situation began to change drastically, especially following the transfer to Lebanon, and in particular to the Sabra, Shatila and Hayy al-Fakhani districts of Beirut, of the Palestinian commands and the military factions.

- The ceiling of the tent, or even of the house, had to remain zinc at best so as to emphasize that refugee life was temporary, regardless of how long it lasted. To cast the ceiling in concrete, for example, was prohibited, since such a ceiling implied settlement and abandonment of the goal of returning to Palestine. And so refugee life remained without a ceiling up till the time of the Revolution, as a consequence of which what had formerly been forbidden was now permitted.

- During the Israeli invasion in the summer of 1982, the district, having been targeted, was almost emptied of its residents. It also became necessary to clear it of the weapons stores, so as to retain hold of the weapons. Yet after the fighters had left and a number of the residents had returned, testimonies combine to demonstrate that people's general tendency was to get rid of weapons rather than retrieve and restore them. Exceptions to this trend were found among some Palestinian organizations whose offices continued to function in the district.

- The residents were told that the United States had issued guarantees regarding their security, but there was no machinery to effect such security or anything like it.

- One of the most significant and widespread pretexts for raiding the Sabra and Shatila 'camps' was the official Israeli claim that 2,500 Palestinian fighters had 'remained' in 'Beirut'. But, as noted above, the combined testimonies of those known as the ''48 men' not only implicitly negate this rumour but originate and end in a different world, one completely unassociated with such rumours. The testimonies concurred on the necessity for all the fighters to leave. As for those men born and raised in Lebanon, who might never return to see their people again, and who included fighters, nurses, teachers, labourers, and so on – these were allowed a humane choice, each being granted the option to stay or to leave. The testimonies also confirm that personal and psychological factors were the prevailing driving force behind the decision made. The main tragedy is that no one, either at the upper level of the commands or elsewhere, had really made plans to ensure the security of the Palestinian communities.

2

The Israeli Army Encircles the District

Just before the fighters left, Brother Abu Ammar (to use the name by which Yasser Arafat was mostly known during the Revolution and Exile periods) gave a specific assurance at the Gaza Hospital in the hearing of a large group of Sabra and Shatila residents. 'Don't worry,' he said. 'I'll ask for the International Forces to be placed at the entry to the camps, for your protection.'[1] Nor was the Chairman of the Palestine Liberation Organization alone in promising this. A number of leaders of Palestinian organizations said similar things, underlining the international agreement and regarding the camp districts as henceforth totally safe for Palestinians.[2]

Such statements were not, however, sufficient to reassure the camps' residents, and women were weeping bitterly throughout the departure days. The same faces would be seen daily in the Mal'ab al-Baladi, near the Beirut Arab University, where fighters would meet on the mornings of departure. Farewells were not confined to relatives; it was farewell, rather, to a poignant episode in the history of the Palestinian people. Despite all that has been said about the mistakes and oversights involved in this episode, it will, for history, be clear testimony to the pangs of an incomplete revolutionary birth.

The Revolution did not recover an inch of the Palestinian occupied lands; yet it brought about unification of a people in the diaspora, and it reinforced the identity of a people previously torn between refuge and the occupying Israeli.

Following the fighters' departure, the most significant event was the assassination of the President-elect, Bashir al-Gemayel, on the evening of Tuesday 14 September. At dawn the following day, Israeli troops marched in and encircled the Sabra and Shatila district. A further 36 hours then elapsed before the arrival of armed Lebanese militias on the Thursday evening. During this period Sabra and Shatila faced the headlong march of events along two opposing lines.

The first line was that of 'peace', as the older men of the camp called it. They sent a delegation to the Israelis to attempt to reassure them that no weapons worth mentioning remained following the fighters' departure. Dozens of women marched for the same purpose.

The second line was that of confronting the occupying Israelis, however meagre the quantity of weapons available. A small number of young people, no more than 20 men and girls, confronted the Israelis here and there, with the few weapons they had in their hands, as a token of their rejection of the Israeli presence.

It was then, while the women were marching in search of the Israeli Command

Centre and the young people were brandishing their weapons at the Israeli soldiers, that the massacre began.

Fear of the unknown

On the evening of 14 September the assassination of the Lebanese President-elect, Bashir al-Gemayel, was announced. The public had been given a report that afternoon of the explosion shaking the Phalangists' headquarters, but there was neither confirmation of survival nor news of death until the government radio station began, some time before ten o'clock in the evening, to broadcast classical music in preparation for the announcement.

A Palestinian teacher at a Relief Agency school, who then lived in the Ras Beirut district, said:

I shall never forget the night of President Bashir's assassination. The moment I heard the news, I was sure Israel would launch a new assault and exploit the situation. I envisaged an occupation of Beirut. I envisaged a major wave of detaining Palestinian and Lebanese men on the pretext of the assassination. But what I never envisaged was a massacre in the camps. It's true I was thinking of them, of our people in the camps, of my pupils, for the whole of the next morning, especially when I heard about the Israeli Army surrounding Sabra and Shatila. But thought of a massacre? Why? Where's the logic? No one with a grain of common sense would suppose there was still an armed force in the camps after all the fighters had left, with the international forces there to watch them leave and see how many there were. But that was the lying pretext they used: that 2,000 fighters had stayed behind. When the massacre had happened, when I'd heard all about the massacre, I realized how stupid I'd been. The massacre was a cause, not an effect.[3]

Just before six o'clock on the morning of Wednesday 15 September, heavy shelling rent the skies of the Sports City and Tariq al-Jadida district – a sign that the Israeli Army had begun its advance into West Beirut. Very soon those living in the Sabra and Shatila district, directly behind the Sports City, found that the Israeli Army had surrounded them. The Israelis also found other routes for their advance within the city. Throughout the day there was shelling, now heavy, now intermittent.

That day, Wednesday, a crowded funeral took place in Bikfaya for the son of the President of the Phalangist Party: Bashir Pierre al-Gemayel, the President-elect. In West Beirut there was bewilderment and a sense of expectancy. Everyone was in front of the television screen, watching the funeral, trying to gather news, wondering. Was it possible the Israelis would enter the whole of Beirut? Would there be any resistance? With the fighters gone and all the weapons from the stores of the Palestinian Resistance and the Lebanese National Movement collected and confiscated by the Lebanese Army, no one held out any hope of a resistance capable of confronting and repelling the Israelis; yet everyone hoped for resistance of some kind, as a token of dignity and self-respect. 'Beirut does not surrender to the aggressor. Beirut may be defeated, but it does not surrender.'

West Beirut had its wish. The city did not surrender. Lebanese men who believed in their country's freedom confronted the Israeli Defence Forces, damaging tanks and killing Israeli soldiers and officers; through the second half of September, between the 14th and the 29th, the occupying presence was not, as the occupiers themselves maintained, a 'promenade'. Still, the Israeli Army effectively achieved its purpose: to occupy an Arab capital, the second after Jerusalem.

The Sabra and Shatila massacre took place on the evening of the second day of occupation, and it lasted for 43 continuous hours. Nor did Israel remotely deny holding effective control over the camps during the massacre days – it had, after all, encircled them from the early hours. Yet it denied any knowledge of a massacre having taken place.

What, then, of the Israeli soldiers and officers who had surrounded the Sabra and Shatila district from dawn on Wednesday? Did they deny or admit knowledge?

Over the full course of events – from the initial establishment of the Israeli siege to its gradual lifting as the days of the massacre passed – these Israeli soldiers and officers had no single, uniform 'viewpoint' on events; their orders and attitudes were in fact various and contradictory. Some monitored events through binoculars, offered assistance to the attacking militias and mocked the pleas of those Palestinians who managed to reach them. Others acted in quite opposite fashion, extending help to Palestinian and Lebanese residents and preventing the killers from carrying out a number of mass murder atrocities. This is demonstrated in residents' testimonies. Testimonies to the Wednesday's events also make it clear that some Israelis were aware of the Lebanese militias' plans to attack Shatila Camp, whereas others were not.

Among those who did know, so it later emerged, was an Israeli soldier who, midway through the Wednesday, had been standing with some other Israeli soldiers near the Sports City. He had a conversation with seven Palestinian men, one of whom gives the following account:

We asked them what we should do. I mean, should we fetch our relatives and families and leave the district? We waited tensely as one of them translated our question into Hebrew so they could all understand it. The answer came firmer and quicker than we'd expected: 'Go back home. Today nobody leaves. Go back home. Don't take your relatives and families away till Friday.'[4]

Several times during the interview he repeated what the Israeli had said: 'Don't take your relatives and families away till Friday.' He was blaming himself because he and his friends had not taken the man's words seriously – or rather because they had failed to understand them. As they understood the matter, they should go back home, and this they did. Only after the massacre did they remember those words. What torment the memory caused them then, and how long and earnestly they analysed what the soldier had said! Why had he told them not to leave before Friday, that specific day? Did he have some notion the massacre would surely be over in a single day – on Thursday, say? Just what was the reason? The narrator himself escaped death because he was not at home that first night; a friend of his had been injured by sniper fire and, with another friend, he rushed the injured man to hospital. Had this young narrator attempted to act on the Israeli soldier's firm advice – 'don't take your relatives and families away till Friday' – he could not have done so since all his relatives had been murdered, with not a single one left by Friday. They had met their end in the first of the 43 hours.

From all I heard, none of those within Sabra and Shatila had any expectation of a massacre, but that did not preclude fear of the unknown. From dawn on Wednesday, as the Israeli Army surrounded the whole district, people's feelings ranged from calmness to fear.

The 'calmness group' pointed out that the Israelis had not interfered with them in the days preceding the siege. Their army had had checkpoints in the Ouza'i district, and others placed close by the Kuwaiti Embassy roundabout; yet Israeli soldiers had made no attempt to harass Palestinians or discover who was there in the camp. They had asked about neither weapons nor fighters. They had not tried to interfere in any way. On the contrary, they had made every effort to keep up warm relations with those walking by, talking to them and giving children biscuits and sweets as a mark of goodwill – even if some had taken the sweets then thrown them away, out of fear.[5] Even checkpoints some way off had played their part in fostering an atmosphere of calm: they had not harassed any Palestinian.[6]

Um Ali al-Biqa'i, a southern Lebanese mother, affirmed that she had felt frightened since the fighters' departure. Her son Rabi', a young employee, would pass by an Israeli checkpoint every day on his way to work and chat with the Israeli soldiers. In the evening he would tell his mother how pleasantly they had talked to him and how kindly they treated the Palestinian children, allowing these to play around them all day. A neighbour – a friend of this woman's from her southern village of Sheb'a – went up to the Israelis on the Wednesday morning and asked them why they had surrounded the camps, given that there were no weapons or fighters in Shatila. 'Should we leave our homes?' she asked. The answer to her, and to others, was always the same: 'Stay where you are. We're here to protect you.'[7]

In point of fact, they totally failed to protect them. Rabi' was among the victims on the second day of the massacre, as were seven of his closest relatives, including his mother's afflicted friend whose fear had led her to approach the Israelis and be given reassurance.

Another southern woman said she had been among those reassured, especially after reports of events in the South, where the Israelis had not, apparently, harassed women, children or the elderly. On the Wednesday the Israelis entered, this woman was standing with the crowds on the public street, near the petrol station between the airport roundabout and the Kuwaiti Embassy roundabout. She watched them come from the nearby Akka (Acre) Hospital and stand at the intersection, telling people: 'Khabibi ["My dear" – Lebanese], don't harm us and we won't harm you either. We're here to protect you.' She had no bread, she went on, and an Israeli soldier came up and offered her a loaf of bread with some cheese for the children. This Israeli soldier fed the woman's children with his own hands. Then, after the massacre, she discovered her husband was among those missing, and though she searched desperately for him she never found him. She never knew whether his fate had been at the hands of Israeli or Lebanese forces.[8]

Um Ahmad Srour, a Palestinian mother of nine, said her husband had not felt in the least afraid, perhaps because he was an employee at the telephone exchange. In the circumstances, any business not linked to the war was reassuring to Palestinians; his job implied no connection with warfare or fighters. She told of what her husband said to his family on the last evening they all met together:

What do we have to be afraid of? Israel's been stationed around Shatila for three days, and we talk to the soldiers and they talk to us. Plus, I'm an old man and they wouldn't do anything to me. I mean, I'm old enough to be their father; do you really think they'd molest me? My brothers in the South are all old men, and no one molested them. Come on … trust in God, you kids, and go to bed.[9]

This was the last thing said by this completely peaceful father on the evening of the first day of the massacre, without any knowledge of what had been happening beyond his home, on the borders of Shatila Camp. Next morning he was one of the first to fall – without any chance to have the killers check up on the nature of his work, that he had been an employee at the telephone exchange. All they needed was an answer to their first question: 'Are you Palestinian?' 'Yes', he answered. 'I'm Palestinian.' Whereupon this utterly harmless Palestinian was gunned down by the killers, along with all the members of his family who were there with him in the small room. Those who survived did so by the will of God – in the common expression, 'by a miracle'.

Many found all talk of fear strange; they had, according to their testimonies, felt quite reassured. Such reassurance had two grounds: first, the withdrawal of the fighters and the absence of weapons within Shatila and the neighbouring district; and second, the Israelis' behaving, on this occasion, in a way that inspired confidence among simple people. The Director of the Gaza Hospital, Aziza Khalidi, confirmed that most of those who sought refuge in the hospital from the Thursday on used this same line of argument.[10]

Another group of the district's residents used an opposite line: that embodying the fear they had felt since the fighters' departure and which had doubled following the assassination of Bashir al-Gemayel. Among this group was a Palestinian mother who sought refuge at the Gaza Hospital with her children on the Wednesday night. On the Thursday morning she went up to some Israeli soldiers standing at a point visible from the hospital. She had a radio with her, and a soldier asked her, rather warily, what it was she was carrying. Once sure it was not a weapon, he spoke reassuringly to her in broken Arabic:

Where are you from? From Burj al-Shamali Camp, you say, in Tyre? Go, go there. Burj al-Shamali is better than Shatila. Go. Tyre is better than here. Why are you here in Beirut? There are terrorists in Beirut. You go to Tyre, go, stay there.[11]

The Israelis raised the level of reassurance through megaphones blaring everywhere: 'Surrender and you won't be harmed – anyone with weapons should hand them over – we won't harass him – everyone stay at home.' People passed on the news that anyone with weapons should surrender them to avert harm from his family and neighbours. Some tried to leave the district on the Wednesday, but few succeeded. The Israelis prevented them.

A Palestinian nurse recounts the experience of neighbours of hers who attempted to escape:

Our neighbours tried to flee. They put their things in the car and came to a checkpoint close to Sabri Hamadeh Palace. When they arrived there, they were stopped and asked: 'Where are you going? Where are you heading for? If you've no weapons, you go back home.' And our neighbour did go back with his family. This incident was repeated with many others. From that we got the feeling that Israel had no intention of entering the camps. What it wanted was to gather weapons.[12]

The Israelis surrounding the Greater Shatila district had little knowledge of it. Some entered the Akka Hospital on the Wednesday to explore the place and ask a number of questions. Dr Sami al-Khatib assured them there were no 'terrorists' in the hospital. The Israelis then (as a nurse at the hospital described)[13] came into the hospital on the Wednesday and Thursday, eating at the cafeteria without permission and giving chocolate and sweets to the children. This did not, however, prevent barbarians breaking into the hospital on the second day of the massacre. As for the doctor who had assured the Israelis there were no 'terrorists' there, he was among those killed, along with a number of patients, doctors and nurses.

An employee in the X-ray department at the Akka Hospital said he had been one of those who felt totally unsafe, especially following the death of the President-elect. He remained frightened throughout that night, on which he had been on duty, and he took notice of every sound outside. He remembers the roaring of the tanks at dawn. Looking west towards the Kuwaiti Embassy and seeing a line of Israeli tanks, he felt his fears had been realized faster than he had expected.[14]

Many testified how they heard the Israelis – or else heard reports of this through relatives and friends – telling people to go back home to the 'camp', by which they meant the camp proper and the parts around it. One such witness was a Palestinian from the Fatah Movement, who said that at noon on the Wednesday he advanced with some other Palestinian men towards an Israeli checkpoint near the Sports City. Horror, he said, was written on their faces – on the faces, that is, of the Israeli soldiers. 'What's going to happen?' the men asked them. They became confused, whereupon the officer in charge came up and said with some firmness: 'Go, *khabibi*, you go to camps, look, we want Murabitoun terrorists. Only Murabitoun terrorists. You all go to camps.'[15]

Words like these left people still more bewildered. Some felt their fears further allayed; for others fear of the unknown grew stronger.

Sabra and Shatila between Thursday dawn and sunset

Many of the residents had noted cars driving around the district since the Thursday morning, their drivers asking suspicious questions about shelters and where these were located. Some residents further affirm they had seen unfamiliar cars on the Wednesday.

A young southern Lebanese wife from Qal'at al-Shaqif, whose house was on the border with Shatila Camp on the east side, reports that there was an Israeli checkpoint near Sabri Hamadeh Palace on the main street. At three o'clock on the Thursday afternoon, she saw masked gunmen passing by her house and was unsure whether these were freedom fighters or attackers. She was hardly likely to try and find out, for, like everyone else, she had heard gunshots outside and was fearful of sniper fire if she left the house to make enquiries. Before her on the table was a bunch of leaflets dropped from planes by the Israelis in the two preceding days and picked up by the family's children. These urged the people of Sabra and Shatila in particular not to put up any resistance: 'Surrender and you won't be harmed.' Although, the young wife continued, she was unsure of the masked gunmen's identity, or of their connection with the leaflets, she was sure some disaster was imminent. It could hardly have been coincidental that a power failure, a total lack of bread and continuous shelling, should all come together on the same day.[16]

A Lebanese man living in Horsh Tabet said that on the Thursday morning he saw just the one car constantly driving around. In it were men with black scarves on their heads and wearing green uniforms. They had not talked to him, but he had seen them talk to other people and had heard them making enquiries about shelters.[17]

A Palestinian woman gave a more detailed description of an incident involving another car:

Everybody was talking about strange cars on the Thursday, but I saw a car on the Wednesday, the same day Shaykh Bashir was buried. I saw a strange car, I don't know its make, but it was white, and there were two people in it dressed in ordinary civilian clothes and asking where the shelters were. I was surprised to see people answer them and point to a shelter. I was sure there'd been an operation to explore the district. Later on I heard other women saying the same thing. A lot of people later started talking about similar cars driving around and asking questions, on the Thursday, driving around and asking, asking about the shelters. No one suspected the car we saw on the Wednesday, except for my husband. He noticed it and told me the car had been going around the district and there was something suspicious about it. And it turned out my husband knew what he was talking about.[18]

Another Palestinian woman, wife of a fighter living in Shatila, near Rawdat al-Shahid Ghassan Kanafani, said:

At noon on the Thursday I saw masked gunmen with scarves on their heads, they were wearing freedom fighters' badges too, maybe to reassure people so no one would know who they were. But it puzzled me to see them going to and fro in front of our house, four or five times maybe. I was taken in by the way they looked and how wary they were, and I went and spoke to them. Three times I spoke to them. They didn't answer or speak to me, not once. I didn't see them speak to anybody. They just

looked at me and kept going. They kept on going back and forth in the quarter. Those people scared me more than the Israeli shelling did.[19]

This witness confirmed that both she and her husband were known to everyone living in the quarter. Had these masked men really been fighters who came to the district regularly, they would certainly have spoken to her. She took their total silence as a clear sign they were reluctant to reveal their dialects, voices or intentions; that they were perhaps informants.[20]

In Sabra, the masked men's behaviour had been somewhat different: more than once they had got out of their car and bought sandwiches and cola. This was affirmed by a girl living in Sabra, who also stated that several of the neighbours had also, on the Thursday, seen a military car with masked people inside. This car had driven regularly around the streets, leading those who lived there to suspect it contained spies.[21]

One witness further said that he had, since half past ten in the morning, seen large and small jeeps driving around the Bir Hasan district and near the Kuwaiti Embassy and the Henri Chehab Barracks. These vehicles clearly displayed the words 'Lebanese Forces', with the Phalangist cedar equally evident. These particular vehicles had not, however, approached Shatila. They were, the witness remarked, not on a reconnaissance mission but rather heralded what was to come. This was how he and his friends had viewed the matter in retrospect, though they could hardly have been aware of its true significance at the time.[22]

This matter of cars seeking out the location of shelters within Greater Shatila was of concern only to those who had seen them and been put on their guard. The matter that deeply disturbed everyone was the absence of many foodstuffs.

On the Thursday morning the streets of the camp and the whole Sabra and Shatila district were thronged with people. There was an air of bewilderment, especially when it was discovered that, simultaneously, bread was totally lacking and the supply of electricity had been cut. Taking everything together – the Israeli siege of the district, the news that the Israeli Army had entered West Beirut through six conduits, the intermittent Israeli shelling of the area and the exchange of gunfire between some local Palestinian and Lebanese and the Israelis – most people did not dare to leave besieged Sabra and Shatila even to look for bread.

As the day advanced, the Israeli Army began a concentrated shelling of Shatila Camp and its immediate vicinity, and people naturally fled to the shelters which quickly became crowded. No one dared return home to fetch food for their children before the shelling eased up.

A little after three in the afternoon, Israeli cannons stationed on sandy hillocks near the Kuwaiti Embassy began an intensified bombardment, shells striking the southern entrance to the camp – the same entrance that was to bear the initial thrust of the massacre in the next few hours. At five o'clock, as the shelling from Israeli vehicles stationed near the Sports City focused on the main street between Sabra and Shatila, the shelters could hold no more people and nor could the Shatila mosque, which had become crammed with women and children treating places of worship as a safe refuge. What horrified people still further was the burning, near the mosque, of the five-storey Mukhallalati building, one of the few tall buildings in the vicinity.[23]

There were marked divisions of opinion among members of the same family: some would rush off to the nearest shelter, while others refused to leave their homes, either from an unfounded notion that the shelling would not last or to avoid the discomfort of the crowded shelters. These latter preferred to remain at home awaiting the unknown, though no one imagined that unknown would be a massacre. These divisions led to different fates for different family members. The fortunate families were those whose members all managed to leave the district, mostly to the north, in the direction of the Beirut Arab University and the Corniche al-Mazra'a, or to the east, close by Sabri Hamadeh Palace. As for the limited number of places within Sabra and Shatila spelling a degree of safety, there were the three

hospitals forming a triangle around the district, the Gaza, Akka and Ma'wa al-Ajaza hospitals, all of which became crowded with incoming families and young men.[24]

A Palestinian nurse told of the terror that engulfed Sabra and Shatila during these hours preceding the massacre:

On the Thursday, around two o'clock, the shelling got very heavy, from two o'clock onwards. Shelling got heavier and heavier, and bombs would fall over and over on the same place. Everyone went to the shelters and no one stayed at home. I mean, those who did stay at home had no shelters nearby.[25]

As for the Palestinian man who, with his friends, was told by the Israeli 'Don't take your relatives and families away till Friday', and who went to take an injured friend to hospital on the Thursday evening, he said he had been surprised by the Israeli Army's withdrawal from the airport roundabout and from near the Akka Hospital in Bir Hasan. He could not, at the time, conceive why they had left so suddenly. He later discovered that they were clearing the way for the Lebanese militias who were coming from the airport to enter Shatila from the Bir Hasan side.[26]

Two events that took place in those final hours before the massacre remain etched in the camp's memory. In each case the outcome was tragic since, as it later emerged, many of those taking part had been killed or abducted. And yet both events sprang from a wish for peace and the avoidance of bloodshed.

The residents of Shatila speak of the first event as the 'peace delegation'; of the second as the 'women's march'. The two following sections recall residents' memories of these.

The peace delegation from Shatila Camp

The shells that had rained down over Shatila and the surrounding district since the Wednesday became progressively more intense on the Thursday. Some people were now seen carrying guns with a view to resistance – young people from the camps and the neighbouring districts, both Palestinian and Lebanese. According to local witnesses who saw them close by the Ali Hamdar Café, and basing numbers on the highest estimate, there were not more than ten men and one girl, most of them under 20 years of age. They were in fact zealous youngsters rather than fully fledged fighters. Some carried a Kalashnikov or an RPG launcher, others carried simple handguns. As the women hurried with their children to the shelters they heaped reproach on these young people, urging them to surrender their weapons and leave the camp or else hide in the houses or shelters. The prevailing feeling among residents was that force should be avoided. The enemies lurking around them were Israeli, and those living in the camp were powerless to confront such an enemy with the fighters gone.

What made things so strange was that this enemy now bombarding the camp and forcing people to seek refuge in the shelters was the very one that had told people 'We're here to protect you.'

What enemy, indeed, ever came to protect its enemy? And the Israelis in particular – those who had founded the State of Israel at the expense of Palestine, and of its people and their rights – what would have led them to protect refugees for whose very refugee status they themselves were responsible? From whom had they come to protect them?

What, then, was the proper response: resistance or surrender? And what was the likely outcome in the two cases? In reality, the situation hardly allowed the Shatila residents any chance for careful reflection and analysis, or even to work out how those apparently come to protect them could shell them in this fashion. How were they to deal with such a paradox?

There was, nevertheless, time for the 'seniors' of the camp to gather hastily and decide what to do in the face of this quite groundless assault. It was customary for these to make decisions at critical times, and all the more so at a crucial time like this.

These seniors, or 'elders' as they were often called, assembled at the house of one of their number, around 40 men being present. In contrast to ordinary social practice, this hastily convened meeting was not attended by invitation. The custom was that, whenever some especially important event occurred, the elders would hasten to consult together at someone's home. News would spread quickly. The meeting, it would be said, was at the home of such-and-such and, since the houses were all within walking distance of one another, those taking part would keep arriving throughout the meeting.

It was also customary for the camp residents to visit these elders both in ordinary circumstances and in crises like the present one. Black coffee was always on hand. Abu Ahmad al-Sa'id's home was, according to Hajj Abu Khodr, one of those in question (he referred, traditionally, to its *diwan*, or reception room). Before they left, Hajj Abu Khodr went on, the commanders of the Palestinian leaderships would gather there. Everyone knew Abu Ahmad al-Sa'id's *diwan*.[27]

Advanced age was not in fact invariable among these elders: if many were over 60, others were still in their forties. And indeed there were two other qualifications, quite apart from age, and no less important for being regarded as an elder: the first was a matter of services the man in question could render to the camp residents, the second related to origins and identity – not the national Palestinian identity but the village one. Those come from each particular village had to have someone to speak on their behalf in 'camp/exile' society; and if there was no representative among the middle-aged then one of the young would be there.

At around two in the afternoon, the elders gathered spontaneously at Abu Kamal Bishr's house in Shatila Camp. The sole issue under discussion was the sending of a delegation to the Israelis to tell them there were no weapons in the camp and to ask them, accordingly, to call a halt to the bombardment. The decision was not unanimous: while most were in favour of sending a delegation, others feared the outcome of such a move, while others rejected the idea outright from apprehension that meeting the Israelis through a delegation might be interpreted as surrender.[28]

There were indeed no angry clashes. Opinions were simply put forward, and it was decided, with very little delay, to form a delegation with the limited mission of telling the Israelis there were no weapons in the camp and that the people were ready to make peace. Some further affirm that the delegation was authorized to tell the Israelis: 'Come into the camp. And if you want to take the camp over, then come and take it over.' The evidence for this is that the delegation elected to carry a white flag to wave as the members approached the Israeli Command Centre.

No delegation was elected as such. Membership was de facto, since no one would have ventured to oppose the voices of these highly respected elders. Whoever was nominated by these at the meeting, or came boldly and confidently forward and possessed the elders' qualities, age, status or wisdom, was a member of the delegation as of right. Those living in Sabra and Shatila invariably speak of the delegation in terms of peaceful intention: they call it, specifically, the Peace Delegation.[29]

Riad Sharqieh was among those attending the meeting. He was one of the few still in his forties, and his membership of the delegation was agreed after a friend from his home town nominated him to go on his behalf. Riad Sharqieh began walking with the other delegation members in front of the camp residents at a little after three in the afternoon. He walked up to the main street, between the airport roundabout and the Kuwaiti Embassy roundabout, with shells still bombarding the camp. At the last moment, though, he decided not to continue, declining to get into the car with the others. This was at around half past three. He described what happened at the meeting:

I was at home when the shelling got fiercer and people started panicking. First I went to the mosque. Then I went to see what the elders were doing. I went to see them with Abu Ahmad al-Sa'id, and we found them at Abu Kamal Bishr's, there were around 40 men. A friend of mine saw me come in and said: 'Here's Abu Muhammad [Riad Sharqieh], he can go instead of me.'

I'd meant to check what was going on. But when I got there, I found things had been sorted out. There was talk of there being more than

five members, and talk of there being more than ten. The number hadn't been agreed on. Abu Ahmad Tawfiq Hishmeh [henceforth 'Abu Ahmad Hishmeh'] was there at the meeting too, and he was all for the number being as large as possible. One important thing I'd like to say, too, is that the people there weren't really agreed on the whole thing. Some of them were against sending a delegation. But those who were for sending a delegation proposed that the men going should ask the Israelis why they were shelling us when we had no armed people there.

The truth is, I felt we were going to the Israelis to tell them 'Kill me.' From the start I didn't want to go. I mean, the elders made me go.[30]

Hasan Abu Ali was not from Shatila but he knew every inch of the district by virtue of his job in the building trade there. He saw the delegation members as they headed south towards the main street joining the airport roundabout with the Kuwaiti Embassy roundabout, with sniper bullets dropping close by them. He said that before they started their march from the camp towards the southern entrance opposite the Akka Hospital, they stopped and told the armed young people to go back from Shatila Main Street. They would not allow them to approach the Ali Hamdar Café, and warned them against taking things too far. Then they went on to the parking lot opposite the Akka Hospital, where Abu Ahmad Hishmeh's car was parked, got into the car and headed towards the Kuwaiti Embassy.[31]

There is more than one story told of men who considered going with the delegation then turned back before it had even moved off. One such story was told by Abu Qassem, an employee at the Ma'wa al-Ajaza Hospital. Initially, he said, his father had intended to go with the delegation. He walked some distance with them, then turned back because the members disagreed over whether the young gunmen had been properly dealt with. Abu Qassem's father was not satisfied with the warning given them by the elders, insisting that a firmer line should have been taken. Abu Qassem refused to give his father's name, ostensibly out of excessive modesty but in fact from exaggerated caution. He gave the reasons for his father's withdrawal as follows:

My father told them as they were leaving, I mean, he was suggesting to them 'Wait, all of you, why the hurry?' Before we go, let's see to these kids still fooling around with their guns from one minute to the next, so that when we get to the Israeli military commander we won't hear him say things like 'How is it you're coming and you still have guys with guns who are resisting?' But the others didn't listen to him, except for one, who said: 'Before you came, we stopped them waving their weapons around, and they promised us they wouldn't come in Shatila Main Street. Look, they're only kids, are the Israelis going to take any notice of kids? Maybe by the time we get to the Command Centre the kids will have got tired of it and stopped.'

My father didn't like the answer. He argued with them then came back halfway through. I'm pretty sure another one turned back halfway as well.[32]

As for Riad Sharqieh, who was taken along by the elders despite himself, he describes the moment the delegation moved off in the car:

I didn't get in Abu Ahmad Hishmeh's car, I went off towards the Akka Hospital while the delegation members were there in front of it. Then there was sniping from the Kuwaiti Embassy and from the bridge. Abu Kamel al-Safsaf was there with me, he stayed behind just like me. Later on he died in the war, God bless his soul, and he's buried in the mosque.[33]

They got in the car and left through the door of the building that belonged to Abu Ahmad Hishmeh, opposite the Akka Hospital. Abu Ahmad Hishmeh had a hotel, and there was a parking area for the Sham garage as well, on the Corniche. They went in through this entrance till they got right to his hotel. Abu Kamel al-Safsaf and I stayed at the Akka Hospital.

I didn't see where the car headed after the Kuwaiti Embassy. The last time I saw it was when it reached the Kuwaiti Embassy, on the slope. Abu Ahmad al-Sa'id had his *kufiyyeh* sticking out of the car door, he wore it coming out like that, and another had stuck a Lebanese flag on the car. And that was the last time I saw them.

I went to Dr Muhammad in the Akka Hospital. Seeing so many people around, I told him: 'Brother, this is a tight corner.' I sheltered in the hospital till sunset, then I came back to al-Horsh to stay with my children.[34]

People began to talk of the return of this or that delegation member on the same day, even before the fate of those who had continued their march was known. Besides Riad Sharqieh and his friend Abu Kamel al-Safsaf there was Abu Kamal Sa'd, who was seen returning from the direction of the Israelis, pale and evidently terrified, some time after three in the afternoon. People tried to find out from him what had happened but he refused to give any answers, simply striding off northward towards Sabra, where things were safer.[35]

Establishing the precise number of delegation members was not easy: each witness insisted his figure was the correct one. Some said there were four, some five, some six, some twelve. All these figures may well be correct in their own way since numbers differed according to whether the delegation had begun its march, or was on the road, or had accomplished its mission (if, that is, the mission was ever carried out).

As'ad, a Shatila resident and one of those testifying that the delegation was initially made up of six members, said the number continuing the march was just four, and he gave their names. He saw the four walking along Shatila Street, and he saw the fifth (that is, Riad Sharqieh) who did not go on. He also saw a sixth whose name he no longer recalled, but was then told that this man had also turned back halfway.[36]

A Lebanese man married to a Palestinian, and among those testifying that the delegation was made up of six men rather than four, specified the members individually to the American writer Ralph Schoenman during the days following the massacre.[37] This Lebanese man may perhaps have been one of those who saw the delegation as it left.

The number of members was not the only matter to provoke discussion before their fate was known. On that same Thursday, while shells were still raining down on the district, another issue was raised among young men angry and upset that these older people should go to the Israelis at all and ask them to call a halt to their bombardment. Such action, they felt, could only be interpreted as capitulation and surrender.

Zakaria al-Shaikh, a Palestinian from Haifa, born and raised in Shatila, was among the zealous men who witnessed the Israeli shelling on the Thursday. He and his friends tried to organize resistance, but in this they failed. On the Thursday afternoon he was at a friend's house in Shatila when the friend's younger brother came in with the dramatic news that a delegation of elders had gone to the Israelis. After recording his own anger and perplexity at this turn of events, Zakaria returned to his impressions following the massacre:

I could not understand why those people had taken this decision. Something was not normal. Were they surrendering to the Israelis? How else could the decision be explained? I wanted to brush off the idea that the camp elders had decided to surrender. I did not want to believe for one second, that Abu Ahmed Said, Abu Ahmed Suwaid, Abu Kamal Saad, or Abu Mohammed Saad, all of whom I knew very well, had decided to surrender.

Abu Ahmed Said was very well known among the people in the camp, both young and old. Many times friendly people from foreign countries who visited the camps had been served Arabic coffee in his special cups decorated with the Palestinian flag. Abu Ahmed Said, that human encyclopaedia of the historic events that had taken place in Palestine, his homeland, and then in Lebanon, over his eighty years, Abu Ahmed Said, surrender? The man who always told the younger generations about the Balfour Declaration, about King Abdullah and King Farouk, about Glubb Pasha, about Hitler, stories about the Ottoman Sultan Abdul Hamid, about the heroism of the Palestinian fighters Izzedin al-Qassam and Abdel Qader Husseini?

And Abu Ahmed Suwaid, whose son had been brought up steeped in Palestinian tradition and taught future generations the lessons of our history, Abu Ahmed Suwaid surrender? Abu Mohammed Saad's eldest son was a prominent doctor who had worked in the camp hospital for years, serving his people as his father has done ...[38]

Seventeen years after the massacre, the freedom fighter Hussein wrote some brief memoirs from a very similar standpoint. He was a leading fighter in the Popular Front for the Liberation of Palestine, heading a group that did actually manage some limited resistance on the Thursday (this is dealt with in a later section on the fighting). He described how the camp elders came to his office to tell him of their idea of forming a delegation:

A group of camp elders came to me (there were, I think, around twelve of them) to say military operations should cease. The Israelis, they said, would not subject a peaceful camp to torment. They themselves would form a delegation to go and see the Israelis in the Sports City. We began a heated argument with them, agreeing, eventually, that each should take the course he thought fit (in other circumstances we might have thought of detaining and imprisoning these people at least).

They would not listen to sense, refusing to see that the Israelis were our enemies and the reason for our whole dilemma; that our struggle with them was one for existence itself, and that they would not, in consequence, show us any mercy.

I learned later that a delegation of these men did in fact go to meet with the Israelis in the Sports City and never came back.[39]

Did the group of twelve elders go to see Hussein before the meeting at Abu Kamal Bishr's? Or was it after? He does not recall exactly when it was, but the probability is that they went to find out his and his comrades' views before their meeting. His resolutely hostile stance would, in that case, have played its part in producing the difference of opinion at the meeting itself, and in making some people so reluctant to proceed that the original twelve was reduced to six.

A more general division of opinion, between the fighting generation of the Revolution and the generation of peaceful elderly people, was natural and to be expected, not only on account of the age gap but because of differences in experience and suffering. Even so, today's peaceful generation had been yesterday's fighting one. Living in Shatila Camp, and also in the Ain al-Hilweh camp and others, were men who had struggled in the Great Revolution in Palestine (from 1936 and 1939). There were also men who had learned struggle in their youth from Shaykh Ezzedinne al-Qassam and borne arms in the name of the principles he evoked to free Palestine from the British Mandate and Zionism alike. Yet here were most of these, in Shatila Camp on Thursday 16 September 1982, showing the banner of surrender rather than resistance. Was their decision based on sound sense? Or was it rather cowardice under the pretext of an inevitable fait accompli?

Hussein, the Popular Front leader, acknowledged the fait accompli. But for that state of affairs, this courageous young fighter would, as he wrote in his memoirs,[40] have been disinclined to let matters proceed.

It was only after the massacre, when bodies had been found and all the evidence unearthed, that Shatila Camp residents were able to confirm the final number and names of the delegation members. Those who went on with their march towards the Israeli Command Centre near the Sports City were, by common consent, four: Saleh Muhammad Abu Sweid, known to everyone as 'Abu Ahmad Sweid'; Abu Hamad Ismail; Abu Ahmad al-Sa'id and Abu Ahmad Hishmeh. The first three were between 60 and 70 years old, while Abu Ahmad Hishmeh, the owner of the car, was in his forties.[41]

When these four men of peace were still alive, it was easy enough for camp residents to recognize and describe them. After their death things became more problematic. When the massacre was over, the bodies of three were found in three separate places, and identification was no simple matter.

According to a doctor from the Palestinian Red Crescent, 'the bodies of the four were found shot, not mutilated, but shot, shot all over'.[42] A fellow-doctor from the Akka Hospital said the bodies were spread along the slope between the Kuwaiti Embassy and the main road.[43] The women of the camp, however, affirmed that the delegation members were slaughtered and dismembered. Um Majed said:

They slaughtered them and put each one in a bag. Abu Ahmad Sweid and Abu Ahmad al-Sa'id, they were close to the Sports City, each one killed with his ID card next to him. And they found Abu Ahmad Sweid's body in front of Intensive Care in a garbage bag. But Abu Ahmad Hishmeh's body was never found, and neither was his car. His sister went there, poor woman, she went and they showed her a dismembered body in a bag, she said: 'Those aren't my brother's clothes, those aren't his clothes, that's not my brother.'[44]

Herein lies the main discrepancy in accounts of how the members of the peace delegation were killed: some state confidently that they were shot, while others testify to their bodies being mutilated. It must in honesty be said that no one witnessed their murder and no one was able to submit an accurate report following the discovery of the three bodies. As for the fourth body, whether or not it was actually discovered, all the evidence points to murder here also. More than one witness saw him go with the delegation, besides confirming him as the owner and driver of the car in which the members rode to their death.

And yet no one knows to this day what precise point the delegation members reached in their brief final journey. Did they ever get to the Israeli Command Centre or did the militias pick them up before they got there? Or were the men handed over to the militias by the Israelis? Did they manage to wave their white flag? Or did death come too quickly? At any rate they were given no chance to speak. They never succeeded in delivering their message to the Israelis that they were a peace delegation, and that there were no arms in the camp with the fighters gone.

The further question obviously remains unanswered. Who killed them? The Israeli Army? The Lebanese Forces militias? Or was it Sa'd Haddad's forces? Or just some unsupervised militia members?

It is still possible that one day someone may provide an answer – one of those who killed them, perhaps, or one of those who watched his friends while they were murdering these four harmless elders. Some person may, for one reason or another, speak out.

However, many things are well enough known about these four men to those living in the camp and the whole district: first and foremost that they were good men. They were not fighters; they were simply good men. Everyone who knew them invoked God's mercy on them and mourned their deaths.

Um Ali al-Biqa'i was one of those who recalled the elders' kindness and helpfulness towards the camp residents. She was from the southern town of Sheb'a, and fate had led her, in the late 1960s, to live with her family in that part of Sabra right alongside Shatila. Her husband was a poor peddler who took worn out clothes to sell in the mountain region. We hear her invoking God's mercy on Abu Ahmad Sweid. His killer remains unknown to this day, but she knew well enough who Abu Ahmad Sweid was. Here is what she had to say:

May God have mercy on the land that embraced Abu Ahmad Sweid. He was a friend to us, a friend more precious than any brother. I swear I think of him all the time, and I grieve for him more than I do for my husband and children.

We got to know Abu Ahmad Sweid soon after we came to the district. We heard how al-Akhdar al-Arabi had been killed by Israel in the South. Al-Akhdar al-Arabi was a hero. That day he was killed in our home town, and they dragged him away.[45] Feelings ran high, and people were giving blood. I was very thin then, even more skinny than I am now. When they started giving blood I was sitting with my neighbour, and we heard they were giving blood.

I went and found Abu Ahmad Sweid sitting at the reception desk in the camp. I went in. He said to me: 'What can I do for you, sister?' I said: 'I want to give blood.' He gazed at me, and said: 'OK, but if we take the blood, we'll have to sacrifice you in return, you're so thin.' I said: 'No, maybe my blood's stronger than my body is, and I want to give with all my heart, even if I needed to take some instead, I'd still want to give.' He said, may God have mercy on him: 'Sister, if you can – I mean there's no obligation – I think it would be better if you gave money, even if it's only five lira. That would be better than giving blood, because you're not strong and you have children to raise.'

I remember I had 25 lira with me, and I went ahead and pulled them out, and he wouldn't take them. I started to swear by God, and so did he, and I wouldn't agree ... I still remember how I went home and cooked *mujaddarra* [a dish of lentils cooked with rice and onion], and then I went back and took the pot to him and told him: 'This is for the fighters.'

And that's how our friendship took off. Whenever something came up, I'd go and see him, and he was always coming to our house. He was more than a brother to Abu Ali [al-Biqa'i], and more than a father to my children.

Once I went to see him to ask for an electricity meter. That was because, after the Resistance started, no government official would give anything to the Lebanese who lived in this district. In the offices they used to tell us 'Go to the Resistance.' I went to the Camp Director, and he wouldn't give me one. He said he only gave them to Palestinians.

I swear to God, I went to him crying, and Abu Ahmad Sweid asked me: 'What's wrong, Um Ali?' ... So I told him. He didn't wait. Next day he went ahead and got me a meter in his son's name, in his son Ahmad's name, his son worked in Libya. He took his son's ration card and got hold of the meter in his son's name. My meter's in the name of Ahmad Sweid.

Days went by, and we started needing water, a water supply. Abu Ahmad Sweid went ahead and got water for our house, in the name of his son Ahmad.

May you rest in Heaven, Abu Ahmad Sweid. May you rest in Heaven.[46]

The women's march and the white flags

As shelling grew fiercer on the Thursday afternoon, as the Akka Hospital became crowded with the hundreds seeking protection, and as fear mounted with the growing numbers of wounded coming to all the hospitals, a number of women at the Akka Hospital conceived the idea of going to the Israelis to assure them they wanted peace and to demand a halt to the shelling of Sabra and Shatila. As discussion rose higher, one of the men who had sought refuge at the hospital began spurring them on and volunteered to go along with them. According to another report, he was the one who actually initiated the plan. Here is what a witness, Riad Sharqieh, had to say:

A man came to the Akka Hospital. He was wearing a pair of shorts and an unbuttoned short sleeve shirt. He was around 40, or a bit less maybe. He said, 'Come on, all of you, come on, let's go, the military are at the Kuwaiti Embassy.' This man was Lebanese, he went ahead and took everybody along, for a demonstration it was understood. They made flags for them there in the hospital, while I and Dr Muhammad, God have mercy on him, were sitting there. They made them white flags and they made the wood supports, and nearly 70 or 80 women, boys and girls went out, mostly they were women and children.[47]

The women and children's march took off from the Akka Hospital and the area round about and headed east towards the airport roundabout. From there the women approached the bridge on the airport road, where there was an Israeli checkpoint. The women did not, beyond doubt, neglect to raise the flags – and yet the Israelis began firing.

Sa'ida, one of the demonstrators and a worker at the Akka Hospital, tells how one of them called out loudly: 'Where are you going? There's nothing, *khabibi*, where are you going? There's nothing, go home. What's going on? Get out of here, get out of here, go home. Do you hear?' Then the voice became louder, and stronger and rougher: 'I just want one of you, I'll talk to just one of you, the rest can wait some way off.' A woman went along, with a man who had escorted the march, and they explained how shells were raining down on their houses and their families' houses, even though there was no resistance in Sabra and Shatila. He, though, would promise them nothing. Instead he looked at the crowd and said: 'Come on then, go up, there's a head man at the Kuwaiti Embassy.'[48]

The women went back with their children, along the same road, as the officer had said, to meet this Israeli superior near the Kuwaiti Embassy. It was, as Sa'ida recalls, a little after five in the afternoon. She recalls, too, how the street was full of gunmen in their dozens.

The distance between the Israeli checkpoint and the Kuwaiti Embassy, which the women's march had reached, would normally be a five-minute walk. This time, though, it took a good deal longer, because the march, in which around 50 women and children and a few men were taking part, coincided with the entry of the armed militias into Shatila. There was no way the women could have interpreted these movements, or the meaning of such exchanges between the gunmen as: 'You go in from here, we'll do it from there', or the significance of the jogging groups of dozens of gunmen, each entering an entrance or an alley or heading towards the Sports City (in order, so it later emerged, to enter the alleys of Greater Shatila from that side). How could these women possibly have known the men were bustling in to kill their people and relatives in their homes? The massacre had not started yet. No voices, no screams, no gunshots.

On one point the women's testimonies were clear and unanimous: these gunmen were not Israelis but Lebanese from the Christian militias. They could be sure of that from their dialects as they talked together, and from the names by which they called one another: 'Georges', 'Maroun', 'Michel'.

The massacre was, in fact, about to begin. The militias themselves were moving back and forth; according to Sa'ida, they numbered in their hundreds overall. None of the advancing militias, however, harassed anyone on the women's march – perhaps because they knew their primary mission was inside, within the borders drawn.

Near the wall of Jam'iyyat al-Ina'ash, opposite the Kuwaiti Embassy, was a group of militia remaining behind for guard surveillance duty. They ordered the women to stop, and here it was that the march ended.

At this point more than one gunman approached the women, yelling: 'Where are the men with you?' One of the women stepped forward and replied loudly: 'We want to say just a few words, just one word. We came to say there are a lot of people, including children, at the Akka Hospital who are being frightened by the shelling.' The reply came quick and firm: 'That's enough. Keep your mouth shut. Just sit down there and keep quiet. Where are the men?'

A few elderly men had escorted the march. The whole march, in fact, included only two or three men fit to bear arms. When the militiaman in charge pointed to two men who had been standing side by side, telling them to come forward, a number of women told him these were Lebanese civilians who were escorting them to the Israeli Command Centre. But the head militiaman appeared not to have heard. The gunmen shouted: 'Put your hands up!' They complied. The gunmen masked their faces, then took the men off towards the Sports City. The men walked away, step by step, then finally faded from sight. So it was that two men whose names the witnesses did not even know simply disappeared. Their fate remains unknown.[49]

However, the residents of Bir Hasan spoke of these men to the foreign press immediately after the massacre. They were, they said, a father and his son. The father was called Sayed, and he worked at the petrol station near the Akka Hospital. His son was called Hasan.[50] Why, how and when they escorted the march remains unknown, but the answer seems clear from the location of the petrol station, which was close to the Akka Hospital. The two men must have seen the women leaving the Akka Hospital with their white flags, and, from enthusiasm and a sense of chivalry, decided to escort them.

As for the man who encouraged the women to march at the hospital and who, according to the witness, 'was wearing a pair of shorts and an unbuttoned short sleeve shirt', it is not known how far he escorted the march itself. Did he leave it before it reached the wall of Jam'iyyat al-Ina'ash? Or did the militiamen somehow miss him? What is known, on the authority of the same witness, is that he returned home to Bir Hasan after things had cooled down.[51]

The white flags raised by the women in token of the march's aims infuriated the attacking militiamen who took the pieces of white cotton and trampled them underfoot, with the words:

So you've brought flags along. How nice! Why didn't you bring the Palestinian flag as well? Brought white flags? Sit down there. And stay sitting … Once we've finished here, if there aren't any terrorists, we'll get you out. But if there are terrorists, then woe betide you. We'll take you off.[52]

During the hour they were detained, which felt like several hours, the gunmen ordered the women and children to stand against the wall: Lebanese to one side, Palestinians to the other. This served to show that the majority had actually been Lebanese, but these latter received no preferential treatment. The gunmen remained arrogant and suspicious of the Lebanese women's identities: 'If anyone isn't telling the truth, we'll know from the dialect. We know how Palestinians talk. Tell the truth, or you'll regret it.'

When it came to the turn of one fat middle-aged woman, she answered boldly: 'I'm Palestinian and I'm not denying my origins. If people deny their origins, they're not worthy of having them.'[53]

The questioning went on. Then, suddenly, one of the gunmen shouted at the women and children:

Quiet, all of you, not another word. Keep quiet and get out of here, quick. No one stop or look back. Keep going, straight ahead, straight on. If anyone does any different, we'll pile them up and throw them down here.[54]

The women began running furiously. When some of them failed to keep up, Sa'ida heard one man say to his friends: 'Let's take them upstairs and finish them off.' Then she saw a gunman come running up and heard him say to the others: 'Come on, quick, get them away, before an Israeli tank comes.' The women's fate was determined in that moment. Some ran off, crying to be saved, along the bumpy sandy road behind the Sports City, but strong military hands seized them and dragged them towards the narrow alleys, while others managed to cross the Sports City Corniche with their children and reach the vicinity of the United Nations building, where they were once more ordered to stop. A woman cried out and begged to be allowed to go and feed her small children, whom she had left behind at home, but she was not treated any differently.

As for Sa'ida, one of those describing the women's march, she told how, near the United Nations building, she found a number of the women to be missing. They had, she thought, gone into the alleys amid the panic-stricken flight and the gunmen's fear of an Israeli tank arriving.[55] This was correct up to a point; what she had not imagined was that these women had been subjected to rape and murder,[56] and that she and the others taken to the United Nations building had been a good deal more fortunate. They were taken to a large truck parked there and forced to get in.

So it was that the women's march ended, and so the fate of the women themselves was decided. Some were raped; some killed; some abducted.

At around seven in the evening, with flares sweeping the sky, a large truck drove off carrying dozens of women and children. In addition to the women 'guilty' of taking part in the march, there were a number of women and girls who had committed the 'crime' of seeking refuge in a shelter. The shelter in question was that close by Jam'iyyat al-Ina'ash, which happened to be among the first subjected to attack. The women were forced to leave with their hands on their heads. One group was taken towards the alleys, another forced to walk to the truck, which took them away.

As for the truck and its passengers, that is another story.

Active resistance to the besieging Israeli Army

In contrast to the attempts of the camp's elders or of the women's march to tell the Israeli Command that the camp contained neither weapons nor fighters, the inclination of some young men was to confront the Israelis no matter what the outcome might be. The Israeli siege was not carried out without resistance from those able to provide it.

Who were these people? Were they Palestinians only, or Palestinians and Lebanese combined? How many were they, and what weapons did they have? Where did confrontation take place, and was there a coordinated plan for it? And how could witnesses be reached with a view to finding out what actually happened?

It was noted in the Introduction that interviews with victims' relatives and other witnesses were conducted on an ad hoc basis, without the need for pre-planning or specific selection. The event was both a general experience and a recent one, and witnesses' recognition of how important it was to record the dramatic happenings in a proper historical way was the key to evoking sharp memories and profound feelings.

As such, any one interview could be followed by others, based only on the names and events involved. Yet there remained one group not immediately accessible, and that was the freedom fighters. Not only were these very limited in number, they also preferred to keep out of sight of the press following the massacre. The only way to reach them was through comrades and friends who had previous knowledge of them and would know where to find them. It so happened that certain of these latter, who worked on the Oral History Project in its first stage (between 1982 and 1984), were able to conduct interviews with some of the freedom fighters on a basis of mutual friendship and trust.

Such interviews were nonetheless few at this stage and not sufficient, in consequence, to shed the full necessary light on the nature of the resistance and the extent of its effectiveness. I therefore decided, during the second stage of the project (between 1998 and 2001), to return and finalize the interviews along the same lines – using, that is, someone working on the project who was also friend to a number of the fighters – till all the pieces of the jigsaw had been collected.

Most of the fighters were young, some of them under 20. The oldest, Hajj Abu Hisham, was in his forties. When asked whether any leaderships had met to decide how to act in the event of the Israeli Army advancing and besieging the district, he answered as follows:

After the fighters left, there was no one there except the families ... Leaderships? What leaderships? I didn't see anything ... No. If anyone tells you we stood up ... and that we fought, that's exaggerating things ... You know, there are a lot of people exaggerating 17 years on, but we don't exaggerate. The ideology of the Front [Popular Front for the Liberation of Palestine – PFLP] is geared to fighting the Israelis. I mean, when the Israelis came and they were here, here they were drinking tea at the Akka Hospital, why shouldn't we disturb their rest? ...

I mean, on that day we, the Popular Front, stood firm. Not many fighters stayed, not many, there were seven or eight of us, no more, and there were some other people with us ...

The true history of the massacre is, we saw what we tell, and what we didn't see we don't tell, and what we heard we say we heard.[57]

The testimonies of Hajj Abu Hisham and others who carried arms and fought, men and boys, and the testimonies of residents who witnessed what happened therefore remain the only reliable source with regard to active resistance.

There were four places witnessing such confrontation: Hayy al-Horsh, Hayy Farhat, Hayy al-Fakhani and Hayy al-Doukhi. Hayy al-Fakhani lies beyond the northern borders of Sabra, but active resistance there related to Sabra and Shatila specifically rather than to West Beirut in general, mainly because the Israeli plan treated Hayy al-Fakhani as lying within the ambit of the besieged camps. It was stated in the Hebrew press that the Israeli Army had, on the Thursday, finalized the encirclement of the refugee camps in the districts of Sabra, Shatila and al-Fakhani.[58]

Conflicting accounts have been given as to the availability of weapons. Some believe there were no weapons, others that Kalashnikovs were available to some young men.

Comrade Hussein, the Popular Front leader, told of his concern over the camp's security. His picture of the situation is vivid and realistic:

There was no committee or organization responsible for the security of the camp. But the camp was already divided due to the presence of the Palestinian factions and their original positions. For example, the axis of the Popular Front extended from Sabri Hamadeh Palace up to al-Horsh, where it had a location opposite the Akka Hospital. Hayy Farhat belonged to the Arab Front, and so on ...

The situation was like a military style 'every man for himself', as all the leaderships had either left by sea or disappeared into the residential quarters of the city, away from the camps.

It was frustrating from a psychological point of view; the departure of the fighters and the Revolution from Beirut had left things in an agitated state, to say nothing of facing the unknown, which was bitter at best.[59]

Hajj Abu Hisham, the other member of the Front and the oldest of the fighters,

testified that there had been skirmishes and clashes since the Israelis began their siege of the Shatila district, and that this was what had caused people to hurry off, if they could, to some safer place. As for the Thursday morning, a comrade of his who was in charge of the weapons stores had called and asked him what weapons were available. Here the narrator explains the situation:

After the withdrawal, I mean, after the fighters had left, we started to give the Murabitoun weapons, and we gave the Socialists, and we gave the Movement, the Amal Movement. There were no Hezbullah then. We gave and gave to other parties, and they were all tough people.

Now, the man in charge asked me: 'Can you get weapons for the guys?' ... I told him: 'If anyone can do it, then I will.'

I had my car with me, I went to Eisha Bakkar, I went there and spoke with a guy who was a leader at the Communist Labour Party. I told him I'm so-and-so and this is the way things are. He said to me 'You've got them, come along with me' ... It was the other way round, we started getting weapons from other people, we started taking from them ... I swear, I went twice or three times, myself, we had a four-wheel drive, a Toyota we used to fill with weapons ...[60]

The weaponry fetched by Hajj Abu Hisham and Abu Ra'ed from the Lebanese patriot parties was used solely in Hayy al-Horsh. Each quarter had its own particular situation with respect to weapons: that in Hayy al-Fakhani and Hayy al-Doukhi was different, since there the fighters used weapons they were able to bring from their houses and nearby offices. At Hayy Farhat, too, there was no need to fetch new weapons as there was a store there. Since the quality of weapons concealed in it was insufficient for confrontation and defiance, it was decided to blow it up. This will be discussed later.

Hayy al-Horsh

The first missiles launched at the Israeli Army from Shatila came from the Horsh district opposite the Akka Hospital. The fighters who launched them were not actually ready: some were at a routine meeting at the office of the Popular Front, others still at home. When they were surprised by the arrival of the Israeli tanks they simply took whatever weapons were to hand.

Comrade Hussein narrates how he heard, on the Thursday, of the concentration of Israeli Forces under the Cola bridge, threw on his clothes then sped off with some of his comrades to the Cola area where they found the situation to be normal. Then, returning towards Shatila Camp, they came face to face with Mirkava tanks near the Engineering College of Beirut Arab University. They accordingly changed direction, to Sabra Street, and from there to the Horsh district where the political office of the Front was situated.[61]

When Comrade Hussein and those with him reached the office, others were already there. Each had his own account of what he had done or seen. One of these was Abu Ra'ed, who told how he had learned of the Israeli Army units' advance from a Palestinian woman who had come, horrified, into the office:

This woman came, agitated and frightened, and started saying: 'The Israelis have reached Sabri Hamadeh Palace, and you're just sitting here.' Well, we said: 'You really mean that?' ...

So anyway ... I went with another comrade, we were in civilian clothes, till we'd nearly reached the Security building. I mean, we saw it, there it all was, a Mirkava and soldiers. We didn't have any weapons. We were just reconnoitring. It was just a reaction to what the woman had told us. Now we'd made sure, we raced off to our office, the political office, and we met three comrades from the Leadership of the Front [Hussein, the leading fighter, and those with him had reached the office while Abu Ra'ed was out on reconnaissance] ...

I told them: 'Comrades, the Israelis have reached Sabri Hamadeh Palace.' 'What are you talking about?' they said. I said: 'It's true, I tell you.' So Comrade Hussein said: 'Go and find out this and that from the guys.' You understand? There were particular people I went looking for. I found them. One of them was my brother-in-law, there were four in all.

The important thing is, we came to a decision ... In under fifteen or twenty minutes, there were three B7s and one lot of RPG shells in the office. We had five or six Kalashnikovs hidden as well, and a machine-gun. But the ammunition wasn't enough

for a proper battle, just for around ten minutes of light fighting. Each had three or four rounds at the most.

Anyway, Comrade Hussein said: 'We'll fight them, guys ... We won't let them come in the camp. Here they are and here's our chance, I mean they've come to us, just like al-Hakim [Dr George Habash] said, just how they wanted us to: they've come, and we'll fight them ...'[62]

When the first batch of weapons reached the Front's office, a number of men, around 17, had already gathered there. Not all belonged to the Popular Front: there was a *shibl* (young fighter) from Fatah, and also a girl from Fatah, both of whom bore themselves well.

Hussein gave his instructions to Abu Ra'ed and the others: they were to go on reconnaissance to an office of the Front near the Akka Hospital, to assess the possibilities of combating the enemy on a hit-and-run basis. Abu Ra'ed gave the following account:

We went, three comrades and me, we had a B7 and three Kalashnikovs, and we each had two grenades, hand grenades. We were masked, covered with red *kufiyyehs*, like Palestinians [the narrator was Lebanese]. Only our eyes were visible, because there were spies around us, as you know.

Before we got to our office, around 70 or 100 metres off, the man in charge of the four of us said to me: 'Put your weapons down and go to the Akka Hospital, and check where the Israelis are.'

So I put my weapons down and he stayed, along with the other two guys. I was walking just like any other civilian – I mean a Lebanese one, sorry! I walked along quite naturally, and I reached the office. The office is on the street, after all. I was walking down the street, and I looked around and saw the Israeli Army at the entrance to Shatila, right on the Kuwaiti Embassy slope. I looked towards the airport bridge and there was a tank which had protected itself by turning and pointing its gun towards Ghobairi Square. How did we know that? Because later we got closer and made sure. Anyway, I went down and stood with the civilians for around five minutes. The Akka Hospital was full of people, men and women – as you know, it was a war situation and people were looking for refuge in the shelters at the hospital, no one was going to attack a hospital. I talked to them, and there were a lot of them whom I knew well.[63]

As they were returning from this reconnaissance, and while Abu Ra'ed was approaching the Zouk office between the Communist Party office and the Husseiniyieh, at the beginning of al-Horsh, he saw a Fatah *shibl* who was known in Shatila standing at the entrance to the Husseiniyieh. He was obviously alone and about to fight without talking to anyone or receiving instructions from anyone. As Abu Ra'ed took a few steps forward, he saw a large group of what he assumed were Israelis walking down the main street, coming from the airport bridge towards the Kuwaiti Embassy. There were ten or twelve of them, and in front of them were striding two masked men – their role, clearly, was to show the 'soldiers' the way. Abu Ra'ed provides the following description of these 'soldiers' and the two spies ahead of them:

You know how everything happens in a flash. Anyway, I swear to God, I started running forward just like that. The Israelis were telling me: 'Hey, you, get back.' So, I swear to God, I got back somehow, or got round, I don't know. All I know is I heard myself screaming at this *shibl* of ours: 'Hey, Hani, the Israelis are right there.' You see? I went off and walked towards the guys, our comrades. I heard an explosion, a bomb exploding, it sounded like a hand grenade. So I started yelling from some way off, before I saw anyone in the Horsh alleys: 'Hey, such-and-such, hey, such-and-such, the Israelis are here!' 'They're trying to get in al-Horsh!' I don't know how, I just said it like that.

We found out later it was Hani who'd flung a grenade at the men walking along. At the same moment, or a matter of a minute, I mean, or maybe half a minute, that guy from Fatah, the *shibl*, had exploded a phosphorus bomb. I mean, they were knocked out, they were screwed, as they say.[64]

As Abu Ra'ed hurried back to assure his comrades in al-Horsh that he had seen 'the Israelis' with his own eyes, he received the instruction to go back to the Akka Hospital. This time, though, he went armed, along with another armed comrade of his, equipped with a B7. The mission was to set up a high ambush overlooking the Israelis in the airport bridge area with the aim of hitting an Israeli tank. He gives the following account:

We wanted to see if we could hit a tank. The point is, Comrade Hussein and I went down and saw them there at the bridge. Anyway, my dear friend, that's when it started. He started shooting this way, I started shooting that way. Don't forget, we were standing on the road and we knew we could have been killed or wounded ... Later on, we moved back a bit to our office, which was four or five metres off the road.

So we started shooting our guns and they started artillery fire, and smoky fire as well, against us and the whole line, the whole Horsh line, and into the Horsh interior. That's the point, we started shooting our guns and they started artillery shelling ...[65]

So it was that the battle began.

In the meantime five or six fighters had reached the Popular Front office one after the other. These were from the Front itself and from Fatah. A small group, including the present witness Abu Ra'ed, Comrade Hatem, the Fatah girl 'Sister Fatima' and Comrade Butros [Farid al-Khatib], who was leading the group, went off. Two clashes took place in the first minutes as shells and gunfire were heard from both sides. Then three of them moved on towards the mass cemetery (as the place came to be known later). They had gone no more than 70 metres past the Front centre when they saw an Israeli military truck full of soldiers, heading from the airport roundabout towards the Kuwaiti Embassy. The truck fired at al-Horsh – fire the men interpreted as precautionary, though it was certainly not random shelling. Comrade Hatem made an attempt to hit the truck:

Comrade Hatem was 50 or 60 metres away from us. Unluckily for him and us, he raised the B7 to try and blow up the tank, which was exposed, I mean, if it had only worked for him, it would have been a massacre for the Israelis. What we saw instead was an M16 coming from the Kuwaiti Embassy. There wasn't all the building you see on this street now. Anyway, he was hit by a shot, here on his cheek, and he fell to the ground. We quickly pulled him away. The Israelis in the tank seemed to have noticed something, and they started strafing the Horsh district. That's how it was. By then we'd pulled Comrade Hatem away, as I told you, and handed him over to some civilians who were standing there, I don't know who, actually. We knew there were just a few of us fighters who didn't want to leave the centre. That's how it was. We'd reckoned they'd get in, but we hadn't reckoned, I swear, that they'd get control of the highways, cut the district off, and come into the alleys.[66]

Comrade Butros and the fighter Fatima, along with two or three others, went on firing towards an elevated site near the Kuwaiti Embassy, which was a garrison for anti-aircraft artillery during the war. Then, as the Israelis began heavy artillery shelling, shelling stopped from the resistance fighters' side. Aircraft were also spotted, flying low as they normally did to nullify the risk of resistance anti-aircraft, and there were sham raids designed to strike terror. At the same time the smoky shelling intensified, leading the fighters to conclude that the Israelis wanted to pull out their casualties following Hani's grenade attack.

During the 'battle', other fighters had arrived piecemeal at al-Horsh Popular Front office, till the number of fighters between the office and the ambush set up by the men on the perimeter of al-Horsh – over a distance of 200–300 metres, that is – neared 20. Sporadic fighting continued for around two hours, in the following fashion:

The point is, my dear friend, we fought for around two hours, not all the time, right through, but maybe a quarter or half an hour was calm and the rest was fighting. So the battles cooled down a bit on both sides because they needed to pull out their victims and casualties. I'm not saying I killed anyone. I shot at the soldiers; whether or not anyone was hit I don't know. I won't exaggerate and swear to you that someone fell down in front of me, like in the movies, you know. But I should think I must surely have hit. I mean, you couldn't have missed, even if you'd covered your eyes and just shot at the street, there were so many soldiers. At the end of the day things cooled down a bit. We dug a trench, in just a few minutes, maybe, just a few minutes, at the entrance to the Husseiniyieh. We had a flower shop downstairs whose upper corner overlooked a road leading into Bir Hasan, it goes between Akka Hospital and La Geralda. So there I put my weapons down and sat down – things had cooled down, as I told you. Abu Ramzi

al-Shafi'i and Walid Ghanem were sitting next to me.

Anyway, I took a way that goes around between La Geralda and the Akka Hospital, towards Bir Hasan, because we were saying the Israelis were everywhere now, all this happened on the first day. I saw one, two and three who made it through. I was on the alert now, I mean, I started getting ready. So I was sitting in a small sandy barricade we'd dug quickly, as I told you. How we dug it I don't know, it was like setting up an ambush, that's how it was … So I saw there were getting to be more and more of them, and they were around 150 metres away from me. They were jogging with stuff on their backs, you know, it was their ammunition and equipment. Each one was carrying around 20 kilos. Anyway, they were around seven or eight 'Israeli' soldiers, and getting more. They were crossing in groups. There was a palace near Bir Hasan. They'd been hiding behind that and moving, step by step, wherever it was they were heading; they weren't coming here towards Al-Jala' Street. And I couldn't describe our feelings when we found out later, when everything was over, that those men had been going to commit a massacre. Later on we found out they'd been Lebanese Forces and Sa'd Haddad …[67]

The comrades returned and assembled at the Front's office. One of the fighters came with Comrade Butros to tell them they had managed to hit an officer and two or three soldiers, who had been standing on top of the hill near the Kuwaiti Embassy, confident they were safe there. They had been looking through binoculars, and their superior had been in various positions pointing with a stick. The comrades struck them with a B7 missile and gunfire, and there was returning fire from several sides.

With the day almost over, the group of fighters was still fighting in al-Horsh in the belief they were fighting just the Israelis; in fact it is certain that, from the Wednesday up till the Thursday evening, the only Israeli soldiers were those in Israeli vehicles. The Israeli Army's role, during its siege, was to pepper the district with grenades and rockets with a view to forcing residents down into the shelters; which is in fact what happened. As for the soldiers in the Israeli truck, it is difficult to establish whether they were Israelis or Lebanese, as some militia members did in fact arrive in Israeli vehicles, while others arrived in those of the Lebanese Forces. As for those described by Abu Ra'ed as having walked in groups of seven or eight, the description matches that of the Lebanese Forces in their attempt to advance through Kuwaiti Embassy Street, though it would not have crossed the mind of someone like Abu Ra'ed that these could be other than Israelis. Even so, Abu Ra'ed's testimony that he had heard speech in broken Arabic, of the kind normally spoken by Israeli Jews, implies that there had been Israeli soldiers with them – although their precise number and role remains unclear. (See Abu Ra'ed's testimony for the Friday, Chapter 4, pp. 120–1.)

There were reinforced concrete barricades in the Horsh district, but these gave no protection against tanks: the concrete was no more than forty centimetres thick, and the Israeli tanks could simply smash their way through. The fighters therefore sought to stay away from these and keep moving around. Comrade Hussein's instructions were that each one should fire one full or half round before taking up a new position, so leaving the attackers in suspense and reluctant to advance. At the front door of the Popular Front were the same fighters who had assembled two hours earlier. There was also the group of four friends, including their spokesman Abu Ra'ed.

Abu Ra'ed then heard, from people going home for food before returning to take refuge at the Akka Hospital, how Comrade Hani had hit a half-track for the second time. Hani was well known in the quarter, and so were his comrades at the Popular Front on account of their having an office there and of their close contact with residents. This PFLP organization was especially notable for including numbers of Lebanese members. The latter were, indeed, in the majority among the approximately 100 fighters it numbered just prior to the invasion. At this crucial hour, though, there were only a few, since a new 'war' had not been expected.

Suddenly someone came to report that a Popular Front member had been wounded not far from the Kuwaiti Embassy. Enquiries were made about his dress and appearance. Was he dark-skinned? Had he been wearing a blue sweater and jeans? When an affirmative reply was given, they knew Comrade Butros had been wounded.[68] His real name was Farid al-Khatib. He was a prime example of a courageous freedom fighter.

According to Hajj Abu Hisham, the first in the Popular Front to be killed on the Thursday was Jamal Barakeh, a man from the ambulance service. After his death, his comrades continued to transport the wounded to hospital in the mistaken belief that the attackers had been Israelis. His testimony about the fighters dwells mainly on the brave young Fatah woman Sister Fatima.

At the start there were around seven or eight, including a young woman I have the very highest regard for.

This young woman came dressed in a pair of tight trousers and a blouse. She stood staring at us, I recognized her. She said: 'I want to fight, I want to be with you.'

And in fact this brave young woman carried the ammunition on her side and started shooting. And all the other seven or eight fellows, may God reward their efforts, and they're still alive, thank God, did things no one else could have brought off, and this young woman was with them.

During that time, while they were getting in [on the Thursday evening], there was no shelling of the camp. Those who came in were on foot, and they were killing whole families, so we found out later … So the people who'd stayed with us, where were they to hide, in the mosque? And where were we? At the political office in al-Horsh …[69]

Night was now falling, and they all agreed to meet next morning. Comrade Hussein left the district with a few of his comrades, and most of the men from the Popular Front preferred not to spend the night at the office as they would normally have done since it was on a wide street and was well known and easily accessible. The group of four spent the night instead at Comrade Abu Ramzi al-Shafi'i's, inside the camp, while others went to their own homes within Shatila. They were virtually certain no one would be able to enter through the alleys, and even if they did it would be easier to defend themselves here than elsewhere.

Hayy Farhat

In the Horsh district an exchange of fire was heard from the relative vicinity of Hayy Farhat. This, the Popular Front realized, was probably happening near the office of the Arab Liberation Front, near Sabri Hamadeh Palace, and a group of four went there to discover what was going on and to offer support.

The group got into the grounds of the Military College, which had been reduced to a wreck during the invasion by the Israeli air force. There the four men heard the sound of a B7 grenade and saw pieces of flying metal, and discovered that the resistance fighters had been in Sabri Hamadeh Palace, fronting on to the public highway. A few seconds later they saw metal fragments being scattered nearby and recognized these as parts of an Israeli vehicle. This fired their spirits; the grenade must, they felt sure, have been fired by their comrades of the Arab Front, and they hurried to provide any assistance needed. Making their way swiftly to the office of the Arab Front a few metres off, they found, they estimated, around 15 of their comrades, led by Comrade Mansour, famous as being, in Palestinian slang, a *zghort* ('tough guy') – or *qabaday* in colloquial Lebanese.

The state of affairs around the Arab Front centre at Hayy Farhat was quite different from that around the Popular Front centre at Hayy al-Horsh. In the latter case the 'soldiers' had made no attempt at a concentrated advance, being content to pull away their wounded or dead. There was, by contrast, continuous shelling towards Sabri Hamadeh Palace, on the Arab Front centre and around it.

It was clear to the fighters that confronting an 'advancing army', however heroically, with the limited weapons available would only lead to further loss of life. When they were virtually sure of the enemy's ability to break into the camp through the so-called Sabri Hamadeh Palace side, they had no choice but to consider an alternative plan. This was quickly conceived and as quickly approved by all the fighters: to blow up a weapons store of the Arab Front which was full of grenade rockets, Katiochas and artillery ammunition.

While the fighters of the Arab and Popular Fronts were debating the practicalities of this – precisely who was to do it, and how and when – they realized a 14.5 cannon, on a Russian truck being driven by a brave and celebrated fighter and with another fighter concealed behind it, had arrived nearby. The driver approached with his truck, up to the middle of Kuwaiti Embassy Street. Then, as he reached the airport bridge, the concealed fighter rose and began firing at the tank that had been bombarding Hayy Farhat a short while back. As the witness said: 'He emptied them, bub, bub, bub, bub … four cylinders, and for sure he was hitting everything in front of him, and all us fighters got up behind him with our Kalashnikovs, and we all hit.'[70]

Following this operation a new move became imperative. There should, everyone agreed, be a withdrawal but no flight. Fighters of the Arab Front told their friends and neighbours of the Popular Front that they would do best to return to their office within al-Horsh. This would avoid too great a concentration of fighters in one place, such as would enable the attackers to wipe them out from the air or through intensive artillery bombardment. As one of them said, 'I mean, they could literally plough us, it would spell disaster for all of us to be here together.' The comrades of the Popular Front, persuaded by this argument, returned to their office but resolved nevertheless to keep moving between Sabri Hamadeh Palace and the Arab Front centre, so that they in turn could be sure of their comrades' movements and offer any necessary assistance.

The Arab Front fighters lay awake that night planning to blow up the store and so make the Israelis think, from the prolonged blasts, that resistance was fierce and well supplied with weapons.

Hayy al-Fakhani

Testimonies regarding the fighting in Hayy al-Fakhani differ from their counterparts in both Hayy al-Horsh and Hayy Farhat – though it should be said that, while four interviews were obtained as to the fighting in the quarter, conducted by four of those taking part in the Oral History Project, none of these latter were able to gain access to any local leaders in al-Fakhani. It later emerged that there was in fact no unified local command in any case: simply, any man able to get hold of a weapon resisted. The gist of the testimonies deals with the significant fighting near the Engineering College of Beirut Arab University.

The first testimony is from a Fatah fighter, obtained by a friend of his in the same organization. The fighter asked his friend not to reveal his identity, so for the purposes of this volume I shall call him 'Ibrahim Baroudi'.

Ibrahim talked of his surveillance of specific spots where the Israelis had been since the beginning of their siege of Sabra and Shatila. From the early hours, he said, they had become concentrated in three main positions: the Akka Hospital, the Kuwaiti Embassy and the Engineering College. He gave the following account of the armed skirmish he saw near the Engineering College at nine o'clock on the Thursday morning:

Just before nine o'clock, there was an armed skirmish involving people who had some sense of honour, they went out to fight the Israeli forces with the weapons they had available, Kalashnikovs or RPGs. The battle went on all day and all night, but it cooled down after an Israeli retreat ...[71]

The nature of the clashes and of the resistance in general led Ibrahim to conclude that there was no senior command in al-Fakhani, and other testimonies confirm this. The witness tells repeatedly how he saw many *ashbal*, young fighters, in this particular spot, and he also confirmed the central importance of the Engineering College, behind which the Israelis eventually retreated. On the Thursday evening Ibrahim headed towards the Akka Hospital to sound things out, and he described what he saw:

At around five o'clock on the Thursday evening I made for the Akka Hospital area, and found no Israelis at all round about. There were people hiding in the hospital. I was surprised to see the Israelis retreat like that, I found it odd. I went back to the camp, to the main street, at around half past five ...[72]

It was Ibrahim who, from within Hayy al-Doukhi, contrived to confront the killers on the evening of the first day. We shall return to this later in the section on Hayy al-Doukhi below.

The second testimony regarding Hayy al-Fakhani comes from another Fatah fighter, Abu Imad, who was not, however, for reasons he explains, able to take any active part in the fighting. He also relates an experience he had, similar to Ibrahim's, on the Thursday morning. He had, he said, been at home when he was visited by a friend, who asked him to go along to al-Fakhani to reconnoitre the situation:

So we were in the middle of the camp, between Sabra and Shatila. We got out, we didn't have any weapons with us, and we went to reconnoitre. When we got into al-Fakhani, we saw an Israeli tank had made it there – that was on the Thursday.

There were five guys and one girl with us, they wanted to hit the tank. A Palestinian woman, who used to live in al-Fakhani, came screaming. When she screamed, the Israelis on the tank heard us and they pointed the gun and fired two shells at the building. The shells went through to the back of the building. We retreated a bit, back to the Gaza Hospital ... then, [later on] we moved back to Sabra. Between Sabra and Shatila, a bloodstained woman came saying the Phalangists were slaughtering people – and I didn't believe her! ...

If we'd thought it was true, do you think we would have let them do it, slaughter people? All I remember is friends of mine dragging me off to the shelter, and saying: 'Everybody's in the shelters now ...'[73]

The third testimony comes from Zainab Saqallah, a Palestinian woman who lived near the Beirut Arab University area. On the Thursday morning, she said, at around half past five, she had been forced into the shelter by the ceaseless Israeli shelling:

I left the house at half past five, with shells falling like a rainstorm ... I went to the shelter, there was shelling from Israel that wouldn't stop. And the streets were full of zealous young men armed with RPGs and Kalashnikovs ... but it was obviously zeal without any planning.[74]

This woman invited three young men from the district to come and talk about what happened in al-Fakhani. They testified, in sum, how they saw Israeli tanks at the buildings opposite the university, known as the Sadeq buildings; they had come to a halt at building number 3, right on the corner of al-Razi bookshop. One said he had seen a damaged tank, and he also described the resistance fighters at al-Fakhani as having been zealous young men, clearly lacking in co-ordination. He further noted the presence of two girls with them.[75]

The fourth testimony comes from a Palestinian fighter, Ali Murad, who played his part in confronting the Israelis near the Arab University. He spoke of the confusion prevalent among the men and among the residents generally, especially after hearing that enemy forces had entered in the direction of the Sports City. He describes the men's feelings, along with the events of the Thursday night, as follows:

Weapons, there were weapons there. But at the same time there was confusion, I mean, there were guys but they weren't organized, I mean, they didn't know what to do. All they knew was that there was an enemy, Israel, and it was getting closer, and they started wondering what the Israelis were going to do to us. I was one of the guys on the Fakhani side, and we were all armed. Yeah, there were arms, the guys were there, most were Palestinian, but there were Lebanese too – there were some from the Communist Party, and there was an organization called Al-Afwaj al-Arabiya, and Ansar al-Thawra, and there were Murabitoun. But they were individuals, you couldn't say they were organized at all, under any local command in charge of them.

That night, Thursday, we found out later it was the first night of the massacre, we saw flare shells when the night came. We saw them from the Fakhani side, to the south side of Beirut, over Shatila Camp. There were flare shells, a lot of them, we started saying maybe they'd get in. We had no idea they were massacring people, but after about three or four hours, people started getting out, they were coming towards al-Fakhani. They were running off, up the slope. We asked them: 'What's the matter?' They said: 'There's a massacre, the Israelis are massacring people …'[76]

This had to be investigated, and Ali Murad accordingly rushed with a group of other men towards Sabra, where they found no trace of a massacre, and from there they headed towards Shatila Camp. By then night had fallen. Their progress through the alleys of Shatila on that first night will be returned to later.

Hayy al-Doukhi

As the members of the peace delegation composed of men from the camp were heading towards the Israeli Forces Command Centre, there were, as noted earlier, some young men with Kalashnikovs on Shatila Main Street, notably in the vicinity of the Ali Hamdar Café. The members approached them, telling them not to take things too far, and even, in some cases, urging them to hold back completely. These elderly men clearly took a paternalist attitude towards the young ones and, equally, they were well enough aware that the zealous youngsters were powerless to halt the blockading Israeli forces. They were even more aware of the Israeli Army's ability to identify the type of bullets fired at them and see that these were fired simply in a spirit of anger and dignified resistance.

What the elderly members did not realize was what had actually been planned for Sabra and Shatila. They could never remotely have imagined that they themselves would be murdered one by one, while the young men, for their part, would go on resisting for several hours afterwards.

Ibrahim Baroudi, the fighter who took part in the resistance at Hayy al-Fakhani, had a different view of the young men from that held by the elderly delegation: he both supported them and co-operated with them, as will be demonstrated in the later description of the events of Thursday and Friday, the first and second days. He had, as we have seen, left Hayy al-Fakhani on the Thursday evening and headed towards the Akka Hospital. There he found, to his surprise, that the Israelis had withdrawn from some of their earlier positions. He made for Shatila around half past five.[77]

Ibrahim would be the first and last to combat the attacking forces, knowing them to be Lebanese and not Israeli Forces. This will be further described in Chapter 3.

The Israeli role in preparing the militias' entry

The massacre could clearly not have taken place without Israeli preparation. The elements of this preparation may be summarized as follows:

- The siege of the whole Sabra and Shatila district, making entry and exit subject to Israeli wishes – the Israelis did in fact prevent people from leaving. The question has to be asked, why were women and children stopped if the goal was, as stated, to seek out 'armed terrorists'?
- The spreading of a false and deliberately deceptive atmosphere of tranquillity among the residents of Sabra and Shatila, both Palestinian and Lebanese. It does appear, indeed, that some Israeli soldiers had no knowledge of the coming event and that they did not therefore tell people to return home with the conscious intention of sending them to their deaths. Such soldiers were, however, in a minority. The statements of others imply a knowledge of what was about to take place, and these latter soldiers had a corresponding interest in keeping people together and restricting them to the area under siege, that is, the Sabra and Shatila district.
- The insinuation that surrender of weapons was the sole requirement, and that any who surrendered them could return home safe and unmolested. Statements to this effect were spread by means of leaflets and announced through megaphones.
- The concentrated shelling that forced residents to run for the shelters, which then provided an ideal place for massacre. Why, after all, should a so-called 'protective' force carry out shelling of this kind? Does such shelling kill only 'terrorists'?
- The co-ordination of the Israelis with the Lebanese militia teams before the massacre, as demonstrated in questions about the location of shelters, put to residents by 'strangers' in 'strange cars'. This became evident, subsequently, through the ceaseless Israeli shelling that forced residents to gather in these shelters.

(It was later confirmed that those taking refuge there were not only subjected to mass killing, but were actually the first to be killed.)

- The withdrawal of the Israeli Army from positions in the immediate proximity of Sabra and Shatila, especially around the perimeter of the Akka Hospital. This withdrawal had quite clearly been programmed in advance so as to give the attacking militias a free hand to enter from that side and bear the sole liability. The whole 'drama' could thus be enacted as though the Israeli forces had seen and heard nothing. There was nothing, after all, to link them directly with the event.
- The halting of the concentrated Israeli shelling, and of the sniping, before the killers entered, together with the lighting up of the district as darkness fell, turning night into day.
- The permission given to several hundred members of the armed militias to enter the camp and the district as a whole, ostensibly in search of 2,500 armed men. How can such a pretext possibly be credible? Israel did not deny knowledge of the Lebanese Forces' entry in search of fighters, or 'terrorists' as it called them. Had Israel really believed in the existence of 2,500 fighters, could their elimination or capture have been effected by a mere few hundred militiamen – 600, according to the highest estimate, on that first day?

Conclusion

- President Bashir al-Gemayel was assassinated on the afternoon of Tuesday 14 September 1982. As dawn broke on the Wednesday, Israeli forces entered Beirut by a number of routes, and, just before six in the morning, massive explosions began to be heard in the Sports City district. Israeli Forces were advancing to tighten their grip on the Sabra, Shatila and al-Fakhani districts.
- The feelings of the inhabitants, Palestinian and Lebanese, ranged between tranquillity and terror. Those reassured had been witnesses of the Israeli invasion of South Lebanon, where occupation

soldiers had not harassed unarmed civilians or harmed women, the elderly or children. As for those who were frightened, either their feelings were instinctive or they had noted the logical links between three things: the cutting off of supplies of bread and electricity, the ceaseless and unjustified shelling of secure residential quarters, and the prevention of people from leaving.

- From the Thursday morning on, the Israeli artillery began to focus shelling on the district. As the day went on, shelling grew so intense that shelters, hospitals and mosque, the places normally regarded as safe, became crowded with residents. Yet it is against all reason to suppose such shelling would eliminate 'fighters', wherever these might be. It was rather intended to strike terror in residents and force them to seek refuge in the shelters. The reason for this would be revealed on the first day of the massacre – in the first hours, indeed.

- A delegation formed of men from the camp and known as the peace delegation attempted to reach the Israeli Command Centre on the Thursday afternoon. Its mission was to inform the Israelis that there were no weapons worth mentioning in the camp and that the residents had no wish to fight. None of the members returned.

- Dozens of women and their children marched in a demonstration from the Akka Hospital to the Israeli Command Centre, to ask them to halt the shelling since there were no weapons or 'terrorists'. This demonstration coincided with the entry of the Lebanese Forces just before the Thursday evening. Those taking part were finally abducted in trucks, or raped or killed in the alleys behind the Sports City.

- The greater part of the Palestinian freedom fighters had left Lebanon completely. As for those from the ' '48 group' who remained in Beirut – in accordance with the Habib Agreement itself – even most of these had not, given the prevailing circumstances, returned to the camps in September 1982.

- There was no local, unified command in the Sabra and Shatila district, but rather the local offices of some organizations and fronts. Some of these offices had been locked up following the departure of leading figures, others were still manned by people fighting on. It was these who contrived to raise some resistance and to distribute arms among unarmed local men who knocked at their doors asking for weapons.

- The groups carrying out the resistance were to be found in four quarters: Hayy al-Horsh, Hayy Farhat, Hayy al-Fakhani and Hayy al-Doukhi. Despite the small geographical area involved, not every group of fighters knew of the existence of the others. There were two reasons for this: first, the lack of a unified command; and second, the actual nature of the resistance, which was effectively a collection of spontaneous reactions.

- According to the testimonies of residents and fighters, the total number of those actively resisting the blockading Israeli Forces on the Thursday in the four focal areas was around 60 men and five girls. Of these only a limited sub-group comprised trained fighters; the majority were simply zealous young people in whom enthusiasm outran actual combat abilities.

- The Israeli Command besieging the district should have realized, from the nature of the resistance and the types of weapons being used, that those opposing them were mostly zealous young people rather than professional fighters. They should have been able to make a correct assessment of the numbers involved: a few dozen in all, professionally trained only in isolated cases.

- When the Lebanese militias began to break into Shatila on the Thursday evening, the 'combat' situation between those resisting and the Israeli Forces was as follows: in Hayy Farhat the fighting had stopped completely; in Hayy al-Horsh the fighters continued into the early hours, brandishing their guns at the marching gunmen in the belief they were Israelis, but the fighting had stopped completely by seven o'clock; in

Hayy al-Fakhani fighting, in the form of sporadic skirmishes, was first and last against Israeli Forces outside the Sabra and Shatila district; in Hayy al-Doukhi there were skirmishes initiated by zealous young men against the Israelis; Kalashnikovs were fired in the air from the besieged district to demonstrate their presence. Was there any possibility of a Kalashnikov bullet reaching from there to, say, the Sports City street, where the closest tanks had been?

- In sum, resistance in the four focal areas on the Thursday should have been such as to persuade the blockading Israeli Forces, and therefore their commanders, that rumours of seasoned fighters remaining behind in violation of the Habib Agreement were unfounded.

- The Israeli Army radio station in Tel Aviv was the first source to broadcast a report on active resistance to the Israeli Forces besieging Shatila, having, on the Thursday, before the entry of the armed militias, provided a report through its correspondent Arad Nir to the effect that the Israeli Army had achieved complete control of West Beirut by the evening, and describing the resistance encountered as scattered, undisciplined and of the hit-and-run type. As for the Sabra and Shatila district specifically, mention was made only of Horsh Tabet, where resistance to the Israeli Army was reported to

have been centred. As for the final situation, it was stated in the report that the Israeli Army would leave the mission of 'cleansing' the Sabra and Shatila district ('cleansing' it of 'terrorists', that is) to the 'Christian Phalangists'.[78] This was so much as to say that the mission of these Phalangists was to 'cleanse' the district of around 15 men, those who had been carrying Kalashnikovs at Horsh Tabet on the Thursday evening, and only a minority of whom were professional fighters.

- The report broadcast to the public by this Israeli Army station was not, of course, the sole Israeli report. Many others were sent, by various means, from Israeli officers to their superiors, and these are not at present available for research. It should be noted, however, that the Israeli Army radio station would have been heard by decision-makers in Israel, in both the government and the army. These knew well enough that there were no organized fighters within Sabra and Shatila, whether in their thousands, hundreds or dozens.

- Why, then, did the Israeli Minister of Defence at that time, Ariel Sharon, issue the directive whereby Israeli Forces occupying Beirut were to give free passage to the Lebanese militias and provide them with all assistance to enter – on the pretext that they were to seek out 2,500 so-called 'terrorists'? Why was this done? Why?

3

Thursday 16 September 1982

Testimonies differ with respect to the hour the massacre began, and this is natural enough given that individual witnesses report what they saw in their own particular street or quarter. Some residents saw the militias as they were gathering themselves for the attack, whereas others were actually surprised in their own homes. As such, the hour for entry ranges, among the dozens of testimonies, between five o'clock and half past six on the evening of Thursday 16 September. All, however, agree that the horrific initial hour was around sunset.

The entrances used on the first day were numerous, and were all located between the south and west sides. On the south side, there were the entrances on Kuwaiti Embassy Street, between the airport roundabout and the Kuwaiti Embassy itself, between the districts of Bir Hasan and southern Greater Shatila. On the west were those entrances on the rear street of the Sports City, separating the latter from the western part of Greater Shatila. In both cases the entrances were narrow streets or alleys, with the exception of Shatila Main Street, which intersects with Kuwaiti Embassy Street halfway down, then goes on north to Sabra.

This chapter deals with the way the armed militias entered and embarked on their atrocities from the early hours, murdering

innocent civilians indiscriminately, without regard to nationality, age or sex. It further describes the limited attempts at resistance carried out by a single fighter and by a group of men who had been gathered throughout the day at Hayy al-Doukhi. As for resistance to the Israelis, at Hayy Farhat and Hayy al-Horsh, this was already over when the attacking militias entered.

There were significant numbers of testimonies regarding the first day and the personal experiences and tragedies involved were correspondingly numerous. From these first-day testimonies – or rather from those of the first few hours – I have selected 24 accounts which, taken together, give a clear overview of the events in question.

Some of these accounts are sufficient in themselves, ending on this same night or indeed at a particular hour or minute. Others need supplementary treatment, and I shall return to these in the later chapters of this first part of the book; in conjunction, that is, with events of the second or third days, or in connection with the subsequent search for victims. If some accounts remain without sequel, that is in the nature of massacres.

The basic aim of selection, on this or the following days, is to place various experience within the overall tragedy; many accounts were in fact excluded to avoid repetition. The objective is not merely to collect and supply accounts but to provide a fully integrated picture. As for witnesses' first names, some of these are authentic and some not, according to the narrator's preference.

Sabra and Shatila immediately before the massacre

As we saw in Chapter 1, artillery fire continued to mount throughout the Thursday; the Israeli Forces blockading the district went on till they had made sure the streets were virtually empty and most residents had sought refuge in the shelters or in their homes. It occurred to no one that this shelling was simply paving the way for something still more horrifying. It was perfectly natural, on the contrary, to see the shelling, however intense it grew, as an end in itself – that, after all, was the way Israeli Forces had acted throughout their summer siege of Beirut. Such were people's thoughts.

By sunset residents were anxiously awaiting the return of the 'peace delegation'. Fear and despair were rising now. Just what had happened to these people? Had they reached the Israeli Command Centre? And if they had done so and delivered their message, that the camp residents wanted no fighting, then why should the barbaric shelling continue? It was days before people in Sabra and Shatila finally realized that none of the delegation would return.

Those who had known of the women's march were far fewer in number, mainly because this had arisen spontaneously at the Akka Hospital, whereas the issue of the delegation had been debated for more than an hour within the camp. Those who did know, however, were profoundly anxious. Was it conceivable anyone would molest women and children carrying white flags? It was some days before those asking such a question discovered the truth: that with massacres the impossible becomes possible and everything is permitted.

By sunset, then, residents were mostly either in the shelters or at home, the streets almost empty apart from a handful of

vigilant freedom fighters. Most fighters had in fact left the district, since resistance to Israeli artillery at night, even had the bombardment continued, would have been impossible. They had arranged to return and meet up again in the morning.

With the power supply cut off, the transistor radio was the key to information. A typical family would gather and listen, wondering what the next day would bring. It occurred to no one to wonder what would happen that night.

We know from residents' testimonies that most had gone without their lunch. Thus while the assailants were first preparing their attack then actually launching it, countless families were sitting down to a combined lunch and supper, while some mothers were still busy preparing food. Still other people were seeking out a route protected from shelling and sniping which would allow them to reach their houses close by the shelter, whence they would return with milk and some food for the youngsters at least.

The shelling died down at last. Then light began to fill the skies of Sabra and Shatila. Many wondering at the strange event found no answer that night. But those living in Hayy al-Horsh and Hayy al-Gharbi, and the districts round about, had no time to ponder the mystery. They were the first victims.

The only Greater Shatila residents enjoying relative security that night were those who, during the hours of Israeli shelling, had managed to reach the protection of the three surrounding hospitals, Akka, Gaza and Ma'wa al-Ajaza – apart, that is, from those, still luckier, who had contrived to flee the whole district or seek refuge at the Kuwaiti Embassy. A Lebanese sergeant, then responsible for protecting the Kuwaiti Embassy, told me he had at his disposal five members of the Lebanese Army and a Sudanese cook. He described how Shatila residents in their dozens sought refuge in the embassy on the Tuesday and Wednesday, fleeing the Israeli shelling. The total number was around 150, mostly women and children.

We spread them through the various hiding places and they stayed with us for five days, during which we let none of them out for their own safety; we knew there were dozens of Israeli tanks at the Sultan Ibrahim restaurant by the seashore, and we had the feeling something was going to happen. I recall how one middle-aged father got out in spite of me, I couldn't stop him, he wanted to make sure his daughter was all right; and this father died.

All through those days we fed them from our food, the military's.

But then on Thursday, at around four or five in the afternoon, I saw the Lebanese Forces gathering. I recognized them straight away, I wasn't taken in at all, even if they were trying to make people think they were military personnel like us. Several of them tried to come in the embassy, but we stopped them. Then they came back and said they wanted some water to drink, didn't we have any water? We told them we had water. We gave them some. I'll never forget how, while they were drinking, they started laughing and said: 'Tomorrow you'll be hearing some pleasant news, it'll make you happy.'[1]

News there was indeed on the following day, but it was far from pleasant.

Those who had sought safety at the Kuwaiti Embassy would stay there throughout the massacre, receiving full protection, just as hundreds of others, seeking refuge at the Henri Chehab barracks behind the embassy, would receive similar protection on that day and in the bloody days to come.

Armed militias at the entrances to Shatila

A lady whose house lay on a mountain road on the outskirts of the town of Aramoun told me how, on the Thursday afternoon, she saw convoys of cars and military vehicles descending from Kfar Shima, from the Tinol intersection, towards the airport; there were also tanks and armoured vehicles. About one in five of the vehicles was Israeli. That same evening her brother told her how those vehicles had indeed settled at the airport and the airport roundabout, eventually leaving just before sunset. Being high up on the slope, all night long they were able to see and wonder at the flare shells flooding the skies of Beirut opposite them. What was going on? Why these lights? And there was a further question. What was the mission of those gunmen, whose number she and her husband estimated at 1,000–1,500?[2]

The above witness was a cultured Lebanese poet not prone to exaggerate. Our discussion actually came about coincidentally, around four months after the event. What she said was so strange I could scarcely believe it. How could all that high level coordination and preparation possibly have taken place without any publication or broadcasting in Beirut? It was not easy at that time to gain access to foreign newspapers. However, when I eventually managed to study what these had had to say about the massacre, I discovered that the account of my poet friend from Aramoun agreed with much of what had been published in newspapers outside Lebanon.

Residents of the Shuwaifat district, speaking with the *Washington Post* correspondent Loren Jenkins, told how, at three o'clock on the Thursday afternoon, they had seen a convoy of trucks and jeeps bearing the sign of the Sa'd Haddad militias passing through Shuwaifat. These had then continued along a road controlled by the Israeli Army, leading to the south end of the western runway of Beirut airport, parallel to the coastal strip, where there were Israeli military positions. At the same time, another convoy of vehicles transporting soldiers from East Beirut arrived, then turned along the same airport road. The sign of the Lebanese Forces (a circle within a triangle, bearing the letters 'MP') was visible throughout, and next to the sign was an arrow showing the direction of advance.

When the two convoys had been observed for around two hours on the south side of the airport, hundreds of gunmen in the uniform of the Christian Lebanese militias moved from the airport towards Bir Hasan, near the Kuwaiti Embassy roundabout. From there they curved towards the coast, setting up headquarters in the College of Business Administration, near the roundabout itself.[3]

The account of the *New York Times* correspondent, Thomas Friedman, agreed with that of Loren Jenkins regarding the militias' arrival at the airport. The two writers based their accounts on the same sources, namely the testimonies of Shuwaifat residents. The second, however, differed from the first over the number heading from the airport towards Shatila Camp: according to the first, there were around 1,200 members in Lebanese Forces uniform, all heading towards the target area; whereas the second said that not all of them left, adding that sources within the Lebanese Army supported the residents' statements.[4]

The number of members most commonly cited in the various references was around 600. This is the estimated figure for those who entered Shatila on the Thursday evening.[5]

Residents of Bir Hasan, the district opposite Shatila, told the writer Amnon Kapeliouk how, at four o'clock in the afternoon, they saw 25 military vehicles filled with armed men going towards the Kuwaiti Embassy.[6] This implies they were going to the Forces' Command Centre to gather prior to attack, for the entry itself did not take place at four o'clock.

Journalist Robert Fisk based his account on the testimony of two Lebanese officers who had spoken to him, while holding maps, in an army operations room near the place. Since they were not officially supposed to be talking to him, they asked that their names and ranks remain undisclosed. Nevertheless, they wanted to talk to him because, as one of them said: 'You should know just what happened here.'

The second officer, pointing through the window to the airport, said: 'I saw hundreds of men and trucks coming from there last Thursday. It was just before the militias went into the camp.'

The first confirmed this, saying that large numbers had been gathering near the Israeli Command Centre. They were, he added, standing there with their weapons and had the badge of the Lebanese Forces on their vehicles. He then corrected himself; anyone, he said, could have painted a badge on a jeep. He ended by saying that he had seen two Israeli Army jeeps carrying militia members to enable them to enter the camp.[7]

The centre of the armed Christian Lebanese militias was not far from that of the Israeli Command, which had already positioned itself near the Kuwaiti Embassy roundabout, on the west side, where it had occupied one of three similar buildings; these had originally lodged Lebanese officers, who had been forced to leave them, along with their families, due to the war. These three buildings were located opposite the Sports City; more precisely, opposite the old Turf Club. The boulevard separating them was known as Camille Chamoun Sports City Boulevard, or the Sports City Boulevard.

The Israeli centre was located at the nearest elevation from which activities within the camp could have been monitored, bearing in mind (as noted previously) that the site slopes progressively from the hill behind the Sports City to the interior of Shatila Camp and Horsh Tabet. Moreover, the building itself comprised six floors, allowing a person standing on the roof to observe the camp district rather in the manner of a panoramic painting, before even considering the use of modern binoculars and night cameras.

At around half past six, people began to see convoys of soldiers without initially being able to determine their identity. Then as night approached, flare shells were launched over the district to the accompaniment of terrified shrieks. The massacre had begun.

As we have seen, the armed forces did not, that Thursday sunset, enter Greater Shatila from a single point. The various entries and alleys used were as follows:

- The west side of the Sports City, coming down from the hill behind the Sports City opposite to the camp and arriving in Hayy Ersal and Hayy al-Gharbi.
- The south-west side, that is, that of the Kuwaiti Embassy, where they entered near Madrasat al-Ina'ash, and of the hill, arriving in Hayy Ersal.
- The south side, that is, that of the Bir Hasan district, where some groups halted while others began to cross Embassy Street (the street between the airport roundabout and the Kuwaiti Embassy) to reach the districts targeted, in the first case Horsh Tabet and Hayy al-Miqdad, through various accesses.
- The east side, through which their planned access failed, perhaps due to a

major explosion in a weapons store near Ard Jalloul.

- One final side remained, namely the north side of Sabra Main Street. Here, however, they did not attempt access in view of the major geographic and demographic difficulties involved. Entry here would not be direct from a public boulevard, like that of the Airport or Camille Chamoun; it would rather have been necessary to penetrate such crowded quarters of Beirut as Tariq al-Jadida and al-Fakhani.

This last side could, it is true, have been part of an entry schedule, given that Israeli tanks were, throughout the Thursday, trying to advance from the Sports City Corniche towards Hayy al-Fakhani, where fighters were resisting with handguns and RPGs. As we saw in Chapter 2, however, the last point of their advance was near al-Razi bookshop and, since it was not in the Israeli Forces' interests to penetrate deep into the residential quarters, they restricted their goal to tightening their overall grip on Sabra, Shatila and al-Fakhani. Even this, indeed, was clearly not achieved in full, and a loophole remained on the Tariq al-Jadida side, adjacent to Sabra, throughout the following bloody days: the north side of Sabra remained as a gateway through which people could flee.[8]

Testimonies with regard to invasion through the south and west entrances

How did they enter? Or, rather, how did they invade?

Their entry into any given part was marked by caution; they did not know exactly where they were, especially as they were still outside the Shatila district. Some testimonies note how the intruders had not the smallest knowledge of the Bir Hasan district opposite Greater Shatila. They also had no clear instructions as to what to do. In other districts, by contrast, they clearly knew exactly what they were to do: they began killing families indiscriminately, young and old, Lebanese and Palestinian.

The six sets of accounts provided below will show the manner of entry or invasion

into the Bir Hasan district and Henri Chehab Barracks Street, both outside Greater Shatila. There were also the districts of Hayy al-Gharbi, Hayy Ersal behind the Sports City, Hayy al-Miqdad and Hayy Farhat, which is part of the Horsh district; all these lie within Greater Shatila. As for the timing, this coincided with the first hour of the entry or invasion.

Account 1: Witnesses to the entry into the Bir Hasan district

Um Ayman, in Bir Hasan, was bathing her four-year-old child and calling to her two-year-old to stay by her. At this point her sister-in-law knocked at the door to ask them to come to her home in the adjacent Ba'jour building, behind the Akka Hospital, and Um Ayman at once agreed. Some seconds later she heard a woman's voice outside, screaming: 'They're coming, they're coming! The Jews are coming in here!' The child, still covered with soap and water, slipped away from his mother, but she, taking a grip on herself, called to him to come back inside. Then she rushed to fetch the first aid kit, always ready in case of emergency, and which also contained the ID cards and the battery-powered torch so indispensable when the power was cut.

While she was going out of the door, Um Ayman says, she saw them coming from Al-Murouj school. There was a huge crowd of them, no fewer than 200 armed men.

With them she saw five masked men walking in a line, protected by a group of gunmen. These men were also in military uniform and their masks were black. The masked men said nothing as she watched them walk towards the camp through the other street, near the Al-Sumoud school. They entered from there, then kept on going down. Um Ayman, unable to control herself any longer, cried out: 'What's happening?' 'Nothing,' they replied. 'Everyone out in the street. Everyone out!' 'There's no one here except me,' she told them. The gunman repeated: 'Everyone out!'

They said very little initially, and Um Ayman could not tell who they were. She did, though, notice some confusion. They split into two groups: one headed towards

Shatila Camp and entered Horsh Tabet, the other spread around the buildings in Bir Hasan.

Around 75 residents of Bir Hasan came out from their homes. Of these only two families were Palestinian; the rest were Lebanese, Syrians and Kurds. Um Ayman herself was Syrian, married to a Palestinian.

They lined them up against the wall near the Ba'jour building. Then they said: 'Women stand at the back, men and old people in front of them, children right at the front.' Terrified women said: 'For God's sake, what are you going to do with us?' 'Fetch your clothes', one of them said, 'and we'll take you to the Akka Hospital.' At this point another gunman answered: 'Why clothes? Forget the clothes.' 'Come on, then,' the first man said. 'Forget the clothes.' Then just as people were getting up to go to the Akka Hospital the gunmen were joined by a new member who told them: 'Stay there. Stay sitting where you are. Tell us. Are there any terrorists here with you?' Um Ayman, keeping a grip on herself, went on watching as they argued and even contradicted one another.[9]

Um Wassim, a neighbour, friend and relative of Um Ayman's, was a mother of three children, the eldest twelve years old, and she lived through the same hours in the same place. She was married to the older brother of Um Ayman's husband. The testimonies were recorded at two separate interviews but their memories related to the same incident.

Um Wassim was a Palestinian from al-Khalisa, later called Keryat Shmona by the Israelis. Her husband was lying injured in the Gaza Hospital, but she could not go to him on the Thursday because of the shelling and sniping. She had contented herself with stopping by her brother and mother's house, near Hayy al-Miqdad, to advise them to be careful, as if caution ever stood in the way of fate. This was the last time she was to see her mother, brother and his family. She said:

When they came into the district it was obvious they didn't know it at all. When they first came, they were more than 100, and they came from the direction of Al-Murouj school. We knew they were

going to come any moment, but we didn't know where we were supposed to go. Some people said they'd come here from the airport, I saw them coming from the Kuwaiti Embassy district too; one group went towards Horsh Tabet, and another went inside Bir Hasan. They were the ones who'd been surrounding the district.

Once they got in, they started shooting at the people in the school, Al-Murouj school. They saw people running, so they started shooting in the air … and after they'd lined us up against the wall, my little daughter Jihan started telling the gunman who had his gun pointed at us: 'May God protect you, don't kill us.' And one of the neighbours told him: 'I'm Lebanese, friend.' So he said to him: 'What? Lebanese? Lebanese now, are you? You weren't Lebanese to start with. Line up here, I'm going to do this … and I'm going to do that to you … now you're all going to see …' When some of the women screamed, and the kids started crying, one of the men yelled at them: 'Shut up. Anyone screams, I'll kill them.'

Our concern now was to try and quieten them down.[10]

While the mother was speaking, eleven-year-old Jihan's gaze never left her face. Then the child said: 'I told him not to kill me. He had a beard, and his voice was loud.'

The grandfather watched his granddaughter proudly. A 70-year-old man who worked as a guard at the Ba'jour building, he viewed the whole affair ironically, and became famous for having challenged the gunmen. He said as follows:

Around seven or half past seven, something like that, I saw them coming, fully armed. He said: 'Sit down', and people sat down. 'Why aren't you sitting down?' he said to me. 'I don't want to sit down', I said. 'If you want to shoot, go ahead.' 'What are you?' he asked me. 'Palestinian from '48,' I told him. 'I'm from the heart of Palestine.' One of them jumped up and said: 'Shoot them. Shoot them and let's get rid of them.' So then one of them, who seemed to be in charge, he had his face turned away and I couldn't see him, but I heard his voice, he said: 'I've no orders to shoot them yet.'

So now this superior went off and was away for a while, then he came back and said: 'Let them go. Come on, let them go.' And that's what happened.

It was getting on for nine or ten o'clock at night. We all went off and tried to find some safety inside the building. Then this man, the one who'd said he didn't have any orders to shoot us, he came back himself to make sure there weren't any terrorists in the building. He was talking to me, and I couldn't make out his face in the darkness. 'You, old man,' he said, 'help me by not letting anyone go out.' They went on watching over us, all night long. At dawn, we sensed they'd gone to the other building.[11]

Um Ayman went on to recall their abnormal state. When, she said, they rounded up the Bir Hasan people in the street, a woman said to them: 'May God protect you, I want to give my son some water.' One of them said furiously: 'No water. You don't give him any water. We went three days without water. Your son can go without water.'[12]

Um Ayman also described what took place in an adjacent building, where not a single Palestinian lived; all the inhabitants were Lebanese. The gunmen, she said, asked them detailed questions about the houses at the end of the street, which used to be called the 'camp', having been a headquarters for the freedom fighters. The residents assured them the fighters had left. Then the man in charge of the gunmen went back to ask her neighbour: 'Tell me … how far are we from Sabra?' 'Sabra's in another district', he was told. The man in charge then went on to ask about the locations of Sabri Hamadeh Palace, Shatila Camp and the airport roundabout. He then checked up that they were actually in Bir Hasan and that this latter was not in fact a camp for Palestinians. When the detained residents all assured him Bir Hasan was not a camp, he communicated with his superiors on a walkie-talkie. 'Sir,' he said, 'we're in the Bir Hasan district now. What are we to do, sir?'

Within seconds his superior's directives were clear: they were to split into two groups, one to continue on inside, towards the southern district, the other to remain at Bir Hasan. And so it happened.[13]

At the Ba'jour building, where the grandfather, the guard of the building, was hiding with his grandchildren and daughters-in-law, Um Ayman and Um Wassim had ample time, after the children had fallen into a fearful and exhausted sleep, for reflection on the matter.

Why had the men not gone ahead and killed them? Was it perhaps because Bir Hasan was not a camp? But they were Palestinians even so, so why hadn't they killed them? Was there some specific reason? It emerged in the days that followed that others in Bir Hasan actually had been killed. Why should they have been spared?

Will the secret behind their survival be revealed one day?

Account 2: Two witnesses to the entry in Barracks Street

The man was doorman of a building near the Henri Chehab barracks, and they killed him in the first hour. There are no family witnesses as to his death but we have the accounts of two neighbours.

The first of these witnesses was Harbeh Barakat ('Barakat' is a pseudonym used or the purposes of this volume), a woman who had been driven out from Tall al-Za'tar to Damour, before being once more relocated, in the course of the war, to Bir Hasan, opposite Henri Chehab Barracks and the Golf Club. Finally this latest Israeli invasion had driven her to the Cinéma Concorde in Verdun Street, where groups of displaced people occupied the large reinforced buildings there. Following the fighters' departure, she returned home to find shattered glass and torn off doors. Her two brothers were abroad. She had just one widowed sister in Beirut, and the two were living together.

Harbeh had seen the Israelis' deployment over recent days but had not, like some other witnesses, encountered their exaggerated reassurances. On the contrary, she said, they had been checking on everybody and ordering anyone they suspected or anyone standing on a balcony to 'come on down'. The person so summoned would then go down to be checked. They seemed to be everywhere, she said, and they remained there at the barracks till the Lebanese Army returned and took possession once more. It was the army, returning in dozens, that instilled some kind of calm in the people.

Harbeh is positive the attacking gunmen were from the Lebanese and Sa'd Haddad's Forces, on account of the white shirts many wore beneath their green military uniforms with the signs of the Lebanese Forces or Sa'd Haddad printed on them, and also because of the many trucks bearing the names either 'Al-Quwat al-Lubnaniyieh' or 'Sa'd Haddad'. Those in the trucks got off and entered the barracks, saying they wanted a drink of water. They were told there was no water at the barracks, that water would not be given to anyone. With that they entered all the neighbouring buildings, bringing the people down to the shelters and starting to terrorize them with axes, knives and guns, as if they had split up into groups for the purpose of instilling terror. She says:

They came in their dozens. Some of them were beating people, others were killing, others were looking for attractive girls.

There was a neighbour of ours, a doorman, a Palestinian from Lubia, called Kheir. I knew him, but I don't know his father's name or his last name. Kheir had a good-looking wife. When they broke in, they were six gunmen, they started using dirty language with his wife and told her to go up with them to the third floor. She was tough. She took off her shoe and hit them with it and said: 'You contemptible people, shame on you, aren't you ashamed of yourselves?' They didn't hit her or force her, they just said: 'Stay here then, we'll take your husband to the third floor and settle things with him.'

Kheir's cousin was standing there, so they went ahead and tied him up, they tied his arms and legs to the wall and told him if he moved or made a sound they'd come back with an axe and hack his head from his body. They went upstairs with her husband, calling out to one another: 'Muhammed, Ahmad, come on, Abdallah ...' They reached the second floor, then stopped. Some of them came down and told her again: 'If you won't come with us, we'll settle things with your husband on the third floor.' She screamed at them again and spat in their faces: 'Shame on you.' So they told her: 'OK, we're going to make you very happy, you and your husband. God keep him for you, this hero of yours.'

The woman kept on waiting, thinking they were questioning her husband. It went on for a long time. And we, on the road, didn't dare move either or go anywhere. We were waiting for someone to come and question us, or else for a chance to run off. The gunmen were in their dozens and they were all over the place, surrounding the shops and inside the homes. We heard them calling for a Baalbek man from the neighbourhood to stop. Then we suddenly heard a woman screaming at the top of her voice: 'Hey, people, save us. People, Kheir's been found killed on the third floor.'

We didn't dare go upstairs. But God sent good people. Two Lebanese men came; they went upstairs, pulled him out and laid his body in front of the building. It turned out they'd hit him on the head with an axe and shot him through his nostrils with a silencer, then they'd stamped on his neck. Then they'd gone off through an exit different from the place they'd used to get in, the door of the shelter.

His wife was in a terrible state. I know his wife. She's Lebanese, and she has a three-year-old daughter. She came and said to me: 'I want to go to the Israelis. I beg you. I beg you. Will you come with me, Harbeh?' I told her: 'I'll go with you. It won't be any worse than death, after all.'

We reached the first Israeli point on our way, I mean Barracks Street or Golf Street. Just as we were going in, his wife saw one of the gunmen who'd broken into her house, sitting with the Israelis. It was the one who'd said things to her. She went ahead and told them what had happened. When she pointed to the gunman, she said this man had been one of them, and that he'd said such-and-such things to her. But he denied it.

So I told the Israeli officer: 'Why are you just standing there? I mean, he's the one who killed the man.'

I'd seen this same officer on the first day the Israelis came in, and I'd asked him: 'Should we go to Sabra?' He said to me: 'Don't go to Sabra and Shatila. If you go to Sabra and Shatila, you'll die ...' This time, though, in a room crowded with soldiers and the Forces of course, this Israeli answered me: 'We've nothing to do with this.' And they were getting their things together to quit this point in Bir Hasan.

So we went back to the army at the barracks. May God reward them, the soldiers at the barracks helped us carry him. But they said: 'We've no orders to stop them. And anyway, we can't put soldiers at every building. Get your things together and come to the barracks.'

And that's what happened. We went to look for safety at the army barracks. There were a lot of Palestinians with us at the barracks.[14]

The second witness, Amaal al-Dirawi, another neighbour, went on to criticize

Kheir's wife's behaviour in ordinary times for having always been 'coquettish and dressed up'. This would not, however, have stopped Amaal from being a truthful witness of events, and her story did not in fact differ significantly from Harbeh's. Moreover, Amaal went on to confirm, with expressions of the greatest admiration, the courage of Kheir's wife. 'His wife grabbed her slippers', she said, 'and started hitting them ...'[15]

Amaal and her family were unable to seek shelter in the Henri Chehab Barracks, as Harbeh and others had done. Their destiny, very different from that of her two neighbours', would be revealed on the following day.

Night spread through Bir Hasan, on the Barracks Road, by the Golf Club, and through all the other parts. But peoples' destinies differed at any given spot in the same district. A number of people were killed near the Akka Hospital, while at the Ba'jour building, near the same hospital, others were kept safe till morning.

Every small street, indeed, saw different fates. Every group of militias had 'interests' different from the others' interests. And there were quite marked differences between the moods of the various killers.

Account 3: A witness to the entry into Hayy al-Gharbi

Hind, a southern Lebanese woman, was well known for her strong personality and sharp intelligence. She was married to a southerner, who was not related to her, when she was just 14 years old; but she gained experience of life and, by virtue of her husband's work, experience of living abroad. She had given birth to nine children in her 20 years of marriage, during which she and her family had been subjected to various crises: her young daughter died during the Israeli invasion of the South in 1978, and her house was destroyed during the Israeli invasion of 1982.

Just before the fighters left Beirut, Hind came in search of a small house, even if no more than two rooms. She agreed with her husband that each should search around the Sabra and Shatila perimeter, and she eventually found herself in the district behind the Sports City, which was almost deserted at the time. To her surprise she found a man sitting alone, and, going up to him, she made enquiries about a house:

'I'm from the South. May God preserve you, is there some room where we can stay? I'm looking for a home, and so's my husband, we'll settle as soon as one of us strikes lucky.' 'You're welcome,' he told me, 'instead of a single room, you can have four. Go upstairs, there's a home, and you're welcome.' 'Where are you from?' I asked him. 'From God's vast lands ...' he said. 'From the way you speak,' I said, 'you're from this district.' 'Quite right,' he said, 'I am from this district. I'm from the Arab countries. I'm Palestinian. Come on, sister, bring your husband and children and come and make your home here.'

Anyway, he gave me blankets and a couch. There were two military type bunks too, which were still inside. 'Take them,' he said. 'They're yours. I'll get some food in for your children.'

I tell you, he kept his word to me. He did go off and fetch food for my children, and told me not to worry. In the next couple of days the Resistance left. When the Resistance left, we settled in. I never saw him again, and I never found out his name. But several times he sent the things he'd promised to send me from their stores, with some young men. He hadn't bought them, I knew, but it was right of him to remember us in those harsh times they were going through.

The house where we stayed had been reinforced by the men who used it before. Obviously they were freedom fighters. Anyway, we stayed. And they elected the President of the Republic. We thought there might be some stability now ... but after Bashir al-Gemayel was killed, you could hardly say we felt secure.[16]

When, on the Thursday, Israeli Forces surrounded the district and began their bombardment in preparation for what was to come, Hind's husband was in the South, visiting his sick mother and fetching bread and any other food available there.

The shelling intensified at noon and through the afternoon. Hind began to calm her children, then to assure them (from her experience as a southerner) that the Israelis had not molested women and children when it occupied the South. Wishing to assure the Israelis there were no fighters or other men in the house, she went out carrying her broom – for no one, surely, would find anything suspicious in the sight of a woman sweeping in front of her house.

Hind's house was located in the upper part of Hayy al-Gharbi on the street separating it from the Sports City, a sandy street parallel to Camille Chamoun Boulevard. Hind was able to look over the famous field and swimming pool from her roof.

On that first night, the strategic position of Hind's home meant she actually witnessed the entry of dozens of gunmen as they came down from the sandy street towards Hayy al-Gharbi, and Hayy Ersal immediately to the south. They came down, she said, like jinn:

I went out of the house with the broom in my hand. Then I saw around 50 or 60 fellows coming through the Sports City, near the swimming pool, and I heard them speak in Lebanese dialect. One would say, 'Come on, Georges', or 'Come on, Elias' … I mean, they were all speaking in Arabic … They were walking along with the bulldozers flattening behind them. They were bulldozing to open up the road. I got scared then and wondered what was going to happen.

It was sunset. Maybe around half past six in the evening. But you'd have thought it was the middle of the day. I went out and told myself, they won't do anything to me because I'm a southerner, and you can tell southern women a long way off! I started picking up sheets of paper from the ground and putting them in the cart.

My kids had mixed feelings about going outside the house. I told them to go out, let them see there were kids here. Then all of a sudden, I tell you, I heard a voice screaming at my kids: 'Come here!' When they came up to us, wanting to take my kids away from me, I screamed; I screamed and made my kids run away, I got them to go down through the window from the other side. So they shot at me. They hit me in the leg. I was hit and in a good deal of pain, but thank God I didn't die, for the kids' sake. You can still see the bullet mark on my leg.

As the blood started flowing from my leg, the pain got worse. There was nothing to stop the bleeding, so I took the scarf off my head. I mean, you can say, thank God we wear a scarf. It's good we have this head covering, I mean, you need it. I took it off and wrapped it around my leg. I didn't

wrap over the bullet itself, but a bit higher to stop the bleeding. Then I started to loosen the knot gradually, to avoid any internal bleeding. I went around the house and came in from a different place, from the steps.[17]

Hind had once worked as a nurse and so had professional training and experience, but this time she was nurse and patient in one. After she had crawled home she gave herself an injection to stop the bleeding, while calming her children. Whenever her daughter coughed, she would place a handkerchief over the girl's mouth for fear the men would hear the sound and come to the house.

She did not dare light a candle. They were not aware, she was certain, that anyone was at home there, since she had made them think she had fled with her children, north through the alleys. Clearly no gunmen had reached there yet – nor indeed would they, even later.

All night long screaming was heard from Hayy al-Gharbi, from the bottom of the hill behind the Sports City. Hind could hear the cries for help:

I'd hear them say: 'For God's sake, what have I done wrong?' And I'd hear them say to them: 'You're such-and-such … you've no respect for God.' And they'd go ahead and slaughter them. One of them told him: 'I'm a Lebanese, I'm from the South.' So he used dirty language back to her, what shall I say, things you can't repeat. When they went to slaughter someone, he'd bellow like a bull. They'd catch him and slaughter him. They'd slaughter each group all together, at the same time. Then they'd put them in the bulldozer, which would fling them out, pour sand over them, and drive over them. They'd leave them without any burial, then go and get some more. It was a night that almost made me lose my mind. They were killing women, little girls, old people, young people …[18]

Hind was talking in her home, and I was listening to her with a friend of mine who was a television photographer. He had been the first to hear her account after the massacre was over, and he took me to meet her. Hind wanted to continue her talk on the roof of her house, to which she had managed to creep, alone, on that first horrific night. The three of us went up on to the roof. At the time, Hind told me, there had been blankets hung over the sides of the roof which made a barrier to prevent them seeing her. As she continued with her account, she pointed to the houses and places down the slope behind the Sports City, in the part known as Hayy al-Gharbi:

I looked down and saw them slaughtering people: one would use an axe to dash out someone's brains, which would fly off to the side; another would come and shoot him with a Kalashnikov. Believe me, really, it was unbelievable. They'd slaughter them – then shoot them – you could hear the shots. I saw everything, I mean, the flares were so bright I could have seen a needle even. Besides, I was higher up than they were, I could see them, they couldn't see me.[19]

Hind had the time to be sure the bulldozers she saw that night were four in number. The nearest, she said, had Hebrew inscriptions on it. She also saw all four bulldozers in operation, large and small. She could not, however, count how many times the bulldozers did their work. At the same time she was anxious for her children, fearing the men would kill them all if they found a way to them.

This mother and nurse witnessed the rape of little girls, and the ripping of an unborn baby from its mother's belly. She gave more than one account of people she did not know; later we discovered the identity of those who had suffered by comparing Hind's descriptions with testimonies supplied by the families of victims and volunteers at the humanitarian institutions.

Hind, the only witness to the men's entry through the rear of the Sports City, did not sleep that night. Whenever she mentioned her husband, she prayed God would bring him back safe. Did God answer her prayers?

Account 4: A postponed testimony from Hayy Ersal

Um Nabil was the mother of three children, a boy and two girls, the younger of whom was just one year old. Her house lay at the heart of Hayy Ersal, next to Hayy al-Gharbi at the bottom of the hill, behind the Sports City, accessible from more than one alley.

Um Nabil herself did not, however, see them break in as Hind did, since she had managed to flee before five in the evening.

Um Nabil had become afraid on account of the heavy shelling in the afternoon, and she also feared for her children, who could no longer bear the noise of the Israeli shells. Her fears rose still higher when a neighbour of theirs was killed by a piece of Israeli shrapnel, and she asked her husband – who was a driver and owned a car – to take them to her aunt's house. He managed, with some difficulty, to get the car out of the alley, which had been narrowed by the presence of a number of other cars whose owners could not get to work on the Thursday. When Um Nabil heard the car approaching, it sounded like music to her ears. She recalled her conversation with her husband as he rushed up:

'Shall I bring anything along?' I asked him. 'Just the clothes you've got ready for the kids', he answered. I'd packed a small suitcase for them. He took us to al-Houri Street at Tariq al-Jadida, where my aunt lives. When we got near the Co-op supermarket, a grenade was launched. When it exploded, he said to me: 'Well, do you want to go back?' 'No,' I said, 'my God, go back? For God's sake, I couldn't wait to get here. Please. There are shelters here.'

We reached my aunt's house. She generally spent the summer at Aley, and as far as I knew she'd be there then. 'Go and check if she's at home', he told me. I went to check and found her at home. 'Take the kids and go', he told me. 'I'll get the milk and the bottles.'

I knew the milk and the bottles were just a pretext. We'd had neighbours with us at home and they'd asked to be brought along. I'd explained my aunt's house was small, just the two rooms, and they were two families; her son might be with her, and we might not find her at home anyway. But my husband, Abu Nabil, told them: 'Stay here, and I'll come back and pick you up.'

I'd sensed something. Plenty of times he'd left me at the shelter with the kids and I hadn't been scared. This time, though, I got really scared. I started begging him to stay with us, but he wouldn't agree, he said he had to keep his promise to the neighbours. He promised to come back quickly.[20]

The first night passed, and Abu Nabil never came back. No one knew then that a massacre had taken place; Um Nabil would know nothing of her husband till everything was over.

She had fled from the shelling. And he had returned without regard to it, to keep his promise to the neighbours and rescue them, just as he had his wife and children. Did he manage to rescue the neighbours? Or himself? Would he ever be able to testify to us, later, as to what had happened?

Account 5: Neighbours' testimonies from the forefront of Shatila

Ahmad Khatib was a young student in 1982. By origin he was from al-Khalisa in northern Palestine, by birth from al-Nabatiyyeh in southern Lebanon. His father had built a house in al-Nabatiyyeh, but they had left it in the wake of the 1978 invasion of the South and moved to Shatila. They lived at the forefront of Shatila, on the Kuwaiti Embassy Street side. He was part of a numerous family, including ten brothers and sisters, but two were missing on this particular day: the eldest brother, who was working abroad, and the eldest sister, who had been abducted one day at a Phalangist checkpoint.

Ahmad's home lay near Shatila Main Street, on the eastern side. The parents, grandmother and remaining eight brothers and sisters lived all together in this small house, which was next to the houses of the al-Miqdad family. His father was a vegetable and cigarette seller, one of the most popular occupations among the camp residents.

According to Ahmad, Israeli shelling had, by four on the Thursday afternoon, become quite unbelievably heavy. Most shells, though, were falling on parts of the camp where no one was living, or where most residents had not yet returned.

Ahmad was not at home at the time; he was with some friends of his, counting the number of grenades exploding and generally discussing things. Suddenly – between five and six o'clock, while the shelling was still fierce – a piece of shrapnel flew nearby and struck Walid, one of the men, and Ahmad and the others took him off to the Gaza Hospital. There he saw hundreds of people who had sought refuge, especially from Sabra. Then, while he was waiting for

his friend's operation to finish, people from Shatila entered the hospital, screaming: 'They've come into the camp! The Israelis have come into the camp!'[21]

Ahmad was astonished at this, having been among those actually reassured by the Israeli blockade. Soon, though, a friend of his, with the pale face of one who had barely escaped death, came in and told him shakily:

It's not true, Ahmad. It's not the Israelis coming in, it's the Phalangists. The moment they got in the house, I slammed the door in their faces and ran off, I jumped over the wall. My brother managed to run off with me, that's my brother there, standing by the door. God saved us, Ahmad. If you'd only seen how many shots they fired at us, but we'd already made it over the wall and they didn't hit us. But I've no idea what's happened to my family. What do you say to that, Ahmad?[22]

The two friends barely slept that night, neither knowing what had happened to his family. There was in fact a vast difference in their fates – life and death.

Ahmad was one of the seven comrades who had been told by that Israeli officer on the Wednesday: 'Go back home. No one's to leave today. Go back home. But on Friday, take your people and families and leave.'[23]

Just what had the Israeli been talking about? Some of the neighbours told how they had seen the gunmen killing Ahmad's family on the doorstep of their house in the first hour of the massacre.[24] This means that, if Ahmad had managed to reach his home on that Friday, he would not have found even the bodies of his parents, brothers and sisters. A single corpse remained as witness on the doorstep: the grandmother's. The other nine, his two parents and seven of his brothers and sisters, were gone.

Account 6: A witness from Hayy al-Miqdad

Whenever the massacre of Sabra and Shatila is mentioned, the tragedy of the al-Miqdad family, an extended Lebanese family, takes priority over all others. Several branches of the family had found their way to Horsh Tabet, where they lived in the Hayy al-Miqdad quarter, at the very beginning of Shatila Main Street on the Embassy Street side. This made Hayy al-Miqdad among the first quarters invaded on the Thursday, with no avowed motive other than killing.

A few have survived from the al-Miqdad family. One of these is Hussein al-Miqdad, who escaped death thanks to his wife's insistence that he flee. Here is his account, given before a group of reporters when the massacre was over:

I was going to the market to buy milk for my small baby and provisions for my family; the shelling was getting heavier and the gunfire was getting louder. I tried to find some protection in an old shelter, which had been largely wrecked by earlier shelling from the enemy air force. I couldn't stand the bad smell, so I came out, to find the stores were closed and there was no one walking in the streets.

The shelling died down for around a quarter of an hour. I saw people running in all directions and screaming, but I simply didn't understand what was happening.

The shop owners quickly shut up their shops; some ran without shutting them behind them. For a few moments I stood there in the middle of the road, not knowing where to go, but I woke when a woman started tugging at my shirt and screaming: 'Run ... they're slaughtering everybody ... why are you standing there like an idiot?' She shot out these words ... I tried to look around, to see what was happening, but she'd disappeared in the crowds, so I decided to go back home.

My wife asked me what was going on. 'I don't know', I told her. 'They're slaughtering everybody. That's what they told me.' 'Slaughtering them?' she answered. 'Why? Are they sheep?' 'I don't know,' I said. 'They're just slaughtering them!' Then she yelled at me: 'Why are you standing there like an idiot? We have to get out of here.'

'I'm not leaving', I said. 'You go ahead, take your children with you, wherever you want; this is my house, I sweated and spat blood to build it ...' I was interrupted by the screaming of a woman begging for mercy for her child. My wife shoved me. 'We've got to get out of here, now', she said. 'They're killing people. Can't you hear?'

I tried to pick up one of my children, but she insisted I had to get out at once. 'I'll carry my son,' I told her, 'and you carry Khadija and Amaal.'

'I'll carry them all ...' she said. 'You run. Go on.'

'I answered her appeal and her tears ... but I was going slowly, I didn't get very far from the house ... suddenly I heard someone shouting, loudly: 'Stop, or we'll shoot.'

I tried to look round. I heard shots. I saw a military man, and I started running. I heard him say: 'Stop right there', but I didn't. I kept on running, till I felt a weight in my left leg and a warm liquid flowing over it. I caught up with the fleeing women and children and old people, who started looking at me, and one of them asked me: 'Are you hurt? You're bleeding. You have to go to the hospital.'[25]

Hussein al-Miqdad spent three days at the hospital. Afterwards he found they had bayoneted his children and stabbed his wife to death. However, his cousin, who brought the news to him, reassured him that they had managed to bury his family. Location and burial of victims was a privilege not available to everyone.

The number of victims in the al-Miqdad family was greater than that in any other. No fewer than 30 died.

Not too far from the homes of the al-Miqdad family, and from that of Ahmad, mentioned in the Account 5, there was a huge rubber tree with wide, bright green leaves. This tree protected a middle-aged shaykh, awarded this title for holiness rather than age. The gunmen's attack took this shaykh by surprise as he was walking down the road, and so he hurried to climb the tree and hide among the branches. Here he remained concealed through the night and a good part of the following day, till he was sure no checkers or killers were left. This shaykh witnessed the killing not only of Ahmad's family but of all the neighbouring families, including the al-Miqdad family.[26]

The aim in the first hours of that first night, at that main entry to Shatila, at all the entries to al-Horsh and all the places entered earlier, was, quite simply, to kill everyone: child and adult, man and woman, Palestinian and Lebanese – whoever came to hand among the residents of the quarter.

Testimonies from the shelters

The most significant feature of that first night's invasion can be summed up in two words: 'the shelters'. The attacking gunmen made straight for the places where shelters were located; and this confirmed the presence of the masked informants who were noted in Account 1 and will be mentioned further in subsequent testimonies. It is also proof of the significance of all those strange cars driving through Shatila under the protection of the Israeli siege, their passengers enquiring as to where the shelters were to be found.

The shelters were normally crowded with women, children and the elderly. They might, it is true, also be crowded with men at times, but they remained the last resort for the responsible freedom fighter. In view of this, why should attacking gunmen, come looking for 'other' gunmen, invade the shelters first? This is the question that remains unanswered, pending the completion of the whole picture.

From testimonies related to the shelters, I have selected the six accounts provided below. These are not, nevertheless, in any sense comprehensive; confirmation of the barbarism to which civilians at various other shelters were subjected will be noted in later chapters. Mention should be made, too, of ventures by responsible and honourable citizens to save those within the shelters from invasion by the attackers and from a consequent horrific fate. We shall discuss such rescue efforts later in this chapter (pp. 100–1).

Account 7: From the shelter to the truck

Thunaya Amin ('Amin' is a pseudonym used for the purposes of this volume), a Lebanese woman married to a Palestinian, told of how, on the very first night, she and other women were abducted from the shelter next to her house, which stood halfway down Shatila Main Street. She said:

It was evening already, darkness had come. We thought they were coming to the shelter to hide like the rest of us. Instead they stood outside while we stayed there inside the shelter, grabbing a bite to eat after a whole day without food. There was no bread. At noon there was nothing; my husband said, 'Let's have lunch', and I said, 'But there's no bread', and I sat down and started baking. Just as the bread was ready they started

firing shells, and finally a shell fell close to us, shrapnel fell on us. So we went down to the shelter at half past one. There we stayed from half past one till six or seven o'clock, then they started coming towards us. Who did we think they were? As I told you, we thought they were people who were lost and wanted to come and hide in the shelter.

Of course, the door of the shelter was open. We heard one of them yelling at one of our men: 'You're here, you're all here, you sons of bitches, you killed Bashir al-Gemayel, you sons of bitches, and you've made all these tunnels, and you're sitting here, come on, get out here and let's see … come on … men line up on one side and women on the other. Come on, walk in line from here, and another from there, women in the middle.' They dragged us on to the road to a spot not far from the Kuwaiti Embassy. And they went ahead and started up this truck and they got us, the women, into the truck. This man said to my husband: 'Are you Lebanese or Palestinian?' 'I'm Palestinian', he told them. 'How old are you?' 'Fifty-two,' he said. 'Why are you sitting down?' he said. 'I told you to stand where you are, give me the girl.' Then he handed me the girl and put us all on the truck. We were a load of around 40 women. Then they started it up. As for my husband, they left him on the street, and I didn't know what happened next.[27]

They were, Thunaya states, taken to the East Side, to a spot beyond Sin al-Fil, then brought back and left at al-Ouza'i. The decision to bring them back was no easy matter, as she describes:

There were four Palestinians with us. I didn't tell you before, my husband's Palestinian but I'm Lebanese. And we were saying to these four Palestinian women who'd been abducted along with us: 'Don't you open your mouths, don't say a word. We'll talk for you.' Right through the trip, we pretended this one had a bad headache, and that one was getting horribly sick. They were asking the Palestinians all the time: 'Tell us, how many fighters do you have in Shatila? Where are the fighters? Where are the weapons?' 'Listen brother,' we told him, 'this one's dumb, if you spend the whole night talking, you won't get a word out of her.' He said: 'You've only just turned deaf and dumb. Have you all become Lebanese as well? Do you all come from Marja'youn, or the South, or Baalbek?'

But when they got us to a command post of theirs, we heard their superior say: 'What's this, why are you bringing us women? We don't want women. Why are you bringing them?'

And so they took us back to al-Ouza'i and threw us off there. But there was no one to bring us water, or food, or blankets. Actually, one man did ask us to come and eat. But which of us could have eaten, when we were all worried about our men?[28]

Sa'ida, one of the women who had taken part in the women's march, was also among those forced to get on the truck. She recalls how they brought other women, who had not been on the march, and put them on the truck too. There were around 40, some with children. There were also two men, one Lebanese and the other Palestinian, the latter being her brother. Her decription of the abduction confirms Thunaya's account:

They grabbed us and put us all on top of one another in the vehicle, a big cargo truck; I'd know it today if I saw it … Just as we got in, a Lebanese man stood up and said to the gunmen guarding us: 'I know Sa'd Haddad, I know him personally.' The man in charge of the truck started yelling at him and cursing Sa'd Haddad. A bit later he turned to one of us and told her: 'I saw your photo with Abu Ammar in the newspaper. I saw you, so don't try and get out of it.' The poor woman started to cry and swear it wasn't true. She told him: 'I swear to God, I'm Lebanese.'

We stayed in the vehicle for around an hour … then they got us to a very tall building with posters of Bashir al-Gemayel over it, and the truck went inside, so we knew the whole building belonged to them, it was obvious. They stopped us, and we heard someone ask: 'Are there any men with you?' We were still in the truck, and we heard them congratulating and kissing one another. 'That's great,' they were saying, 'really great, you've brought us Palestinians. Now we'll suck out their blood.'

One of them got on the truck, looked around, and said: 'Where are the men? Aren't there any men?' I was fat, and I was hiding my brother so no one could see him; the other, Lebanese, fellow was thin like a sissy, but the poor fellow stood there and swore he was Lebanese but he'd left his ID card at home. We just heard the Phalangist say: 'Get down, you.' We saw them kicking him about and hitting him, and we didn't know what happened to him after that. Then one of their superiors looked at us – I mean, he seemed to be a superior – and he said

to the ones who'd brought us in the truck: 'What's this? What are you bringing women and children for? Go on, take them back where you found them, bring us some men, so we can suck out their blood.' Another one looked up, and said: 'Wait a second, isn't there a pretty one you can give us? Where are the pretty ones?'

We prayed to God we'd get back quickly. They didn't give us a drop of water. We asked for water, we were thirsty. They just wouldn't agree. They kept on cursing us.

They took us back by a different road. It was a road I hadn't seen before. It was an up-and-down road. Maybe they took us to al-Ashrafieh, I don't know. But I know the men with us were changed on the road. I mean, they were replaced by others. When we reached al-Ouza'i, the new guards asked us again, before they put us down: 'Which of you are Palestinians?' And then a Lebanese woman started telling us: 'Curse you, Palestinians. It's all your fault.'

In the end they put us down at al-Ouza'i, it was around nine or ten at night by then. From there we saw the flare shells still being shot. But we didn't hear any shelling. We stayed there till two in the morning, with the children shivering from cold and hunger. No one in the district opened his doors to us.[29]

The women and children stayed there till morning. Had it not been for a degree of mercy from some of them, some of the 'Phalangists' as Sa'ida said, they would not have had a blanket or any sense of safety. Some were quite different from the rest.

In the morning these women had to return to look for their families.

Account 8: The 150 at Abu Yasser's shelter

Abu Yasser's shelter lay to the left of an alley branching off from Shatila Main Street, for someone coming from the south.

The shelter was named after its owner, Abu Yasser, a man of Syrian origin who had built it for his family and, of course, for the immediate neighbours. Constructed without pre-planning, it was considered a small one by the standards of the district – not one of those built to accommodate very large numbers of residents.

On that Thursday, Abu Yasser's shelter became crowded with neighbours, and with the neighbours of neighbours, who had fled the Israeli shelling. Abu Yasser was a generous, kind-hearted man who would turn no one away from his shelter.

When the militias entered, or rather invaded, Abu Yasser's shelter was one of the first places they reached. How did they get there? And who exactly were these people who, just minutes after their entry into Shatila, found their way to a small shelter in a narrow alley, in the heart of al-Horsh – when their main mission, after all, was to search for armed Palestinian fighters who had, apparently, failed to move on to the new places of exile?

Who could have contrived such a thing unless guided by the masked informants, whose entry into the Bir Hasan district was described in Um Ayman's testimony, and by so many others too?

Um Ali al-Biqa'i was among those who had fled to Abu Yasser's shelter. Her home was less than 20 metres away, so that she was an immediate neighbour rather than one of those come from further off.

It was almost six in the evening when one of her daughters came in with the news. 'Listen,' she told everyone, 'the Israelis and the Phalangists have got in, and they're killing the men!'

Chaos erupted. Um Fadi, Um Ali's eldest daughter, who was married to her cousin and had rushed to the shelter with her husband, children and mother, jumped up and began attacking her younger sister in front of everyone. 'Be quiet,' she cried, 'stop spreading rumours! The Israelis wouldn't do any such thing, and nor would the Phalangists. Stop stirring up rumours and terrifying people. Don't be afraid, all of you.'

Um Ali could not decide between her two daughters. The younger had, she knew, intelligence and courage; and she could see that her older daughter, the children's mother, was frightened for all her denials. The latter, as usual throughout the shelling and the horror, was reluctant to leave the shelter. Looking round, Um Ali guessed there were about 150 children with their mothers. She told herself, in a spirit of faith: 'May God do as He wills. Whatever happens to these children will happen equally to my grandchildren.' Um Ali left the shelter with her head high.

The Israelis had launched so many flare shells, Um Ali said, that it was like walking in daylight rather than at night. What, she began to wonder, was about to happen?

Um Fadi followed her to the road and began tugging at her dress, begging her to return to the shelter and stay with her and the children. The mother, however, had made her decision. It was imperative to return to her home, which was filled with people, both family and guests.

The owner of the house, Abu Ali al-Biqa'i, spoke in the light of experience. 'Go to sleep, everyone,' he said, 'and trust in God. Israel won't do anything. Once they're in, people won't put up any resistance. Everyone should stay at home.' Abu Ali, however, wasn't at home next day, as he had supposed he would be. This was to be his last night there.

Next morning, their relative, whose home was right next to Abu Yasser's shelter, came by and told them of the screams of the women and children the night before. They had been shrieking: 'Please, hand us over to the Red Cross!' He had heard the voice of their daughter, Um Fadi, screaming: 'Abu Fadi, come and help us. You people, hand us over to the Red Cross. For God's sake, we're Lebanese, don't shoot us!'[30] The relative knew the voice well enough.

Um Ali had one thing at least to thank God for: that there was someone to tell her of her daughter's last moments. There were many victims from Abu Yasser's shelter whose last words, or manner of death, were never revealed. The bodies of some were found, but not of others.

The instant the killers reached the door of the small shelter they yelled at everyone to leave at once. They had no ears for Um Fadi's appeal, or for anyone else's.

How different the fates were of those who came out from Abu Yasser's shelter! Death in massacre is not identical in every case. There is no truth in what a poet once said: 'Many are the causes, but death is one.'

Three kinds of fate were swiftly devised by the killers.

The first fate was one instantly delivered by the arrogant assailants: to be shot out of hand, or else dragged, dead or alive, to Abu Jamal's garage, close by Shatila Main Street.

The second was reserved for the men ordered to stand against a nearby wall, in anticipation of what was to come.

The third was reserved for the women and children ordered to walk towards the Main Street, and from there on south towards Embassy Street, being taken, so the killers told them, to the Akka Hospital. Just why should they be taken there? The women and children, though, believed this. They had indeed no other option.

The killers did not take them to the Akka Hospital. They made them halt where the mass cemetery is located today, on a spot where no building stands. Some they took to a nearby petrol station. Others remained in the square itself, and there they were all shot, women and children – at the hands of those whose declared mission was to search out Palestinian fighters and armed men who had failed to travel with the rest to the new places of exile! The bodies were left exposed.

As for the men lined up against the wall, their fate was to be shot after the women and children had been moved some way off.

Massacres are not totally without mercy. The women were spared the sight of the men being killed. They simply heard the firing, which was relentlessly heavy, for those who fell were not only the occupants of Abu Yasser's shelter but a number of Horsh Tabet residents ordered by the killers to leave their houses and stand against the wall. Everyone stood there, to receive a hail of bullets.

Massacres are not totally without mercy, for death by a bullet is a good deal more merciful than death by other means.

The will of God alone determined the survival of a very small number of people here and there among the men lined against the wall inside al-Horsh, and among the women and children on the site of the mass cemetery. We shall return to these people's stories later; they are the ones who described to us what took place at Abu Yasser's shelter and inside al-Horsh. Yet there were whole families with no survivors at all to tell of what occurred.

The family that lost most members was the al-Muhammad family, one of those that had sought out Abu Yasser's shelter.

The al-Muhammad family came from Sehmata village, in the Akka county of northern Palestine, and they lived in Greater Shatila not far from Abu Yasser's shelter. As the al-Miqdad family was famous for losing most members overall, so that of al-Muhammad became famous for suffering the greatest loss within the nuclear family. The parents and nine of the eleven sons and daughters were wiped out.

The only survivors were the married daughter Maha and the eldest son Zuhair, who had both been away from the house. All those who had been at home and sought out Abu Yasser's shelter, from the parents Khaled and Fatima down to two-year-old Samir, were killed: eleven from a single family.[31]

So why were they cut down? Why, too, was the shelter's middle-aged owner, Abu Yasser himself, killed along with them? He was innocent of the crime of being Palestinian – or even of being Lebanese and living close to Palestinians!

Account 9: A mother and her children

Abu Yasser's shelter, small as it was, contained so many victims, and each one has a story.

The family of Ahmad Muhammad Hammoud sought refuge there like so many of the other neighbours. Before they went down into it, though, there had been a discussion between the father and the mother, the latter striving to persuade her husband to go and find immediate safety at the Gaza Hospital. The Israelis, she had heard, had been killing men, whereas she and the three children would be in no danger at the shelter. Her husband, finally convinced, succeeded in reaching the Gaza Hospital. She and the three children made it safely to Abu Yasser's shelter. The sky was alight with flare shells.

This family was among the last to reach the shelter, finding, indeed, barely a spot to settle themselves down. It was, according to the narrator, between half past six and seven in the evening.

Seven gunmen came into the shelter, deaf to all appeals for mercy, or to the screams or the children's crying. The moment they entered they began shooting in all directions, leaving many dead on the ground. Then they ordered the men to stand against the infamous 'wall of death' and dragged the women off to Shatila Main Street.

The end for Ahmad Muhammad Hammoud's family came at Abu Jamal's garage, on Shatila Main Street. There the killers excelled themselves in the variety of the deaths dealt out to the women and children.

This matter must, however, await the stage of search for the victims. Whoever was found was found, and whoever was lost was lost, as people like Ahmad Muhammad Hammoud began searching for the remains of his wife and children, and Um Ali al-Biqa'i for the remains of her daughter and grandchildren.

A witness from Shatila reports what he saw in front of the garage on the Saturday:

The bodies were there in front of the garage, one next to the other, each one killed in a different way. It was unbelievable. I've never in my whole life seen anything like that. Some women had been butchered with knives. Some women had been strangled. Some women had been burned. Some women had been shot.[32]

Account 10: A witness to the invasion of a shelter

The girl who provided the following account was the only survivor from her whole family.

She saw what happened, and she was the first to talk immediately after the massacre, while civil defence workers were still lifting the rubble. The girl spoke to the United Press correspondent Jack Rayden, who – as he stated in the introduction to his interview – withheld her name for her own safety. The interview took place in a tent erected on the site of the massacre, in the presence of a superior of the Lebanese Civil Defence Force.

The shelter in question was likewise unspecified, but it was one of those at Hayy Ersal. The girl said:

There were five of us in the family, and they were all killed. I'll never forget that Thursday afternoon, I was in a hiding place with a friend of mine, and we decided to get out because it was difficult to breathe

in there. We took one look at the district and saw the edges of the camp being turned into a hell; some people were jumping from the roofs. I rushed back to our hiding place with my friend and told the neighbours and my family we'd seen Kata'eb soldiers.

Everyone in the shelter went outside. They went towards the soldiers carrying white flags, but the soldiers didn't take the slightest notice and fired at the men and women; the children were screaming. When I saw all that, those women and children killed by the soldiers' firing, I ran and hid in the bathroom.

Later on I saw the soldiers going inside the camp and firing at random, then they dragged the women and children to a spot near our house, after they'd killed their husbands and sons. I lifted my head and tried to see where they'd gone, but a soldier saw me peering out through the window and shot at me, and he told a lady to come in and fetch me. When the lady came in, she told me to come out and not be frightened. I did as she said. I'd spent more than five hours there, and I nearly suffocated because of the bad smells.

Some soldiers came up and flashed a light on me, to check who I was, and one of them told me to sit down and asked me: 'Are you Palestinian?' I answered: 'Yes.' My nine-month-old baby cousin was screaming next to me. The soldier yelled in my face: 'Why's he crying?' He didn't wait for a reply, but just pointed his gun at the baby, and shot and hit him in the shoulder … I started crying, and told him this baby was the only one who'd survived from my family, then I saw the soldier grab the baby up by his feet and tear him in two.[33]

The writer Amnon Kapeliouk provides a supplement to the girl's story. When her feeble-minded uncle, Faisal, arrived, and they decided to kill him, he asked for mercy and she begged them to spare him.[34]

They did in fact leave him alive that night. But why? Was it in response to her plea or for some other reason?

And on the following day, would the killers leave her uncle alive, or would they kill him? What of her? And what of the fate of those inside the neighbouring shelters?

Account 11: They killed him before he was born

Amaal, a Palestinian girl from Shatila, was dumb. Nevertheless, she had a desire for life and was resolutely aspiring.

At the beginning of 1982, Amaal was married to a Palestinian man who understood her needs. Her friends were happy at the marriage, including a foreign friend working in the social field.

Mary and Amaal first came across one another during the invasion. Amaal was then experiencing the life of the displaced at one of the al-Hamra shelters, some way off from Shatila. Mary made constant visits to the places where these people lived; and, meeting Amaal, she contrived to communicate with her through gestures and sentiments. Amaal was proficient in typing, and she also knew English, her new friend's language, quite well.

Amaal was pregnant when they met, and Mary understood from her that she longed to become the mother of a baby girl, whom she would pamper just as her mother had pampered her when she was a baby. Mary promised to visit Amaal in Shatila whenever she came to Lebanon on her social work.

Mary's first visit came in the aftermath of the Israeli invasion. She arrived, in fact, just before the fortieth-day commemoration of the martyrs of Sabra and Shatila, and so had no immediate opportunity to ask Amaal just what had happened. Aware of Arab customs and traditions, Mary wished to attend the painful fortieth day, and decided to search for her friend afterwards.

There, at the mass cemetery, this foreign friend met Amaal's mother, whom she had come to know quite well before. Amaal's mother spoke to her; and the friend, who had come to see Amaal, found only a story.

This foreign social worker and researcher, who declined to be identified ('Mary' is an alias we agreed on), wrote Amaal's story down; then she simply went on writing. She heard accounts in Arabic, which she knew, then wrote them down in English. Amaal's story was the seventh of a total of 13 testimonies she collected and recorded, and she provided me with a photocopy in her handwriting:

I saw Amaal's mother dressed in black from head to toe, pale in face. When I asked her the matter she told me the story of Amaal with tears hanging on her cheeks. Many people who talked to me were by now dry-eyed, but the tears of Amaal's mother will never dry up. She told me:

'Amaal and her husband were hiding in one of the shelters of Shatila, when the Phalangists entered. They killed her husband with a big axe before her eyes. They saw that she was pregnant, being in her eighth month, but their hearts were devoid of even an iota of mercy. They cut off her husband's right hand and threw it in front of her. Then her turn came. They brought a big knife, thrust it in her pregnant belly, they took out the baby while they were laughing. Amaal could not take it anymore, she fell down, breathing her last breaths. After they were certain of the baby's death they threw it beside her, and maybe he died from the first thrust. They did not bother to carry her corpse as they did with many corpses ... It was very important to them to leave evidence behind to let people see their doings.'[35]

Many people in Shatila told Amaal's story, but her tragedy was not unique. Killing children and unborn babies was commonplace in this massacre.

Account 12: Testimony of a twelve-year-old boy

Munir was a Palestinian boy who somehow survived Abu Yasser's shelter. Three times they tried to kill him, but he survived.

When the forces of tyranny descended on the small shelter, Munir was a twelve-year-old pupil at the Jalil (Galilee) school. It is a Palestinian custom to name schools, hospitals and other institutions after occupied cities, villages and towns, or indeed unoccupied ones, in an attempt to keep their memory alive for the coming generations. In Beirut there were the Haifa, Akka (Acre), Gaza and Nassira (Nazareth) hospitals. In Shatila Camp there were the Jericho and Jalil schools. In Sabra there were the Jaffa, Ras al-Tin, Bak'a, Ya'bod, Ramallah, Afula, Haifa, and Himmeh schools.[36] Here, then, was Munir, who attended the Jalil school in Shatila, and managed, even though he said little in the interview, to convince us of his thorough knowledge of Jalil in northern Palestine. About Jalil he did speak a little.

The neighbour who accompanied Munir to the interview did most of the talking. I had to verify what he was saying by looking into Munir's eyes; he only nodded to show his agreement in response to a specific request of mine. Were my questions troubling him so much?

Our talk was taking place, I recalled, eight months after the massacre. I was in fact being deeply unfair to this handsome, silent, suffering boy. Had I for a moment reflected on the number of press interviews where Munir had spoken – or held back from speaking – I should not have requested an interview with him.

The neighbour, who worked at Ma'wa al-Ajaza Hospital, said:

Munir was at home in Shatila, near Horsh Tabet, with his mother and sisters and brothers. When the shelling got heavy on the Thursday afternoon, Munir's family split up like all the other Palestinian families. The men would go to the nearest hospital for protection, and the women and children would go to the nearest shelter. And that's what happened here. Munir's older brother, uncle and brother-in-law came to us at Ma'wa al-Ajaza, while the rest of the family fled to Abu Yasser's shelter. The shelter was full of women and children, and Munir was with his mother, two sisters and two brothers. What now? Shall I go on? Don't you want to say something, Munir?

I'll go on, I know what happened as if I'd been there with them. By seven o'clock, night had turned to day thanks to the flare shells. The gunmen yelled at the door of the shelter, telling everybody to get out. They lined the men up against the wall, and they told the women and children: 'Walk away from here.' The gunmen, who'd stayed with the men, beat them and then killed them. Munir looked around and saw them fall to the ground. Isn't that what happened, Munir?

The women and children reached a nearby petrol station. They left them waiting for about an hour. Some people say they went off to have some supper. Others say they went to kill other groups. Then they came back and they shot at everyone without sparing a single woman or child. When they all fell to the ground, one yelled at them: 'If any of you are injured, we'll take her to the hospital. Get up and you'll see.' Anyone who tried to get up was shot from head to foot. They started flashing strong torches on them. The light was strong enough already! But they wanted to make quite sure, and maybe there were some places in shadow, with not enough light.

But ... I've skipped something, Munir's mother was going to get up when she heard they'd take them to the hospital, but Munir, may God protect him, told her: 'Don't get up, mother, they're lying.'

Are you going to leave me to say everything, Munir?[37]

Munir had to pretend to be dead so as to survive. All night he stayed there next to his mother and sisters, not knowing they were gone for good. He did not even know if he would be able to flee next day.

I pondered my interview with Munir more than any other. This was the first time I would talk to someone of his age who had lived through the massacre. I thought of taking him a gift – but what could I take? A book? A colouring and drawing book? A toy? I thought of a small transistor radio, and my doubts somehow vanished. The whole of Beirut had switched over to transistors because of the constant electricity cuts. When I gave it to him at the end of the interview, I had to tell him what was there inside the box, wrapped in coloured paper, but he showed no reaction. Did he like the gift? Or was he silent by habit now? I don't know.

Before I said goodbye to them at the entrance to the lift, accompanied by my friend and the landlady who had acted as host for the interview, I remembered the most important question of all. I expected no answer, but I asked in any case:

Munir, one day you'll grow up and you'll be able to carry weapons. Do you have thoughts of revenge? Will you kill the way they did you? Or will you forgive them? What do you think you might do?

For the first time Munir spoke out clearly and boldly, showing a strong personality: 'No. No. I'd never think of revenge by killing children the way they killed us. What did the children do wrong?'[38]

More than 17 years later, Munir came to Beirut from Washington, a well-built, courteous young man, like the boy but a little more talkative. I had seen him more than once in the United States in the intervening years.

On that particular visit, at the end of the summer of 2000, I asked him to go with me to Shatila, so that we could walk along the same road. Perhaps there was something more he would like to say now – though he was firm he would not. We went along with a friend who knew the district well.

Munir stood in silence before the door of Abu Yasser's shelter. The pain was evident on his face. Long moments passed, then he said: 'I don't know. Maybe that's the door. Can it be? Can it be so small?'

I looked at the friend for help, but he did not know either. He knew the public streets well enough, but not the shelters. He had relied on Munir for those. We had to return a few days later, accompanied this time by a fourth person: Munir's brother-in-law, who was well acquainted with the place.

We entered Shatila Main Street, via Kuwaiti Embassy Street, on foot. We turned right at one of the alleys, then, without thinking, followed behind his brother-in-law, who stopped at a small door on the left. 'Have you forgotten, Munir?' he asked.

It was the same entrance at which Munir had stood a few days earlier – unable to imagine, perhaps, how dozens could have come out through this small door to the places of death. He said nothing.

It was his relative who spoke. He pointed to the wall opposite and said: 'They killed them at this wall. There was blood all over the wall when we got back ...'

With that we walked back along Shatila Main Street, towards the Akka Hospital. I had no questions.

As we approached the square of the mass cemetery, the Cemetery of the Martyrs of Sabra and Shatila, Munir did not stop. Instead, still walking, he said in a low, jerky voice, as though talking to himself:

After they shot us, we were all down on the ground, and they were going back and forth, and they were saying: 'If any of you are still alive, we'll have mercy and pity and take them to the hospital. Come on, you can tell us.'

Munir said no more after that. None of us asked him what happened afterwards, because we all knew.

The four of us, Munir, his relative, the friend familiar with the place and I, were walking along the main street of the site of a late twentieth-century massacre – between

two lines of greengrocers that had not existed then. We had to endure a car honking here, some peddlers calling out for customers there, or else the blaring of some new, popular song from some cart. We heard it all, without being aware of it almost. We were waiting for whatever Munir wanted to say, and he started talking, of his own free will, while we walked along together:

If anyone moaned, or believed them and said they needed an ambulance, she'd be rescued with shots and finished off there and then.

I ... what really disturbed me wasn't just the death all around me. I ... didn't know for sure whether my mother and sisters and brother had died. I knew most of the people round me had died. And it's true I was afraid of dying myself. But ... what disturbed me so very much was that they were laughing, getting drunk and enjoying themselves all night long. They threw blankets on us and left us there till morning. All night long I could hear the voices of girls crying and screaming: 'For God's sake, leave us alone.' I mean ... I can't remember how many girls they raped. The girls' voices, with their fear and pain, you can't ever forget them.[39]

Paul Morris, a British doctor, treated Munir as soon as he arrived at the hospital next day, on the Friday, and kept him under observation over the following months. During a talk at an American lady's house, on the campus of the American University of Beirut in spring 1983, he told me: 'He'll smile a little, play football once in a while, but he doesn't react spontaneously like others of his age, except just occasionally.' Then the doctor banged on the table, and said: 'The lad has to be saved. He has to leave the district, if only for a while, to recover himself.'[40]

Account 13: A boy's testimony that never reached us

Mufid, a Palestinian boy, was among the first people who fled to Abu Yasser's shelter. A few years older than his brother Munir, he regarded himself, at 15, as already a man.

Twice they tried to kill him. Did Mufid survive, or did he die? And if he died, how exactly did it happen?

The first time they tried to kill him was on that Thursday when the crowds who had been dragged from Abu Yasser's shelter were walking along Shatila Main Street, heading, so they were told by the gunmen, south towards the Akka Hospital, but actually towards the mass cemetery square.

Mufid was with his mother, and with his sisters and brothers: Aida, Mu'in, Fadya, Iman and Munir. He was among dozens of people he knew; but he knew nothing of those who were pointing guns at them and had no idea why these should want to kill them. He had no belief, however, in the claim that the gunmen were taking them to the Akka Hospital. He had heard with his own ears the shots that had killed his neighbours and loved ones.

Mufid's testimony never reached us, and no doubt it never will in the conventional sense; but we do not need it to be certain of his intelligence or of his awareness of the fate awaiting a march like this, made up of women and children and controlled by guns.

Mufid gave his mother a farewell look, then, in the twinkling of an eye, flung himself through the herded crowds, striving to flee as fast as he could.

The killers saw him and shouted at him to stay where he was. Then they fired, hitting him. Yet he managed to keep on running, despite a serious wound in the upper thigh.[41]

When I interviewed his, twelve-year-old brother Munir (see Account 12, p. 91), he said not a word about Mufid, although the Lebanese press had written a great deal about him. Yet as we were walking along Shatila Main Street 17 years later, going towards the Akka Hospital, Munir suddenly pointed ahead and said:

The last time I saw my brother Mufid was on this street. He was running off on his own, he was older than I was and maybe he realized what was going to happen to us, and they shot at him, but we didn't know then what had happened to him.[42]

That was the first episode of Mufid's story, which saw him melting into the crowds and alleys. As for the second episode, it found Mufid hiding under the pine trees near the Akka Hospital on the evening of the same day. This indicated that, despite his wound, he had been able to cross Kuwaiti Embassy Street and reach the other side. He had not, however, had the strength to get to the hospital by himself, falling from exhaustion nearby in the shadow of the pine trees.

Colin Smith, correspondent for the *Observer*, elaborated on this second episode as he had heard it from the hospital nurses. A number of injured people had, he said, sought out the same spot as Mufid. Some had been killed off there, but others had managed, with the assistance of some nurses and women, to reach the hospital. Mufid had been one of these.

Just before the Thursday evening, the Akka Hospital was becoming crammed with people seeking protection from the shelling; numbers were growing all the time. When Mufid arrived on his stretcher there was scarcely room to move on the ground floor, and those carrying him had difficulty clearing a way for the stretcher to make it to the nearest operating theatre[43] where he received medical attention. The doctor who told me of Mufid's arrival, as he himself heard it from a colleague, no longer recalls whether they operated on him or decided first aid would be sufficient.[44]

On that first night Mufid's luck was far better than Munir's: he received care at the Akka Hospital and spent the night under the protection of the International Red Cross (this is how people seeking refuge at hospitals customarily thought of themselves), while Munir was out in the open with the dead, scarcely daring to breathe for fear they would come running to kill him off.

What, though, of the following day? Who was to be the lucky one then? What a difference tiny plays of chance make in the cauldron of a massacre! How shall we ever retrieve Mufid's testimony?

Testimonies concerning the 'wall of death'

The 'wall of death' close to Abu Yasser's shelter was not the only one of the Sabra and Shatila massacre, but it may have been the first among a series of similar operations over the three days as a whole.

Had everyone who stood there been destined to die from the gunshots, there would have been no one left to tell of the 'wall of death'. The perfect crime, however, does not exist even in massacres.

Moreover, had the bulldozers succeeded in covering all traces of the crimes, photographers would have found nothing, when the three days were over, to substantiate the witness statements that follow.

Finally, had the consciences of a number of people not remained intact, there could have been no one like the scrupulous writer David Lamb, who wrote of the 'walls of death' in connection with the events of the first night in particular. He said:

Entire families were slain. Groups consisting of 10–20 people were lined up against walls and sprayed with bullets. Mothers died while clutching their babies. All men appeared to be shot in the back. Five youths of fighting age were tied to a pickup truck and dragged through the streets before being shot.[45]

Account 14: 14 bullets in his body

Mustafa Habrat was an intelligent labourer who first became aware of the imminent danger when he noted the otherwise inexplicable lights that had turned night into day. He knew the perpetrators were not Israelis but rather criminal killers under Israeli protection, and he knew too that the true black night was not the physical darkness but rather the injustice. Knowing these things, he was considering the possibility of detention and prison, but no more than that.

Mustafa gave his Algerian wife the ID cards, official papers and whatever money he had. Then he said goodbye to her, telling her to look after the children. He added just a few words: 'They might take me away.' His wife realized things were dangerous but was not sure of the extent of the danger.

They left him no time to say anything more to his wife, beyond those few words. Nor did they leave him time to flee, since Mustafa's house was near the edge of al-Horsh, next to Shatila, and this was the part that saw more bullets and bodies than any. And they arrived, like aliens sprung suddenly from all parts.

A close friend of Mustafa's describes the scene as he heard it from him:

Mustafa's in Germany now, may God heal him. He told me how they came and captured him and lined him up against the wall with all the other men. A few seconds later shots were rattling out. His wife and three children had already fallen dead on the ground before the criminals turned to the men. He knew at once, he said, that they were gone. He knew instantly, from his small daughter's screams, that they were dead ... and so he lost control and jumped forward at the gunmen standing there in front of him. They were quicker than him. They shot him, and went on shooting him. He lay there on the ground. And they thought he was dead.

His eldest daughter was six years old, his youngest son was still a baby, they all died. And his wife died too.

Mustafa wasn't the only one. They took him along with 20 other men. They lined them against the wall and fired at them. They were all hit.

He told me:

'After midnight, on the next day, I got up. I'd been either asleep or unconscious, I don't know. There was a fat guy over me, I told him to move off. But he didn't. I guessed he must be dead. I sensed there was something happening on the road, and I didn't dare move for fear they'd see I was alive and shoot me ... I stayed down and didn't move, and I kept praying, all night long ... God ... Have mercy on me.'[46]

Account 15: They killed us twice

Hamza was a Lebanese man from the southern village of Majdal Zoun. After their house had been destroyed by Israeli shelling, his family moved on to Horsh Tabet where they bought a small house.

If you asked Hamza how many there were in his family, he would reply, with a bewildered air: 'There are four of us. I mean ... there used to be seven, now there are four.' Should you go on to ask him where the others were now, he would answer briefly, astonished at the question: 'In the massacre ... here.'

Hamza and his family stayed at Majdal Zoun through the invasion, but when the war was over – when, as people commonly said, 'the fighters had left' – he and his family returned to Horsh Tabet, near Shatila. They were happy to find the house had not been seriously hit.

Hamza affirmed that the shelling became more intense through the whole district on the Thursday between half past two and half past six. Later the conventional shelling abated considerably, but flare shells began filling the skies. Although Hamza had been among those noting strange faces in the district that day, and although there was obviously some reason for the lights he said were 'strange and indescribable', Hamza and his family, being simple citizens, failed to make any connection between the two incidents. They simply sat on their small front balcony, drinking tea and saying: 'Thank God the shelling's died down!'

It was half past seven when they were overtaken by a group of gunmen yelling 'Put your hands up!' They did so. Hamza realized at once that these men were Lebanese and had come to kill. He knew they were Lebanese from their dialects and from the yellow badge on their green uniforms, inscribed 'Al-Kata'eb al-Lubnaniyieh'. He did not notice any other badge on their shoulders but, he said, remembered their faces well and would have been able to pick out any of the men from a thousand.

While the gunmen were vying with one another in cursing and insulting the inhabitants in a variety of ways, Hamza, his family and the neighbours were going down to the street as ordered. Some of the neighbours had, like Hamza's own family, been sitting out in front of their houses, while others had been indoors. Hamza gives the following account:

Once we reached the street, they said: 'OK ... men on one side, women on the other.'

When they first got us together, there were around 30 women and children, the residents kept on coming down and joining the group. There were 27 of us men, lined up against the wall. First they started beating us, flinging us to the ground, cursing us and stamping on our heads. They took our ID cards as well. I mean they definitely saw I was Lebanese but I didn't dare say a word while they were there, nor did my father and brother; none of us said a word. After the beating they told us to stand and face the wall. We did. They said to the women: 'We'll send them on after you, we'll let them go after a bit. You go on ahead.'

The women and children were led down to where the road leads. There used to be a petrol station there. That's the place where they killed people later on. They killed the women and children. I didn't see it with my own eyes because they'd already fired at us, but that's according to a little boy who only just made it. He told us when God spared his life and he got back home safe. [He is referring to the boy Munir; see Account 12, above.] That's how we found out later that my mother and sisters were all gone.

When the women had got a little way off, they told us they wanted to search us. But they didn't. They shot us instead. One of them would keep on firing at us, then lean his arm on the edge of the wall to rest for a bit, then a bit later he'd start shooting again. If he was still tired, there were others who went on. They were around 15 men. I was standing nearly at the end of the line, there were just two beyond me. When they started firing from a distance, I looked around and saw people crumpling up, dying. So I told myself to crumple as well. I threw myself to the ground before they could hit me, and they thought I was dead. I stayed down for around five or ten minutes.

They came up to shoot and kill us, they came up to finish us off while we were down on the ground. While they were doing it, they hit me in the lower part of the leg. But the bullet went straight in and out, and that's what helped me.[47]

Hamza added that his father was also hit but did not die. His brother Abbas, however, was among the first to die. He also remembered some of the neighbours he knew on that 'wall of death'. Abu Yasser and his family were, he said, all killed, as were two other neighbours whose names he did not know. Another man was also killed with all his children, and six Pakistanis and two Syrians were killed.[48]

Hamza waited till the killers had gone before he got up with his wounded leg. He recalled:

I felt it when they left. An injured guy next to me had put his head on the sand. 'Have they gone?' I asked him. He said 'Get up and see.' I did. But he was still afraid to get up, or maybe he couldn't.

I thought, what shall I do? I decided the best thing to do was go home and hide there. I limped home and got in the house. I was afraid, naturally. But what else could I have done? I took off the shirt that was all stained with blood, I took off my shoe, and I bandaged my leg. It was around half past nine then. I saw my sister coming from the Akka Hospital, and she found my father was still alive. I told them to take my father, that I'd be able to manage on my own. So I walked to the hospital by myself, behind them.[49]

Hamza related what had been happening to everyone he saw at the Akka Hospital. People were horrified. But what was to be done?

His most difficult moment, he said, was after he had got back home to hide and heard a wounded man screaming: 'Give me some water! Give me some water!' No one hiding in their homes, Hamza continued with evident anguish, dared take him a glass of water.

Hamza, this man from Majdal Zoun, could never forget how he failed to take a wounded man a drink of water at a time when he himself was in the direst need of someone to comfort him. He knew, in those moments, that his father was also injured and that his brother, mother and sisters all must have died.

Account 16: When both killer and victim fled

Randa was in the shelter of the Akka Hospital on the Thursday afternoon. She had gone there in search of medication for her neighbours rather than for protection but when she found her older brother there and he told her to stay with him, she did so. Then her other brother came to tell them of a massacre at the camp but rejected his sister's plea to stay there with them till things cooled down. At half past eight another man came to tell of a massacre on the streets. Randa could hardly believe this but feared for her parents in case it might be true.

An elderly woman accompanied her along the road and they got in together through the alley close to the shelter of Fatah 17 – opposite to the garage that they, as she would say, 'had brought down on its people'. She went on towards her parents' house at Horsh Tabet, walking, as she later discovered, through the same alleys that had been traversed by the killers. By then,

though, these had left. Randa could not have known that a single grenade launched at the killers had caused them to flee the Horsh alleys through which she was now passing, and that, otherwise, she would have faced death like her family and others. One thing nonetheless struck her as abnormal: the sight of some men in hurried flight through an alleyway.

Randa was the sister of Hamza, who was at that moment alone at home, bandaging his wound. She describes what she saw in al-Horsh:

As I came into al-Horsh I saw dead people all over the streets. Everything had changed. There were men still running and shouting: 'People, there's a massacre', and I turned to the victims, I heard some people moaning, others screaming in pain, and I started saying to myself, whispering: 'I beg You, God, have mercy. I beg You, have mercy.' I saw all the victims and I stared at them, and God gave me patience. I and the woman with me started counting them, on the two sides. They were so many, it was pointless trying to count.

As I was looking around I saw my father, and he saw me and heard me, he called to me. My father was lying over the victims and he was moaning with pain. I went up to him and said: 'God is great, father, God is great. He won't abandon us, father.' He said to me: 'You won't be able to pick me up. Get me an ambulance, daughter.'

I couldn't think of anything but my father. I went back to the Akka Hospital and told them there were victims and casualties, and we needed a rescue team to get my father. I told them as well there were a lot of others who needed an ambulance. There were a lot of men there but no one would agree to come along. Even the nurses didn't believe me. One of them said 'Get some blood on your finger, then we'll believe you.' What blood on my finger, when I'd seen the victims piled up in the street? Why should I need blood on my finger to make a nurse believe me, when I'd left my father dying?

Finally my sister, my sister-in-law and the elderly woman, the one who'd been there with me earlier, came along.

When we got back there, we found some of the victims still alive. One would be saying: 'Get me some water.' Another would be saying: 'Get us some help. I beg you, get us up.' I didn't have the strength to go to my house and get some water.

My only thought was to get my father to the hospital. As for my brother Abbas, I knew by then he must be dead. I took his watch from his wrist, and knew who he was from the watch. Oh God, he'd been thrown down in the middle of the road.

My father was halfway between being conscious and unconscious. He told us later they'd run off after someone had launched a grenade at them. He said the Phalangists kept on running, and the ones who launched the grenade ran as well. As a result, al-Horsh, from the middle of it up to Embassy Street ... became completely empty.[50]

The family walked towards the Akka Hospital, the shocked daughter carrying her wounded father, supported by those who had joined her, and the injured son following the convoy. As they walked along, not a sound came from Horsh Tabet. It was as though it was a different district from the one that had resisted the Israelis up to a few hours earlier, or witnessed the most barbaric mass murder just an hour or two before. The silence of death lay over everything. There were, though, no killer bands left, and there were also survivors among the victims, appealing for water or trying to flee, including those subjected to two murder attempts and who had evidently not been killed by the gunmen.

Randa's injured father had been right when he said that both killer and victim had fled. Another witness, from the side of the killers, testified that they had indeed all fled. The witness in question did not identify himself, but, according to the magazine *Der Spiegel*, which published his testimony, his name is recorded in its archives.

This attacker said:

Suddenly we heard gunshots. In the northern part of the Shatila Camp some of the Palestinian men had reinforced themselves. They launched a bazooka at our group.

A colleague of mine lost his left arm, and we had to withdraw.

We gave up any thought of accomplishing the mission within three hours ...[51]

Who, then, launched an RPG shell and emptied the whole Horsh district of the armed killers, so allowing Randa to return from the hospital to rescue her injured father? What we learn definitely from the attacker's

testimony is the source of the grenade, which came from the north side; and we have confirmation, too, that they fled.

Yet as the small family convoy headed towards the Akka Hospital, those family members who had fallen as victims were still on the streets. The body of Abbas, the eldest son, remained there until his uncle arrived on the Saturday and transported it to Majdal Zoun, where the village gave him a proper martyr's burial. As for the mother and her two daughters, Najah and Nuha, their bodies were never found but they were presumed to be among the victims.

The confrontation at Hayy al-Doukhi

The armed confrontations that took place on the Thursday between the resistance fighters of Hayy Farhat and the Israelis were over, as we saw in the previous chapter, following the hitting of the tank; the confrontations at al-Horsh were likewise over following the injury to Comrade Butros [Farid al-Khatib]. As a consequence, the resistance fighters, apart from the small number who spent the night in Shatila Camp, had withdrawn beyond the district boundaries. They learned of the militias' atrocities only on the following day.

It was an irony the resistance fighters would never forget. They had assumed without a second thought that those men seen in the distance, wearing military uniforms were Israelis. Now it emerged that they were, after all, Lebanese militias about to invade Shatila and carry out a massacre.

The fighters numbered around 15 at the hour al-Khatib was wounded. Their plan, quickly agreed upon following his injury, was to rest that night, since they anticipated the Israelis would launch only artillery fire to which they had no means of retaliation. They would then reassemble next morning and resume the confrontation with individual weapons as they had done the previous day.

The gunmen of the Lebanese militias entered through the borders and alleys of al-Horsh, al-Miqdad, Hayy al-Gharbi and Hayy Ersal and embarked on their mass killing and torture of civilians. The survivors of this were the first to spread the horrifying news. There was not a single superior at the Hayy al-Horsh office or that of Hayy Farhat on the Thursday evening; the Resistance had resolved to keep away from the offices, supposing the Israeli artillery fire would reach these first.

One single fighter, who had resisted individually at Hayy al-Fakhani on the Thursday, decided to go into Sabra and Shatila at the end of the day to discover what had been happening there. This was the fighter we have called Ibrahim.

He alone was to confront the attacking militias on Shatila Main Street. He was with a group of men who had zealously carried their weapons and made the residents fearful of Israeli retaliation. Only these would, through the night, remain awake and on guard, leading the attackers to feel they were under surveillance.

The single fighter

Ibrahim Baroudi had left Hayy al-Fakhani and gone on to the Akka Hospital where he found, to his surprise, that the Israelis had withdrawn from some of their earlier positions. Now, at sunset, he entered Shatila through the Main Street opposite the Akka Hospital. Surprised by the sound of intensive gunfire within al-Horsh, he increased his pace, no doubt not realizing that an attack by Lebanese armed militias had even started on the right, towards al-Horsh, let alone that the attackers had reached Abu Yasser's shelter by the time he himself reached Hayy al-Doukhi. At those very moments, in fact, they were dragging people from the shelter, shooting at their leisure, ordering the men to line up against walls and the women and children to walk towards the Akka Hospital, towards their deaths.

Arriving in Hayy al-Doukhi, Ibrahim found his friend Hasan covered with blood. 'They've come in,' he was told at once. 'They're wiping us out.' 'Who?' Ibrahim asked. 'The Israelis?' 'No,' Hasan replied, 'these are Lebanese.'

Ibrahim went straight to a house where he and some of his Fatah comrades hid individual weapons, seized a Kalashnikov and stood near the al-Doukhi crossroads. He could see the attackers now, leading the crowd of women and children along the

Main Street, heading south. Ibrahim was barricaded behind them to the north.

He fired several shots in the air and the attackers stopped at the crossroads leading to Sabri Hamadeh Palace. He was in no position to fire at them direct, being, as he explained, fearful for the safety of the people, who he thought were attempting to escape:

I couldn't fire direct because people were running in front of me. After a bit they'd fled into the distance, near today's mass cemetery. I skirmished with them, with the attackers, for almost 15 minutes. They were screaming 'Give up your weapons' and insulting my mother, saying '——', and repeating 'Give up your weapons.'

I shouted over to them: 'If you're real men, come and get them.' I went on shooting for a quarter of an hour. I couldn't know the results of the firing. Whether or not any of them was hit, I don't know. But after quarter of an hour I started withdrawing, through the houses … I had no ammunition left.[52]

While Ibrahim could not know the effect of his firing, it appears that he did indeed hit some. This was attested to by the twelve-year-old boy Munir.

Munir was, as stated earlier, among the dozens of women and children dragged from Abu Yasser's shelter and forced to walk south along Shatila Main Street near the mass cemetery. Ibrahim could not have known they were walking under coercion rather than fleeing. In fact, far from evading death, they were going towards it.

When he was still a boy Munir told me nothing of this final march. Later, however, during his visit to Beirut at the end of the summer of 2000, and while we were walking on that road, he twice volunteered details.

First, he recalled the flare shells flooding the sky, as though night had turned to day; adding that he remembered screaming and cursing, but could not be sure who had been screaming at whom.

The second time he told how he saw three militiamen, or maybe four, falling at different points along the street. He said:

We were walking along this very street, we were walking like sheep. No one dared look back. They were telling us they were taking us to the Akka

Hospital. We believed them. But no. They didn't take us to the Akka Hospital.

Munir seemed in his own world, looking straight ahead as though we other three were not there. After some moments of unbroken silence, he said:

I remember now. It was while we were walking along here. I counted three or four of the gunmen who'd attacked us, I counted them when they fell. Did they die? Perhaps. I can't be sure. Maybe one of them died, maybe two. What I do know is, they were hit from the upper side.

Munir pointed to the north where the al-Doukhi crossroads had been, 200 metres from the Ali Hamdar Café. It was from the first crossroads that the freedom fighter Ibrahim had been firing his Kalashnikov at the militias. Wishing, however, to be sure, I asked him how someone could have fired from that position with civilians in the middle of the road. His answer was immediate:

They were walking, the militias I mean, guarding us on the upper side of the street. [He pointed to the Sports City side of the street.] They were telling us 'Go on, keep walking, keep going towards the Akka Hospital.' I don't remember whether the fighters who'd been shooting did it down the middle of the street. No, they were shooting to the upper side of the street, here. I remember clearly now, one of the men who'd been giving orders shouted at the other militiamen as loud as he could: 'For God's sake, Robert, don't shoot from where you are, a bullet might hit us. Three of our men are down.'[53]

The first conclusion we may reach from the memories of Ibrahim and Munir is that individual resistance had some impact. The second is that, while the gunmen were herding the people southwards, there were others heading north. These were the ones Ibrahim had taunted before stopping their advance. Third, we may conclude that one or more of the gunmen may actually have been shot down by mistake, by fire from their fellow militiamen.

Saving those in the shelters

Ibrahim Baroudi came upon the brave and zealous men near the Hamdar Café, and told them to await his return there. He realized

that, with his ammunition almost exhausted and no time to work out a precise strategy, he could not continue fighting alone. As a brave fighter, and also aware and responsible, he judged it most useful to strive to save the people in the various shelters, which, he realized, the armed militias might invade at any moment. He supposed, he said, that they had already begun to do so, as was indeed the case.

Ibrahim started going from one shelter to another, telling people to leave calmly and head north. He went, among others, to the shelter of the Jalil school, about 50 metres before the mosque. He knew that people must have sought protection there, as they habitually did in dangerous situations.

Finding around 200 men, women and children in the shelter, he told them of the massacre and was immediately believed. He was a well known fighter and, in the colloquial expression, 'those like him are not subject to discussion'. He told how he gave them firm and calm instructions:

'Listen carefully. All we have between them and us is a wall, nothing more. I don't want to hear a single voice. Wait for me near the mosque, till I come. If you make a sound, we'll all be wiped out, because there are more of them.'

'Let's not forget, either, the Israeli forces have been lighting up the camp. Every half minute there's been a flare shell, along with light from mortars and the air force.' People responded to what I said. They headed towards the mosque. I advanced a bit, through the houses, and I found three houses full of people. I got them out and went back. We took them to the Gaza Hospital.[54]

Ibrahim was not alone in his thought of saving those in the shelters. There was also the nurse Um Rabi', who did exactly as he did, knowing nothing of the tragedy her family was suffering while she was rescuing others. Like Ibrahim she led people to the Gaza Hospital, which provided the nearest refuge.

It also emerged that hundreds of residents on that first night had sought refuge at the Henri Chehab Barracks. A Lebanese officer there said:

On the Thursday evening, women, children and elderly men – around five hundred – came to me here at the barracks, and begged us to protect them against the Lebanese militias who'd been killing people at the camp. They said those people had come to kill them. We couldn't believe them, but we took care of them through the night, and lodged them behind the barracks, under our soldiers' protection.[55]

Account 17: From the shelter to the Gaza Hospital

'My father was killed in the Tall al-Za'tar massacre,' Um Rabi' would say, 'and my mother and brother were killed in the Shatila massacre.'

The residents of the camp find nothing surprising in the tragedy of a particular family losing this or that person at Tall al-Za'tar or Shatila. Every family has lost its martyrs in battles or massacres.

Palestinians have grown used to telling or listening, as if, indeed, there were no difference between the situation of teller and listener. This is what makes Um Rabi''s account of things so matter-of-fact, as though she were hardly telling you her father had been killed in Tall al-Za'tar and her mother and brother killed in Shatila – rather as if she were saying they came from al-Khalisa, or that she worked as a nurse at the Akka Hospital.

For all that, Um Rabi' provided a still more accurate description of the flare shells:

At around six in the evening the flare shells really started. I mean, they'd launched flare shells in the past, but not like that. Then they got more and more, they became so many. At the start they'd waited for the flare to go off, then launched a fresh one. Now they started launching them in groups of three or four, and that lit up the whole district, as if the sun was shining. Whenever a shell came down it would start up a fire straight away. A house near ours was set on fire just like that. Everyone at the shelter door started watching it, and they tried to go and put it out, but they couldn't, they were sure another shell was going to fall.

During that time, my three brothers and I were at home preparing supper, we'd gone the whole day with nothing to eat. There was no bread, and we'd got very hungry. We were worried, though, and we had no real appetite. But we got in and started preparing some food. Less than five minutes

after I'd gone in the house and started boiling a pot of tea, the lights began to get brighter and brighter. My brothers were still standing outside. I told them to get in before a shell came down on them, and they did. About five minutes later we heard a voice outside; it sounded like an argument of some sort, with screaming, and so we got out. My brother was the first to get out; he yelled at me: 'Come on, come on ... The Phalangists are here ... Come on, listen to what they're saying!'

Our house was near Abu Yasser's house and his shelter. I mean, what could we say? There were dozens in the shelter: men, women and children. There were even more Lebanese there than Palestinians. Um Yasser was there, so were Um Rida, Um Fadi, Um Ja'far and Um Ali [al-Biqa'i]; they were all Lebanese. We'd been with them just a little while back. We'd been in the shelter with them, my brothers and I.

The moment I looked, I heard orders and yelling: 'Turn your face to the wall, you, turn your face to the wall.' He said to him: 'May God preserve you, I'm Lebanese ... I'm not Palestinian.' He told him: 'Lebanese or Palestinian, what are you doing here, living with the Palestinians? Turn your face to the wall and put your hands up, now.' And he started lining the men up, one after the other.

They saw me. 'Come on,' my brother said, 'let's run for it.' We got back inside, dressed, and got ready to run. My brothers were faster than I was: they'd already started running. But they saw them running and shot at them straight off. One of them said: 'Stop running, you, stand right there.' My brothers had already made it. I stood still and he couldn't but see me. I didn't move, I thought he'd either call out to me or shoot me. So I stood still and stared at him, and he stared back. Then he got busy with the people he was lining against the wall, to make sure no one ran off. I thought of going back indoors and running off from another side. I went back, opened the door and got out from the other side, and I could hear unbelievably heavy shooting. I said to myself, 'He must surely have killed all the men he'd lined up against the wall.' We found out later that was just what happened. [This was the 'wall of death' described above, pp. 94–6.]

I went straight to the Gaza Hospital. It was between half past six and seven o'clock. On the road, I saw our neighbours spending the evening and laughing: Um Akram, her daughter Dalal, and their neighbours were spending the evening talking and laughing, none of them knew what was going on. And yet Um Akram's house was less than ten metres from the shelter [Abu Yasser's shelter]! But I was afraid to go in and tell them for fear he'd surprise me and come out from the second side.

While I was walking I found another shelter full of people, mostly civilian guys just standing there as if nothing was happening. They were looking at the flare shells. 'Quick,' I told them, 'get out, there are armed Phalangists and Israelis, they're killing all the men in front of Abu Yasser's shelter.' The men went crazy, they didn't think it was possible. Anyway, I took them and got out with them. The women and children got out too. And we all went on to the Gaza Hospital.[56]

Um Rabi' was first and foremost a nurse, who had saved dozens of people. She would not, while taking everyone to the Gaza Hospital (as if they could not have found the way themselves), have thought of her own imminent tragedy.

At Abu Yasser's shelter, where she had heard the shots, were her brother and mother, together with her cousin with her children and mother, but she kept reassuring herself through the night that the gunmen would never kill women and children. As for her brother, he was still a boy of 15; he was not a grown fighter. How could they possibly kill him? She thanked God her husband had left with the fighters.

It was next morning before she could find someone to ask about her family. Her neighbour Um Akram, the first to examine the victims, had already discovered the truth, and the two women met on the stairway of the Gaza Hospital and talked together.[57]

A group of men with Kalashnikovs

Just one group maintained its position on the Thursday evening, and this was the group seen near the Ali Hamdar Café, to the north of the al-Doukhi junction. They thought it good to fire from a distance, to let the Israelis know there were some fighting men in the district. These were the same men who had evoked protest from the camp elders who had told them not to 'fool around' with weapons and so give the enemy the impression the camp was still crammed with gunmen and Resistance fighters. They were, as stated earlier, zealous

lads rather than professional fighters. Still, they were zealous enough not to abandon their position even when they learned the invaders were armed militias committing massacre.

The group comprised barely seven or eight young men, Palestinian and Lebanese, and there were also one or two girls, one of whom had attracted attention by carrying the RPG on her shoulder most of the time. It was the first group to make an appearance in the whole Sabra and Shatila district, and it was the last to remain in place, on the Friday morning.

Residents near al-Doukhi and the Ali Hamdar Café recall two significant facts vis-à-vis this group. The first was the fighters' use of a tall building, the well known Mukhallalati building, for firing and protection, which led Israeli troops to retaliate and concentrate artillery fire there, setting the building on fire. The second was the young men's detonation, on their own account, of a weapons store, commonly known as the 'studio store' since there had been a photographic studio in the same building.

A Palestinian mother living 'on the borderline between Sabra and Shatila' was one of those who had seen them near the Ali Hamdar Café, and she gave an account of them:

We could see everything. There were shells being launched from the building in front of our house, right opposite to us. They launched shells at the building and it was set on fire. My daughter, the neighbours and I went down to watch. The Israelis must have sensed there was shelling coming from the building.

As for the store, people blew it up deliberately. Some young men were passing, and I asked them what was going on. They told us not to worry, we're the ones, they said, who set it on fire, that way if Israel wants to get in, or even get hold of some weapons, it'll know there are people resisting ...[58]

Her daughter also spoke of this group, stressing the importance of the detonation of the weapons store near their house. It had, she assured us, been blown up deliberately; so she had been told by some men she knew from the Palestine Liberation Army:

The ones I saw were a bunch of young fellows. They were coming together; I saw them, standing next to our house. They opened up a clothing store of the Liberation Army, brought out the *kufiyyeh*s and started masking themselves. Even the people here were telling them to go away because they didn't want any trouble, they started cursing them. There was a masked girl with them too … They had RPGs and Kalashnikovs. They were right at the entrance to the camp, and we could see them from the balcony. They went on resisting.

What sort of resistance was it?

They were firing bullets and RPGs in the air till Friday morning. We didn't hear a single shot after that. Those fellows were under 20; they were between 17 and 20.[59]

Clearly the surrounding forces did not view these young men's zeal as of any great importance; nor indeed would any intelligent non-military observer have done so. They were not, Dr Paul Morris said, professional fighters, and he added that he saw, from the Gaza Hospital, no more than 15 men changing positions and moving around the same circle rather than specifically targeting. Watching them on the Thursday evening, he recognized many of their faces and was sure they were not professional fighters. In any case, he went on, no one had expected the camps to come under attack.[60]

As for Ibrahim Baroudi, he did, as noted, come across the group, telling them to await his return from his mission to try and save those seeking protection in the shelters. Here is what he had to say:

On my way, I ran into some guys who'd taken up a position near the Café al-Sharq [that is, the Ali Hamdar Café; there is a cinema called al-Sharq in the same building and both names are used]. It was past seven o'clock. They were Palestinian guys with two Lebanese girls: the mayor's daughters. They'd already come into the Trumba district. These guys had decided they were going to fight Israel. When I got there, I told them such-and-such was happening, and I told them: 'Wait for me … I'll be back.' And that's what they did. Meanwhile I'd taken a group of civilians to the Gaza Hospital. I put them in there and went back and found the guys still

waiting. A set of four guys stayed with me. They were all from the camp, and no one could get inside there.

We started advancing between the houses, up to al-Ashbal training camp, where we had a skirmish with them.

There were casualties on the ground. We tried to lift them, and we did manage to lift two women. I went to lift a guy, a guy who'd been injured. We tried to give them first aid, but the woman died. The guy … he died too. He was from the camp, from the Sarris family, I think his name was Jamal Sarris.

At around ten I went back and got deep into the houses up to al-Horsh. I got the people out of their houses, telling them there'd been a massacre, such-and-such had happened, and we went back … at around ten at night. I told people to wait for me near the mosque [known as the Shatila mosque], because there were some guys around there.[61]

So it was that Ibrahim and these other men, who had found support from him, strove hard to demonstrate their presence without fear or retreat, but also without progress beyond that. Ibrahim alone realized that such demonstration of presence was the extent of their possible achievement, and it did indeed have some effect for, as we shall see, the attacking militias' advance in the north on that first night was limited in its scope.

The mystery of the RPG shell

A number of testimonies confirm that the attackers swiftly evacuated the Horsh district following the launching of an RPG shell. Before being struck by this they had had ample time to kill the men near Abu Yasser's shelter and to bring people out from their houses to face their fate. They had, indeed, had time to fill the alleys with bodies. It is certain, however, that they were no longer there after the RPG shell was launched. It is not known precisely when this launching occurred, though everything indicates a time around nine in the evening. Nor is it known who launched the shell.

There are two possibilities regarding this shell. The first is that the one launching it was a man resolved to resist on his own initiative, or with some friends, and such an analysis cannot be ruled out. The second is that he was one of the men from the Kalashnikov group which had been resented by the camp inhabitants but had won the approval of Ibrahim, who had asked them to wait for him near the Ali Hamdar Café and returned to them after rescuing those in the Jalil shelter. What we do not know is whether these young men did simply wait for him or whether they launched the shell during his absence. They were, after all, in a position from which to strike, especially if they had stationed themselves in Shatila Street itself or on the opposite side; and they did have an RPG.

This latter possibility finds support from the attacker's testimony, referred to in Account 16 above. He specified the northern direction, and admitted that he and his fellow militiamen had fled as a result of the shell.[62]

At any rate, the direct consequences of the anonymous resistance fighter's shell were: first, the flight of the attacking gunmen from the Horsh district; second, as noted in Account 16, the survival of some of the wounded; third, an opportunity for the camp residents to leave, since the evacuation of Hayy al-Horsh and Hayy Farhat had now granted the small camp a chance of survival.

Testimonies regarding the first night

The five stories that follow, relating to the first night, serve to supplement the framework of earlier testimonies to the invasion, the shelters and the wall of death – testimonies, let it be reiterated, that not only describe the torture and savagery committed against the residents from the first hours, but show, beyond all doubt, how far the primary mission of these attacking gunmen was from any search for professional freedom fighters.

Account 18: A bomb on a house full of people

Nawal Husari was a nurse who enjoyed her job. She would take a day off only if she was seriously sick, or if there was a situation like that on the Thursday, when Israeli shelling was especially heavy and moving from one place to another involved mortal danger.

Her house lay near Shatila Main Street, close by a bicycle shop; the entrance to the camp was in fact located there. Her house was, as she said, 'on the edge of the camp'.

Around half past five Nawal went out into the street to buy some food. She would not allow any of her brothers or sisters to go out, and her word was law in the house. She said:

The moment I left the house, I saw them, slaughtering people like sheep, not far from where I was. I was back inside the house in a second. There were so many of them. I didn't count them. There must have been hundreds. The instant I was inside, I shrieked: 'Come on, out, these people coming in aren't Israelis, they're gunmen, slaughtering people!' My brothers and sisters kept their heads. I can't recall what each one said, but they agreed those doing this couldn't be from the Lebanese Army, because the army would advance with tanks and jeeps. Each one picked up one or two children and ran for it. There are a number of alleys in the camp. As for me, I picked up my two little nephews and ran.

We left the door open, no one cared or gave a thought to locking it. One of my brothers was barefoot; he had no time to put on his shoes. Even my mother, who's a hajjeh [a woman who has made the pilgrimage to Mecca], started running without a scarf over her head. We hid first at our neighbours', the Aidi family, and told them to leave the house. There was one man among them, Ahmad, who came along with us, together with his wife and three little kids. But his mother, his pregnant sister, his four brothers and sisters, their father and their two brothers-in-law, they didn't run. We did, and so did the rest of the neighbours who'd seen what had happened. But there was no one left to tell the others. Everyone asked God to protect his own self, and wanted to save himself.

When we reached the heart of the camp, we went into a shelter. The people, who were flocking in, were talking of people being slaughtered inside their houses, and being hit with axes. The moment we could start running again, we ran to the Gaza Hospital.

I don't remember when we reached the Gaza Hospital, it was at night.

Our heads were still spinning, after all …

After just half an hour, our neighbours came into the hospital. The criminals had thrown a bomb at their house while they were there inside. I heard what happened.

They knocked at their door. No one opened. They got frightened, and threw a bomb at the house. Three men and two little children died. The mother was injured but still conscious when I went up and asked her: 'What happened, neighbour?'

She said: 'They killed Moussa.'

Later on … the mother died from her wounds.[63]

Among the victims, Nawal recalled, was a man from the Matar family, together with his sister-in-law. These were Palestinians, and they had also been hiding a Syrian neighbour of theirs, whose name she did not know. But she knew Moussa Aidi, and the two men, Syrian and Palestinian, were brothers-in-law. All these died, and so did Um Matar.

Nawal's story was not yet over:

Um Matar had seven children, and her children were hiding at the neighbours'. As for Moussa Aidi's brother [her brother-in-law], whose name was Sa'id, he was outside, just coming into the house. They saw his shoulder from behind, and started to curse and swear; they didn't give him a chance, they fired a machine-gun with a silencer at him, and he died. It was Sa'id's wife who told me what happened to him, she's a friend of mine, a Lebanese, and she has two kids, Rabi' and Muhammad. When she saw how they'd killed her husband, she went straight off and hid under the bed with her kids, afraid they'd get in and kill them.[64]

Nawal's story was still not over. Her main source of anguish was that no one at the hospital would believe her; they refused to believe her or anyone else, even those whose houses had been bombed. Some of the doctors said Nawal was mad. The Hospital Director, who held her tenderly, appeared to believe what Nawal was saying,[65] but this was just a means of comfort – she did not believe her in reality.[66]

Account 19: The first searcher for the victims

Um Akram was a mother of nine children, the youngest four years old, and the wife of a freedom fighter who did not leave Lebanon. He was one of those who had lived there since 1948, and took pride in saying 'We're freedom fighters.'

For all his pride in this, Abu Akram hurried to the Gaza Hospital along with his children before six o'clock on the Thursday afternoon. His wife and small daughters stayed at home, as did the grandmother, Abu Akram's mother.

Um Akram had been one of those horrified by the masked gunmen who went back and forth in Shatila, saying not a word to anyone. She said:

Our house is right by Rawdat al-Shahid Ghassan Kanafani. The garden was full of people and children. When I came, they told me: 'Come and hide in the shelter.' 'No,' I told them. 'I want to stay at home, in case anyone goes in there.' So I put the kids in the shelter and I stayed at home.

A bit later the mother-in-law of my eldest married daughter, Dalal, came. 'For God's sake,' she said, 'I'm going to stay with you.' 'You're welcome', I told her. A bit later, we heard screaming, shooting, and voices saying: 'Oh God … oh God!' That was on the Thursday night, and it was still quite light.

Dalal came running into the alley. There was a shelter where she'd managed to hide. When she came out, she thought it was over, and God forbid what she saw in front of her. She saw around 16 men in military uniform standing there. They started yelling at the men: 'You, come out … You, come out.' So the men started coming out of the shelter.

There were women and children there in the shelter, not just men. My little kids were in the shelter too. I'd say there were around 300 people.[67]

Dalal described the same scene:

I was afraid to stay in the shelter, quite naturally, because once we ran off while Israel was shelling and a nine-storey building collapsed on the shelter and no one in the shelter survived. When I heard the screaming I started running, and I could hear shots. I stuck to the wall so I wouldn't be hit by a bullet. I looked around and saw about 16 men carrying weapons, dressed in green, in army uniform, I mean, and speaking in Lebanese dialect: 'Come out, you, you're happy, are you, Bashir al-Gemayel's dead? Come out, you. You, all of you, come out.' When I heard that, I wouldn't go any closer, I went straight to my parents'. I saw my mother-in-law at my mother's, and I told her: 'Mother, my children and my husband could be in terrible danger ... I left them back there at the shelter ...'

I had three children, I left behind a three-year-old girl and a two-year-old boy, with their father. When I got out, I was carrying the youngest, the newborn baby, in my arms.

My mother-in-law went straight off, we couldn't stop her. She said: 'I'm going to see my son and my little grandchildren.' Then she ran off. Half an hour passed and she hadn't come back. Suddenly a woman from the quarter came running, her feet all stained with blood, and she had her four-year-old boy with her. She'd been stepping over the blood spilling out from the men. She was like a madwoman, and she lifted up her arms and said: 'God's my witness! Why do you still have the gate and door wide open? Go and see those men lying dead, everywhere!'

The moment I heard her say that, I lost my nerve completely, I couldn't move; I thought my children must have been killed! My husband must have been killed! My mother-in-law must have been killed! Who else do you want me to mention? Suddenly, I found myself begging the woman: 'Please, stay with us.' She came in, and we shut the gate, turned off the lights and went into the middle room. She got up, and said: 'Don't say a word. Let's just trust in God.'

We spent the whole night living on our nerves. We really didn't dare talk.[68]

The mother went on:

Next morning we got some news from a fellow who'd been standing guard at the shelter door, where he could see without being seen. He told us there'd been four gunmen, among those who'd been killing and beating people, going up the steps to our roof, going up and down all night long. They were taking binoculars up with them. He said to me as well: 'Thank God you're safe, it's a good thing they never realized there was someone at home. But you mustn't stay at home, they're still slaughtering people and they're just coming to your district.'

I had the youngest with me. The men had gone with their father, but the rest of my children, and my grandchildren, were in the shelter.[69]

On the Friday morning, at exactly five o'clock, Um Akram went to look for her

children among the victims. She may well have been the first of those looking for victims in the massacre, which was still known to relatively few. Even those who had heard about it, some only metres away from the mass killing and torture, had refused to believe it.

Man supposes the death of loved ones to be the worst and most painful news that can come in his life. Yet in massacres he learns that death itself can become a mere piece of news, while everything revolving around it is absolute brutality and unforgettable pain.

Account 20: Awaiting death

Shahira lived in Shatila, in the front part of the camp, or on the edge, as people also say. They had, she said, been spending the evening at the home of her aunt, Um As'ad, who lived close by. They had, however, heard and known nothing.

Shahira did not recall exactly when her sister Aida left to fetch her brother's passport and a sum of 2,000 Lebanese pounds. The two houses were adjacent. But suddenly they heard her screaming at the top of her voice. The father rushed out to check on her and found her dead.

Shahira said:

You're asking us, are you, whether we knew they'd killed them? How could we not have known? Of course we did. But who could have gone out? Who would have dared go near a window? I mean, my father was killed the instant he went out. We stayed all night, waiting for the dawn to come.[70]

The hope was that morning would break and the family would be able to bury its dead. But whoever said burial was permitted in massacres?

Next morning came the savage attack on the other members of the family, who had spent the night sitting with death. Those who had waited for morning to bury their dead now themselves became bodies awaiting burial.

Account 21: A father and his daughter

On that mad Thursday, each member of the family in this account, which lived on the edge of the camp, had his or her particular viewpoint.

The mother, unable to bear the Israeli shelling during the day, had hurried off to the Gaza Hospital, but the young daughter Afaf refused to flee. She was weary of constant flight and the refugee life. Only a few days had passed since their final return home, after they had earlier been forced to move to Hamra Street.

The father, Muhammad Mahmoud Sa'd, had been born in Palestine in the early 1930s. Refusing to leave his house as his wife had done, he stayed with his daughter, though his reasons were different from hers. He was convinced the house was safer than the hospital shelter, which was crammed with people as far as the public street. Nor was he wrong, for there was no longer room to set foot anywhere in the Gaza Hospital, let alone the shelter.

The son tried to persuade his father to flee the district; there were, he said, reports of the militias killing people in their homes. But the father refused to believe this.

The mother, quoting the neighbours but also inspired by her own memories, said:

They told me later the attackers had been 15 armed men. Some were armed with axes, others with guns like Kalashnikovs.

My daughter was wearing a very beautiful dress. Her brother had brought it for her as a gift when he came back from Saudi Arabia. He always brought gifts and dresses for his sister, whenever he travelled. But ... the misery of what was fated to come!

What did they say to them? No one knows. The whole thing was over in just a few minutes. But this is what they told me ...

They shot my daughter dead. The bullets ripped her chest. They threw tinplate on her too; why, I don't know ... My daughter looked like an angel, in the prettiest dress she'd ever worn in her life ...

We never found out what happened to her father. We had a long wait to find out. I wish I hadn't left the house. I wish we'd all died together.[71]

Account 22: No one would believe us

Yusra and her husband heard a woman screaming in the street: 'Run, you people! The Phalangists have got to al-Horsh, the Embassy and al-Ina'ash. Run! The Phalangists are killing people!' Yusra and her husband believed what they had heard. It

was essential the family should split up. Her husband took his sons to the Gaza Hospital and told her to go straight to the shelter with the other children. The time was around half past five in the evening.

The husband said:

We couldn't take the main road to the hospital. We went through the narrow alleys; the alleys are always safer at times like that. On our way we saw a lot of people from the camp, and we told them everything we'd heard, but no one believed us. Just the opposite. They said: 'There's no truth in it, you're trying to demoralize us. You're serving Israel, talking like that.' Still, we went on to the hospital, where we met all kinds of people; we told them, and we got the same answer as we'd had from the Shatila people.

While we were at the hospital, we started hearing the noise of explosions, one after the other. At first we didn't realize what was going on. Then we found the studio store, which belonged to the Sa'iqa, was being blown up and shells were flying. That added to the horror for people, and for the attacking gunmen too. But who blew up the store I never found out.[72]

His wife's experience was a different one. When, she said, her children became hungry, and she saw the other women going to fetch food for their own children, she felt emboldened and asked a neighbour who had been sitting next to her in the shelter: 'Could you lend me your torch?' The neighbour courageously told her he would not let her go alone. He got up, and they left together.

When she reached her house on the edge of the main street, she knocked at her neighbour's to learn what was happening. The neighbour would not open, but answered from inside. 'Go away, may God help you. You don't know I'm here.' This neighbour, Yusra added, stayed at home with her children, making not a sound, through all the days of the massacre. No one knew they were there and in consequence they were unharmed.

Yusra went off home. As she was putting the key in the lock one of the gunmen suddenly started yelling, in Lebanese dialect: 'Who's there, you sons of ——, stay where you are!' Yusra, panic-stricken, left the key in the lock and ran, and so did the neighbour escorting her, each in a different direction. The gunman's cursing was better than his aim; he emptied a full round but hit neither, thanks also to the narrow alleys.

The mother took her hungry children from the shelter and met the neighbour who had helped with his torch. Expressing her happiness that he had emerged safe, she told him that, come what may, she was going to the Gaza Hospital with her children.

At the Gaza Hospital she saw her husband, who told her, to her amazement: 'Don't talk to anyone. No one's prepared to believe anything!'[73]

Limits of the first-night penetrations

In the course of their attack on the first night, the armed militias came in through the south and west entries to a number of quarters of Greater Shatila: Hayy Farhat, al-Miqdad and al-Horsh, east of Shatila Main Street, and Ersal and al-Gharbi, west of the street. They did not, however, penetrate to the interior of Shatila, nor did they reach Sabra. They did not, in fact, even reach the imaginary line between Shatila and Sabra.

It would not have been feasible for the militias to enter by the roads and alleys at night had it not been for the continuous light provided by the surrounding Israeli forces. Israeli sources admitted the existence of this, claiming it to have been indispensable for the achievement of the desired aim: the capture of the Palestinian fighters said to have remained behind in Sabra and Shatila. Sharon, the Israeli Defence Minister, stated that his forces had been firing flare shells from 81 mm artillery in response to a request by the Lebanese Forces, with a view to lighting their way.[74]

Most Israeli newspapers published the facts of the matter clearly. The Israeli Army, they said, fired flare shells throughout the night to light up the camps for the militias. According to one Israeli artillery soldier, his unit was firing two flare shells every two minutes all through the night, from dusk till dawn, with a view to supporting the Christian militias. He added that further flare shells were fired from planes.[75]

The testimonies below reveal the limits of penetration by the attacking forces on the north and east sides, despite Israeli support and the lighting that turned night into day.

Account 23: The three friends

They were three friends, in the habit of drinking small glasses of white araq, the favourite Lebanese drink, openly and straightforwardly, near the Ali Hamdar Café. As a matter of fact, though, they were not Lebanese but Palestinians. They were considered *zghortiyah* in Palestinian argot, *qabadayat* in Lebanese, the words carrying implications of courage.

They were preparing a simple meat kebab for the grill, and, being the humorous men they were, were spending their evening laughing and joking. They could hardly have known a massacre had begun in al-Horsh. One of these three friends described the kind of thing that happened, repeatedly, to the camp residents: while Qassem, one of the three, was grilling, he heard someone call out to him: 'You, come here … come here, you … over here.'

Qassem turned to him and said loudly: 'If you're a *qabaday*, you come here.'

In the event neither approached the other. To begin with, Qassem and his friends supposed the men in question were Israelis, and Qassem was actually apprehensive about getting closer. As for those who had called out, and were actually not Israelis but some of the armed attackers, they were equally apprehensive, given that this was the first group to have challenged them without fear. Taunting invitations were exchanged, but neither approached the other.

At this point, Muhammad al-Nabulsi, another of the three, decided the other men were simply trying to provoke them to test their mettle, and he hurried to fetch a Kalashnikov kept by for reassurance rather than for use. Going to the middle of the street, he said to the original caller: 'Who are you, then? God? God forgive me, who are you?'

This *qabaday* Muhammad supposed that those in front of him were merely young men fooling around; after all, he and his friends were well known in the district. The attackers, though, were of a different order. They sprayed Muhammad with shots and he fell dead on the ground.

The two other friends, now realizing the seriousness of the situation, ran off into the camp alleys, from which shots now began to ring out towards the main street. The murderous attackers now discovered, in their turn, that this was no joke, that they would be unwise to go any further.

Did the gunfire from within the camp come from *qabadayat* like the three friends, or was it from zealous young men? It hardly matters in practice. What is important is that it protected dozens, even hundreds inside the camp. The proof of this is that the attackers stopped there on the edge, on that night, about 20 metres south of the Ali Hamdar Café. They advanced not one step following the death of Muhammad al-Nabulsi.[76]

This story has been passed on in various versions. Some of the camp residents swear that Muhammad brandished his Kalashnikov there in the middle of the street and told them: 'Don't you know who I am? Don't you know I'm the brother of the two famous al-Nabulsi wrestlers?' Did they really give him a chance to say that? Or did these people suppose Muhammad al-Nabulsi was in the habit of boasting about his two champion wrestler brothers? It is only human to react with horror to the sight of a loved one lying helpless in the street, and some came forward to affirm he had actually said those words.

A number note how Muhammad al-Nabulsi's corpse lay in the middle of the street for days before it was picked up and given a proper burial.

Account 24: The steadfast family from Qal'at al-Shaqif

Who was Hajj Abu Ali Ajami? He was the smiling hajj, who never talked without smiling or laughing; a pious man who read the Quran daily. He was also the father of eleven children, seven boys and four girls. When the girls were married, each lived close to her parents in Hayy Farhat on the edge of Shatila Camp; one to the south, the rest to the east.

If you asked the smiling hajj where he came from, the answer would be immediate: 'We're from Qal'at al-Shaqif.'

As far as the hajj was concerned, no place in Lebanon was lovelier than Qal'at al-Shaqif. He might be living in Beirut for the moment, but eventually he would be returning to his southern stronghold. He said:

Nowhere's more beautiful than al-Qal'a. No, I'm not from Arnoun. I'm from the heart of al-Qal'a, from al-Qal'a itself. You have to pass through the middle of Arnoun before you reach al-Qal'a. Al-Qal'a's on the mountain, while the village is underneath. Al-Shaqif has the best climate, dry air, you won't find a better climate anywhere. During the invasion no one stayed in the village, it was being shelled constantly. They used to drag any family outside, then blow up the house. From the mid-1970s there was really nobody. Now people have started going back. A lot of people's homes were destroyed. But still people have started going back. So will we, God willing.[77]

For Hajj Abu Ali, who had twice performed the pilgrimage to Mecca, Beirut could never take the place of his southern village. Nor did he reflect why destiny had drawn him to this particular spot. He was not the type of man to philosophize about things; he was easygoing, and this was the source of his popularity among his neighbours.

He never closed his door on anyone, and all the more so on the first night of the massacre. The neighbours all sought protection at Hajj Abu Ali's home, and eventually there were more than 30 taking refuge there.

His daughter Fatima Ajami tells of that night:

My mother told us to go and sit downstairs, on the ground floor, I mean, so we wouldn't be hurt if something happened above us. We went downstairs and we got lunch ready. It was nearly four in the afternoon and we still hadn't had lunch. Just as we'd set the plates, I swear to God, and I was starting to put the bread out – you should say bread crumbs really, because there was no bread then – we heard a grenade explode at the door, an Israeli grenade we supposed. So we went inside. Several of our neighbours were hit.

The sun went down. Instead, there were those eerie flare shells. We started to hear screaming and crying, but we thought people were getting hit by the shelling and sniping. No one thought of a massacre. In no time all our neighbours were there. Our house is separate from the rest; it has an outside gate that's normally kept locked. Our Palestinian and Iraqi neighbours, and Lebanese too, came and hid at our place. Some Pakistani labourers came too; the poor fellows didn't speak a word of Arabic except 'Allahu Akbar – Allahu Akbar' ['God is great']. My father didn't stop anyone coming in. He went and fetched some woollen blankets and told them: 'Sit down and don't worry.' There wasn't a corner of the house unoccupied, even the bathrooms.

It was almost ten o'clock at night now. There was constant knocking on the door. We didn't open. We just wouldn't. We thought whoever was knocking must have been some Palestinian fighters looking for shelter, and the Israelis would trace them and take us all in. That's what we thought. A Palestinian neighbour got quite scared and said: 'I beg you, close that gate, lock it, otherwise the fighters might get in here and there'd be a real problem. Don't open the door, please; if armed guys get in here and ask for shelter, we'll all be wiped out.' My father told her: 'Don't worry, neighbour; look, I'm going to sit on the staircase.'

I watched my father all night long. He was sitting on the staircase, crying and reading the Quran. We were all praying God would help us through the situation. We didn't know then there was a massacre going on outside, which had reached the next street.[78]

As for why the hajj spent his night on the staircase, he said:

I sat and started praying to Almighty God: 'Oh God, may it please You to keep them away from us.' I thought if they were to come and see me first, they wouldn't go looking for my children, they'd leave them alone; I mean, they'd take me instead … so I sat and waited for them. When they rapped on the door and got no answer, they may have thought there was no one there. Maybe. I don't know. Maybe God kept them away. As for us, we didn't hear their voices at all. They didn't say anything. We only heard the knocking.

I stayed up all night. I heard all kinds of screaming outside, and I heard people saying there was slaughter going on. When they said that, I couldn't stay there inside. I thought, let the Israelis kill me instead of breaking in and killing my children in

front of me. I sat on this staircase and started to pray to God to blind their sight. And thank God. God had mercy on us.[79]

After the rapping on the door, his daughter Fatima Ajami took her children from their beds and hid them under the wide sink, where she laid some sheets and had them spend the rest of the night. It would, she thought, cross no one's mind that there might be children, underneath the sink; if the criminals got in, they might kill her but they would not touch her children, so she reasoned.

As for Hajjeh Um Ali, who had accompanied her husband on his two pilgrimages to Mecca, she heard voices outside as her husband did, and knew they were killing people. To save the children's lives, she told them to hurry and hide in a pool on the roof if they sensed someone was breaking in. The pool was, it was true, filled with water, but wasn't that better than facing death?

It was a dreadful night indeed. When dawn broke at last, Um Ali discovered that their neighbour's roof had been burned by a flare shell, the house of a neighbour had likewise been burned, and the street was filled with bodies. People had been forced to flee.[80]

Those living in Hayy Farhat still talk of Hajj Abu Ali. People like him saved dozens from death.

Shatila Camp at night

It was noted earlier how the freedom fighter Ibrahim, along with members of the Kalashnikov group, worked calmly on that first night to remove people from their homes in the heart of Shatila Camp. As for the residents themselves, a number were aware of the massacre in any case and rushed outdoors. So things continued till the Friday morning, by which time most of the residents were actually outside the borders.

There was no single leadership – not even a local and popular one – that had felt a direct responsibility to maintain vigilance and to keep abreast of developments hour by hour – or indeed minute by minute – from the time the Israeli siege of the Shatila district began, with everyone knowing that the camp specifically was the 'wanted head'. Nevertheless, there were those who felt personally responsible, either by virtue of their presence in the district or because of their nationalist feelings and moral conscience. These accordingly went to the camp at night in an attempt to discover what was happening and to help others as best they could. The testimonies of these people are substantiated by what has been stated above concerning the near total evacuation of the camp on the first night.

Ali Murad was one of those who fought at Hayy al-Fakhani. He was also one of those who picked up their guns and headed towards Shatila at around eight o'clock in the evening, when they heard the rumours about what had been happening there. He said:

A number of guys went to see what could be done, and I was with them. But I can't wander alone in Shatila Camp. I mean, there are narrow alleys. That's why we took a guy from the camp along with us. He was with us at al-Fakhani. He'd walk and we'd follow behind. Some people were still getting out; we'd ask them: 'What's going on?' They'd say: 'The Israelis are massacring people.' Whenever we got closer, people would say: 'Keep going, keep going.'

We crossed the whole camp without seeing even a slaughtered chicken. There was nothing, there was nothing clear yet. We got to the end of the camp, on the other edge of the camp, in the al-Doukhi direction, on the al-Doukhi edge. We didn't go on any further. I was one of those who didn't. But it was obvious there was shooting over towards al-Horsh, where there was noise everywhere ... We were totally confused by then. Everybody was confused. No one knew what to do or where to go. No one knew anything. Even the guy from the camp, the one who was with us, didn't know what was going on.

We went back. We had no other option, frankly. There was nothing we could do. All I can say is, there were no skirmishes or massacres in the camp.[81]

Another man, Hasan Abu Ali, was not a professional fighter. He carried no gun, nor indeed was he a Shatila resident. He just happened to be in the district on that day,

by virtue of his job. He could, he said, have returned to his home, which was outside the district where he worked, from the Gaza Hospital side; but he preferred, in the circumstances, to stay and make any contribution he could. He was one of those who walked in Shatila Camp on the first night, and he testified that it was almost evacuated after ten o'clock. As for those who protected the residents, or stopped the attacking gunmen penetrating deeper into the camp by night, as they had done at Hayy Farhat or Hayy al-Gharbi, Hasan Abu Ali's thoughts were as follows:

We didn't see any of the military resistance we were used to. There were no skirmishes. We didn't sense there was any serious resistance at all.

Maybe there was when Muhammad al-Nabulsi took up the Kalashnikov to scare the attackers off, even though he'd never shot at anybody. I'm sure he thought they were from the district and when they fired at him, he fired back, and he was killed on the spot. Maybe there was the group of young fellows too, who were shooting near the [Ali] Hamdar Café. We saw those. I felt sorry for them, I was afraid they might be wiped out by a grenade at any moment. I'd say those guys might have stopped the massacre reaching the interior.

The attacker, even if he was out to massacre people and backed up by Israeli protection, would lose his nerve facing the unknown ... The guys' shots from inside the camp, after al-Nabulsi's death, must have scared the attackers off, otherwise why would they have stopped when the constant lighting had turned night into day?

The militias obviously thought they'd be carrying on next morning. But there was no one left in the camp next morning. Those who had stayed managed to get out through the Sabri Hamadeh Palace side or the Gaza Hospital side. When the militias made it through to the Gaza Hospital itself, on the third day, there was no one left in the camp.[82]

As'ad was a man from Shatila who worked at the Gaza Hospital. He entered the camp with another man who worked at the hospital's Accident and Emergency Unit, and there was a third with them to help carry the wounded. They all entered between half past eight and nine o'clock in the evening, gave first aid to two people they found in the street, then walked on. There was no sign of a massacre inside the camp.

As'ad reached his home right at the corner of Shatila Camp, separated by just one house from the street leading to Sabri Hamadeh Palace and by just one road from Shatila Main Street. He saw no sign of the massacre on these borders, and concluded that the attackers must have come to a complete halt ahead of the al-Doukhi cross-roads on the first night.[83] This conclusion was correct.

The end of the first day

- The massacre could not have begun in the first place had it not been for the Israeli preparation and protection. This preparation began through the spreading of a false sense of security, starting with the setting up of the Israeli checkpoints in the Ouza'i and Bir Hasan districts. Then, since the Wednesday morning and the direct siege of the Camp district, some Israeli soldiers had contrived to reinforce this air of security, though this actually ran counter to their intermittent shelling, which in turn forced people to stay inside on the Wednesday and Thursday. From the Thursday noon onwards, the shelling intensified, forcing people to go down into the shelters until these were completely full. The shelters were the attackers' first target.
- Just as it grew dark, the phase of full Israeli co-operation began through the launching of flare shells that turned night into day. These shells also set fire to numerous houses.
- The Israelis called a halt to the shelling of the district only for the brief period that coincided with the entry of the attackers through a number of access points. However, they swiftly resumed their intermittent shelling thereafter, selecting spots where there were no attackers; by so doing, they forced those already in the shelters to remain there and those not yet in the shelters to go there.
- The attackers did not know the alleys of the district. This obstacle was, however, circumvented by virtue of the constant lights, the earlier activities of the masked informants and the bulldozing of roads from the very first hours.
- Some of those living in Shatila Camp and Sabra spent their first night without knowledge of a massacre.
- Some were unable to sleep from a sense, or a foreboding, that crimes were being committed outside, and accordingly locked their doors. None of them dared even to light a candle.
- Some managed to flee, either to the nearby hospitals – Gaza, Akka and Ma'wa al-Ajaza – or to the Henri Chehab Barracks, the Kuwaiti Embassy or outside the district through the northern side.
- Of those who sought refuge in the shelters, a number faced mass killing, others were abducted, others survived by sheer chance.
- The killers did not discriminate between Lebanese and Palestinians; indeed, they made no distinction of nationality, sex or age.
- Everyone was a target, and there was no time for questions. When some of the victims informed the attackers that they were Lebanese, their punishment was death because they had voluntarily lived alongside Palestinians.
- Despite the attackers' enquiries about 'terrorists' in certain places, their behaviour from the moment they entered the district suggested that their mission was not to search out 'terrorists' but to kill the innocent.
- From the early hours, the attackers had ample time not only to kill but also to rape, rob and torture victims before killing them.
- All the following districts were made arenas for the massacre in the early hours or on the first day: al-Horsh, including such component quarters as Hayy al-Miqdad, Hayy Farhat and the parts behind the Sports City such as Hayy Ersal and Hayy al-Gharbi, together with the Main Street between its intersection with Kuwaiti Embassy Street and a point about 20 metres ahead of the Ali Hamdar Café.

- None of the attackers entered Shatila Camp itself, nor did any reach the Sabra district.
- While it has been said that the attackers had insufficient time to enter the camp, the more significant reason was the resistance, albeit limited, that they met: the detonation of the studio store; the confrontation from the Hayy al-Doukhi freedom fighter; and the grenade launched from the northern side of al-Horsh, causing the attackers to flee.
- At dawn on the Friday, the bodies of victims lay all over the Shatila district except in the camp itself.
- On the first day whole families were wiped out.
- It later emerged that the number of those killed on the first day exceeded that for the following two days. Nevertheless, the number might have been double what it was but for five factors:

1. The opportunity for many people to flee towards the north or seek refuge in the hospitals.
2. The success of the virtually spontaneous and strictly limited resistance in halting the advance towards the camp.

The detonation of the store was in fact a sign of the limitation of this resistance rather than its strength.
3. The help provided by the Lebanese Army, which sheltered hundreds of residents at the Henri Chehab Barracks or inside the Kuwaiti Embassy.
4. A few people realized the importance of evacuating the shelters and managed to move people to some safer place. It was confirmed that the shelter locations were a deliberate target for the attackers; some they definitely entered with previous knowledge of their existence, others they entered by chance.
5. Some of the attackers held back from committing mass or individual murder, differences and contradictions in their attitudes being apparent from the first night. The attitude of some differed from that of the majority. Whereas the majority simply killed every person that came their way, a minority held back from killing Palestinian families. These cases were sufficiently limited in number to be labelled 'exceptions to the rule', but they did in fact exist.

4

Friday 17 September 1982

By early Friday morning the attackers had already received essential support and penetrated the area. Shatila was filled with blaring calls: 'Surrender and you won't be harmed.'

Nevertheless, anyone who could have passed through the Shatila district and seen the roads and alleys filled with bodies would have discovered soon enough what this promise amounted to. As for the terrified people cramming the shelters, a few were able to flee, but the rest were killed either inside the shelter itself, in front of it, against the wall opposite, or at the end of the alley – apart, that is, from some shelters that were still full of people on the Friday and faced the same various fates as those the day before.

If the Thursday night was that of liquidation in the shelters, Friday saw the invasion of the Akka Hospital, and 'walls of death', no longer deemed sufficient, were supplemented by pits. Even so, new means were found of breaking into shelters; in more than one case people were burned by phosphorus bombs or shot dead while still inside. The attackers did not in fact make significant advances on the Friday. Yet mass and individual killing, accompanied by torture, actually went beyond what had taken place on the previous day.

Various testimonies note how the Israelis witnessed the mass killing operations in the pits, or else knew of these and other atrocities through residents' complaints. The Israelis' reactions were mixed: some refused to help whereas others, on a number of occasions, intervened to prevent mass killings.

Accounts in this chapter supplement those for the previous day, comprising ten accounts dealing with the tragedies of whole families. One might have thought, indeed, that the obliteration of families was the prime aim of the whole bloody affair.

The attackers failed to enter the small Shatila Camp on this day, and would have found no one had they done so. Most residents had left during the evening, and those who had not managed to do so, or had remained initially ignorant of the massacre, had left through the north or north-east side by the morning.

The Israelis, as noted above, had apparently asked the killers to leave on the Friday. However, this request – assuming it was indeed made – was not complied with, either by the killers themselves or by the Israeli Forces who were besieging the area and were in a position to pull the militias out.

Shatila between five and seven in the morning

Abu Jamal, the Palestinian garage owner quoted earlier, noted as follows:

On the Thursday they still hadn't got to Shatila Camp. They'd reached the middle of Shatila Main Street, no further. The last point they reached was the al-Doukhi shop, a wholesale and retail store. Al-Doukhi, the shop owner, was killed on the Thursday night, God bless his soul.[1]

This witness's garage was located halfway down Shatila Main Street, on the right-hand side coming from the Kuwaiti Embassy. He did not live in Shatila but, having worked there since the 1960s, knew every stone of the place. When people were eventually allowed to return and check on their houses and shops, he found the attackers had brought down the sturdy front part of his garage. He also found dozens of victims in front of it.

This witness's conclusion, based also on what he had heard from others, was replicated in further eye-witness testimonies. Photographers and reporters were in fact barred until the Saturday when the killers had left, but the human eye is credible enough.

There were five testimonies to the events of the Friday morning between five and seven o'clock, and these provide a panorama of Shatila during the hours in question.

The first testimony was supplied by Thunaya Amin, one of the women who had been abducted from the shelter on the previous night and had returned to al-Ouza'i (see the account of the women's march in Chapter 2, pp. 58–61). Not knowing a massacre had taken place, she had returned to look for her husband and, passing by Abu Jamal's garage, was able to confirm that its front part was still undestroyed on the Friday morning. She described what she saw:

It was half past six in the morning, there was no one at all on Shatila Main Street, not a soul; we didn't even see a chicken. You wished you could see someone walking along the road, but there was nobody. I walked and reached Abu Jamal's garage half way down the street, and it still hadn't been damaged at all. I don't know when they came back

and knocked it down. Later on, when everything was over, we saw it knocked down.

… When they heard the noise of an engine, they started coming down from the top end [that is, from Hayy Ersal], and from the front of al-Horsh, from all different directions; you could see, there were so many of them, like ants. They started shooting at us and shouting: 'Where are you going, you ——s, you whores, where are you going?'

We told them we'd been taken to al-Ouza'i and spent the night there, and that we'd asked Mr Nadim for permission to go and fetch milk for our children. Then one of them said: '—— you and —— whoever sent you. Come along to the Command Centre. Come on!' They came and walked alongside us in two lines, one this side, one the other; there we were in the middle, being led along. If anyone fell behind, they either kicked her or hit her with the butt of their gun.

On our way to the Command Centre, that was past the Kuwaiti Embassy going towards the sea – it still wasn't seven o'clock – we passed by the shelter where we'd been, I mean, where they'd taken us from the night before. We didn't dare look, I swear, because anyone looking here or there would be told to look straight ahead and not look round. But even without looking round, we could see people lying in the streets. We found Um Muhammad, Hussein's mother, next to Abu Afif's house, she was lying flat on her stomach, shot. And at Abu Bassam's house, there they'd shot Um Bassam and her children on the doorstep. They hadn't done anything to the houses yet, no houses had been knocked down at all, nothing like that. The houses we went by were all still standing.[2]

The second testimony was from another woman who had taken part in the Thursday's women's march (see Account 7, p. 86). She and her mother were also among those abducted and taken to al-Ouza'i, and she too had experienced trying to return to Shatila on the Friday morning. She said:

It was five o'clock, dawn was just breaking, when a Lebanese woman jumped up and said: 'You're Palestinians, you go your way and we'll go ours. If they see you with us, they'll kill us all. You stay. We'll go first, we Lebanese, then you Palestinians go.'

We wouldn't agree. We started walking. They walked in one direction, we walked in another. The poor children were running in front of us.

We went from al-Ouza'i to Bir Hasan. We kept on walking till we reached the Henri Chehab Barracks. We saw the Lebanese Army, one of the soldiers asked: 'Where are you going?' We told him: 'We were trying to get away from the shelling, now we're going back home. Is there some problem?' 'No,' he said. 'There's no problem.' A bit later, another Lebanese soldier, just getting in a car, came up and asked us: 'Where are you going?' 'We're going back to our homes in Shatila', we said. 'Is there some problem?' The soldier said: 'Don't go there. Don't go to Sabra and Shatila. You'll die if you do. Go back, for your own good.'

We were sure he was telling the truth. Even so, we thought we'd go and risk our lives there rather than stay where we were, where they could just come and slaughter us.

We walked on to the start of Shatila Street. We wanted to cross at the Abu Hasan Salameh statue. They started sniping at us and shelling us.

… God saved us, and we went on walking.

… As we got closer to al-Horsh, and then to the camp, we saw there was no one in the camp, not a soul, no sound, nothing. Were could we go? We thought, let's go to the Akka Hospital. Actually, my mother and I work at the Akka. We started running, one behind the other, towards the Akka. The sniping went on round us. When we got to the hospital, it was just before seven in the morning.[3]

The third testimony came from the Lebanese policeman mentioned earlier as one of the people guarding the Kuwaiti Embassy, when he and his comrades protected anyone seeking refuge there. This policeman was standing in front of the embassy on the Friday morning when a Palestinian woman took hold of him, screaming: 'You're killing us! You're killing us!' When he refused to believe what she was saying, she told him: 'Come with me.' Then she took him to the entrance to the camp in Kuwaiti Embassy Street. He described what he saw:

On the main street, in front of each house, there were five or six bodies. I went to check the upper quarter. There again each house had its five or six bodies. It was obviously done either with silencers or knives, or by burning. At the front of the upper camp, there was a girl of 14 or 15 whose breast they'd taken off with a knife, as well as shooting her in the chest. She still wasn't dead. The Red Cross

took her to the nearest centre in Mar Michel. The ones who carried her there were two men from the military.

I saw a man, too, killed on a chair. They'd tied him up and hit him on the head with an axe. The Forces were there at the end of the street, you could tell them by their green uniform.[4]

The fourth testimony was that of the Palestinian freedom fighter Ibrahim Baroudi, who had realized from the first night that armed resistance was impossible and had focused his efforts on saving anyone he could from among those seeking protection in the shelters (see Chapter 3). His testimony for the Friday morning confirmed that of the policeman above. He said:

On the Friday morning I went deep into the camp, as far as al-Ashbal camp, myself and four other guys. We found the body of a man called Jamal Barakeh. He'd been shot some way from there; he'd run from the Main Street through the alleys till he fell. There was no one to pick him up. We took him and sent him to the Gaza Hospital … It turned out bulldozers had been pulling down the houses over the people they'd been killing. Don't ask how many people had been killed in Shatila Main Street, and in the alleys we went into in al-Horsh.[5]

The fifth testimony was from Um Akram, who had been the first to search for victims (see Account 19, p. 105; p. 222). She had been looking for her children since five in the morning, and, unable to find them, had gone on scouring the alleys. She had only given up, finally, through a fear of fainting with no one to rescue her.

This is how Um Akram described the devastated Shatila district between five and seven on the Friday morning:

At the start of the road, the start of the alley, I mean from where we first went in at Abu Ahmad Srour's up to Abu As'ad's, up to Rashida's, I saw about 150 bodies, not counting those at the shelter. The alleys were full of victims too. Each way I looked, I'd find five or six victims. I was walking without notic-ing almost. Do you know the alleys going to the Akka Hospital, at al-Horsh? I walked through all of them: I'd go in at one alley and out at another. Every alley I went into there were victims. Some had been crushed under the carts that sell kerosene. As I was passing by Rashida's, there was a cart with six men stuck under it. Whether they'd put them there or collected their bodies, or whether the men themselves had piled one on top of another out of panic, I don't know.

I nearly fainted in the Doukhi alley especially: it was children there, along with women mostly, they'd all been killed in the street and in the alleys. Just by al-Doukhi, there's an alley that goes up, isn't there? I got halfway through the alley that goes up to Moussa's house, but when I saw so many victims, everything started spinning round me, I couldn't control my nerves because of all the things I'd been seeing. I was afraid the dizziness would make me ill. I went back and then made straight for the Gaza Hospital, I didn't go on.

But I forgot one thing. At Hayy Ersal there were dead people stacked on top of each other. It was obvious bulldozers had been at work, piling up people. I saw the marks of the bulldozer on the road. I looked for houses I knew but I couldn't find them. At Ersal I saw houses they'd managed to pull down and get rid of in a single night. They were killing and bulldozing at the same time.[6]

Um Akram said she heard the megaphones calling 'Surrender and you won't be harmed', and that she'd meant to give herself up so as to be safe. With her, she continued, were ten women, young men and children, and they'd assembled their papers ready for surrender. However, her nephew came and whispered in her ear:

Don't go. Don't get yourself into this, aunt. It's all a trick, aunt. There's no surrender or anything of the sort. They're taking people to the Sports City and killing them there. Listen to me, aunt.[7]

His aunt listened to him and held back; as for the other people, she did not know. That Friday, she said, was like doomsday.

*　*　*

We noted how Hind, in her testimony at Hayy al-Gharbi (see Account 3, p. 81), had described the attackers as digging out a new road behind the Sports City, leading towards Hayy Ersal. This was confirmed by a Palestinian woman in her testimony for the Friday morning, as the gunmen were forcibly leading them to the Sports City: 'We saw a bulldozer digging out a road from the Sports City down to the camp. They were laying gravel so they could march over it. It was quite obvious they'd started the road digging before the Friday morning.'[8]

Another Palestinian woman among those forced, on the same day, to walk under guard along the same road from Shatila Main Street to the Sports City, through Hayy Ersal, reported as follows:

The bulldozer was pulling down the houses and covering the victims with backfill. There were two men who'd carry the victims and take them to a big pit. These two men weren't from the attackers. Some of those who were walking with us knew them. When they'd finished transporting the bodies, the killers rewarded them by killing them. Alas for them![9]

If we compare the first five testimonies above, about events of the early morning, with the two subsequent ones about the later forced walk to the Sports City, it becomes clear that the bulldozing of houses did not take place over a single night, but was rather an ongoing operation.

In the first testimony, Thunaya Amin said that the houses she had seen on the way to the Kuwaiti Embassy were still standing just as they always had been; these, though, were the very houses bulldozed subsequently. At the same time, Um Akram, in the fifth testimony, told how the killing, demolition and bulldozing at Hayy Ersal took place consecutively at night. In the two final testimonies, from Hayy Ersal itself, two Palestinian women affirmed how, during their forced walk with other residents to the Sports City, bulldozers were doing their work in front of them.

In fact the landmarks of Greater Shatila were changing from morning to evening, and even from hour to hour. Houses were being destroyed and bodies were being swallowed up by the bulldozers.

The attacker and the defender

Who exactly were the attackers? Who were the militias that invaded Shatila? This cannot be comprehensively answered within a single section, but must rather emerge through the book as a whole. The answer was begun in the previous chapter by references to the armed militias at the entrances to Shatila, and continued, in that chapter, in the light of testimonies about the incursion through the southern and western entrances; and it will continue to be answered up to the last pages. This section serves as a supplement to previous statements and deals with the situation of the attackers between the first night and the first morning, along with the situation of the defenders.

An Israeli soldier described the attackers to the *Jerusalem Post* correspondent, Abraham Rabinovich, as they were when they broke in on the Thursday evening. Although, he said, they were ostensibly set for a battle, the way they were organized suggested otherwise: they were manifestly split up into groups. One of them had boasted: 'We're going to kill terrorists.' As for what happened after they entered Shatila, this Israeli said they heard no exchange of fire beyond a brief initial period.[10]

Other soldiers told the same correspondent how, during the night, a militiaman came to the nearest Israeli point and asked for a stretcher in order to bring away wounded militia colleagues. One of them asked him what was going on and he answered that, so far, they had killed 250 terrorists. After he had left, the soldiers had all laughed. He must have been counting civilians, they said, since they had heard no exchange of gunfire.[11]

According to *Time* magazine, resistance did exist, but it was scattered. Referring to the attackers as 'Hobeika's men', *Time* mentioned that these had asked the Israelis for further lighting and artillery shelling, then had come to ask for assistance to evacuate their wounded. By dawn on the Friday, their commander, Elie Hobeika, had received permission to call up two additional battalions (though it subsequently emerged that only one was used).[12]

By sunrise the attackers had already brought in jeeps and other vehicles, including bulldozers. An Israeli soldier who was among those watching the scene said they had all supposed the bulldozers were being brought in to demolish houses, but that they were actually used (as they discovered later) to bury bodies.[13]

One of the attackers was not in fact from among Hobeika's men. He identified himself subsequently, to *Der Spiegel*, as part of Al-Numour al-Ahrar, adding that they had, however, all been wearing the official Phalangist uniform. Furthermore, he said, more than twelve Israelis wearing the green Phalangist uniform had joined them from the Wednesday, the day on which they assembled and were given instructions at Wadi Shahrour, near Beirut. He described these Israelis as having been fluent in Arabic, apart from the sound 'ha'', which they pronounced 'kha''. He did not omit to mention the officers' explanation: 'The Israeli friends who will be joining you will be going on their own initiative, without their army's knowledge. They will facilitate your mission.'[14]

The most significant instructions given to the attackers were that everything should be carried out silently. As such, bayonets and knives were to be used, with gunfire avoided as far as possible, so as not to attract residents' attention. Most important of all, everything was to be carried out within just three hours![15] Somehow these three hours stretched into three days. Why and how this happened will be revealed as events unfolded hour by hour.

By the Friday morning the attackers were all set to complete the mission. Some had gone by truck, during the night, to rest at al-Hadath town before returning in the morning.[16] Others had arrived with the new convoys in the early morning.[17] Still others had spent the night on the massacre site, completing as much of their mission as the night would permit (this will be discussed further in Chapter 6). Only a minority of the victims were ever found and identified; the majority had disappeared without trace. The search revealed, nevertheless, residual signs of the attackers' work: in front of the houses, on the tables, even on the walls.

Such was the visible picture they provided. As for the invisible one, the fact is that these were no ghosts but rather guerrillas belonging to local Lebanese leaderships which were in turn subject to the command besieging Sabra and Shatila: that of the Israeli Army, regarded as the most powerful striking force in the Middle East.

The whole of West Beirut had come under Israeli occupation. And in order to carry out their missions, declared and undeclared, the attackers obtained everything they needed through the forces besieging the popular district known as the Sabra and Shatila camps.

What precisely was it the attackers needed? Lighting? Tightening their grip? The securing of entrances and exits? Artillery? Trucks and other vehicles? Bulldozers? Ammunition? Food? Drink? All this was assured to an extent that met their full expectations, and to an extent, too, that compels reflection. What was left for the attackers to do but use their weapons?

Let us move now from the attackers to the defenders, those supposed to be there on the other side. Who exactly were they?

I shall not discuss here the rumours of fighters numbered in their thousands; such rumours can be simply refuted by the facts. Nor will I repeat earlier material about such defenders as were in fact found, numbering a few dozen at most and largely from the district, who hastily took hold of the nearest available weapons and acted together as they could. I shall rather content myself with drawing a comparison between attacker and defender at the leadership level.

The typical defender, living in Sabra and Shatila and (whether Palestinian or Lebanese) identified, mentally and spiritually, with the Palestine Revolution, was without leadership on any level during those lost days. He had no connection of any kind with the upper leadership abroad, since all means of communication had been severed. Equally, he had no connection with any who were left among the members of the Palestinian faction leaderships, who were logically supposed to be still in Lebanon, especially in al-Beka'a and the North (without any breach of the famous Habib Agreement). As such, the situation permitted no one to reach out to anyone; those besieged inside Sabra and Shatila had to decide what to do on their own initiative.

There was, furthermore, no local leadership responsible for the security of the camp or adjacent areas. There were just local offices subordinate to some particular front or party. Some of these were now completely closed; others had started to open on a day-to-day basis following the departure of the fighters, with anyone left merely coming in to deal with routine matters.

In two of the four quarters that saw resistance, albeit limited, to the Israeli Forces, men took up weapons, as we have seen, with no command or commanders to lead or guide them. These were Hayy al-Fakhani and Hayy al-Doukhi. Hayy Farhat, on the other hand, had an office of the Arab Front, and Hayy al-Horsh an office of the Popular Front. In these latter quarters, in other words, men had a door on which they could knock to ask for a weapon to enable them to defend their families and homes against the besieging Israeli Forces.

The Thursday was over, and so was the fighting at both Hayy Farhat and Hayy al-Horsh. The commanders from the Arab Front and Popular Front offices had left, hoping, as we have seen, to meet on the following day. Their decision was based on the immense difficulty they anticipated in fighting the Israeli Forces at night, when only artillery fire was to be expected.

That night, though, there was an infantry attack after all, moving from one alley to the next and from one house to the next – but not by the Israeli Forces, whose inclination was always to hold back from night assaults on camps, leaving such missions to others.

One can hardly speak of any defence against these other attackers on the first night; just an exchange of fire, for a quarter of an hour, from the Hayy al-Doukhi side, when a courageous freedom fighter went on firing till his ammunition ran out. This man, with some other brave men he found round about, went on guarding the camp through the night.

What, then, of the Friday? What of the residual resistance by those defenders who were left, without backup, against bloodthirsty criminals backed by besieging military forces from an army comprising, by common consent, the most powerful strike force in the Middle East region – the same forces that had reassured people with claims that they had come to protect them? Did any resistance get underway before a withdrawal took place?

The defenders' retreat

Just as resistance to the Israeli Forces had a different beginning in each of the four quarters in question, so the end was different in each case. As in chapter 2, we shall deal with the quarters one by one.

Hayy al-Horsh

In al-Horsh, as we have seen, one section of the group confronting the Israelis on the Thursday had left the whole Shatila district, while another had remained inside. Retaliation against Israeli artillery fire at night had been discounted due to the crippling difficulties involved, and no one had anticipated anything more than a resumption of such artillery.

As dawn began to break on the Friday morning, Abu Ra'ed and his small group – the four members who had stayed with him inside Shatila Camp – had already begun a cautious reconnaissance. Near the Popular Front office, they saw a blood-stained woman and asked her what was wrong. She told them, in a broken voice: 'The Israelis are slaughtering people, right here at the entrance to Shatila Street.'

The men were utterly shocked. This was not something they had been expecting. Abu al-Ra'ed described these moments, as they discussed events:

'So what are we going to do?'

There was total turmoil. So they were slaughtering people, stabbing with knives, hitting with axes ... I won't say we panicked, it wasn't that, but it was a shock. No one had expected massacres to happen. No one had been expecting this. Killing civilians? Just like that? In that kind of way?

'What about it, then? Are we going to fight?'

'We want to face them', they said. I swear to God they did.

We were still inside al-Horsh, near the office of the Nidal Front. When we reached our house, just underneath our window, we saw a woman called Um Ja'far, from Majdal Zoun, whose house was ten metres from ours, right at the back. She and her daughter had been flung down on the ground. Her head had been hacked off, along with the eyes and the hair. Her daughter – I think it was her daughter; we couldn't identify her exactly, though I'd known her well enough – had been killed the same way, poor girl.

Now, up to then we'd seen no Israelis, but we were sure now the story was true; a massacre had been going on, and was still going on. There was the Mhanna family too: there was the mother and her daughter, and her son as well, if I remember ... They'd all been hit by axes, killed in the most brutal way ...

I went on with just two men, the four of us didn't stay together ... This is getting really distressing, I can't talk any more ...[18]

Abu Ra'ed's voice changed, but he did go on talking. Among the victims on the ground, he said, he saw Abu Rida and Um Ja'far's brother, from Majdal Zoun, and he saw the latter's son. He saw other bodies too, in front of an amusement centre that belonged to Abu al-Issa. By a wall near a garage, he saw five or six people who had been 'lined up and shot'. For all that, though, they had not yet seen a single attacker.

Abu Ra'ed and his group walked on till they were inside al-Horsh, at a small underground shelter able to accommodate barely 50 or 60 people, not too far from Um Ja'far's. It was accessible only to those who knew where it was; residents called it the 'secret shelter'. They began to approach in order to check on it and make sure everyone there was all right, but before they reached it they were surprised by the sound of gunfire. Stopping and looking towards Shatila Main Street, they saw soldiers in identical uniforms accompanied by others in civilian clothes. At first glance they supposed them all to be Israelis.

As the fighters gazed at the attacking armed soldiers, a phosphorus bomb fell in the shelter doorway. There was an explosion, then a blazing fire as the whole shelter began to burn. The fighters, enraged, fired at the attackers, and a skirmish took place over several minutes with no one knowing if any of the attackers had been hit. The fighters no longer felt sure, as they had on the previous day, of just where the Israelis were likely to appear.

Abu Ra'ed could not forget the victims' screams after the phosphorus bomb had exploded at the entrance to the shelter:

... I mean, the instant the phosphorus bomb was launched at the shelter underneath, everything was set on fire. The shelter, and everybody in it, was set on fire ... and we heard screaming. Oh, God, what screams they were. We saw them in those moments, while they were launching the bomb, and we fired at them. There were around four of us, and she was with us, I suddenly saw her standing there with us; it was [Sister] Fatima, I swear to God it was Fatima. She was a bit fat, short and dark-haired. She was still alive then.

We fired. We skirmished with them for about ten minutes, maybe less.

... Of course, we heard them calling out to each other, names like 'Tony', 'Sa'id', 'Pierre' and 'Robert' ... In those moments I heard some Hebrew too, particularly in the seconds when the phosphorus bomb was launched. I looked at them and heard the Jewish language, I heard Hebrew ...[19]

The fighters made a random withdrawal from one alley to the next but quickly realized that, however deep they went into the alleys, they would not face their Israeli enemies – the mission of these latter was beyond the camp district and its perimeter. They realized, too, that the Hebrew they had heard was not the language of the majority of the killers.

Realization only dawned in fact after they had been assured by everyone they met that a massacre had indeed been taking place, starting at sunset the previous day. The attackers, they learned, were Lebanese aided by informants with a good knowledge of the streets and alleys, but with some Israelis perhaps accompanying them. Where, after all, had the Hebrew speakers come from?

Abu Ra'ed confirmed the informants' role:

Even now we were getting lost in the camp, even in the front part. There are alleys I still don't know, and remember, I think of myself as being from the camp. I've been here for several years. I live here, and I've come to know the camp better than its own people. Even so, there are some alleys that

make me feel as if I'm going into them for the first time. So it's impossible all this could have happened at night, or even during the day, without help from informants.[20]

It was still before noon on the Friday. The fighters checked their ammunition and found it was almost completely exhausted; there was not enough even for a one-minute fight.

When they reached the office they found four more comrades there. They also discovered the office had been completely emptied of weapons and ammunition. There were just 40 hand grenades for defensive purposes, on top, of course, of the weapons and ammunition that had been distributed to those who had asked for them the day before.

'Let's go and ask our brothers at the Arab Front', one of them said. 'They must have weapons, and they'll give us some.' 'They're arranging to blow up their store', another said. The first man had nothing more to say.

A few minutes later a series of explosions was heard. The men, knowing the source of these, made a calm withdrawal, leaving behind, between the office walls, the Kalash-nikovs they had with them, along with one B7 rocket launcher.

Having no one to command them, they had agreed among themselves, when the fighters left, that each should make his own decision as to what to do. Should he go to his family, if they themselves were still there, or should he leave? And, if he left, where should he go?

They agreed, finally, to go to the Abdul Nasser mosque on the Corniche al-Mazra'a. There were just eight of them, each carrying one or two hand grenades for self-defence and protection against capture by the Israelis. They were not to know that the Murabitoun radio station building inside the mosque was now, like the PLO office on the Corniche al-Mazra'a itself, under occupation.

As for the group of men that had left at the start of the night, intending to return next morning, they too had learned of events. In consequence, Comrade Hussein, the man in charge, made the decision not to return to the camp.[21]

The total number of people fighting or carrying weapons at Hayy al-Horsh from the Wednesday to the Friday totalled around 25, in separate groups and at various times. Only a handful were trained, the others bearing arms for the first time. All these acted under the direction of the people at the Popular Front office at al-Horsh. Just seven or eight were actually members of the Popular Front. The political identity of the rest remained largely unknown, but their residence was not in question: they were all from the camp and the neighbouring district, either Palestinian or Lebanese. The group included some gypsy men from among the original residents of al-Horsh. Nothing had been heard of most of these since the previous night, and it was assumed they had left the district.

Nothing definite was known, either, of the fate of the one girl, known as 'Sister Fatima', who had carried weapons with the Horsh group. This courageous girl from Fatah had, on the Thursday, come alone to the Popular Front office to ask for weapons. Had she fallen as a martyr?

There are witnesses that Fatima used her weapon, and to the fact that she was alongside Farid al-Khatib, near the entrance to Shatila, when he was wounded on the Thursday afternoon. She was also seen on the Friday morning alongside Abu Ra'ed's group, near the small shelter burned out by a phosphorus bomb. From these last moments, though, no one saw Fatima again.

A phosphorus bomb had been launched on a small shelter full of people; and no one was likely to make enquiries of another person at a moment like that. At any rate, she was not seen again anywhere in the camp. It was said her parents went to live in Damascus, where they had relatives. Did Sister Fatima join them? Or did she stay with her comrades, who had found their final resting place deep in the earth?

People other than Sister Fatima died as martyrs, with even their first names unknown. The young *shibl* who fought with the other *shibl*, Zaher al-Sa'di,[22] on the Thursday, was never identified. Witnesses remembered well enough, though, how he launched a phosphorus bomb at the Israelis,

while Zaher launched four hand grenades. One of them recalled, too, the last time he saw him, on the Thursday, walking in front of the Communist Party office. All he knew was that the lad was 14 years old and that 'we heard the *shibl* from Fatah died as a martyr'.[23]

Hayy Farhat

The main resistance at Hayy Farhat took place against the Israelis on the Thursday, when the defenders shelled the besieging forces with a 14.5 artillery weapon on a truck. The confrontation, as we saw in Chapter 2, lasted around a quarter of an hour. Beyond that there was no active resistance, the truck itself, driven by a man from the Arab Front, having left the district subsequently. This man's comrades remained vigilant, guarding the celebrated Hayy Farhat weapons store, but, unlike their Popular Front comrades in neighbouring Hayy al-Horsh, they did not move beyond their office.

The superiors at the Arab Front office took the decision to blow up the store, should this be judged necessary, as early as the Thursday. However, they lacked an expert to carry this out under the present circumstances. The most qualified person available was a fighter from the Popular Front, who prepared the necessary explosive and set it in place so that the guards would need to do no more than detonate it at the proper time. The 'expert' himself then returned to his group at Hayy al-Horsh, where he was later injured. There was no infirmary nearby, but a nurse managed to give him initial treatment in her house before he was eventually taken to the Gaza Hospital.

The detonation stemmed from a fear that the attackers would invade Hayy Farhat and seize what remained in the weapons store, including Grad rockets. The store was accordingly blown up before noon on the Friday while the attacking killers were busy in other places around Shatila and Sabra, dragging people from their homes and leading them forcibly towards the Sports City, the trucks or the death pits. As the charge was detonated, rockets began to explode in all directions, and it was around a quarter of an hour before the sounds of violent explosion at last began to fade.[24]

Hayy al-Fakhani

The Fakhani district lies beyond the perimeter of Sabra and Shatila; the attackers had in fact had no intention of going there, but it was the district where the Israelis first arrived. The resistance fighters there hurried to take up their weapons; and, the district being well populated, their number exceeded that of fighters in the other quarters. However, as was revealed in the testimony of the freedom fighter Ali Murad (see Chapter 2, pp. 67–9), they had neither leadership, clearly prescribed roles nor popular support. We have already heard of Ali's night inspection of Shatila. Here is his account of the 'fighting' in al-Fakhani following his return there:

The Israelis advanced as soon as dawn broke. We saw them, they appeared and advanced on a tank, came right up the slope and approached the edge of the Engineering College from the south. I mean, they ended up ahead of the parking garage to the right of the University, just a bit ahead of it, that's where the tank stopped.

There was a guy with us who took the initiative and fired a B7 rocket at it. The Israelis started to fire back. There was damage, and skirmishes. You might call all Thursday and Friday's skirmishes the hit-and-run sort. The Israelis retreated to the front of the Sports City. Then, every hour or two, we'd see them coming back, getting close to the Engineering College, and so we'd go back and launch an assault, and they'd retaliate, and so it was all quick attacks.

Two of our guys died, I remember the name of one them: Issam al-Yassir …[25]

The men bearing arms at Hayy al-Fakhani belonged, as we have seen, to various parties and organizations. Although they were under no command or direction, this was not in fact the main reason for their final withdrawal from the confrontation. The freedom fighter Ali provided the two main reasons, simply and straightforwardly:

Two days after the Israeli siege, on the third day, Friday, we were all pretty confused, and we didn't know what to do. Here at al-Fakhani, there were already two, maybe three tanks, and we started hearing this or that part of Beirut had fallen, and so we were all bewildered finally, didn't know what was going on.

At the same time, and this was the most important thing, some of the people living in the district were starting to resent us, I mean, may God forgive them, they thought we were causing damage to the district. So, after they'd closed the entrance doors of their buildings in our faces, we'd no justification for staying there. Who were we defending?

In the end we withdrew to the Sabra district; I mean we went from al-Fakhani towards Sabra – al-Dana, because we used to live around there …[26]

Hayy al-Doukhi

The freedom fighter Ibrahim Baroudi had, as we saw in Chapter 3, stood alone to stop the advance of the attackers in Hayy al-Doukhi, saved people in the shelters and lent his assistance to the Kalashnikov men. We have also seen, in this present chapter, his testimony as to events in Shatila between five and seven on the Friday morning. He was a level-headed fighter. On the Friday he took his weapon and led a limited skirmish near al-Ashbal training camp, hearing sounds which he took to be from armoured vehicles but which actually came from bulldozers demolishing houses, with their owners inside, in the wake of the killing.

Resistance undoubtedly ended before noon on the Friday, but it is difficult to know precisely when, especially as a number of men continued to carry their Kalashnikovs, most courageously, for several hours more, fully aware they had no way of stopping the massacre.

A number of reporters managed to reach al-Doukhi from the north at noon on Friday, and they talked with Ibrahim who gave the following account:

By midday, several foreign reporters had arrived from the Gaza Hospital side. There was an Arab reporter with them, and he told me: 'I want to take photographs of what's going on.' 'Unfortunately,' I told him, 'we've withdrawn from our positions; there won't be any fight, there are only a few of us. You can get as far as the Ali Hamdar Café and take photos of the massacre actually happening, and there are people still carrying their weapons, I mean, guys who just won't let go of their weapons.' ... 'That can't be true,' he said. 'I find that hard to believe.' So I told him: 'Come on and I'll show you.'

I took him to the Ali Hamdar Café, and from there we climbed up on to the roof of one of the buildings, and he took photos of people lying killed on the ground. I think he took other photos of four people carrying out killings in the street. The reporters spoke French, but of course that doesn't necessarily mean they were French, I didn't know their nationalities.

They were the reporters who went to the French Ambassador and told him such-and-such.

The French Ambassador came on the Friday but he couldn't get in, so he went back and started working on the basis that there'd been a massacre and it had to be stopped.[27]

It is difficult, in fact, to speak of any real resistance on the Friday. The men who went on firing near the Ali Hamdar Café in the southern part of Shatila Street were simply trying to mislead the attackers into supposing a stand was still being made. On that day, in fact, the sole videotape taken by a television photographer (frequently said, subsequently, to be Danish) clearly shows three men standing and firing in turns. They were courageous but not professional. One of them would approach the beginning of the street and fire a rapid hail of bullets in the air. The picture did not show any target. Then the one who had shot would withdraw and reload the Kalashnikov in a manifestly unprofessional manner, while another moved towards the street, with extreme caution, to do, in his turn, what his comrade had just done.[28]

Five Shatila residents, in a single session, watched this videotape with a view to identifying the men in question. They did so by name, commenting that they were brave young men aged between 17 and 20, but that not one of them was a professional fighter.

It may be that the photographer who made this sole videotape was the one who had been directed by Ibrahim Baroudi at noon on the Friday. These courageous young men were the last to fire, albeit in the air, with the aim of showing there was someone there.

* * *

When reporters were permitted to enter the district, when events were over at last, one of the first on the scene was the British journalist Robert Fisk. He covered the same entry point where the al-Doukhi men had been standing, and he covered every alley of the massacre. The headline of his famous article was almost an article in itself: 'Down Every Alleyway ... Women, Young Men, Babies – Lying Where They Had Been Knifed or Machine Gunned to Death.'

Robert Fisk described the signs of the 'fighting' near Sabra mosque (he meant the Shatila Camp mosque) and the al-Doukhi road. He said that the road was strewn with spent cartridges, and that some of the equipment he found, of Soviet manufacture, was being used by Palestinians. There had, he said, been fighting in the alleyway in question; then he added that he had found, flung down on the ground, a wooden Kalashnikov which turned out, on closer inspection, to be a child's toy.[29]

Among those who witnessed the aftermath of the massacre, and testified as to what they had seen, was the French writer Jean Genet. His succinct sentences provide an effective rejoinder to the 'battle' myth that circulated following the release of the Kahan Report:

What happened to the weapons responsible for all these bodies? And what of the weapons of those who defended themselves? In the part of the camp that I visited, I saw only two unused anti-tank weapons.[30]

The incursion into the Akka Hospital

The most significant event on the Friday morning was the incursion into the Akka Hospital, which, after being inoperative through the days of the invasion, had recently returned to its normal activities.

Hundreds of residents had sought protection at the hospital, but all had left by dawn, before the incursion took place. As for the regular hospital occupants – patients, doctors and nurses, both Arab and foreign – each of these had, during these crucial hours, to face their own particular fate.

Returning to work at the hospital

The Akka Hospital, founded in the mid-1970s, was a five-storey building sited on Kuwaiti Embassy Street, opposite Horsh Shatila. It included a large underground shelter and a ground floor also serving as a shelter and divided into departments for surgery, treatment, emergencies, X-rays and clinics. Above the ground floor were clinics, the administration department and the patient wards, containing a total of 60 beds.

In the early stages of the Israeli invasion, the Akka Hospital, despite its limited capacity, played a significant role in taking in the wounded, especially from the airport district, the patients in question being from various Palestinian and Lebanese factions, and from the Syrian Forces.

The hospital was struck during the invasion but the damage was not too extensive; patients had in fact been moved from the first to the ground floor. As the invasion and siege of Beirut continued, the Palestinian Red Crescent deemed it appropriate to commission field hospitals and infirmaries in safer areas of Ras Beirut. The Akka Hospital was regarded as particularly unsafe, partly because its site made it subject to continual bombardment and partly because of its proximity to a petrol station, which, if it took a direct hit, might set the whole hospital ablaze. As such the hospital became a mere outpatient centre, most employees moving to newer Ras Beirut hospitals, notably the Lahout Hospital, established at the Lahout school in al-Sidani Street, parallel to and between Bliss and Hamra Streets.

After the end of the war and the departure of the Palestinian and Syrian fighters from Lebanon, life at the Akka Hospital began to return to normal, and volunteers from the Lebanese Red Cross came to play their part in its renewal. No one imagined the Israelis might return to the district. By mid-September, all normal activities had been resumed at the Akka Hospital, and there were even a number of foreign doctors and nurses now working there.[31]

An employee in the X-ray department, who declined to be named, proudly introduced himself as being from the city of Akka (Acre) by origin and from Sabra by birth. As for his joining the hospital he had, he said, always been keen to study medicine but, as a Palestinian refugee, could never even have dreamed of the possibility. As a child he had received preliminary education at the Ya'bod school, affiliated to the UNRWA and sited in al-Dik alley in Sabra. Then he had received intermediate education at the Jalil school, again affiliated to the UNRWA, in Shatila. Eventually he had completed his secondary education at Ras al-Nabe' public school, affiliated to the Lebanese Ministry of Education. His only means of specialization thereafter was to enter a nursing school founded by the Palestinian Red Crescent. This comprised four departments – nursing, laboratory, pharmacy and X-ray – and he had opted for the last. Crescent doctors provided theoretical courses, and the practical courses were provided by a German institute in Hamra Street. Since graduating in 1978, he had worked in the X-ray department at the Akka Hospital, and had been the employee on duty the day the Israeli tanks surrounded Sabra and Shatila, on the dawn of Wednesday 15 September.[32]

His shift, he said, was from eight in the evening till eight in the morning. That evening he had spent with his colleagues, talking of the murder of Shaykh Bashir. Everyone suspected something was about to happen. But what exactly? No one was sure. At around four o'clock on the Wednesday morning he was wide awake and on duty when he heard the roaring of the tanks as they approached the Sports City. He got up, looked towards the Kuwaiti Embassy and, seeing the advancing Israeli tanks, called the doctor on night duty to show him what was happening. The doctor looked, shook his head, and remarked that he should wait till eight in the morning, then change shifts with whoever was next on duty.

At exactly eight o'clock, the X-ray employee changed shifts with his counterpart on the day shift, then left the hospital and went home to Sabra. He would not, however, be able to return to the Akka Hospital; he would rather remain in Sabra and witness what took place there on the Saturday.[33]

Nuzha, a Palestinian nurse who had worked at the Red Crescent since 1979, said the Israelis had come to the Akka Hospital several times since the siege began, on the pretext of ensuring there were no 'terrorists' there. Dr Sami al-Khatib would tell them there was no one there apart from patients and the medical staff. More than once, she said, they had come, eaten at the cafeteria without permission, then gone up to the first floor to see the patients. They never neglected to bring chocolate and sweets for the children.[34] It need hardly be said that the Israeli soldiers had no need of the hospital cafeteria. They simply wished to know what was on hand at the hospital, or what was going on there, and this they contrived to do.

Marjaleena (Maria), a Finnish nurse and the wife of Urabi, an Egyptian employee, testified that Wednesday was a relatively normal day at the hospital. They had opened the clinic and received 20 patients, from whom they heard that the Israelis had been advancing towards the camps and that some had reached al-Fakhani. The Palestinian nurses and patients had, Maria noticed, become frightened. Nevertheless, work at the clinic was not affected: they went on receiving patients, most suffering from minor ailments like flu, or from small wounds, or whose bandages needed changing. Shots could be heard outside, and explosions from the direction of the camps. That night the shelling intensified, and the hospital received those who had been injured, along with dozens of people from the camps seeking protection and shelter. To avert danger from the shelling, it was decided to spend the night on the ground floor.[35]

Nuzha, the Palestinian nurse, also said that hundreds of families had sought refuge at the Akka Hospital, especially on the Thursday, with everyone fleeing from the shelling. In the evening, news began to arrive: not just of casualties from the constant shelling but of direct killing.

Among the injured was a young Lebanese man from the South. The attackers had sprayed him with bullets, along with a group of other men ordered to stand facing the wall. He, though, had only been hit twice, in the leg, and had subsequently managed to reach the hospital (see Account 15, p. 95). His wounded father had also managed to reach the hospital (see Account 16, p. 97). Both had spoken of the mass killing they had witnessed but, the nurse affirmed, no one at the hospital had believed this.[36]

Ann Sunde, a Norwegian nurse and one of the specialists in social work, confirmed all this. She had visited Beirut more than once. During the summer of the invasion, however, she had started working at the hospitals, since these were the primary workplace for rescuing casualties and the injured. She had been at the Akka Hospital that same night and said the hospital had received a father and his son, who had been hit in the feet, at around half past eight in the evening. The father had also been hit in the chest. Those in charge had thought it best to send the father on to the Gaza Hospital, which was better equipped for major cases. This, however, proved to be impossible, and accordingly a Sri Lankan doctor, together with a Norwegian and a French nurse, conducted an emergency operation. In the middle of this, the electricity generator failed due to a shortage of fuel and the operation had to be finished by candlelight. The mains electricity had, she said, been cut for many hours.[37]

Ann Sunde told of a girl who, during the father's operation, had been weeping hysterically at the bottom of the stairs. She called her, calmed her down and asked what was wrong. The girl told her she lived at al-Horsh and that a large number of Palestinians and Lebanese had been gunned down against a wall, her father and brother among them. A little later it dawned on Ann Sunde that the man undergoing the candlelight operation was the girl's father, and that the girl herself, despite her desperate state, had managed to rescue him and bring him to the hospital. Even then neither Ann nor anybody else at the Akka Hospital was able to comprehend that a genuine massacre had been taking place, at the hands of Lebanese Phalangists, and that those supposed to be Israelis entering the camps were actually Lebanese militiamen. The doctors' judgement, she said, had been that the whole thing was merely some local quarrel or matter of personal revenge! A little later another wounded man arrived, and Dr Sami al-Khatib went to treat him.[38]

The Akka Hospital on the Friday morning

Ann Sunde woke at five in the morning. A little later she heard through the megaphones that people should return to their homes from wherever they were and should place any weapons they possessed in front of the houses. The calls were in Arabic, and her colleagues translated them for her. Residents who had sought shelter at the hospital quickly began to leave. Some said they were returning to Shatila, others that they were going to Burj al-Barajneh Camp.[39]

Since the early hours of the Friday morning, therefore, the hospital had been almost completely emptied of the hundreds who – as confirmed by a number of women in their testimonies – had sought refuge there. Among the witnesses was Um Kamal who, on the Friday, had personally seen the bands of gunmen and heard their threats, and so had returned to the hospital to urge everyone to leave at once (see Account 33, p. 155).[40] Sa'ida, one of those taking part in the women's march, and driven in the truck to the eastern districts (see Account 7, p. 86), also testified as to what she had seen at the Akka Hospital early that morning. She had, she said, managed, despite the shooting and sniping, to reach the Akka Hospital between six and seven o'clock, together with her mother, who was also a hospital worker. She described the terror that had spread among the people at the hospital and the shelter:

A lot of people were still there. Some started saying: 'Come on, let's all make a run for it.' Others, though, were saying: 'Don't worry, everyone, there's nothing, I swear.' Then we saw a woman arrive, screaming: 'There's a massacre. Run, before they come to the Akka Hospital.' I didn't know the woman, but I heard them say: 'Did you hear what

Um Kamal just said?' I looked round and saw some people still sitting there. 'We're staying here', they were saying. 'There's nothing.' But at the hospital entrance there were casualties being admitted.

In no time, people were flocking out, one behind the other. One man said: 'Keep in groups.' I heard it but didn't know who it was. We got up and started walking till we reached the bridge on the airport highway. But there they started launching grenades at us; we stopped. My mother couldn't keep up with us but we all fled – myself, my sister and my little brothers. We went on running till we reached Bir al-Abed. There we found people walking normally back and forth not knowing what was going on.[41]

Ann Sunde said that, at eight in the morning, she had attended a meeting of doctors and nurses to discuss what should be done. Should they flee or stay? They decided to stay. The two nurses who had been on duty through the night went to rest and get some sleep, the work being divided among the rest. Two nurses, one of whom was French, stayed to work in Emergency, whereas the Australian nurses Mary and Gene stayed to look after the disabled children. Two Arab nurses stayed in the basement, and one or two on the upper floor.[42]

A Palestinian doctor who declined to be identified supplied a testimony in accordance with Ann's above. The hospital administration, he said, held a meeting of the medical staff between eight and nine in the morning. One group was in favour of leaving, another of remaining steadfastly at their posts. Finally it was decided not to leave. The worst they were expecting, the doctor said, was to be detained by the Israelis. In any case, he went on, they supposed they would be captured easily enough if they left the hospital, surrounded as they were on all sides. It was safer for everyone, especially the Palestinians, to remain within the hospital limits.[43]

Indeed, this same doctor, who was also a senior doctor at the hospital, even refused to evacuate the sick children, against the advice of Dr Sami al-Khatib and others. He was among the first to leave the hospital, with three others, the moment the attackers burst in.[44]

He made no effort to conceal this. He told me he had actually left with another doctor and two other employees just before the Lebanese Forces entered through the Jacobian building. The four men entered this building, then went out through another door, where Israelis were present and did not harass them. A young man then came forward and drove them to Haret Hreik.[45] All the doctors and nurses who fled the hospital were able to escape, apart from Dr Ali Uthman.

The most significant event at the Akka Hospital on the morning of this long day crammed with tragedies was the murder of Urabi, an Egyptian employee in the X-ray department. He was the very model of a popular and hard-working employee, and everyone who knew him wept at his death. According to Nurse Nuzha, at ten in the morning Urabi went to fetch a car. Others say he fled for his life. There is agreement, though, on how Urabi met his end: as he was going out, by the side of the hospital facing the petrol station, he was gunned down. At the same time, an Egyptian worker who had gone out to buy a packet of cigarettes for Dr Sami was sniped at the hospital entrance and she too died.[46]

The anonymous senior doctor said Urabi was killed straight after the meeting they had held. He was struck by a bullet in the liver, and also suffered a wound to the right side of the face, fracture of the left leg and fracture of the joint. It was clear, the doctor added, that Urabi had been killed not just by the bullets but by splinters from a grenade.[47]

Ann Sunde said she knew nothing of Urabi's death at the time, as her attention had been caught by a fire that had broken out in the upper part of a house behind the petrol station. At that moment, a man came in with serious injuries. He had been standing by the petrol station, and he it was who told them that two others had been hit there. Could Urabi have been one of them?

Urabi was not just a close friend of Ann's but a model colleague, with whom she had worked in the scanner department. She had frequently had tea with him and his wife Maria at the hospital. They were among those she loved most in Beirut.

The French nurse, intending to identify the casualties at the petrol station, went up to the emergency room and laid himself flat till he was able to make out a body lying parallel to the emergency department entrance. He told his colleagues it was not Urabi. Ann, in turn, made an attempt to identify the other casualty but was unable to do so. She then crawled to the balcony and, raising her head a little over the balustrade, managed to see the man hit and lying on the ground. When she saw how tall he was, she was reassured. 'No,' she thought, 'that's not Urabi. That man's a lot taller.'[48]

Dr Sami al-Khatib's main concern was to bring in the two men injured at the petrol station so as to save them, or one of them at least. Hearing the noise of a car outside, he immediately sent someone to enquire whose it was; it was in fact being driven by a woman they did not know. They called to her and she immediately agreed to give them her car for humanitarian purposes. An Egyptian worker from the hospital kitchen then came and drove the car, with Ann and Nurse Erica in the back so that their heads would not be visible. The worker drove the car somewhat to the right, then crossed the road to have cover from the houses before finally turning back round to the petrol station. When the three arrived they found the man lying there was in fact Urabi. Ann described these moments:

I don't know why he'd looked taller from the hospital balcony.

Urabi had been gone for some time, and hadn't told his wife where he was going.

We recognized him from his clothes and the bag he was carrying. His face, though, was unrecognizable. The whole left cheek had been blown away.[49] I don't know what kind of bullets they used. There was multiple bleeding from several parts of his body. Erica and I managed to drag him to the car … In the emergency room I took a look at his watch … I saw it read exactly 10:51. We put his personal belongings to one side. Just as the doctor had finished shrouding him and had gone to tell his wife of what had happened, we saw a gunman standing by the door …[50]

Urabi's wife, Nurse Maria, told of the last time she had seen her husband. She had, she said, been discussing the situation with him as they drank coffee on the Friday morning: they had been expecting a tense day, especially after those seeking refuge had left the hospital, having heard through the megaphones that everyone should return home, that nothing was going to happen. Maria was anticipating problems in treating patients due to a shortage of medical equipment. An injured man came in, she said, at around nine in the morning; an Egyptian who worked at the nearby petrol station. She heard him speaking about her husband but did not fully understand what he was saying, though it was clear to her something had happened. She went to the emergency room, then to the Intensive Care Unit where the Norwegian team was, but failed to find anything. She learned nothing, indeed, until the Sri Lankan doctor, Dr Rasha, came and told her that her husband Urabi had died from injuries caused by shots and the explosion.

This wife, who had come from the frost of Finland to a hell that would not end even when the war itself ended, said: 'I had a feeling the whole world was collapsing.'[51]

A Norwegian at the Akka Hospital

The attackers burst in at eleven in the morning, tense and looking left and right in search of 'terrorists'. During their time in the hospital that day, they had ample time to deal with everyone there, whether doctors, workers or patients. Their treatment of people varied, sometimes according to nationality, sometimes to mood: it ranged from friendliness to torture, rape and vicious killing.

The French nurse Erica was the first to spot their arrival, and she hurried to summon Dr Sami. He and those around him came quickly to find a gunman leading a group through the main entrance, shouting in a disturbingly jerky and violent way as if expecting armed opposition. Ann ventured to ask if she could fetch her passport, but the man would not allow this. She asked him, in her limited Arabic, who they were. They answered, in English, that they were Phalangists. She then asked the two gunmen who were standing in front of her what they

were looking for and the answer came that they were looking for soldiers, fighters or terrorists. She could not confirm which actual word was used, but she remembered her answer: that there was not a single armed soldier in the building, that all were civilians. Also, there were no weapons whatsoever. The second gunman took in what she was saying and allowed her to go and fetch her passport.[52]

Meanwhile, other gunmen were assembling the nurses and all the hospital workers. The Norwegian nurse Astrid Barkved was still asleep in her room, exhausted after the long night shift. As she opened her eyes, she saw them standing by her head; they told her they were Phalangists, but she noticed no badges on their clothes. Soon afterwards she heard these soldiers yelling from one room to another, looking for Palestinian soldiers.[53]

The Norwegian nurse Astrid, along with the Australian nurse, stayed to watch over the children, while Nurse Gene stayed to watch over the disabled, and Ann left the hospital, guarded by a gunman who had loaded his gun and had it ready for use if necessary. The gunmen were tensed up, not believing the hospital contained no fighters, and contradictory orders were being issued. Outside one gunman told her in an imperative tone: 'Come here.' Simultaneously, another gunman told her: 'Stay where you are.' Ann had a calm and strong personality. Taking a grip on herself, she asked them, in English: 'Who am I supposed to obey? You're contradicting one another. If I do what either of you says, I'll be in trouble.' With that she was told to leave, which she did. Walking alongside her was the Egyptian worker who, a short while back, had driven the car to bring Urabi's body into the hospital, and others were walking there too. It was quickly noticed that foreigners were walking in one line, Palestinians in another.

Looking up the street, Ann saw gunmen sitting in front of the houses of Horsh Tabet, as far as the main entrance to Shatila. There were, she thought, around 15 gunmen, with five or six more at the roundabout. At the intersection of the main street (Kuwaiti Embassy Street) and the entrance to Shatila sat another group of 10–15 gunmen. Between these checkpoints Ann showed her passport, and, when they had made sure she was a foreigner, they said there was no problem.[54]

The First Secretary at the Norwegian Embassy arrived to pick up the Norwegian members of the hospital's medical body, and the gunmen allowed him to do so. Would Ann agree, though, before being assured of her other colleagues' safety? In those critical moments she was also grief-stricken and furious at Urabi's death. How could she forget he was lying there dead in the emergency department, and that others were threatened with the same fate, even if the First Secretary had come to protect his compatriots? Perhaps, though, he was right. Ann described these moments as follows:

The decision was one of the most difficult of my life, and I had to take it in a split second. Should I get in the car with him? Should I let go of my friends and leave the place, or should I stay?

I couldn't have known what was going to happen. The group of soldiers [the militias] had been polite, and we didn't know then what had actually happened in the camps. Instinctively, and without thinking, I found myself in the car.

When they allowed us to return to the hospital, they let us take Astrid along too, and they let me fetch my bag, which, very importantly, had in it some films from my previous days. I asked them if we could take the children along; they agreed, and we took four of them. There was a fifth child there in the room that we didn't dare take along in view of his critical condition; he needed an ambulance.[55]

One of the contradictions among the gunmen themselves was that one asked, in French, whether the Norwegian Chargé d'Affaires had a car big enough to take the rest of the children. He was told there was no such car, and the Norwegian asked, in turn: 'Do you have a car to take the rest of the children?' The gunman answered that they did not. An agreement was finally reached that the Norwegians would return to fetch the rest of the children. But there would be no children to take along later.

On the way back, Ann Sunde noted the disappearance of all her friends and colleagues who had been stopped near the entrance to Shatila. She also noticed a large truck facing the airport roundabout and half filled with youths and men. She examined their faces closely but found no one she knew.

The diplomatic car eventually reached the American University Hospital, whose administration at first refused to admit the children because of the critical nature of their cases. Ann had no intention of revealing the children's identity and the fact that they were from the Akka Hospital, because she did not know to whom she was talking. She finally persuaded them by proposing that a nurse should stay to look after the children, and Nurse Astrid accordingly remained there.[56]

Ann Sunde's experience at the Akka Hospital ended only for a fresh experience to begin, immediately, at the Gaza Hospital – she being 'the Norwegian' who managed to reach there and tell them what had been happening at the Akka Hospital.

A Palestinian at the Akka Hospital

The experience of Nuzha, the Palestinian nurse, was very different from that of the Norwegian Ann. Their days began indeed in similar fashion: both had just finished their morning shower when they heard the megaphones calling on people to surrender. From then on, though, things went very differently for the pair.

Nuzha was still getting dressed and, as she heard the calls, began for the first time to realize the danger of the situation. She said:

The Red Crescent residence was in a neighbouring building, on the fourth floor. I looked around and I heard them shouting through the megaphone. I can see the megaphone now, with its white speaker and the red handle at the back. They started yelling, saying 'Surrender and you won't be harmed. If there are terrorists, or if there's something no one dares give up, then throw your weapons into the street and run. If you're frightened, then throw the weapons and run.'[57]

Nuzha finished dressing then went down close by the hospital, where she saw Dr Sami. 'For God's sake, Dr Sami,' she said, 'let's run for it.' 'Nuzha,' Dr Sami answered, 'the Israelis came into the South, and your family live in the South. Did the Israelis harass them? Harass the women and children, I mean? They didn't.' The doctor, Nuzha realized, refused to believe the people there were Phalangists, not Israelis. She described her despair during those moments:

I started crying and hugging the doctor, and kissing his hands, so he'd let us run for it. But he'd have none of it. He asked: 'How can we possibly cut and run?' So we stayed there till they reached us.

Dr Sami was shrouding Urabi. His shirt was soaked with blood. 'Go upstairs, Nuzha,' he told me, 'and find me a clean shirt to put on.' I told him: 'I don't dare, Doctor', and I started crying. 'I swear,' he said, meaning to spur me on, 'if you don't go up, I'll throw you out of the window. Are you so short of courage?' 'I'm not a coward, Doctor,' I answered, 'but I'm scared, because those are Phalangists, not Israelis …'

Sensing they'd come in through the emergency entrance, I found myself, without thinking, running out through the second one. There were three of my women friends with me. We were all running together, and we had a small child with us, who we took along.

On the road we saw an Israeli tank; we told them what had happened to us in the hospital, and the cases that had come in, about the way people were being shot and slaughtered. The Israelis started laughing at us. They said: 'Move on … move on … khabibi, don't be frightened.'[58]

Nuzha and her friends reached Burj al-Barajneh Camp where they spent the night. Next day she returned to the hospital to fetch her ID card, her bag and what was left from her monthly salary, as she did not have enough money to get to Tyre, where her people lived. However, she found no one she knew at the hospital. There was no one there. She came across some men from the Lebanese Red Cross who asked her why she was crying. When they discovered she was a nurse, some of them escorted her to the nurses' residential quarters on the fourth floor. There Nuzha found her bag, emptied of the ID card and the rest of her salary.

Nuzha did not hesitate; rather she felt a sense of her responsibility as a nurse. She no longer thought of fleeing to Tyre but decided to stay and began investigating what had happened at the hospital.[59]

A Lebanese at the Akka Hospital

A young Lebanese woman's experience was totally different again from that of the two earlier, Norwegian and Palestinian women at the hospital. This was the experience of Randa, who had saved her injured father (see Account 16, p. 97) and had spent the night together with him at the Akka Hospital after his operation by candlelight on the Thursday night.

Randa witnessed the gunmen's behaviour from the time they entered the Akka Hospital. According to her testimony, she was not treated politely as the foreigners were, but, on the other hand, they had been less harsh with her than with the Palestinians.

Randa was standing by the door, and in no time found them filling the entrance. 'They took us by surprise,' she said, 'and started pushing us around and dragging us downstairs.' They were very numerous, especially taking into account the ones standing outside, from the petrol station up to the hospital. Randa thanked God those taking refuge in the hospital shelter had left it; otherwise the disaster would have been greater still. She said:

When they first came in, I ran to my father and told him: 'The Israelis have come, father.' But they were behind me, and said: 'No. We're Sa'd Haddad and Phalangists.'

One of them came and sat next to me on my father's bed. 'Don't be afraid,' he told me. 'We're Lebanese, like you.' I told him: 'But you've been killing us. Why have you been killing us? Here are my father and brother, injured. I have a brother who was killed, and I'm sure his body's still lying there on the ground. And we still don't know what happened to my mother and sisters.'

'But we didn't go into the Horsh district at all', he told me.

Of course I knew he was lying. Even if he hadn't actually gone in himself, other friends of his certainly had. What can I say? Time passed, and they'd be asking now for coffee, now for tea, or else ordering us to get up and bring them some water to drink. At first they didn't frighten us; but even if they were laughing and joking with us, they still treated us like servants.

One of them tried to get through on the intercom and couldn't, or maybe he was trying me out to see if I was familiar with it. 'Come on,' he told me, 'get through and talk.' I told him: 'I've only been here since yesterday, I don't know how to use the intercom. Anyway, I'm Lebanese, not Palestinian.' 'We know you're Lebanese,' he said, 'but why do you live with them?' I said to him: 'Do you think we can afford to rent a house for 1,000–2,000 lira? God help us, we're all girls, and we all work and help out my father.'[60]

Randa did not see anyone killed in front of her, but she heard the shots when they killed Nurse Intissar. She told of another nurse who had managed to survive. She had told them she would return immediately with some water, then took them by surprise and flung herself outside. Some people then helped her, getting her into a car that drove her to Haret Hreik.

By three o'clock Randa felt at the end of her tether. She pretended she was hungry, and they told her: 'We'll get you some food; besides, you said you'd stay till five.' She replied that she was going to her uncle's at al-Shayah, where she was expected. If she had decided to get out, leaving her father and brother, it was from fear of their boorish manners and the obscene words they used in front of her. Some were behaving so badly she feared a fate similar to that of people whose stories she had heard. Almighty God, she told herself, would protect her father and brother, while she was incapable of doing it alone. She also managed to save a Palestinian girl she took with her as she left. The girl was, she claimed, a Lebanese she had known back in her village in the South. The girl had already torn up her ID card and burned it.

Once outside, both breathed a deep sigh of relief. What attracted their attention, however, was that the Israelis had left from beneath the airport bridge.[61]

The nurses' fate

A Lebanese nurse at the Akka Hospital gave the following account to the *Libération* correspondent Maya Thabet:

At eleven o'clock, some men broke into the hospital … They were speaking Arabic and English … They were extremely tense, and, in a military manner, they told all the foreign workers at the hospital, more than eleven doctors and nurses, to leave with their hands in the air … Two nurses stayed to look after eight injured and five disabled children, and other, newborn children remained there as well.

At the entrance to Shatila, an Israeli officer told us to go back and close the hospital on the injured and the victims, but they kept a Palestinian doctor who was with us, and we haven't seen him since. [She was referring to Dr Sami al-Khatib.]

We went back to the hospital and found four injured people had been abducted, but the two nurses were still there. In the afternoon, the Red Cross delegation came to check on us and take down our names; that's when we found the two nurses had disappeared. The doctor told us he'd seen the gunmen strangle the nurses behind the building.

One of the Palestinian nurses was with us. She went looking for her sister who'd gone to try and find protection in a house near the hospital, only to find her naked and smeared with blood … and strangled to death.[62]

Tony Asmar ('Asmar' is a pseudonym used for the purposes of this volume), a Lebanese citizen living in a building near the Akka Hospital, told how he returned to check on his house, having been away throughout the Israeli siege of Beirut. His enforced absence stemmed from the fact that he was a Christian; for the logic of sectarian civil war dictates, everywhere, the residential segregation of each and every sect, and this was no less the case in Lebanon.

Tony told how he had been compelled to seek protection inside his home, as there had been a number of gunmen outside pointing their machine-guns towards the hospital. Just as he saw these through his window, so he was able to watch what happened to two nurses from the Akka Hospital. He saw the first nurse when he went to open the door to observe events outside: she was squatting at a corner of the steps, petrified with terror. He invited her to seek refuge inside his house, but she pointed to the other side, from which shots were being fired. A whole hour passed; then, emboldened, he opened a side window, and there he saw a number of soldiers raping another nurse. She was screaming breathlessly for help, and she was crying. He saw the end of the crime: they shot her dead.[63]

Two further hours passed, during which the killers returned to a terrified nurse, bound her, raped her and left. Tony went back to open the door to check what had happened to her, and found her there, transformed to a victim and flung into the alleyway. As he was praying for her, as he had done for her colleague, bullets began raining from a spot nearby, and he was hit in the right leg. Looking to where the shots were coming from, he discovered the person who had shot at him was one of his own relatives. The man in charge of the group ordered the gunman to finish Tony off. However, the relative had now, in his turn, realized his victim's identity and refused to do so. But for this coincidence, Tony would not have survived.[64]

It is possible that the second nurse was the same one found in the shelter of the neighbouring building, the building where the witness Tony lived. However, it was not easy to identify her body. She was eventually identified by her hair and sandals, and it was obvious she had been raped to death.[65]

As for Nurse Intissar, she may have been one of the two nurses whose fate Tony witnessed. The X-ray employee told what happened to Intissar based on hearsay from colleagues at the hospital; they reported how the gunmen forced her into the shelter, tugged her by the hair and brought her to the ground screaming and begging to be killed – which they did, but only after raping her several times. When they had finished their work, they dragged her to the petrol station, where she held on desperately to the petrol pump. In the words of one of her colleagues: 'She seized hold of the thing people used to fill up with petrol, kept hold of it, and they took aim at her. They shot her to bits.'[66]

Nurse Nuzha, who had managed to flee and return, told how she was asked to go to the American University Hospital to identify her colleague Intissar's body, as no one from the latter's family was in Beirut – they lived in Tripoli. Accordingly she went and identified her:

The nurse they killed was my friend [Nurse] Intissar. I used to sleep in the same room as her. I told her to run with me, but she wouldn't, because she wanted to stay with a Lebanese girl called Sana' who worked with us; Intissar was saying, if they came in and questioned her, she'd tell them she was Lebanese from Baalbek.

But when they went in, they identified her as Palestinian. They identified her from her dialect, straight away. They attacked her, and they killed her. She didn't spare them. She cursed them and resisted as hard as she could. Some people heard it and told me.

I wish I hadn't gone to identify the body. There's nothing harder than seeing someone dear to you disfigured to that extent. But how could I not go and identify my friend? How could she have died with no one to see her and confirm who she was? May God bless her soul.[67]

The doctors' and workers' fate

The doctors' fate was no less brutal than that of the nurses. Two of them were tortured and killed: Dr Ali Uthman and Dr Sami al-Khatib. Both were Palestinian.

Dr Ali Uthman was married to a Soviet woman and they had one son. He was among the group of doctors and workers at the hospital that were summoned at the very start. When they yelled at him, telling him to come up, he asked to be able to go into the hospital and fetch his wife. Supposing, obviously, that she was Palestinian, and therefore a new prey, they allowed him to go. The moment he entered the hospital, he jumped from the window into the garden overlooked by the Jacobian building. He fell, however, on a previously broken leg, and as a consequence could not run quickly. He began walking slowly, step by step, till he entered the Jacobian building, found its owner in the entrance and told him he needed to hide there. The two men knew one another, and he was able to conceal himself on the fourth floor.

Jacobian subsequently told some employees at the Akka Hospital how the gunmen had come and asked if someone had hidden in his building, to which he replied: 'I don't know.' He had 300,000 lira with him, which they seized, and they searched the building.[68]

They found Dr Uthman on the fourth floor. The X-ray employee gave the following account:

They went up and took Dr Uthman. They subjected him to unspeakable torture. I mean, there's an eye-witness, and she's still around. She saw them with her own eyes. She spoke to me, and said she saw his teeth broken and pulled out. She saw them, too, as they dragged him along the ground. He was screaming and saying: 'I beg you ...' To this day nothing's known for certain about Dr Ali Uthman. People say they killed him; which is the obvious thing. But no body was ever found! Dr Sami al-Khatib's body wasn't found either. It was never, ever found.[69]

One piece of evidence linked to Dr Ali Uthman's death was in fact found: the piece of metal set in his artificial leg. When this was found on the road, they knew he had been killed. Dr Ali Uthman was an intern who had completed his studies in the Soviet Union and returned to Beirut, with his Soviet wife and their only son, at the end of 1981. He was in his mid-thirties, a dedicated and much liked doctor.[70]

As for Dr Sami al-Khatib, he was one of those who left the hospital in accordance with the Lebanese Forces' instructions. Not far from where the workers had been assembled, the First Secretary at the Norwegian Embassy was standing and negotiating with the gunmen regarding the evacuation of the Norwegian citizens.

Ann Sunde said that, during the conversation, she noticed Dr Sami al-Khatib had been separated from the group and taken to the main Shatila entrance. She went straight towards him. There he stood facing the wall, next to 15 others, side by side. As she got close, she heard him ask the gunmen to let him return to the hospital, since he was the only paediatrician and the hospital needed him on account of the many child patients. Ann heard them ask one another about her, in Arabic: 'Who is she?' She answered that she was a Norwegian nurse. At that the gunmen told her, in English: 'Go, now, to where your group is standing.' Dr Sami told her: 'Don't worry. Go back, please.'[71]

Ann went back to where the foreigners were standing, segregated from the Palestinians despite herself.

As was noted above, the Norwegian Chargé d'Affaires and his fellow Norwegians were allowed to return to the hospital to rescue some children; they did so, and managed to save four disabled children. Yet the instant the diplomatic car had left the hospital towards al-Ouza'i, Ann turned to where her colleagues from the medical body had been standing, and saw no one. Dr Sami al-Khatib and the others had disappeared; the Palestinians had disappeared. According to Ann, others maintained they had seen Dr Sami at the Sports City, and someone said that he had seen him and that he had been brutally tortured before being killed.[72]

Were the bodies of Dr Sami al-Khatib or Dr Ali Uthman among those flung into the Sports City pool? Eye-witnesses from some distance off judged this to be so because they had seen the bodies of four men in white gowns floating on the surface of the shallow pool.

Some Red Crescent employees were, however, of a different opinion: namely, that the rescue workers were also dressed in white gowns. Three of these were killed while in an ambulance; and it is possible that one or all of the bodies were thrown into the pool. People from the Red Crescent always bracket the names of the three martyrs together: Ziad Ma'rouf, Nizar al-Sadeq and Jihad al-Hajj. They were three friends in life and three comrades in death.[73] Whenever Nurse Nuzha is asked about the relatives she lost in the massacre, she says she lost many. After a time, the listener discovers that, strictly speaking, she lost no one from among her relatives but rather from among her colleagues. She said:

Three of them were closer to me than any other. I lost Nizar, and I lost Jihad, and I lost Ziad. They were all killed in the massacre. The three of them were rescue workers, and Nizar's rank was first aid officer. They were transporting an injured man named Hatem to the Gaza Hospital. They reached the Gaza and handed over the injured man, and on the way back they were killed, in the middle of the road. The vehicle they had with them was from the

Red Cross, and it had the Red Cross sign on it. But we didn't know they'd died till the following day. There was no communication between us and the Gaza Hospital. Communications had been cut, and we couldn't make any inquiries about them.[74]

Among the victims of the medical staff and workers of the Akka Hospital were two doctors, two nurses, three rescue workers, an employee, a cook and a guard. The rest of the victims were patients, mainly children.

As for the foreigners, some of these returned on the same day, among them the Finn Maria Urabi, whose Egyptian husband had been killed: she was among the group taken for questioning the moment the killers entered the hospital. Following the interrogation, near the entrance to Shatila, the gunmen showed special consideration towards the foreigners. They set a blanket on the ground for them to sit on, offered them cigarettes and chewing gum, and expressed concern at their exposure to the fierce sun over their heads. But when the foreigners asked how long they were to be kept there, no answer was forthcoming. Then a decision was taken to release them, for fear the Israelis would suppose they had been detaining them. When the foreigners asked where they were to go, the gunman simply shrugged his shoulders. The foreigners told them, accordingly, that they would return to the hospital and asked that Dr Sami al-Khatib should return with them, because he was indispensable to the hospital; but the request was declined. Maria then saw the crowds of detainees walking along in lines with their hands held above their heads.

As for the gunmen who had occupied the hospital, and were still there inside, they were furious when they saw them returning to care for the children and other patients, speaking offensively to them and abusing them for working with Palestinians. They also asked them whether they were Communists, or from the Baader-Meinhof group, and who had sent them; to which the people answered that they were Christians and represented various humanitarian organizations.[75]

The gunmen allowed the foreign medical team to remain only on the ground floor, where there were still five disabled children

and one child from the children's hospital. The rest of the patients were on the first floor; they numbered eight, and with them there were a Palestinian and a Lebanese nurse. The Sri Lankan, Dr Rasha, also stayed with the patients, but not for long.

Even with the foreigners these gunmen's behaviour was, according to Maria, highly contradictory. 'One moment,' she said, 'they were extremely aggressive; the next, ready to do anything to help us.'[76]

There was one foreign doctor to whom the gunmen meted out special treatment, intending to harm him and leaving him alone on the sixth floor as a preliminary step. This was the Sri Lankan doctor, Dr Rasha. It transpired that one of the gunmen had held the doctor as a hostage, threatening to kill him if a certain nurse, whom he had promised himself, had not returned by seven in the evening. This was the same nurse who had begged Ann Sunde to take her along with her. The Norwegian team had been unable to comply, but she had in any case managed to flee. Only divine providence saved the doctor, through the medium of an Israeli whom the doctor had treated in the South while working there. The Israeli ordered the militiaman to release Dr Rasha, then told the doctor: 'Go to East Beirut and leave the country at once.'[77] According to another account, they threatened to kill Dr Rasha unless he handed them a sum of money.[78] Eventually the doctor was saved, along with the others, when the Red Cross arrived.

The militias had clearly left the hospital, perhaps temporarily, at around three o'clock, for the International Red Cross found no one when they arrived there in the afternoon. On the other hand, the fire that broke out at the hospital later suggests that someone had returned with the intention of burning it down.

Delegates from the International Red Cross came twice to save whoever was still in the hospital. The first time was around two in the afternoon; they had tried unsuccessfully, they said, to come in the morning. They promised to return in the afternoon, and managed to keep their promise at half past four. According to Maria, there were just four patients on the first floor, whose fate she never knew. The Red Cross took the patients to the Najjar Hospital and handed over the children, along with the nurse, to an Amal centre.[79] Hamza confirmed that he and his father had been among the lucky ones rescued, and he recalled that it was half past three in the afternoon when they reached the Najjar Hospital.[80]

Tony Jamil ('Jamil' is a pseudonym used for the purposes of this volume) was one of the rescue workers in the Lebanese Red Cross unit that escorted the International Red Cross to the Akka Hospital on the Friday afternoon. They had, he said, received a call that three had died at the Akka Hospital and that they should go and fetch them. Since Sabra Street was blocked, they had to go via the Ouza'i road. There they were confronted by checkpoints, but it 'went all right', although they were stopped in dangerous spots exposed to shelling. The International Red Cross representative would get out and speak to the Israelis in charge. At the Tayyouneh checkpoint they had to step out draped in Red Cross flags to convince the soldiers they really were rescue workers.

When they reached the Akka Hospital they heard intensive gunfire and shelling. This surprised them, as they knew all the weapons had been handed over. Why the shooting? Who was fighting whom? Tony said:

When we entered the Akka Hospital, we discovered that the dead people we were going to fetch had not died from shelling, or anything of that kind, but as a result of gunshots fired at point-blank range. They'd died like the ones we saw later in the massacre. We were still at the Akka Hospital while the massacre was happening, but we weren't aware of it.

We found later that the group [that is, the armed militias] had left the Akka, found their way to the interior and reached Sabra. That day, I still recall quite clearly, we removed, from the Akka group, the bodies of two women, a doctor, and a labourer of Egyptian nationality who had worked at a petrol station. We carried them. They'd disfigured them badly: the nurses and the doctor had been killed, and so had the Egyptian. We took them. We also carried with us around six or seven patients, most of them elderly.[81]

The children's fate

The Norwegian Chargé d'Affaires and the Norwegian team saved four disabled children, and the International Red Cross saved some others. But where did the rest of the children go? What of the disabled among them? The patients? The newborns? Were they killed? And how? Where were the corpses?

According to the X-ray employee, the children had been put to bed in the shelter, for their protection, and that is where they killed them. The International Red Cross subsequently handed them over to the Gaza Hospital.[82]

The British doctor Paul Morris appeared in a video film made at the Gaza Hospital on the Friday, carrying the bodies of newborn babies to the morgue and showing them to the photographers. Whose bodies were these exactly?[83]

Nurse Nuzha said that, when she returned to the hospital on the Saturday, she asked the Lebanese Red Cross volunteers what had happened at the children's department of the Akka Hospital. They had not even known of its existence. She took them there and they found no one – conclusive evidence, as far as she was concerned, that they had killed the children:

Next day we found a child flung outside in the garden. We went back to Sabra and found some children we'd treated. I mean, we could recognize them when we saw them.

Some children were around a year old, some three, some four, and there was one paralysed child who couldn't move; they'd killed him with an axe.

Maybe they killed them and flung them into Sabra so it wouldn't be said they'd killed child patients in a hospital.[84]

Aziza Khalidi, Director of the Gaza Hospital, told of a report by International Red Cross rescue workers who arrived at the Akka Hospital on the Friday, to the effect that they had seen a small child dead as a result of burning.[85]

Um Akram, the first to search for victims, said: 'When the Phalangists entered the Akka on the Friday morning, they took all the babies in the incubators, the premature ones, I mean; and they killed them.'[86]

The hajj who escaped death (Hajj Mahmoud Rukn), as reported in Account 39 (p. 190), he thanked God for his survival and for several days assisted the Red Cross and Civil Defence men in searching for victims. When, he said, they unlocked the door of a shelter in Hayy Ersal, he saw, among the piles, around a dozen bodies of infants in their first months and premature babies.[87] It is not certain whether all these bodies were babies from the Akka Hospital. But babies they certainly were.

As for the Akka Hospital, Nurse Nuzha said she saw it burned when she returned on the Saturday afternoon. All the curtains were burned; the refrigerator was smashed on the floor; the food supplies had been dumped and trampled; the glass was shattered; and the picture of Dr Fathi Arafat had been broken and bore the marks of stamping. In addition, three victims at the hospital still lay unburied, the cafeteria had been destroyed, along with all the evidence that they had been eating and drinking there all night long; and the mattresses had been removed and laid outside, where some had slept that night.[88]

Completion of accounts from the first day

Each day had its own particular tragedies and accounts, but those of the first day did not end with the day itself. For some of the people figuring in them, the bitter ordeal continued into the following day, the fate of their loved ones still unknown and their questions still unanswered. The accounts of those for whom Friday meant further tragedy, waiting and questioning are treated below.

Hind, the witness to the entry into Hayy al-Gharbi (see Account 3, p. 81), remained with her children in her home behind the Sports City throughout the Friday and Saturday, not daring to leave. When she felt pain from her leg, where it had been struck by a bullet from the attackers, she took a painkiller and prayed to God to bring her husband back safely.[89]

Um Nabil, from Account 4 (p. 83), went on waiting with her three children at her aunt's house, which she felt to be safe.

Knowing of the massacre, she did not dare go home. Her fear for her husband was greater than Hind's fear for hers, since Hind's husband had gone to the South on a family visit and there was hope his mother would keep him for a while longer. As for Um Nabil's husband, he had returned home to Hayy Ersal on the Thursday afternoon to rescue his neighbours and to bring back the milk and the bottle for his newborn baby.

Intissar was educated, calm and pious; she remained there at her aunt's, hoping her husband would come at any moment. She was sure even so, from what people had been saying, that the killers had broken in at six in the evening – the very time her husband was returning home.[90]

Would Abu Nabil return to his wife and children? Would he return to testify?

Ahmad Khatib, the sole survivor from his family in Account 5 (p. 84), had, it will be remembered, taken an injured friend of his to the Gaza Hospital on the Thursday evening, and had spent his night in an agony of anxiety over the fate of his family who had been at the forefront of Shatila near Hayy al-Miqdad. Having left the hospital on the Friday morning, he tried in vain to enter Shatila, then, returning, went through Ard Jalloul to the airport roundabout, hoping to find a way in through the main entrance at Kuwaiti Embassy Street. However, he found bands of Phalangists on the airport bridge and at around one o'clock he had to turn back once more.

An hour later he made a further attempt, but without success. As he arrived at the Gaza Hospital he was surprised to find that the hundreds who had sought refuge there were leaving, and to see patients in the streets waiting for the Red Cross to come and rescue them. He then went to take part in the great march, which headed towards the Corniche al-Mazra'a. The Israeli soldiers, however, would not allow them to proceed, under pretext of curfew.[91]

Ahmad had a long wait to endure before he finally learned of his parents' fate.

As for the girl who had survived alone among her family, and whose name was not published in the newspapers (see Account 10, p. 90), she had thanked God the attackers had not killed her Uncle Faisal. He was, though, to live just one day more. Here is her account of the last day of his life:

In the morning, some trucks came. The Phalangist soldiers put the victims' bodies inside and told my Uncle Faisal to help them. As he was lifting the bodies, he found his mother's among them and burst into tears. Then the loaded trucks headed for the Sports City, where they buried the victims in a mass grave. The soldiers arrested those who were left and told us to wait inside the Sports City. After they'd gone, I tried to run off, with some others who were with me.[92]

This suffering girl sought, quite wonderfully, to help others in her own hour of greatest need. Seeing her neighbours' daughter, a two-year-old baby, buried alive under her mother's body in the Sports City, she picked her up. After the Phalangist militias had shot the people at the Sports City, Israeli soldiers moved in to save those still alive and take them to the Sanaye' district.

The terrified girl spent the night at the American University Hospital. Then, next day, she returned with the prime objective of finding her Uncle Faisal and searching for her parents' bodies. When, though, she eventually found her Uncle Faisal, he was a lifeless corpse riddled with bullets.[93]

Her uncle had, as we have seen, been forced to assist in lifting the bodies into the trucks. They saw him weeping for his mother, who lay amid the piles; with no mercy for his mental or physical state, they shot him dead.

Was it conceivable that someone of his limited mental capacities could have borne arms and fought? Perhaps, in practice, death was a mercy for him. Nevertheless, when they killed him, it was not from mercy but from the mere lust to kill.

Munir, the lad who, in Account 12 (p. 91), had said he would not seek revenge by killing children, realized next morning, while he himself was still lying on the ground among the piled bodies of women and children, that he had lost his mother, brother and three sisters. He had no choice but to go on feigning death.

The wounded boy could not hide his trembling when someone came to cover the bodies with blankets, and the gunman quickly shot him; but once more he was destined to live. Munir had hidden his face in his hands, and the second bullet, aimed at his head, merely cut his forefinger. Believing, for the second time, that he was dead, they covered him with a blanket. If a person is destined to remain alive, even the cruellest criminals cannot put an end to his life.

The moment Munir was finally able to get up, he sought refuge in the nearest house to change his bloodstained clothes. Then they burst into the house and yelled at him: 'Who are you? Speak up! Are you Lebanese or Palestinian?' Munir found himself answering, in a trembling voice: 'I'm Lebanese.'[94]

Could Munir be said to have lied? Had he told them 'I'm Palestinian', he would have met his death: 'If you'd been Palestinian,' they told him, 'we would have killed you.' Was it a lie?

After they had left, the wounded boy looked for a shirt in the house, though, with no one to help him, it was half an hour before he was able to find one and put it on. Then, looking out through the window, he decided it would be possible to leave.

He walked fast, eager to reach the camp. Someone saw him and shouted: 'Stop right there.' But he moved on, as fast as he could. The gunman fired a quick shot at him, but, by God's will, this just grazed his left cheek.[95]

Munir walked on alone till he met some men from the camp who rescued him. They took him to the Gaza Hospital, which, on the Friday, was still carrying out operations; he was in fact the last person to be operated on.

Who, though, could save him from being haunted, over a whole lifetime, from this night spent in the street with the dead? Who would save him from people's questions, when they met him for the first time: 'What happened to your finger? Where did you get that scar on your cheek? Have you been a fighter? Which war? Where?'

Mufid, the 15-year-old brother of Munir who, on the Thursday evening, had sped away from the 'march towards death' (see Account 13, p. 93) – and who had been shot at and hit during his flight, then saved by doctors at the Akka Hospital, where he spent the night – had to face the killers next day when they burst into the hospital. We have three testimonies regarding him, from three members of a single family.

Mufid had spent the night next to an elderly man from Majdal Zoun: Hajj Ali F., one of those lined up and machine-gunned at the 'wall of death' in al-Horsh. This latter was the father rescued by his daughter, in Account 16 (p. 97). According to this compassionate father, the wounded young man had a back injury; other testimonies affirmed he had been hit in the upper thigh. In either case, he did not run and could not have done so even if he wanted to.

One of the killers actually boasted to this father: 'Remember the guy who was lying next to you? We hit him in the street with an axe.'

Hajj Ali F.'s son, Hamza, was also a witness. He was lying injured in the same room, and he it was who said (see Account 15, p. 95) 'they killed us twice'. When, Hamza said, the killers found him lying there in his bed, they did not harass him, realizing he was Lebanese. Then Mufid Muhammad was asked: 'And you? What are you?' He told them: 'I'm Palestinian.' At that they seized him and ordered him roughly to get out of bed. Then they killed him in the street, near the petrol station.

Hamza heard from them about other killings. They were, he noted, in an abnormal state, cursing incessantly. Inside the hospital, they killed some people and left others alone. They spared an elderly Palestinian, but killed Mufid Muhammad.[96]

Hamza was deeply affected by Mufid's death for he himself was just two years older; the only difference otherwise was Hamza's Lebanese nationality. Those two facts – age and nationality – were the only ones the killers were concerned to know about the pair. Then they killed one and spared the other.

Randa added to her father's and brother's testimonies. She still, she said, remembered this arrogant killer. He was halfway between short and medium in height, aged 20–22. She could have picked him out from among dozens.[97]

On the Friday morning while the killers were dragging Mufid from his bed at the Akka Hospital to his death, simply because he told them 'I'm Palestinian', his younger brother Munir was striving to flee through the alleys of Shatila – having received three bullets from three separate bands, and having survived certain death at the hands of a fourth by stammering out the words 'I'm Lebanese.'

The testimony of Mufid – lying wounded at the Akka Hospital, not knowing whether his mother, three sisters and two brothers were dead or alive, not knowing whether his older brother had made it to the Ma'wa al-Ajaza Hospital the night before – reached us through three people who had been with him in the same room: a father, his son and his daughter. Each of them affirmed that Mufid had said no more than two words: 'I'm Palestinian.'

Does anyone still expect a testimony from Mufid himself?

Mustafa, one of those who had stood against the wall of death, in Account 14 (p. 95), and who had also spent his night among the dead, was seriously wounded, unable to move. All he could remember was the screams of his youngest daughter while his wife and children were being shot.

On the Friday morning, God's mercy came through a tormented mother who was roaming the alleys searching for her daughter, a girl newly wed and pregnant. This mother, Samiha Abbas Hijazi, had no option but to search through the bodies, though the neighbours with her in the shelter had urged her not to go out, telling her the street was still being shelled. These neighbours did not believe her when she said she was going to fetch food for the children. It was still just six in the morning. She was, they all realized, just waiting for it to be light enough to search for her daughter.

There, among the piles of bodies, she heard the sound of moaning. Then Mustafa began calling to her in a low voice, begging her to save him. She said:

I looked over the first part of the street and saw the piled up bodies. Some still had heads, some didn't. The men were all on top of each other. Suddenly,

I heard someone moaning, saying: 'I beg you, for your children's sake, come and help me.' I went up to him, and I recognized Mustafa, I recognized him straight away, and I found his wife and children killed on their doorstep, not that far from where he was. I started screaming: 'Anyone who loves God, who worships God, come and help me save this man!'

I thought, maybe if I save this man, God will send me someone to save my daughter. I went and picked the man up, with a Syrian and a Lebanese helping me. We picked Mustafa up and started running, while everybody else was still in the shelter. I thought I'd tell them what had happened, so they'd run off. There were around 400 people, including women and children. I yelled at them to go, and I grabbed my little son's hand in one hand and my daughter's in another, and the elder girl walked along next to me; and these two men were carrying the wounded man, and we all went to the Gaza Hospital …[98]

Samiha Abbas Hijazi had no time to tell the people in charge at the hospital what had happened to Mustafa. She was sure he could talk. And she told them so: 'He has a tongue, doesn't he? and I have a daughter to find.'[99] This was her first concern, and she believed heaven would send someone to save her daughter just as she had saved Mustafa.

Mustafa was one of those discharged from the Gaza Hospital under the protection of the International Red Cross. The bullets, though, were still in his body. A friend of his, who saw him both at the hospital on the Friday and subsequently, said he no longer had proper use of his hand and as a result could no longer practise his profession as a plumber, at which (his friend proudly concluded) he had been notably skilled and proficient.

Mustafa eventually sought refuge in Germany.[100]

Um Rabi', the nurse who, on the Thursday night, began rescuing people from the shelters (see Account 17, p. 101), met her neighbour Um Akram on the steps of the Gaza Hospital on the Friday morning. 'For God's sake, dear neighbour,' she said, 'what happened? Have you seen my mother? Have you seen my brother?' Um Akram, the first

to search for the victims – just returned, indeed, from looking for her family in the alleys – asked: 'Where was your mother, my dear? Where? At Abu Yasser's shelter?' Um Rabi' confirmed that her mother and brother had indeed been there. Um Akram then told her as follows:

In the morning, I passed by Abu Yasser's shelter and found the men all killed and piled up on top of each other, in the street near the shelter. But I didn't find anyone in the shelter itself.

My dear, it was clear they'd taken the people out of the shelter. But there were women and children in the shelter. Where had they taken them? I looked around, everywhere. I found they'd taken the women to the Darwish Garage and killed them there. I'm so sorry, my dear.[101]

Um Rabi' found her mother and 15-year-old brother were gone – not, like her husband, with the guerrillas, but gone for good. The night before, even while she had been leading people to safety at the Gaza Hospital, her mother and younger brother had been facing death, and she had known nothing of it. Now those who had sought refuge at the hospital took flight once more, outside the district.

Um Rabi' was one of those who fled to Hamad Street. On the Friday evening she tried to persuade as many people as possible to accompany her to the Israelis, to let them know what was happening. However, this did not happen for a number of reasons – most significantly on account of disagreement among the fugitives themselves.[102]

There was also, though, an inner voice telling her: 'Why bother to complain anyway? What good would that do? Wouldn't the Israelis know about it if they wanted to know? Wouldn't the press know if it wanted to know? Wouldn't God know? Oh God, we seek Your forgiveness and Mercy.'

Complaint to any but God is humiliating.

Shahira lived through the experience of awaiting death (see Account 20, p. 106), and remained sleepless in the home of her aunt, Um As'ad. The attackers had, she knew, killed her sister Aida, along with her father, but she was not daring to admit it to herself.

On the Friday morning, she said, about 20 gunmen came to their house. Some stood by the windows, some by the doors, some by the steps, carrying guns. They began by smashing the glass. Then they took the women and children out, keeping the men in the house. She added:

The streets were filled with victims. As we came out, we saw my father and my sister Aida in front of the house. My father had been shot dead, and Aida had been almost torn apart. Her face was disfigured. I screamed when I saw her. The Phalangist soldier told me: 'Get out of here or I'll kill you on top of her.' My little children started screaming when they saw their Aunt Aida killed. 'Mother,' they said, 'look at Aunt Aida.'

Wherever we walked, we saw bodies. One of those I remember was Muhammad al-Nabulsi [see Account 23, p. 108], God bless his soul, and there were a lot of others I didn't know.

They kept us captive in the Sports City, in one room. There were a lot of us. They had guards over us. When the children got thirsty and hungry and started crying, one of the guards let us go and buy some food and water from the shop. 'Go on, then,' he said, 'go there and come back.' We went, but we didn't go back. We ran off and didn't go back home till it was all over.

I wish … I wish we'd never gone back.[103]

Hajjeh Um Ali (see Account 24, p. 109), who had hidden more than 30 neighbours and others seeking refuge, opened the front gate of her house just before six in the morning and began walking down the short alley. When she reached the end and looked around, she found the next street filled with bodies and approached in case anyone needed help. The killers, though, saw her and sent a hail of bullets towards her. She retreated swiftly, sheltered by the neighbours' wall. The megaphones were still blaring out: 'Surrender and you won't be harmed.'

The street down which Hajjeh Um Ali had looked was the same one at whose wall the killers had lined up the youths and men, having taken them from their houses and Abu Yasser's shelter. It was also the street Randa had reached when she rescued her father the night before, and had seen no one in the whole neighbourhood – the attackers having fled after resistance fighters had launched an RPG shell (see Account 16, p. 97).

Now, on the Friday morning, the gunmen had returned, stronger and more numerous than ever. But the family of Hajj Abu Ali Ajami, the cheerful, pious man from Qal'at al-Shaqif, had no need to run through the alleys now occupied by the attackers. They had managed to flee east, through the Sabri Hamadeh Palace side, whence they had found their way to al-Shayah. Once there, they found the whole district had become shut off just after their departure.[104]

Testimonies from the second day

The second day began with bodies flung everywhere and with torn-down houses covering the tell-tale signs of whole families murdered the night before. The mega-phones were still blaring: 'Surrender and you won't be harmed.' So loud were the calls, and so ubiquitous, that they were heard by a Palestinian woman in Bir Hasan. Men were told to come out from their houses, lay down their arms and leave the doors of their houses open. Women and children were being told to return home.[105] In reality events hardly allowed them to return.

On this Friday, crowds of people were being marched towards the Sports City. Many went voluntarily, either from fear or because they believed the message relayed through the megaphones. Many others, however, were frightened and began locking themselves in, or else rushed in search of a way out.

The killers' calls were, needless to say, quite disingenuous. No one had his ID card returned with the words: 'Here's your card. Go back home.' Some of the Israelis, in contrast, said nothing else. In fact, they were the dominant force in the Sports City and the district round about.

From the testimonies of the second day, I have selected ten accounts that vie with their first-day counterparts in terms of the brutality and mutilation involved. They differ on one point in that they refer to what occurred in the middle of the day – as if there were any difference in massacres by day or night.

Testimonies regarding the killing and abduction of families

The attacker from Al-Numour al-Ahrar had, it may be recalled, quoted a remark of his superiors on the Wednesday in Wadi al-Shahrour while he was being prepared for the attack, to the effect that the operation would take no longer than three hours.

In fact the operation lasted throughout the following day too. Nor did it even end with this second day, which was, however, especially characterized by escalating violence and attacks on entire families. This will be evident from the events of the eight accounts immediately below.

Account 25: Um Ahmad's family

Um Ahmad Srour was from the village of al-Na'imah in the Safad region, but had left there when she was just five years old. However, she married a man from her village and had nine children.

On the evening of the first day, her two older sons went out to make enquiries as to what was about to happen, while their seven brothers and sisters remained in their parents' house, on the borders of the camp, near Sabra.

Um Ahmad, frightened, wished to seek protection at the nearby shelter, but her husband thought this unnecessary. An employee of the telephone centre, he was sure his job, to say nothing of his age, would protect him from any harm at the hands of the Israelis. More important still, his brothers living in the South had not been detained or even questioned by the Israelis. There the Israelis had only sought out young men.

Um Ahmad's chief memories of the Thursday were of the total lack of bread. She had accordingly prepared *mujaddarra* for the children, in the hope the lentils would fill them up a little. Somehow a car passed through just before sunset from which someone was loudly offering bread for sale, so she fetched a bag of it for the children then went to bed happy in the knowledge that there would at least be bread for breakfast next day. She was far less reassured about what might be about to happen. She recalled the fierce, ominous lights and the intermittent shelling that had finally ceased and allowed them some sleep.

On the Friday morning, before seven o'clock, Um Ahmad was in the kitchen, boiling some tea and preparing breakfast, when her neighbour Laila came in. The latter had been alone since her husband left the country, and had spent the night there at Um Ahmad's urgent insistence. She refused, though, to stay beyond the night, insisting on returning home despite any incursions that might have taken place. She was fearful nevertheless, going up on to Um Ahmad's roof and holding on to the hand of her neighbour's son, to assure herself the street was safe and to discover what was happening.

Immediately, one of the gunmen caught sight of them. 'You whore,' he yelled, 'you slut, where did you come from? Did you come yourself or did God send you down from the sky? Come down here, you ——s ... come on down. Come out of that house or we'll bring it down on your heads. Come down here.'

The neighbour went down, crying out: 'Um Ahmad, Abu Ahmad, they've come here! Ask the boy who was with me. Ask him!'[106]

There was no time for questions. The yells for them to open the door were growing louder, and the attackers were also attempting to get in through the neighbours' house. Abu Ahmad Srour, who had remained calm, decided to open the door. Getting up, he said: 'All right, brothers, here I am.' They marched in, more as if descending on some deserted island than entering an inhabited house.

'Where have you been hiding yourselves?' they yelled. 'What nationality are you, you ——?'

'I'm Palestinian,' Abu Ahmad replied.

'And your neighbour, you ——', they went on. 'What nationality's he?'

'My neighbour's from Baalbek,' Abu Ahmad said, 'and that's where he is now. He's an old man, in any case ...'

'Whose are those pictures on the walls, you son of a bitch?' one of them broke in. 'They're your eldest sons, aren't they? Where did they go?'

The father remained calm. 'Those are pictures of my nephews', he answered. 'They were staying with us, and now they've gone back to their parents in Sidon.'

No one will ever know whether or not the attackers believed what Abu Ahmad had said. They had already given their orders before he could finish his sentence. 'All right, all right, everyone out, come out with your hands above your heads.'

They all went out as ordered, with more than ten gunmen in front of them and behind them. The only ones left were two children hiding in the bathroom, of whose existence the gunmen remained unaware. Even the parents did not miss them. Who would miss anyone at a time like that, even his own children?

Um Ahmad said:

They made us go out. We left the house open. We had the birth certificates and identity cards ready, and told them they could see the papers if they wanted to. Some of them looked at them. Others only kept yelling: 'All right, come on out.' We all went out with our hands above our heads; even little Shadia raised her hands the way we did. They walked us to the start of the alley; then, I don't know why, they changed their minds. They said: 'All right, go back home.' We did. They took us back in and said: 'All right, line up against the wall.'

I swear they made us stand with our hands up, and they started shooting. They started with the girls and me. I fell to the ground. I felt as if my back had been ripped apart and I thought I was dead and gone. My eldest daughter got hit too, with the splinter still in her hand and shoulder and back. Since that day my daughter Su'ad [Srour] has been paralysed, and my daughter Nuhad was injured. All the others were killed; they were all killed. I heard Farid say: 'Father, they're coming for me.' They hit him and dashed his brains out. I felt little Shadia turning around me, saying, 'Mummy, mummy'. They took her and hit her, and her soul departed straight away.

As soon as they'd gone, we started moving our legs to find out who was dead and who was still alive. It was then I realized Isma'il and Maher had gone and hidden in the bathroom. God saved them. I saw too that my middle daughter Nuhad was injured but could walk, whereas Su'ad couldn't. I went with her two brothers and tried to pick her

up, but we couldn't, they'd shot four bullets at Su'ad, some in the back, and they paralysed her. She couldn't move, let alone stand. 'Mother,' she said, 'my legs are gone. Take my brothers and get them out if you can, run with my brothers, mother.'

I took the children and got out, and the last time I laid eyes on Abu Ahmad, he had the ID card in his hand ready to give them. But they shot him before he could hand them his papers.

We ran out in the street like mad people. The two children, the older one, Maher, was mature enough, 13 years old, so he grabbed his younger brother Isma'il, who was six, and they went and hid at the neighbours'. I saw them just three or four days later. I went on running with my daughter with the scarf over my head, stained with my little daughter's blood and spattered brains.[107]

Um Ahmad was not alone when she came to my house on 22 February 1983, five months after the massacre, to describe what had happened. A friend of her husband's, who had told me of her tragedy, escorted her to the appointment. He it was who had introduced me to a large number of Sabra and Shatila residents, but he did not introduce another woman who had come along with Um Ahmad. There was no need to ask: the other woman also belonged quite obviously to the 'group with memories'. She was draped in black, tall and erect, but said not a word. She listened to Um Ahmad intently, as though hearing everything for the first time, though she was certainly aware of everything that had happened. Her own story I did not know. What I noticed, though, was that she was weeping all the time Um Ahmad spoke. Um Ahmad herself shed just one or two tears. As I listened to Um Ahmad, my eyes were on the woman accompanying her, whose silent tears were eloquent.

Um Ahmad continued the account of her escape with her daughter:

I thought of knocking at some neighbours' door. Where should I go? We had some Lebanese neighbours, I went and said to her: 'You're Lebanese, and they won't come to you. Come with us, let's go out together.' 'We're not going anywhere', the neighbour told me. 'We're staying at home.' So I said: 'Hide us in your house, I beg you, where are we to go?' As I talked to her, blood was dripping on the floor … She told me: 'My dear neighbour, for God's sake, go to the hospital.'[108]

Unable to control myself, I found myself saying angrily: 'For heaven's sake! How could that happen? She wouldn't help you, when you were in a state like that? Tell me, Um Ahmad, did you meet her after all this happened? Did you talk? Did she offer any sort of apology?'

Um Ahmad did not answer. She said nothing.

The woman accompanying her was, I noticed, weeping once more, I did not know why. I stopped the tape recorder and turned to her. 'Excuse me, sister,' I said, 'we still haven't been introduced. Did I say something to upset you?' She made no reply.

I turned to the man who had escorted them, sensing he knew more of matters than I did. He too remained resolutely silent.

Then Um Ahmad's companion spoke at last; for the first time I heard her voice in my home. 'I'm her neighbour,' she said calmly.

Still Um Ahmad's story of the Friday was not finished. Leaving her neighbours' house with her daughter – in a half-crazed state, though she had such a reputation for being level-headed – she made for the Gaza Hospital. She began screaming to all the Palestinians she saw, urging them to leave their homes because they were going to be killed. The climax came when she arrived at the hospital. No one there would even forget the way she yelled:

What's the matter with you all? Why are you still here? Woe to you, you're armed, and you're just standing here? In front of the hospital? Go and see how people are piled up in the streets. They're killing people in their homes! You men, you're carrying arms and you're still standing there, in front of the hospital? Woe to you![109]

Um Ahmad was, she admitted, yelling at them like a madwoman. She said, too, that she felt no one believed her, that no one responded to her or even asked her to tell them what was going on. She was terrified the killers would return to the hospital. So the moment they had finished bandaging her daughter's wounds, and her own, she left the place, seeking refuge for the two of them in the nearest building.

Did she think of her daughter, lying unconscious among the dead? Of course she did. But what could she have done?

At one point it occurred to her that they had not asked her husband about his job. Would they have released them, had they discovered and confirmed that he was employed at the telephone centre, and not a fighter in Fatah's ranks? But they had killed him without even asking him.

At one point, too, she thought about her neighbour Laila, who had been killed along with them, and invoked God's mercy on her.

She did not, it appears, give too much thought to what happened to her two sons, Isma'il and Maher, after they left the bathroom, where they had hidden while the criminals were wiping out the entire family.

The reunion of whoever was left from the family took place three days later.

Account 26: Um Ali's family

Um Ali al-Biqa'i was the woman I saw weeping in my home while Um Ahmad was describing her tragedy – the same woman who had told Um Ahmad, 'My dear neighbour, for God's sake, go to the hospital', refusing to admit her to her house.

She was also the same woman we heard, during the account of the peace delegation in Chapter 2, asking God to have mercy on the delegation member Abu Ahmad Sweid, who had been such a good friend to her husband and family since their arrival in Shatila.

She was a Sheba'i southern Lebanese who liked Palestinians as neighbours and, by virtue of this neighbourhood, faced the same destiny. Um Ali's turn to speak, and Um Ahmad Srour's to listen, came during our meeting of 22 February 1983.

On the Thursday night when I left Abu Yasser's shelter and went back home, leaving my daughter Um Fadi behind, I'd put all my trust in Almighty God. I'd no way of knowing what was going to happen. If I had known, I wouldn't have left her behind at the shelter. We had guests back at our house and we spent the night there, but no one could sleep …

On the Friday morning, we were told they'd taken away all the women and children. I swear, my daughter had four … forgive me, God. My daughter, I tell you, was worth almost a tribe on her own. My heart cries out for her. I thought there'd been gunmen in the camp. Actually there weren't any gunmen there, but we'd heard some shots and thought there were gunmen.

I picked up my scarf and was just going out in the street to tell people, 'For God's sake, these are Israelis, they won't do anything. In the South they didn't do anything to the women and children. Just raise white flags, don't do anything, and no one will touch you.'

Just then I felt my son Rabi' grabbing my hand. 'Quiet', he was telling me. 'Not a word, mother. Don't go out, mother. I've heard Abu Yasser and a lot of others were killed in front of the shelter. And mother, I heard they took my sister, Um Fadi, and her children, and Abu Fadi, and no one's seen them since.' 'But, son,' I told him, 'they wouldn't harass your sister or her children. How could they possibly harass Lebanese, or harm them?' So my son told me about our other neighbours who'd been killed at our neighbour Sa'id's, how Sa'id himself had been slaughtered on his doorstep, and he went on begging me not to leave the house. Then, he started begging me to let him run to save his own life. He was afraid of being shot, because he was a man. 'Son,' I started saying, 'they'll think you're a fugitive. We're Lebanese, we have our ID cards.'

We stayed till half past seven in the morning. Then our neighbour Um Ahmad stopped by. She came in, covered in blood, her and her daughter. She said: 'Please hide me.' I told her: 'For heaven's sake, look at the blood on you, what do you mean, we hide you, what can we do for you? They'll come and find us. They're killing, aren't they? They'll find you here and kill us all. Please, go to the hospital, maybe you can make it there and have your wounds bandaged.' 'They're not harassing people with Lebanese cards,' the woman told me. Five minutes later she left.

My husband came in from outside. 'Why did you tell her that?' he asked. 'Why did you throw the woman out? She has only God to turn to, and so have we, how could you let her go?' I told him: 'For heaven's sake, her blood was staining the floor. If they come, they'll think there's been fighting here. How can I freeze her blood? Didn't you see her blood, and her daughter's, how it was flowing out?' He kept on saying: 'Woe to you, how could you let her go?' And he started clapping his hands in his anguish, one hand over the other.[110]

The couple's argument was resolved as the calls outside became louder: 'Surrender … you won't be harmed.' Whereupon the whole family went out to surrender.

Um Ali al-Biqa'i, Abu Ali al-Biqa'i, their daughters and their young green-eyed son, Rabi', an employee at the Hasna' printing company, who had never carried a gun in his life, went out, as did the guests staying with them. Um Ali named these latter three or four times during the meeting and, as the horrific episode began, she brought in their neighbours' names too:

As we got out into the street, we saw our Palestinian neighbours and the people who'd been hiding. We saw Qassem Abu Harb's wife and the Awdeh family. All our neighbours came in a group when they heard our voices. Then there was an 80-year-old neighbour from Arab al-Maslakh with us, an Egyptian woman, and a Syrian-Lebanese woman. They lined up the Lebanese on one side and the Palestinians on the other.

Then we saw one of them calling on a man and asking them: 'Do you recognize these faces? Do you have any idea who they are?'

We didn't know what he told him; but they ordered us to walk, men apart from the women. I asked them: 'Where are you taking my son?' And I yelled: 'Rabi'! Just listen to me, son.' Rabi' turned to me and kept on walking with the men. Just then I saw my husband begging the gunman, telling him: 'For God's sake, let me go to the shelter to see my daughter and her children.' He let him go. But what did he find? My husband found no one at the shelter. He saw the victims in front of the shelter, and they were all men. By the time the old man had come back, my son, my husband's nephew, my son-in-law, Dib al-Hinawi from Sheb'a, and the old man next to us, Hussein Younes, had all crossed to the other side. They took them in pairs to another alley.

As we were walking along, one of them saw my daughter, who was a beautiful young girl, 16 years old. 'Are you Lebanese?' he asked her. 'Give me your card.' He grabbed the card and started trying to get her in a house nearby. I shrieked at him: 'Where are you taking my daughter?' I caught hold of the girl and pulled her into the women's group, then I went for him and snatched the card out of his hand. He hit my thumb with his bayonet and said: 'You're going to die.' When he hit me, I felt as though my hand had been cut off. It started trembling.

There we were in the street, the people were walking as if it was doomsday. We saw the victims and walked past them. We saw the men from the Aidi family and their son-in-law. They were all heaped up like logs. We passed by a garage too, owned by someone called Abu Jamal, where my daughter had been killed and heaped up along with her children. But we didn't see them then. The garage was still standing. They took us to the Sports City near al-Ina'ash, that's where they put us …

A tough, brave Palestinian girl had come to visit her sister, poor girl. This girl lived in Sidon. They took hold of her and grabbed her blouse, then they ripped off her pants, they did that, but she was brave, a lioness, she started hitting them right and left – there were four of them, and she stopped them getting her on the ground. As the girl was resisting, a woman with a child told them: 'Shame on you, she's a young woman, don't you have sisters?' Then one of them took his pistol, shot the woman from behind, and sent her to the ground, and her child fell and started crying.

Near the Ina'ash school we saw a southern man, from al-Khiam; he was one of them, someone we know, and we knew his family too. So my daughter told him who we were. The man didn't hold back. In fact, he started helping us. He brought some food, bread, cheese, halva and *labneh* [a thick yogurt], and he told us: 'Don't be afraid.' At the same time there were two others whistling and saying out loud: 'We'll haunt you to Saudi Arabia. We'll haunt you to Yemen. We'll haunt you up to God. You Arabs are a worthless bunch. We'll haunt you wherever you go.'

They wouldn't leave us alone. We told the man who'd helped us about the tough girl. He went and rescued her. When he got there he found her naked, and hit on the back and in the stomach. But they hadn't managed to get her on the ground. This man, who went to get her, found a woman killed too, who had a bag with a striped gown in it, and he took this and handed it to the girl, saying: 'Cover yourself up, sister.' Then he turned his back, and then he pulled her out and brought her to the Sports City.

He told us what had happened. I told him I didn't care any more what happened to my son or husband. 'I beg you,' I told him, 'I'm ready to kneel down, please get these two girls through. Think of them as your sisters.'

Again, he did help. 'Keep walking,' he told us, 'and go on past the Sports City.'[111]

Um Ali could not believe she had made it through with her daughters. She went past the Sports City to the Lebanese Red Cross centre, arriving some time before midday. She gave their names and described everything that had happened to them. Their names were taken down, and they were told they would be released if they had been held captive. From there, she made it to the Hélou Barracks where she told the officers in charge what had happened in Sabra and Shatila. A liaison officer called the Command Centre and reported what Um Ali had said, but the man in charge there replied that the woman must be senile. He said this loud enough for Um Ali to hear.

Um Ali had not yet finished with her humanitarian mission. She left her daughters with a family she knew in the Hélou Barracks district, then started telling the Israeli soldiers on every tank she encountered what was happening. She intended to go to the Command Centre too, but her legs failed her and she fell on the sand near the Beirut Hospital in the Janah district.

An Israeli soldier saw her and came to bring her some water, drinking himself first to reassure her the water was pure. He spoke a little Arabic. 'Take water,' he told her. 'Take water. Beirut water is good.'

Um Ali burst into tears and told him what had happened. The soldier began weeping with her, and told her:

'Hajjeh, these are Lebanese commandos, these are commandos. We didn't do anything. We don't kill and we don't go to Sabra. We have nothing to do with Sabra and we don't dare to go down there, we have no orders. But tomorrow, if they are prisoners, we will go down and get them.'

'Hajjeh, will you come back tomorrow?'[112]

Um Ali could gain no news of her son, her husband and the guests who had been at her house on the Friday. Accordingly she rushed to save others who had no knowledge of events.

Reaching the Gaza Hospital, she began screaming and asking about her daughter Um Fadi and her children, in case they had been injured and someone had brought them to the hospital. She hardly expected to find anyone, but she made the attempt nevertheless.

She found around 300 Palestinian men, and yelled at them:

'You Palestinians, woe to you, what are you doing here? They'll come and kill you now, right there. Come along to Qulailat, come on, come with me to Qulailat. Don't you want someone to protect you? Who else is there to defend you?'

I swear I didn't know myself any more. Where did I get such a loud voice from?

Some of them believed her: about 100 men left the hospital. It was still only half past one.

Whenever Um Ali al-Biqa'i became impassioned she would speak of her young, sensitive, green-eyed son Rabi' who, as she repeated a number of times, worked at *Al-Hasna'* – a women's magazine, not a political one!

Rabi' ... how could I ever forget Rabi', even for a single day? ... He had such beautiful eyes. 'Mother,' he'd tell me, 'I'm your heir.' I'd say: 'What do I have to leave you, son?' And he'd say: 'I have your affection. I've inherited affection from you, mother.'

Ikram, too – Um Fadi – she was the sort of girl you wouldn't forget. She was so loving, she'd help me with my work even if she was sick. Once Ikram was sick for a whole year. I stayed with her till the last moment, when she passed away.[113]

Um Ali realized, deep down, that she had lost both Rabi' and Ikram, along with her grandchildren, husband and son-in-law. What she had not reckoned with was the bitter pain she was to undergo in searching for them.

Account 27: The one who survived – simply to testify

27 October 1982, was the memorial day for the Sabra and Shatila massacre, 40 days having passed. People and sympathizers gathered at the mass cemetery to shed a tear and recite some Quranic verses.

'Mary' (the name we agreed on for the purposes of publication) was, as we have seen, a foreign woman working in the social field. She had been to Lebanon a number of times in the course of her work, most recently during the invasion, and she was also a friend to several Palestinian families. After the massacre she returned alone to Beirut for work and personal reasons combined, and took a red rose to place on the mass cemetery.

Seeing a 14-year-old girl standing alone with a picture in her hand, Mary went over to her. The girl gazed at her for a few moments, then remembered her from the time she had gone to visit them in one of Verdun buildings, in the midst of the invasion. When, as people were dispersing, Mary asked her what was wrong, the girl stepped aside and told her story right through, without waiting to be asked – as if she had only been waiting for someone to come and listen:

On Friday morning, we were at home. My father, brother, and a neighbor of ours were drinking coffee ... My mother had gone to Saida [Sidon] to inquire about my older brother, who had been detained by the Israelis in 'Ansar' prison since the beginning of the invasion.

They barely finished drinking the coffee, when we heard the door almost getting broken. We instantly saw four gunmen from the Quwat. In front of the house, we saw six others standing. They had machine guns and a lot of knives and axes, and they ordered us to walk to the Sport City. All the way they were kicking us around with their legs and the rifles. My father tried to give me some money, in case something would happen. But immediately as he put his hand in his pocket, someone hit his hand with the bottom of the gun, and they took all the money he had.

All the way to the Sports City, the roads were filled with victims, they forced us to walk on them, and they threatened to kill us if we didn't; and we walked on the victims.

When we arrived at the Sports City, it was overcrowded. The Quwat and the Israelis had brought them all. Among them was a group of guys who had been put by the Phalangist Forces in a very big pit. There was also a big truck getting ready to dump sand over them and to bury them alive. Once they finished doing so, in front of our eyes, we knew that our turn was next. At those moments, and after seeing all that, I developed exactly the same feeling that is described by the expression 'the blood froze in my veins'. It didn't cross my mind at all that the more hideous scene was yet to come, and that I would see how they would kill my father and brother. They had spared me intentionally, so that I see how they would kill them.

One of them brought a knife. He gave it to my father and told him: 'Go ahead and kill your son,' but another interfered: 'We had vowed to kill them with our own hands. Give me the knife. I'll slaughter him myself.' He took the knife and cut my brother's neck from the back. In addition, he threw him to the ground while his blood was dripping. He left him to bleed till the last breath.

I could take it no longer. I couldn't hear their voices or look at them. So I fell to the ground, unconscious. They started to spray water over me and said: 'Get up now, so that you see how your father is going to be killed. Then you can fall down unconscious as much as you please.'

They started shooting at my father. Bullets came from more than one side. My father was thin, and so he couldn't take much before falling to the ground giving away his last breath.

I then thought that my turn had come. As I was about to say my prayers and raise my eyes to the sky, I heard them laugh at me and say: 'We won't kill you. We'll leave you alive so that you go and tell everything that happened in front of you. Come on, go ...'[114]

The girl did as they had wished, describing what had happened to everyone she saw.

Mary decided to write the girl's story, the first story she had heard since returning to Beirut – though not the last.

This social worker took care to visit everyone she had known; listening to them and easing their pain. With a tear in her eyes, she handed me a photocopy of the 13 accounts, which she had written down by hand.

Our meeting took place at the house of another foreign woman friend, who brought us together in 1985.

Account 28: Um Walid's family

Um Walid and her family were hiding in one of the rooms at their home in Shatila, on the borders of the camp near Hayy Farhat, supposing they would be protected from the heavy Israeli shelling. Nor, in a sense, were they wrong, for it was hardly likely they would be exposed to any shelling when this could just as easily have struck the attackers themselves.

Suddenly, they heard pounding on the door. The members of the family huddled together, and Um Walid said to her husband: 'Who's that at the door? They must be coming to kill us. Don't open, whatever you do! If they think there's no one here, maybe they'll go away.'

Her husband gave a reasoned reply:

Don't worry. I've never hurt anyone in all my life. I haven't been a fighter either ... I'm a businessman, and I've got all the papers and the bank credentials to show that.

Don't worry. I'll show them all my papers, and there's no way they'll harm us.[115]

The knocking, however, became harder still, and Um Walid heard a voice yelling: 'Open the door, or we'll break it down.' In fact they were given no chance to open. The door was broken down, and five gunmen armed with machine-guns, axes and knives burst in. They were all tall and strongly built, and they ordered the inhabitants to march in front of them to the Sports City.

Um Walid recalled what happened:

My husband told them he had nothing to do with the fighters, that he was a businessman. He handed over all his papers. In a flash, they ripped up all the papers and threw them down on the ground. They only left his savings account book, and they ordered him to sign it, so they could go back and take out all the money. They asked as well about any money and jewellery we kept at home, and they took it all. There was even a gold chain round the neck of my son, a three-year-old boy. They almost strangled him trying to pull it off. I begged them to leave him alone, while I unlocked the chain and gave it to them.

When there was nothing left worth stealing, they shouted: 'Now we'll go to the City.'

The ones who went to the City were the children, my mother, my sister and myself. They ordered the men to stay there at home. Those who stayed were my husband, my eldest son, my brother-in-law and my brothers, three young men.

On the way to the City, we saw hundreds of bodies. They ordered us to step over them, or else they'd kill us and throw us down like them. A lot of the bodies were in an indescribable state, some were burned, while others were pierced by bullets fired at point blank range. I was sure we were going to be killed, and I thought of all the loved ones I'd left behind at home. Had they killed them? What had happened?

We reached the City. We saw them all from close up. We saw them bragging about the badges on their shoulders. I realized they were Lebanese Forces. When we got there, some of them were eating, laughing and drinking alcohol. The bottles were there in front of them, and a lot of them were drunk.

One of them said: 'Here's another Palestinian family. What shall we do with them?' Another said: 'This one's for the big pit, this one and any more like them. We'll put them in and dump sand over them.'

I looked upward and around, I saw we were among the first to have reached the City. I found hundreds of people walking and getting to where we were. I tried to find my family, but I couldn't make anyone out, there were so many people and so far away.

There was an explosion near us. I thought it was a bomb. A woman standing next to me said it was an explosion. I saw people falling and dying in front of me. I heard the drunks burst out laughing too, as people were falling and dying. There was a second explosion, or a second mine maybe – this Sports City was mined right through the war. So, it gave us the chance to run. I ran.

The same day I went back home. I thought maybe someone was hurt and needed help, or maybe I wouldn't find anyone, if they'd been taken prisoner.

I got home, and all I found was bodies lying on the ground. They'd killed them all. All of them. Never in my life, in any television film, in the darkest jungles anywhere, could I have imagined anything more savage.

My husband didn't have a head. They'd cut off his head and thrown it between his son's legs. They'd cut off my son's arm and thrown it on the shoulder of his uncle, who'd been killed next to him. My other brother's head was sliced in half from a heavy blow from an axe.

I couldn't take any more. I fainted. But my mother was tougher. She was the one who gathered the bodies together and found people to bear them next day, for burial in the mass cemetery.

They buried them, it's true … But there are no names left. There's no grave to weep at.[116]

Account 29: Families without names

When asked for her name, so that it could be set down with her account, the woman who gave this account shook her head and answered: 'What does it matter whether I tell you or not? Aren't Palestinians just numbers in the UNRWA files?'

When asked how many members of her family she had lost, there were tears in her eyes as she answered, shaking her hand to imply they were many. 'I lost nearly all my family,' she said. 'There wasn't a single battle where we didn't lose someone. It's the tragedy of a nation.'

When asked about what she had seen during the three bloody days, her voice changed. She adjusted her position, giving the impression the talk would be a long one, then slowly started relating what had happened to her at the shelter at Hayy al-Horsh, where she miraculously survived the certain death she faced, along with everyone else, on that first night:

We were in the shelter on the Thursday night without any food or any water to drink. I thought of going to fetch some food, because the night was just like day, with all the flare shells over the camp. But I didn't dare go. I stayed sitting on the shelter step till Friday morning came.

When dawn came I felt my courage coming back, and I went over by the mosque, to buy some food. There I saw an injured man pleading for help, because he hadn't been able to reach the Gaza Hospital. He told me the main street had been blocked. I went to the hospital, through the alleys, to look for my son. On the way, I met someone who told me they'd killed a lot of people. It didn't cross my mind there'd been any killing. I thought straight away of my family I'd left behind at the shelter, and I thought my son would be fine with all the other people looking for protection at the hospital. No one was going to invade a hospital. So I ran back to the shelter. While I was running, three of the Lebanese Forces, armed with machine guns, spotted me. They stopped me and ordered me to walk to the Sports City.

At the end of the street, I saw a jeep and a tank belonging to the Forces. As I looked around, I saw an old man breathing his last. A bomb suddenly blew up by us. We'd been standing in a long line. A lot of us died, and a lot got injured. I wasn't harmed, and so I went straight back to the shelter to try and find out about my family. I saw no one in the street, except for a little girl who was crying and calling for her mother.

I reached the shelter, which was filled with bodies, but I didn't see anyone from my family.

They'd killed them all in the middle of the day.

Two days later I went to Shatila, to the place where the Red Cross used to be, and where they'd put the victims ready for mass burial. I saw a lot of victims covered with blankets. I started lifting them. I saw the body of an old woman draped in black. Was she my mother maybe? Her face wasn't recognizable any more. I tried to think, how many women had there been dressed in black, in the shelter? How many women had been mourning people they'd lost in the war? There was no way I could remember them all.

No one gave me a death certificate for anyone from my family. The Red Cross hadn't seen their cards. They hadn't recorded their names.

The last time I saw them was at the shelter.[117]

Was the witness right when she declined to give her name, on the grounds that Palestinians were merely numbers at the UNRWA?

She was not remotely surprised at having obtained no death certificates for her parents, given that the Red Cross had not seen their 'cards' and, in consequence, did not even know their numbers. Had they seen the cards, and read their numbers, they could also have known the names if they wished, since these were printed on the cards.

The sole survivor of the family was effectively saying that when they were alive they were numbers. Are their names going to come back when they're dead? Can anyone tell her how many Palestinian families were there in that shelter? How many Lebanese families? Can anyone tell her the difference between one person with a UNRWA number on his card, which they ripped up, and another with a cedar of Lebanon, which they refused to recognize?

All those who died were just numbers.

Account 30: Abu Mahmoud's family

Abu Mahmoud lived on the outskirts of Shatila, on the border with Sabra. He was quite popular among those in Sabra and

Shatila, especially with young people, as he owned a bicycle shop.

When his first wife died, he married Mariam, who loved the children of his first wife and cared for them so well that she was generally known as Um Mahmoud. When her first son, Hasan, was born, some continued to call her Um Mahmoud, while others began to call her Um Hasan, but she will be referred to as Mariam Abu Harb in this volume. The couple were at the head of a close-knit, loving family.

The lady of the house was the first to sense, from the Thursday evening on, that some danger was imminent, and – though she could hardly have been aware of the implications of this – she decided early on the Friday morning to flee with her husband and children. However, the moment she looked through the window, at six o'clock, she saw the street filled with armed militias and no longer dared to contemplate escape.

It was not long before the gunmen began rapping on the family's door. Mariam said:

Four armed soldiers came marching in. They had the Lebanese Forces sign on their chests, and there were five others standing and waiting for them at the street entrance to the house. They took us all out. They put my husband and eldest son to one side, and my little children, the girls and myself to another.

My daughter had been carrying a bag we used to call the 'war bag', which had clothes for my little six-month-old baby. This time I'd put in it all our money, gold, documents for the house, ID cards, cheques, bills and insurance policies. One of them soon took hold of the bag and started throwing the clothes in the street. He took the money and the gold, and divided it between himself and the man with him, there in front of me … Then he saw my ring and my watch, and told me: 'Hand them over. We're wild about gold.' Another one snatched the earrings from my little daughter's ears. When he was finally sure there was nothing left to steal, he said: 'Come on, then. Get moving.'

On the way to the Sports City, there were around 400 Phalangist soldiers sitting on what later became a mass grave. They were sitting on mattresses, and some of them were lying down as if they were at home. But they made us walk on the right, and go through Hayy Ersal to the Sports City.

On the way I saw a woman who'd been killed while still clutching her three children, all dead, to her breast. We saw men as well who'd been stabbed and bodies that had been cut apart. They were piling up the bodies so the bulldozer could come and cover them with gravel.

My daughter Samar was 17 years old. I suddenly saw one of them trying to take her away from me. I begged him to leave her alone, but he wouldn't. I started pulling her by one arm, while he pulled the other, and I was shouting at him. 'Don't think I'm going to let my daughter go', I said. 'Kill us all together. Kill us all, right now.' He started laughing at me. 'You know how to make a rebellion too, do you?' he said. We kept up our noise till one of his superiors came up, and asked: 'What's the matter with you?' I told him: 'This soldier's trying to take my daughter away.' So the superior yelled at him: 'Let her go.' Even so, we'd hardly walked any distance before he started chasing after us, trying to take her away again.

This time, though, one of the men with him came and rescued her. The man took his revenge by kicking me, but I moved off quickly, I walked fast, with my daughter and the children, while he was spraying us with dust and shooting between our legs.

We reached the Sports City. They started cursing and laughing at us, and they told us: 'Get over there.' We went where we'd been told. We found a sewage pit filled with victims, chopped heads, hands and legs.

When I saw this, I ran to the upper part of the Sports City; I ran to an Israeli tank filled with Israeli soldiers. I told them about the victims, about the Phalangists, and how they'd been slaughtering people. 'Get away from here', they told me. 'Get away from us. We've nothing to do with this.'

We went back, not knowing where to go or what to do. We heard an Israeli yell: 'Get back! Go back!' So we ran to the Cola bridge.[118]

Mariam was one of the women who went to try and tell the senior Lebanese officials of what was happening. Yet they could find satisfaction from no one on that Friday afternoon. The Prime Minister, Shafiq al-Wazzan, told them he was not prepared to go to the district while the Israelis were still there. Nor could they even see the ex-Prime Minister, Sa'eb Slam, as the guards intervened, telling them he was asleep.[119]

On the following morning, Mariam met at the Cola bridge with groups of men standing there and talking, with no notion of what had been happening. She told them of everything she had seen, about the Phalangists slaughtering people, and told them: 'Don't go to the camp.' When the men had taken in what she was saying, some answered: 'How can we run off and not help our people in the camp?' Soon they were divided among themselves. Some listened to her and decided not to go to the camp, others insisted they should go there.

When Mariam returned home, she discovered the tragedy not only in her present family home – the killing of her husband and her young son Hasan – but of killing within her own original family. Mariam was the sister of the 'four victim brothers', whose fate is described below.

Account 31: The four victim brothers

The conversation with Um Muhammad Aidi took place at her home in Hayy Farhat, and Abu Jamal, both as a neighbour and as a friend of her deceased husband, took part in the talk. But for him, indeed, it would have been impossible for me to discover the full details of what happened, since the lady of the house was still in a state of shock, despite her strong character, solid spirit and pride at having been a mature woman during the days of the Great Revolution in Palestine.

Pictures of the sons so cruelly murdered were hanging on the walls of the small living room. The walls were, indeed, covered with pictures. Um Muhammad seldom spoke without pointing to a picture or gazing at it.

Um Muhammad belonged to the generation that remembered Palestine well. Married in 1937, when she was 13, she was from Shafa Amr in the Haifa district. Her husband was from Lubia in the Tabariyya district, but had been brought up in Haifa. Details of origin and upbringing meant a great deal to this generation. Knowledge of every yard, every tree, every village, defined their memories. What could be dearer than such memories, to those who had lost their homeland?

Um Muhammad and her family emigrated to South Lebanon, living in the town of al-Ghaziyya. She could not recall the year they left al-Ghaziyya and came to Shatila, where they rented a place at Hayy Farhat. She only remembered they had come in the 1960s.

Her sons worked at various jobs. As for Abu Muhammad himself, he had been a stonemason till forced into retirement by age and fatigue. As for the number of children, Um Muhammad said, with astonishing simplicity: 'I used to have seven boys and four girls, now I have just three boys and three girls.' Shatila residents, though, do not find it easy to speak of Um Muhammad's disaster. She was famous as being the 'Mother of the Four Martyrs'.

Some things, nevertheless, Um Muhammad set out in a manner far from simple, among them her sons' professions, which ranged from employee, to laundry worker, to blacksmith, to student, to fighter. She would become excited as she started talking about her sons, merely pointing to each one's picture on the wall, without mentioning names. At last she said, pointing to a particular one:

This one joined the Popular Committee, then later he left it. He had no gun, nothing. Only this one [she pointed to another picture], he had three, not just one. If all the men had had weapons, no one could have got into the camp. Our bad luck was to have no weapons.[120]

Um Muhammad learned of what had happened on the Friday. She was not a witness – and this was a source of anguish to her – since she was among those who had fled to the Gaza Hospital, along with 13 other relatives and family members. Had they not done so they would all have faced the same fate. It was, she said, only the fact of artillery shells destroying a two-storey house quite close by, at half past two on the Thursday afternoon, that induced her to flee.

Um Muhammad refused to make any comparison between the events of the Thursday and those of the Friday. She felt the whole chain of events in the massacre to be one continuous unit, and perhaps she was right. Out of respect for her feelings on this, we shall tell her story as she herself wished.

Um Muhammad reported details related to her sons and husband as though she had been the sole witness. The neighbour, meanwhile, confirmed what she said and added supplementary details Um Muhammad had overlooked. Even when her daughter-in-law, the first witness and main describer of the event, intervened with details concerning her own husband, the final word remained Um Muhammad's:

At six o'clock on the Thursday, my son Sa'id was on the doorstep. A short man yelled at him: 'Come out here, you son of a bitch.' Sa'id answered: 'All right then', and he turned with his hands up. I swear to God, my son Sa'id could have beaten ten like him, but he thought the man was an Israeli who wanted to question him. It didn't cross his mind he'd been fooled. That's how I see it. The short man showered him with bullets. My son fell under the vegetable cart. We found him dead with one of his hands raised, the other hand under his head. Sa'id had bought the cart and started selling vegetables the day the fighters left. His wife saw everything. She went and hid with the children.

My son Moussa was at the shelter, and they started yelling: 'Come out and give yourselves up.' He got out and tried to escape through the alley in front of the house, where his brother had been killed. They saw him, and surrounded him on two sides. Moussa was carrying his baby daughter who was 13 months old. When he saw them killing people, he knew he was going to die. He looked around and saw Um Hussein, a woman he knew, and told her: 'Take your son's daughter.' And he was going to hand his daughter to her. Um Hussein didn't understand him. In fact, she thought that if the girl stayed with him, they wouldn't kill him, for her sake. He, though, was sure they'd kill them both. 'That's not my son's daughter', she said. 'Look,' she told them, 'I'm Lebanese and he's Palestinian.' 'I'm telling you,' he said to her, 'take her … take her, hajjeh', but she just wouldn't agree to take her, still thinking they'd let him go for his daughter's sake.

They didn't give him a second. They showered him, while he was carrying the milk bottles and the can for his daughters. He had twin girls. They took all his money too. He'd taken his payment from Um Saleh for fixing her son's house. After they'd shot him dead and robbed him, they mutilated the body and crushed it with the balcony.

What can we say, each one was killed in a different way. My son's brother-in-law, for example, was shot with 30 bullets.

My daughter Mariam was the first to see her brothers Sa'id and Moussa killed, in two different corners. She fainted over them. This daughter of mine had already suffered a terrible loss, because her husband, Qassem Abu Harb, whom they called Abu Mahmoud, had been killed too. He used to sell bicycles, and he was well off. They went ahead and stripped her of all the gold and money, and she was saying all the while: 'I beg you, take anything you want, but don't kill my husband.' But they killed him, and they killed her son. They took them away and killed them.

As for us here at home, there were my husband and my other children. Those stayed till morning. They were on the first floor at their brother Sa'id's.

Just as morning was breaking on the Friday, there they were. When they broke the door open and came in, they started calling for my husband and children by name. 'Ibrahim, Abu Muhammad, come on out.' When they did, they told them: 'There's still Hussein, where is he?' Hussein came out, and they took them off, at half past six in the morning.[121]

Towards the end of her account, Um Muhammad went on to enumerate the victims of the Thursday and Friday.

Between the sunset of one day and the morning of the next, this patiently suffering woman lost four of her children, her husband, her son-in-law, her grandson and two other in-laws. She lost them all. Had she remained at home with the other children, she herself would not have been alive to miss them.

At the end she had still not counted her baby granddaughter, Moussa's daughter, among the victims. When I asked what had happened to the child, her face brightened in a smile:

She's alive, pretty as a flower. May God preserve her. When her father thrust her at the hajjeh, who wouldn't take her, one of the gunmen hit the woman in the back with the butt of his rifle. 'Um Muhammad,' she told me, 'I fell down on the ground. Your son looked at me and said, "Take her, hajjeh." I took her and thrust her on a Palestinian woman who knows you, Um Ghanem. She said, "For God's sake, stay away from me." '

What can I say? This Um Ghanem had a son who'd been killed too, and she was in a wretched state. She went and put the girl in the mosque. The

people there recognized her and brought her to us. She was stained all over with blood. The poor baby, women were flinging her from hand to hand as her father was being killed.

If you could only see her now, pretty as a flower.[122]

Account 32: The four abducted brothers

Pictures of abducted young men and women vary only with the location. In essentials they are the same.

There are mothers, wives and sisters demonstrating in their hundreds, carrying pictures of loved ones abducted or missing, in this capital or that. Even the pictures of the demonstrators are not so very different, as if the pain had made peoples' clothing one. Usually it is black, but even where there is coloured material with some design, grief leaves only a small margin for variation. True grief unites not just hearts but many other things, and one common feature is indifference to appearance. Women go on marches that are alike in appearance and in the appeals made. Their scarves are bound tight on their heads, or else their heads are uncovered, as they walk in row after row, carrying the pictures of their sons, daughters and abducted loved ones.

Meanwhile we, the spectators, watch the television or, browsing through the newspapers, see the pictures among other pictures. We see the loved ones held up by hands or pinned on chests, in pictures with splendid, firm frames to keep the pictures from being lost. Isn't it enough, after all, that those portrayed in the pictures have been lost?

Has it ever occurred to us, at some time or another, to count the capitals and other cities where there have been demonstrations calling for the return of the abducted to their homes? We have nothing but the pictures – the pictures, that is, of those carrying pictures. The time came when I could no longer make out the difference between two demonstrations, one in Argentina and another in Beirut, till I read what was written on the pictures.

The story of the four abducted brothers from the Dirawi family became quite famous. There was not one demonstration or gathering where their mother was not there in the forefront, carrying on her chest four pictures, for her four abducted sons.

Amaal al-Dirawi, the wife of one of the four, Mansour al-Dirawi, told me what had happened. She had lived for a time in the Bir Hasan district near the Kuwaiti Embassy and in these critical times had been responsible for her husband's nephews, her sister-in-law being sick in hospital. Amaal herself had just the one baby girl. When she mentioned the four brothers, who lived next to one another in apartments for the displaced, she would also invariably mention their neighbour, who had come from the camp, out of fear, to stay with them. Amaal had been surprised to see her neighbour so afraid; but, on that Friday morning, she herself had felt an indefinable sense of fear. She said:

We heard them call out to us, tell us all to come out with the men. All at once I found myself shivering. I forgot about my husband and thought of my daughter. That's the truth. My daughter was being bottle-fed then. 'I beg you,' I said, 'my daughter needs feeding. If you take me out without letting me get the bottle, my daughter's going to die in my arms.' I implored them. 'For God's sake. Just let me go and fetch a bottle for the girl.' To be honest, I can remember one of them telling me: 'All right, all right.' They took my husband and all his brothers, and I went up and fetched the bottle for my daughter and came back down. All the time I was carrying my daughter, holding on to her, scared to death someone might take her away from me. She was only eight months old.

To be frank ... I was more worried about my daughter than my husband, because he was a man, after all, and he could look after himself, but my daughter was just a little baby.

They took all us women out. They made us go upstairs together with the men. Suddenly, I saw a Lebanese neighbour of ours come and tell them: 'Look, for God's sake, you've taken the men, what do you want with the women and children, and there are babies with them?' They asked him: 'Where are you from?' He said: 'I'm Lebanese.' The moment he told him he was Lebanese, the gunman slapped his face. Then, a moment later, he thought things over. 'All right, then,' he said, 'take the women inside. But if you go out, even if you are Lebanese, we'll take you along. Take the women and get out of here.'

So this good neighbour ended up saving us. But the moment we got inside the building, he told me: 'Listen, my dear, just pick up your children, take your clothes and get out of here. I can't protect you if someone comes in wanting to harm us, they'd shoot me, then shoot you.'

And so we all left. Our neighbour, who'd come looking for protection with us, had four children, and my sister-in-law had two ... we even took the doorman's son along, because none of his family were around.[123]

Amaal stopped several times to mention the date, first to jog her memory, then to confirm that it was Friday 17 September, at eight in the morning. This concurred with other testimonies:

From eight till two in the afternoon they kept dragging us out. We passed by the truck and saw them there. We saw the four: my husband and my three brothers-in-law. The truck had been parked on the slope by the Kuwaiti Embassy, towards St Simon and St Michel, by the sea. There's a United Nations centre there, further down. We saw them beating them up. They took out my older brother-in-law and started beating him up. My husband was beaten in the truck, as we watched.

They asked us: 'Where are you going?' We said: 'We're going to al-Burj, to my uncle's.' 'Are there any more men at home?' they asked. 'No,' we said, 'there aren't. You've taken them all.'

Then we decided we ought to go and complain to the Israelis, maybe they'd help.

We went to an Israeli centre near the Bahraini Embassy. The building's to the left of the UN centre, and further down the road there are buildings and villas, and there are the Libyan and Bahraini Embassies. We went and complained to the officer, and we begged him and started crying, but he said: 'We can't do anything. These are Sa'd Haddad.' He didn't say Phalangists. He knew Arabic, although he had an interpreter with him. The last thing he said was: 'You're terrorists, you're terrorists.'

We went out from there, and we found a car, I don't know what make it was, but there were two gunmen inside it. We'd given up hope, and we started complaining to them and crying. They asked us: 'Where are you from?' We said: 'We're Palestinians.' The moment they heard the word 'Palestinians', oh God, that did it. One of them pulled out an M16, or maybe it was a Kalashnikov, and told the Israelis: 'Shoot them, they're terrorists.'

Believe me, you people, I don't know how we managed to run ... how we got into one building and got out of another ... We were afraid to look back, in case they were behind us ... We kept walking and walking, till God helped us and we reached Burj al-Barajneh Camp, where my uncle lived.

It's been 18 months now without any news, we don't know anything about them. More than once we've been tricked by people, and we've paid money, but ... no news.[124]

Amaal also spoke of the others abducted in the same truck. Among them were the building contractor Abu Fayez Zaghloul, his son Ahmad Zaghloul, and others. She remembered the shape of the truck, which she described as being like large army trucks, open, without a canopy and with three steel bars on the sides. There was also a steel rod against which they would stand those abducted so as to kick them. You could tell, simply from their faces, that they had been subjected to beating and kicking.

As Amaal spoke of her tragedy, she said, in a pained and condemnatory tone, that 18 months had now passed and none had returned. Little did any of us know that 18 years would pass, and the world would reach the twenty-first century, with still no information forthcoming on the fate of her husband Mansour and his brothers Aziz, Ibrahim and Ahmad, the four sons of Faisal al-Dirawi. Nothing was ever discovered of the fate of hundreds of others who were abducted, or who disappeared, over those three days.

Testimonies regarding families saved by Israelis

The above accounts include numerous examples of Palestinians going to complain to the Israelis, and of the latter refusing to listen, professing themselves unconcerned or abruptly telling people to leave.

These testimonies ranged from that of Mariam – who was told: 'Go away from here, go away, we've nothing to do with anything' – to that of Amaal, who, along with the women and children accompanying her, were told: 'You're terrorists, you're terrorists.' On the other hand, there was the testimony of Um Ali, who, in contrast to her counterparts, encountered an Israeli soldier who came to her unprompted when he saw her fall, then calmed her and assured her, 'We'll go and fetch them if they're prisoners, hajjeh', then asked her to return next day.

The two accounts below deal with Israeli officers and soldiers who could not endure the sight of militiamen on the verge of committing mass killings at the pits and took the initiative to stop these crimes.

Account 33: Near the Kuwaiti Embassy

Um Kamal was a Lebanese mother of twelve children, living in the Horsh district. It was less than a five-minute walk from her house to the Akka Hospital, via Kuwaiti Embassy Street and a few alleys in the forefront of al-Horsh.

She had taken her children to the Akka Hospital to spend the Thursday there. Then, in the evening, when she returned alone to fetch some food, one of her neighbours told her how she had heard guns being fired but supposed they must belong to the Resistance. Um Kamal, however, disagreed. The way she had described the shooting, she told her neighbour, suggested not the Resistance but rather the Israelis and the Phalangists. Her sense of these things was, she said, never wrong.

As she was hurrying back to the hospital she ran into another neighbour, Um Yousef, who complained that the Israelis had harmed her husband. The woman herself was dripping blood. Um Kamal gave her first aid with what means she had available, then went on to the hospital, where she told people what she had seen. Then she led the Palestinian men who had believed her to the airport bridge. Her children she left at the hospital, confident no one would harm any Lebanese.

Waking at half past four in the morning, Um Kamal began once more to urge the men to flee, assuring everyone that women and children would not be harmed. Her adolescent children were also among those who had left. She herself entrusted herself to God and walked home to fetch food, confident no one would harass a woman striving to feed her children. She excused the hospital staff on this score, since, with so many people there, no one could have fed anyone. She said:

In the morning, at around half past five maybe, I reached the front entrance of the Akka Hospital. Seeing no one at the first turn, I started walking. Excuse me; my plastic slippers started making a noise, and they heard it and started saying to one another: 'Here she is.' Actually, they hadn't been waiting for me in particular, but for anyone passing by so early in the morning. I started looking round and found them lined up in two rows, on the two sides. You could have counted grains of sand easier than counting them, there were so many men standing there, with their weapons.

I said to them: 'What do you mean, son, here she is? For God's sake, I'm Lebanese, may God protect you all.' One of them yelled in my face: 'No. You're a terrorist bitch! Come here! Come over here! Georges, put her over with the others.'

I still couldn't understand what was going on. I went over to him and said: 'Son, what others do you want me to go with? Can you see any artillery piece on my shoulder or a gun in my hand? No, my dear, may God bless you. I'm not a terrorist. In any case, where could we flee to? We're displaced people. We're staying with others. For us, any hour and any minute can spell death. Fear God, you men, I'm the mother of twelve children.'[125]

The gunmen asked her a number of questions, trying to find out about everybody who had been in the shelter of the Akka Hospital, and whether there had been any armed 'terrorists'. The 'negotiations' between her and them resulted in the demand that she go back into the hospital to fetch her children, as evidence of her good faith; otherwise, they said, they would follow her and kill them. Two of them followed her up to the entrance of the Akka Hospital. She had no choice but to comply; but, being a decent woman who sought good for the others as well as for her children, and although ordered to be quick, found time to warn those hiding in the hospital and advise them to leave at once. Then she hurried back with the children and stood there with them, where the original talk with the gunmen had taken place. She had ten of her children with her – the two eldest having fled – as well as an Egyptian woman with four children. Thus there were, as Um Kamal affirmed, 16 people in all.

It was still not six o'clock. The gunmen ordered this small human convoy to throw whatever they had down on the ground. Then came an immediate second order: that they should all put their hands up. Unable to bear being insulted in front of her children and in front of the Egyptian woman who had sought protection through her, Um Kamal told them: 'Look, son, we're not terrorists.' 'Don't call me "son"!' the man shouted. She saw, finally, how things stood. 'As you like,' she said, 'as you like.' She put her hands up and walked as she had been told to.

Then, after a few seconds, she realized she had thrown down the ID cards with the other things. Accordingly, she asked if she could go back a little way and pick them up. One of them yelled at her to keep moving, but another told him to let her go back. Um Kamal took advantage of this to say:

'You say I'm a terrorist. You don't know whether I'm a terrorist, or even who I am, and if you shoot me now, you'll never know who I am. You'll waste my life without knowing anything. But if someone dies with his card in his hand, people will know who he is, and his family will come and take him and bury him.'

'Go on, then,' he broke in angrily, 'be quick about it.'

As I picked up the cards, I saw they'd moved forward with the children and got some way ahead. I started to hurry behind my children, while the gunmen were still behind me. I caught up with the children at the forefront of Hayy Ersal. I saw nothing in the street, but from the Ersal border on, God forbid, I saw the victims in piles. The victims were on the two sides, and I was walking in the middle. When I saw them, I got frightened. They'd put dirt on this one, a blanket on that one, or rubbish on this one or that. There was blood all over; the whole ground was blood. I kept stepping in blood as if I was stepping in water. One of my little children screamed in terror when he saw a victim still looking upwards. The gunman cocked his gun in his direction, and my son pleaded – 'I beg you' – and I don't know how it went off without shooting. God is great. We went on walking, and I was carrying a child in my arms, with the rest of my children on ahead of me. We walked till we reached the door of the Kuwaiti Embassy.

Across from there was someone sitting on a chair behind a dark table, throwing orders at people. The table was outdoors, below a house full of victims, with more victims below it. Near the table were more victims, and on the table, if you can believe it, there was food and drink. This man, sitting like a peacock, was talking in Egyptian dialect, and I didn't find out any more about him. As we stood there in front of him, he turned towards the children and said: 'Well, I must say ... good, good.' Then he burst out laughing and started pointing at the pretty girls, along with the others who were there with him ...

They brought a Palestinian woman with three children to join us, and two or three others. I know there were 23 of us when they made us stand under the hill of sand, by the pit. Beside us was a bulldozer, a big one. The two gunmen who'd brought us were standing next to the driver of the bulldozer, I don't know what they were telling him ... We were standing where they'd been burying the victims; in other words, they meant to bury us rather than take us out and be merciful. We were standing on a small slope, and they told us, 'get in a line', so we did. The gunman stood in front of us and was ready to start shooting.

I was last in the line, facing the street in other words. Suddenly, I saw someone who seemed to have come out of the blue, and I heard him yelling and telling him in English, 'No ... no ... no ... no ...', and he raised his forefinger to confirm the 'No ... no ...' My little daughter came closer to me and I told her: 'Don't be frightened, child, maybe God hasn't destined us to die.'

Let me tell the truth, you people. Let me tell the truth. The one who saved us was an Israeli. And although he was an Israeli, I pray to God to protect him and his children against death just as he protected our children and us, even if he was an Israeli.

The Israeli didn't leave us till he was sure they'd finally let us go. To get rid of us, they started yelling: 'Don't come back. Go off to the sea. Run off to the sea.'

I was afraid they'd come and shoot us in the back. I said to myself, 'Now they'll kill us'. But as I got closer, walking with my children, I didn't feel afraid any more. It wasn't a matter of courage. It wasn't courage, or anything of that sort. That's how God judges man and grants him patience and endurance, so he doesn't die before it's time for him to die.[126]

Um Kamal admitted that for several months after the three bloody days she was too frightened to sleep. The image of the gunman standing in front of them, his gun cocked and ready to shoot, remained fixed in her mind.

Um Kamal was a pious, God-fearing woman, and all her talk was mingled with religious references. When the meeting was over and we said goodbye to one another at the front door of her house, I could not forget her final words and her last, heartfelt appeal: 'Now, will you tell people what happened? God be with you. May God and Ali be with you. May God and Ali be with you.'

Account 34: At the Sports City

Um Ghazi Madi was proud of having been already eight years old when her parents left Palestine – that she knew Palestine. Her house was near Dar al-Doukhi, which has become a landmark of the massacre on Shatila Main Street.

Um Ghazi was being visited by her married daughter who lived in Tyre; the latter had come, with her two babies, for the 40-day mourning for her sister, who had been a victim at the Akar building when the Israelis blew it up using the (internationally banned) vacuum bomb.

The mother had never recovered from the loss of her daughter; she could not forget her for a moment and mentioned her constantly as she spoke, even at the height of her talk about the massacre. The pretext for the bombing was that Chairman Yasser Arafat had been on the ground floor of the building, chairing an important meeting. In fact he was not there – or perhaps, just possibly, he had been there and had left a little before the explosion. The outcome, in any case, was the total destruction of the building and the death of 250 of its residents, her daughter among them.

When Um Ghazi began talking of the events of the Thursday evening, she spoke confidently of the time: 'On the Thursday, between half past five and six o'clock, the Israelis came in.' Should anyone dispute this – saying she must surely know it wasn't the Israelis – she would reply firmly:

But for the Israelis, they would never have got in. Who else could have backed them up? Not the Israelis? I know they were Lebanese, and they were dressed in official army uniform, with Lebanese Phalangist Forces badges. I can't read, but my daughter can. I was getting supper ready. There were little children who needed to eat. Suddenly, I heard my daughter say, 'Kata'eb ... Kata'eb, Kata'eb,' so I looked through the window and saw them chasing Abu Ibrahim, up from the Doukhi house, and they were yelling at him: 'Hey, hey you ... you son of a bitch ... come back here ... we're going to kill you!'

What disaster was waiting for us? My husband has paralysis, he can't walk. We were all of us sitting round him that evening. First of all my son and son-in-law picked him up and took him in, so he could sleep inside in the bedroom. We went into the bedroom too, locked the door and sat up till morning.

As you'd expect, none of us could sleep. We spent the whole night asking ourselves what we should do. There was no way, I knew, for my husband to get out with us in his wheelchair. What should we do? Then I thought, he was a disabled man, they couldn't possibly do anything to him. I said to myself, 'I'd better hide the money we'd been saving, leave it with Abu Ghazi' [the name by which Um Ghazi called her husband, Younes Madi]. That was safer than keeping the money with us, as we didn't know what was going to happen ...

Next morning we heard them calling out. They were calling our names. To start with, I thought maybe they were people we knew. I peeped through the door to see who was outside and I saw a dark, bald man with big sunglasses, dressed in a short-sleeved white shirt. He was standing at the door with four of the Kata'eb. From the outside, they could see the living room and the pictures on the wall, and I heard them talking. One of the Kata'eb asked him, pointing at the pictures: 'Whose house is this?' And the bald man said: 'Younes Madi's.' Then he asked him: 'What do his children do?' And he told him: 'They're with Fatah.' Finally, he asked: 'And what does the father do?' And he answered: 'He used to be with Fatah, but now he's sick and asleep inside.'

I saw they had my nephew's picture with them, it was upside down, and the man asked him about the picture: 'What about Saleh al-Titi, how is he related to them?' He told him: 'He's the nephew of Um Ghazi, the woman of the house.'

He finished his questions. Then they went back and called: 'Younes Madi, come on out. Saleh al-Titi, come on out.'[127]

The bald informant was quite correct. Saleh was indeed Um Ghazi's nephew, and he had been visiting his aunt. He was also making preparations for his wedding, scheduled to take place following the Eid.

By sheer coincidence, a man was passing by; they shouted to him to stop, but he did not do so. Um Ghazi saw him running, then she saw them pursuing him, as though they had completely forgotten about the Madi family. She also heard the man's voice as he screamed in pain: 'Oh, mother!' Then the voice faded away.

Naive as she was, Um Ghazi supposed the man had been detained or locked in 'the room'. It did not occur to her that he had been butchered. What concerned her more was that, having been distracted in this way, the men had not returned.

Um Ghazi gave little thought to the fate of this man, whose final words had been a call to his mother. Indeed, she returned to the task of preparing food for the family, as it was now almost noon. Her daughter's children were ravenous, and she had to cook for both children and adults. The saucepan was still on the stove when the family decided to submit to the calls for surrender:

The megaphones were calling: 'Surrender ... you won't be harmed.' It was midday already. My husband and son-in-law both said: 'You, women, go and give yourselves up. You go on ahead and we'll follow.'

We went out and gave ourselves up. We found them asking in surprise: 'Where have you come from?' We told them: 'We were at home. Where could we go?' And they said: 'Well, maybe there's an underground tunnel.' We told them: 'We swear, there's no tunnel. There's a sick man sleeping in the inner room, and we're sitting round him.' Then they said: 'You women, you stay outside. We'll deal with you outside. All the men, go inside', and they made my daughter's little son go in along with the men. So I told them: 'That's not a boy, that's a girl, her name's Hamdeh.' The boy had long hair, because his mother had let his hair grow, she hadn't cut his hair like a boy's. They couldn't agree about it. Then one said to the other: 'Let her bring her along.' He turned to me and said: 'Go and fetch her.'

When my daughter saw that, she said to one of them: 'For heaven's sake, I beg you, my husband and my brothers, for the Prophet's sake.' He told her: 'Go to hell, go to hell, you bitch. What prophet? Come on out.' And he hit her. I ran and snatched her from him, while he was just getting ready to go in the house.

I can't count how many were going in ... The whole room inside was full, so was the hallway, and so was the whole house.[128]

Amid all the turmoil of the killers' bursting into the house, Um Ghazi contrived to get in too, wishing to bid farewell to her paralysed husband and hand him their life savings, the sum of 8,000 Lebanese pounds. 'You're sick,' she told him, 'and they won't do you any harm. But we're going to face death. Goodbye, Abu Ghazi ... we're going to die.'

Um Ghazi was not attempting to draw sympathy from her husband, who actually needed it more himself; she simply wanted to tell him they were 'going to face death', something of which she had been sure since she heard their words, 'we'll deal with you outside'. The paralysed man, however, reasoned that it would be best not to keep the whole amount. 'Take a thousand pounds,' he said, 'and keep it with you. You may have to go somewhere eventually.' At that Abu Ghazi could not hold back from weeping. Was it for himself or for his family? His wife placed the bundle of 8,000 pounds in the pocket of his blue-striped pyjamas.

Guarded by four gunmen, two in front and two behind, Um Ghazi's convoy of women and children began to march forward; yet the dreadful nature of the march did not prevent Um Ghazi's eyes from seeing the houses of friends and relatives. On the way she saw Um Fahed's body, and also that of her daughter's sister-in-law. The daughter had actually left for Damascus with her husband and the fighters, and so her sister-in-law had come to live in the house.

The hardest thing this family had to endure along the way was the possible loss of little Mahmoud, or 'Hamdeh'; this eleven-year-old boy had to carry his niece, but he fell and that was how they discovered he was a boy. They set him against a wall to gun him down, but finally held back after getting hold of all the money they possibly could.

The convoy, along with its four guards, reached the Sports City, where, on the field, she saw a bulldozer digging out a large trench. The gunmen then told them: 'You're all going down in this pit.' Um Ghazi went on with her recollections:

There were my daughters, Um Mahmoud – my son-in-law's aunt – the children and myself. There were a lot of women and children at the City. But we couldn't see further down. He said again: 'You're all going down in there.' The one driving the bulldozer lifted the shovel and filled it with sand. The gunmen came and were going to drag us down. So I told them: 'I beg you, for heaven's sake, just a drink of water.' My daughter started screaming and one of them started beating her. She had 3,000 pounds in her purse. He grabbed the purse and asked: 'How much is there in here?' She said: 'Only 3,000 pounds, for God's sake; take it all, but just don't kill my husband and brothers.' And he said to her: 'You're afraid someone's going to kill them? We don't want to kill them, we don't want to harm them.' And the money distracted his attention, and there was no time left for him to throw us in the pit. Just at that moment, a car came up delivering water for the people in the Sports City.

It was God's mercy. The official in the car was an Israeli. While he was in the car, he saw how this Phalangist was beating my daughter and snatching her purse and her money, with her little son sitting on her lap. The Israeli yelled out loudly, in English, pointing to the pit: 'No, no.' Then he pointed to the Sports City, and told them again they should all go there.

The armed thief started cursing and damning our religion, but he gave in to the Israeli anyway. We went to the City and stayed there from two in the afternoon till seven in the evening.

In the evening, they started getting active again and lined us up. We thought, if they lined us up, that meant they were going to let us go. But they stood, two on the outside and two on the inside, and they raised their guns at us. Once again the Israelis saved us. Seven Israeli cars arrived; there were a lot of them. We saw how the Israelis took them aside, and started talking and whispering with them. After a little while, an Israeli Jew who spoke the barest Arabic, with a heavy accent, came up and said to us: 'Girls. You know Fakhani? Go on. Go on. No return to your houses. If you go back … you die. Go to Fakhani.'

And we did run to al-Fakhani; we had to. The criminals were behind us all the way. They were afraid of the Israeli, but when we got a bit further the bullets started spraying us like rain. They couldn't bear the thought that God had saved us from their hands.

The trouble was that Um Mahmoud was fat and couldn't walk fast, and she started pleading with me: 'I beg you, Um Ghazi, don't leave me.' And my daughter turned back to protect us, although it was she and her children who really needed protecting. 'Please, daughter,' I told her, 'run with the children. We'll catch up with you.' The bullets kept on chasing us like rain. I told myself we were going to die for sure, we'd never make it.

Just as we reached the street, we saw an Israeli car that had been following us. The man inside it said: 'Why are you still walking outside? You could be killed any moment.' I said to him: 'I beg you, sir, let this old woman get in. Take her just to the bridge.' He said: 'Madam, that way's Kata'eb, this way's Israel. I can't go that way.' … I left the woman on the road and started yelling at the girls: 'Girls, girls, wait, wait, stop! Where are you going, you wretched creatures? To the Kata'eb?' They said: 'What do you mean, to the Kata'eb?' I told them the Israeli had just said so, and we stood there confused, not knowing what to do.

I swear … the women couldn't agree about it. I was dithering about where to go, standing there under the Cola bridge. There were maybe 20 of us women, still standing under the bridge. The bullets were still showering us, shooting from here, shooting from there. We didn't know how to get out of the situation. I looked up a little way, and I saw a man sitting close to the Arab University. I went to talk to him, with the girls frightened and yelling he might be a Kata'eb. I felt he couldn't be a Kata'eb, and I told my daughter: 'If I'm to die, I'll die, and if I'm to live, I'll live.' And we worked out some signals so I could let them know what was happening.

I walked up to the young man sitting there. He looked like an Arab, and he wasn't wearing a military uniform. I said to him: 'Hello, brother.' 'Hello, sister,' he said. I said to him: 'Brother, I need to know, are there any Kata'eb here?' The young man laughed and said: 'No, sister, there aren't any Kata'eb here. I'm Syrian. If there'd been any Kata'eb, you wouldn't have seen me here. I live here. Just three days ago the Israelis came here, then they left.'[129]

The group of women and children spent the night in the corridors of the Beirut Arab University. Twice they had escaped almost certain death: the first time from the death pit at noon, and the second time, in the evening, from the bullets pursuing them from the City up to the bridge.

As for the ones Um Ghazi had left behind at home, they found no one to save them from death. Um Ghazi spent the whole night waiting for morning to come so she could return home to check on her husband, older children, guests and neighbours. Then when she did return on the Sunday morning and saw what she saw, she realized how merciful those criminals had been who killed her daughter in the Akar building. There the people had died within seconds, and the vacuum bomb had aroused no terrified forebodings and tortured no one.

The end of the second day

- Of the three days, the Friday was the longest in terms of suffering, lasting a full 24 hours; in contrast to the Thursday – where the terror lasted around six hours, from sunset till midnight – and the final day – where it lasted around 13 hours, from midnight to one in the afternoon.
- The second day passed without the gunmen being able to enter either Shatila Camp or the Sabra district. They did, however, manage to advance slightly further along Shatila Main Street, up to the borders with Sabra. They also entered some houses in Hayy Farhat, on the right-hand side of the street.
- Flight from the camp itself was possible from the northern side, particularly through the Gaza Hospital side, which they did not reach before the Saturday.
- Some of those forcibly taken to the Sports City managed to flee, since guarding so many detainees was no simple operation.

- A number of families remained at home, not leaving at all. It transpired that the attackers supposed these houses to be empty.
- Referred to as 'the battle' by the Kahan Report, this second and longest day was more associated with retreat than with fighting: there were only two limited skirmishes, lasting just a few minutes, between attackers and defenders. The first was at Hayy al-Horsh and the second at Hayy al-Doukhi.
- Mass and individual murders continued, mainly inside houses, in some alleys, in the vicinity of the Kuwaiti Embassy and inside the Sports City.
- The bulldozers went on working still more intensively, their mission being to demolish houses over the bodies inside and to bury as many bodies as possible in pits already dug for the purpose.
- At the beginning of the day many women tried, individually, to search for victims, but were unable to discover anything. Their subsequent testimonies revealed, nevertheless, the point the massacre had reached.
- On the Friday the killing of families continued. Many families were exterminated in the middle of the day. The killers were no longer tense; all the Friday mass killings took place in the full knowledge of what they were doing.
- The mass killing took place not only in lines in the alleys, or inside shelters, as on the Thursday night. They were also carried out in pits either caused by the Israeli air force during the invasion or dug specifically for the purpose. There were a number of spots for killing of this kind, either through shooting or by burying the victims alive.
- On the Friday the crimes of rape continued. These were normally followed up by killing, especially in the case of Palestinian women.
- Many survived the day by sheer chance. But many also survived because people helped one another.
- The attacking gunmen put Palestinians and Lebanese in separate lines. It emerged later, however, from testimonies and from victims' names and nationalities, that the separation was merely artificial.
- The attackers' treatment of foreigners was marked out by a degree of respect. They made no attempt to harm them, but rather facilitated their departure.
- The Friday saw countless examples of Israeli soldiers' and officers' disregard for residents' complaints; they heard these with expressions of irritation and anger. That is not, however, to deny that humane attitudes were adopted by other Israeli soldiers and officers on a number of occasions. In these human situations, some Israeli guards prevented the committing of mass murder. There was, in other words, an evident discrepancy in the behaviour of members of the Israeli Army.
- Regardless of whether Israelis witnessed and prevented criminal activities, or whether they even refused to believe the statements of fugitives and were ruthless in their response, such contradictory attitudes, on the human and political levels, suggests that the Israelis knew what was happening. It seems likely that the soldiers in question, whatever their attitude, would normally have reported the matters to their superiors.
- There is no evidence that every Israeli soldier or officer who personally witnessed the attackers' mass killing operations at the pits, and who actively prevented them as happened near the Kuwaiti Embassy or inside the Sports City, did in fact report to his superiors. On the other hand, a witness from the Horsh district testified to having heard Hebrew spoken among the attackers, which points to knowledge, on the part of the Israelis, of what had been taking place. Further evidence is provided by a guerrilla from Al-Numour al-Ahrar, who testified that twelve Israelis, dressed in the Lebanese Forces uniform, had come and offered his group assistance from the Wednesday on; it was said that they had come to assist without their superiors' knowledge.
- The role of informants was more apparent than on the first day. Some residents were able to describe such informants in detail.

- The Friday might be characterized as 'hospital day'. The International Red Cross evacuated patients from the Gaza Hospital, as it had done at the Akka Hospital, but only after the militias had entered.
- The incursion into the Akka Hospital was characterized by a remarkable discrepancy between the treatment of foreigners, on the one hand, and, on the other, of Lebanese and Palestinians. A number of Palestinian doctors, nurses and patients were brutally killed.

5

Saturday 18 September 1982

According to a subsequent statement by Israeli officials, the attackers had been instructed to withdraw on the Saturday morning. However, the withdrawal was not concluded from Sabra and Shatila specifically before noon, and from the district as a whole before the afternoon. Moreover, this third day witnessed all the kinds of aggression against residents that had been carried out on the two previous days; it was, indeed, characterized by especially savage and brutal abductions and mass killings. It was also marked out by the degree of deliberate humiliation imposed, this reaching its peak on the long road of the 'final march', with the gunmen driving people along like sheep.

Even as dawn broke on the Saturday, residents were being rounded up from the alleys and side streets of both Sabra and Shatila – though not from the camp itself and its inner alleys, which the attackers were unable to enter. Had they, indeed, got into Shatila Camp on this third day they would have found it quite deserted. The main assembly points, from daybreak onwards, were at Sabra Square and in front of the Palestinian Red Crescent centre. A little after seven o'clock the 'final march' began from Sabra Square, continuing through Sabra Street, through Shatila Main Street, then on towards the Kuwaiti Embassy and, finally, from the Embassy roundabout straight on to the Sports City.

On this day the Israelis played a major role, reflected both in the continual blaring of megaphones, telling people to head towards the football field, and in the questioning of hundreds of local residents – following which some, though not all, were allowed to return home.

During the first part of the day, the most significant event was the incursion into the Gaza Hospital. This, though, differed from the parallel incursion into the Akka Hospital, in that the gunmen found only members of the foreign medical body, who were likewise ordered to take part in the 'final march'; though, in their case, towards the Command Centre of the Lebanese Forces for questioning, then, subsequently, towards the neighbouring Israeli Command Centre.

Sabra and Shatila between four and seven in the morning

Residents of Sabra, even those living near Shatila or on its borders, were still unaware of what had been happening. This is hardly surprising given the circumstances. There had been no announcements; the constant Israeli shelling, which preceded the advance of the militias, had forced people to stay indoors, and the attackers themselves only reached the edge of Shatila and Sabra Square on this third day.

Here, nevertheless, are three testimonies from residents who learned the news with total astonishment, as if Sabra had been located on some remote island rather than on the border with Shatila.

The first testimony comes from Um Majed, a hardy Palestinian mother who lived in Sabra Main Street near the imaginary line dividing Sabra and Shatila. Leaving her house with her daughter-in-law at six in the morning, she found nothing out of the ordinary in the Main Street. She had no notion there had been gunmen in the alleys of Sabra and that these had begun to round people up, let alone that there had been a massacre. Um Majed said:

At six o'clock I went to the camp to check if there was any bread. My son's children were living with me then; they needed food, so I asked my daughter-in-law to go with me to look for some bread. For three whole days we'd been frying dough to get by. We did go to the camp, but we didn't find anyone – there was no one at all, the whole camp had turned into a ghost town.

I looked up the road and saw several Doshkas [machine-guns] and RPGs, thrown down on the ground. I wondered what was wrong; for God's sake, those guys must really have been afraid of something if they'd thrown down their weapons like that. But who'd throw down his weapons anyway? Were they men carrying arms or a bunch of kids? As God's my judge, I hadn't heard so much as a word of any massacre, and no one would have dreamed Shatila Camp would be deserted like that.

God help us. Who did I see lying on the ground in front of me? It was Fidda, the daughter of Nafiz's son, I saw her suddenly, they'd dragged her off and slaughtered her. I walked a bit further and saw a man from the Sharqawi family, running. So I asked him: 'Why are you running like that?' He said: 'The Israelis are here.' My daughter-in-law and I decided we'd go to the Corniche and fill a couple of containers with water, and we did that and came back.

But I didn't go home. I stayed on the corner. 'We've made it out', I told my daughter-in-law. 'Go back home with the water and bring another container to fill up, the water may be off for a while yet.' She went, but she didn't come back. I waited a long time for her, then I walked as far as the entrance to the [Ali Hamdar] Café, and I saw the 'army' on both sides.

They didn't say anything to me, but I could see something was wrong. I went upstairs – we live high up – and I saw the doors were open. There was no one there at home – not my daughter-in-law, or my daughter, or the children. I called out their names, but no one answered. Why had they all gone out like that, and left the doors open?[1]

It was now approaching seven in the morning. The third day of the massacre was already actively underway, and still everyone, including even this courageous Palestinian mother, was unable to comprehend what was actually happening. Briefly leaving her home, she went straight up to the gunmen, supposing them to be from the Lebanese Army, and asked, in Palestinian dialect: 'What's wrong, son?' They simply laughed at her, and one of them made to hit her with the butt of his Kalashnikov. His colleague, however, pushed him to one side and pointed in the direction she should walk. She walked some way till she reached the Red Crescent centre, and there an appalling sight met her eyes. Had the earth suddenly opened and produced all the residents of Sabra and Shatila? Why were they all assembled here at this spot?

There, among the throng, she found her daughter, daughter-in-law and grandchildren. She stood with those standing there, then sat down with some of the others, awaiting the unknown.[2]

The second testimony comes from a laundry equipment repair man, who lived in al-Dik alley, one of the Sabra alleys where the gunmen had arrived quite early and started shouting, telling residents to come down straight away. Although an early riser and used to the sounds of early morning, he found it strange to hear a clamour like this at such an hour; looking at his watch he found it was just four in the morning. But – as he said later to a friend of his, who happened to be among those summoned at seven o'clock – there was no choice but to comply.[3]

This talk between the two friends took place at Sabra Square, where they had been assembled with hundreds of neighbours and other residents. Many sought the answers to questions, but few ventured to try and provide them, especially as the glances and rifles of the gunmen would be directed towards anyone heard whispering. The minutes passed like hours, the haphazard assembly swelling all the while, the whispering rising, but with nothing of any great significance said.

The third testimony comes from the employee in the X-ray department at the Akka Hospital, mentioned in the previous chapter. He lived in Sabra but failed to hear the summons as the others did, perhaps because he was so sound asleep or perhaps because the attackers did not actually reach his street and his home before seven in the morning.

This employee, waking just before seven, was surprised to find an aunt of his from the Barbir district standing there in the street and calling out to him. 'I've come to fetch you, nephew', she said. 'There's a lot happening, and you're a young man. You shouldn't be staying here.' His aunt was, he knew, a level-headed woman not liable to be swayed by rumours. He took what she said seriously and waved his hand to indicate he was coming down. On his way downstairs, he met an old friend of his who had come to pick him up in his car. There was little time for discussion. 'Right,' he told his friend, 'I'll come with you. But my aunt's downstairs, we must take her along too.' 'You've heard, I suppose', his friend said in a low tone, 'that they've got as far as the Gaza Hospital?'

They reached the street, where the aunt, there just moments before, had vanished. In a moment they almost found themselves face to face with an armed man. 'Stop right there, you two', he told them arrogantly. 'Where are you going?' The X-ray employee answered, without thinking: 'We're going to fill up with water.' The gunman gave a sneering smile. 'So', he said, his dialect making it clear enough he was Lebanese rather than Israeli, 'where are your containers? Going to fetch water, are you, without any containers?' 'The containers are in the entrance', the employee said. 'You son of a bitch', the gunman yelled. 'You're going to fetch water, and you don't even have any shoes or slippers on? Stop all this rubbish, both of you, and start walking. Go on, off to Shatila.'[4]

As they walked along side by side, the two friends noticed the streets were now crowded with people and gunmen. They heard another gunman, too, telling people to leave their houses open and come down. They weren't, they said, going to hurt anyone.

'This is unbelievable', one of them said. In no time they reached the Gaza Hospital, where Dr Paul Morris was standing and talking to a group of gunmen. The X-ray department employee knew Dr Morris well, since they had both worked at the Lahout Centre, the hospital brought into being during the invasion. He also knew some of the nurses, but did not, in those moments, dare to slacken his pace. Nor did he dare contemplate flight down the street leading to Ard Jalloul. Dozens had fled down it on the two previous days; now, though, it was crammed with gunmen ready to forestall any further attempts at escape. He weighed the chances of getting away at the vegetable market where there were a number of alleys – only to find two or three gunmen standing at the entrance to each, blocking off all possibility.

As they walked along, as slowly as they could, a jeep containing armed men with MP badges on their sleeves passed close by. The gunmen exchanged some words with them, then the driver said: 'Come on, get in. Stop strolling along like that.'

The remaining distance was hardly worth the ride. Almost at once they reached the Red Crescent centre, where the two friends found that everyone they knew from Sabra and Shatila was already there. They had all been rounded up, but no one had the least idea why, or where they were going.

Some people, the two were told, had been there since five in the morning, with still no end to the waiting. The second witness above, the repair man, was one of these. Although a friend since childhood, he asked the X-ray employee to stand apart, since the latter's post was at the Akka Hospital; he was, in other words, employed by the Red Crescent, which was affiliated to the PLO, and so was – as he put it – a Palestinian institution, despite its humanitarian role. Expressing his fear that the attackers would take their revenge on all of them, he concluded:

Don't hold it against me. Look, they're pointing at you! Maybe they already know you work at the PLO. Please, get over on the other side. For God's sake, don't hold it against me. Life's precious.[5]

Saturday was indeed like doomsday.

The incursion into the Gaza Hospital

The incursion into the Gaza Hospital took place at around seven on the Saturday morning. News of what had happened at the Akka Hospital the day before had been transmitted that same day, along with news of what had happened and was still happening in Shatila. Before the Friday was over, therefore, all those seeking refuge had left the hospital, as had the Palestinian and Lebanese medical staff and most of the patients; the latter either with their families or with the International Red Cross. All that remained, when the incursion took place, was a small number of patients, together with the team of foreign doctors and nurses, who had unanimously refused to leave, preferring to remain to protect the patients and the hospital.

The significance of the Gaza Hospital

Among the group of hospitals established by the Palestinian Red Crescent in Beirut, three were of special importance: the Gaza Hospital in Sabra, specially designed with a view to future development; the Akka Hospital, incorporated within a large building in the Bir Hasan district; and the Sumoud Hospital at Haret Hreik, which was in reality nothing more than an adapted underground garage. These three were known as the 'triangle', and of the three the Gaza was considered the top hospital with regard to size, quality of construction and general significance: it was not only of central importance in itself but served as the link with a number of Lebanese hospitals, particularly the nearby Ma'wa al-Ajaza Hospital sited in the street, known as Ghana Street, connecting the Sports City with Sabra Square.[6]

The Gaza Hospital had been relocated several times before being finally settled in Sabra, at the time the nationalist leader from Sidon, Ma'rouf Sa'd, was killed. If asked, indeed, in which year the hospital was set up, senior workers at the hospital would habitually say not 1975, but the year of the assassination of Ma'rouf Sa'd, who had been one of the most popular leaders among the refugees in Sidon and indeed in the whole of Lebanon.[7] The original site had been at the airport roundabout, the second at al-Hazmiyyeh – where it was known as al-Quds Hospital – the third at the present Sabra location. When, in the past, shelling had grown especially fierce, the hospital services had been transferred to the Beirut Arab University in Hayy al-Fakhani.[8]

Construction at the Gaza Hospital took off in the mid-1970s. The surveyor, Jubran Abdallah Jubran, constructed two separate buildings, facing one another, with the main one comprising ten floors. He also had the walls built in reinforced concrete as a safeguard in the event of wars and other emergencies. Work on the second wing had begun on 26 January 1982, on the anniversary of the Crescent's foundation. This new building had been designed to double the capacity, being equipped, eventually, with around 100 beds.[9]

Hasan Abu Ali, one of those in charge of the foundation works at the Gaza Hospital, told how, when the Israeli bombardment of the Sports City began on 4 June 1982, at a time when he himself was standing inside the hospital with a group of labourers to whom he was paying out wages, everyone felt the structure tremble for all its bulk and solidity. He accordingly told the labourers to hurry to one of the large shelters that were a special feature of the hospital. Yet however solidly built, and however spacious its shelters, could any building act as a shield against a massacre? Such was the reflection of the works supervisor, surveyor Jubran's right-hand man, as he painfully recalled the days of the massacre.[10]

Those overseeing the Palestinian Red Crescent were keen not only to construct solid hospital buildings and establish infirmaries (there were, in all, 13 infirmaries and clinics spread through West Beirut and linked to the Gaza Hospital) but also to speed up the development of hospital services, especially at the Gaza Hospital. However, barely two months after the development plan had been initiated, the Israeli invasion began, and the officials at the Red Crescent were consequently obliged to reduce the work at the Gaza Hospital in particular, given its location in the heart of the Sabra district; to compensate, as we have seen, they set up temporary and field hospitals in more secure districts in Ras Beirut.

Work at the Gaza Hospital did not come to a total halt during the invasion. A good-sized medical team remained; more indeed than patients strictly needed, especially as most had now been transferred to the other newly established temporary hospitals. Those patients who did stay, numbering no more than 20, had an underground ward set up for their protection.

If the number of patients was small, however, those seeking refuge in the hospital shelters were far more numerous; these latter amounted to almost 300, and the hospital provided food and shelter for them throughout the days of the invasion. At night the hospital, powered by its own electric generators, could be seen shining like a star, in stark contrast to the bumpy roads and thick darkness all around it.[11]

By early September, life at the hospital had returned to normal. It was, however, in need of a new medical body. A number of international humanitarian organizations responded to the Palestinian Red Crescent's request, sending doctors who had been working at various centres in West Beirut. The foreign organizations were, indeed, the prime force in putting the hospital back on track. Their staff, including doctors and nurses, now amounted to around 20 men and women of various nationalities: from Britain, Ireland, France, Germany, Holland, Norway, Sweden, Denmark, Finland, Singapore and the United States.[12]

One day before the incursion, a Danish television crew made a videotape of the interior of the Gaza Hospital, showing just how busy the hospital was at this time. According to Dr Paul Morris, this crew, from Vision News, arrived at half past ten or eleven o'clock on the Friday morning, then came for the second time a few hours later, in answer to a request from the Norwegian Embassy; he also noted the arrival of an official from the embassy. The videotape bore witness to the very large numbers of people seeking protection at the Gaza Hospital, and to the casualties and ongoing operations, throughout the time a massacre was taking place in Shatila and the surrounding area. These photographers could hardly have guessed that, if they had come back a third time at sunset, they would have found that most of those seeking refuge were now gone.[13]

The hospital/shelter

People began seeking refuge at the Gaza Hospital on the Wednesday – in other words as soon as the Israeli Forces began their siege of the Sabra and Shatila district. In the course of that day 200–300 of those living nearby came to look for protection there.

On the Thursday substantial numbers of families and individuals began to flee to the hospital; some did so to avoid danger, while others, having seen the danger with their own eyes, contrived to get away with the aid of divine providence.

Then, on the Thursday evening and on Friday, a number of men and women went to urge dozens of those in the shelters to leave at once and move on to the Gaza Hospital. We saw in Account 17 (p. 101) how an Akka Hospital nurse took it upon herself to get a large group out from one shelter, while a fighter moved to save the people in another, regarding the preservation of lives as the noblest course of action at that critical time. The Gaza Hospital was now the 'shelter'.

During the bloody Thursday night, hundreds of nearby residents remained there; in the hospital shelters themselves, on the staircases, even on the surrounding sandy areas. Though many hardly slept, their fear did not extend beyond the shelling to any apprehension of a massacre. Even those who had come crying out and warning – that the Phalangists were in the camps, that Sa'd Haddad was in the camps, that they were killing and slaughtering – were regarded as merely hysterical.

Those seeking protection continued to arrive through the Thursday and Friday, swelling the numbers considerably. Initially there was no one to make a count, since the main efforts were directed towards treating the injured and the casualties.[14] Estimates were provided, nevertheless, by members of the foreign medical staff. In her testimony given to the Nordic Commission in Oslo, the Norwegian nurse Vera Talseth said that the number had been between 1,500 and 2,000, most being women, children and the elderly, and that they had been utterly terrified. Given the sights they described, there was every excuse for such feelings.[15]

The American nurse Ellen Siegel gave an estimate of double this. Testifying to the Kahan Commission, she said those seeking protection at the hospital on the Thursday night numbered almost 4,000, half of these being inside the hospital and half outside, mostly spending the night in the large yard in front of the hospital.[16] It may be that Vera Talseth was referring solely to those inside the hospital, and that this accounts for the discrepancy. In any case the number was undoubtedly changing from one hour to the next. The Hospital Director, Aziza Khalidi, supplied a figure of 2,000 to the International Red Cross at noon on the Friday, and she herself went back on that same day and told the people to leave the hospital for their own safety. Eventually, as we shall see, there was no one left.

The injured began to arrive from two o'clock on the Thursday afternoon, and the operating theatre was in continuous action thereafter till the Friday evening. There was a constant flow of arrivals by day and night alike, and it was clear most of the Thursday's casualties had been struck by bullets. Some local men had assisted the Crescent rescue workers, first in searching for casualties through the nearby streets and other places as far as the Ashbal Camp and then in bringing these casualties to the hospital. The rescue workers informed the hospital officials that the nearest Israeli point was that close to the Sabri Hamadeh Palace, but did not report the presence of Lebanese militias, since they had seen none. This was natural enough given that the attackers had not as yet penetrated far into Shatila or Sabra. According to Aziza Khalidi, records showed around 50 casualties admitted to the hospital between two on the Thursday afternoon and five on the Friday morning.[17] Dr Paul Morris's figure was around 100 casualties, but this was clearly based on observation and estimate rather than official records; a number of casualties would not, in such circumstances, have been recorded following completion of their treatment.[18]

The testimony of Dr Per Maehlumschlagen, as supplied to the Nordic Commission in Oslo, both confirmed and supplemented the main points noted by Khalidi and Morris:

From the 15 September … we received civilians who were wounded with almost no break until Friday afternoon. On Thursday 16 September we received about 100 civilian wounded, about 80 per cent were children or women. Nearly all of them were wounded by bullets, gun shot. There were only few wounded by shrapnel. The ambulances could not move because there was shooting, and the only people who came into the hospital were those carried by others; so we concluded that these wounded people were just the people around the hospital area.[19]

The Singaporean doctor Dr Swee Chai Ang testified to the MacBride Commission that most casualties admitted on the Wednesday had been hit by splinters and brought in by their families. On the Thursday major cases resulting from stray gunshots had begun to arrive, struck mainly in the jaw, the head or the stomach, and the number of occupied beds had risen in the course of the day from 45 to 82, necessitating the transfer of 30 cases to the Makased Hospital. The mortuary filled up just as quickly. She also, she said, had pictures of the corpses. This doctor (who before coming to Lebanon had supposed all Palestinians to be terrorists) added that she had become deeply fearful she might be killed before having the chance to testify. In the most significant part of her testimony, she said it had been obvious to her, from the casualties, that the gunmen had entered the houses of the Sabra and Shatila residents and fired inside them.[20]

The British doctor Paul Morris's testimony to the Kahan Commission supported

Dr Swee's statement. He was certain, he said, that on the Friday casualties had been fired at from close range. The injured themselves, who were arriving at the rate of around ten every half-hour, described what had happened to them. The initial problem faced by the doctors was which cases should be given priority. In response to Judge Kahan's question as to what had happened on the Friday, Dr Morris said that as far as they were concerned there was no distinction between the Thursday and Friday, since they were operating, continuously and without a break, from the Thursday afternoon till the Friday morning at around ten or eleven o'clock. (We shall see later, however, that there were other doctors who continued to operate up till the Friday evening.) That should not, he added, be taken to imply that casualties had completely ceased to arrive; a limited number had arrived on the Friday afternoon and evening, between five and seven o'clock.[21]

Most firmly imprinted on the memory of the hospital was the tragic sight of the injured boy Milad Farouk, who told them, weeping, how the gunmen had killed his mother, father and brothers. While being operated on, he was screaming: 'Don't cut off my leg ...'[22] Milad Farouk's case was actually the first sign for the doctors that something abnormal had been going on in the camp. So two of the doctors, Maehlumschlagen and Witsoe, told Thomas Friedman, and they also mentioned the boy's account of how members of the Christian Lebanese militias had broken into his house and killed his family, including his newborn baby brother.[23]

There was also the sight of Um Ahmad Srour and her daughter, both wounded (see Account 25, p. 142). Um Ahmad told everyone of her family's fate but did not beat her face or weep hysterically; she gave her account with deep pain but without tears, and this led some level-headed people to believe her and conclude that there actually had been a massacre – though even then there were others who refused to do so.[24]

As for Samiha Abbas Hijazi, the woman who rescued the injured man in Account 14 (pp. 95, 139), she brought in this man,

Mustafa al-Habrat, and resumed her search for her daughter Zainab, confident he would speak. And so he did.[25]

Friday was to see not only the arrival of casualties but the departure of both casualties and patients, since all those families with relatives at the hospital had hurriedly come to fetch them. By noon on the Friday, many of those seeking refuge at the hospital had fled it, heading northwards, but there were still a few hundred when the southern woman Um Ali al-Biqa'i was going around searching for the lost members of her family; when she reached the hospital at one in the afternoon, she shouted at those men who had still not fled: 'You Palestinians, woe to you, what are you doing here? They'll come and kill you now, right there ...'[26] (see Account 26, p. 144). Others had likewise arrived and given similar warnings, till the hospital was finally emptied of the people who had sought protection there, along with most of the patients.

A number of those leaving the Gaza Hospital took part in a major demonstration near the Corniche al-Mazra'a, in an attempt to convince the Israelis that the Lebanese Phalangists and the Sa'd Haddad group were killing people in Sabra and Shatila, and that their only aim in trying to cross the Corniche was to reach a place of safety. But all was in vain. They were sternly instructed to return whence they had come.[27] Some added, in their testimonies, that an Israeli tank had directed its gun towards the demonstrators, forcing them to retreat.[28]

The decision to evacuate the hospital

At around ten o'clock on the Friday morning, Aziza Khalidi went to the International Red Cross Centre to request medical aid for the Gaza Hospital. At the same time, she informed the officials there of the presence of a foreign medical team comprising 22 doctors and nurses from various European nations and the United States, providing a list of their names which the Red Cross could in turn hand over to the Israelis, who would then assume responsibility for the foreigners' protection. She further told them there were around 2,000 seeking refuge.

She then returned to the hospital at around midday.[29]

While the Director was absent on this mission, Dr Swee Chai Ang was making a round of the hospital. According to her, the situation had deteriorated by the Friday morning; she added that the Intensive Care Unit, devoted to the care of patients operated on within the past two days, had become overloaded with highly critical cases. When she asked Dr Morris for a brief report at least, he took her to the mortuary, which was full of bodies. Many casualties had died before there was any chance to operate and the place was so small that the bodies – of elderly men, children and women – had simply had to be stacked one on top of the other.

The ground floor was also overcrowded. Some people there were wounded and awaiting treatment, others silent and trembling with fear. Still unaware of the massacre outside, Dr Swee Chai Ang could not comprehend such a level of anxiety. The children stuck to her, calling her 'the brave doctor', a name she commented on as follows: 'I wasn't brave at all, merely uninformed. Anyway, I'd been working so hard I had no time to be afraid.'[30]

After returning from the International Red Cross at noon, Aziza Khalidi realized the situation had grown worse and, assembling all the Arab members of the medical team, doctors and nurses in the surgery room, she told them to leave the hospital. They should all, she said, look to themselves, as she could take no responsibility for anyone. 'Leave at once', she said. 'I don't want to find any of you here in the hospital.' 'But where are we to go?' they asked. 'Go wherever you want', she said. 'Just don't stay at the hospital.' She also assured them that the entire foreign medical team would stay on to work at the hospital and that she, by virtue of her position, would remain with them till the International Red Cross arrived.[31] This message reached the crowds seeking protection inside the hospital and they began to leave accordingly. News of the massacre in Shatila had also leaked out to them from more than one source.

Ann Sunde, as we saw in the previous chapter, had ensured that the four disabled children were transferred from the Akka Hospital to the American University Hospital in the Norwegian diplomatic car. She then went to the Gaza Hospital, accompanied by the First Secretary at the Norwegian Embassy, by a different route – via UNESCO, al-Fakhani and the Beirut Arab University – so as to warn them and discover what was needed. None of the Israelis, she said, had stopped them on the way, and they had sensed nothing out of the ordinary.[32] In fact the massacre had not reached those alleys at all. The setting for the massacre, as will be seen, somewhat resembled a peninsula, and in such circumstances a boat that cruises close to the shore is rarely in a position to discover events on land.

Ann Sunde met with Aziza Khalidi and briefed her on what had occurred at the Akka Hospital; this happened, coincidentally, at the time when there were also reporters at the hospital, including Norwegian radio and television correspondents who met with the Norwegian First Secretary and received first-hand information from him. The Norwegian doctors also asked Ann to make contact with the International Red Cross and hand them a list of the necessary items.[33]

Khalidi confirmed that she had learned from Ann Sunde of all that had taken place at the Akka Hospital. She knew, in consequence, that those who had carried out the attacks and killings there were Phalangists. Nevertheless, she had, she said, heard nothing of the massacres within Sabra or Shatila.[34]

Neither witness was being disingenuous. Ann Sunde kept nothing back, and, if she made no mention of events outside the Akka Hospital, this was for the simple reason that she too knew nothing, having passed through none of the massacre streets.

From the Gaza Hospital, Ann Sunde made immediately for the International Red Cross centre and submitted the Norwegian doctors' requests. She then went on to the Norwegian Embassy, where the Chargé d'Affaires and a Norwegian reporter told her of what they had just seen in the southern part of the camp – they had had to stop there as a result of the heavy shelling and wait inside the car. Inside the 'camp', about 150 metres away, they had seen a bulldozer with around eight or ten bodies, as well as hacked off limbs, some still adhering to the sharp edge on the front. The moment he reached his Embassy, the Chargé d'Affaires sent a telex and made his report to the Minister of Foreign Affairs.[35]

For the second time, the two Norwegian men returned to the Gaza Hospital, accompanied by Ann Sunde, who had a further request from Aziza Khalidi regarding the necessity of a mission from the Red Cross to supervise the evacuation of children and critical cases from the hospital.[36]

Artillery fire was constant throughout the Friday, although it was fiercer at some times than at others. In the afternoon it grew so intense that windows broke and doors slammed. When smoke began to seep into the hospital, those in charge were obliged to transfer all casualties and patients from the fourth to the first floor. Even here they hardly felt any safer, keeping close to the walls for protection as though the hospital were about to be shelled at any moment.[37]

At around half past four in the afternoon, Khalidi held a meeting with the foreign team. Regrettably, she told them, she must now depart, leaving the hospital in their charge. She would, she said, tell the Red Cross of their presence there. In fact, the International Red Cross team, bringing with it medical equipment, medicines, food supplies and five foreign health workers, arrived at six o'clock.[38]

Khalidi had already, at noon, informed the Red Cross of the 82 patients and 2,000 displaced persons at the hospital. By six, however, all the latter had left, as had most of the patients; the Red Cross had to evacuate only a small number of patients together with seven children. This happened between half past six and seven in the evening. Khalidi left with them in the role of a Red Cross rescue worker, leaving the remainder of the patients in the care of the foreign team.[39]

Vera Talseth was one of the nurses who stayed. She said in her testimony in Oslo that 40 patients, 24 doctors and nurses and a small number of Lebanese had remained there at the hospital.[40]

It is not clear how Talseth could be so sure that the Arabs who stayed were Lebanese as opposed to Palestinian. Possibly they themselves said this, not wishing to admit their Palestinian identity for fear of putting pressure on the foreign team, who were now the sole protectors of the hospital and its occupants. As Palestinians, they had been officially and publicly told to leave the hospital. If they failed to do so, this would either have been because they had nowhere to go in the present circumstances or because one or more had relatives among the patients and wished to stay close by them. Who can be sure of the truth? But it is quite clear from the testimonies of the doctors and of residents standing on the Sabra–Shatila road that these Arab workers, who left the Gaza Hospital with the foreign team, were killed along the way, and that they were Palestinians. This will be discussed further in Account 35 (p. 184).

One of the most significant occurrences at the hospital on the Friday was the Norwegian doctors' refusal to save themselves by accompanying their Embassy's Chargé d'Affaires when the latter arrived a second time with the International Red Cross mission that had come to evacuate the hospital.[41] They opted to remain with their colleagues and their patients.

The last night at the hospital

None of the foreign team could have known that night would be the last, though the imminent danger was clear enough. They felt as though they had been forgotten on some remote island, with no one asking about them. Even when they tuned in to the radio news, they failed to learn of what had been taking place outside just a few metres away. Nor had they any idea who was responsible for the bombardment. When the American nurse Ellen Siegel was asked what they had learned from the various radio stations, she said:

All I knew from the radio was that Grace Kelly had died and all Monaco was in mourning; Bashir Gemayel had been assassinated, and that Israel was in West Beirut and occupying the Soviet Embassy. But I knew that something was going on in that camp, and that nobody was bothering with us. Where was the International Red Cross, where was the American Ambassador, where was the UN, the news media – what in the world was going on here?[42]

Ellen Siegel was in the Intensive Care Unit on the Friday evening when two well-dressed men arrived, their clean and starched shirts a sign they had not been involved in any field operation. They were also shaved and their hair was neatly combed. One of them (his sleepy eyes suggesting, she thought, that he might have been taking hashish) spoke to her and, having only a limited knowledge of English, asked whether anyone there spoke German. When she sharply asked him what he wanted, he answered, in his limited English, that he wished to know whether the Phalangists would be returning at nine o'clock next morning to kill the Palestinian children. She asked him a second time and received the same answer. The nurse affirmed that there were no Palestinians at the hospital; all the workers were foreign, and there was in fact one German female worker. She called this German woman, who heard the same questions and gave the same answers. The man spoke good German, the worker said, but in the academic style commonly taught in schools. It was not a native manner of speaking.[43]

The evening was relatively quiet, despite the noise from machine-guns and shelling, which was in fact sufficient to make the glass crack and shatter in the Intensive Care Unit. Some of the patients chose to leave, preferring the risk of this to the risk of staying.

Dr Swee Chai Ang performed the last three operations, one of them on a twelve-year-old boy shot three times and left for dead on the Friday morning, managing through divine providence to reach the hospital. He had been hit in the arm, foot and index finger. When finally able to talk, he had said, 'They were Israelis, Phalangists and Sa'd Haddad', before going into shock. This wounded boy, Dr Swee said, eventually survived.[44] The boy, as Dr Morris confirmed, was Munir.[45] (See Account 12, p. 91.)

Subsequently, when 30 years old, Munir himself described those critical moments at the Gaza Hospital. He had, he said, run as fast as his pain and his wounds would allow him and at last had met a man who instantly recognized him and carried him on his shoulders to the hospital. Beyond that he remembered nothing, had no memory of having spoken and given the identity of those who had fired at him and the others. He had quickly fainted, but he remembered the operating theatre and having seen people wearing white gowns.[46]

The two final operations were on a mother and her small child, who had been hit while playing with his friends. The mother's case was the more serious, but both needed blood, and both were of the same blood type, of which there was only one unit available at the hospital. Dr Swee decided to give the transfusion to the mother on account of her more critical state but, while she was discussing the matter with the nurse, the mother overheard and her maternal instinct led her to understand. She begged them to give the blood to her son, and her final request was for a tranquillizer, which she was given, while her son received the blood. The mother died that night. The boy was saved.[47]

This was Dr Swee's final operation at the Gaza Hospital; she was one of the surgeons who had worked continuously over the past days. Between 15 and 18 September, she recalled, she had spent 72 hours, almost without break, operating on the patients who had been flowing in. Whenever she left the operating theatre on the lower floor her immediate and urgent task was to examine the new wounded before making a swift decision about who should be operated on next.[48]

When I interviewed Dr Paul Morris at length at an American professor's house on the American University campus, this British doctor was being pursued by the security authorities as one whose residence in the country was no longer considered desirable. His residence permit had not been renewed and as such he was regarded as being in Lebanon illegally and could no longer move around. In fact I had some considerable difficulty in locating him. The professor's wife received us in her house at night so that his arrival would not attract attention. I asked him about that last night at the hospital but he spoke of this only in a desultory way. He was far more concerned about what had happened generally at the hospital, and soon he had moved on to the subject of the future of Palestinian children. This was his prime concern. As for what had happened specifically on that night, he was content to say that he had barely slept, had examined the patients a number of times, thought continually of what the next day might bring, and reflected on the operations that needed to be carried out next morning. He did not, though, speak of his most important experience that night.

It was Dr Swee who actually spoke of the private preoccupations of her colleague Dr Morris, the man she regarded as a model for all of them in terms of patience, endurance, self-control and unstinting effort. His whole life was his humanitarian work, and vice versa. That night, however, he was just like any ordinary man.

That night, so Dr Swee noted in her diaries, he had written a letter to his wife Mary and asked her to deliver this should any harm befall him. Realizing how deep his fears were, she decided to try and soothe him. 'Hey, Paul', she said, 'you're talking as though you're going to die. You're joking, aren't you?' Paul Morris was, however, quite serious. She took the letter without further comment, promising to do as he had requested.[49]

That evening, before the multinational team of doctors and nurses went off to sleep, they held a meeting in which they discussed the possibility of the Israelis, or Haddad's group, or the Phalangists, coming to the hospital, considering what they should do in this event. After some discussion they decided priority should be given to negotiation in the interest of patients' lives and safety.[50]

The doctors marched off for questioning

The doctors' and nurses' testimonies differ with respect to the exact time the gunmen arrived at the hospital. Some said they had seen them standing in front of the hospital at a quarter to seven in the morning; others that they had arrived at seven o'clock or half past seven. According to some there were five gunmen leading the group; according to others there were ten. What all testimonies agreed on, however, was that the gunmen who stayed outside were more numerous than the group that actually advanced on the hospital.

At this early hour, the doctors began to respond to the summons that they should come out and assemble in front of the hospital.

According to the testimony of Dr Juhani Pajula, in Oslo, five Lebanese gunmen arrived at the Gaza Hospital at half past seven on the Saturday morning, introducing themselves as members of the Lebanese Forces. They were equipped with helmets, machine-guns and a radio. The man in charge of the group said that every foreigner working in the medical field should come out of the hospital. This was merely 'for a routine check'. There were still six patients in a critical condition in the Intensive Care Unit, and 32 other patients. The doctors asked the gunmen that two of the nurses should stay to care for the patients, and the gunmen agreed to this.[51]

Nurse Ellen Siegel said that one of the hospital workers woke her at seven in the morning, after the attackers had arrived. The moment she looked through the window, she saw a whole army of combatants; when she went down, she saw about ten soldiers very neatly and smartly dressed, with 'Lebanese Forces' written on their clothes. Siegel confirmed what a number of her colleagues had said earlier, regarding the gunmen's permission for two nurses to remain at the hospital. She had also, she said, had to assure them twice that she was not Lebanese.[52]

How many foreigners were actually taken off for questioning? According to some testimonies, these numbered 18 doctors and nurses, of both sexes; others spoke of 20 or 22. The difference may perhaps spring from whether or not numbers included workers brought in by the International Red Cross on the Friday evening, or whether or not the two members left at the hospital were taken into account. More importantly, it should be borne in mind that in such circumstances numbers are frequently given as final when in fact they are simply estimates from memory.

The members of the foreign team walked from the Gaza Hospital to the Main Street, which had, at the time of the Palestinian factions, been known as Abu Hasan Salameh Street. They walked south as far as the intersection of Sabra–Shatila Street with Kuwaiti Embassy Street, where the gunmen forced them to turn right towards the Kuwaiti Embassy then on towards the sea where, on the left, the Lebanese Forces headquarters was situated.

The foreigners' testimonies concerning incidents on the way were similar, and they supplemented one another.

Dr Juhani Pajula said that his first impression of Shatila, as they went down its main street, was of significant new destruction. There were houses burned and blown up, the roads contained pits produced by explosives, bullets were strewn here and there, three bodies had been thrown to the side of the road, and a large bulldozer had collected all the rubble, making a series of sizeable heaps.[53]

Nurse Ellen Siegel said that there had, all the way, been gunshots from both sides of the road, and she had walked with her head down to avoid being hit. Killing had, she believed, still been going on while they were walking. At one point she looked to the right and saw three bodies: one of a man shot in the head, one of a veiled woman and one with a cover over it. She also saw hundreds of Palestinians, both camp residents and medical care workers, sitting on the two sides of the road. Some stood up and greeted the medical team with a victory sign. Behind these, too, were people who worked at the hospital and knew the doctors and nurses quite well. They began pointing affectionately towards the team, trying to approach, but the 'soldiers', as she called them, prevented them from doing so.

Siegel also said that, the more they walked, the more new 'soldiers' appeared in front of them. These, though, were of unkempt appearance and wore cheap clothes without badges. One was wearing a beret, and alongside him was a woman 'soldier'. She was pretty, and she had cold blue eyes and long curly hair. They both shouted at the foreign medical team, in English:

You're dirty. You're not Christians. Christians don't treat terrorists who kill other Christians. You're Baader-Meinhof, Communists, Socialists, dirty people.[54]

Two things attracted Ellen Siegel's attention. The first was that the gunmen had a number of walkie-talkie devices; the second was the presence of bulldozers at the end of the main street, which had the right of way over pedestrians so that the team had to wait at several points while they passed through. It was clear a number of houses had already been bulldozed, making the road wider than before.[55]

As for Siegel's colleague Dr Swee, what most attracted her attention was that the guards escorting them were replaced four times on the way. She saw a number of militiamen without any distinguishing badges; merely a green uniform along with baseball caps. As for her observations on the walk as a whole, she testified before the MacBride Commission that she had seen, at the sides of the street, five or six bodies that had apparently been lying there for a long time. She also saw three huge bulldozers that were tearing down the houses of the camp and reducing them to rubble. She was perhaps (she continued) imagining things, but she thought there might have been bodies in among the rubble.[56] She later added to this picture in her diaries:

Large bulldozers were at work tearing down shelled buildings and burying bodies inside them. I could hardly recognize the camps. The houses were now heaps of rubble. Within the rubble, I could see newly-hung curtains and pictures. The dynamited, partially bulldozed homes still had fresh paint on them.

… I thought of all those who died, and the ones rounded up by the gunmen on the roadside. From the terror in their faces, they knew they were going to be killed once we left them. Suddenly I found myself wishing that the PLO fighters had not been evacuated. They could have defended their people!

I felt myself getting angrier and angrier as we were marched further down the road. A doctor is a doctor, but a doctor is also a human being.[57]

What happened immediately before the questioning? Ellen Siegel gave the following description:

At the end of Rue Sabra, we turned right and they told us to take off our white lab coats. Then they lined us up against a brick wall, filled with bullet holes. About 40 or 50 soldiers, with their rifles aimed, stood in front of us, one by one, and everything was very quiet. These soldiers were dressed in Lebanese Forces uniforms. They're frightening looking; the look in their eyes is scary. I really thought this was it. I said to the woman next to me: 'Do you think we're going to die?' She said: 'Yes, I think we might.' I think all of us felt that this might be the end. It is very interesting what you think about at that point. Do you think about the great loves in your life, or do you think you want to scream and say don't kill me, do you want to cry? But you don't do anything, you just stand there. And you think 'nobody will know that I'm dead, I'll just die in this heap, in this Palestinian refugee camp, even the Palestinians won't know I'm dead'. You think nobody is going to know that you're dead.

This lasted a couple of minutes. Then most of the soldiers went back into the camp, one by one, with their guns cocked. The rest marched us up the street past the Kuwaiti Embassy to the roundabout. Just past the Kuwaiti Embassy was a clearly visible Israeli soldier, in uniform, with three Hebrew letters on his lapel. I didn't get near him, because I was frightened; I thought since I'm Jewish I shouldn't get too near the Israelis. The Israeli soldier talked to a couple of people in our group – I don't know what he said – then he disappeared. We continued our march with the same soldiers ...[58]

Ellen Siegel was asked whether she thought the Israelis had seen them while they were standing against the wall:

Absolutely. Clearly we were not camp people, we were wearing green and white, we were blonde haired and light skinned. I believe the Israelis saved our lives. I believe that the Phalangists and Haddad (if they were also there) would have killed us because they're crazed, and I do believe, in all honesty, that our lives were saved by the Israelis.[59]

The Irish doctor Phil McKenna, being closer to the Israeli soldier, was able to hear what he said. He had, she testified, appeared suddenly in front of them, from nowhere, and asked: 'Where are they taking you?' They answered that they were being taken to the next building down, and they asked that an Israeli official should come at once.[60]

As for the scene where the gunmen pointed their rifles at the doctors to make them think they were going to kill them, Dr Swee said that she was, in those moments, engaged in a furious argument with them, so that she was not fully aware of what was happening. All she could think about was that these gunmen had dragged them from the hospital so as to be able to kill the patients. Later, however, she learned from friends that the gunmen had ordered them to hand over all their possessions, take off their white uniforms and stand against the wall.

There were two bulldozers ready to bring the wall down on top of them. There was also a group of soldiers standing in front of them with machine-guns, as if about to shoot them all. When she heard this from her colleagues, she remembered how she too had taken off her white uniform and walked towards the wall. Her concern was to look beyond the moderately high wall to see if the bulldozers were trying to eridicate the bodies piled up behind. But, as she herself described it, her extreme anger blinded her sight. Also, if she took little notice of the militiamen pointing their guns at them as if about to execute them, no doubt she had reasoned that such things were intended to instil fear; so utterly furious was she that morning that she was beyond fear.[61]

The questioning of the foreign doctors and nurses

The militiamen assembled them behind the United Nations building, and there the questioning began. The doctors and nurses were ordered to sit down on the ground. Their passports were also confiscated.

The gunmen began with a show of emollience. They themselves, they said, were Christians, who had killed no one; they also expressed interest in the doctors' backgrounds and families. This was followed by repeated questioning, with the same questions asked. During this period, a Palestinian boy, injured in the chest and neck, was brought into the yard and the militiamen began to treat his wounds, as if to show their civilized attitude even towards Palestinians. Dr Juhani Pajula commented that the boy was obviously quaking with terror when they eventually took him away.[62]

Dr Paul Morris actually approached the boy to watch the work of the doctor treating him, but they thrust him aside. All he was able to see was four small, separate wounds from which fresh blood was seeping. This he found strange. The only possible explanation, he felt, was that someone had given the boy cuts in four different places just before handing him over.[63]

Dr Phil McKenna said that some of them were questioned in German, others in English. A 'woman soldier' came and expressed her utter astonishment that they were all Christians working for the Middle East Council of Churches, yet were working with Palestinians at the Gaza Hospital. How, she asked, was that possible? She further asked whether they had volunteered for the work or had been sent on the instructions of others? Why had they not been working in East Beirut? At Mother Teresa's home for children, for instance?[64]

Dr Swee described the Forces woman as having been pretty with black curly hair and cold blue eyes, which matches Ellen Siegel's description of the 'soldier' who intercepted them while they were being taken for interrogation. Her character also matched. She became utterly furious when she discovered the Singaporean Dr Swee was Christian, yelling at her: 'You're a Christian and you dare to help Palestinians! You're just dirty!'[65]

This yard, at the headquarters of the Lebanese Forces, provided abundant evidence of an Israeli presence: Hebrew newspapers, along with food cans, beer cans and bottles of alcoholic drink, all made in Israel. The dates of the Hebrew newspapers lying around ranged between 15 and 17 September. Still more important was that the men of the Lebanese Forces did nothing

without consulting an Israeli officer, either directly or over a radio.[66]

After questioning that lasted an hour and a half, the militiamen returned the team members' passports and told them they would be passed on to the Israeli Command Centre, which was in a different building about 150 metres away.[67]

Ten minutes after their arrival there, a crew from Israeli Television arrived, along with Israeli soldiers carrying cartons with bottles of water, pears and bread. The crew then took shots of the medical team while they were eating. The Israelis showed no interest whatever in the doctors; they did not even ask what they were doing at the Command Centre.

The Saturday was Rosh Hashana, the Jewish New Year, and thus there were large numbers of young soldiers going in and out of the Command Centre with *yarmulkes* on their heads.[68] Ellen Siegel commented that – being Jewish herself – she found the sight intolerable in these particular circumstances.[69]

The testimonies of Dr Swee Chai Ang and Ellen Siegel complement one another. The former wrote in her diaries that they had, at the Command Centre, met with an Israeli officer who told them not to worry, that he would do everything in his power to help them and their patients. With the Israeli Television cameras running, the Israelis also gave them food and water. The building comprised six floors, which would, she concluded, undoubtedly have facilitated surveillance of anyone in the camp. She also heard from them that 'they're trying to protect us from the Haddads', and she described further how a number of the gunmen were outside at that time harassing one of the girls of the medical team who worked as a physiotherapist, trying to take her away by force. When the doctors complained to the Israelis, an Israeli officer went out and immediately put a stop to it. Whether the militias were Phalangist or Sa'd Haddad, Dr Swee remarked, it was obvious they were taking orders direct from the Israelis.[70]

The medical team asked the Israelis that some of the team should be allowed to return to the Gaza Hospital to attend to the patients. Just three men were permitted to go: two doctors and a nurse. When Dr Swee talked to these subsequently, she learned that a colonel had taken them to the Sports City. There, after the doctors had demanded some kind of security – anything, they said, might happen to them – this officer wrote a safe-conduct permit for them in Hebrew. 'Don't worry', he told them, 'this pass will get you through the whole camp.' The doctor refused to take the document. The Haddads, he said, read Arabic, and the permit must be written in that language. 'Don't worry', the Colonel said again. 'just show it to the Haddads, you'll get through.' Still, though, the doctor insisted, till the colonel finally relented and summoned someone to write the permit in Arabic. From there they went on to the hospital with the permit in their hand,[71] transported by a United Nations vehicle that took them direct to the hospital.[72]

Dr Phil McKenna's testimony in Oslo confirmed the above means of transport to the hospital. She also noted how, when the Israeli officer offered to take the three of them to the Sports City, he added that he and his colleagues had no authority beyond that point. Anything after that was outside their jurisdiction.[73]

Dr McKenna further said that, when the officer handed the three the permit, she had told him: 'No one will understand this. You need to write it in Arabic.' 'No, it's OK', the officer had answered, 'it will be understood.' She had insisted, nevertheless, that the permit be made out again, in Arabic, and the others had done likewise. They had had to wait five minutes for someone who knew Arabic to come and write it.[74]

Dr Paul Morris affirmed that the permit, originally in Hebrew, had also been made out in English but that the doctors insisted on having it written in Arabic, especially after they had heard three times, while at the Israeli Command Centre, that those who had entered the camp were Sa'd Haddad's men, who had Arabic as their mother tongue.[75]

Around 16 or 17 doctors and nurses were still there at the Command Centre, and they asked to be taken into the city. The Israelis refused to take them to the Hamra district because of the risks involved, but did agree to take them to the Corniche al-Bahr. Ellen Siegel, who knew Beirut better than the others, got in the first jeep, while the rest got in a smaller jeep, and they were given a ride to a spot not far from the American Embassy, where they learned that the International Red Cross had returned to the Gaza Hospital and transferred the patients to other hospitals. Accordingly, the doctors went to these hospitals during the afternoon and examined the patients.[76]

The 'final march' to the Sports City

As the residents of Shatila had been forcibly marched to the Sports City on the Friday morning, so those of Sabra were marched on the Saturday. There were, nonetheless, certain differences. First, the gunmen, on reaching the heart of Sabra, were able to round up many more people than they had the day before. Second, they were fully aware that Saturday was their last day, and they exerted themselves to exploit what little time remained by maximizing the killings and abductions. Third, the number of bulldozers, and therefore the work they did, was doubled on this day, and their activities were carried out more openly.

The first stage of the 'final march'
The 'final march' began between seven and half past seven in the morning; individual people recalled the starting time according to their position in the march or to their particular memory. No one, though, realized what was going to happen.

Megaphones were calling out for the surrender of weapons and for people to go to the Sports City, just as they had done earlier. More people were marched than on the previous day, when it was presumed by some that no one had remained at home. What added to the people's astonishment was the sight of the group of foreign doctors and nurses walking along the same road. They were not, however, allowed to approach the team.

Hajj Mahmoud Rukn, a virtuous and pious man from Sabra, was one of the people thus marched along to an unknown fate. With his beard – long left uncut, his long white gown and the skullcap on his head, he seemed more like a holy man than the professional house painter he was. Hajj Mahmoud never minded if someone called him 'the shaykh'; it was, after all, a seemly, indeed holy title. And perhaps these gunmen, whose intentions were still unclear, might respect him accordingly. Could a holy man fail to be respected?

Early that morning, Hajj Mahmoud had heard a pounding on his door; on opening it he had found gunmen there in front of him, yelling to know why he had not obeyed the summons and come down into the street. This he now did, thanking God he had managed to seize his rosary and packet of cigarettes. He added:

I swear to God. We'd all of us look down the street and see people being driven along like sheep. The Kata'eb were walking on both sides, with their machine-guns and ammunition. It was a sight you couldn't ever imagine. But we survived it all. I was afraid of what might happen, frankly, when I saw them driving the foreign doctors along. It's true they showed them some respect, but they were still marching them by force.

We walked along Sabra–Shatila Main Street towards Bir Hasan and the Akka Hospital, and we reached the Ali Hamdar Café and crossed less than 25 metres further down. Then the alleys began, and we started seeing things you'd never believe possible. Passing the entrance to one alley, we saw an elderly man and an elderly woman, whose scarf they'd ripped off. They'd both been killed; one with an axe, the other shot. The marrow of the woman's bones was exposed. We saw it because she'd been unveiled. The two bodies had been booby-trapped too.

When I first saw all that, I said, 'Oh God! Oh God!', then he yelled at me: 'Don't go any closer, you son of a bitch.' Why? Was it likely I was going to go any closer? As I looked, I saw the edge of the bomb appearing under the body. They'd put a bomb there, you could see it easily, and taken out the safety catch; the man had a bomb put under his body too, just like the woman. Her head was over his. All that was at the forefront of the camp, and I said: 'I testify that there is no God but God, and I testify that Muhammad is the messenger of God.' Of course, to be honest, I said it silently, and I kept on saying to myself: 'Allahu Akbar, isn't there

anyone to stand up to them? Where's the National Movement? Are we sheep, or what?' Up to then, I tell you, we still had no idea there'd been a massacre. We'd heard they'd been slaughtering people at the camp on the Thursday and Friday, but we hadn't believed it … They'd said it wasn't Israel but Sa'd Haddad. We hadn't believed it …

On the way, we saw a single house in which they'd found 21 bodies: women, children, old people and young men. I mean, they were obviously all from the same family. For God's sake, I can't say any more. It was the most dreadful street I ever walked down in my life.

Suddenly, they said: 'Stop right here.' So we did.

They started calling people out, and each one would go where he was told to go. My group happened to be at the end of the street, I mean, before Sabra–Shatila Street crosses with Akka Hospital Street, about 25 metres before. We stood still. One of them said: 'Right, keep standing like that.' But we couldn't do it, so he came back and yelled: 'You, you son of a bitch … you, all of you, sit down right here, by the side of the road.' So we did that. After he'd rounded up a lot of people, this same man came back and yelled: 'Stand up, you … all of you, stand up.' We did, we gathered on the two pavements.[77]

The employee from the X-ray department, who had been the first to see the Israeli vehicles at dawn on the Wednesday and who had had no time to pick up his slippers on the morning of this long day, now had time enough to observe the street and the area round about. He was walking along barefoot, unkempt and unshaven, in worn-out trousers like a labourer's on a building site. It was some time before he could put his hand on a pair of plastic slippers – probably a victim's.

The employee was becoming overwhelmingly concerned about his appearance. Would they not, seeing how shabby he looked, simply spray him with bullets? How were people like these going to be persuaded he was an educated man, an employee at the Red Crescent? In the X-ray department? But on reflection, would it be wise to tell them? Might they not be furious if they learned he worked for the Palestinian Red Crescent – just as his friend had told him in Sabra Square? All these things had to be considered.

Even so, fear for himself did not stop him noticing the victims lying in the street. He was, after all, a human being first and foremost. He spoke with anguish of the twelve victims he counted personally, whose bodies he saw with his own eyes, up to the time they reached Abu Hasan Salameh Square. These, obviously, were only the ones that happened to be close to the entrance to alleys.

Soon after they reached the Square, the militias told men to stand to one side and women to the other. He recalled:

We stood near the Abu Hasan Salameh statue. Within 15 minutes, or a bit later, a Lebanese Forces Land-Rover arrived and a man in a green uniform got out. He was neither fat nor thin; middle sized, with a beard, and he had on a cap and a pair of dark glasses. He was obviously someone of senior rank. They said through the megaphone: 'Clap your hands for the chief, you bastards.' So we clapped our hands for the chief. The bulldozers were making so much noise I could hardly hear what he was saying ... They tried to take away a friend of mine, a nurse at the Gaza Hospital, but Dr Paul Morris told them the man was one of us, so they brought him back. The man heard what this 'chief' was saying. I gathered from him later that the man had been cursing Abu Ammar, the Palestinians and the whole leadership, and singing the praises of Reagan, Begin, Bashir al-Gemayel and their group. But we didn't know his name.[78]

Siham Balqis, a girl from Sabra who endured this 'final march' along with Hajj Mahmoud, the Crescent employee and countless others, described the same places over the same hours. Eight months later, she and I walked together from Sabra Square up to the heart of the Sports City, and she gave her recollections of the painful day in a low voice, so that no one would hear. It was not difficult to note four differences between the final march and our own walk together, along the same route.

The first difference was that it took us around half an hour to cover the distance, whereas the final march had lasted the whole morning, up till noon on that bloody Saturday. Humiliation, questioning, mass killings and open abductions, in the presence of live witnesses, made so much time necessary.

The second difference was the deep prevailing silence as we walked along alone, in contrast to the cries and turmoil that had been all around eight months before.

The third difference was between, on the one hand, the freedom to cry out and scream with pain in the midst of the massacre, and, on the other, the lack of freedom to do so now, at the painful memory of what those three days had produced. We were walking along the same route, but, at that time, the very mention of the word 'massacre' was forbidden.

This brings us to the fourth difference which was, quite simply, the difference between openness and concealment. Throughout the 43 hours in question, those armed and murderous attackers, on whose shoulders were written 'Lebanese Forces' or 'Sa'd Haddad', had been driving great numbers of people back and forth. As we walked eight months later, there was, in contrast, nothing beyond a Lebanese Army checkpoint. Yet for all that, there was still a powerful sense of prevailing fear. As I walked with Siham, we met a Palestinian woman I had interviewed a few months before, and this woman took me to one side and whispered, pointing to one of the soldiers: 'You see that soldier standing next to the vehicle? He was one of the men in the massacre. The two with him are quite all right.'

The spectacle surely needs no comment. 'That man', pointed out eight months later, and protected behind his official military uniform, had only recently been wearing the uniform of a militia to which he had openly belonged. Yesterday he had been a killer; today he was a guardian of the public order, on behalf of the government. His primary mission was to implement the secret orders of his organization: to bury the news and agonies of the massacre, just as its victims had been buried.

As we resumed our walk, I asked Siham: 'Did you hear what Um Ali [Samiha Abbas Hijazi] said there? Was it true?' She answered in a low tone:

Yes, it's true. This isn't the first time, you know, that we've seen men who took part in the massacre as soldiers in the army. Some women and girls come across them quite often at checkpoints outside the district, at al-Hamra or al-Raouché. Girls who work there have come back plenty of times, crying and crying, and told us they've seen one of them that day, at a checkpoint.[79]

We went on with our walk in relative silence, while the tape recorder in my bag, which I had contrived to leave running, was doing its work; and we passed through the checkpoint without harassment. We then approached the mass cemetery. Siham pointed to the Red Crescent centre and said:

I swear to God, at the front door of the Crescent, people were falling over one another. They'd rounded up about a thousand people, women, boys and girls, and brought us here, up as far as the Abu Hasan Salameh statue, just to the right of us here; and here, they told us to stand, women to one side and men to the other. They started lining us up, separately. Suddenly one of them said: 'Would you like to join up with us? Of course you wouldn't. You're only interested in joining up with your "freedom fighters", not with us.' He seemed to be talking to himself, then he'd come back and yell: 'Come on, clap, clap.' Then another one said: 'Say, down with Abu Ammar.' No one answered, of course they didn't. 'Say, down with Abu Ammar.' No one answered. He went back to what he'd been saying before: 'Join up with us? Of course you wouldn't.' And he went back, as if he was talking to himself. There are those who say some people repeated what they wanted them to, but I didn't hear anything ...

There's another thing I saw I never told you about before, the most horrible one of all. There was an elderly woman who used to work as a janitor at the Crescent. She was fond of Abu Ammar, and when she saw the gunmen, she thought the fighters had come back. So she went ahead and started singing Abu Ammar's praises, with not the least idea of what she was doing. They just went and cut her mouth with a knife, from here up to the ear, and then they killed her.[80]

Killings and abductions
Siham Balqis spoke of more than the clapping and the slogans. She had realized quickly enough that all this violence and uproar was merely a front for the day's main objective: namely, the abduction of as many people as possible during those final hours. She said:

While the clapping was going on, while they had us all distracted, they were pulling people away. They were pulling away anyone they felt like. One moment we'd see someone standing somewhere, and a moment later he'd be gone. It froze the blood in our veins ...[81]

Hajj Mahmoud Rukn also testified to the vehicles crammed with abducted people. He said:

While we were standing by the [Abu Hasan Salameh] statue, later on, we saw some jeeps loaded with men we'd left at the beginning of the alley. There were some big loaded Land-Rovers, like the ones the British Army used to use, bigger maybe. All those men were taken off, and none of them ever came back.[82]

As we were walking in the same street along which the Sabra and Shatila residents had been driven, Siham said:

The bulldozers were going backwards and forwards. By the way, let me tell you something, they meant to gun everyone down, and the bulldozer was ready. I mean, the bulldozer was digging and wrecking, right there in front of them ... To start with, we thought it was clearing the street, taking the rubble away ... Then, later on, we saw the results of the bulldozers' work ...[83]

In a similar testimony, Hajj Mahmoud Rukn provided further details on the bulldozers:

They made us sit on the ground, all the while we could hear the bulldozers doing their digging; we stayed like that, and it looked as if they were just waiting for the bulldozers to finish – which they did; we saw them. We started to sense they were getting the pits ready for us, to kill us all and round the massacre off. After all, if they went on killing us one by one, they'd never finish us all. Still, they'd already killed more than 20 or 30 people; and we saw them, I saw them when they killed the poor nurse, the old woman, and the pregnant woman's husband, how many more do you want me to say?

All the time, while they were killing the men one by one, they were telling us: 'Say it, long live ... long live Al-Kata'eb al-Lubnaniyieh ...' Then one would come and say, 'Clap, you sons of bitches', and we would, 'Dance', and we would. We danced, everybody did, I swear to God, that's what happened.

Now, when they'd just finished digging and killed the pregnant woman's husband, a bulldozer stopped at the Ali Hamdar Café and turned back towards us, its blade was as wide as the road was, it was wider and bigger than any I've ever seen. There was another one too, parked at the round-about where there'd been people, and it turned round and faced us, and they brought two Doshkas too, and some machine-guns on trucks. They were about 25 metres apart; all the gunmen turned to the other pavement, they transferred the people on the east pavement and brought them all over to ours, and then they turned towards us, cocked their guns and stood up. It was obvious they were waiting for some signal.

But … God is great. At one point we suddenly saw a vehicle coming, and I looked in it and saw some military personnel – they seemed to be senior officers. One of them raised his arm to tell them to stop.

It's true they didn't launch the Doshkas at us. But after that general had stopped them killing us, I saw them take seven or eight men to the bulldozer and make them stand there. I've no idea what happened to them after that. That dark man who used to work for Abu al-Hawl was with them; he was a pious man, he really was, he'd been on pilgrimage twice. I don't know whether or not they killed them afterwards. At that time they separated the men from the women; even a ten-year-old boy would be dumped with the men.

They went and brought some trucks, those big ones, like the ones the British Army used to use, and they started dragging men away and putting them inside. That was when the biggest abductions of the whole massacre happened. Of course the abduction never stopped all through, I know that, but the biggest abduction happened then. I saw them, with my own eyes, putting 40 or 50 men in three trucks, from those who'd been rounded up from behind the hills near the embassy. I've no idea how many more they managed to abduct later; I can only say what I saw.

I recognized some of the people put in the trucks. There was Abu Yassin, the guard at the Dana mosque, an old man, who'd happened to be stand-ing by his window. They asked him: 'Where are you from?' 'I'm Syrian', he told them. They said: 'Come down here, you. Come on down.' And he ended up

being one of the people taken away in the trucks. But we didn't hear them gun him down.

There was another man too, one I had a lot of respect for, who was gone as well. This one was wearing a suit, and he was carrying his ID card in his hand. They came and asked him, I heard them: 'Where are you from?' He said: 'I'm Palestinian.' And he asked again: 'Where from?' And he answered: 'From Egypt.' He asked again: 'From the Liberation Army?' And he replied: 'Yeah, yes.' He asked again: 'From the Ain Jalout Forces, right?' And he answered again: 'Yeah …' And that was where the talk stopped and the orders started. He told him, 'Get in the truck', and they took him away. He was gone, and he never turned up again.

Out of everyone, maybe he was the only one from the Ain Jalout Forces. But, what can you say, it was his bad luck. I'll never forget how brave he was.

As for us, they started making us walk in groups of eight, one row at a time. When we reached the Corniche, we saw trucks with 'Al-Quwat al-Lubnaniyieh' written on them.

We found out later, from friends of ours, that they'd taken a lot of people, in other trucks, to other places.[84]

As we walked towards the Kuwaiti Embassy, near the hill that was there at the time, Siham Balqis said:

Here, close to the hill, or behind it rather, one of them would come, and he'd pick out a man at random and tell him: 'Crawl on the ground, here in front of us.' Whether they wouldn't crawl or did crawl, they were shot. Three were shot, and the women started screaming and shouting … and so the Israelis came; they'd been close by those trees, a bit higher up at the start of the street, near the Kuwaiti Embassy, which shows they saw everything.

Anyway, we were getting close to Markaz Ina'ash al-Mukhayyam al-Filastini, here to the right of us; there'd been a shelter behind, with around five hundred people in it. They were all gone. They'd all gone on the first day.[85]

The abductions never actually stopped, though they were overshadowed by talk of the killing, which was more tangible, no matter how hard the killers strove to conceal the signs through demolition and rubble. As for the abducted people themselves, the intention was, from the first, to move them out of the district, after which no trace of their fate would be found: no body, not so much as a shoe, or belt, or ID card.

And yet the human memory remains both the starting point and the end point in the search for those abducted and missing. In addition to the above testimonies, we have that of Nurse Harbeh Barakat, a resident of Barracks Street, who had sought refuge at the Henri Chehab Barracks for two weeks at the time of the massacre. On the Saturday, she said, she saw six large trucks passing along Barracks Street, each containing 30 or 40 young men. Three had passed first, then a further three, loaded with young men as the first had been.[86]

There were other trucks, loaded not just with young men but with women and girls. The abduction of women on the Thursday evening has already been noted in Chapter 3. As for the truck that appears in the videotape shot by the Danish photographer, this was, according to a television photographer at Vision News, Muhammad Awwad, produced secretly in the middle part of Friday.[87] The sight that remains unforgettable for anyone viewing the video is that of a girl who was inside a truck parked not far from the entrance to Shatila near the Kuwaiti Embassy. She was calling to a militiaman, pointing to another truck and entreating him: 'Let us stay with our cousins.'[88]

Where is this girl today? Where are her cousins? Where are the countless numbers of those abducted and missing?

The minefields

As the crowds were approaching the Sports City, they received a series of orders to move on inside, to the football field. An Israeli officer's voice was being amplified through the loudspeakers. He was not aware that a hidden camera lens had captured him, sight and sound together: 'Anyone carrying guns or explosives should bring them, together with a white flag, and move on to the football field at the Sports City.'

The voice become louder: 'Listen, don't be afraid, we're not going to kill anyone … Give up the weapons and explosives, then that's it. We've warned you … Hand over the weapons and come to the football field at the Sports City, carrying white cloths, and you won't be harmed.'

A break, then the voice returned: 'This is your last chance, I'm telling you … Your first and last chance … If the country isn't cleaned up now, it never will be …'[89]

The moans and cries and wails of the women grew ever louder. As the Israelis were calling for the surrender of weapons and the women were wailing, guards from the Forces were thrusting people this way and that, striking them with the butts of their rifles and yelling at them: 'Come on, you sons of bitches, walk. Walk, you son of a bitch. All of you, come on.'

Hajj Mahmoud Rukn described the scene as follows:

All the way, as we were walking, there was beating, pushing and kicking. They had no consideration at all for people who were disabled. The bastards wouldn't let us carry Abu Ghazi Akkili, who was half paralysed from diving. There wasn't a shred of decency.

We had an argument with them. The Israeli officer, we said, was telling us to go to the football field, while they were determined to make us go through a minefield. I had about twelve rows ahead of me. But they just wouldn't agree, they made fun of us every way they could, I tell you, then they yelled: 'We told you, go through here.'

And a mine went off.

Six got killed and six got injured. All the little kids in Sabra and Shatila cried over one of the wounded, a well known, pious hajj. He used to sell small pieces of grated coconut, he'd wander from one alley to the next, calling: 'It's tasty … it's tasty.' He'd sell it at five pennies a piece, and the kids would buy it and have something sweet to enjoy. The poor man was at the front of the line. His leg got struck while a splinter hit him in the neck and finished him off.

People started screaming: 'Look out … It's a minefield, everywhere here!'[90]

This minefield was the space between the Sports City building and the swimming pool, where a good deal of rubble had built up from buildings blown up during the war – so much that a number of hills had been formed. The place had already been sown with mines in the past, and now new ones had been added. At this point, the people refused to go further into the minefield, challenging the gunmen to kill them on the spot. Hajj Mahmoud spoke on their behalf:

'The Israeli commander told you to take us to the football field, he didn't tell you to make us go through here.' He said: 'What's in here then, you?' I told him: 'You've seen already. You mined this ground so you could kill people, there's no way we're going through here.' He said: 'If you don't want to go through, then lie down on the ground, you sons of bitches. Lie down, you sons of bitches. Let's see what you're made of, you sons of bitches.'

I turned round halfway, to the back of one of the wounded, and I heard someone calling out to the man from the Kuwaiti Embassy side: 'Anton! What's the matter, what's the matter?' He told him: 'Nothing, just a dozen of the sons of bitches got hit. There are six dead and six injured.' The other said: '—— them, that's the end of them with any luck. Get the rest of them in there.' And the other man answered: 'They won't go, and the Israelis have seen us.'[91]

The sound of the megaphone returned to drown out everything, calling everyone to get up and go towards the football field or the UNESCO building, where there was an Israeli centre. People complied, and Hajj Mahmoud described these moments:

We got up, but we couldn't walk. Our knees were hurting. The fact is, every step we took made us feel as if our knees were wrapped in lead, and we just couldn't walk. Some of us felt our legs giving way, others felt completely paralysed ... We started walking again, but we were all of us scared to death about any mines along the way. But, glory be to God, He gave me strength from His own strength, I forgot all the beating I'd had [see Account 39, p. 190], I started walking between the rows, telling people how to walk. I was telling them: 'You people, don't walk over anywhere that's covered with sand, don't walk over anywhere that's not walked over already. Walk on solid ground, where there are marks of shoes, or tank treads, or tyre marks; that's where you need to walk. If you see a small pit, jump over it, don't walk through it.'

I stayed there ahead of them, and still God gave me strength, till we reached the UNESCO centre; there I looked at my watch and saw it was 11:30.[92]

The end of the 'final march'
The Israelis told the people standing there, who had just arrived from the minefield, to delegate one person to speak on their behalf. Abu Zuheir al-Akkili asked Hajj Mahmoud Rukn to speak, and the Israeli said: 'Go on then, hajj. They've delegated you to speak for everyone.'

After a slight hesitation, Hajj Mahmoud spoke. 'The Phalangists and Sa'd Haddad,' he began, 'have come in ...' 'No, no, sir,' the Israeli broke in. 'Not Haddad, not Sa'd Haddad, these are Phalangists. Sa'd Haddad doesn't come here; besides, he wouldn't do this, Sa'd Haddad's like Israel.'

There was uproar, and some people took advantage of this to run off. 'Please!' the Israeli said. 'Calm down. Calm down! You're now in the hands of the Israeli Defence Army. You're safe now, and we ask you all to calm down. The Israeli Defence Army will see to it that you're made comfortable. They'll provide you with food and water, but, please, calm down, then we'll see what needs to be done.'

The Israeli repeated this phrase – 'then we'll see what needs to be done' – three times. Tanks and troop carriers approached the barricade, to ensure no one could escape. It was not possible, even so, to restrict such great numbers of people. Chaos reigned, as though doomsday had come, and over 1,000 people (1,500, some say) were able to flee. These returned to Sabra.

The Israelis provided those still there with bread, water and apples.[93] These people were, nevertheless, subjected to questioning.

Testimonies from the third day

The third day was also the final one, operations ceasing officially – according to subsequent hearsay – at ten in the morning. According to these times, the massacre would have lasted for 40 hours; from sunset on Thursday till Saturday some time before noon. On the basis of testimonies we have obtained, however, it is beyond doubt that the killing and abduction went on till after twelve noon; it is not clear at what exact point these things stopped. We have seen how atrocities were still being committed near the Kuwaiti Embassy and the Sports City just before noon, and the aggressors' vehicles were still to be seen driving freely through the district up till one o'clock. As such, the massacre may be said to have lasted for 43 hours.

More important than the time factor was the psychological one. The accounts of the Saturday, even those of noon on Saturday, all show the attackers behaving as though they were there to stay; the manner of the killing and abduction did not suggest, even for an instant, that they were going to end their operations within, say, an hour or so. They were acting as though they had just entered the massacre ground rather than being about to leave it.

On this third day, the residents of Sabra and Shatila had no means of returning to check on what had happened. What, finally, could people so afflicted do except wait, till they could finally get in with others to search for their victims? For this reason accounts developed in the two preceding chapters are not finalized until Chapter 6.

Two kinds of spectacle formed the basis for the testimonies of the third day: the first involved the killing, described in five accounts below, which went on in a still more barbaric and savage fashion than on the preceding days; the second involved abduction, described in a further two accounts, which dramatically exceeded even the earlier abductions.

All these were killed
Throughout the route along which residents were obliged to walk on their 'final march', the killings never stopped, either on the individual or the mass level. A distinction can scarcely be made between the two sets of operations, carried out in the clear light of day. The noteworthy feature, however, is the attitude of the Israelis, who could no longer hide behind the claim of 'not having known', 'not having heard' or 'not having seen', with a consequent 'inability to testify'.

Account 35: Who was the killer?
The Sabra and Shatila residents were accompanied on that 'final march' along Sabra–Shatila Street by the foreign doctors and nurses. Yet how different the experiences of the two groups were!

The foreigners' experience was marked by an outward show of respect. Any danger to which they were exposed was incidental and exceptional, and in fact they all emerged safe and sound. The experience of the local residents, in contrast, involved serious danger and the facing of death, particularly for the Palestinians among them.

Arab workers with the foreign medical team were very few in number. Two left the hospital with the team itself, while others joined it at the outset of the march, seeking protection with the foreigners. We cannot be sure precisely how many of these latter there were, but there were four or five. Some were killed, and the rest joined the huge crowds when they realized that staying with the medical team actually meant a certain death sentence. For those people spread out on the two sides of the whole, long street, life and death were like two horses wagered on in a race.

Seven people partially witnessed the killing of a Palestinian walking with the doctors. Five of these were foreigners, two residents of Sabra. Although the incident took place over just a few minutes, each witness provided a separate account. These accounts match in certain parts, differ in others, suggesting that they might refer to more than one incident and more than one victim. All the stories, nevertheless, involved the killing of a human being, whose crime was his identity and his belonging to a homeland called Palestine.

The first witness was Dr Phil McKenna, an Irish national who had volunteered to work at the Gaza Hospital from July to October 1982. The following is what she stated in evidence before the MacBride Commission:

I'd like to make a point here. By Saturday morning and by late Friday evening, all the Palestinian staff had left the hospital at our request and with our full approval. All of them, except for two teenage boys. And when the staff of the hospital met on the steps, before the 'Lebanese Forces', these two Palestinians came with us, introduced themselves, showed their identity cards, and they were welcomed in Arabic. Together we all walked down through [S]hatila where the civilians were gathered in groups on either side of the road. About three or four hundred yards beyond that, one of the Palestinians was taken out of the group and brought behind us. And a German girl and myself looked behind. She said 'Where are you taking him?' And they replied 'Mind your own business, we're doing our duty, just like you're doing your duty'. And about ten seconds later we heard shots. That boy is now dead.[94]

The second witness was Dr Swee Chai Ang from Singapore, who had left her British husband in London and come out on a humanitarian mission in early September. She it was who, before arriving in Lebanon, had supposed all Palestinians to be terrorists. Subsequently, however, she chose to work at the Gaza Hospital specifically, having discovered that it was dedicated to the care of everyone without exception, and also provided its services free of charge. She wrote as follows in her diaries:

A Palestinian employee of the PRCS [Palestinian Red Crescent Society] had come along with us from Gaza Hospital, but was discovered almost immediately, taken away and killed. It was as though they had been instructed to kill Palestinians but not foreigners, and kept to their orders.[95]

The third witness was Dr Juhani Pajula, from Finland, who was working at the hospital during the months of August and September. He testified as follows in Oslo:

At 7.50 a.m., surrounded by the soldiers, we started to walk towards [S]hatila camp – 18 foreign health workers, one Syrian and one Palestinian volunteer who had spent the night in the hospital.

… The men seemed to be gathered in small groups. I could identify some workers at the hospital among the people, for instance the cook of the hospital. We were walking through this mass of people and the Syrian volunteer joined us.

After we had passed this mass of people they tried to follow us. This was prevented by the soldiers. The soldiers noticed the Palestinian volunteer who was still with us and asked him to show his identification card. After that they tore off his white jacket, beat him on his face and took him into a side street. After ten seconds we could hear shooting.[96]

The fourth witness was the elderly Palestinian man from Sabra, Hajj Mahmoud Rukn. He stated the following in his

testimony for the Oral History Project:

As we were walking along the road, they brought some foreign doctors from the Gaza Hospital, and with them was a man called Khalil, a male nurse dressed like a surgeon. There was a gynaecologist from the Gaza Hospital too, who I knew, I think she was Swedish; she was walking normally alongside me, and they let them stand right next to me.

A hefty gunman, dressed in civilian clothes and armed with a Kalashnikov, went up and said to him: 'Come here, you, what are you?' He said: 'I'm a doctor.' Perhaps he said what the foreigners had told him to say, so they'd let him go, poor guy.

They made us stand so we could watch how they were going to kill him. When he told them he was a doctor, they said to him: 'Did you see how many children were killed here because of ceilings falling in, from the shelling during the night? Go and look at them.' I swear to God, I heard that with my own ears – he was just close by; that's what the gunman told him, word for word. So he went, and he must have sensed he was going to be finished off while he was walking, because he raised his finger [to say his final prayers] there in the middle of the street; but he reached a wrecked house where there were several bodies under the ceiling … you could see two dead children. At that instant he must have sensed again he was going to perish, and God inspired him to raise his finger again, and they went ahead, they fired nine times and shot into his body from head to foot. To start with, he fell on his face, then on to his back, with his finger still raised.

This nurse was called Khalil. His brother, Abu Ismat, and his four children, from the camp, were all wiped out, all wiped out. He'd lived in the camp, while Abu Ismat had lived across from the Dana mosque, in the first Sabra alley. He was taken away too … God bless your soul, Khalil.

When they called for me later to identify his body, I did it. I went out of duty: he'd been killed there in front of us. God bless your soul, Khalil.[97]

The fifth witness was the American nurse Ellen Siegel, who reported in a press interview what she had testified before the Kahan Commission:

I saw hundreds of Palestinians from the camp, and healthcare workers, sitting on both sides of the road under guard. We recognized some; some got up and gave us a 'V' sign. A young man, who somehow got a white lab coat, joined us, but they stopped him. A German nurse told me what happened: she saw a soldier take his ID, take off his coat, slap him around, and then take him around the corner from where she heard a shot. Behind us we saw people who had been working at the hospital who pointed at us, but the soldiers wouldn't let them come over to us.[98]

The sixth witness was a Palestinian girl from Sabra, Siham Balqis. She stated the following in her testimony for the Oral History project:

By Saturday morning they'd rounded us up, and it was as if doomsday had come: everyone was there, all the people we knew. Anyway, after they'd gone on ahead of us to the Gaza Hospital, they brought back the foreign doctors and nurses, less than half an hour afterwards: they walked and passed right by us. Among the doctors there was a Palestinian, tall and strongly built; I'm not sure just what his job was, but he wasn't a doctor. Anyway, he had a white coat on and he was walking with the doctors, so they'd suppose he was a doctor.

Anyway, we don't know if someone informed on him, or maybe they saw from the look of him that he wasn't a foreigner. They took him to one side and shot him, through and through. They gunned him down right there in front of us, at about half past seven.[99]

The seventh witness was Dr Maehlum-schlagen, whose testimony was notable for his statement that there were actually two Palestinian nurses who had joined the team as a means of protecting themselves. He stated that the killers had dragged one of them away while he was standing with the doctors; they had demanded his ID card, taken him to one side, then killed him – the doctor heard the gunshots. As for the second (the doctor reported), he had, according to other witnesses, been taken away by the killers some time later, but his fate remained unknown.[100]

All the accounts, then, agree both on the victim's connection with the Gaza Hospital and with his Palestinian nationality. They disagree, however, on two points: age and occupation.

Taking age first, the difference in appearance between a young man and a father of young men is obvious enough, and this suggests that at least two victims had been seized from the team of doctors and nurses. Had Dr Maehlumschlagen specified the age of each of the two nurses, he would have settled the matter.

As for the man's occupation, one of the witnesses stated categorically that he was a nurse, while another testimony spoke of him as a cook.

It was said that the other two young men were volunteers, and that one of them worked at the Palestinian Red Crescent. There was a moment at which they were both asked by the gunmen, at the hospital entrance, to present their identity cards, following which they were, as Dr Phil McKenna reported, treated in a welcoming manner. This is in fact in harmony with other testimonies provided by a number of doctors who confirmed that the group had come to the hospital and addressed people calmly and reasonably; they had harassed no one and had clearly been concerned about their reputation. The guards were, however, replaced four times along the way, and each replacement led to a deterioration in treatment. In any case, as the march went on, the firing of bullets prevailed over 'good name'.

It must be remembered that the fourth witness, who lived in Sabra, identified Nurse Khalil and subsequently supplied us with his name. He actually saw the man being killed, and he it was who identified the body. In contrast, no one supplied even the first name of the man who worked at the Red Crescent.

Why, one might ask, should there be so much discussion about the death of a single Palestinian, or even two or three, when hundreds of Palestinians, Lebanese and people of other nationalities were killed and remained anonymous, with no one even to testify as witnesses to their deaths?

There is one very good reason for this discussion of the nurse dressed in a white gown and walking with the doctors, or the account of that other Palestinian man who sought protection with the foreigners, and that is that both demonstrate clearly how the objectives of the massacre were not in fact related to a search for Palestinian guerrillas, but were rather to hunt down Palestinians in general – any Palestinian. Even doctors, nurses or rescue workers were all on the wanted list, as long as the nationality fitted.

Had Nurse Khalil heard about the killing of Dr Ali Uthman, or of Dr Sami al-Khatib, at the Akka Hospital, he would not have sought protection with the foreigners. He would have realized that the matter had nothing to do with wearing, or not wearing, a doctor's white coat. It was a matter of belonging to a country called Palestine.

Perhaps if Nurse Khalil had had a little more time for reflection, he would have realized there was no security for people of his kind; not when those who had occupied his homeland of Palestine were, at that very moment, besieging him with their tanks, even in his eventual, humble exile in Sabra and Shatila.

Just what way out was there finally? Do we need to ask the question 'Who was the killer'?

Account 36: Nameless children

There was no way of discovering these children's names. They were killed not in a single incident, but in various incidents in a number of places. I have selected three from among the stories of children who were killed and who remained nameless.

The first incident (A) was reported by Nurse Ellen Siegel, Dr Swee Chai Ang and a Palestinian teacher, Huda A.

Siegel said that, while the attackers were taking the team members for questioning, and they were walking along Sabra Street with countless others, a woman with a baby in her arms came through the crowds and handed her child to Dr Swee Chai Ang. Dr Swee took the baby and carried him, but only for a few moments; one of the 'soldiers' came and told her to hand him back to the woman. Ellen Siegel commented as follows:

It is strange how people respond. I didn't do anything, and no one else did either. It's a second in your life – everyone wanted to do something, but we just didn't. It was very painful to watch.[101]

Dr Swee herself also described the incident, telling how a desperate mother came and handed her the newborn baby boy, whom she managed to carry for just a moment before one of the gunmen came and pulled him violently off. She told, too, of how, when she returned to Lebanon, she scoured the camps but was unable to find either the mother or her baby.[102]

It so happened that Huda A., a teacher, was among the people walking along on that tragic day. When she read the diaries of the 'Chinese doctor', as Dr Swee was commonly referred to in the camp, she felt it was her duty to search for the mother and baby. She made enquiries among many residents, neighbours and friends, but met with no successs. Then later, by sheer chance, she learned, through a Lebanese friend living in Sabra, what had happened to the pair.

This friend had, as he told her, been effectively an eye-witness. He had been walking in the line and had seen how the gunmen forced the doctor to return the baby to his mother. The witness had deliberately slowed down so as to learn the fate of the pair, all the more so as the baby had appeared to bear a strong resemblance to his own small nephew.

The gunmen had, he said, taken them off to a concealed spot where they were no longer visible to him, then killed them once the foreign doctors were far enough off. He had not seen the act with his own eyes, but he knew what had happened from the screams of the mother, who had begged them rather to kill her but spare her son; he was just a baby, she said, and God would protect him. He knew next, when the baby's crying suddenly stopped, that they had killed him first; then he knew from the tormented mother's cries, which again were silenced suddenly after a few moments, that they killed her second.[103]

So both baby and mother died. Neither his name nor hers is known. It is as if the whole story had a beginning and no more.

The second incident (B) was described by a man from Shatila who was among the people taken away on the Saturday morning. He told how, as they approached the Sports City and the minefield, a mine not too far away from him exploded. Like all the rest of them being driven along, he felt himself to be in grave danger. The crowds, though, went on walking.

Among them, he went on, was a man carrying a percussion grenade, which he was keeping hidden for the right moment. He launched it, finally, when there was just a short distance between the crowds and the 'Forces'. It made a tremendous noise and there was chaos and turmoil among the people, which in turn led to retreat and flight on the part of the 'Forces' gunmen along with a large group of people. Whoever could contrive to do so ran off.

The narrator grew calmer. Of course, he said, percussion grenades were harmless, as everyone knew. There was, though, a small child walking alongside his father, and both took fright. The child, terrified by the noise of the grenade, grabbed his father's shirt. Suddenly, after walking a further few minutes, he fell to the ground. Possibly he bumped into something or someone, or perhaps the fright itself had been sufficient cause. The narrator was not sure of the reason. What he did know was that this little boy died. He could never forget the sight of the father carrying him, dead, when, a short time before, he had been holding his hand as they walked side by side.

No one had been able to offer condolences to the child's parents since no one had known the father's name or address. All the narrator could remember was that the father was an Egyptian labourer. He met him occasionally in the Sabra market, where they would greet one another. He recalled, too, how the greengrocers liked the man and would talk to him in Egyptian dialect: 'How are you doing today? The same with us, we don't want any Camp David either ...'

After the people had returned home, the narrator made enquiries about the labourer, among the Sabra greengrocers, and was told the man had gone back to Egypt and never returned.[104]

The third incident (C) was reported by Huda A. who, as noted above, had confirmed the death of the baby and his mother. By virtue of her job in the social and educational fields, she received frequent news and confidences from many of the camp residents. She lost no relatives in the massacre, but had earlier lost two brothers at Tall al-Za'tar. What, I asked her, had been her worst moments on that 'final march'? Or what sights had been the most appalling? I have never forgotten her answer:

There was one particular sight I'll never forget. Maybe I've read or heard about even more barbaric scenes, but you asked me about what I'd seen personally. I've heard about them knifing and cutting up children. And yet what I saw was more abominable still.

As we were walking along, I mean, on the way to the Sports City, there were bulldozers tearing down houses and putting backfill over the corpses, and I saw arms and legs on the bulldozers. They were agonizing sights, yet the most heart-rending one, as far as I'm concerned, was the remains of a little baby on the tread of a tank. I tell you, it was a little baby. I'll never forget the sight. A tank running over a baby?

A newborn baby, just born, couldn't have been dropped on to the street: they must have killed him, along with his mother. Maybe he was gunned down first, and then they ran over him with the tank. What I do know is I couldn't sleep for months afterwards. All I could think of was how brutal people could be.

Just how ... just how can the Palestinian people bear what happened? I swear, if I'd seen it happening in front of my eyes, if I'd seen the tank and how it was running over the baby, I would have attacked it myself. If you do nothing against injustice, then you're just conniving with the people who cause it.[105]

Account 37: Testimony regarding victim number 36

All those forced to take part in the 'final march' spoke of murders the killers themselves made no attempt to conceal – making every effort, indeed, to draw people's attention to them. As for the number of victims, witnesses gave their own individual testimony as to what they saw.

One man from Sabra told how, throughout the march, he had had no fears for his family: his three grown-up sons were working in Kuwait, and there was no one in Beirut to cause him concern. He rather feared for his neighbours and countrymen, and began to feel it was his duty to keep his eyes open and try to take in just what was happening around him.

He talked of the death pits, noting two of them in particular, one bigger than the other. He also described the killing of men, youths and women. These deaths he witnessed one by one, and he elaborated on the final one he saw:

Where I was standing, near the Abu Hasan Salameh statue, people were piled up on each other, there were people all over the street. There was one woman who was pregnant, in her ninth month, with a very big belly, and her husband and two sons and one little daughter were close by too. One of them picked her out, without any warning, and told her: 'Come here, you bitch. Come on, clap, you sons of bitches, you ...' 'Brother,' the poor woman said, 'what am I supposed to do. Can't you see I'm pregnant?'

He went on cursing her, then he called to her husband and said: 'Come here, you ... stand here and clap. And you, dance.'

They made her dance, they laughed at her, and when they'd finally worn her out, she fell to the ground sweating. He brought her husband and told him: 'Get down, you son of a bitch. Get down, kneel.' And he did, he got down, he knelt, till his head was touching his knees. I saw all that with my own eyes, as God's the witness to every word we speak. That pregnant woman's husband was killed right there in front of us. There were about 20 or 30 witnesses. All of us round the woman saw what happened.

I was counting the victims. Most of them were gunned down, but some were knifed, like that poor woman who started singing for Abu Ammar. I was counting the ones who were killed in front of us, or who I saw being taken on the road.

They'd killed 35 people before they killed the pregnant woman's husband. He was number 36.[106]

Account 38: He lived to tell what happened – then died

Hajj Abu Sulaiman was a resident of Nahr al-Bared Camp in Tripoli, and had come to visit relatives in Burj al-Barajneh and Shatila. One of the militia groups, which had set up a checkpoint on the airport road, captured him and decided he was 'fair game'; he had, they felt, gone out of his way to find them, saving them the trouble of searching him out.

Hajj Abu Sulaiman was unable to identify the people at the checkpoint, but he did realize they were Lebanese. He told them, with naive honesty, that he was going to Shatila to visit relatives. A Palestinian going to Shatila; a crime indeed. Palestinians should rather be leaving Shatila – and going to hell.

They would, they said, take him to Shatila. Such was their sympathy for this artless old man they had picked up! Later, when he had finally regained consciousness and speech, he said he thought the day had probably been Saturday – he could not recall exactly. The details he provided confirmed that it was indeed Saturday.

These armed men had lied to him. Solicitous he should not miss his chance of taking part in the 'great march', they took him not to Shatila, to visit his relatives, but to the Sports City. At the entrance to Shatila, they let him out of the vehicle and insolently ordered him to walk with the crowds. He walked as he had been told to. He saw corpses piled, here and there, all the way to the Sports City.

To humiliate him still further, they threw his *kufiyyeh* down on the ground close by him, and he stayed there for four long hours, under the burning sun, begging to be given his *kufiyyeh* back so as to have some protection from the heat. They did not respond.

This simple old man had still not taken in just what was happening; and so, when he still insisted on having his *kufiyyeh* back, there was no option but to kill him, simply to be rid of him. A group of armed men, one of them with a knife, came and took hold of the man, laughing all the while. Then the man with the knife took on the job of dispatching him.

It was as simple as that: they stabbed him, then dumped him in a nearby pit to die slowly, should he still have any spark of life left. In fact he was still alive and was conscious enough to understand, at last, what was going on.

Whenever a gunman passed the pit, he pretended to be dead. Only when he was sure they were far enough off did he come out of the pit, running blindly till he came near an Israeli troop carrier. There an officer saw him, dripping with blood, and said: 'Come with us, hajj. We'll treat you in Israel, get in.'

At that Hajj Abu Sulaiman regained full consciousness. Looking at the Israeli, he said, 'No – no', then went on walking till he fell down and was still. He came to again, finally, at the Hôtel Dieu, but was told not to try to speak.

The International Red Cross rescue workers had brought him to the hospital, where, following instructions from their superiors, they reported that the Palestinian casualty in question was linked to their organization. His relatives searched high and low for him, then, finding no trace, supposed he was 'gone in the massacre'.

Hajj Abu Sulaiman was well liked and respected by his relatives, who were spread through a number of camps in Lebanon, and these wished, accordingly, to arrange for formal expressions of condolence in keeping with his standing. Indeed, those at Burj al-Barajneh did not wait for arrangements to be made in Tripoli, given that the hajj had been lost in Beirut.

Ten days after that Saturday, the condolences began at the Burj al-Barajneh Camp. While his wife and relatives were receiving those bringing comfort, the man responsible for delivering the camp mail came and asked for the hajjeh, Hajj Abu Sulaiman's wife. She must, he insisted, come along with him as there was a girl at his home waiting with a letter. How could the deceased's wife leave at such a time? Nevertheless, she felt bound to go with him.

There she met a Lebanese girl who was, she said, the sister of Hanna Diab, who owned the shops for sanitary supplies in Burj al-Barajneh. The girl introduced herself in this way so as to inspire confidence, for Hajjeh Um Sulaiman would certainly be familiar with these places, which were well known in al-Burj. She then reassured the hajjeh, telling her that her husband was still alive in the Hôtel Dieu, though his situation was critical and he was living on artificial respiration.

At dawn next day, Hajjeh Um Sulaiman went to the Hôtel Dieu with her daughter to visit her husband and the visits continued. Then, two weeks later, the daughter went to the International Red Cross centre to ask that her father be transferred to the Gaza Hospital, which was now functioning again. He was transferred accordingly.

For three months he was unable to speak, though he contrived, through signs, to report all that had happened to him. Then, suddenly, the Hajj Abu Sulaiman began to talk again. He spelled out, clearly now, what he had indicated before, adding those things he had previously been unable to express. The man who cut him down was, he said, called Ahmad, and one of those who had seized him and flung him in the pit was called Hussein. These were the names they had used to one another.

Hajj Abu Sulaiman repeated many times what had happened to him, his wife urging him all the while not to tire himself. However he was already worn out enough by life's injustice. He talked for just three days, then he died.[107]

Account 39: The death pit

The place was opposite the Kuwaiti Embassy. The time was eleven o'clock on the morning of Saturday 18 September 1982. As for the setting, it seemed like doomsday.

People were waiting in their hundreds for their turn to be questioned, or simply to be flung into the death pit without any questioning, or to finish their 'final march' towards the Sports City. Alongside the killers – or interrogators as they tried to make themselves appear – stood the informants. These were people from Sabra and Shatila. A short distance away Land-Rovers were parked, ready and waiting to transport 'undesirables' into oblivion, following interrogations that lasted one or two minutes, or, in some cases, went no further than a shake of the head from a single informant, or perhaps from a couple of them.

Not far from the place where the interrogations took place, and visible to the Israelis with the naked eye, were a number of pits referred to by witnesses as the 'death pits'. There, early on the Friday morning, an

Israeli soldier or officer saw the killers ordering women and children to get down into one of these pits (see Account 33, p. 155), and rushed over shouting to them to stop, which they did. On the Saturday, it appears, there was no one to put an end to similar mass killings of men and youths.

There was one large pit and there were two of medium size, to cater for numbers of the 'undesirables', driving them on to a fate known rather than unknown – to death, that is to say, rather than abduction. There was disagreement as to how the largest pit was formed: whether it was the product of air force shelling in the course of the invasion or the direct result of the bulldozers' work. The latter would naturally be significant, implying special preparation for a specific goal. Some witnesses preferred to combine the two, being of the opinion that the bulldozers supplemented the original devastation, with a view to making room for larger numbers of victims to be driven to their end.

Many similar pits were reported, in many other places, by various men and women. It should also be borne in mind that such reports stemmed from those who, providentially, had been saved from the pits for one reason or another. Those who entered the pits no longer had the ability to speak.

The crucial importance of Hajj Mahmoud Rukn's account springs from the fact that he was – to the best of my knowledge – the only person who entered the depths of the death pit and came out alive. He told me exactly what happened.

Hajj Mahmoud had believed, misguidedly, that his long white gown, his 50 years and his long beard, together with his cap and the rosary in his hand, would preclude any accusation of being a guerrilla, whether representing Fatah, the Popular Front or any other Front. His confidence was, it emerged, unfounded. While counting the beads on his rosary and murmuring holy verses, he heard the interrogator – or killer – say: 'You, come here … come here … you, hajj. What do you do, hajj?'

Hajj Mahmoud, who had undertaken the pilgrimage twice, solely at his own expense, had worked in various occupations ranging from work at the port to painting on construction sites, and had also been with the Egyptian Army defending Palestine in 1948. How was he to answer? He only remembered answering, without thinking: 'I serve the houses of God.'

At this the interrogator asked a fellow-militiaman: 'What does that mean? What is it, serving the houses of God?'

'It means', the other man said, 'serving the church and the mosque.'

The first questioner said nothing. Instead, as Hajj Mahmoud recalled ever afterwards, he gave a disdainful wave of the hand, then, as the line of people approached the main pit, condescended to rise and fling Hajj Mahmoud personally into the pit. Hajj Mahmoud gave the following account:

There were 17 people in the pit already; I was the eighteenth. Don't ask me how I managed to count them. I've always been quick at counting. I figured there were seventeen of them as I was falling in. The pit was round, like a plate or a deep pot of soup on a dinner table. It was backfilled with sand, but the sand looked different: it seemed like a stiff dough, on account of so many people being killed in the pit. The mud at the bottom of the pit hadn't dried, there was so much blood it was still soft. There were four military troop-carriers near the pit. They weren't armoured vehicles, they were half-tracks, like the ones the Israeli Army had: two wheels at the front and a chain at the back, and they were joined together, back-to-back …

It was very hot that day, it was a burning hell, and we were covered in sweat – we'd been walking since early morning, and it was nearly eleven by then. As the line was moving up to the Sports City, I was the only one picked out by that man and thrown into the pit. He started trampling my head and saying: 'To hell with you, you son of a bitch, just you lift your head one centimetre and I'll make a sieve out of you.' He had a Kalashnikov and two rounds of ammunition with him. What can I say? I said my last prayers. I'd been praying silently ever since they picked me up at the edge of the camp, and I'd submitted totally to God's will, there was no way out.

The hardest thing I saw, the hardest thing I had to suffer, I mean, was almost choking from the smell, of soil and blood mixed – there's no smell as bad as the smell of human blood. How can

I describe it, it's like the smell from a leaky bottle of butane gas, only worse. What I mean is, the smell gets to you and makes you want to throw up. And on top of that, I couldn't move at all, he was on top of me, his boots were hurting my head. May God take vengeance on him! The gown's still stained with blood; I still keep it.

He was still yelling at me: 'Ask God's house to come and save you, you ——.' Then he'd ask again: 'What did you say your job was? Serve God's houses, do you? OK, you son of a bitch, what's your name?' I answered, without thinking: 'My name's Mahmoud Hasan.' I didn't give my real family name then, when I was so near death, I don't know why.

Oh … there's one very important thing I should mention. As I was going down into the pit, I saw someone I'd known from the time he was a small child; his name was Elias. I'd worked with his father, and we'd visited one another in the past, and we'd eaten together. His father had a high regard for me. For all that, though, his father was with the Kata'eb, and so, when things changed, I didn't see any more of him. The years went by, and Elias grew up. And now, there he was, standing with a lot of other men, surrounded by 20 armoured vehicles; no, actually they were half-tracks, and they were all parked on the road.

Of course, I recognized him the moment I laid eyes on him, but I was hidden from him. I felt, though, that he was staring at me, wondering whether it was me or not.

Then I heard Elias say: 'I beg you, Robert, I'm ready to kneel and kiss your feet, may no harm ever come near you, please.' Then the other one said: 'What are you talking about, Lillo?' When I heard the second man call him Lillo, I was quite sure it was Elias, though he was a big, strong man now; he'd grown a lot. He said: 'Just do one thing for me, Robert.' The other man said: 'What?' Elias said: 'This hajj, the last one here. For the sake of your honour, this man raised me, I swear on my honour and yours, my father and mother and I have visited him, and we've eaten with him at home. I'll never forget this favour. I beg you, Robert.'

'Robert!' I'll never forget that name, may God send him to hell. He told me: 'Get up, you ——.' He got hold of me, pulled me up by the shoulder till it nearly broke and threw me down on the ground. Then Elias told me to get up quickly, before anyone came, and we started walking. The other one, may God send him to hell, had been trampling on my head and neck and humiliating me. The line ahead of us was walking towards the Sports City, and Elias and I walked to catch up with it.

After I'd gone just one or two steps, I heard the shooting: 'too, too, too, too, too …' I turned my head towards the pit and just froze on the spot. They were shooting them all. I just froze, and I thought, now he'll come back and finish me off. I'd seen them with my own eyes, how they killed the Nurse Khalil while his back was turned to them. How could I walk? Then Elias was there, pulling me away, and he said: 'Don't look back, go on, just walk.'

I started walking in spite of myself. I felt as if my back was broken from the stamping boots of that evil Robert, may God send him straight to hell. Then Elias told me, holding my hand there on the road: 'The Israelis will take charge of you now, and no one will come near you after that.' With that Elias left me.

I staggered over to the line, and I saw they were facing the side where the officers' houses were, opposite the Sports' City. What a line it was! It stretched from the backfilling near the embassy right up to the Sports' City.[108]

All these were abducted

It is well enough known now that abductions continued throughout that last day; that military trucks and jeeps were actually waiting by the sides of the roads round about to carry those abducted off to the unknown.

There were no fixed rules. Some people were taken after undergoing a form of trial a few minutes long; others were forced to crawl or jump, in a way designed, no doubt, to allow the interrogator to gauge the extent of their terrorism. Some were asked just a single question, or two, in the midst of the massacre, then ordered to move this way or that. There were even some who were dragged off to one of the trucks in response to a mere nod of the head from an informant. Finally, there were those abducted, in front of their families and neighbours, without any questions at all. This was how Sami Shaker Natat was abducted on the Saturday, after he had been forced to walk in that 'final march' with his father, family and neighbours. By the time they had reached the Rehab petrol station, it was clear the killers' destination was the Kuwaiti Embassy. Then, suddenly, the march came to a halt, as some of the killers' vehicles stopped and those in them got out and started seizing men from the crowd. No one could get any answer as to where they were taking them or why.

Shaker Natat was one of the people being driven along, and his young son Sami had been walking alongside him. Now the narrator, the father, Shaker Natat, trudged on to the Kuwaiti Embassy, while his son Sami was borne off to the unknown, not to return.[109]

Both the following accounts relate to the Saturday, the first to the morning, the second to noon.

Account 40: People called him 'Uthman'

Uthman was not a Palestinian, nor was he a fighter. He used to work at the Gaza Hospital. They abducted him, nevertheless, on that Saturday.

Uthman, a black African man, was well liked among the hospital workers for his invariably courteous and pleasant manner. What led Palestinians to like him, however, led others to abduct him.

Uthman's worst crime, perhaps, was to suppose his British citizenship would afford him protection against the killers. He was, may God forgive him, lacking in experience, unaware that passports and other national documents cut no ice on the sites of massacres, where citizenship is defined solely by place of residence. For the killers he was a 'terrorist', indistinguishable from those other 'terrorists' with whom he had come to live and work.

He was no terrorist. He was a devout Muslim, and this it was that had led his friends at the Gaza Hospital, and in Shatila, to call him 'Uthman' – which was not his real name, as set down on his British passport. Nor did this passport carry any mention of his religious faith.

What actually happened to Uthman? No one knows. Perhaps he said, without thinking, 'in the name of God, the Compassionate, the Merciful', or 'God is great', as he was inclined to do. A friend who worked with him at the Gaza Hospital gave the following account:

Uthman worked with us on the building site. He was tough and cheerful, and he loved to laugh. He spoke good Arabic too. I remember telling him he ought to leave when the fighters did, and I wondered why he wasn't afraid of staying on in the country. I tried to persuade him – he was a British citizen, I told him, and once he was out he could go to any country he wanted. His answer was always the same. He could go off any time he wanted anyway, and it wouldn't be right to leave us in the middle of the building work.

On the Saturday when they came and rounded up the Sabra people from the streets, they took him along too. 'I'm British', he told them. 'Get moving', they answered. 'Just keep your mouth shut and start walking.'

Uthman had to go. They put him in a vehicle and off they went. None of the people taken with Uthman ever came back. And Uthman never came back either.[110]

Another young man, who worked at the Palestinian Red Crescent and knew Uthman, heard what they were saying:

I heard them ask him: 'What do you do? Electrician? At the Gaza Hospital? We'd better give you a blood test then, and find out what group you are. You're one of the mercenaries. We'd better give you a blood test. Come on, come out, you son of a bitch.'

There were a lot of their military jeeps nearby, they'd put dozens of people in them and taken them off. Uthman went with them and never came back.[111]

Uthman had always supposed no one would detain him; he was, after all, one of those privileged people with embassies of the kind that would follow up on their citizens. This was something he had repeated constantly to his friends.

He had made a simple mistake. It had not occurred to him that he might be killed or abducted before his embassy ever came to know of him and so have something to work on. The thinnest of lines often divides a simple mistake from a fatal one.

None of his friends knew whether or not the British Embassy did subsequently learn of the matter. When I asked them why they had not taken it on themselves to inform the embassy, they said: 'We never knew his name. People called him "Uthman".'

Account 41: The 'field courts' massacre

This story involves the abduction of a young man on that bloody Saturday, the narrator being a young neighbour of his who was standing in line near the Abu Hasan Salameh statue.

According to this narrator, the gunmen were summoning people from the crowd, especially the young men. They would yell at a particular person, who would go over to them, then vanish behind the hill, where those closest could see him being taken off to one of the waiting Land-Rovers. Once a vehicle was full up, and the engine started, these men would disappear – the kind of disappearance that rivals death itself in lonely isolation.

The abductors wore military uniform with MP badges on their shoulders, and they were heavily armed. Each member carried an M16 machine-gun along with a couple of Doshkas, and some – about a quarter, the narrator estimated – also had axes. He gave the following description:

There ... by the Abu Hasan Salameh statue, they were detaining people.

We stood in line, in single file. I guessed my number in the line must be around 100 – that's about how many people there were ahead of me. In front of me was a neighbour of ours from Sabra, a tall, dark fellow with frizzy dark hair. Most of those ahead of us were young fellows, and there were a few older men too.

Looking back, I reckoned there were around a thousand people behind me. They still hadn't separated Palestinians from Lebanese. I thought, if they did that before my turn came, I'd be dead for sure. Behind me were some Lebanese guys who weren't too worried. One of them said to his friend: 'We're Lebanese, they won't do anything to us.'

Our neighbour's turn came, and he stood there, without moving. There were 30 or 40 gunmen in front of us, they were all standing except for one who was sitting on a high bench. Any one of the 30 or 40 gunmen might pick out any one of us, at random, and say: 'Come here, you son of a bitch.' The one who was called over had to obey and go up the hill.

It varied, according to the way they felt. I mean, they'd just pick people out as they felt like. None of us could know whether or not he'd be called over. They called our neighbour, and he went up to them.

When he called our neighbour, though, I thought it was actually me he was calling. I got close and started shaking, and he said: 'What are you doing here, you son of a bitch? Who told you to come? I was calling that other one, the one who launches B7s.' And he turned to the militiaman with him and said: 'That's a surefire launcher, get him.'[112]

This neighbour, the narrator affirmed, had never launched a B7. He was actually a car repair worker, and the chief breadwinner for his family. He had seven younger brothers and sisters, and he worked to support his father. He was an 18-year-old Palestinian from the Nasser family.

The narrator mentioned the Nasser family name without thinking, but asked that his own name should not be published under any circumstances. It was for this reason too that he declined to give his neighbour's first name. He went on as follows:

I noticed there were two people giving him orders. One of them said: 'Get down in there, you son of a bitch.'

There were some people lying inside a pit they'd dug. Those lying there had already been killed. There was a hill above it, I mean, the pit was right underneath the hill. One of them told him to get down in the pit, but then, straight away, another one told him, 'Go there, right there', meaning he should go up to the top of the hill.

I looked inside the pit and saw several guys lying there, and others who were still shaking. There were others, too, lying on top of the hill, maybe those ones hadn't been shot yet, or perhaps they had and some of them were dead, I could hear their voices: 'I beg you, don't kill me. For God's sake, for Muhammad's sake.'

Our neighbour started shaking too, then one of them told the other: 'No ... no ... bring this one here. Why did you tell him to go and lie down there? Get him. Come here, come on.'

I looked at him, not realizing it would be the last time I saw him. I looked to see where they were taking him, and I saw they'd made him stand on a sort of bench with his face turned towards the airport. I could see him clearly, he was no more than twelve metres away, but I never found out what happened to him in the end.[113]

When, a few minutes later, the narrator's turn came, they asked him the familar question: 'Are you Lebanese or Palestinian?' Trying hard not to shake, he said: 'Lebanese.' When they asked for his ID card, he claimed to have left it at home. In fact the card was in his pocket, but they had failed to notice it when beating and searching him. His trousers were made of a thick fabric suitable for physical work, and he had contrived to thrust the card deep into a pocket. When they told him to come closer, he discovered something which, intent on watching his neighbour, he had not noticed earlier: the presence of three informants apparently unconcerned to hide their appearance. All were without masks, and they were giving their opinion on each person about to be interrogated. The local residents recognized all three: one Palestinian and two Lebanese. As it happened, all three shook their heads to indicate the narrator was unknown to them; and so he survived.

Nevertheless, being saved from the pit, in which he saw men in their death throes, and from the abduction that had been his neighbour's fate, did not imply ultimate survival. He had still to pass the running and crawling test. One of the killers welcomed him by shaking his shoulder violently and greeting him ironically in familiar Palestinian dialect. Then he seized hold of him, and the narrator was sure he was about to die. But at that point he heard another gunman telling the first: 'No, Tony, let him go, he isn't one of that Palestinian lot. But let's give him a beating he'll never forget, for living with them.' And so he was given the 'appropriate' treatment, after which he was told to clear out and go back to the line. This he was quick enough to do, and he walked on with everyone else, to the Sports City.[114]

Thus the narrator survived death and abduction alike. He nonetheless failed to survive a guilty conscience. When they had asked him, 'Palestinian or Lebanese?', he had denied he was Palestinian. This was his first anguish. His second anguish sprang from his inability to hear what they had said to his neighbour. From a distance of twelve metres he had seen well enough, but had failed to hear the full exchange of words. He had, he said, managed to hear some things – or at least thought he had heard them – but had missed others.

He did not, for example, learn why they were so sure the man had launched B7s. This issue at least was resolved when a friend told him subsequently: 'I know your friend, he wouldn't even know how to carry a B7, I only wish they'd tried him out ...'

An irrevocable 'guilty' verdict had been reached even before the man was summoned. Was he not, in the narrator's words, 'a tall, dark fellow, with frizzy dark hair' – or, to put it bluntly, 'Palestinian'?

In the wake of those unforgettable days, the narrator would regularly wake sweating, and crying out: 'They took him, right in front of my eyes – they took him!'

His neighbour, the family breadwinner, was not the only one to have been seized in front of him. The others, though, had been strangers, whereas this neighbour he had known and cared about; it was not easy for him to forget the moment the man had vanished. Perhaps they had asked his neighbour too the question, 'Palestinian or Lebanese?' If they had, he would certainly have answered: 'Palestinian.' It might be, of course, that they had not asked. But then why had they abducted him?

The tormented narrator, unable to sleep now, would ponder deeply. Even if it had been proved that his friend launched B7s, that would still not constitute a legitimate charge against someone whose land had been stolen by enemies who had then built a state on it. But it could not be proved in any case. And indeed, either way, who gave that person sitting on the bench the right to judge people? Who had appointed him to head such a 'field court'? What kind of court was that, just a few metres away from pits where murders were being committed, a few metres in front of a hill that was the scene of torture and abduction? What kind of verdicts were those reached after just a few minutes of haphazard hearings and the nod of a head from an informant?

The question remains, why did they detain – in the language of massacres, 'abduct' – this young man from the Nasser family? The question remains unanswered, the account without clear conclusion.

A list exists of the names of victims and those missing, released by the Lebanese Dar al-Fatwa in 1983. On it are the names of two abducted young men from the Nasser family, named Hamza and Taysir.[115] The list compiled by the Committee for the Families of those Abducted and Missing in Lebanon, released in the same year, included, under the heading 'various nationalities', the name 'Jamal Ibrahim Nasser'.[116] This list was published by *Al-Safir* newspaper.[117]

As part of the investigation I myself launched, between 1998 and 1999, into the fate of those abducted, one of the research team visited Ibrahim Nasser's home. Just one question was asked, and one answer received. Jamal Ibrahim Nasser had not returned.[118]

At the Sports City

The Sports City formed a kind of common location for the militia members and the Israeli Army. As such, it was easy enough, during the first two days, for the Israelis to monitor what was going on in the City's yards and fields – including all the killing, the torture, the death pits, the minefields over which people were forced to step. We shall begin, in this connection, with what happened on the fields of the City from Saturday noon, the time the Israelis began their questioning and investigations. These fields were the only place capable of accommodating the hundreds of people involved, who had indeed reached thousands before, as we saw earlier, the explosion of a mine enabled some to escape.

It was here at the Sports City, then, that the Israelis undertook preliminary questioning, with investigators and informants spread out among the people. However, higher level questioning took place opposite the City, on the other side of the Boulevard Camille Chamoun, where the Israeli Command used the UNESCO building as an intelligence and interrogation centre. There serious suspects were pulled in and subjected to open questioning, beneath the burning sun, in the spacious yard on the north side of the building, in large pits formed by Israeli air force shelling.

Hajj Mahmoud Rukn told of what happened to him at noon on the Saturday, after the Israelis had given them bread, apples and water:

But who had the appetite to eat? I took a piece of bread because I'd had nothing to eat since morning. I felt the blood had dried in my veins from all the things I'd seen. Besides, I was a smoker; thank God, I had a packet with me. The bread was plain and baked with milk. I started chewing and drinking water, and I finally managed to get it down …

After half an hour or so, we saw two Israeli tanks arrive, along with military vehicles and civilian cars. I looked at my watch and saw the time was between twelve and quarter past, no later.

That fat guy with the big head and belly, wasn't that Sharon? I saw a man coming who looked just like Sharon, and the tanks were on full alert. But I didn't look round any more after I saw the Hamdan guy, Rajab Hamdan's son.

That man's father had enlisted along with us in the Arab League Forces, in the Egyptian Army, but later on he defected and went to Israel, where he became a big intelligence officer; now he's living paralysed in Yaffa [Jaffa].

Rajab's son was an intelligence officer too, and he had dark glasses on. I knew him well enough, because two years before the invasion I visited my brother on the West Bank, and we saw him there. They run a modern taxi service. The father started off in intelligence, and now his son had followed him. I don't recall the son's name, but I do know he was born in Yaffa. Rajab Hamdan's son wasn't alone, there were other spies: there was one cross-eyed guy, another who laughed the whole time, and another who used to be a shoe-shiner.

Of course, there were no chairs for us to sit on. We were spread out all over. One was sitting on an empty bag, another on a sack of supplies, another one on a stone. But when they arrived, the Intelligence men told us all to gather in one place, and we did. From then on, one or other of the men in dark glasses would just wag his finger for one of us to come forward. The first man they took was my brother-in-law, my wife's brother.

He asked him: 'What's your name?' He answered: 'Muhammad al-Masri.' Then he asked again: 'What's your father's name?' And he answered again: 'Tawfiq al-Masri, but my father's dead.' The officer went on: 'How old are you?' He answered: 'Nineteen.' Then he asked: 'Where was your father from?' He answered: 'From Yaffa.' At that the officer smiled and said: 'I'm from there too.'

The man asking the questions was Rajab Hamdan's son. He told him: 'Don't worry, *habibi* ["my dear" – Arabic]. Where do you live?' He said: 'In Sabra Street.' And the other man asked: 'Where exactly?' He answered: 'Near the Dana mosque, in al-Dik alley.' The last question was: 'What do you do?' And he said: 'I own a garage.'

A garage? What kind of suspicious job is that? The moment he said the word, the officer yelled at him: 'Out! get out!'[119]

All the time the questioning was going on, large numbers of Lebanese residents, who had been arrested at al-Mal'ab al-Baladi, were arriving at the Sports City. They started coming at around one o'clock, and finally numbered 700–800. There were also some Palestinians among them.

They had been instructed to go to the Sports City to have their ID cards stamped. In reality, they might have to face interrogation the moment they arrived – a movement of the finger by any of the informants would be enough to have someone brought forward. As a result several dozen ended up being told to move on to the interrogation centre opposite the UNESCO building. The rest, the majority, were told at about three in the afternoon to go back home and return next day, when their cards would be stamped.[120]

While people were being massed together in this fashion, an Israeli officer with a megaphone was shouting at the top of his voice, telling anyone with weapons or ammunition to move towards the football field. He urged them to be quick, and kept repeating: 'Don't be afraid, we won't harm you, you won't be in any danger.' Then he ended: 'This is your first and last chance. If the country isn't cleaned up now, it never will be.'[121]

Siham Balqis was one of those who walked to the Sports City on the Saturday. She described how Sa'd Haddad's men – after the mine had gone off and any who could had escaped in the resulting chaos – started shouting at the women to go home, since only men would be questioned. When, however, she saw her brother Salah standing with some other men and waiting his turn to be questioned, she decided to stay and see what was going to happen to him and the others. She heard some people, an Israeli Army group apparently, ordering the men to assemble on the football field. Siham managed to return home to fetch her brother's card, and, with some difficulty and after talking to a number of Israelis, finally contrived to pass it on to him. Arriving at noon, in a spot from which she could overlook the men, she was able to make a rough count, which exceeded Hajj Mahmoud Rukn's estimate: there were, she said, more than 50 men and youths.

In the afternoon, Siham stopped an Israeli officer who was passing in his car along the boulevard, and told him they had been detaining her brother for hours without cause. Her brother was, she added, a mechanic in a workshop for cars. Had he ever been a guerrilla, he would surely have left with the fighters. The officer told her this was untrue, that her brother had already confessed; to which she replied that any such confession must have been extorted by torture, from which he had been willing to take any way out. It was, she pointed out, easy enough for them to verify what she was saying. He asked her how. 'Give him a broken-down car', she answered, 'and see how he repairs it in no time.'

At sunset interrogations were still going on, but it was no longer possible to remain there, and Siham and her mother returned to their home in Sabra. A little later, her brother arrived in a state of exhaustion. The Israelis had, he told them, kept his card and had told him and the others to come back next day, to have their cards stamped and returned.

He told them what had happened. The Israelis had summoned people and told them to crawl and go down into the pits. If ever they suspected someone, because he wasn't crawling in the right way, they would stamp on his head and all over his body.

Describing his own particular experience, he said an inspector who spoke good Arabic had accused him of belonging to the Democratic Front, and they had given him a severe beating as a result. He had, however, refused to confess anything; at which they had threatened to hand him over to the Phalangists, who would, they said, certainly be able to wring a confession from him. In the end, unable to take any more, he had said he was a mechanic working at a garage for the Liberation Front. They then used this to accuse him of having repaired the cars of 'terrorists'. As such he must know these people, and would be able to say where weapons were stored. He assured them he had no knowledge of any particular place.

Next day, on the Sunday, Siham and her brother Salah Balqis returned to the Sports City. The district was full of rumours about the return of Sa'd Haddad's men, but vanguards of the Lebanese Army were approaching the City and taking up position there. Siham rushed up to a Lebanese officer and told him she had a brother who was still being detained, though innocent of any charge. The man advised her to report the matter immediately to the Red Cross before the latter's withdrawal had been finalized. Otherwise her brother would be taken off to the South, where anything might happen to him, or else they might take him to the Ansar Detention Camp. The officer then assured her the Lebanese Army was to be stationed at the Sports City, and that the Israelis would be making a full withdrawal. Siham did not, however, need to inform the Red Cross as her brother returned at noon, with his card bearing an Israeli stamp.[122]

Muhammad al-Misri, the garage owner who had also been detained at the yard opposite the UNESCO building, returned and told his brother-in-law, Hajj Mahmoud, of the torture and humiliation he had undergone. They had, he affirmed, gone on questioning him till ten at night; he had finally managed to convince them of his 'innocence' by insisting they accompany him to see his simple garage, which he had set up just six months earlier. They had kept him all day long under the burning sun, with questions and accusations being fired at him by more than ten officers and informants. When they suspected someone,

they would subject him to a more severe test, flinging him into a big pit formed by air force shelling, in which there were various types of bomb. If a man should cry that there was a cluster bomb in the pit, the Israelis would straightaway pull him out and deal out more serious punishment; for anyone who could recognize a cluster bomb was presumed to be a fighter, and had to be imprisoned accordingly.[123]

According to Hajj Mahmoud Rukn, the number of men detained at noon on the Saturday was close on 30, while Siham's estimate (based on her brother's) for those detained at sunset approached 50. Of all these just three or four, Salah and Muhammad among them, returned.

What happened to the others? It was said they ended up in the Ansar prison – detained without any specific charge, in contravention of all international law obliging an occupying army to work to preserve the lives and freedom of those occupied.

But did Sharon, or any other Israeli official, admit that any such thing had occurred? Almost as soon as the massacre was over, it was stated in local newspapers that the Israeli forces had imprisoned residents of the 'two camps', and of the neighbouring area, in massive numbers. According to foreign correspondents, the number of those detained by the Israelis was as high as 1,000 or 1,500 people, some of whom were later released, while others continued to be held.[124]

No one was able to calculate the exact figure, all the more so as any total had to include those abducted by the armed militias, hauled into trucks and military vehicles in broad daylight under the irrefutable pretext that they were 'terrorists'.

Did the Israelis take charge of those they allowed the armed militias to abduct? If so, where are they now? And if they left them in the militias' custody, the same question imposes itself. Where are they?

Account 42: A conversation between an Israeli and a Palestinian

The first man was an officer in the Israeli Army, whose rank was not made specific – though the narrator was sure it must have been quite a senior one, for the Israeli soldiers who filled the yard between Dar al-Mu'allimin and the UNESCO building, at noon that Saturday, obeyed his orders to the letter. Saturday noon was, it will be recalled, the time when the Lebanese militias were supposed to be getting ready to leave, while the Israelis were still summoning people to gather at the Sports City, as well as rounding off their interrogations, stamping ID cards and concluding various other matters.

The second man was Hajj Mahmoud Rukn, a Palestinian from Sabra, who looked much older than his 50 years. This pious man had faced the rigours of the 'final march', on which he had had to endure various kinds of beating and humiliation; he was in fact the self-same man who had survived the death pit half an hour before. Now he described what happened to him while he was standing in line, waiting for his turn to be questioned once more, by the Israelis this time.

Before the interrogation itself, there was a conversation between this man and the Israeli officer. It took place in Arabic, the narrator's mother tongue and a language acquired by the other man, as a Jew who had been born in Palestine.

The Israeli officer, whose name was Rami, took Hajj Mahmoud to one side to ensure his words would not be heard by others. 'Please, hajj', he said, 'I'd like to talk to you.'

Why in heaven's name, Hajj Mahmoud wondered fearfully, had he been singled out from among all these crowds? Could the man be from Israeli Intelligence? He must be, surely? Or was he just an ordinary army officer doing his job? Perhaps he had chosen him because the latter had been the one to speak on behalf of all these people some time before – he supposed Hajj Mahmoud must have special knowledge. Or had he picked him out, maybe, because there was blood staining his white gown, a sign that something dramatic had happened?

Whatever the reason, the Israeli officer left Hajj Mahmoud little time to ponder. 'Hajj', he said, 'tell me, please, what's happening? What's going on? For God's sake, speak up. For God's sake, hajj, I swear, by my religion, I won't repeat anything you tell me. For God's sake, talk to me.'

Hajj Mahmoud plunged in accordingly, and the following conversation took place:

'The Kata'eb came, attacked the camps, and took some of the people away in their vehicles, right in front of our eyes. We had no idea where they were taking them. I personally witnessed the killing of innocent men and women. They killed a woman nine months pregnant; they killed children. With my own eyes I saw 36 people killed. Seventeen were killed in the pit I came out from. What more do I need to say? I tell you, they were heaping people up in the pits, killing them one on top of the other. Go up towards the Kuwaiti Embassy, you'll see the victims piled up right in front of it.'

'All right, hajj, tell me, how many did they take away in the vehicles?'

'There were four big vehicles. Each one held 20–25 people, and they came from behind the sandy hills. That was what I saw myself. I don't know how many more were taken.'[125]

The officer began to summon colleagues over his radio, and shortly afterwards four military jeeps and a large car arrived. The officer went off with them for a time, then returned and resumed his talk with Hajj Mahmoud:

'All right, hajj, go on. Just trust me.'

'God willing. But tell me, which town in Palestine are you from?'

'I'm from Israel, hajj. I was born in Yaffo, and I live in a settlement near Ramallah. Do you know Yaffo?'

'The Yaffo I know is Yaffa. In English, I gather, it's called Jaffa.'

'Where was it again? Where did you say a pregnant woman was killed?'

'If only all they'd done was kill her ... If only ...'

Hajj Mahmoud went on to describe all the incidents he had personally witnessed, while the officer listened, interposed questions and wept. Hajj Mahmoud continued with his account of the meeting:

I swear to God, I swear to God ... he started crying, his tears were dropping on the ground, then he turned his face away to hide his tears. He wiped his tears away, turned to me, and said:

'It's all right, hajj, you needn't worry. I won't repeat a word of this to anyone.'[126]

Should the officer, Rami, have reported this? Told his superiors what he had heard from Hajj Mahmoud? Or should he have said nothing? Surely he should have reported it. But did he?

The puzzling question, in any case, remains. How could such a senior officer, as Hajj Mahmoud described him, have failed to know of all the things that had happened on the Thursday and Friday? On this score Hajj Mahmoud's answer was immediate. The officer's questions, he said, led him to believe the man had come to Beirut, or to the Sports City at least, only recently. This was the conclusion he had drawn, though he could provide no evidence for it.

When, however, I asked Hajj Mahmoud if he had any objection to my publishing his conversation with the officer, he did not hesitate. 'Of course I agree', he said. 'I'm sure of every word I said.'

The end of the third day

- From Wednesday on, people had been streaming to seek refuge at the Gaza Hospital, their numbers finally approaching a couple of thousand. Casualties began to arrive in large numbers from midday on the Thursday, and the hospital was soon a hive of activity.
- By Friday sunset there was almost dead silence at the hospital. All those seeking protection had left, a considerable number of patients and casualties had likewise left with their families, and further casualties had been evacuated by the International Red Cross. All that remained, finally, was a few patients together with the foreign doctors and nurses, who had refused to leave *en bloc*.
- On the third day, the gunmen reached the square and alleys of Sabra, where they began shouting and summoning people from their houses. Between dawn and seven in the morning, the residents of Sabra and Shatila were assembled in Sabra Main Square, in front of the Palestinian Red Crescent; then the day began.
- At about seven in the morning, the attacking gunmen reached the Gaza

Hospital, which did not, however, experience an incursion similar to that at the Akka Hospital; the foreign doctors and nurses came out as told by the gunmen and succeeded in convincing them there was no one at the hospital beyond a few patients. They also persuaded them that a small number of the medical team should remain to care for these patients.

- The gunmen led the medical team along the same crowded road with the residents of Sabra and Shatila. When they reached the headquarters of the Lebanese Forces, they were initially questioned, then taken on to the Israeli headquarters, whence they were able to return home; and some, indeed, actually managed to return to the hospital.
- A 'final march' took place, with great crowds forced to take part, along the whole of Shatila Main Street to the heart of the Sports City. In more than one place they were forced to stop, to endure humiliation and to witness haphazard murder and abduction.
- The Saturday's testimonies suggest the gunmen were not acting as though they supposed this to be the final day – their behaviour implied, indeed, that they were there to stay. Even at noon the mass killing in the death pits hardly suggested they were in their final hour. Torture, murder and abduction continued to the end.
- There was extensive killing on the final day and the militiamen made no attempt to conceal the death pits outside Sabra and Shatila, near the Kuwaiti Embassy and inside the Sports City, within the sight of the Israelis. Nevertheless, abduction remained the first priority, those seized being put in trucks and military jeeps and taken off to a fate that remains unknown to this day.
- For their part, the Israelis were no mere spectators on the Saturday. They played a significant role in questioning young men in front of the Sports City and in stamping ID cards. Some of those questioned were able to return home that night, but others have never returned.

6

The Killer and the Victim

Massacres are characterized alike by the obvious and the covert. The killers leave behind horrific evidence and sights, sufficient to cause a vehement outcry. Yet at the same time they conceal evidence and the bodies of victims, to an extent that searchers must strive hard to fit all the pieces of the jigsaw together.

The official Lebanese report concluded that a 'battle' had taken place. The official Israeli report was ready enough to avoid this word, but was equally at pains to avoid the word 'massacre'; the decidedly contradictory terms chosen to describe the events were 'combat operations' and 'acts of slaughter'.

The distinction between a 'battle' and a 'massacre' is clear enough, the most significant difference being that between openness and secrecy. Battles, by their nature, dictate the publication of all available news, documents and photographs, whether on the part of the victor or the vanquished; the former takes pride in victory, while the latter seeks to justify defeat.

In ancient times, historians would take on the additional role of witness, accompanying armies and commanders with a view to observing battles from close range and providing a detailed description. Now, in our own times, and especially since the birth of modern mass communications and satellite systems, news of battle finds its way into homes everywhere, through television or the Internet.

Details of massacres are a quite different matter. Even where images can be beamed on the spot, such images remain exclusive to those supervising them – and the primary goal of the supervisors is to promote secrecy rather than public information.

The Israelis will certainly have used satellites at Sabra and Shatila. Yet – in marked contrast, for instance, to the media-serving role of American satellites during both Gulf Wars – the results were not placed at the disposal of journalists. They were rather devoted to facilitating operations that remain 'secret' even now. By the same token, the full objectives of the constant illumination, supplied both by the Israeli artillery from their positions on the western and southern borders of the camps and by planes flying directly over the district, have remained undisclosed. The one avowed aim was to assist the attacking gunmen, enabling them to distinguish, swiftly and clearly, between 'terrorists' and civilians.

To this day the question has not been properly discussed. Did the Israeli Army compile photographic records of the massacre? One would surely expect them to have done so. If they did, where are the photographs now? And if they took no photographs, then why not?

As for the attacking gunmen, they were not fighters but killers. There is a wide gulf between the two. A fighter takes pride in his principles, courage and actions. A killer of unarmed women, children, old people and youths has, in contrast, no interest in revealing his identity. Even if he does so to boast, his statement is linked to an immediate setting, and his statements are liable to change from one day to the next. What a killer says today, he may deny tomorrow.

Sabra and Shatila was prototypical of a massacre combining the two extremes. The very killers who boasted of their activities in the field, whether before residents or among themselves in the days following the tragic event, subsequently reconsidered their positions and revoked their testimonies.

Yet the insistence of those Lebanese elements accused of the massacre, and the subsequent insistence of various Israeli sources, that what had occurred was a 'battle' was accompanied by none of the openness characterizing true battles. There was a conspicuous lack of various items that mark a battle: maps, documents, photographs, the names of the fighters on the two sides – or of the leaders, at least – and the names of those who fell on the two sides. Is it conceivable that those falling in battle should be from one side only?

The primary aim of this chapter is to establish that what took place on the site of Sabra and Shatila between 16 and 18 September 1982 was indeed a massacre and not a battle, and that in consequence there were not two sides but rather killers and victims.

The testimonies within this chapter fall into three broad categories: the first set comprises testimonies and writings of the journalists, writers and photographers who first had access to the massacre site and consequently were the first to speak of the victims; the second comprises the testimonies of rescue workers from the various humanitarian organizations who spent two whole weeks clearing rubble and searching for victims; the third comprises the testimonies of families of the victims themselves, who were actually able to see the killers and the killing, abduction and torture they carried out, and also to see the signs left

behind in their homes, on walls and in the features of the people they had lost.

The families of the victims spoke out; their testimonies in this chapter supplement the tragedies and accounts of those three bloody days. There are, in addition, accounts provided by four people who went to search for their loved ones. The testimonies in this chapter supply clear descriptions, and they point to the identity of the killers.

The first to enter

According to Israeli sources, the final instructions issued to the attackers were to withdraw at ten on the Saturday morning. As the previous chapter revealed, however, no withdrawal actually began till the afternoon; the attackers had left Sabra and Shatila by noon, but were still on the southwest boundaries of Shatila near the Kuwaiti Embassy, actively involved in killing and abduction. It is not clear at what precise hour the 'massacre trials', haphazardly conducted by the hill opposite the embassy, finally came to an end. There are, however, people to testify that these were still continuing at midday, with the queue still quite long. Also, there are eye-witnesses to dozens of militiamen, in their armoured vehicles, being still on Shatila's south-west borders at two in the afternoon.

Brief news of the massacre had leaked out to the media; but when the foreign correspondents hurried to file their reports they discovered that the phone and telex lines had been completely out of order since eight in the morning. Some, in consequence, had to go to Damascus in order to contact their newspapers and agencies, while others went to the Israeli press centre near B'abda, from where, as the American writer David Lamb later said,[1] they freely distributed news of the massacre.

When the attackers left, the Israeli Army was still besieging the district and questioning residents at the Sports City. Foreign journalists and photographers were nevertheless able to gain access, and were in fact the first people to enter the 'forbidden zone'.

Ryuichi Hirokawa, a Japanese reporter and photographer, did not wait for the departure of the armed militias. He was the first to attempt entry, from half past eight on the Saturday morning. Attempting to enter the camps from the north side – with the sound of bulldozers and gunshots still quite audible – he found his way blocked by two Israeli tanks. He told the Israelis he was a Japanese reporter, but they denied him access and forced him to withdraw. He tried again, from the east side this time, only to find himself blocked here as well. His final alternative was from the south, where firing was still audible, but where there was also no one to stop him; nor did he find anyone on the massacre site. He had obviously entered through Horsh Tabet, opposite the Akka Hospital; Horsh Tabet had been one of the first places exposed to the massacre, on the Thursday evening, but was now completely deserted.

A short while afterwards an adolescent called to Hirokawa and told him Sa'd Haddad's group had committed a massacre. He refused, however, to accompany the journalist; he appeared quite frightened and fled straight away after giving the information. Hirokawa therefore had no choice but to enter alone. Describing the killing of families and the attempts to hide the crime, he wrote as follows:

Entering a garage, I saw tens of people lying dead one on top of the other. I walked up a small incline, then turned around. In a small alley I saw the bodies of seven or eight women and children, sprawled on the ground.

Descending again, I reached the garden of a house where I found all the members of a family massacred. It looked as though a bulldozer had attempted to hide these bodies. The dead body of a child, of about two years old, was thrown beside the rubble. The child was, I supposed, alive right up to the end, since the killers had not hidden the body beneath the bulldozed rubble.

In the next alley I found the bodies of two more children, a girl and a boy, both around five years of age.

Near them a woman's body, probably that of their mother, had been covered with the rubble by a bulldozer. The rubble did not cover her completely, and some parts of her body could be seen. The girl was wearing toy earrings. The boy

was wearing something like a chain around his neck. He seemed to have been strangled with this chain, as his neck appeared swollen with congested blood.[2]

In the days that followed, a number of further scenes were conveyed, through articles or photographs, by writers and photographers from various European and American countries. The sights portrayed were both similar and different. It was Jean Genet who, in his article, drew a comparison between the photographic image and that conveyed by an eye-witness. Having, on the Sunday, walked through what remained of Sabra and Shatila and personally witnessed the aftermath of the massacre, he noted the following:

A photograph has two dimensions, so does a television screen; neither can be walked through. From one wall of the street to the other, bent or arched, with their feet pushing against one wall and their heads pressing against the other, the black and bloated corpses that I had to step over were all Palestinians and Lebanese. For me, as for what remained of the population, walking through Shatila and Sabra resembled a game of hopscotch. Sometimes a dead child blocked the streets: they were so small, so narrow, and the dead so numerous.[3]

During his visit Genet paused to examine 40 victims. He provided a detailed description of the first victim he saw:

The first corpse I saw was that of a man fifty or sixty years old. He would have had a shock of white hair if a wound (an axe blow, it seemed to me) hadn't split his skull. Part of the blackened brain was on the ground, next to the head. The whole body was lying in a pool of black and clotted blood. The belt was unbuckled, a single button held the pants. The dead man's feet and legs were bare and black, purple and blue; perhaps he had been taken by surprise at night or at dawn. Was he running away? He was lying in a little alley immediately to the right of the entry to Shatila camp which is across from the Kuwaiti Embassy.[4]

A number of further writers described the various spectacles, all of them showing victims to have been taken by surprise and killed indiscriminately. One of the first to register his observations was the British writer Robert Fisk:

Down every alleyway, there were corpses – women, young men, babies and grand-parents …

Each corridor through the rubble produced more bodies … There were signs of hastily-dug mass graves …

There were more bodies on the main road. 'That was my neighbour Mr. Nouri,' a woman shouted at me. 'He was ninety.' And there in a pile of garbage on the pavement beside her lay a very old man with a thin grey beard and a small woollen hat still on his head. Another old man lay by his front door in his pyjamas, slaughtered as he ran in terror for safety a few hours earlier.[5]

In a radio interview, the *Washington Post* correspondent Loren Jenkins said:

It looks like something out of someone's worst dream. Buildings broken, bodies lying in the street, people in alley ways crumpled in great big piles. Walls where 8 or 9 people have been lined up and shot and they've fallen down. Seeing in a family that was shot near a courtyard, obviously the man had come to answer the gate and was shot right there and the woman that was shot right next to him, she still had her dinner plates in her hand crumpled on the ground; babies in diapers next to them with bullet holes in their heads. Bodies that have been booby trapped, grenades placed under them, so when people come in to pick them up, they're going to get killed too. It's just a horror, it's just hard to imagine.[6]

Ian Glover-James of the *Daily Telegraph* was more concerned with describing the gunshots, which ruled out any notion of a battle. What had occurred was clearly killing at close range:

Everywhere there were 'tableaux' of death.

An entire family – parents, two children and a baby – were sprawled in one of the tiny concrete homes, sprayed with machine bullets through the front door …

Eight men lay dead, their bodies piled on top of one another in front of a concrete wall. They had been lined up and shot. The bullet holes were fresh in the concrete at chest height. They ranged from teenagers to middle-aged men.

A family huddled nearby. Two children aged about eight were spread-eagled with bullet holes in

their heads. Their parents were shot dead in rubble alongside.

Another family in the neighbouring home had spilled out of their doorway in their last terrified moments of life.

The bodies included a baby of about one year, lying with a woman and five other bodies, some hanging upside-down over a broken wall, where the killers caught them as they tried to run.[7]

The American photographer Mya Shone and her husband Ralph Schoenman were among the first people to get in. In contrast to what was published in the newspapers, Mya Shone produced a whole series of clear, high-quality slides. As she projected these on the wall in my home, she spoke as follows to me and a number of my friends:

Look at those. Ropes were tied to the victims' hands and feet, and then they were dragged. Men were taken around corners, shot, and cut to pieces by knives and axes. Tractors were used to run over them.

Look.

The aged weren't spared. These two men were killed during the forced march on Saturday morning.[8]

Everyone spoke of the stench from the dead people – a stench not only mentioned by articles but captured by photographs and videotapes in scenes of people covering their noses with handkerchiefs. Mark Fineman from the *Philadelphia Inquirer* was among those to write of the smell:

The smell was unmistakable; it was the smell of death.

It rose yesterday with the black clouds of flies and the stench of month-old garbage all along the demolished main road through the Palestinian refugee camp called Shatila.

It filled the lungs and the very pores of the reporters and photographers and Red Cross workers who descended on the nearby deserted camp in the wake of the slaughter of hundreds of unarmed Palestinian men, women and children.

So bad was the reek that the women who were making their way out of the camp with the tiny bundles that were their worldly possessions were forced to tie cloths across their noses and mouths.[9]

In this same land of pain and defeat from which he wrote of freedom, Jean Genet also noted the stench. He was in fact referring to the freedom of flies rather than that of humans; hardly surprising, since, if there were freedom for suppressed nations, there would have been no massacre in the first place. He wrote:

The smell is probably familiar to old people; it didn't bother me. But there were so many flies. If I lifted the handkerchief or the Arab newspaper placed over a head, I disturbed them. Infuriated by my action, they swarmed onto the back of my hand and tried to feed there.[10]

This eye-witness writer entered a wrecked three-room house, and whichever room he moved to he found piled-up bodies. In the third room he found four bodies piled on a single bed, as if each victim had taken it upon himself to protect the one beneath; the bodies seemed like shields. 'This pile of shields,' he wrote, 'smelled strongly, but it didn't smell bad. The smell and the flies had, so it seemed, gotten used to me. I no longer disturbed anything in these ruins, in this quiet.'[11] After leaving the house he spoke of the men who were with him and, once more, about the stench. 'The three young men were waiting fairly far from the house with handkerchiefs over their noses.'[12] After walking here and there for four hours, he returned to the subject one last time:

Here are the bodies I saw last, on Sunday, about two o'clock in the afternoon, when the International Red Cross came in with its bulldozers. The stench of death was coming neither from a house nor a victim: my body, my being, seemed to emit it.[13]

The search for the victims

The search for the victims might have been expected to begin immediately the massacre was over. This, though, was not the case. The killers remained in the district till the Saturday afternoon, while the Israeli Army, for its part, was still besieging the district, checking cars, questioning residents and stamping ID cards.

Nonetheless, there had been an attempt to enter on the Friday, the second day of the massacre, by young men from the Scouts of Al-Risala al-Islamiyieh, who had come in

two ambulances as soon as they heard the news, but they had found their way barred by an Israeli tank still stationed across the street opposite the Akka Hospital, and had been forced to return.[14]

There had also, on the Saturday, been various attempts to enter by the International Red Cross, but these had been aborted by the attackers themselves, who had still not completely left the massacre site. At eleven in the morning, Ibrahim Baroudi, a man from Shatila, saw the French Ambassador, accompanied by a Red Cross team. Along with some other men, Ibrahim had therefore taken the initiative and gone along with the Ambassador and the team as far as Bir Hasan, where they managed to rescue a wounded man and take him in the ambulance. They had then walked back to the camp, where panic reigned as people began to return to check on their families and homes. Suddenly, the panic took further hold and people started running and shrieking at the rescue workers: 'Get back, get back!' It emerged that a group from the Lebanese Forces had also been approaching, from some distance off, and this led everyone to flee, including the Ambassador and the drivers of the ambulances.[15]

Ibrahim's testimony matches those of two Lebanese Red Cross rescue workers who both affirmed that they had, along with their colleagues, attempted to enter on the Saturday but had failed to do so. Search operations did not, they added, begin until the Sunday.[16]

In confirmation of the above, *Al-Nahar* wrote that a Red Cross rescue team had attempted to enter Sabra and Shatila on the Saturday morning, but had not succeeded in getting in to do its work. The Lebanese government (it continued) had then decided the army should enter the district on the Sunday morning, to ensure security and facilitate rescue operations and the search for victims.[17]

Ma'moun, a young man from the Lebanese Civil Defence, spoke of how they entered on that Sunday morning. They had, he said, parked their vehicles near the Akka Hospital, where they found the district to be empty and the Israeli Army beginning to withdraw. They had to wait for half an hour until all the Israeli tanks had gone, then the first rescue workers, from various humanitarian organizations, began to enter with the Lebanese vanguard.[18] The narrator was referring, presumably, to the Israelis' exit from near the southern entrances, since the Israeli Army was still present on the edge of the Sports City all through the Sunday, conducting investigations and stamping ID cards.

By noon, 1,500 Lebanese soldiers were spread through the massacre site and the surrounding area. Sabra and Shatila were now protected by the Lebanese Army under the command of Colonel Marcel Prince, who quickly began to co-operate with the various rescue teams and facilitate their operations. One of these, undertaken by representatives of the Red Cross and members of the army, was to prepare lists of the names of survivors, whose statements furnished, in their turn, the basis for lists of those missing.[19]

Such, at least, was the plan. But what actually happened within the massacre area? Where did the rescue teams succeed in carrying out effective work, and where did they fail? And did they in fact compile accurate lists of victims and of those missing?

The humanitarian organizations

During the summer months, which had witnessed the Israeli invasion of Lebanon and the siege of Beirut, the cutting of water and electricity supplies, and the Israeli Army's hellish bombardment of the capital from land, sea and air – using such internationally banned weapons as cluster, vacuum and phosphorus bombs[20] – hundreds of Beirutis had volunteered to serve with the humanitarian organizations. Some of these had previous experience, while others' first experience was during the invasion itself; these latter began by taking intensive courses in first aid before joining one of the organizations. When asked subsequently about their experience of field rescue work, these young men and women were unanimous and emphatic: their work in Sabra and Shatila was memorable beyond any other.

There were eleven humanitarian organizations (at least) involved in the clearing of rubble and the search for victims.

These were, in alphabetical order: the Civil Defence of the Amal Movement; the Civil Defence of Al-Makased al-Islamiyieh; the Civil Defence of the Scouts of Al-Risala al-Islamiyieh; the International Red Cross; the Lebanese Civil Defence; the Lebanese Red Cross; the Organization of Al-Iss'af al-Sha'bi; the Scouts of Al-Tarbiya al-Wataniyieh; the Scouts of Al-Urouba; the Union of Al-Shabiba al-Islamiyieh; and the United Front of Ras Beirut.

In addition, then, to the International Red Cross (an international organization), the Lebanese Red Cross (one of its branches) and the Lebanese Civil Defence (officially recognized as a public institution), there were various civil organizations involved. Some of these last had, however, previously co-ordinated their efforts under the umbrella of the Organization of Civil Defence Volunteers, commonly known as the Volunteer Committee. This committee, which was subject to the jurisdiction of the Lebanese Civil Defence, was headed by Fu'ad Rustom, and he it was who took responsibility for the search for victims. He immediately dispatched all the organizations of the Volunteer Committee to the massacre site, and also issued a mission permit to each of the private organizations that had come swiftly forward to offer their humanitarian services. This was because the area had become an effective military zone and permits were therefore necessary to enter it.

The work began, and went on for two full weeks. In many cases the organizations worked day and night, a number of them even erecting field tents for accommodation. There were, it was estimated, some hundreds of rescue workers. In the crucial first days, each organization comprised 50–100 members, if not more, with female volunteers playing their full parts. A noteworthy feature was the volunteers' relative youth: some were under 20; some even under 18.

A Danish documentary film included scenes of clearance and burial, and these bore witness to the ceaseless efforts of the various teams involved and the high level of co-operation between them.[21]

From the testimonies of the rescue volunteers

The Oral History Project of Sabra and Shatila included the testimonies of 24 rescue workers affiliated to various humanitarian organizations who contributed to the crucial and difficult search for victims.

There was general agreement among them that they had never in their lives witnessed such savagery; this being marked, most distinctively, by the killing of babies and whole families, the backfilling over corpses using bulldozers, the booby-trapping of bodies lying on the ground (so that they would blow up if anyone came to lift them), and the mutilation of victims' faces with caustic solutions, rendering identification difficult or even impossible.

They also noted in their testimonies how Lebanese photographers and reporters had been prevented from entering, especially on that first Sunday, while their foreign counterparts, as their photographs and articles showed, were going about freely. Over the following days, however, a degree of 'leniency' was shown to Lebanese photographers, leading to the publication of a number of photographs in local newspapers.

I shall, first of all, provide part of the rescuers' testimonies dealing with the early hours of the gruelling mission and the spectacles that remain imprinted on their memories.

Imad, a rescuer from the Organization of Al-Iss'af al-Sha'bi, drew a comparison between the ferocity of the massacre and that of the civil war:

As soon as the news was broadcast, I headed for Sabra and Shatila with some members of Al-Iss'af al-Sha'bi. Believe me, none of us had ever seen anything like it before, however ugly the Lebanese civil war had been. For the first time we saw roads littered with corpses, horribly stacked one on top of the other ... Some of them had quite clearly been mutilated and others killed, either cut down or directly shot ...

Really, what horrifies you, and fills you with anguish, is to see a baby under two months old, not hurt by an explosion, or a grenade, or air force shelling or whatever, but simply cut from ear to ear ...[22]

Hajj Maysam, from the Scouts of Al-Risala al-Islamiyieh, spoke of the killing of an entire family, and also of the harassment of Lebanese photographers:

When we first got in, we saw the people gathering in the square. We rushed into the alleys. The Lebanese Army had been imposing a lot of restrictions: reporters weren't allowed to go in, and taking photographs wasn't allowed. I smuggled the Al-Safir journalist in, inside the ambulance, I got him in ...

We went into a house ... I'll never forget the sight. The members of a Palestinian family were sitting round in a circle; they'd been eating supper. Apparently they'd had no idea a massacre was going on. Their house was in one of the branch alleys, inside al-Horsh, near the Akka Hospital road. There was a father, I remember, sitting there, and next to him was a mother, very fat, and there were five children sitting there in front of them. It was the first time I'd seen a massacre like that – you just couldn't believe it! It was obvious they'd all been machine-gunned; there wasn't a single one left, not one.

What got to me was the sight of a boy still holding a fork in his hand; the boy had died, with his fork still in his hand.

I said to the reporter who was with us: 'Please, take some photos, take them.'

We moved on to another sight: there was a group of 13 people who'd been forced to line up against the wall, then they'd been gunned down. You could still see the bullet marks on their bodies, the blood had stained the walls, and they were all on the ground, meaning they'd been gunned down while they were standing; you could see the shots on the walls. We saw that close to the camp ... I carried those 13 bodies away myself, with my own hands.

Suddenly, we heard a foreign woman from the Red Cross call to the Lebanese Army, telling them we were taking pictures, and the army came and confiscated the film. Earlier on, we'd hidden all the films that were finished in the ambulance. We managed to hide five films we distributed to the agencies the same day.

They asked the photographer: 'How did you get in? Who got you in?' He said: 'I went in by myself.'

The photo of the group gunned down against the wall was on that last film, the one that was confiscated.[23]

Wafiq, from the Civil Defence of Al-Makased al-Islamiyieh, spoke of the killings of women and children and of the booby-trapped bodies:

I was one of the first to go in there ... We had instructions from our leadership not to touch anything we saw, we weren't to touch anything without orders. Thank God, the instructions were spot on, because the bodies were booby-trapped. Some members from other Civil Defence teams tried to lift bodies without noticing some of them had been booby-trapped, and they went off ...

I tell you, we saw such things as we'd never seen before: hundreds of bodies flung here and there, and they were all swollen and booby-trapped; every body had a bomb or something like that inside it. We saw it all along the Sabra Camp road, up as far as the border of Bir Hasan with the Akka Hospital.

We saw so many dreadful things. There were a lot of children in a horrifying state. I swear, there were mostly women and children. There were old people too, but what stood out was the women and children ... In a single family, we'd see a woman and her children, we'd see a grandmother along with her children and grandchildren, and we'd see the old men and the younger ones. There were a few men, we saw a lot of old men, but what stuck out with the victims was the women and children ...[24]

Ma'moun, of the Volunteer Committee, supplied details of a friend of his who had survived a booby-trap placed beneath one body:

We wanted to go back, we were worn out after working all day long. The guys came, and it's lucky they were so exhausted. There were four guys going to carry one body, one at each corner. While they were lifting it, the bomb underneath it started twisting, the safety catch was already released, and I saw it and told them to let go, I yelled and told them to let go ... I was afraid it would blow up, we reported it to the army straight away.[25]

Nuhad Israwi ('Israwi' is a pseudonym used for the purposes of this volume), an official at the Civil Defence of Al-Makased al-Islamiyieh, also spoke of the children and booby-trapped bodies, drawing a comparison between Sabra and Shatila and Deir Yassin (the Arab village in Palestine which, in 1948, was subjected to a brutal unprovoked attack by Zionist Irgun forces, and its

inhabitants butchered or forced to flee):

As members and leaders of a Civil Defence Force, we've taken part in a fair number of rescue operations, and we've seen plenty of disasters. Whenever we saw an old man, or an old woman, or a young man, or a girl, in the Sabra and Shatila massacre, some of their bodies mutilated, we'd lift them up and clear all the rubble away, because we thought it was our humanitarian duty.

But that doesn't mean we weren't affected or we didn't weep, especially when we saw the small children, that was what really hurt us deeply, so much so that one of us had to stop work for a time ... He couldn't go on, he went away for a few days and then he came back.

Frankly, I tell you, Sabra and Shatila put the Deir Yassin massacre completely in the shade.

When we first arrived, there were bodies thrown down on the ground. We went up to check on them, and we saw the killers had booby-trapped them with hand grenades. The hand grenade was attached in such a way that if the body was turned over the safety catch would be released and it would go off in a matter of five or six seconds. And so I told Colonel Marcel, who'd been delegated to carry out the humanitarian mission by the Lebanese Army, that the army should send in a specialist bomb disposal team. There was no way we could work, as a Civil Defence force from Al-Makased or anywhere else, till the bombs had been disabled.

We waited for nearly four hours, then this team arrived and inspected the bodies, and they disabled a lot of bombs.[26]

Hasan Hamzawi ('Hamzawi' is a pseudonym used for the purposes of this volume), from the Scouts of Al-Tarbiya al-Wataniyieh, spoke of the various methods of killing and, again, of the booby-trapped bodies:

When we first got in we saw people who'd been killed in all different ways. The first thing was the mass shooting, which we saw at the forefront of the camp. The victims had been put against the wall with their backs turned, and the killers had shot them all in the back, and they were all piled on top of one another ...

One of the witnesses, who's gone mad now, described how the martyrs were shaking and dripping blood. She saw the killers when they gathered and killed the first group on the edge of the camp. We saw some people who'd been hit on the head with axes; they'd chopped off some people's heads so you couldn't see their eyes and noses any more. There was one whose intestines they'd blown up, they'd put bombs in and blown him up; we're still wondering how it happened. We don't understand the burning either. You'd see a clean corpse with no marks except a burned belly, and we didn't know how it was done. Some people say they used butane gas bottles fixed with a straw to make a flame and burn bellies, but no one knew how it was done.

We'd get in a house and find a woman with the unborn child taken from her and thrown on to the ground ... We'd see bodies with grenades attached to them, to kill us off too. If we hadn't noticed them, we would have had casualties. We really kept our eyes open working at the massacre. Our group found six bodies with time bombs attached to them, I mean, the bomb would go off just as you were pulling the body ...

We were really careful, we'd try and disable the bomb on the basis it must have been wired. We'd pull the body out just as the bomb was unwired, and along with others we managed to pull a lot out.[27]

Shawqi, from the United Front of Ras Beirut, spoke of the booby-traps and the savage killing of children – he himself was a secondary school student:

The killing of children was the most appalling thing any human being could ever have imagined. There was a house that had been brought down on some small children; I can tell you exactly where it was. About a 100 metres past Sabra Square, there's a street with a house at the end of it, to the right, that's where the house was brought down on the kids. It was close to the two dead horses in Sabra, everyone knows that photo. On the outside the house was completely wrecked, and everyone we saw there was little kids. The first kid we lifted out had had his head split in five pieces. That was the most savage thing I saw in that house.

And then, the most critical moments for me were when I was going into a garden to make a search. I was on my own, but when I'd taken just four steps, I heard a woman yell: 'Stop, right there. You're going over a minefield. You'll have to walk slowly.' Coming back, I stepped on the same places I'd used going in.

The woman was right, because the French team came later on and detonated the mine.

There were a lot of mined roads up to the Sports City. Not even the Red Cross dared go in. We knew there'd been bodies in the swimming pool, and we were afraid to go out to them. But when the French soldiers came, they helped detonate the bombs.[28]

Ziad, from the Union of Al-Shabiba al-Islamiyieh, spoke of the nature and various difficulties of the work, and of how photographers were prevented from going in:

People knew the army had come in, so they started going back to see what had happened to their houses and families and neighbours. They found them all lying on the ground: some had been gunned down, others axed, others knifed; we still have a knife that was used in the massacre.

On the first day our job was to pick up the victims whose bodies you could see there on the roads.

We had no idea how much work there was still waiting for us, or how many people there were lying dead under the rubble, the bodies we couldn't see.

We set up a field centre inside the camp. We slept there, in Sabra. We stayed for two weeks in a camp specially reserved for the committees, so we could work in shifts and the work could go on without any break. One group would go in the morning, and another would go in the afternoon. There were days when we had to turn on searchlights and work at night, to be able to take away all the bodies. The longer the bodies stayed there, the more smell, epidemics and infections were released. We were using anti-odour chemicals all over Sabra.

... One small comment I'd like to make here: they wouldn't let photographers take pictures of the bodies, and we think that was a mistake. The bodies should have been photographed so the international public could be informed, especially as there were Lebanese civilians among them ... We helped photographers, as well, to take shots for their various magazines.[29]

The rumours of Sa'd Haddad's return

According to those who, during the search for victims, recorded their observations and impressions of the massacre, their worst experience of all concerned rumours of the return of Sa'd Haddad.

It was clear enough when the search was over that these had in fact been rumours only. At the time, nevertheless, people believed them; the panic would spread and everyone, rescue workers included, would flee, leaving no one there but the victims.

Shawqi, the young rescue worker mentioned earlier who fled before starting work, spoke of his and his colleagues' experience:

On the Sunday, once we knew some of the Red Cross had made it into Sabra and Shatila, we felt reassured we could go too. We were still worried even so, as we started, and we had green clothes on.

We went in through al-Fakhani and the Arab University side. We arrived on the Sunday, at ten in the morning. As we were going in, we saw everybody running and screaming: 'Sa'd Haddad's here! Sa'd Haddad's here!'

We took off as well.

When we reached the Cola roundabout we saw some army soldiers there. We stayed in the vehicles close to them.

At noon, another rumour started going around …

We had to wait till the afternoon before we could go back, then we worked till night without a break …[30]

In his testimony, Hajj Maysam – who had led the rescue workers of the Scouts of Al-Risala al-Islamiyieh – emphasized that two rumours had spread on the Sunday, not just one:

There were two rumours on Sunday; there was one in the morning and another one between half past two and three in the afternoon.

I tell you frankly, there was no one left after the rumours. Hardly anyone stayed. Even the Red Cross people took off, but they came back when they saw us working.

On the Monday a third rumour started going round, again that Sa'd Haddad was back. There was no one left. What happened was horrifying, just the way you'd imagine Judgement Day, with people rushing in all different directions; people were utterly terrified that day. They ran up to Burj Abu Haidar, and al-Ghobairi, and other districts a long way from the camp, and so there was panic all over the different districts, not just in the camps.[31]

One of the few not to believe the rumours was Hajj Mahmoud Rukn, a 50-year-old man from Sabra who had lost no one from his family but, from humanitarian motives, wanted to contribute to the search and rescue efforts. He confirmed Hajj Maysam's account of the rumours:

On Sunday, I saw a man standing by a car the colour of cumin, and he was saying: 'Get back, it's Sa'd Haddad! Get back, it's Sa'd Haddad!'

There weren't a lot of people in the camp, there were just a few going back and forth, some were checking the bodies, looking for members of their family. All the streets were still covered with heads, arms, legs, hair, other body parts, and they'd started covering them up …

I was standing by the hill … To start with I didn't move, but when I saw people running down both sides of the streets, I thought maybe they were coming in through another entrance. Hellish thoughts took hold of me.

And so I ran off too …

I went back on Monday, they'd covered up a lot of people by then … and they'd started laying the bodies out on the ground, there were around 300 of them. The Sa'd Haddad rumours started going round again, and straight away people started running. But earlier I'd seen an engineering team from the Lebanese Army, I'd recognized them by their uniform, it was official Lebanese Army's; they'd come in to disable and detonate mines, there were around ten of them …[32]

The rumours, as the Tuesday's newspapers confirmed, had their source in the intervention of the army's engineering team, accompanied by a military force, to search for mines. Eventually (the newspapers further noted) these rumours had spread to all parts of West Beirut.[33]

Yet the rumours did not cease even when the search operations had been completed. After returning to their homes, residents continued to live in constant fear, especially as there was continual talk of Sa'd Haddad's return.[34]

However, the rumour eclipsing all others before it was the one that spread at sunset on the fortieth day after the massacre, running through Sabra, Shatila and all the neighbouring quarters and causing people to flee in utter panic. An eye-witness who lived in the Revolutionary Judiciary building behind the Sports City said people were running in vast numbers, all seeking to escape. The French and Italian soldiers from the multinational forces did their best to reassure them. 'I saw an agonized Palestinian father,' this eye-witness said, 'who, not knowing what he was doing, grabbed a Lebanese soldier by his shirt, yelling: "Are you Lebanese Army or Sa'd Haddad?" The young soldier tried to calm him down. "I swear by God, uncle," he told him, "I'm Lebanese Army." '[35]

A full week after the fortieth day, a Palestinian mother, hearing that Sa'd Haddad was about to return, warned her neighbours then went into her house to fetch her children and leave. Two Lebanese soldiers assigned as guards went in, and the woman subsequently gave an account of her conversation with one of them:

He said to me: 'What's the matter, hajjeh? Who told you there's going to be a massacre?' I said: 'I've just run into two guys on the road, they told me ...' He said: 'Hajjeh, just tell me who they are, we'll cut the tongue of anyone who starts up rumours. There's no massacre or anything like it. Sleep here at home, sister, and don't be frightened.'

We calmed down after that. The army kept going back and forth in the district where we are now. They started patrolling every evening.[36]

It is possible to trace every rumour back to some underlying cause. It has already been noted how the rumour of Sunday 19 September began when people saw a group of military engineers or commandos and mistook them for militias. Two points, nevertheless, merit further analysis.

The first point is that the rumours always specifically concerned Sa'd Haddad's forces. Not once did they name the Lebanese Forces, even though members of the Lebanese Forces were considerably more numerous in the massacre than those of Sa'd Haddad's; added to which (and people knew this perfectly well) the leadership was theirs alone, not Sa'd Haddad's. If, then, the misconception had sprung merely from confusion of members of the army with those of the militias, the panic-stricken people would have been more likely to cry

out about 'the Lebanese Forces'. The constant repetition of 'Sa'd Haddad' shows how those sowing the rumours brought in Sa'd Haddad specifically, while also instilling fear with the aim of making people leave the district at once.

The second point is that these rumours did not result only in the flight of residents and rescuers. The most significant outcome was revealed next day when the families of victims returned to find their loved ones had been taken away and buried – thereby removing all trace of them and making it impossible to register their names.

It was in the Lebanese Forces' interest both to shift full liability for the massacre on to another party and to reduce the number of civilian victims, in order to demonstrate that this had indeed been a 'battle' rather than a massacre.

For all that, the rumours remain one of the mysteries of Sabra and Shatila to this day.

The bulldozers and their contrary missions

The bulldozers had played a prominent role during the Sabra and Shatila massacre. Once the massacre was over, their role became totally different – indeed the ironic reverse of before. During those three bloody days, the bulldozers had been used to cover victims beneath the rubble; now their job was to search for victims.

There were many bulldozers during the massacre, mostly Israeli-made. In the subsequent stage there were very few of them, and these belonged to the humanitarian organizations. The most active and mobile bulldozer belonged to Al-Makased al-Islamiyieh.

The most significant references to bulldozers were contained in the Kahan Report, the articles of foreign authors and journalists, and the testimonies of the victims' families and the rescue workers.

According to the Kahan Report, a meeting was held between the Israelis and the Lebanese Forces, at the latter's headquarters in Beirut, at around four o'clock on the Friday afternoon (the second day of the massacre). There the Forces' representatives asked the Israeli Army for a bulldozer to enable them to remove all illegitimate buildings, and the Israeli Chief of Staff decided the request was reasonable, especially as he had long heard of the presence of illegitimate Palestinian quarters. He therefore approved the request.[37]

We may note, however, that, while the text spoke of a single bulldozer requested, multiple bulldozers were in fact issued. There is nothing intrinsically very surprising about this. What was odd was the late time at which the request was made, at four o'clock on the second day of the massacre, when the Israelis were asking them (at the same meeting) to be out completely by five o'clock on the Saturday morning, in view of American pressure. By what rationale was the 'removal of illegitimate buildings' – as both parties referred to the process – to be postponed till the final night? Was there really time for the Lebanese Forces militia to distinguish clearly between 'legitimate' and 'illegitimate' buildings? Did they have maps? Or was their aim rather the indiscriminate removal of buildings and the whole district? If the last, then they would have had to start doing this from the early hours of the Thursday evening onward – which is, in fact, precisely what they did. Then they covered up the matter by submitting a request for a bulldozer, as though they were only then going to begin the demolition operation! The Kahan Report did not – officially – investigate the delay involved in making such a key request.

The fact of the matter is that bulldozers were available in large numbers from the early hours onwards. What is more, they were used not only to demolish houses and shops but also to bring houses down on top of their owners, to dig trenches, to transport and backfill corpses, and to conceal, as far as possible, all traces of the massacre.

Had the Kahan Report paused to consider Dr Paul Morris's testimony, which he submitted to the Kahan Commission in person, it would, at the very least, have drawn a comparison between the numbers involved in his account, which spoke of the use of ten bulldozers on the Saturday morning, and the Forces' request for a 'single one' at the meeting at four on the Friday afternoon. Is it conceivable that these

ten bulldozers suddenly appeared on the final night?

Dr Morris's testimony included his observations on the time, during the Saturday morning, when he and his medical colleagues at the Gaza Hospital were walking along Sabra–Shatila Street on their way to be questioned:

General Efrat: On the way through the camps you have seen bulldozers?
Dr. Morris: Yes.
General Efrat: How many?
Dr. Morris: Ten or more.
General Efrat: Ten or more.
Dr. Morris: Ten or more. I noticed at least ten. I mean there may be more. There were bulldozers working down the lower part, the lower half of the street. And also at the end of the street, at the cross roads, at the very bottom of Rue Sabra, at the exit from the camps where there was a water hydrant. I particularly noticed a bulldozer there because that was where the people used to collect water from and that had been completely flattened. The bulldozer was working on there. There were some behind it. And there were some on either side of the street.
General Efrat: What were they doing?
Dr. Morris: Some of them were moving just mounds of earth and some of them simply pushing houses down.[38]

General Efrat's repetition of the phrase suggests his astonishment at the presence of ten bulldozers; which was understandable enough, especially since, as a member of the Investigatory Commission, he must have reviewed the details of the Friday's meeting between the Forces and the Israelis. General Efrat and his two colleagues on the commission could have verified the significance and function of the bulldozers from two other witnesses appearing before them: Dr Swee Chai Ang and Nurse Ellen Siegel, each of whom had something to say on the matter (their statements in this regard being subsequently published). In the event, the final commission report excluded any indication as to the actual role of bulldozers in the massacre.

The plain fact is that the demolition of houses was not something intrinsically 'legitimate', as the Forces' representatives had claimed, but rather an illegitimate and inhuman means of burying victims beneath the rubble.

The Israeli journalist Ben-Yishay reported on the Friday afternoon meeting between the Israelis, led by General Etan, and the Forces. The details conveyed in his report do not, however, correspond to those subsequently published in the Kahan Report. Quoting Israeli officers, he said the Forces had requested two bulldozers in order to remove 'obstacles and obstructions' at the camps, but that the General had turned this down (the Kahan Report, in contrast, affirms that the General welcomed the idea as a means of removing the illegitimate houses). He then added that the Phalangists had received a single Israeli bulldozer after the meeting, but that he did not know who had authorized this. The bulldozer then broke down, forcing the Phalangists to cover up the bodies and remove the houses using another, which they had also managed to obtain on the Friday evening.[39]

Apart from Ben-Yishay, foreign correspondents were less concerned with the means by which the Phalangists had contrived to obtain the bulldozers than with subsequent activities. Thomas Friedman wrote that, judging by the number of buildings removed or largely demolished, the objective was evidently to transform the district into a place uninhabitable for returning survivors. Regarding the operations of the bulldozers, he noted:

Many buildings were bulldozed atop the bodies inside them. Some bodies were bulldozed into huge sandpiles, with arms and legs poking out in spots. In some areas the militia men made neat piles of rubble and corrugated iron shields to hide the corpses.[40]

As for Robert Fisk, who covered the Sabra and Shatila case extensively, he said of the bulldozers:

There were signs of hastily-dug mass graves.
… The blood was still wet on the ground.
… There was another trackway deeper inside the camp where a bulldozer had left its tracks in the mud. We followed these tracks until we came to one hundred square yards of newly ploughed earth. Flies carpeted the ground and there was a familiar, fine, sweet smell in the air.

We looked at this place, all of us suspected what none of us would ever find out, that this was a mass grave. A diplomat driving down the road outside the camp some hours earlier had seen a bulldozer with a dozen corpses in its scoop. Who dug this earth with such efficiency? Who drove the bulldozer? We could not find out.[41]

A *Newsweek* article compiled by a number of correspondents substantiated the diplomat's testimony regarding the bulldozers' departure from the camp, loaded with bodies. It stated:

Witnesses said that on Friday afternoon they saw bulldozers rumble out of Sabra, their scoops filled with bodies. At some point the bulldozers dug out a mass grave outside the west wall of Sabra, about 200 paces from the Israeli command post. When Wilkinson [a *Newsweek* reporter] found the grave later, limbs of at least three bodies were sticking out.[42]

In any case, the testimonies of victims' families, involving as they did the early hours of the massacre, precede both the Kahan Report and the foreign press. A number of these were provided earlier, and I shall therefore simply pause at a small number of testimonies relating to the Thursday evening and Friday morning – prior, that is, to General Etan's meeting with the Forces at half past four on the Friday afternoon. The implication of the Kahan Report was that, when the Forces made their request for a bulldozer to demolish illegitimate houses, they had had no bulldozers earlier and so had not yet operated any.

I shall note, first, the testimony of Hind, the woman who lived just behind the Sports City. She it was who, on the Thursday evening, saw four bulldozers operating together near her house at Hayy al-Gharbi, and she it was, too, who stated that she had been able to make out Hebrew writings on the bulldozers closest to her (see Account 3, p. 81). Seven months after the massacre, as we walked together along the dirt road between her small house and the Sports City, Hind explained to me how the bulldozers had been operating on that first night, covering up bodies and digging up roads:

They'd dug big trenches, which they filled with victims ... They were digging and burying bodies at the same time, with the bulldozer. If you'd only seen how much they did, how much they dug here alone, you wouldn't have believed it all happened in just one night. You would have thought they must have been working for a month ...

They were slaughtering and burying people in the pit. I was on the roof of my house, watching them from behind the hanging blankets. I could see them, but they couldn't see me.

... All the houses here were wrecked by the bulldozers from that first night ... There are still bodies underneath.

There were bulldozers digging new roads too. You see that road? There used to be a sandy hill there. They took away the sand and dug the road. When you reach the end of that road, you turn right and you come to the mass grave.

They came in through different entrances. But even so, they dug a lot of roads, let's walk on and I'll show you another road ...

You see that pit here? It was completely filled with bodies. They brought them all with the bulldozer and threw them in here, dozens of them. Later on the Civil Defence took them all out and wrapped them in nylon bags.[43]

In Um Akram's testimony about the Friday morning (see Chapter 4, pp. 116–17), we saw how, at that early hour, the witness noted the distinct marks of bulldozers on the roads of Hayy Ersal. Seeing that a number of houses she knew were no longer there, it was obvious enough to her that demolition was taking place. She further noted that killing and removal was happening at the same time.

Testimonies from many different places agree that the demolition of houses was continuous. One of these was from the woman (see Chapter 4, p. 117) who, on the Friday morning, was dragged along with the crowds to the Sports City. She testified how, on the road between Shatila Street and Hayy Ersal, all the way to the Sports City, she saw the bulldozers wrecking houses and backfilling over the victims, in front of everybody.

As for the type of bulldozer used, an eye-witness from among those driven off for questioning told how he saw them on the Saturday morning:

There were three types of bulldozer I saw. There was a special one for demolishing houses, that one was unstoppable, it destroyed the whole house; the second one surfaced or opened up the road; and the third was the rotating sort, it scooped things away. So, each one was a type on its own, and the attackers worked them all at the same time, and they were all yellow. There were some trenches too, which had obviously been dug before the Saturday. But not all the bulldozers were brought in by the Israelis; I saw some others the militias had brought in, and they were backfilling over the victims, right there in front of us all.[44]

Um Majed, a Palestinian mother, saw the demolition and confirmed that the bulldozers' primary mission was the shameless burial of people in front of everyone. She was one of those forced to walk on the Saturday, and she described what she saw while standing near the Kuwaiti Embassy:

I saw how they machine-gunned them in the pit, from the Bir Hasan side. There used to be a sandy hill there, and the pit was behind the hill; I mean, the whole area there was like a pit, lower down than the hill, we saw how they machine-gunned 15 people there. They put them together and they machine-gunned them. Then they brought the bulldozer and dumped the backfill. I saw them, with my own eyes, shooting them, and the bulldozer dumping backfill over them.

That's what I saw, but after we'd gone, quite a few of the people who were still there told me the militias took them to Khaldé afterwards.[45]

A local witness made a link between the pits created by the Israeli air force in the course of the invasion and those created by the bulldozers during the massacre. He said:

The pit I'm talking about is inside the Sports City. The militias there machine-gunned the people who'd come out to surrender. They'd shoot anyone, too, who made a second move; and there were times when they buried people alive.

This pit's opposite the Sports City, next to Jam'iyyat al-Ina'ash; it had been made by an air force rocket.

But there were other pits the militias had dug, and we saw them being prepared. The bulldozers were digging deep trenches, in rather a strange way; and later on they'd put all the victims in them.

I also, with my own eyes, saw the bulldozer digging up the road and wrecking the houses ... it even tore down the shops over the people. They got them inside the shops, then they tore them down over their heads.[46]

Abu Jamal, the owner of the garage in Shatila Street, told how, on the Saturday, he had seen a huge Israeli bulldozer, odd-looking and olive-green in colour, at the entrance to Shatila. It had seemed like a mountain, and could, he added with bitter sarcasm, have shovelled up the whole of Beirut, let alone Shatila. We noted in Chapter 1 Abu Jamal's description of Shatila Main Street, so crowded and brimming with life before the invasion. We have also seen, through a number of testimonies, how residents returning to Sabra and Shatila after the departure of the fighters did not find the destruction of houses and public places they had been expecting. Yet just as the place was returning to normal, the massacre took place. Five months later, Abu Jamal walked with me down Shatila Street, pointing out sites where houses had been destroyed with not a trace left behind. We began our walk from the south side, up towards Sabra, with Abu Jamal deep in talk about people and places:

Everyone who lived in this house here was wiped out. Everyone who lived in that house opposite was wiped out, there was no one left. That's Abu Yasser's house; that's Abu Ali's house, everyone there went too. That's his car, poor fellow; it's still parked here. May God bless his soul. That's Youssef's house; his father, mother, grandmother and brother all died. Abu Saber and Um Saber were never found either, nor were their children. May God bless their souls. Their bodies were never found; they were backfilled along with the others. May God bless their souls. Those who lived in the houses right down there, they were all wiped out ... That's Hayy Ersal, where the road starts; oh God, so many people died there, may God rest their souls ...

All those people were killed during the massacre. The bulldozer was right behind them on the road, the militias would do their work, then the bulldozer would do its job. As I told you, this district had some of the finest houses and buildings. A lot of the people we knew stayed there under the rubble because no one could get them out.

There's a whole section there, to the right, and they did away with it all, along with shops six or seven metres long. My garage was 25 metres long; they took out ten metres then they tried to strike deeper and tear it down over the dozens of people they'd shot in the garage entrance on the first night. There was a man who climbed up into that famous big rubber tree and stayed there; he was there all night, watching what they were doing. He told me that himself, and he told me how they didn't pull down the garage to start with, but came back and did it next day ...[47]

As search operations proceeded, rescue workers were able to see the results of the bulldozers' work. Nuhad Israwi said:

We realized a lot of the bodies, babies' bodies especially, had been buried in advance. In other words, there were bulldozers from the start; we could see the marks of their wheels, and the chain was there – we got there first, there was no one ahead of us. So there were bulldozers there; they dug and put down a lot of corpses and later they came back and dumped backfill over them; we found those bodies while we were working.[48]

After the massacre, the bulldozer's task was the reverse of what it had been before; it turned to removing the backfill so as to find victims and – as the rescue workers repeatedly stressed – provide them with a decent burial rather than leaving them buried anonymously deep in the earth, and leaving memory of them to fade away. Rescue worker Fayez, from the United Front of Ras Beirut, described how the militias had used the bulldozers:

I was working near the Sports City from above, along with Captain Ghassan, and we were watching to see whether there'd been pits and bodies in the City. He was working on one bulldozer and I was working on another. All at once the bulldozer blade started working, up till then we'd thought there was nothing. The second time, it brought up 25 bodies, all sliced in pieces. I screamed, I was shocked ... I nearly choked.

There was a woman and her children, and there was a family along with their neighbours; around 27 people all together, and I saw them in the pit.

Later we found another pit ...

If you ask me, there are pits we still haven't found yet, because the pit we saw had been there for a couple of weeks or so ...

Then we were given instructions to stop the work, and leave everything, it was over. That was because the bodies had decomposed completely by then, or because they'd taken enough bodies away ...[49]

Even the lifting out of bodies with bulldozers was no comfortable matter for the rescue workers, though they realized there was no other way. Rescue worker Ma'moun, of the Lebanese Civil Defence, described how they used the bulldozers to collect bodies:

There were dozens of bodies in some of the narrow streets. We started getting them out with the Al-Makased al-Islamiyieh bulldozer. Imagine a bulldozer taking out backfill, stones and gravel, then it started taking out bodies. There were a good number of them, and they were all swollen.[50]

The Danish photographer (whose name I have not been able to obtain) took some shots of the lifting of bodies with the bulldozer, which was operating very carefully under the constant guidance of the rescue workers; these latter, on the spot, would instruct the driver to stop whenever there was concern a body might be ripped or an arm or a leg disfigured.[51]

The burial of the victims

For a full two weeks, burial went on alongside the search for victims. This does not mean, however, that every victim was (in the words of the rescue workers) 'honourably' buried, if buried at all. This was due to circumstances beyond the best efforts of everyone on the massacre site. There were various reasons.

First, it was simply not possible to reach all the vast numbers of people who had been buried beneath the rubble of their homes, or had been dumped in mass graves specially dug during the massacre, or whose bodies had remained stacked on the bulldozers, before being removed altogether, as a diplomat and others have testified above.

Second, the harmful rumours about the return of 'Sa'd Haddad' or 'Sa'd Haddad's

men' had a significant effect, leading people to flee in panic. This in turn resulted (especially after the Sunday's rumour) in the mass burial of a great many victims whose names or exact numbers were unknown. Various people returned on the Monday morning to find their loved ones no longer there, and were subsequently told everyone was in the mass cemetery – though the cemetery had not, in point of fact, been dug yet. This, in turn, indicates that many people were buried on the Sunday evening without any religious formalities, knowledge of names, or identification of the place.

Third, search operations were halted after two weeks, for various reasons – among them the intention of closing the book on Sabra and Shatila at the earliest possible opportunity.

Despite all these factors, many people did manage to transfer and bury their family victims in several Beiruti cemeteries: Rawdat al-Shahidein, al-Shuhada and al-Bashoura. In addition to this, dozens of victims were taken off to their respective towns or villages, particularly to Baalbek, Tyre, Majdal Zoun and Bra'sheit.

Even so, there were, according to a significant number of Palestinians, many who were unable to transfer or bury their dead relatives, either because there was no family member left to do so, or because whoever was left had insufficient money, or because people had fled on account of the rumours and returned to find the victims gone.

The 'Danish video' covering the days of the search captured the most tragic, heartrending scenes, such as bodies laid in a line, or women removing the cover from this body or that in an attempt to identify their loved ones. On the Monday (so the scenes revealed), more than 80 bodies remained unidentified and, at the end of the day, the majority of the bodies were buried unknown, for whole families had been wiped out. Those watching the tape could hear a woman's voice crying: 'Alas for people and their right to live, don't they have a right to live?'[52]

Those who remained unidentified, or whose people could not afford to transfer them for burial, were interred in what later became known as the mass cemetery. This lies in the forefront of Shatila, to the right for someone entering from the south side. The establishment of such a cemetery during these harsh times was a delicate matter and required some kind of religious accompaniment, all the more so as there were those calling for immediate burial without prayer or formality so as to save time and prevent the spread of disease. Hajj Maysam, who was in charge of the Al-Risala al-Islamiyieh Civil Defence, explained how the decision to dig the mass cemetery was reached:

We had a clash with the Lebanese Army and the Civil Defence Force regarding the method of burial. We have a public religious law, and Muslims should be buried in accordance with it.

We found the Lebanese Army, along with the Red Cross, were determined to bring in bulldozers and finish with burials on the spot, without any prayers. Like everyone else, we'd been working all through Monday, till those Sa'd Haddad rumours started spreading; after that there wasn't a soul left in the street except us. The day was nearly over.

Mr Fu'ad Rustom arrived and told us: 'The situation's very dangerous; the guys want to leave.' I told him: 'We can't leave.' He said: 'Will you take the responsibility?' I said: 'We're ready to do that.'

We went to see the Lebanese Army, and an officer told us the only option was to lift out the bodies with the bulldozers. 'At this moment,' I said, 'I've got 70 young Al-Risala men with me, and we're all ready to die if we have to. All these victims should be buried in an honourable manner.' He answered: 'Where are you going to take all these people?'

As far as I could estimate, after watching all day, there were still 1,400 bodies. All the while he was talking to me, I was thinking, how could we bury them all? A lot, I knew, had been taken by their people during the day, al-Miqdad people and others. So I answered: 'We'll bring bulldozers and have them dig very deep into empty ground, and we'll bring a shaykh and ask him to perform pre-burial prayers.'[53]

The young men of Al-Risala al-Islamiyieh decided to make swift contact with high-level religious authorities: they contacted Shaykh Muhammad Shams al-Din, the Vice-President of the Higher Islamic Shi'ite Council and a man known for his sharp mind and fatherly authority, and al-Sayyed Muhammad Hasan Fadlallah, the widely known and highly respected Islamic authority. Both were of the opinion that religious formalities for the victims should be set in train without delay. Fu'ad Rustom, the Head of the Civil Defence Force, sent an immediate call to Shaykh Salman al-Khalil, who arrived at four o'clock on the Monday afternoon to pray over the victims' souls.

The work that had been halted following the rumours now resumed. The Red Cross members had made ready to leave, but when they saw the Al-Risala al-Islamiyieh men working, they returned to help them; and so night was turned into day.

Hajj Maysam elaborated on the work:

We had to bury no fewer than 800 victims, most of them Palestinians.

Shaykh Salman wouldn't permit the burial of men and women in a common grave, with no barrier; this was on strictly religious grounds. So, we started making multiple levels, putting lime on to the decomposed bodies, and laying bodies next to one another in tens and twelves. Shaykh Salman would then make a group prayer for every batch of ten, for a full five minutes. His brother, Shaykh Ja'far al-Khalil, would help him with the prayers, taking it in turns, it was such a tedious job.

There was no chance of shrouding; we'd just cover the victims with blankets, add lime and finish the burial. We added lime to avoid any bad effects from so many bodies being there together, one on top of the other. Lime absorbs bacteria.

So by sunset on Monday, we started the burial work.

In the mass cemetery alone there were 700 or 800 bodies.[54]

Shaykh Salman al-Khalil kept brief diaries of the invasion and the massacre, and these included the following entry with regard to the burial:

On Saturday, my brother Hajj Ja'far and I completed the burial of the Sabra and Shatila victims at Rawdat al-Shahidein; there were almost twenty of these on the first day.

On Sunday, we buried a good many of them. Then, on Monday, September 20, 1982, we buried and performed prayers over twenty-seven bodies in a single section; they were all members of the

Miqdad family. At a quarter past four that afternoon, I went to the Sabra and Shatila Camp, at the request of the Civil Defence and the Scouts of al-Risala, and I performed prayers for almost a hundred victims: babies, women and the elderly. I performed prayers twice for the men and once for the women. I returned home at five o'clock that evening, in an exhausted state.

The Civil Defence called for me again on Tuesday, to go to Sabra and Shatila, and I performed prayers for seventy-five victims, men, women and children. The French Ambassador was there on that day, and I had a talk with him. I then returned with the young men to Rawdat al-Shahidein, buried a number of victims, and arranged for the transfer of others to the South and Baalbek, in cars …

… I performed prayers for five hundred victims over a period of five days …[55]

Nuhad Israwi, the man in charge of the Al-Makased al-Islamiyieh Civil Defence, also spoke of the mass cemetery:

We arranged for a mass cemetery. Sometimes a crisis calls for desperate measures.

We covered all the bodies; and we regarded them all as martyrs' bodies, that's why we didn't wash them. We buried them still bloodstained, as they were, but we covered them all and put them down in the mass cemetery, and we also fenced the place … and we placed wreaths of flowers …[56]

Supplements to accounts of the three days

Forty-two accounts have been provided concerning events of the three bloody days, and some of these were left without any final conclusion.

Some who had lost relatives still lived in hope of finding them when the massacre was over. Others had found their loved ones dead, either whole or in pieces. Yet others had failed to find them, or, in some cases, any trace of them. As such, the accounts were not over even when searches had come to an end, and tragedy was aggravated further by people's inability to prove their relatives' death.

Houses had been brought down on the heads of their inhabitants by bulldozers, after which the bulldozers had gone on to remove what remained of the houses, along with the victims, and flung them elsewhere. How were relatives supposed to find the victims' ID cards? What means did they have of demonstrating matters to officials?

Account 1 (p. 77) involved witnesses to the gunmen's entry into Bir Hasan at sunset on the Thursday. The account was remarkable in both its beginning and its end.

The beginning was remarkable in that none of the narrators or witnesses was killed, abducted or tortured. One of those trapped inside the Ba'jour building had, it will be remembered, even challenged them, telling them proudly: 'If you want to shoot, go ahead … [I'm a] Palestinian from '48. I'm from the heart of Palestine.' A militiaman had leaped up and urged a colleague to gun down these Palestinians and be rid of them; but the other militiaman had refused to fire at the residents, claiming he had no orders to do so.

That guard at the Ba'jour building, the brave grandfather who, on the Thursday evening, had escaped death with his grandchildren and daughters-in-law, Um Wassim and Um Ayman, had numerous times sat with his family wondering why they had been spared in this way.

The months passed, following those three bloody days. Then, finally, news came through a neighbour of theirs, Abu Muhammad Sudaini ('Sudaini' is a pseudonym used for the purposes of this volume), who had also been one of those trapped along with them. Um Ayman gives the following account of what this neighbour told them.

Abu Muhammad [Sudaini] told us how, one day, when he was standing by the side of the road in Sidon, someone suddenly came up behind him and tapped him on the shoulder. Abu Muhammad turned round but didn't recognize the man. Then the man asked: 'Don't you recognize me?' Abu Muhammad answered: 'I do … and I don't.' 'I'm your friend ——,' the man said, 'from Jall al-Dib, don't you remember me?' At this point Abu Muhammad did remember him. 'I do now,' he said. 'Now … I do … but sometimes, as years pass, people go their different ways.'

The man asked again: 'Weren't you in the Ba'jour building on that first day?' Abu Muhammad was quite puzzled now. 'That's right,' he said. 'How did you know?' That was when the man said: 'I was in charge of the group; and there was no way I could shoot you, after all the good old days we'd shared. But I didn't want you to see my face, so I turned away and said I didn't have any orders.'[57]

This was a truly extraordinary story, from beginning to end. However, one question remains: are 'the good old days' necessary before one man can show another that touch of humanity that marks mankind out from God's other creatures?

In Account 3 (p. 81) we saw how Hind, having been hit in the leg in front of her house, had managed to bring her children back home by making the attackers think they had fled from the other side. Now she spent the whole three days hoping for her husband's safe return from his visit to his mother in the South.

The moment Hind was sure people had started leaving their homes again, she went out to look for her husband. She searched for two days before she eventually found him lying, with dozens of others, near the mass cemetery:

He was all swollen, he looked pitiful. I couldn't even identify him from his clothes. There was dirt all over his clothes, and it wasn't just him you couldn't make out, it was everyone. We identified him from a mark he had on his head, it was like a date. I got closer to him, but still couldn't see his face. I just couldn't see him, they'd ripped open his face, or maybe they'd poured acid over them, who knows? But I identified him straight away from his mark … and what do you think happened then?

I started screaming, without realizing it. My children came and started crying over their father. And while I was still recovering from the shock, I saw my three cousins, three men, or bodies lying there rather, next to my husband …[58]

When she had calmed down a little, Hind told me her aunt was a Lebanese married to a Palestinian. Her cousins were Walid, Mahmoud and Muhammad Harb.

When I asked her whether she had learned, later, the date of her husband's return from the South, she said he had returned on the first evening: 'he arrived along with the massacre'. She also discovered, subsequently, that her mother-in-law

had baked some special bread, for her and the children. She knew her daughter-in-law was fond of this bread, and was aware, too, that bread of any kind was now impossible to find in Beirut, so she had insisted that her son take a large loaf of bread and a big container of yogurt. And her son, for his part, had insisted on returning that same night, to be sure of getting the bread and yogurt to the children.

Account 4 (p. 83) concerned Um Nabil the wife who, from the Thursday evening, sat waiting for her husband Abu Nabil, along with their three children, at the home of her aunt; he himself having returned home to Hayy Ersal to fetch milk for his newborn child. Her mother and aunt would not allow her to return herself and check, but she was naturally deeply anxious something had happened to him. 'How can he be safe?' she kept asking her aunt. 'All this time, and he still hasn't come. It doesn't make sense.' Once aware, though, of some of the things that had been taking place, she insisted on going home despite her aunt's advice, heading from the north through Sabra. A dreadful sight awaited her. She said:

I could never, ever have imagined the sight in front of me. The men were dumped there on the ground; some had been hit with axes, others had been shot, and I saw with my own eyes how booby-traps had been taken out from under them, from under their heads, that was just before the Doukhi shop.

I wanted to cross the road, to get home to Hayy Ersal, but I couldn't find the entrance to the quarter any more; people were just piled on top of one another. So, I kept walking till I found the main entrance. And now, where was our house, for God's sake? All the houses round us were more or less intact. But what had they done with mine? They'd gathered all the rubble and put it there inside, they'd torn down all the walls and the ceiling, they hadn't left anything but the pillars. I looked towards one corner and saw the television, that's how I knew it was our house, and I started screaming: 'Abu Nabil!'

There was no one in the quarter, I was all by myself, screaming, there wasn't a living soul … I went to ask at the Akka Hospital, but there was no one there. There were a lot of gunmen near the

Kuwaiti Embassy, and I didn't dare go near. Where could I ask?

My son was six weeks old and needed milk. I went back home, and found the milk and the bottles still there, so I took them and went back to my aunt's.

I ran into some foreign reporters on the way, and they went with me to my aunt's. I told them what had happened, and one of them gave me 100 lira for the children; I was still hardly conscious …

Next day I went back and came across an old woman, who asked me: 'What's wrong, daughter?' I said: 'I've lost my husband, I can't find any trace of him.' She said: 'There's one there, go and check.'

I did. I found a man lying there, without a head, without any clothes either. All he had on was a bathing suit. May God punish them for what they did to him; they'd bulldozed him along with everything else, and I couldn't see his head, or legs, or arms. All I could see was a dismembered body with a bathing suit; may God punish them.

May God bless his soul; he'd taken a shower on the Thursday and asked me for the bathing suit, he always felt more comfortable that way …[59]

The wife's agony was far from over. She still needed a bulldozer to remove the slab of masonry that had fallen on her husband. The men of the Civil Defence had to keep her to one side. Having removed the slab, they assured her they had made a thorough search but found nothing more.

On the third day, Um Nabil began to search on her own account and found parts of his head and hair that permitted further identification. With the evidence now beyond doubt, she fell into a faint.

Um Nabil could not understand why her house had been torn down while her neighbours' had not. Her neighbour, in whose home I conducted the interview with Um Nabil, shook her head and said: 'Do you want to know, Um Nabil, why they were so vindictive towards your husband and hacked him to pieces like that? You won't believe us when we tell you.' Then the neighbour turned towards me and said, with great firmness:

Abu Nabil resisted. He was the only one in the whole district, in all Hayy Ersal, who grabbed a Kalashnikov, and resisted. He used the handful of bullets and 14 mm pistol he had with him.

Um Nabil has never been sure whether her husband really did resist. He kept the Kalashnikov and pistol at home, she told me, and this had been completely bulldozed, including the place where he kept the guns. She couldn't be sure.

Had the guns really been lost through the bulldozing? Was it just a coincidence, or had they rather decided to bulldoze the house because her husband was armed and resisted? To answer that would truly need a postponed testimony from Hayy Ersal.

In Account 5 (p. 84) we saw how Ahmad Khatib had been with friends on the Thursday afternoon when the Israeli shells had begun to fall on Shatila, and had taken one of these friends to the Gaza Hospital when the latter had been struck by a splinter. When he left his house, he said, his family had still been at home. That evening at the hospital he met a neighbour who told him everyone had gone to the shelter for protection against the increased bombardment; she herself had been there with them. When, however, the killers had come and put men to one side and women and children to the other, she had managed to flee unnoticed to the Gaza Hospital.

Ahmad, the sole survivor of his family, spoke calmly and rationally; most of his answers were concise. He only grew impassioned when I asked him about the family members he had lost – and whether he had managed to recover the bodies. He had, he answered, found none of them: his parents, grandmother, and seven brothers and sisters were all gone. Not satisfied with this, he went on to repeat their full names, one after the other. He began with his father's, mother's and grandmother's names; then, when he reached his brothers' and sisters', he uttered their first, middle and last names as if he were in a courtroom: 'Saber Ali Khatib, Hussein Ali Khatib, Nader Ali Khatib, Munther Ali Khatib, Maryam Ali Khatib, Amina Ali Khatib, Imtithal Ali Khatib.' He gazed into the distance, his voice fading slowly, then began to speak very calmly, as though to himself:

My little sister was only seven years old. They're all gone. We didn't find a single one of my family's bodies. And they kept asking me for proof. There was no body; no ID card in the pocket; no proof. I couldn't register them in the Red Cross records. I didn't find any proof.[60]

One body was in fact found: that of the grandmother. Her daughter Khadija, Ahmad's aunt, identified her from a photograph of the victims on the front page of the Sunday newspapers – from her clothes, the face not being visible. A second daughter also identified her on the massacre site, again through the clothes.[61]

In Account 15 (p. 95) we saw how Hamza, having escaped the 'wall of death' together with his father, realized that his brother Abbas had been killed near the wall and that his mother and sisters must also have been killed. Who, though, can ever know the whole truth in the midst of a massacre?

Hamza and his father spent the night at the Akka Hospital, being among the witnesses to the incursion on the Friday morning, before being removed to the Najjar Hospital, along with others, by the Red Cross.

Once he had heard the news, an uncle of Hamza's came from their distant village of Majdal Zoun and, arriving at al-Horsh, saw the body of his 18-year-old nephew Abbas lying on the gravel near the house and the infamous wall. The man wept at the sight; then he took the boy's body to Majdal Zoun. He buried him there, and the entire village turned out to pay their last respects.

This happened on the same day as the rumours of the return of Sa'd Haddad, and he was therefore in no position to try to learn of the others' fate. Even when the family eventually managed to return home, they never knew just what had happened to the young sisters, Najah and Nuha, or to their mother.[62]

After the massacre, however, Fatima Ajami, a neighbour of Najah and Nuha who came from Qal'at al-Shaqif, told how local people had described seeing the two sisters' bodies near the Fatah petrol station. The victims had had their ID cards in their hands.

Where are the bodies now, and the cards? Neither the Red Cross nor the men of the Civil Defence had the chance to see what the eye-witnesses had seen. The bodies they found, perhaps, but no family members on the spot to identify them. Subsequent testimonies were deemed unacceptable.

And where were those family members? The head of the family was (let us remind ourselves) lying injured in the Najjar Hospital, accompanied by his son Hamza. As for the uncle, caught up in the Sa'd Haddad rumours, he was able only to hurry away with the body of Abbas, for burial in Majdal Zoun. The names of Najah Fayyad and Nuha Fayyad were not mentioned in the official lists.

Events after the massacre were, in a sense, no less brutal than the massacre itself. If the massacre denied these people their right to live, what happened after it denied them the right to die.

In Account 17 (p. 101) we left Um Rabi', the nurse who had saved dozens of people, standing on the hospital staircase on the Friday morning asking her neighbour Um Akram about her mother and brother, and learning that all those in Abu Yasser's shelter had been killed.

Like others, she had tried to get in on the Saturday and failed. Now, on the Sunday morning, she tried again, entering through the Dana mosque side and reaching the café at the Sharq cinema intersection. She said:

When I got in, the Lebanese Army was everywhere. Bodies were piled on both sides of the road, underneath the dirt and rubble. Some were buried, some you could see, some you couldn't see at all – they'd been covered from both sides. I went on, though the stench was unbearable. And all I saw was children piled one on top of the other. Their ages ranged from three to five years; some didn't have heads any more, others had their legs ripped off …

A soldier saw me and asked me where I was going. I told him I was going home and pointed to the entrance to the alley. He told me to go in through another alley, as there were other soldiers who wouldn't let me go any further. I turned back and went in through another alley, as he said, and finally reached our house, near Abu Yasser's shelter. The first thing I saw was five bodies near the shelter.

It wasn't nine o'clock yet, and everything was quiet, not a sound anywhere, the whole camp was empty. I plucked up courage and took a look at the bodies; the killers had tied them with a rope.

A man passed by me, and he asked me: 'Sister, where's Abu Yasser's shelter?' I said: 'There's the shelter in front of you, and there's Abu Yasser himself.' Abu Yasser was still lying on the ground, just a dead body like all the others. I asked the man to go into the shelter and see if there was anyone there, and he did that for me. He was away for five minutes, then he came back and told me there was no one.[63]

Um Rabi' reached Abu Hasan Salameh Square where, by her estimation, more than 200 bodies had accumulated. She could not identify her mother, brother, aunt or any of her neighbours. She then headed for the Darwish garage, where the militias had taken people and where, as she had been told by Um Akram, mass killing had been carried out. But it was, she discovered, impossible to identify anyone, as the garage itself had been brought down over the victims.

In Account 19 (p. 105) we saw how Um Akram was the first to search for the victims, starting as early as dawn on the Friday. She was in fact the last to gain knowledge of the victims in her family.

Having once made sure her family was safe at Al-Zarif school, Um Akram began making daily visits to the squares and alleys where victims were lying, searching for her missing relatives. Each day she would pass the spot where the militias had brought down the Darwish garage over the people they had killed.

On the fourth day, the Red Cross finally managed to remove the rubble there and bring out the bodies. Um Akram was looking for four in particular: those of her two grandchildren (her daughter's children), and those of their father and grandmother. Now that all the bodily remains had been collected in a heap, even Um Akram, a woman known for her courage and balance, was utterly stunned. Those were limbs, not bodies.

'Oh God, we beg Your forgiveness!' After all she had been through, was Um Akram right or wrong to persist in the search for the victims in her family? Might it not have been better if the picture of the children had remained, lively and smiling in the grandmother's memories? Now the picture had been changed for a pile of limbs. Um Akram thanked God for having saved her youngest grandchild and her daughter, the child's mother, who had refused to stay in the shelter.[64]

Massacres are not wars triggered by bombardment, where people find protection in shelters. In massacres, shelters, far from protecting the innocent, are themselves agents of death – the first targets on the killers' maps.

In Account 20 (p. 106) the Abu Rudaineh family's tragedy had not ended on the Thursday evening or even on the Friday. When the killers forced Shahira and her children to walk to the Sports City, she saw her sister Aida killed; and the children saw their aunt and shrieked: 'Mother, look at Aunt Aida!' As for her father, Shahira had known nothing till she returned home. She it was then who said: 'I wish … I wish we'd never gone back.'

On returning, Shahira discovered that her beloved sister Aida was not the only one to have been killed; they had also killed her husband Mahmoud Abu al-Dib, her father Muhammad Abu Rudaineh, her brother Kayed and her cousin Shawkat.

One thing, at least, Shahira could do that countless others could not: that is, bury her dead family members in the Shuhada cemetery, in graves where she could later go to mourn. She managed to bury them all except for her sister Aida, who had already been taken to the mass cemetery by the Civil Defence.

Shahira went constantly to the mass cemetery, invoking God's mercy on her sister and all the other victims sleeping there beneath the earth.[65]

Muhammad Mahmoud Sa'd's wife (see Account 21 (p. 106)) experienced a double tragedy. Returning home she saw how the militias had killed her beautiful daughter Afaf. Then, finding no trace of her husband after four whole days of searching, she found him flung down in the street, his body decomposing.

Now began the problem of removing the body for burial. Those in charge at the Gaza

Hospital refused her request for an escort and a stretcher on the grounds that all the bodies had been booby-trapped – though it later emerged that this particular one had not been. She then turned to the Red Cross, who helped her remove the body, so allowing her to bury her husband and mourn him.[66]

Again, this was more than some of her neighbours and friends were able to do. Often, indeed, they would envy her. One neighbour even once said: 'You should thank God your husband has a grave you can visit.'

With regard to Account 25 (p. 142) Um Ahmad Srour remained in hiding with her daughter Nuhad, awaiting the right time to return home; both had been injured.

As for her daughter Su'ad, struck by four bullets that left her immobile and thus unable to flee with her mother and sister, she had remained lying on the floor with all the victims from her family, her father, little sister, and other brothers and sisters; the only one left alive.[67] There she stayed until the Sunday, when Lebanese soldiers entered the house and rescued her.

Everyone from Sabra and Shatila had a story, but Su'ad Srour had more than one. Indeed it was after the soldiers had rescued her and taken her to hospital that the story really began: a story shifting between Lebanon and the outside world, especially Cyprus, where she underwent a number of surgical operations.

At the end of it all Su'ad was able to walk again, with the aid of a crutch. Physical wounds were, though, more easily treated than psychological ones.

In Account 26 (p. 144) Um Ali al-Biqa'i, from the southern Sheb'a village, was the only one who, on the Saturday, went off to search for her loved ones: her husband, her two children Rabi' and Ikram, her grandchildren and her son-in-law. She found none of them.

On the Sunday, she returned with one of her daughters. Whenever she heard of a pile of victims set down in this or that spot, she would go and look. At last she heard her daughter's scream: 'Mother, there's my father [Abu Ali al-Biqa'i]! Mother, there's my brother-in-law! Mother, there's Rabi', under the pickup!' Her mother rushed to catch up with her, and afterwards described the dreadful sight that met her eyes:

Abu Ali was clutching his ID card in his hand, there was still blood on the card. The packet of cigarettes was in his hand too. They'd shot him dead and hit him on the head with an axe, and he'd fallen as if he was praying. He was a pious man and never missed his prayers. He'd go short of sleep so as not to miss the morning prayer.

'And Rabi'? What kind of state was my son Rabi' in? They'd chased after him and run him over with the pickup. Rabi' had had his white shirt and white shoes on, and he was holding on to his ID, 75 lira, and an ID from the publishing firm where he worked …

As for Ikram, the daughter, Um Ali finally found her after three more days of weary search.

We found Ikram near Abu Jamal's garage, just opposite the Fatah petrol station. She was lying there along with 50 other women. Um Karem was there, and the one with the eight children, and there was Um Yasser too, the owner of the shelter, with three children. Um Yasser's handbag, and her husband's ID card and hers, were still there with her …

Five months have passed now. People's spattered brains are still there on the walls of the garage, like yeast. The traces couldn't be wiped off.

Along with my daughter Ikram were her 15-year-old daughter Fadia al-Beka'i, her fair ten-year-old son Imad, eight-year-old son Shadi, and six-year-old Wissam.

… One of my daughter's sons didn't have any head, or arms, or legs. I identified him from the belt I'd given him as a present, and from his corduroy trousers; and I identified my daughter from her dress. She'd been shot in the head, and her face was mutilated, I couldn't recognize her. I couldn't recognize her second son either. All her children had been oddly mutilated.

Ikram, Um Fadi, and her husband Saleh [Abu Fadi] too, were all gone. May God bless his soul; he was such a good man.

They let us bury them in the Shuhada cemetery.[68]

Um Ali went on in surprisingly calm fashion, speaking so low she was almost whispering: 'I thank God for leaving me Kamel and Fadi, Ikram's little children. They're still with me, and I'm raising them.'

With regard to Account 30 (p. 150) Mariam Abu Harb, a capable woman, had very much taken after her strong mother, Um Muhammad Aidi, the mother of the four martyrs. Mariam had lost her husband and son, but not her mental balance or sympathy with others. She recounted her personal tragedy – her inability even to bury her son – but paused to consider others' tragedies too. She said:

We buried my husband at the Shuhada cemetery on Sunday. We couldn't take my son too, there was only room for one person in the car. And in the end I couldn't bury my son at all, because, when we came to fetch his body, everyone was running and screaming: 'Sa'd Haddad! Sa'd Haddad's here! Sa'd Haddad's here!'

We ran off with everyone else. And when we came back next day we found the Civil Defence had buried him in the mass cemetery.[69]

Even at the height of her tragedy, Mariam could not forget how much she had wept for Fidda, one of her neighbours in Shatila. It filled her with anguish to see Fidda flung down on the ground, in front of her house:

When I finally got back home, the first thing I saw was poor Fidda, killed right there in front of our house. She was carrying a few loaves of bread she must have been taking to her children.

Her arm was still stretched out, as if she wanted to go on carrying the bread to the children.[70]

Let us return for a moment to Um Muhammad Aidi, mother of Mariam Abu Harb and the four who were killed without even being asked who they were.

Um Muhammad Aidi, whose tragedy was told in Account 31 (p. 151) was held back from entering on the Sunday by members of the Lebanese Army. She contrived to enter even so, along with her oldest daughter, through a prickly cactus garden; no one noticed them. As they approached the house her daughter cried out: 'Mother, there's Moussa, I've found him …'

The mother approached and found her son's head blackened and twice the size. She looked around for his brothers but found only Sa'id, who was close by. She also found her grandson near his Uncle Sa'id. Of her two other children and her husband there was no trace.[71]

Um Muhammad Aidi was left with nothing except pictures on the wall. This was the mother who talked to me in her home about all her children in the pictures, without mentioning any of their names. She spoke proudly and without tears, pointing to the pictures.

In Account 34 (p. 157) we saw how Um Ghazi, together with her daughter and grandchildren, had twice escaped death, surviving both the death pit in the heart of the City and the gunshots that pursued them as far as Cola Square. On the Sunday she was at the American University Hospital, and, hearing that entrance to the zone was now finally permitted, she made preparations to leave.

By chance she met with Munira, a neighbour of hers, who told her without preamble that her husband and children had been killed. Um Ghazi became hysterical at the news and started screaming. Then she went out to the street in search of a taxi, which a policeman helped her to find. The driver, however, refused to go to Shatila at any price whatever, and asked for 75 lira to go to the Shuhada cemetery. Um Ghazi, giving in, drove off with him, supposing she would end up giving him more. There was still money in the pocket of the blue-striped pyjamas Abu Ghazi had been wearing when she said goodbye to him on the Friday morning.

During the afternoon there was a curfew in the district, declared after the rumours had spread of Sa'd Haddad's return. Nevertheless, Um Ghazi made it home, and might well have wished she had not done so.

All her young sons, Ahmad, Madi and Muhammad Madi, had been killed. The oldest had been 19, the youngest 15. Even her paralysed husband, Younes Madi, had found no mercy. Her son-in-law Hussein al-Ali, whom she recalled as though he had been one of her sons, had been killed along with the rest. 'He was so young,' she said. 'So dreadful, he was just 23 years old.' She then went on to speak of her beloved nephew Saleh al-Titi.

Um Ghazi stopped at this point, as if unable to believe just what she had seen. Then suddenly she began once more, telling how the killers had burned and chopped her young son, making sure to throw his chopped feet down in front of him. Um Ghazi could never forget the sight.

Nor would she ever forget Prime Minister Shafiq al-Wazzan's visit to Shatila on the Monday. 'Come and see with your own eyes …' she shouted. 'You're the one who told Abu Ammar it would be all right, told him he needn't worry, you'd see the Palestinians were protected. Did you protect us, Wazzan?' At this point, she went on, some soldiers began assaulting her, but they were stopped by Prime Minister Wazzan who told them to let her go. Um Ghazi went on with her memories: 'I swear to God, the Prime Minister started crying, a Japanese photographer was taking shots, and his eyes were like pools of fire.'[72]

Even before she lost all these people, Um Ghazi had lost her oldest son Ghazi, who had fallen as a martyr in Jordan. She had also, during the invasion, lost her young daughter, who had died in the Akar building when it was struck by an Israeli vacuum bomb and almost instantaneously reduced to rubble.

Um Ghazi's tragedy was not confined to the death of her children. She also lacked any grave for them where she could visit and mourn. She went on:

It was destined I shouldn't find their graves. Ghazi died in Jordan without a grave; and Aisha died in the Akar building without a grave; and now, have all these died too, and I don't know where their graves are? Who's going to help me? There aren't any men left at home.

The Civil Defence wouldn't take anyone for burial unless you could tell them that you'd done the digging and got everything ready … My cousin came and told me we should go and dig a grave ourselves. My 17-year-old son and her daughter were born in the same week, so we thought of burying them together. At least then there'd be a grave for one of my children. I said to them: 'When you were alive, I always wanted to see you married; now you're dead, we'll still do it for you.' And I started singing … and went on till we reached the cemetery.

We buried them next to one another. They placed her daughter on top of a sister of hers who'd died a long time before. And we buried my son and his father next to one another. But all the rest were buried in the mass cemetery.[73]

Um Ghazi did not return home to spend the night. There was no one left there except ghosts.

Some testimonies from the rubble

Many people had stories to tell from the midst of the rubble. The rubble was removed, but that was not the end of the stories.

Women searching for their loved ones were an everyday sight. I have selected just four testimonies here, provided by women seeking those they had lost: a brother, a husband, a mother or a daughter.

Account 43: Looking for her brother

Not being a resident of Shatila, Um Isma'il heard of the horrifying events only after they had taken place. When she did finally hear, she hurried to try and find out what had happened to her brother, who was not in fact a resident either but would go each day to his work as an employee at the forefront of Shatila.

Um Isma'il searched among the piles of victims, men, women and children. She examined more than 40 bodies, then, having failed to find her brother, returned home at the end of the day.

When Monday morning came (or possibly Tuesday morning, she no longer recalled), she returned to Shatila and by chance met a neighbour of her brother's. She said:

I went and asked her: 'Please, have you seen my brother Abu Majed?' She said: 'Our friend Abu Majed was with us. We were all sitting together in a group, and we all ran off together. We ran east, and he ran north. Go and check further north.'

I walked up to an alley where there was a tree. It was there, by the tree, that they'd slaughtered him. They'd stabbed him in the stomach and pierced him with a bayonet, or something, I don't know what. There were three other men lying dead next to him. I started screaming: 'My dear brother ... my dear brother!'

The photographers came and started taking pictures and recording my voice. I still couldn't believe it when I finally managed to pull myself together and go running out of there ...

I'm not just mourning for my brother but for the other dreadful sights I saw.

At the beginning of the alley there was a house with a staircase. The people had been sticking close to the staircase for protection. The killers just went ahead and gunned them down. The victims are still there, the floor's still stained with blood and footprints. Some other people had been hiding by a steel gate, and the killers shot them all; they were all piled up one on top of the other.

Still no one had taken anyone out of that alley.[74]

Um Isma'il had already reported her brother to the Red Cross, as a missing person. They promised to look for him, but later said they had found no one.

She now returned and told them she had found her brother's body. They asked for his ID card, which had been on a stone by the body, but had, according to neighbours, been lost. Um Isma'il had no idea who had taken it. It may have been someone intending to keep it safe. Still, she had no answer to give the Red Cross as to where the card was or who had taken it.

Next day, she was told the Red Cross representative had been asking for her, to verify her brother's identity – while she herself had been away, actually trying to find any available document that would certify this. As a result the name vanished from the records of victims. Or perhaps it would be more accurate to say he was never registered there to begin with.

His name was initially recorded, certainly, as one of those missing. But no official ever asked for these records of missing persons. It was as though they had never existed.

To this day, even the number of those reported missing is not known. Shaykh Salman al-Khalil could only deduce it:

On the fourth day, when I went in with the Scouts of Al-Risala, the Amal Movement and the Lebanese Red Cross, the Red Cross had already been taking down some names.

My eyes fell on one of their notebooks. There were more than 50 sheets of paper in it, each page divided into two columns with names. If we calculate just ten names per column, that still adds up to more than 2,000 people.[75]

Account 44: Looking for her husband

Amina went to try and find out what had happened to her husband. The worst she conceived was that he might have been detained by some group (he was a well known Palestinian man), or perhaps struck by a splinter or a sniper's bullet. She decided, though, to begin by making enquiries at the Gaza Hospital.

Though still only 22, she was the mother of four children, and, like most people, she was exhausted by the war that had been going on all through the summer. She had still not settled in her Shatila home, or even finished the repair work, when the Israeli Forces besieged the area. She feared for her children and begged her husband to leave home; and this time he gave in and agreed. They were, it emerged, among the few who made it out through Sabra's northern entrance. They spent the days of the massacre in a shelter in the Haret Hreik district, which was regarded up to then as relatively safe.

Amina recalled how the shelling intensified on the Thursday, before slackening considerably on the Friday. She thereupon pressed her husband to return home to fetch food and clothes for the children. He went as she asked, but failed (as she had also asked) to return quickly. By the Saturday, news of the massacre had spread. But Amina's friend, who knew of her husband's trip to Shatila, was careful to see that Amina was not told what was happening.

Amina began to grow impatient. Nor could she understand why her friend was sticking so close to her, preventing her, among other things, from going to Shatila to make sure all was well with her husband. After two days she crept off, leaving her children in the care of the doorman's wife.

She was surprised to see the large numbers of soldiers but took their presence as a positive sign; no doubt these would ensure the camp's safety, as had happened at Burj al-Barajneh. She had taken no more than a few steps from the entrance to Sabra when a group of women, all dressed in black, stopped her and expressed their condolences.

She stared at them in astonishment, wondering who was the object of these condolences, and surprised, too, to see them in black. Where, she asked, had they been? On hearing from one of the women what had happened to each one of them, Amina almost fainted. Then, remembering the condolences had only begun when they caught sight of her, she asked why this had been. There was silence for a few moments. Then Amina's neighbour Salwa embraced her and kissed her, and told her that her own husband had also been killed in the massacre.

What was this calm talk of a 'massacre'? It was the first time she had heard the shocking word, and the first she had heard of her husband's death. How had it happened? And why?

The women went on to supply details while she stood supporting herself against a wall. Her husband, she learned, had never made it home; he had been stopped on the way (one of the women indicated the place), and witnesses had seen him searched, stripped of his money and personal documents, then, quite simply, forced to stand against a wall before being gunned down.

The killers, they told her, had been from the Lebanese Forces. On her insistence the women provided her with further details. After killing him and flinging him to the ground, they had turned him over to be sure he was dead, then placed a zinc board over him.

So where was he now? Amina thought that God must have sent these women to lead her to her husband's body so that she could bury him. Too distraught to speak coherently, she begged them, through signs, to take her to where the body was.

Salwa, taking her aside, spoke gently to her. 'Don't you see, Amina,' she said, 'that we're all dressed in black? I still haven't found my mother. Your husband was buried in the mass cemetery. Our neighbour,

Um Hussein, saw him and recited the Fatiha [the opening chapter of the Quran] for his soul. And I promise you there was a shaykh who prayed over him and all the others who perished.'[76]

It was the first time Amina had ever heard of something called a 'mass cemetery'. She wanted to ask further questions but there was no time left for talk or tears – no time, perhaps, even to escape, for panic-stricken cries about the return of Sa'd Haddad's group had begun to fill the district. The women scattered in search of safety, and Amina could hardly believe it when she found herself safe back in Haret Hreik with her four children. Hugging them, she burst into floods of tears – this being one thing still permitted in the shelters.

Account 45: Looking for her mother

Afifa A.'s story was common enough in Palestinian circles: that of a typical family where tragedy was born anew with every invasion or war, the children taken from one place of exile to the next.

As Afifa was growing up, all she knew was that she was from Palestine and that Tall al-Za'tar was an alternative, temporary place in which to live till she returned to her country. But in the summer of 1976, in the course of the so-called 'two-year war', the camp was besieged for two whole months, and at the end of it 3,000 of those living there were martyred or missing. Afifa's family had borne the full brunt of this: her father and three of her four brothers were gone, and the remnants of the family – the mother, a son and two daughters – were forced to seek a new refuge elsewhere.

When she was told to go with her family to Damour, where there were vacant houses, the desperate mother had no time to reflect on the matter – that those living in Damour had left, just as her own family was about to leave. Thoughts of that kind were a luxury for people in their situation. The head of the household simply had to soldier on, however harsh things were. And so Afifa's family moved to Damour.

Afifa was waiting desperately for the day when she could rent a room or two, anywhere in Beirut, just to bring an end to the constant movement and humiliation. She was ready enough to work as a maid, to earn some money and build up some savings, and this kept her from losing hope.

When the Israeli invasion came in June 1982, the family left for Beirut carrying whatever they could with them. There were, so Afifa was told, some displaced people just like them in the Raouché district, and there she and the family eventually stayed all through the months of the invasion. After the fighters had left, however, she stayed not a day longer, picking up what remained of her belongings and making for the nearby part of Sabra and Shatila, where she settled down – again temporarily – in an apartment in the Fakhani district formerly lived in by fighters who had now left. For the first time Afifa felt some sense of security, since the place was, in her own words, 'near where our people are and not too far from the Sports City'.

The family had been there scarcely two weeks when the Israeli Army besieged Sabra and Shatila. The family members remained where they were, refusing to leave their homes even though they could hear the Israeli shells raining down.

As the shelling grew fiercer on the Thursday, the power was cut and there was not a loaf of bread left in the house. Afifa asked her mother that they should leave for a safer district, but her mother shook her head. 'Where can we go?' she asked. 'With the fighters gone, we won't find anyone willing to take us. I'm staying here with my people. Whatever happens to them happens to all of us.'

The discussion within the family grew more heated. It was the mother who finally put an end to it. 'All right', she said. 'I'll leave, the way you want to, but I won't go anywhere except Shatila. I'll go to my cousin's. And then whatever happens, happens. Any of you who don't want to come with me can go where you like.'

The family split accordingly. Afifa and her brother, refusing to go to Shatila, went to Hamad Street where, throughout the massacre, they stayed with dozens of other fugitives. Her sister, though, preferred to join her mother rather than leave her on her own.

Only on the Sunday were people permitted to go and check on their relatives. Afifa went with her brother, and their attempted entry was naturally through the Sabra side, close to Hamad Street. When, though, they discovered how blocked the routes were, and when they heard the army was allowing no one to enter, they decided on alternative means.

Afifa reached the Fatah petrol station, and there, on the road, she found scattered limbs and also ID cards – her mother's and sister's among them. At that point she decided not to go on to their relatives' house in Shatila and began instead to search in the nearby piles of bodies. She said:

When I saw the cards scattered on the road, I thought they must belong to the people who were lying there. Maybe the killer had collected the cards to identify the people, or to gain time, while he was assembling all the victims in some yard. I can't say what day my mother and sister were killed; what I do know is there were a lot of murdered people those cards belonged to, and I was the only one searching around at that hour.

I found my mother and sister; the killers had showered them with bullets in the most fearful way, and their bodies were mutilated. I dragged them off to a place near a tree at al-Horsh, and I thought, my brother should be here any moment, or maybe someone else I know from the camp might come – I wasn't able to bury them alone. As I was dragging them, I checked the time and found it was three in the afternoon. I stayed there waiting for someone to turn up and help me, till half past five, but no one came.

I definitely remember it was half past five, because I was looking at my watch when I heard people shrieking: 'Sa'd Haddad! … Sa'd Haddad!' I had no choice, I had to leave my dead mother and sister behind and run off with all the others, who were streaming out from every side, and running. I'd never seen people running like that before; they were like a stream, running and screaming, in total panic …[77]

Afifa never did succeed in burying her mother and sister. Nor was she ever able to learn where they were finally buried. Probably, she thought, they had been interred in the mass cemetery; that at least was what she was told when she made enquiries the following day.

Nor was Afifa able to register her mother's and sister's deaths in the official records, the ID cards she had found being regarded as insufficient evidence. There were simply no witnesses or bodies.

Nor could she blame her brother for taking so long; she only saw him, so she said, 'a few months later' – she was not sure exactly when. He had not fled, nor had he been in hiding. Like her, he had been searching for his mother and sister on that Sunday; but members of the Lebanese Army had arrested him and dragged him off for questioning. What was a Palestinian doing among the piles of victims? What was he doing in Sabra and Shatila?

They dragged him off in a truck, as they did dozens of others in those days filled with the stench of death. As a Palestinian man, he was guilty till proved innocent; and it took him some months to prove that innocence.

Account 46: Looking for her daughter

When the Israelis besieged Sabra and Shatila, Samiha Abbas Hijazi, a Lebanese married to a Palestinian of the Idilbi family, went to the house of her newly-wed, pregnant daughter Zainab Hassan Idilbi near the Sports City, to persuade her to come and stay with her in Shatila, the heart of Shatila being generally regarded as the safest place to be. The bride's mother-in-law, however, would not allow her to leave. Samiha gave the following account:

My daughter's house was the highest one, right underneath the Sports City. I went to get her; she was pregnant, she couldn't put up with hardships. Her mother-in-law told me: 'Why, do you have your own personal god?' 'God forgive me,' I said, 'there's no need to talk in that high-and-mighty way. It's just that maybe things are safer where we are. You're right under the City, the Israelis are just a step away. We're inside al-Horsh, we're further off.' She said: 'No.'

I went back again on Thursday, hoping she might relent. I wanted them all to come and stay with us. She said: 'Listen, take your daughter, but my son stays here with me.'[78]

Samiha did not spend that first night with her children at home in al-Horsh, but in the shelter of the nearby school. Then, just before six on the Friday morning, she prepared to leave, paying no heed to the other women crowding the shelter. She wanted, she said, to fetch food for her children. A few seconds later, she was in the street – intending not to fetch food but to hurry to her daughter's. But how was she to get there? To her astonishment, the streets were piled with bodies.

In the street near Abu Yasser's shelter, she heard a man moaning for help. This was Mustafa Habrat, the man who had spent the night among the dead (see Account 14, p. 95). Two other men rushed to answer Samiha's call and carried the wounded man to the Gaza Hospital.

Samiha believed Almighty God would reward her by sending someone to save her daughter, just as she had saved the wounded man. Days went by, however, and there was still no trace of her daughter or anyone from her son-in-law's family. Had the earth simply swallowed them up? Just who had buried her daughter, her son-in-law and the whole family? Clearly, all the neighbours had been killed. But where had the bodies gone?

She spent eight whole days searching for her daughter. Every time she heard of a pit she would inform the Civil Defence, so they could go and search for those inside it. At last she learned of a pit near the Sports City, which had become accessible only after the removal of mines, and there she found her daughter.

Samiha was a friend of Um Ali al-Beka'i, the sad, resigned Lebanese mother who had lost eight of her family (see Account 26, p. 144), and the two came to my home together. Um Ali al-Beka'i related how, after finding the bodies of her own loved ones, she could not let her friend go on looking for her daughter alone, and accompanied her on her search. Samiha would carry Zainab's picture on her lapel as she moved from one pit to the next, and ask, house by house, whether anyone had seen her.

Samiha mentions all who were killed with her daughter, naming them one by one: first her daughter Zainab, the four-months pregnant bride, then her son-in-law Fahd Ali Haidar, together with his mother Kulthoum Muhammad Salameh, his brother Fu'ad, and his half-sister Samia with her two children, Mahmoud and Tareq. Of Samia's children the sole survivor was the two-year-old baby girl.

Returning to her daughter's neighbours, she confirmed they had all been killed. She had found 21 bodies in the pit, among whom were Um Faysal, together with her son Faysal, her grandson Khodor, another grandson from her other son, her daughter-in-law Fatima Ahmad Sarriya, her daughter-in-law Nahed Sa'd, and her son Ibrahim; there was also Um Issam; there was the southern woman Um Muhammad, who was married to a Syrian; and there were Abu Nayef and Um Nayef.

Nahed Sa'd had, she said, been nine months pregnant. They had killed her and removed the foetus. She also learned from a girl who had witnessed the crime that the baby had been cut in two pieces just as he was making his first cry. The will to live was no match for the killers.

Samiha was not content to enumerate the names but provided further details, especially of where the bodies were found:

There were 21 in the pit. I found another three in a pit in the military camp [the former training camp], and I found another two at the side of the camp, killed near the shelter, making five altogether. And I found Abu Nayef and his daughter a little further down the road. Then there were Saleh al-Titi and his cousin, one on top of the other, behind al-Doukhi's place; and al-Doukhi himself was killed too, I mean, near the Fatah military camp there were more than 15 bodies collected together; those ones must have been shot in the alleys ...

I asked her, 'How was Zainab when you found her?'

Apparently ignoring the question, she went on with her account – as if to say she was mourning for everyone, not just her daughter:

It was one of the pits made by the air force. Before they killed them, they took them out of the shelter, everyone knew it was Fatah's, a huge shelter behind the City. The house was actually near the shelter. They lifted them to the City with bulldozers and buried them there, in the pit I told you about.

'Some people told me later how my daughter's mother-in-law came out with other women, carrying a white flag. They thought the ones who'd come

were Israelis, who wouldn't kill women. My son-in-law, Fahd, came out along with his mother; and ended up being one of the first killed. The killers had hit him and cut him in three pieces. He didn't have a head when I buried him. He still had his card in his pocket, and he'd been wearing a watch my daughter had given him once, I knew it well enough.

Zainab – you asked me about Zainab?

They'd shot her in the face with caustic bullets. My daughter hadn't been touched afterwards, and she was covered with a pyjama ... but Samia, my daughter's sister-in-law, was completely naked, stripped of all her clothes, with only very short covers on her.

They'd all been shot in the head. My daughter's mother-in-law's brain had spilled out, and it was the same with her brother-in-law, who'd been shot straight in the head.

All this happened on the Friday [24 September]. I asked God to lead me to my daughter. There was a little girl, Um Faysal's granddaughter, she was the only one in her family who survived; she was 14 years old, her name was Hana' Wahbeh, and she told me how the killers had put them on the steps and threatened to kill anyone who screamed. When they killed her husband Fahd, my daughter did scream, so one of them went ahead and shot her in the face, and the others with him carried on and shot all the women. Maybe my daughter's scream did make them kill her first, but it protected her against their vile behaviour. It's unbelievable what they did to those women ...

Zainab, my daughter ... you asked me about my daughter.

Her whole face was burned by the bullets ... I recognized my daughter from her pyjama and her long hair. When they put her on the bulldozer, her hair was all spoiled. When I saw my daughter, I fainted ...

Hana' Wahbeh said they laid the victims down, then booby-trapped them. That was why the expert wouldn't go and search with me, and he told me there was no one near the Sports City anyway. But in the end he changed his mind and went with me and some others to the City. They defused the booby-traps under the bodies, then they brought the bulldozers and started digging with them, and straight away the corpses appeared.

You asked me about my daughter ...[79]

She had, she said, taken her daughter Zainab and buried her on 24 September; and this date was confirmed by the following day's edition of *Al-Safir* which reported that Civil Defence teams engaged in the removal of rubble at the Sabra and Shatila camps had found 19 new bodies in a mass grave set up in a dirt area near the Sports City. Some reports also noted the extermination of a single family. Of the 19 bodies, 17 had been identified and the names had been listed as follows:

Nahed Sa'd, nine months pregnant, Lebanese.
Fatima Ahmad Sarriya, 23 years.
Her son Ibrahim Khalil Wehbeh, 9 months, Palestinian.
Najla' Sa'id Taha. Palestinian, 67 years.
Ahmad al-Moughrabi, 25 years, Syrian.
Kulthoum Muhammad Salameh, 55 years, Lebanese.
Fahd Ali Haidar (Kulthoum's son), 19 years.
Zainab Hassan Idilbi, wife of Fahd.
Fu'ad [Ali Haidar], brother of Fahd, 13 years.
Samia, sister of Fahd Haidar, 25 years.
Tareq Muhammad Titi, 5 years, son of Samia.
Mahmoud, two months, son of Samia.
Um Issam, further identity unknown, 30 years.
Mariam, 7 years, daughter of Um Issam.
Suzan, 5 years, daughter of Um Issam.
Jinan, 3 years, daughter of Um Issam.
Baby girl, one year and a half, name unknown, Um Issam's daughter.
Man.
Baby, 3 years.[80]

The question remains, if the press had been allowed to enter, monitor and publish names and figures in the first days, as it subsequently was on 24 September before the infamous 'air force pit' near the Sports City, would the daily newspapers not have become a major source of the victims' identities?

Newspaper reports are there for posterity. As for the lists of names established by various institutions – international humanitarian, official, and national – these still remain unpublished, after a space of 20 years.

The killers

What did the survivors know of the killers? What did the killers leave behind? And what evidence of the killers did the journalists and rescue workers find?

Were all the attackers in fact killers? Or did some individual attackers, at one point or another, preserve some spark of humanity? And will the day finally come when the killer speaks out?

The killers as seen by eye-witnesses

How did the inhabitants of Sabra and Shatila describe these armed attackers? How did they describe their clothes and weapons? What did they say about their language or dialect? And which militias were they certain were there?

A nurse from al-Khalisa, who worked at the Akka Hospital, whose father had been killed at Tall al-Za'tar, and whose mother and brother had been among the victims of the massacre, said: 'The ones I saw wore an ordinary green military uniform, and were equipped with ammunition and Kalashnikov, along with a dagger at the waist.'[81] Another nurse from al-Khalisa, who worked at the Gaza Hospital and had lost two of her brothers at Tall al-Za'tar, said: 'The uniform was all the same military-style green. They obviously belonged to a single group.'[82]

One, who had witnessed the killing of her sister and father in the early hours of the massacre, said: 'They were dressed like the army, and they had badges with "Lebanese Forces" written on them.'[83] Another witness reported on the Saturday's 'final march', before she had learned of her father's murder on the first day of the massacre: 'They weren't all dressed the same. Some uniforms were speckled and some were solid green. Some very neat and tidy, and some were quite worn out.'[84]

A mother from the South, who discovered after the massacre that she had lost eight members of her family, described the attackers seen in the street on the Friday: 'It was the Lebanese Forces uniform with the cedar on the lapel, but some had straps on.'[85]

A young man from the village of Majdal Zoun, who had survived what would have been inevitable death on the Thursday evening, reported: 'They were wearing green uniforms with a yellow slogan saying "Al-Kata'eb al-Lubnaniyieh".' When this eye-witness was asked whether he meant 'Al-Quwat al-Lubnaniyieh', he replied: 'No. I'm sure. Al-Kata'eb al-Lubnaniyieh'.' He had, he said, paid no attention to the shoulders but had read what was written on the lapels: 'Al-Kata'eb al-Lubnaniyieh'.[86]

A girl from al-Khalisa, who had spent her life moving with her parents from one place to another on account of wars, said: 'They had a shirt underneath their military uniform, and on the white shirt "Al-Quwat al-Lubnaniyieh" was written, and on the others it was "Sa'd Haddad".'[87]

A tile worker, who had been among the displaced people from Tall al-Za'tar and had lost two brothers there, reported: 'They had "Hizb al-Kata'eb al-Lubnaniyieh" written on their helmets.'[88]

Three members of the foreign medical team gave their own description of those they saw on the Saturday morning at the Gaza Hospital. The following is extracted from the American nurse Ellen Siegel's testimony before the Kahan Commission: 'There were maybe ten soldiers dressed in very clean, tidy uniforms. Written in their lapels was "Al-Quwat al-Lubnaniyieh" [Lebanese Forces].'[89] And the following comes from the Singaporean doctor Swee's testimony before the MacBride Commission: 'They had two Arabic words on green uniforms, the Lebanese crest on one arm, and some of them had a blue triangle. Others had yellow insignia on their pockets.'[90]

And in response to Judge Kahan's question, 'Can you describe the soldiers for us?', we quote the following from the British doctor Paul Morris's testimony:

One with a radio … He was wearing a lightish grey, whitish kind of helmet, the same shape as the Israeli army wear. He was very neatly dressed, very cleanly dressed, wearing lightish green uniform, trousers and shirt were matching. There were five of these soldiers. They were wearing also the canvas type belts and canvas type webbing which they held, held their radio and other things on with. And also black boots. But no puttees. The trousers were

tapered at the bottom so they fit into their boots … There was some Arabic inscription on certainly all five uniforms …[91]

Of special interest was the testimony of a Syrian woman married to a Palestinian: not only for its close detail but because it included descriptions of the first troops to enter through the Bir Hasan district from the first hour. She said:

They were all armed soldiers, dressed in green uniforms without badges. And all the uniforms were very new and neat, without a speck of the dust you usually see on soldiers' uniforms. Their shoes were polished and shiny too. There were nearly 200 men altogether, then they split up, one part went to Shatila and the other stayed at Bir Hasan.

But there's another important thing I'd like to put on record. There was one small group among the people, who kept their weapons pointed at us, who didn't say a word. They didn't talk to us at all, the way the others did. I could make out five or six who didn't say anything. They were dressed in green uniforms, just like the others, but they were different – some had beards and coloured eyes, and they were mostly tall and young.

I suspected they weren't Lebanese, because they didn't say anything. We didn't hear their voices, or their language or dialect. That's no good reason, I know, to suppose they weren't Arabs, but I noticed another difference that might be significant – I noticed a difference between their headwear. The ones who talked to us had ordinary military head-wear, their helmets were the round type you pull with a peak, and they were thin and tall, a kind of cap in other words, and they were green like the uniform. But the headgear of the ones who didn't say a word to us, they weren't like the others'; they were different. They were made of fabric and wider, rounder and shorter than the others, and they didn't have the extra beret.[92]

More than 30 of the testimonies related to the oral history project of Sabra and Shatila dealt with the attacking gunmen's uniform. The testimonies of residents who saw the gunmen can be summarized as follows:

- The uniform was the ordinary military green one, like that of the Lebanese Forces, but some gunmen had a speckled one.

- There were badges on some gunmen's lapels or shoulders, or on the tops of their sleeves. Some had 'Al-Quwat al-Lubnaniyieh' on them; on others it was 'Al-Kata'eb al-Lubnaniyieh'; 'Quwat Sa'd Haddad' was written on some gunmen's shoulders; and the cedar was to be seen on still other uniforms.
- Some gunmen had the same military green uniform, but without any badges at all.
- As for headgear, some had red berets, whereas others had black ones; and the shape of the berets was not always the same. Some gunmen were uncovered.
- A majority part were wearing military boots.
- The uniforms of some were neatly pressed and gave the impression of being worn for the first time. Others, in contrast, gave the impression their wearers had been on duty for days.

The testimony of a member of the attacking militias, published by the German magazine *Der Spiegel*, conforms to the testimonies noted above. In the interview this man noted that the uniform of most was the official Kata'eb one, but he added something the surviving eye-witnesses could not have known: the common uniform most of them wore did not, he said, imply that they actually belonged to the Kata'eb or Quwat al-Lubnaniyieh. The narrator made no bones of his membership of Al-Numour al-Ahrar, and there were, he said, other Numour members too, though they were fewer in number than the other attackers. They had, as instructed, put on Kata'eb militia clothes.[93]

Also in conformity with the testimonies were the interviews conducted with local eye-witnesses by the German correspondent Karl Buchalla in the week following the massacre. He interviewed Bassam Hijab, a Palestinian man who lived in West Beirut and witnessed the massacre by chance, having come to Beirut for a family visit just a few weeks before. Bassam's description accorded with the Syrian woman's description given above. He had, he said, personally witnessed the way in which around two

hundred men, dressed in full military uniform, had lined up in the Bir Hasan district opposite the two camps; these had entered Shatila Main Street at around half past six on the Thursday evening. But he also affirmed the presence of Sa'd Haddad's men, who he had seen to be wearing Israeli military uniform with one additional feature: a knot on their chests representing the Lebanese cedar.[94]

One of the photographers managed to capture Sa'd Haddad's gunmen as they were leaving the camp on Friday, the badge visible on their shoulders. The American television station ABC broadcast this,[95] then the same shots were included in a number of videotapes on the massacre taken from the original ABC film. While all this took place, Sa'd Haddad himself was vehemently denying that he or any of his men had any connection whatever with the massacre, even threatening to take action against the ABC correspondents should they ever dare to return to Lebanon.

The killers' weapons

Most of the testimonies dealing with the gunmen's uniforms also made observations on the weapons they had been carrying. Indeed, many of those who had witnessed the massacre, or seen the marks of it while searching for victims afterwards, were able to supply considerable detail on this score.

One Palestinian man, who had been trained in the use of arms in training camps in the South, said: 'The weapons used in the massacre included M16 machine-guns, axes, bayonets and knives.'[96] The al-Khalisa girl who had wandered from place to place with her family said: 'I saw them. They were carrying axes, knives and pistols.'[97] The nurse at the Gaza Hospital, who was also from al-Khalisa, said:

On Thursday, on the first night, they all did their killing using silencers. They used axes too. They did that where a lot of the people were hiding, people could hear the screams but they didn't hear any shooting.[98]

A Palestinian mother, whose husband had been killed in Sabra and Shatila along with several of her children, said:

Of course they were carrying axes. They'd fixed white axes with short handles to their waists; these axes were of the hand-size grip type. A lot of them were carrying Kalashnikovs too. What do you call them, M16s. Oh, God, if you could have seen the state I was in that day! They were carrying rifles, I know.[99]

A southern woman, who was one of the first to see them on the Thursday night, having watched them all night from her roof, said:

I swear to God, they were hitting them with axes, and I heard people yelling out and begging them to stop. But they fired a lot of shots too; not all the shots were from silencers. There was a lot of noisy gunfire – why not, when they couldn't care less about anybody?[100]

The tile worker displaced from Tall al-Za'tar described an axe whose user had failed to remove it from the victim's head:

I saw one man who'd been killed – axed on the head. We were trying to open the door, but we couldn't. The victim had been hit with an axe, which stretched to the door and stayed stuck in his head. I saw this axe in Sabra.[101]

The southern woman who had lost eight of her family described the attackers she saw on the Friday when they were dragging the women and children towards the Sports City and the men and boys elsewhere:

While they were herding us along on the Friday, we saw them on the road carrying M16 guns, Kalashnikovs, axes and daggers. And I tell you, when we went to look for our relatives among the victims after the massacre, we saw things you'd never believe. We saw people who'd been strangled with ropes, we saw others who'd been burned. How do we know whether the killers burned them or killed them first? Anyway, why are you asking me about their weapons? There are knives that can kill you with a single stab, but there are others that can cut a little child into four or five pieces; and we saw that with our own eyes. Now, isn't there a difference between the two knives? God forgive me.[102]

Finally, let us examine more closely one of the testimonies describing the weapons of the attacking gunmen at noon on the Saturday,

when, according to the Kahan Report, the killers were supposed to have been gone for some hours. The narrator was one of those held for questioning in front of the Kuwaiti Embassy, where he saw comrades of his being dragged to the trucks or vanishing into the pits or behind the hill, where he could no longer see their final fate. The eye-witness related as follows:

There were some people without any shirts on. They had ropes and axes on them, they'd fixed them to their bare skin, I swear that's what I saw. They'd hung the ropes round their necks. The axes were separate from the ropes, I mean, the axes weren't tied to the ropes. I mean, those ones who didn't have shirts had a sort of net of ropes on their chests.

Most of them had let their beards grow, and a lot of them were huge …

Some of them were carrying their guns in their hands; I mean, they had an M16, and there were two Doshkas with them.

And some were in military uniform with an MP badge, 'Al-Quwat al-Lubnaniyieh'. How could we have recognized them otherwise?[103]

There is, in the testimonies, a consensus as to the most significant individual weapons used: guns with silencers, regular pistols, M16 rifles, Kalashnikovs, axes, knives, daggers, bayonets and ropes, together with the shells launched on to houses to force people to leave their homes, the explosives used to blow up houses after killing the inhabitants, and the booby-traps placed with the victims to ensure the continuation of the massacre even after it had apparently ended.

The killers' language

The predominant language used among the killers was Arabic. There were, however, some gunmen who spoke foreign languages: French, English, German and Hebrew were all heard. There were also some who did not speak at all. Nevertheless, those speaking foreign languages, or remaining silent, were a small minority.

The most significant of the foreign languages heard, albeit rarely, was Hebrew; for this might indicate an active Israeli presence. As for other languages, there are several possible explanations. Some of the attackers might habitually have used these, Lebanon being a country whose citizens take pride in mastering (for example) French, English, German or Spanish in preference to their own Arabic. Another explanation is people's adaptation to foreign languages in their daily lives, through television and conversation; large numbers of shop owners, as any tourist will quickly discover, post signs only in English or French. A final explanation might lie in the necessity of communicating with the Israelis – if these were in fact present – using a common language. The Israelis also habitually speak more than one language, though for reasons different from those of their Lebanese counterparts; the foreign language – German, say, or French – might actually have been the Israeli soldier's mother tongue before he or his parents came to Israel.

As for the prevalent Arabic language, this was in the various local Lebanese dialects, making it simple to assess from which area or religious sect the speaker came.

When initially questioned on the point, residents spoke simply of 'Lebanese dialect'. When, however, they were asked to provide specific details, they mentioned the dialects of people from certain areas, which included Christian East Beirut, the South, Damour, Maron al-Ras, al-Khiam and Baalbek. They would also sometimes specify the 'sect': dialect and geography combined to reveal the majority of the attackers as Maronite Christians, while the minority included other Christians and Shi'ite Muslims, who were to be found in areas controlled by Sa'd Haddad.[104]

The names heard shed still more light on sectarian affiliation, suggesting once more a Christian majority and a Muslim minority. The attackers called one another by names such as 'Tony', 'Johnny', 'Elias', 'Abbas', 'Muhammad', 'Hasan', 'Maron' and 'Georges'.

Some believed these were not the attackers' real names. Such names as 'Abbas', 'Hasan' or 'Muhammad' were, they thought, used merely for camouflage, to suggest that the killers included Muslims in their numbers. Perhaps such camouflage did exist,

but that does not rule out the possibility that some names were authentic. This latter point is confirmed through a number of specific testimonies where narrators not only repeated the names they heard but affirmed previous knowledge of the person in question.

What the killers left behind

Sabra and Shatila was not a 'perfect crime' with regard to concealment of evidence and proof. And the question remains in any case, how far had the armed killers really sought to carry out a perfect crime? Had they made any serious effort to conceal the signs of the massacre?

Something of the kind was certainly attempted; or, to be more precise, the 'mastermind' or overall 'planner' had tried to give the impression not of a massacre but of a battle between two sides. As such, what the killers chiefly strove to conceal was the enormous number of victims; for it would have been impossible, logically speaking, to kill so many people in a battle between 2,000 'terrorists' and a few hundred attackers. In practice, however, the criminal attackers were unable to conceal the number of dead involved, any more than they could hide other items and evidence – all indicative of a massacre.

The main things left behind by the killers were: weapons, berets, ID cards, Israeli canned food, whisky bottles, beer cans and biscuit boxes. As for the Israelis, who firmly maintained that none of them had entered the massacre area, they had their own items pointing to their presence.

We shall leave it to the testimonies of victims' relatives and of volunteers from the humanitarian organizations to record the items in question.

A young Palestinian man said:

We saw a red beret with the Lebanese cedar on it. There were weapons and ammunition too, made in Israel and used by the Phalangist Party. I'd say the most significant things they left behind were the slogans they put on the walls, on the walls of the Shatila streets. ['The Furn al-Shebbak Forces were here', 'Al-Quwat al-Lubnaniyieh were here.'][105]

Two young men from the Scouts of Al-Tarbiya al-Wataniyieh of the Civil

Defence said:

We were some of the first Civil Defence forces to enter the district. At the Sabra camp we found some military canned food on the ground, like cheese, luncheon meat and various other things. We took all these and kept some as samples, and we still have them. The gunmen had used them, but the cans didn't have any writing on them. We couldn't work out where the ones we found came from, but we're still keeping the samples.[106]

One man from the humanitarian organizations, a member of the Union of Al-Shabiba al-Islamiyieh, found one of the murder weapons. He said:

We saw a lot who'd been killed with knives; the evidence is, we actually found a knife that had been used in the massacre. We still have it, we picked it up on the first day, when the streets were still filled with victims.[107]

A Palestinian man, who had returned home and found no one and nothing but traces of the killers, said:

We found sardine cans at home with Hebrew writing on them, and the Red Cross officials saw them too. The gunmen had made themselves comfortable – they'd cut up a watermelon and eaten it, the leftovers from the melon were still there in the house.[108]

A mother returning to her home in Hayy Ersal found it totally wrecked. She had, though, something to say about what she saw in front of her own house and her neighbours':

There were mattresses all over the front yard; the Kata'eb took the mattresses from the houses, laid them out on the ground and sat on them. They'd lie down and sleep. They took away all the blankets too, they must have been completely cold-blooded.[109]

A nurse who had witnessed the militias' entry on the Thursday described what she saw at her own and her neighbours' houses when she returned:

When we fled the massacre, we stayed at a building near the Hélou Barracks; it was a building without any doors or windows, and we didn't have any clothes, mattresses, blankets or sheets, none at all.

The children with us were wearing the same clothes they had on when we left. We didn't have any food either, we actually had nothing to eat the whole time we were away.

On Saturday, at half past four in the afternoon, I said to my mother: 'Let me go to the Dana petrol station and see whether they've left the camps.' We'd heard the Lebanese Army had gone into the camp district. When I reached the Arab University district, I found soldiers from the Army going in there and taking up position. I was with my neighbour Mariam [Abu Harb], who wanted to take away the bodies of her husband, children and other family. The army soldiers stopped and asked us: 'Where are you going?' We said: 'To Sabra and Shatila.' Then we broke down in tears. They didn't ask anything else at all, they just came up and said: 'All right then, but don't let on you're Palestinian; say you're Lebanese, from the South.'

So we started walking. From almost the moment we got into the district, we saw the bodies scattered on the ground; in the main street, in the houses, in the alleys. We couldn't believe it.

We went into our houses and found they'd been ransacked. The televisions and tape recorders, and the money, they were all gone. And all the things were on top of one another, the supplies, like sugar, crushed wheat and spices, had all been spilled about.

I'd had a few suitcases too, filled with bridal gear, all new; we have a tradition, or custom, from back in the Palestine times, to get things ready for a daughter who's engaged, as her marriage gets nearer. We found all these suitcases had been opened, and the attackers had smeared blood on them with their fingers and knives, then flung them down on the floor. All the clothes were stained with blood.

In front of the house they'd brought out mattresses and chairs, and they'd been drinking coffee. I found the coffee pots still there in the front yard; they'd taken them out of the kitchen and made some coffee, just like that … cold-bloodedly, you could tell.

But they'd brought some of their own food and drink along too. On the floor we found some sardine cans with Hebrew writing on them. And we found a beer can too, with Hebrew writing on it.

We noticed something odd too – the Hebrew biscuit boxes were very light, no heavier than a single match, to make them lighter to carry obviously.

Before I went back, I saw a big knife on our neighbours' doorstep, a black knife, and I asked our neighbour: 'Tell me, is this knife yours?' And she said: 'No.'[110]

In the district adjacent to Shatila Camp on the Horsh side, evidence of the killers' presence was not limited to signs of lying down or resting but also included intoxicants. One witness, who had gone there to check on residents and the district generally, reported as follows:

Well, in front of a house on the edge of the camp, on the Horsh side, there was a vehicle in which I found two boxes that had had whisky and mixed nuts. In other words, they'd come along to kill happily and drink whisky, and couldn't have cared less, they didn't even bother to burn them and hide their crime ... In the same way, they didn't bother to hide the victims here on the edge of the camp. We found six or seven bodies here, run over by a truck, and the killers had brought something like a bulldozer, they were going to dump backfill on them, evidently they wanted to bury them. These bodies were just outside the camp street limits.[111]

As for Um Ali al-Beka'i, she not only saw the food and drink on their tables but went on to provide a detailed description of the 'drinks tables' on the Friday morning, when she was being herded along with her neighbours, towards an unknown fate:

Listen, you people, descendants of Muhammad, here's something you simply won't believe. They hadn't just been drinking during the night, they'd been opening whisky bottles in front of everybody from early on Friday morning. How could anyone drink as early as that, with the bodies right next to him, making a barricade pretty well? I swear, that's what we saw. A lot of them had put the whisky, and the food and other drinks, out on tables. I saw all that as I ran to beg one of them: 'I beg you, where are you taking my son? I beg you, tell me, where?' Nobody answered. They just laughed at me. As I was going back to the queue, I saw those things. I wished now I hadn't pleaded with any of them. I ask you, how can people like that be called proper human beings?[112]

Hajj Mahmoud Rukn, describing the Saturday's forced march, gave an account similar to Um Ali al-Beka'i's for the Friday:

I can't imagine a more dreadful sight. I saw four bodies; and they'd put the whisky and araq [a Lebanese alcoholic beverage, made from grapes] glasses right down next to them. I saw it with my own eyes. They'd killed those four people and mutilated their bodies, then they laid them down and started drinking araq and whisky right next to them. May God curse them; *Allahu Akbar* on them![113]

The food leftovers residents had seen were also seen, along with remaining weapons, by reporters who arrived in the days immediately following the massacre. Thomas Friedman, in the *New York Times*, wrote how correspondents had found boxes containing M16 bullets, which had had Hebrew writing on them. They also found wrapping paper for Israeli-made chocolate biscuits, and leftovers of military rations of American manufacture.[114]

Ron Ben-Yishay wrote that he had, with his own eyes, seen Israeli-made canned food and weapons. The intention, he observed, was to give the impression that the men in question were Haddad's, since it was well known that Sa'd Haddad's group received direct support from the Israeli Army in respect of weapons and equipment.[115]

As for indisputable evidence as to the killers' identity, this includes the actual ID cards some of them carried in their pockets then accidentally dropped and lost during the incursion into the camps. A number of witnesses testified to the presence of both Lebanese and Israeli cards.

The young man who, above, told of the sardine cans in his house said:

On the first day after the massacre, I went into my house and found an identity document marked 'Ikhraj Qaid', which I handed over to the army and Civil Defence; they were there together. It was a Lebanese ID.[116]

Another resident of the massacre site said: 'There's a man called ——, from Bint Jbeil, and his ID document was found. It must have been dropped by accident.'[117] And the director of the Gaza Hospital said:

Two American journalists came after the massacre, I don't remember their names. They showed me a necklace with Hebrew writing on it, including Hebrew good luck prayers on the back. A Palestinian boy had found this necklace and given it to the American journalist. This journalist had another colleague too, they always hung out together …

There's a friend of mine too, who got hold of an Israeli ID card from a man in Shatila Camp. This man had found the card in the street near the camp, right next to it, and she bought it from him and kept it as evidence. I didn't see it with my own eyes. Even so, that friend of mine's quite trustworthy, she's never in her life said anything that wasn't true.[118]

During the first Muslim feast after the massacre, while victims' relatives were at the cemeteries mourning their loved ones, a girl from the Miqdad family stood in front of everyone holding Israeli military helmets with the Star of David on them. Everyone there saw her and heard the furious, hysterical account she gave to the journalists present:

Where did these come from? Where, tell me that? We found these in the houses. Take pictures of me, holding a helmet in each hand. I'm not afraid of anybody. I'm from the Miqdad family. These helmets were found in the houses. That's the flag of Palestine there, look, you see it raised? And I'm telling you, we're Lebanese, and we won't give it up.

Israel claims it had nothing to do with everything that happened. So where did these helmets come from? Where?[119]

The killers' identity and characteristics

Did residents succeed in confirming the killers' identity?

The attacking militias entered the Sabra and Shatila district with badges on their lapels and shoulders; the residents could read well enough, and they had been familiar with such badges throughout the civil wars in Lebanon. They stated that these armed attackers were from Al-Kata'eb al-Lubnaniyieh, the Phalangists (Al-Quwat al-Lubnaniyieh) and Sa'd Haddad's Forces (Quwat Sa'd Haddad). And amid the furious subsequent denials of those responsible for the massacre, there was much talk that the badges might not imply actual membership

of one or another group. This may be true; nevertheless, the identity of the killers was not determined through the badges alone.

There were direct admissions by the gunmen that they belonged to the Lebanese Forces or Sa'd Haddad; and this concurs with much of what local residents heard and with the content of many testimonies. One killer, for instance, would be exultantly boastful about his mission, another would freely proclaim his militia identity with a view to further terrorizing residents, or to avenging himself on Palestinians.

On the Saturday morning, Dr Swee Chai Ang asked the gunmen in front of the Gaza Hospital who they were, and she testified as to their answers before the MacBride Commission:

They said they were from the army. I asked, 'what army'? They replied, 'Lebanese Forces'. Now, I was new to the country and I didn't know what Lebanese Forces meant. Of course, I subsequently found out that Lebanese Forces meant Kataeb.[120]

As we have seen, the attackers gave similar answers to a number of the foreign doctors, making no attempt to deny their identity as they were dragging the doctors off for questioning.

There were local witnesses who knew who the killer was, having actually seen him committing his crimes. Some of these spoke out, as can be seen from a number of the testimonies included above.

Other residents knew but were afraid to speak out. Among these was a witness in his forties, who was standing next to one of the victims on Sunday 19 September. Jean Genet saw him and asked him about the killer, and they talked together in French. Before enlarging on this conversation, Jean Genet embarked on a description of love and death, inspired by these moments when he stood alongside the victim flung down there on the ground:

Love and death. These two words are quickly associated when one of them is written down. I had to go to Shatila to understand the obscenity of love and the obscenity of death. In both cases the body has nothing more to hide; positions, contortions, gestures, signs, even silences belong to one world and to the other. The body of a man of thirty to thirty-five was lying face down. As if the whole body was nothing but a bladder in the shape of a man, it had become so bloated in the sun and through the chemistry of decomposition that the pants were stretched tight as though they were going to burst open at the buttocks and thighs. The only part of the face that I could see was purple and black. Slightly above the knee you could see a thigh wound under the torn fabric. Cause of the wound: a bayonet, a knife, a dagger? Flies on the wound and around it. His head was larger than a watermelon – a black watermelon. I asked his name; he was a Moslem.

'Who is it?'

'A Palestinian,' a man about forty answered in French. 'See what they've done.'

He pulled back the blanket covering the feet and part of the legs. The calves were bare, black and swollen. The feet, in black unlaced army boots, and the ankles of both feet were very tightly bound together by the knot of a strong rope – its strength was obvious – about nine feet long, which I arranged so that Mrs. S (an American) could get a good picture of it. I asked the man of forty if I could see the face.

'If you want to, but look at it yourself.'

'Would you help me to turn his head?'

'No.'

'Did they drag him through the streets with this rope?'

'I don't know, sir.'

'Who tied him up?'

'I don't know, sir.'

'Was it Haddad's men?'

'I don't know.'

'The Israelis?'

'I don't know.'

'The Kataeb?'

'I don't know.'

'Did you know him?'

'Yes.'

'Did you see him die?'

'Yes.'

'Who killed him?'

'I don't know.'

He hastily walked away from the dead man and me. From afar he looked back at me and disappeared into a side street.[121]

This witness was not the only one who feared to tell the truth; dozens of others felt similarly during those crucial days.

But what of the killer's characteristics, or psychology? Were the individuals involved similar, or were there disparities? There was much talk that the killers had all come from Damour, in a spirit of vengeance for what had taken place there – thirsting for revenge, as some said: 'This was Damour's axe.' (Damour, where some Palestinian survivors of the 1976 Tall al-Za'tar massacre had subsequently gone to live, was historically Christian. See Chapter 7.) It was said, again, that they had come to avenge Bashir al-Gemayel's death; and some witnesses quoted the attackers as saying: 'You killed Bashir al-Gemayel. Now we've come to kill you.'

One woman described how they broke into the shelter on the Thursday evening:

I looked out through the shelter door and found around sixteen men there in front of me: 'You, you son of a bitch, all of you, all come here … you're all gloating about Bashir Gemayel's death. Come here and we'll show you.'[122]

Yet such statements do not indicate that the massacre as a whole was intended to avenge Damour, or Bashir al-Gemayel's death. The underlying causes run deeper, the historical resonance is more subtle. It is pointless even so to enlarge on all this, for what can justify a massacre?

Testimonies differed with regard to the attackers' psychological state, and this is natural enough given the nature of an event beyond normal human experience, and given that the gunmen entered in groups over three consecutive days, with the beginning differing from the end. When they first entered Bir Hasan, they were confused and hesitant, unclear even as to where exactly they were. However, they quickly adjusted to the situation of the massacre; any residual guilt or fear was swept away through imitation of those more experienced or senior among them, till the majority had become hardened to the killing of innocent residents: women, children, the elderly and men, either individually or in groups, in the most savage fashion. There were, nevertheless, a few whose experience ran exactly counter to this; who were brutal in the beginning, then stopped later to ask themselves just what they were doing.

Many testified that the killers they saw were not in a normal state. They were constantly drinking intoxicants, smoking hashish, or whatever. Some, as a number of witnesses noted, were under the influence of drink or drugs from the moment they arrived. An officer of the Lebanese Army, who was close and witnessed the massacre, summed the situation up. 'In my view,' he said, 'they were certainly … in an abnormal state.'[123]

Yet there were others whose testimony was precisely contrary: the killers, they said, knew exactly what they were doing, and were acting in cold blood. This can be seen, for example, in the testimony of a Palestinian woman whose sister and father were among the first victims on the Thursday evening. In her view the men were acting in total awareness of what they were doing, and manifesting the utmost contempt and hatred.[124]

There is no real contradiction here; rather there are differences and multiple viewpoints reflecting a difference in individual psychologies. The testimonies were describing the behaviour of hundreds of attackers, who were not in any sense a unified army with a uniform military training; and even if this had been the case, the individuals in question could not possibly have possessed the same psychological make-up. Sometimes, indeed, two testimonies would be contradictory with respect to a single group, or to a single gunman even, because they were describing different circumstances and different moments.

Massacres are to be measured not in days or hours, but in minutes. And the days of the massacre overall were not alone sufficient to determine the characteristics of the murderous attackers. Some killers went on, even after the massacre, seeking out places likely to harbour Palestinians who had left Sabra and Shatila for places felt to offer greater security. An example of this was at Sanaye' Park, where two suspicious-looking men began making periodic visits. Um Majed recounts one such incident:

Two days after the massacre, we went to Sanaye' Park. Where else did we have to go? We used to sleep there at night, along with all our neighbours.

Two men came more than once, they came in a red car, and told everyone they were Kata'eb. One of us got suspicious about them and reported them to the Army, and the officer at the police station told him to let them know the moment the men came back.

And come back they did. One of them came up and started talking to us. I asked him: 'Where are you from?' He said he was from Zahlé. I was standing next to some other women, and we noticed he started sounding frightened. He said: 'I found a Quran and I hid it on me. I'm a Christian from Zahlé. I found a torn piece from the Quran on the ground, and I just couldn't step on it, so I picked it up and put it in my pocket.' And he actually put his hand in his pocket and took out some torn pieces of the Quran he had with him …

I was suspicious; where could he have found torn paper from the Quran on the ground? And something else I found odd about him, why would someone who smoked foreign cigarettes carry cigarette paper to put tobacco in? I thought at first the man must have been taking drugs, especially as his eyes were red, and I asked him: 'Why are your eyes so red?' He said: 'From staying up late, we don't sleep, we spend the nights watching over people to protect them!' He wasn't, by the way, wearing any regular military uniform.

He asked us where we were from, and we said we were from Sabra. And he took a breath, and said: 'What are you doing here then? Is the army going to protect you at Sanaye'?'

While he was still talking some army soldiers came and they pointed their guns at him and took him in. If he'd really belonged to the army, he would have shown them his card.

We found out later what happened to him at the station, from a woman we knew who was with us at Sanaye', and was related to a Lebanese soldier at the station. They questioned him and beat him, she told me, then they saw his undershirt was soaked with dried blood from that day, it was obvious he'd never taken it off since. He went to pieces then, and admitted he was one of the people who'd taken part in Sabra and Shatila. It turned out, as well, he had several different ID cards, including the Kata'eb one. Finally he admitted he was a Kata'eb.

The other man, the one who was with him, he was the same.[125]

Such wandering around places where victims or their relatives were to be found happened repeatedly in Beirut – confirming the commonly held theory that the killer automatically returns to the scene of the crime.

Immediately after the massacre, the gendarmes arrested three armed men from a southern village who were wandering about close to the airport roundabout. When the gendarmes inspected their papers, these turned out to be old documents. The three men denied their identity initially, but confessed, after questioning, that they were from Sa'd Haddad's group – and that they had been there at Sabra and Shatila.[126]

There were indeed attackers at Sabra and Shatila who declined to take part in killing or torturing, but they were few in number. Their stories became known through residents who were acquainted with them from earlier days; this mutual acquaintance was both the reason for the gunmen's mercy towards them and the means of establishing the gunmen's identity.

So it was with one of the southern women during the Friday's march, when she recognized a Muslim Shi'ite man from al-Khiam. She spoke to him and told him of her tragedy; and he responded, not only making no effort to deny his identity, but going on actively to help her: when she told him of a hardy Palestinian girl fallen into the hands of a group of rapists, he went and rescued the girl. This man was from Sa'd Haddad's group.

Then there was the Palestinian hajj who had formerly known a Kata'eb man and his little son – the latter now a grown man and a member of the Lebanese Forces. Under the spur of this old friendship, the young man saved the old hajj's life when he saw him about to be killed along with others in the death pit, before noon on the Saturday. A similar event occurred on the first day, when a Phalangist, come to kill, recognized one of the Palestinians trapped in Bir Hasan, and held back out of consideration for the 'good old days'.

The previous pages contain reference to these and further, limited incidents; but such cases, resulting from pre-existing friendships or relations, were quite few in number. There were also other, very limited incidents springing not from pre-existing relations but from a more general humanity. A few of those supposed to act as killers did not do so; they spared women or children and offered help instead, like 'Monsieur Nadim' in the case of the exhausted women who were piled into the truck and sent back on the Thursday night. There was no indication, nevertheless, that others respected 'Monsieur Nadim's' word. On the contrary, they avenged themselves on these women.

To every rule there is an exception; and even in massacres occasional sparks of humanity are found.

Conclusion

- The first people to enter the massacre area were the foreign journalists and photographers.
- For unknown reasons, Lebanese photographers were banned from taking pictures on the first days but were permitted to do so afterwards.
- The search for victims began only after the Lebanese Army had entered the district and assumed control, on the morning of Sunday 19 September.
- The prominent humanitarian institutions practically involved included the International Red Cross, the Lebanese Red Cross, the Lebanese Civil Defence and at least eight national civil institutions. These worked for two whole weeks, clearing rubble and searching for and burying victims.
- A number of witnesses reported seeing bulldozers leave Sabra and Shatila loaded with bodies, before the attacking militias left Sabra and Shatila.
- A number of rescue workers and reporters testified that whole houses had been brought down over their inhabitants. Rescue workers succeeded in clearing much of the rubble and removing the bodies, but were not able to achieve this everywhere.
- The course of the search revealed a number of mass graves, some of these pits caused by Israeli air force shelling during the invasion, others dug by the militias

using bulldozers. In either case the intention was concealment of the vast quantity of victims' bodies.

- Some Lebanese and Palestinian residents managed to take the bodies of their loved ones and bury them in public cemeteries in Beirut or in their villages or towns of origin.
- Rumours that Sa'd Haddad's forces had returned to carry out a further massacre swept through the district, leading people, including rescue workers, to take flight during the first two days. When they returned on the following morning, most residents could find no trace of their loved ones and were regularly told that these latter had been buried in mass cemeteries to guard against the spread of disease.
- The locations of the graves referred to on the Saturday and Sunday had not been determined. As for the famous mass cemetery, work on this had not yet begun.
- Two rumours, not just one, spread on the Monday, and, as on the two earlier days, large numbers of victims could have been buried in unknown sites. However, the young Civil Defence men of Al-Risala al-Islamiyieh insisted on staying in Sabra and Shatila to conclude the mass burial formalities in accordance with Islamic rules. This was after they had contacted high-level Islamic religious authorities, and had been instructed to begin the formalities, including pre-burial prayers, without delay.
- Excavation work for mass burial was begun, to the right of Shatila for someone entering from the South, after four o'clock on the afternoon of Monday 20 September, and burial and prayers went on for some days.
- Between 700 and 800 victims were buried in the mass cemetery alone.
- The International Red Cross and Lebanese Civil Defence recorded the names of known victims and of those missing and abducted.
- Prior requirements for registration of victims comprised: first, availability and submission of the victim's ID card; second, availability and examination of the body; third, availability of immediate family or other relatives to identify the body. To fulfil these three requirements together was far from easy.
- The International Red Cross, Lebanese Red Cross and Lebanese Civil Defence compiled independent lists of victims. Nevertheless, the names on the three lists as a whole do not comprise all the victims. Most significant among the victims whose names were not listed were: those taken by their families for burial elsewhere; those whose bodies or limbs had vanished beneath the rubble; those that had disappeared in undiscovered graves; those whose bodies had been dragged off to places outside the district; those buried, without any religious formalities, in the two days after the rumours had begun to spread; and those whose bodies had been left exposed and remained unidentified (due, perhaps, to the death of the whole family, or to the impossibility of recognition even by the families of those concerned).
- The International Red Cross, together with other humanitarian organizations, compiled lists for large numbers of those missing. The fate of these was never established, and the lists themselves eventually disappeared.
- Residents' testimonies about the attacking gunmen – involving descriptions, dialects, clothes, weapons, actions, statements, names, boasts and slogans – in conjunction with the testimonies of foreign authors and reporters, indicate that the gunmen were from Al-Kata'eb al-Lubnaniyieh, Al-Quwat al-Lubnaniyieh and Quwat Sa'd Haddad.
- This chapter's initial question, as to whether the affair was a battle or a massacre, is perhaps better replaced by another question. How many massacres, throughout history, have paralleled that of Sabra and Shatila?

Part II

Statistics and Comparisons

Sabra is the crossroads over a body
Sabra is growth of the spirit in a stone.
Sabra? There is no one!
Sabra defines our time for ever.

Mahmoud Darwish
'Praising the High Shadow'

7

Field Study, Spring 1984

Any immediate field study within Sabra and Shatila was simply out of the question. It was impossible even to mention the word 'massacre' openly, let alone enter the zone where the action had taken place and distribute questionnaires or talk to victims' families. There was simply no option but to wait.

As commonly happens in those countries labelled 'Third World', or 'developing' (more decent terms than the previous 'under-developed'), the security situation was liable to change from one day to the next. Such a change occurred in the city of Beirut as of 6 February 1984. Suddenly, what had been almost impossible now became possible, welcomed indeed by the Lebanese men who had begun to guard the Sabra and Shatila district and its vicinity.

Why, in fact, was a field study necessary? The answer is that documentary work was needed to collate the data regarding victims and those abducted, and, at the same time, to compile a full list of names. These were the two main objectives of the study carried out in the spring of 1984.

Field studies are an established method, on the level of theory and practice alike, for gaining reliable access to 'final' or 'near final' figures; and, by their nature, the results of such studies differ fundamentally from official statistics compiled, for the most part, by governments, international committees or official organizations. Partly this is because field studies have no legal backing, and because individual researchers lack the manpower and material resources available to governments and international or official organizations. There is, though, a still more crucial difference, which may be summarized in terms of two major points:

- First, the aim of official statistical compilations is the statistics themselves, and these are normally established by making a thorough survey of a specific territory, country or group, whereas field studies deal with only limited numbers of residents, or whoever, whose situation is under examination.
- Second, field studies are normally more wide-ranging than the statistical survey, requiring as they do the collection of various data about each and every individual, in every relevant group, party, sect or family. They may, indeed, go beyond such individual data collection, in accordance with the necessary objectives of the research and in harmony with the principal questions generally posed at the outset by the researchers in question.

In other words, the significance of the statistical method lies in the retrieval of figures with maximum accuracy and completeness; whereas that of the field study method lies in the utilization of limited statistics for specific patterns, sectors or groups, with a view to establishing percentages for the subjects under investigation (including topics linked to the objectives of the study), and arriving at a comprehensive final analysis.

I was well enough aware of these differences. Nevertheless, I felt that the implementation of a field study (in the spring of 1984) was the sole means of retrieving the largest possible number of names. No official organization, after all, had shown any apparent inclination to undertake the task – even though this might normally have been expected on humane and documentary grounds alike. On the contrary, official efforts had been made to cover up all signs of the massacre.

Aims of the field study

The underlying aim of this field study is not simply to supply scholarly enlightenment in relation to a massacre surrounded by extreme secrecy at the time it occurred and subject to a whole wave of prohibitions once it was over (or, to be strictly accurate, from just a few weeks after it was over, when international media coverage, neither controllable nor ignorable up till then, had finally died down). Nor is the purpose to provide coming generations with a comprehensive account of the massacre, from which the full significance of events might be drawn – a formidable task that would, in any case, be beyond the scope of this work as conceived by the author (see the Introduction).

The principal aims are, first and last, linked to human conscience. Nor is this 'conscience' restricted to the citizens of one people; it extends to all human beings on the face of the earth, who will not tolerate the notion of killing children, pregnant women, the handicapped elderly, or even able-bodied adults with no weapons with which to defend themselves.

To feel sorrow or anguish at others' sorrows, to shed a tear on hearing of an innocent man being killed, to say, 'Poor man, so tragic, how unjust that was' – all this

qualifies a person to be called 'humane'. But to be a human being, in the full sense of the term, also entails assuming responsibility: for preventing injustice, for protecting the innocent, for ensuring no other child is killed, in your own country or anywhere else in the world.

Nevertheless, we citizens of Beirut bear more responsibility for what happened in Sabra and Shatila than anyone else on earth. We are responsible by virtue of our physical nearness. How could it have happened? How could all this barbaric torture and murder have taken place? How could the residents of Sabra and Shatila have been forced to live through death, for 43 unbroken hours, while we, the other Beirutis, remained ignorant of it all? Only at noon on the Saturday did we hear of the massacre – through radio stations in London and Monte Carlo. And Sabra and Shatila lie in the heart of Beirut!

The question remains, why were they killed? And why did we survive, when all were citizens of Beirut? Let us set aside the spurious pretext that there were armed Palestinians within Sabra and Shatila – an allegation which even the Israeli authorities themselves, the Kahan Report, or the Lebanese parties accused of committing the massacre, failed ever to substantiate. Still the question requires an answer. Other Beirutis were not killed, and nor were those living in other Palestinian camps and communities. Just why were the residents of Sabra and Shatila singled out for slaughter? What major differences were there between the residents of Sabra and Shatila and those of, say, Bliss Street, Verdun Street or the Ramlat al-Baida district?

What springs instantly to mind is that the residents of Sabra and Shatila lived in popular, crowded houses, while others lived in luxurious apartments. Was this in fact the crime of the Palestinian victims – that they were not 'wealthy refugees'? That – in contrast to the affluent Palestinians whose retail shops flooded Hamra Street and Ras Beirut – they were not from a class that could afford to live in decent neighbourhoods? Was their crime to have come from Galilee, in northern Palestine, where most of the villages had been wiped clean off the map by Israel, so that they themselves had been driven out of Tarshiha, Deir al-Qasi, Sihmata, Saffourieh, or wherever?

As for the crime of the Lebanese victims, was this, in turn, to have come from Sheb'a, Majdal Zoun, al-Shaqif, Bint Jbeil, and other Lebanese villages? Was the crime of the Arab, Pakistani, Bangladeshi and other nationals that they had come not from Europe or North America, but from Arab and Islamic countries which they had left in an attempt to earn an honest living in Lebanon? In short, was poverty their crime? The poverty that compelled them to live alongside Palestinians, who had received them warmly?

The fact of the matter is that Arab and Muslim labourers from other countries were not the only ones classified as temporary rather than permanent residents of Sabra and Shatila. Over the years various Lebanese and Palestinians had become displaced in the wake of the destructive Israeli shelling of the southern Lebanese villages and Palestinian camps. Others had been victims of the Lebanese civil wars, moving on continually from one place to the next: Sidon, Tyre, Nabatieh, Dikwaneh, Tall al-Za'tar, Burj Hammoud and Karantina. For these, Sabra and Shatila was not, in the autumn of 1982, a final place of residence, but rather a temporary staging post pending the liberation of the South, which would leave southern Lebanese free to go back home, or pending the establishment of a true Palestinian state on Palestinian land which would allow refugees to return.

They were killed, and we remained alive. Was this, then, simply because we had the means to live outside the popular districts? Or was it rather, in the main, because the scope for the attacking killer is always limited? If this scope had been greater, he might, perhaps, have extended his destruction at least to the camps of Burj al-Barajneh and Mar Elias and their surroundings. Were there not, after all, Palestinians in these camps? Would it not have seemed quite natural for some 'terrorists' to be concealed among them? I cannot provide answers to all these questions. Frankly, I do not know.

But of one thing I am certain: had any of us been a resident of Sabra and Shatila, he or she would have faced the same fate.

From Deir Yassin in April 1948 to Jenin in April 2002, Zionist massacres against Palestinian, Lebanese or other Arab people have been unceasing. In Palestine there were the massacres of Qibya, Kafr Qassem and al-Samou'; subsequently, in the late 1960s, there was the massacre of Bahr al-Baqar in Egypt; and in the 1990s there were those of al-Khiam and Qana in Lebanon. Even these are only the prime examples. And, at the heart of this maelstrom of bloody violence, there was Sabra and Shatila.

But let us return to the original question. Why did those who died die, and why did we remain alive? If I cannot provide clear answers to this, then I can at the very least pay the ransom for survival: not money, but rather the will to embark on the laborious process of seeking answers to certain more specific questions. What happened? And why? And how?

The field study team

The chief credit for this study must go to a number of responsible and mature people, both Palestinian and Lebanese, from the Sabra and Shatila district, who not only volunteered, spontaneously and eagerly, to distribute questionnaires to victims' families and their neighbours, but also explained these questionnaires, filling them out in front of respondents and ensuring the latter signed and recorded their precise relation to the victim concerned.

The work began with fewer than ten team members, but it ended with almost 20 including four girls. Each of these would select a friend or relative, thereby ensuring that a further member would contribute and work in another quarter. Many times the interviewees themselves would guide the people to some other home or family; so much so, indeed, that during the six weeks in which the questionnaires were being distributed and filled out in April and May 1984, Sabra and Shatila became a veritable hive of activity, with everyone working together like members of a single family.

While most of the team worked on the distribution, others checked the completed questionnaires for accuracy. The men would go out from their homes to those of neighbours, and from there to other homes in their quarter, working progressively outwards. Everything rested, needless to say, on the mutual trust existing between them and the residents.

The central principle was clear to everyone: what was required was to record data as accurately as possible. There were no preconceptions; rather the firm conviction that exaggeration was to be avoided. Everyone proceeded from a sense of duty towards every victim or abducted person, whether Arab or foreign, old or young, man or woman.

As for verifying the credibility of the information obtained, a matter commonly addressed in studies of this kind by sending a second team member to respondents after an interval of time, the latter method was not necessary here. This was because the oral project I initiated late in 1982, involving the interviewing of dozens of families, had already reached its final stage. In other words, we might say that the process of 'verification' had preceded rather than followed the field study and, what is more, the numbers involved actually exceeded the conventionally requisite 10–30 per cent.[1] In the event of ambiguity, even if partial only, a correction would be made following verification with the people concerned.

As for the specific information sought on the questionnaires, this fell into two categories. The first category dealt with data concerning the particular individual, whether victim or abducted. This included: name; place of residence; nationality; gender; age; religious sect; level of education; profession; financial responsibility towards the family; and fate. For the victim, data further included: date of death; place of death; identification of the body; registration of death. For the abducted person, the data further included: date of abduction; place of abduction; availability of witnesses; identity of abductor.

The second category, in contrast, dealt with data concerning the families, and mainly comprised: place of residence prior to 1948; shifting residence or successive migrations after 1948; number of victims and abducted for each particular family; mass emigration in the aftermath of the massacre.

By the final phase, and following the elimination of duplicate questionnaires (which were inevitable in the early stages), the number of questionnaires had reached 430 for victims and 100 for those abducted.

With respect to those abducted, more names and information could have been compiled but for the human situation with which we found ourselves confronted. So enormous was the number of abducted in all parts of Lebanon, as a result of successive civil wars, that a mother, say, devastated by the abduction of husband, son or daughter, would clutch at the hope that the project might somehow help in finding her loved one. Throughout the first weeks, team members struggled to convince a mother or father that the project applied strictly to Sabra and Shatila.

The result was that hundreds of completed questionnaires contained the names of people abducted at Tall al-Za'tar, or at Christian militia checkpoints at al-Hazmiyeh, on the Damascus highway or on mountain roads. We came to fear, indeed, that the project, for all its humane motives, might result in unintended cruelty as these tormented people began to believe we were involved in a general statistical project and clung to the hope that their loved ones might now be found at last. In the light of this, I elected to limit the number to 100 and to treat this as sufficient for the purposes of analysis.

The team members were careful to record the relationship of the interviewee to the victim or abducted person. The code A1 applied to immediate kin, such as father, mother, sister, wife, and so on; A2 to a relative outside the immediate family, such as uncle, cousin, and so on; A3 to a friend; A4 to a neighbour; A5 to a simple witness. There was no hierarchy in these codes – no implication, say, that the testimony of a father or son should take precedence over that of a friend or simple witness. All information was verified in the interests of the study's overall credibility; to confirm that those approached were indeed linked to the victim or abducted person, as relatives, friends, neighbours or witnesses.

In this regard, the 430 questionnaires involving victims broke down as follows: the A1 type numbered 231 (53.72 per cent); the A2 type, 69 (16.05 per cent); the A3 type, 52 (12.09 per cent); the A4 type, 35 (8.14 per cent); the A5 type, 43 (10.00 per cent).

As for the 100 questionnaires for those abducted, the A1 type numbered 83 (83 per cent); the A2 type, 3 (3 per cent); the A3 type, 2 (2 per cent); the A4 type, 8 (8 per cent); the A5 type, 4 (4 per cent). (See Appendix 1, Table 1.)

When distribution and verification were complete, I had to invest additional time for analysis of the results, for computer equipment at that time was still available only at a few institutions in Beirut, and home computers were virtually unknown. In the following year an expert undertook the task, and as a result the questionnaire contents were converted into tables, numbers and lists of names by the winter of 1985.

In this manner, I finally managed to deliver part of the results and statistics to the 'Israeli Crimes Against the Lebanese and Palestinian Peoples' Convention, which was summoned by the International Committee for Solidarity with the Arab People, in Bonn, Germany, at the end of March 1985.

On the fourth anniversary of the Sabra and Shatila massacre, the novelist Elias Khoury wrote of the tragic event in *Al-Safir*, dedicating to it the educational section for which he was responsible. He was one of the first Lebanese authors, following four years of silence, to declare that the massacre was a historic event and that as such it should be dealt with not just as a matter of specific detail but as one of principle. I was, perhaps, a little surprised when he asked me to take part in writing about the massacre for this special edition. The conclusions I had earlier submitted at the Bonn Convention were thereupon published in an article entitled: 'Isn't it High Time these Victims Spoke Out?' (*Al-Safir*, 17 September 1986).

I then fell silent – like everyone else – before returning to Sabra and Shatila at the end of the twentieth century to complete my study and write the present book.

The archive and the record

The archive for the field study comprised the questionnaires distributed to the residents of Sabra and Shatila; after checking and classification, these, as noted above, numbered 430 and 100 for victims and abducted persons respectively. Each questionnaire was numbered in accordance with its order during the initial stage. Questionnaires for victims were therefore numbered consecutively from 1 to 430. Those for abducted persons were, however, numbered from 501 to 600. The distinction between victim and abducted person therefore became self-evident.

The questionnaires and related files are now retained in an Arab research institution. Before being sent for storage, however, the contents of the documents were copied in full to form a special record, typed under the title 'Record of the Sabra and Shatila Field Study'. This included the information relevant to each victim or abducted person, as contained in the original questionnaires, and the sequential numbers were also retained.

This record is the principal source for the analytical tables contained in this chapter, both for the first list of names in Appendix 2, comprising the names of victims, and for the second list, comprising the names of those abducted.

The victims and the abducted: details of identity

Let us consider, first, the victims of this historic tragedy. Most of those who have written about Sabra and Shatila or addressed television or radio audiences on the subject have in fact largely concentrated on this aspect, the consensus being that those in question were victims of one of the most horrific massacres of the twentieth century.

Nevertheless, the official Israeli statement made no mention whatever of victims, nor did it at any point stop to consider the fate of those abducted. It was characterized, on the contrary, by expressions not used even by a number of the Israeli authors and reporters who were among the first to enter the massacre territory and who were among those covering the case of Sabra and Shatila most intensively in written reports, publications and broadcasts. These latter referred to victims, those abducted and missing, and to a massacre; the official Israeli statement, in contrast, used such terms as 'saboteurs' and 'terrorists'. 'Saboteur' was in fact the standard term at that time, the one reiterated by officers through the blaring megaphones near the Sports City.

Yet were those referred to by their enemies as 'saboteurs' or 'terrorists' not, in reality, perfectly ordinary human beings? Did they not have a community like any other? Did they not have families, children, schools, markets, shops, streets? Even if their 'streets' were actually alleys narrower than the corridors inside some luxurious buildings? Did they not have basil and jasmine in their cramped window spaces, just as they had once had back in Palestine? Did they not have dreams – a life?

The field study is not, however, a narrative description but a collection of numbers and proportions. These are aspects that must be broached if we are to encounter and identify the reality behind the victims and those abducted. When we organized the study in 1984, it was based, as said above, on 430 questionnaires for victims and 100 for those abducted. Now, 20 years after the disaster, no serious hope remains, short of a divine miracle, that the abducted loved ones of so many families will return. As far as contemporary Lebanese history is concerned, the 'abducted' have now become 'victims'.

Before the twentieth century ended, an official Lebanese commission was appointed by the Prime Ministry. Its mission was to register the names of all those abducted on Lebanese soil from the mid-1970s through to the 1990s, and this list was to include two special clauses concerning the identity of the abductors and the place where the person had been abducted, if this was known by the family. This was the first and last serious official effort made to establish the fate of those abducted and missing.

Among the names recorded were some for those abducted and missing in the Sabra and Shatila massacre.

In July 2000, Prime Minister Salim al-Hoss announced that the work of this Investigatory Commission into the Fate of All Those Abducted and Missing had been completed. He further announced that all those who had been registered as abducted and missing were now to be officially regarded as dead. By this means the government had finally laid to rest one of the most complex issues to be raised in Lebanon since the mid-1970s. In a previous report, the commission had in fact announced that the number of abducted and missing throughout the Lebanese territories amounted, according to its statistics, to a total of 2,046 persons, and it had advised the families of these to pursue the proper legal procedures to establish their deaths.[2]

About two years before this announcement, three young men delegated by the field study project went to Sabra and Shatila with the names of the 100 abducted persons from the 1984 questionnaires, paying a visit to the family of each. These visits continued over some months. The main questions asked were: Had there been any news? Had the abducted person returned? Was there any hope that he would?

The answers to the second question were invariable. The person in question had not returned. As to hopes of return, the answers varied. Some parents regarded their son as a de facto victim, repeating several times: 'We consider our son a martyr.' Others still clung to hope: 'Our son must come back. We shall never lose hope.'[3]

Some in the latter category did eventually give up hope, especially after the official government declaration referred to above. Accordingly, they were prepared to register their sons as victims rather than abducted in the lawsuit brought against Sharon to the Belgian judiciary in 2001, through the Lebanese lawyer Chibli Mallat and the two Belgian lawyers Luc Walleyn and Michaël Verhaeghe.[4]

Even now not all parents of those on the list regarded their sons as finally dead. The main fact remains, however. The 100 people in question were abducted during the massacre of 1982 and, for year after year following this event, the main subject of conversation was the fate of those abducted and missing.

It was especially important to analyse the tables for those abducted in a manner independent of the tables for victims, in order to underline any differences between the two groups. Could any significant distinction be made concerning, for instance, nationality, gender or age? And what of the issue unyieldingly asserted both by the besieging Israelis and by the attackers themselves – the search for so-called 'saboteurs'? Were the 100 people abducted after their names and identities were known regarded as being in this category?

The questionnaires for victims or abducted were finally conflated, with just a few variations dictated by the difference in their fates, as identified above. What follows introduces us to victims and abducted with respect to nationality, gender, age, profession and standard of living. All tables referred to in this chapter are located in Appendix 1; all lists of names in Appendix 2.

Nationality

In the midst of this massacre targeting Palestinians, it occurred to few people that those killed actually belonged to twelve nationalities. Palestinians were indeed the most frequent victims, but they were not the only ones.

Of 430 victims, 209 (48.60 per cent) were Palestinians. Next came Lebanese, who numbered 120 (27.91 per cent). Then came those resident in Lebanese territory but (undeservedly) still stateless, their nationality officially under review; these numbered 31 (7.21 per cent). These were followed by: Syrians with 23 (5.35 per cent); Egyptians with 18 (4.19 per cent); Bangladeshis with 6 (1.40 per cent); Jordanians and Turks each with 3 (0.70 per cent); Sudanese, Algerians and Pakistanis, each with 2 (0.47 per cent); and finally Iranians and Tunisians, each with 1 (0.23 per cent).

To these should be added a further 9 (2.09 per cent) whose nationalities were impossible to identify, they having been among the newborn patients or premature babies placed in incubators. The bodies of all these were found either burned or thrown into the backyard of the Akka Hospital or into mass graves. It is difficult to confirm they were all Palestinian babies since the Red Crescent hospitals would also take in Lebanese and patients from all other nationalities. (See Table 2.a.)

As for the 100 people abducted, the number of nationalities was just six, made up as follows: Palestinian 66 (66 per cent); Syrian 13 (13 per cent); Lebanese 11 (11 per cent); stateless 6 (6 per cent); Egyptian 3 (3 per cent); and finally one British – Uthman (see Account 40, p. 193). (See Table 2.b.)

The higher percentage of Palestinians is clear indication both of abductors' awareness of their targets' nationalities and of their preference for abducting Palestinians.

But what of the others – those of Lebanese and other nationalities? Were they really wanted by 'militia justice'? Just what was the charge? Were they all 'saboteurs'? And where was the evidence? What, indeed, of the 66 Palestinians themselves? Were they, in the language of the abductors, 'saboteurs'? Were they all, in the language of Sabra and Shatila and Palestinian society generally, 'fighters'? Or were they simply labourers, employees and people working in vocational fields? I aim to clarify this point below.

Gender

If the massacre had indeed been a battle between two sides then the bulk of the victims would have been male fighters; the proportion of female combatants is, after all, very small. Yet in practice the overwhelming majority of victims were not male combatants but unarmed civilians both male and female.

As regards gender distribution, more than a quarter of the victims were female – a clear enough indication of non-discriminatory killing. (As for the age of those involved, it further becomes evident that the attackers made no distinction between grandfather and grandmother, younger adult man and woman, boy and girl.)

Of the 430 victims, we have 303 (70.47 per cent) clearly male, 112 (26.05 per cent) clearly female. For those of undetermined sex, babies killed or burned, numbered nine. Some unborn babies were deliberately killed along with their mothers – the foetus being, sometimes being torn out of its mother while she was still alive, as 'entertainment' to discover whether the unborn baby was a boy or a girl. Six unborn babies were killed. The number of infants whose sex was undetermined therefore totalled 15 (3.49 per cent).

Calculating from the 415 victims of known gender, we therefore reach (rounded) figures of 73 per cent male and 27 per cent female. Further consideration of victims' ages shows that the females, like the males, were of all ages. It is sufficient, perhaps, to note that, of the 112 victims, 42 were mothers, some of them even grandmothers. (See List of names 1; Table 3.)

As for the 100 abducted, these were all male. It should nonetheless be borne in mind that significant numbers of women were also abducted. This was revealed earlier in the book and further material will be provided later (List of names 4).

Age

Not all the 430 victims were men in their prime, or youths – that is, within the age category from whose ranks modern armies or revolutionary cadres are commonly drawn. The age of victims ranged from unborn babies and children in all stages of childhood, through to young adults, the middle-aged and the elderly. The figures and percentages below (bearing in mind, also, that these include both males and females) hardly require further comment.

Unborn infants: 6 (1.40 per cent)
Infants in their first year: 18 (4.19 per cent)
Child victims aged 2–3: 13 (3.02 per cent)
Child victims aged 4–12: 58 (13.49 per cent)
Victims aged 13–18: 66 (15.35 per cent)
Victims aged 19–30: 105 (24.42 per cent)
Victims aged 31–40: 47 (10.93 per cent)
Victims aged 41–50: 47 (10.93 per cent)
Victims aged 51–60: 29 (6.74 per cent)
Victims aged 61–70: 19 (4.42 per cent)
Victims over the age of 70: 22 (5.12 per cent) (See Table 4.a.)

The total number of children (including unborn infants) up to the age of twelve is therefore 95 (22.09 per cent). They were not solely Palestinians, as at first thought. They comprised 46 Palestinians, 32 Lebanese, 4 Syrians, 2 stateless and a single Egyptian; apart, that is, from the nine children whose nationalities were never disclosed. (See Table 4.b.)

Of the 66 victims aged 13–18 – mostly male students, working teenagers helping to support their families, or female students or girls helping out their mothers at home – there were 34 Palestinians, 21 Lebanese, 5 stateless, 4 Syrians, 1 Egyptian and 1 Jordanian. (See Table 4.c.)

Victims aged 19–50 (male and female combined) totalled 199. The twelve nationalities were distributed as follows: 91 Palestinians, 48 Lebanese, 17 stateless, 16 Egyptians, 11 Syrians, 6 Bangladeshis, and the remaining 10 distributed among Turkish, Jordanian, Algerian, Iranian, Pakistani and Sudanese. (See Table 4.d.)

Older victims, aged 51–70 (male and female combined) totalled 48. The oldest, aged over 70 and extending to 80 or even 90 in some cases, totalled 22. The combined total of 70 (16.28 per cent) ranged over seven nationalities: 37 Palestinians, 19 Lebanese, 7 stateless, 4 Syrians, and one each for Algerian, Sudanese and Tunisian. (See Table 4.e.)

The age distribution in the list of those abducted differs markedly from that for the list of victims in three principal ways.

The first difference is the absence of females; as noted above, the list of those abducted (List of names 2) is the one list where females do not figure. Part I of this book testifies, nonetheless, to the abduction of females, as does List of names 4.

The second difference is the absence of children. The list of 100 abducted starts at the teenage level, that is, age 13 and over. It is only fair to point out that even at Sabra and Shatila newborn infants and small children were not abducted!

The third difference is the absence of elderly over the age of 70, though one man in the age group 60–70 is found on the list.

The number of abducted aged 13–18 was 30 (30 per cent); aged 19–30, 41 (41 per cent);

aged 31–40, 14 (14 per cent); aged 41–50, 8 (8 per cent); aged 51–60, 6 (6 per cent); aged 61–70, 1 (1 per cent). (See Table 5.a.)

It is noticeable that the smallest numbers, with a total of 7 abducted, are for those aged 51–70. Next come teenagers aged up to 18, with 30; while the highest figures, of 63 abducted, are for those aged 19–50. All this implies that abductions, in contrast to killings, were not haphazard.

As for the distribution of nationalities in the various age categories, the number of Palestinians was again high, reaching around two-thirds in each case. Exact percentages were as follows. The 30 in the teenage group aged up to 18 comprised 20 Palestinians, 4 Lebanese, 3 Syrians and 3 stateless. (See Table 5.b.)

The 63 in the group aged 19–50 comprised 41 Palestinians, 7 Lebanese, 8 Syrians, 3 for both stateless and Egyptians, and 1 British. (See Table 5.c.) The remaining 7 in the older or elderly group comprised 5 Palestinians and 2 Syrians. (See Table 5.d.)

The age distribution of victims, from unborn babies to 80-year-olds, provides stark proof for the occurrence of a horrific massacre. In addition, the complete lack of discrimination between nationalities in the various age categories shows that the killing of families was as much an objective as the killing of individuals. Indeed, it goes further – to show that the wiping out of life from this particular spot was also the objective.

Profession

Discovering the professions of the victims and abducted – not just from close relations but from residents generally – was a straight-forward task. Everyone, by and large, knew everyone else. Consider, for instance, the Palestinian owner of the small house in the Horsh district on the outskirts of Shatila who had rented out his house to six men from Bangladesh in search of a livelihood. Asked about these men's ages, he could not say exactly, but testified they were all under 30 years old. Their names he could not recall, but he knew they were from Bangladesh, and he was quite clear about their profession: they were all daily labourers. He was also sure

of their faith and of their honesty: they would all repeat 'Allahu Akbar' at times of prayer or on hearing the sound of a grenade, and they paid him their rent promptly. The owner testified, finally, that he had seen them killed in their beds; it was clear they had been asleep or preparing to sleep.

The question of profession was an open one, since no specific types of profession were listed on the questionnaires. Team members were asked to note down the profession exactly as they heard it, and as a result a whole string of professions emerged, amounting to 34 and 28 for victims and abducted respectively. However, those of the abducted differed from those of victims in only two categories. The total number of professions for victims and abducted combined was therefore 36.

In making my classification, I omitted the names of schools, hospitals or banks at which doctors, nurses or employees worked: 'nurse', for instance, or 'employee' was considered sufficient. All the jobs, it should be said, were regular and humble.

Similar professions were bracketed together (either according to the way people themselves tended to view them or accord-ing to particular institutions at which people worked), numbers in a single such category ranging between two and four. Professions singled out were recorded in separate entries.

From the 430 victims, the total number of those working, male and female combined, was 217. The remaining 213 had no jobs for a variety of reasons. For some – children up to the age of twelve and the elderly – age was the determining factor. More general non-workers included students, housewives, patients or people terminally ill. The percentage of non-working victims was 49.54 per cent, fractionally below half the total number.

As for the 100 abducted, the percentage of those working significantly exceeded that for those not working: no fewer than 80 (80 per cent). The remaining 20 had no jobs for just two of the reasons noted above: one was an old man, the other 19 were school children and students, aged 13 or over. The principal reason for the difference in overall figures lay, obviously, in the absence of women and children.

The distribution in the table of professions is determined simply by the numbers working in a particular profession; there is no attempt to grade the professions in ascending or descending order. The professions listed below relate to male and female victims alike.

Numbers ranged from 1 to 4 in each of the following: teacher; artist/musician; tailor/ weaver/ upholsterer; draughtsman/ designer. Numbers ranged from 6 to 10 in each of the following: doorman/guard/ jockey; mobile kerosene vendor; small tradesman; electrician/telephone repairman; fish vendor/ vegetable vendor/ peddler; barber/baker/cook/butcher.

There were 13 who were involved in two specific different categories of job: the first category comprised those working for the Palestinian Red Crescent as doctor/nurse/ hospital worker; the second category comprised driver/mechanic.

There were 16 who belonged exclusively to the category proudly recorded by their families as 'freedom fighters' (fida'ioun).

As for the larger numbers, these belonged to the categories of employees and workers: 27 employees, and 35 labourers involved on work sites or in furniture manufacture: mason/painter/carpenter/blacksmith. The largest number of all, 51, belonged to people registered as 'freelance workers'.

There were, in addition, 10 victims whose precise profession remained unknown. (See Table 6.a.)

As for those abducted, who were all males, there were 7 who were sole representatives for their category, namely: doorman/ guard/jockey; freedom fighter; Palestinian Red Crescent worker; small tradesman; upholsterer; teacher; unspecified. Between 2 and 4 represented the following professions: shoemaker; employee; plumber; fish vendor/ vegetable vendor/peddler; electrician/tele-phone repairman. There were 7 who represented a single group of professions, namely driver/mechanic, and 17 represented the following professions: mason/painter/ carpenter/blacksmith. The highest number, 34, belonged to 'freelance workers', similar to List of names 1. (See Table 6.b.)

It is hardly surprising to find a popular district like Sabra and Shatila containing very high numbers of labourers, craftsmen, peddlers or street vendors, and very small numbers of doctors, artists and musicians. Such a matter requires no further comment. The significance lies rather in the enormous number of professions, implying as this does the presence of a whole integrated society pulsing with life, with all life's variety and clamour.

This study was not, of course, undertaken as a socio-economic survey. Having said that, the social information obtained nonetheless testifies to the occurrence of a massacre of the most fearful kind. Is it possible that all these varied professions – no fewer than 36 – could be identified in a situation where 'fighters' alone were being sought? We shall in fact deal specifically with 'freedom fighters' later in this chapter.

Standard of living, education and religious sect

The professional situation reflects the general economic one, given that none of the professions noted guaranteed a good or truly adequate income. Even the doctors at the Palestinian Red Crescent, with the prestige of their professional title, had a standard of living not substantially different from other employees; indeed their incomes hardly supported their families. We should note that Palestinian doctors were not officially authorized to work in Lebanon in the first place, this being one of more than 50 professions from which Palestinian refugees were legally barred. The presence of Red Crescent institutions in September 1982 implied nothing more than a continuation of their original presence, which had taken deep root, and had diversified in accordance with the presence of Palestinian revolutionary factions and their leaderships in Lebanon from the early 1970s on.

As for the employees living in Sabra and Shatila, those who were Lebanese worked in various public or private institutions, while Palestinians worked in Palestinian offices or hospitals or in certain Lebanese private institutions. Their jobs were, without exception, simple and even humble.

As for the small tradesmen or shop owners, who prided themselves on being free entrepreneurs (however limited their capital might be), their shops were all within Sabra and Shatila and were run for the benefit of residents of the district itself. The fruit and vegetable market in Sabra did, it is true, attract smart Beiruti women who bought supplies there. Yet the very presence of the market, even at its peak in the 1970s, shows how numerous vendors of vegetables, fruit, meat, chicken or eggs actually were – all from Sabra and Shatila, living in those closely packed dwellings. As for the labourers and craftsmen who made up the largest section, their standard of living was obviously meagre enough.

In fact, nothing on the questionnaire dealt specifically with standard of living. Such a question would have been embarrassing to team members, let alone respondents, and would have been condemned as both intrusive and redundant.

Without going into details, it should be stated that the homes in the Sabra district were slightly more spacious than the crammed units of Shatila. It is also well enough known that Sabra residents, with their slightly higher standard of living, had always behaved somewhat aloofly to their neighbours in Shatila.

It was, nevertheless, of the utmost importance that team members should know something of victims' financial role vis-à-vis their families. How many provided for their families, and how many were dependent on other family members?

Of the victims, 200, male or female, provided for their families; more specifically, they were either the sole major provider or one of two such (students who did part-time jobs to help out their parents and themselves being excluded in this connection). The percentage of these providers from the total of 430 victims was 46.51 per cent. The rest were dependent on other members of their family, either because they were too old or too young to work, or because most housewives devoted their efforts to their home and children, or because students were concentrating on their studies. (See Table 7.a.)

Among those abducted, on the other hand, the percentage of family providers was higher: 70 (70 per cent), all male, fell into this category. This higher rate is further evidence of the abductors' interest in their targets' ages, whether young or middle-aged men. (See Table 7.b.)

As for level of education, figures for victims and abducted show approximate similarities, though some differences are discernible.

For both categories, the highest percentage is for those with elementary education, followed by secondary school graduates, and, in the smallest group (hardly exceeding 1 per cent in either category), those of college level.

The distinctive difference, however, lies in the percentages for technical school education, where victims showed a mere 1.16 per cent as against 12 per cent for those abducted – a self-evident indication that significant numbers of abducted labourers were not simple labourers but the products of technical schools.

A further distinctive difference lies in the percentage of illiterates: 17.44 per cent among the victims, but a mere 5.0 per cent among those abducted. The underlying reason is that victims were from a wider range – including women, the elderly and men in their prime – whereas the abducted were mostly men in their prime, young men and teenagers. (See Table 8.a.)

Figures for level of education among victims and abducted should not be taken as specific indicators for the nature of specifically Palestinian or Lebanese society in Sabra and Shatila. The district was not simply residential but more generally proletarian; as such the figures reflect the educational status of everyone there: Palestinian, Lebanese and other Arab and foreign labourers, some of whom (like most of the Syrians) had come with their families, others of whom had come alone (as was the case with most of the Egyptians, Pakistanis, Bangladeshis and others).

In fact, comparison of general figures with figures for Palestinians (victims and abducted alike) reveals fundamental differences. With secondary education, for instance, that for

Palestinian victims alone was 23.92 per cent, against an overall percentage of 14.65 per cent. As for university-level education (college graduates or students), this was 1.40 per cent for victims overall, but double that for Palestinian victims at 2.87 per cent. A similar tendency is observed for university-level abducted, being 1.52 per cent for Palestinians against 1 per cent overall.

As for the overall percentage of illiterates among victims, male and female, this amounts to 17.44 per cent. Among Palestinians, male and female, this drops to 9.09 per cent; and the decrease becomes still more marked with respect to those abducted, where overall and Palestinian rates amount respectively to 5.0 per cent and 1.52 per cent. (See Tables 8.a and 8.b.)

It is worth noting that parents of victims and those abducted initially found the question about educational level disconcerting, for whatever reason – though they were persuaded easily enough that we were simply doing our best to get to know their loved ones, and co-operated and responded accordingly.

The one question, however, to which they resolutely refused to respond was that involving religious sect. We can provide no convincing reason for posing this question in the first place beyond noting that even we had been frankly overwhelmed by the Lebanese sectarian atmosphere prevailing at the time we were preparing the field study – plus the fact that field studies undertaken in Lebanon tend routinely to contain a separate entry for this. The Sabra and Shatila questionnaires followed this trend, but the answers given by victims' families, and by residents generally, showed the question to be inappropriate.

It was not clear, to begin with, how far this question was being ignored by the families concerned. Only when we began to review the piles of questionnaires did it become apparent. The majority would either leave the section blank or simply write 'Muslim' – in itself a sharply implicit refusal to specify the sect.

We hardly needed to ask to know that those killed or abducted had been Muslims (though we did also know, from people's accounts, that a single Maronite Lebanese had been killed – his crime was to have worked as a doorman just outside Sabra and Shatila, at a building near the Kuwaiti Embassy).

Specifically, responses to this question introduced (as noted above) by custom or common convention were of three kinds: some left the section blank; others supplied the general term 'Islam' or 'Muslim', with the sect unspecified; still others did specify the sect, under one of the three natural and expected categories: Sunni, Shi'ite or Druze.

No percentages will be supplied for these sects, partly because they would be suspect as representing only a part of the victims and those abducted, but also out of respect for the wishes of the people of Sabra and Shatila themselves, whether Lebanese, Palestinian, Arab or foreigner. These popular places were places of love and fraternity, unmarked by any kind of religious or sectarian fanaticism.

The victims and the abducted: details of death

Among the philosophical poetry encountered by Arab students during their studies, whether in Arab capitals or in the villages and the countryside, is the saying, 'There are many reasons for death, but death is one.'

Yet death in massacres is not like death elsewhere. It is more than a simple end, even if it has a single beginning, at a known hour. In this case the beginning was six o'clock, at sunset, on Thursday 16 September 1982. As for the end – officially announced as the Saturday morning, on the third day, but actually at one in the afternoon – there was no sign of an end resembling that to be expected with other disastrous deaths, which are followed, supposedly, by certainty about the victim's fate.

Those in Sabra and Shatila were not the victims of an earthquake or volcanic eruption. They were the victims of a massacre, and it is as though such deaths are two rather than one. The first death is death itself. The second is the denial that death ever occurred; it lies in the search for a lost victim, and in the attempt to establish a number of lost rights for that victim – including the right to die, and, finally, to have a death certificate issued. There were, needless to say, many who died at Sabra and Shatila yet left no remnants for their families to pick up, and were not even granted death certificates.

For all the agonized scenes when the killers first left the place, the signs of the massacre soon began to disappear. And the process began with the victims themselves.

The tragedy of the families was their inability to make an initial confirmation of their loved ones' death. Some found the bodies, others found pieces or limbs, still others found nothing. Some managed to bury their victims, while others simply did not know whether their victims had been buried in the mass cemeteries (as they had been told) or in other places unknown to this day. Some managed to register their victims at the Lebanese Red Cross, the Lebanese Civil Defence or another humanitarian organization, while others failed to convince any organization, humanitarian or official, of the victim's death. They had to be content with registering them as 'missing'.

Twenty years have passed since Sabra and Shatila, and the 'missing' are missing still. Even worse, the lists that once bore their names are themselves now forgotten or lost.

The known fates of victims and abducted

Among the residents of Sabra and Shatila, the question arousing the most enthusiasm was the one about the fate of their loved ones. This was the subject they wished to discuss even before team members brought it up.

In response to the question of whether identification of the body had been possible, by parents, friends or neighbours, it emerged that 294 victims out of the 430 had been identified, while 133 remained neither found nor identified. The remaining 3 had been injured during the massacre and subsequently died. (See Table 9.)

As for those abducted, there were three questions concerning eye-witnesses. Had there been witnesses to the abduction from families or other Sabra and Shatila residents?

Had there been witnesses other than these? Or had there been no witnesses at all?

The first question secured the highest positive response: 78 out of 100 total. There were 12 cases where the abduction had been witnessed or reported by others, and 10 had been witnessed by no one at all – but considerations of general logic, coupled with the specific fact that the men in question had been forced to take part in the Friday or Saturday march before they disappeared along with others, made the fact of their abduction obvious enough. (See Table 10.a.)

Further questions were asked in connection with the abductors: Did interviewees know who had carried out the abduction? Did they have clear suspicions on this score? Or were they simply unaware of the abductor's identity?

In response, 29 (29 per cent) of cases said they were sure the abductors were the 'Lebanese Forces', while 19 (19 per cent) replied that they suspected the 'Lebanese Forces'. The rest, comprising the parents and friends of 52 abducted (52 per cent), said they did not know who the abductors were and had no suspicions on this score. (See Table 10.b.)

This last figure might well seem odd, given that a number of those concerned had actually witnessed the abductions. If, however, we recall the accounts and events in connection with the abductions, as described earlier, in Part I, the credibility of all three responses becomes evident. While some of the killers or abductors (particularly on the Saturday, the third and last day) loudly proclaimed their militia identity out of arrogance or a wish to terrorize, others were at pains to keep this hidden and were wearing uniforms without badges. As for the witnesses themselves, they were simply overwhelmed by the horrific nature of the tragedy and could not, in the event, affirm anything regarding the abductors' identity beyond the general fact that they were all 'Lebanese militias', or 'Christian militias'.

The number of victims and abducted within each family

Every member of the team taking part in the field study was aware from the beginning that certain families had been wholly or largely wiped out. This had been made nakedly clear from published photographs of families whose members had been killed while eating their meal or attempting to flee. In addition, there were articles by the first reporters who entered the district on the Sunday, many of which had focused on family tragedies. Yet in spite of this, it could hardly be known initially how many families had lost more than one member, or what the total number in these cases was.

During the first phase of this work, I supposed the numerous photographs, along with the few videotapes, supplied a fully reliable guide to the tragedies of families wiped out. The photographs showed how the massacre had been directed against families, against these people's simplest types of activity, living quietly in Sabra and Shatila. It had clearly been directed against childhood, against motherhood, and against life itself; the life granted by God to everyone, including these poor people, as attested to by the number of unborn babies killed.

To kill a single individual is in principle as great a crime as to kill 100 or 1,000 people; and I had believed, once, that killing a family, or even several families, was a crime of the same magnitude as killing one or several individuals – for whoever kills unjustifiably once is on the same level as another who kills several times. Now I discovered for the first time that numbers bear a different meaning when it comes to families.

Let me draw some comparisons between the experiences of the Oral History Project and that of the Field Study Project.

In the former phase, the tragic killing of families, as described by survivors, was a source of constant pain to me. Whenever I read once more through the text of a particular interview, or listened repeatedly to a particular tape, some new and painful image, unnoticed before, would rise before my eyes. I could hardly wait for the oral history phase to end. Surely, I thought, the field study phase, involving figures alone, would be less distressing than hearing the voices of tormented people. In fact I was wrong. The figures became, on the contrary, a still more intense source of pain and suffering, carrying still greater implications than the photographs.

After I had compiled the list of victims' names, with careful detail of the relationships within each nuclear family, I realized that the number of families with more than one victim exceeded all expectation. (See List of names 1.)

According to this list, numerous families had lost more than one victim, the number ranging between 2 and 11. Twenty families had each suffered the loss of 2 victims; 13 the loss of 3; another 13 the loss of 4; and 10 the loss of 5. The number of families then at last began to decrease, but with the number of victims, of course, increasing still further: 2 families had each lost 6 victims; 3 families, 7; and 3 families, 9. Finally there were 3 families that had suffered, respectively, the loss of 8, 10 and 11 victims.

The number of families suffering the loss of between 2 and 11 victims totalled 67, while the number of victims killed along with other family members totalled 270 out of the full 430. The average number of victims within each individual family, was, in consequence, 4. (See Table 11.a.)

We checked and re-checked to verify our figures. Never before had I found figures to be more clearly visible than pictures, more firmly retained in the memory, opening up still wider vistas to the imagination. This was the true massacre, the massacre of families.

Moving on now to those abducted, it might at first sight seem we are more obviously concerned with individuals. In fact the figures quite fail to bear this out.

We compiled the list of names for those abducted in the same way as for victims, with details of relationships within the nuclear family. To our surprise, we found that significant numbers of those abducted came from within the same families. (See List of names 2.)

There were 10 families that had each suffered the loss of 2 members abducted; 3, the loss of 3; and finally there were 3 families each suffering the loss of 4 abducted. A total of 16 families therefore suffered the loss of 2–4 members abducted, while the number abducted along with other family members (father, son or brother) totalled 41 out of a total of 100. The average number of abducted within each individual family was therefore 2.56. (See Table 11.b.)

Most of the abductions took place on the Friday and Saturday, which witnessed more horrific events than the first day. It was evident that the abductors had familiarized themselves closely with their targets' identities, and that they had also had ample time to seek out and examine ID cards, asking the card holders any questions they wished. The oral history in Part I makes this clear enough. And as such the joint abduction of a father with his son, or of a father with two or three of his sons, is hardly to be regarded as coincidental.

As for the killing of families – especially on the first day, which saw the highest number of victims – this too was no matter of mere chance. It has been shown how the killers collected the ID cards of a number of people, especially from the men lined up against the 'walls of death', killing the people immediately thereafter – as though the collection process were an end in itself; not something intended for the establishment of names or identities, and clearly not for the purposes of questioning since no one was questioned on the first day. As far as the killers were concerned, the crime was linked not to name, nationality or profession, but rather to the place where a person happened to be at that particular moment – that, by the logic of massacres, was sufficient reason for death. The evidence is that they killed these people even though they had collected their cards, and immediately after collecting them. No distinction was made between Palestinian, Lebanese, Syrian, Egyptian or any other nationality, up to twelve in all.

And what of the families killed on their doorsteps? What difference is there, in the midst of a massacre, between collecting or not collecting ID cards there? Does a child need a card to certify he is a child? Or an 80-year-old man to certify his age? Does a grandmother hiding behind a door, clutching her grandchildren, need a card? Or a pregnant mother, whether inside or outside her house?

Victims and abducted vis-à-vis time, place and fate

In the Sabra and Shatila massacre, place was the prime factor in determining the destiny of any one person or family, though time was of major significance too, especially when linked to place. Each of the three days was different, and no two spots were the same.

The two principal questions in this connection were: Where was the victim killed? And on what day was he or she killed? By the same token, the questions for the relatives of those abducted were: Where did the abduction take place? And on what day?

The first day, Thursday 16 September, saw killing on the largest scale: 56.51 per cent of the total number of killings – more, that is, than on the second and third days combined. On the second day, the percentage decreased to 29.77 per cent, and on the third day, it decreased further to 13.72 per cent.

The significance of the higher number of killings on the first day becomes still more pronounced when we recall that this day lasted, in effect, just a few hours, from sunset at six o'clock, and that, as the oral history shows, the killings had lost some momentum by around ten o'clock and ceased completely some time after that. We are dealing effectively with no more than four hours, and this in itself is eloquent testimony to the indescribable savagery involved – a savagery borne out by figures and percentages. Of the 430 victims, no fewer than 243 (56.51 per cent, as noted) were killed during these four hours, as opposed to 187 (43.49 per cent) killed during the 38 hours that followed, from the Thursday/Friday night till Saturday afternoon.

The first paradox, which becomes apparent through a comparison between killings and abductions vis-à-vis their respective time and place, is that the percentage for abductions follows a precisely contrary pattern: in this case the percentage increased day by day over the three days. The first day accounted for only 8 per cent of total abductions, figures then rising to 33 per cent on the second day, and finally to 59 per cent on the third; higher than for the first two days combined.

These inversely varying percentages are fully in accordance with the nature of the massacre. Taking the killings first, these moved from the phase of random, indiscriminate killing of families and individuals on the first night to a succeeding phase where killings were of no less savagery but involved smaller numbers and percentages, this reduction being linked to the nature of incidents as they developed on the second and third day, which in some ways were similar to those of the first night but in other ways were different. One of the similarities was that a number of the residents were killed at home and in shelters on the Friday, just as had happened on the first night. Friday was, however, marked by what became known in the history of the massacre as the 'march', in which most of the residents of Shatila and the surrounding area were rounded up in the morning and forced to walk towards the Sports City while being subjected to all kinds of questioning, and to abduction and killing. A good proportion of them – particularly women – did manage to flee northwards from the Sports City.

Saturday, on the other hand, saw none of the incursions into homes that marked the two earlier days. It rather witnessed the great 'final march', whose magnitude exceeded that of the day before, with Sabra residents now added to their Shatila neighbours. The crowds were forced to walk all the way to the Sports City while bulldozers finished the demolition of whatever was left of the houses, and the attackers continued with their killing and abduction from the early morning on, starting in Sabra Square.

This day, Saturday, was characterized by mass killings in the death pits, which were more extensive than on the previous day, even though the overall number of victims was less. It was further characterized by 'trials', none of them lasting more than a few minutes, with most of those tried being subsequently thrust on to the trucks parked by the pavement. This maximized the number of abductions on the third day.

The combined percentage for killing and abductions totalled 47.36 per cent on the first day, then dropped to 30.38 per cent and 22.26 per cent on the second and third days respectively. (See Table 12.) It is to be expected that these combined percentages should be weighted in favour of killings, which by their nature involved greater quantities than the abductions. As such, we find the movement of the overall percentage corresponding more closely to that for killings, with the highest percentage found on the first day, before dropping through the second and third days.

If we make a comparison between the material of the oral history and the figures given above, we find conformity between the flow of events described and the increase or reduction in the general figures and percentages of the field study. On the first night, mass killings took place inside and in front of the shelters, and against the walls. As for the tragedies of that first night, the Thursday, Chapter 3 provided 24 accounts, some dealing with incursions and most referring to the tragedies of families; this compared with 10 accounts for Chapter 4 (Friday) and 8 accounts for Chapter 5 (Saturday). The reduction in the number of accounts corresponds to the reduced figures and percentages.

We should note, nevertheless, that this day-by-day reduction in the figures does not, emphatically, imply any reduction in the degree of savagery or violence – these, as reference to the oral history will confirm, were actually increasing steadily. Let us consider, for instance, the nature of the abductions, specifically four accounts dealing with these. One took place on the first night, another on the second day, and the third and fourth on the third day; and the accounts indicate a general escalation in the momentum of operations (see Account 7, p. 86; Account 32, p. 153; Account 40, p. 193; Account 41, p. 194).

Similar tendencies are found in the accounts of individual and mass killings. For all their greater number and their ferocity, on the first day, the subsequent reduction in numbers was not accompanied by any reduction in savagery, as reflected in various kinds of mass killings. Details of the death pits on the Friday and Saturday should make this clear enough (see Account 33, p. 155; Account 34, p. 157; Account 38, p. 189; Account 39, p. 190).

Let us now move on from time to place – consideration of the scenes of killing or abduction being essential, if only as a mark of respect to those who suffered these things.

The three parts of Table 12 are devoted to the first, second and third days respectively. However, the first column of the first part specifies the locations of killings or abductions, sorted neither alphabetically nor in accordance with the number of victims or abducted, but in descending order of their proximity to the Israeli Forces headquarters.

Regarding the Israeli response – as to whether or not the Israeli Army could see what was happening – a uniform impression was given that the killings had all taken place in the heart of Shatila Camp, which was indeed the part most distant from the Israeli Command headquarters. Yet at no time during the three days was the camp itself penetrated by the attackers. Let us for the moment set aside consideration of the various other means that might have been – indeed were – available to the Israeli Army in this regard and which found no mention in the Kahan Report. We shall return to discuss these 'other means' in the final parts of this book. Let us for the moment pause to consider this one point only: the proximity or remoteness of the buildings the Israeli Command acknowledged were used as its headquarters. It was not the case, as stated in the Kahan Report, that the killings all took place in remote spots invisible to the naked eye or even through modern binoculars. Table 12 is revealing in this respect.

According to the Kahan Report, the facing Israeli Command headquarters were on the roof of a five-floor building 200 metres south-west of Shatila Camp. The report stated as follows:

From the roof of the front side Command headquarters, it was possible to have a general view of the camps area, but – as testified by a number of witnesses who we consider to be credible – it was impossible to see what was happening in the alleys of the camp from the roof, not even with the help of double binoculars (120*20), which were available on the roof.[5]

In fact the headquarters building comprised not five floors but six. It was the first (for someone heading from the Cola roundabout to the Kuwaiti Embassy roundabout) of three buildings commonly known as the officers' buildings, and it lay by the side of the road facing the Sports City, exactly opposite the former Turf Club. As for the other building, which was converted into a surveillance point and on whose roof General Yaron ordered the installation of binoculars and surveillance equipment,[6] this again was one of the three buildings, close by the first (the headquarters building) and of the same height (whereas the third building, which lay between the other two and further inwards, comprised only four floors).

As for the distance between the headquarters building and Shatila Camp, this was incorrectly estimated by the Kahan Report as 200 metres. In reality it was more than twice that. In any case, there was no need to focus on the remoteness of the camp alleys since, as noted above, the attacking killers never entered Shatila Camp in the first place. The parts they did enter were the districts adjacent to Shatila Camp, such as Hayy al-Doukhi or Horsh Tabet. The distance between the Israeli Command headquarters and Hayy al-Doukhi was 420 metres; the distance between it and Abu Yasser's shelter in al-Horsh was 475 metres; and the distance between it and the middle of Horsh Tabet was 550 metres. According to the Kahan Report, it would have been difficult to see what was happening in these places; this for various reasons, some of them related to the nature of the alleys or the distance involved.

Nevertheless, the Kahan Report itself allows us to discover that other, closer places than either Horsh Tabet or Hayy al-Doukhi would have been visible. The report states that General Drori was on the roof of the headquarters building at around half past seven on the evening of the first night, and that he was able to observe and follow the combat before leaving at around eight o'clock.[7]

The Kahan Report did not identify the combat location in question. However, the oral history in Part I noted that there was indeed an exchange of gunfire that night, during the same short period specified by

General Drori. This was the skirmish between the single fighter we called Ibrahim and the attackers on Shatila Main Street. Ibrahim went on firing from a Kalashnikov for a quarter of an hour, in a southerly direction, till he ran out of ammunition. Meanwhile the attackers were on the same street, taking along the women and children they had gathered from Abu Yasser's shelter under the pretext of conducting them to the Akka Hospital – though in fact they ended up killing them (see Chapter 3, pp. 98–101).

This must surely have been the 'combat' incident referred to by General Drori; for there was no other exchange of gunfire at this hour or even later (apart from the RPG shell launched from the direction of al-Doukhi, towards al-Horsh, after nine o'clock, causing the attackers to flee the entire Horsh district) (see Chapter 3, pp. 103–4).

Therefore, since Shatila Main Street, on which the exchange of fire had taken place, was easily visible (as was stated in the Kahan Report), then the parts between that street and the headquarters building must of necessity have been visible too. Some have tried to refute this on the grounds of the district's topography. In response to this I will simply cite the statements of a number of foreign reporters who stood on the roof of the headquarters building and affirmed that they had been able to see through, together with statements to the same effect from the Lebanese Army; Dr Labban, a Minister for Social Affairs, said, quoting Lebanese officers, that undoubtedly the area was visible.[8]

As for the three areas that were close to the Israeli headquarters building and were clearly visible, these were as follows. The first area included the sandy yards of the former Turf Club, which lay exactly opposite the officers' buildings used by the Israelis as command and surveillance centres. This sandy area had once been used for horse riding. The distance, along a virtual straight line from the sidewalk of the Sports City Boulevard, parallel with the sandy Turf Club area, to the headquarters, penetrating the boulevard and the square opposite the headquarters building, was 70 metres. On the other hand, the distance between the middle of the sandy Turf Club area and the headquarters building was 130 metres. This implies clear visibility in the stretch between the 70 metres and the 130 metres. Even if we add another 30 metres, extending the stretch up to the end of the sand parallel to Shatila Main Street whose combats were observed by General Drori, visibility remains possible.

The second area was Hayy Ersal, which lay exactly behind the sandy Turf Club area, all the way down to Shatila Main Street, and which was the quarter suffering the highest incidence of rape, torture and killing, especially on the first night. The distance between the centre of Hayy Ersal and the headquarters building was 190 metres, which suggests that visibility was more than possible, especially as the extremities of Hayy Ersal, closest to the sandy Turf Club area, were within 170 metres.

The third area was the sandy yard of the Kuwaiti Embassy, which lay precisely between the Embassy and al-Rehab petrol station on the south-east side, the distance between the centre of this yard and the Israeli Command headquarters building being 260 metres. This yard specifically witnessed mass killings on the third day. The significance of this small area lies in the fact that it actually included an Israeli surveillance centre. This was not mentioned in the Kahan Report. Yet a southern Lebanese woman testified how she had almost been killed, early on the Friday morning, along with her eight children and other children and mothers: a total of 23 people. The arrogant militiamen had ordered this mother, together with the other women and children, to go down into one of the death pits in the Turf Club yard, but fortunately they had been saved by an Israeli soldier who happened to be near the surveillance centre in the Kuwaiti Embassy yard opposite and rushed from there to shout at the militiamen to stop (see Account 33, p. 155). Is it really likely (albeit technically possible) that the surveillance centre was suddenly brought into operation at dawn? At any rate, this mother testified that at least one surveillance centre had been there since early on the Friday morning.

A question arises here. Was a single hour – or let us say three hours – not sufficient for someone like this Israeli soldier, who had refused to countenance the extermination of women and children, to stand up and make himself heard by his superiors? Had the testimony of such a soldier reached them, this should surely have led to the attacking killers being deterred at once; should have put an end to the massacre, sparing Sabra and Shatila a whole day of death. But this did not happen.

Using the figures from Table 12, it is illuminating to consider the number of victims and abducted relative to the three areas mentioned above, where – by the evidence of the Kahan Report itself and of on-site distance measurements – lack of visibility could not possibly have been a factor. There were, indeed, a number of other means whereby the Israelis could have discovered exactly what was going on at Sabra and Shatila. These, however, will be left for the concluding chapter.

On the first day, and more specifically during those four hours on the first night, 27 people were killed in the first area (the Turf Club yard), 62 in the second (Hayy Ersal), and 4 in the third (the Kuwaiti Embassy yard). The victims in these three areas alone – excluding other, remote areas – therefore totalled 93, these amounting to 21.63 per cent of the 430 considered over the full three days. (See Table 12.)

It should be pointed out that considerations of closeness or distance vis-à-vis the Israeli Command headquarters involve more than the Israeli officers' actual positions on the roof of this building or on any of the adjacent officers' buildings. The officers did not reach the roof of the headquarters building by helicopter; they came in armoured vehicles which were still on the adjacent street, the Sports City Boulevard, at least, and were also seen in various other places. It is inconceivable that all these soldiers and drivers should have left their vehicles unguarded. They were also extremely close to the relevant areas. They could not possibly have failed to hear the voices of the victims, which would have been especially loud at Hayy Ersal or on the elevated sandy road (as it was at that time) between the Sports City, Hayy Ersal and Hayy al-Gharbi. Nor, indeed, could the incidents have been missed by their superiors, who were standing on the roofs equipped with their modern binoculars – with the aim, apparently, of showing they saw nothing as well as heard nothing.

In addition, these soldiers were the best qualified to witness the abduction of the women and children, described in Part I. Table 12 includes entries for three people abducted at Hayy Ersal on the first night; these were in fact three women. There were also, as noted earlier, dozens of women and children abducted and forced to get in the truck parked near the Command Centre headquarters of the Lebanese Forces at the College of Business Administration on the St Simon branch road. The attackers further dragged off a large number of women who had taken part in the women's march, stopping these near the centre of Jam'iyyat al-Ina'ash near the Kuwaiti Embassy; then finally dragged off yet another group of women and children from a shelter at Hayy Ersal, ordering these to hurry to the truck parked at the top of the slope in St Simon Street.

These women must, undoubtedly, have passed by Israeli soldiers. How could they have reached the truck, which was near the Lebanese Forces headquarters building just a few metres from its Israeli counterpart, and not have been seen by any of the Israelis at the surveillance point on the roof of the Lebanese Forces headquarters building – particularly by the liaison officer delegated to supervise the militiamen? How could this officer have failed to see the truck parked there at the top of the slope, when all he had to do was look down? How could he have failed to see the abduction itself? Did these women and their children give the appearance of 'saboteurs', to be arrested and taken off (see Account 7, p. 86)? They were, moreover, there on the sidewalk for a considerable period, in their dozens, enough for a full truck load.

The Kahan Report, along with several news articles, made mention of a telephone call between an officer of the Lebanese

Forces, who was at the massacre site, and his superior Elie Hobeika, who was standing on the roof of the Israeli headquarters building at half past seven on the Thursday evening. The officer asked his commander, in Arabic, what he was to do with 50 women and children. Thereupon his commander answered: 'I don't want to hear a question like that again. You know exactly what to do.'[9] Some of the Forces members, standing on the roof with their commander, overheard this conversation and burst out laughing. General Yaron then asked Lieutenant Elul for an explanation of the call, of which he was aware through the communications device. When the latter had given his answer, Yaron went to Elie Hobeika and spoke to him for five minutes in English, but Lieutenant Elul did not hear what they said.[10]

As for General Yaron's testimony to the Kahan Commission, this stated (in essence) that he had understood the matter to involve the killing of 45 'terrorists'.[11] The Kahan Report's main problem was how to resolve the differences, amounting at times to virtual contradiction, between the testimonies, and how to justify the fact that the news did not reach the high-ranking generals.

Another incident, similarly worthy of analysis and in need of justification, was that involving the entry of a Lebanese Forces officer into the dining room at the Israeli headquarters at around eight o'clock on the Thursday evening. He told them they had, up to that time, killed around 300 people, including civilians. He then left the room, but returned a little later and revised the figure from 300 to 120.[12] The Kahan Report made a detailed examination of this and of everyone's testimony regarding it, including General Yaron's. The investigation ended, however, at a point before the 'news' – that civilians were being killed in Sabra and Shatila – reached even the high-ranking generals, let alone the Prime Minister!

A similar incident was encountered in Part I, described by Abraham Rabinovich, the *Jerusalem Post* correspondent who had had the details passed on to him by an Israeli soldier. According to the latter, a militiaman on the Thursday evening, had announced in his and his unit's presence that they had killed 250 *mukharibin* (the Arabic word for saboteurs). After his departure (the informant continued), the soldiers had laughed, sure the man must have been counting civilians, since no gunfire had been heard.[13]

The question remains: Why were these two incidents given such prominence, when the Israelis had, after all, no need of anyone to tell them what was going on?

From the above, we have concluded that the number of victims killed on that first evening, at the three locations nearest to the Israeli headquarters alone, was 93; noting also that this was 21.63 per cent of the total of 430 victims whose cases were examined. Nevertheless, these numbers from the field study are not final. There were 17 sources from which we collected the names of victims, and we contrived, by this means, to arrive at the names of 906 victims killed at Sabra and Shatila (see List of names 3). If, in the light of this, we were to include all those killed in the three areas in question, the number of victims would rise to 196.

Naturally it cannot be guaranteed, given all the circumstances, that this figure is precisely accurate; the number may have been more or less than 196. In any event the numbers involved are substantial – close to 200; and conviction springs from the oral history testimonies, which contain such numerous tragedies for the Thursday night. This is especially true when we recall that the estimate figures are higher than the documented ones.

It is, in the final analysis, extremely unlikely that around 200 people should have been killed at locations so close to the Israeli headquarters without any member of the Israeli military, whether officer or soldier, noticing anything.

The freedom fighter victims: who were they, and how were they killed?

Earlier in this chapter it was revealed that 16 victims were registered by their families and friends as freedom fighters. Some used the term 'fighter', while others insisted on the term '*fida'i*'. Was there a difference between the two at Sabra and Shatila? Or within Palestinian society as a whole?

The word *fida'i* (from a root meaning 'redeemed with one's life', the implication being that these fighters were certain or at least highly likely to pay for their country's liberation with their lives) was already in use when the Revolution initially arose in the Jordanian valleys in the 1960s. Early operations were commonly of the hit-and-run kind. When, however, *fida'i* activity developed to the stage of 'hit and stand', the word *fida'i* itself took on a deeper sense, not simply for Palestinians but for the Arab peoples as a whole. Accordingly, the *kufiyyeh* of the *fida'ioun* – as a symbol of freedom – was worn as a headscarf by most young Arabs, along with others throughout the world who passionately desired freedom.

From the early beginnings of the PLO and the Revolution, which were born together in the mid-1960s, and in the first phase, during which the various Palestinian factions were formed, the word '*fida'i*' was a powerful source of unity in the Palestinian arena, bringing together all the different factions whose goals were united in the interests of liberation. The *fida'i* represented the sole hope of achieving that liberation.

The term 'fighter', on the other hand, was never publicized officially, nor did it have any official starting point such as the PLO, whose army had formerly been known as the Palestine Liberation Army (PLA), and which had contained officers and soldiers of the various ranks, like any other army in the world. There was, furthermore, no way for the term to become widespread in tandem with the Revolution, which specified *fida'i* activity by name, and whose followers were called *fida'ioun*.

The term 'fighter' first arose when the PLO itself was transformed from an organization implemented by official Arab resolution in the mid-1960s to an internationally recognized entity in the mid-1970s. The more embassies or offices the PLO set up in world capitals, particularly during the 1970s, and the more resolutions the General Assembly of the United Nations issued (and there were many of these) to affirm recognition of Palestinian rights, the more the role of the PLO changed from that of regular 'mother organization' to one of preparing for the 'upcoming Palestinian state'. As for the organizational side, vis-à-vis the assemblies of the various Palestinian communities, the PLO became their main umbrella wherever they happened to be. All its offices, institutions, schools and unions were accordingly converted into an organizational mobilization entity broadly similar to that of a 'state', even if no state was formally in existence. In the shadow of these developments, which had all taken place over several years prior to the Oslo Agreement or Madrid Convention, the term 'fighter' gradually replaced the term '*fida'i*'.

One further issue should not be overlooked, and that is a widening of the meaning of the word 'fighter' in the updated Palestinian lexicon, so that it was no longer restricted to the basic 'fighters' alone but also to all workers in the official cadres, including correspondents, drivers, telephone operators, engineers and contractors; a typical one of these would proudly repeat: 'I'm a fighter.' It was enough for him to see the senior officers or the *fida'ioun* on a daily basis and address them as, for instance, 'Brother Abu Youssef' or 'Brother Kamal' (rather than using their military or organizational titles), till he began to feel he himself deserved the title of 'fighter'. Was the logic of the Revolution not, finally, the logic of brotherhood?

In view of this, it did not in the least surprise me to find 16 questionnaires for victims containing 'fighter', '*fida'i*', 'fighter for Palestine' or 'fighter for the return' in the section set aside for 'profession'.

It was relatively simple for us to find out what kind of fighter each of these 16 was. Was he a 'field fighter'? Or was he rather a 'fighter working in the official cadres', ranging from those working in PLO offices themselves, or the offices of factions, to those driving ambulances? Narrowing definitions in this way was perfectly feasible and was in fact done on the basis of observations made by team members who themselves came from Sabra and Shatila and were familiar with the victims in question.

Even so, when I came to transfer the questionnaire data to an independent record for the field study I paused over the 'profession' section, and particularly over the term 'fighter'. What fundamental difference was there, I wondered, with respect to these freedom fighters or their families, between the field fighter and the correspondent, driver or contractor, each of whom had at some time received military training – all the more so in that the Sabra and Shatila community recognized no such differences? Suppose they all knew how to use a weapon, or were even expert in its use? Or suppose, even further, they were all actual fighters? The principal questions then became as follows. Did they have any weapons at that time? If so, had they been able to lay hands on them? And if so, had they been able to fight?

In other words, were these 15 men and one woman, proudly described as fighters by their families, used to fuel the official Israeli claim that a 'battle' had taken place? Such a limited number could not, needless to say, lend credibility to the notion – though it might be argued in theory that further people could have been involved in fighting. Finally, though, this whole myth of a 'battle' has already been disposed of in the oral history in Part I.

Let us stop only to consider each of the 16 'fighter victims' individually. Place of residence and place and date of death must all be taken into account, but only by bringing all these together can we interpret the fate of each individual and determine whether or not any of them had actually managed to fight. In practice we are concerned with events of the first and second days, as it was then that all those entered as 'fighters' had been confirmed as meeting their end.

With regard to any idea of 'battle', it is sufficient to note that these 16 people were unarmed when killed and that there were witnesses to this. God bless that small boy who said not a word when the horror was taking place, but was an eye-witness to the death of his neighbour, the 'fighter', along with his family.

But if the oral history is the main and also the most important source of reference for the massacre, it remains one source only. If we are to answer the 'battle myth' propounded both by the official Lebanese

report (commonly known as the Jermanos Report) and the official Israeli statements, we must stop to consider the deaths of each and every one of the 16 fighters, for in each case the circumstances of death constitute evidence for an impartial court of law (if such a court could be found) that they were victims of a massacre rather than casualties on a battlefield.

One of the lessons we learned from the oral history is that place rather than person is the prime factor in a massacre. People are killed, usually in a treacherous manner, because they happen to be in a certain spot; and this it was that induced me to register the fighters according to their place of residence rather than in alphabetical order or by order of age.

Table 13 deals with all 16 of the 'freedom fighter' victims and provides, for each: name; nationality; age; place of residence; date of death; place of death; identification of body during the search for victims; number of victims in the freedom fighter's family; reference number of the victim in the field study record for Sabra and Shatila.

The nationality entry shows that the fighters comprised 13 Palestinians, two Lebanese and one Jordanian. As for the age entry, this reveals that fighters' ages ranged from a young one of 17 to a much older one of 52; between these were eight aged 19–30, two in their thirties and four in their forties. This age distribution indicates fighting experience, if the men had been able to make use of it.

As for residence, the Horsh district was the most prominent, ten of the 16 being from here – more specifically from the part across from the Akka Hospital; this was the part subjected to the most barbaric attack from the first hours on, if not literally from the first hour itself, and also the part that saw resistance against the Israelis during daylight hours on the Thursday. (These latter, as we have seen, withdrew completely before the day was over.) Al-Horsh witnessed multiple killings and exterminations in the shelters, especially Abu Yasser's, from which everyone was brought out and then killed, apart from the few who providentially survived.

It was al-Horsh, too, that witnessed the mass killings against the 'walls of death', most famously against the one across from Abu Yasser's shelter. There it was, too, that residents were summoned from their homes to meet random gunfire, before the killers surprisingly withdrew in response (as one of their number admitted) to a rocket launched from the north. As concluded earlier, this had probably been launched by a group of zealous hit-and-run fighters, who could hardly have known that a single RPG shell would be sufficient to make the attackers flee the Horsh district – until, at least, they returned next day to continue their murderous work.

However, we need to draw a distinction between place of residence on the one hand and time and place of death on the other, before then considering the number of victims in each particular family.

Of the ten Horsh fighters, seven were killed on the first night, in the first hours even, when there was no fighting anywhere in the district, but rather mass killing. Of the seven, four had in fact sought protection in Abu Yasser's shelter, where they were all killed together along with their families. These fighters were as follows.

Karem Ahmad Jabr Hussein, 17 years old. He was one of nine killed in his family. Killed with him were his mother Salha Hussein; his uncle Abdallah Jabr Hussein, who had been suffering from a chronic disease; his two sisters, Nawal and Su'ad, who was the youngest and only nine years old; and his four brothers, Imad, Fu'ad, Muhammad and Rabi', the youngest of whom was just eleven.

Suhaila Khaled Yousuf Muhammad, 19 years old. She had operated a communications system at one of the offices of the Revolution, but was killed with both her parents on the first night of the massacre. Deprived of her right to defend her people and her parents, she became known instead as a member of the family that had suffered the highest loss in the massacre. Eleven of her family members, seeking protection in Abu Yasser's shelter like all the others, were killed. Suhaila had been the oldest. Also killed were her father, Khaled Yousuf Muhammad; her mother Fatima Sa'ud

Awad; her two brothers, Akram and Samer, who was two years old, and six sisters: Sana', Baha', Laila, Iman, Manal and Ahlam, who was the youngest and still an infant.

Nur Eddine Sa'ud Awad, 25 years old. He was one of the well accredited brave young men, but, hardly aware of what was going on in al-Horsh, he hurried with his younger brothers and sisters, thinking to protect them in Abu Yasser's shelter. All four, however, were killed. They were, in order of age: Nur Eddine himself, Muyassar, Fatima, and Hussein, who was still just two years old.

Shihadeh Ahmad Shoufani, 28 years old. His house was near Abu Yasser's shelter, and it was natural for the family to seek protection there. No one, after all, had issued warnings of a possible massacre, nor had anyone called on him to carry his weapons. He took his children and went to the shelter with his wife Dalal, who, unable to bear the situation, returned home with her infant child. Those in the shelter were killed en masse, this fighter Shihadeh Ahmad Shoufani among them, along with his daughter Wafa', aged four, and his son Ahmad, aged two. His mother Thunaya Shoufani, who had rushed to the shelter to be with her son and grandchildren, was also killed.

Identification of the bodies was not possible in every case: some had been deliberately buried beneath the rubble before the search operations started, while others had been buried before their families arrived on the first search days, after the successive rumours about the coming of Sa'd Haddad's men. Some bodies were in fact identified, others were not; either because they had been lost, or because they were mutilated to an extent that rendered identification impossible.

Of the four victims listed above, the last two, Nur Eddine Sa'ud Awad and Shihadeh Ahmad Shoufani, were identified. Karem Hussein and all nine members of his family were among those whose bodies were never found. As for Suhaila Muhammad, the bodies of her father and mother were found, but those of the nine children, including Suhaila, were not.

Three further Horsh residents were killed in various places in the district on the first night: two with their families and one alone. These were as follows.

Muhammad Salim Nazzal, 33 years old. This courageous man was one of those ordered to line up against the wall. The place where he died in al-Horsh saw a number of further victims. His body was found and identified.

Muhammad Hussein Freijeh, 40 years old. He had always been regarded by his friends as both brave and level-headed. But fate denied him the honour of the martyr's death he had always told his friends he wished for. He died with his 13-year-old son Khaled. The bodies of both father and son were found.

Saleh Dakhil Qadi, 52 years old. He was the oldest victim among the fighters, and a householder, killed together with his children, the oldest and youngest of whom were 18 and ten respectively. There were three sons and one daughter: Bassam, Ibtisam, Husam and Issam. All the Qadi victims were found.

Next morning, on the Friday, the attacking killers returned to the Horsh district from which they had fled the night before. That morning three of the fighters, either local men or guests from outside, died. These were as follows.

Saleh Hussein al-Titi, 21 years old. He had come from Tyre with his parents on a family visit to his aunt Um Ghazi Madi, whose house was in al-Horsh on the edge of Shatila Camp. Saleh was known to the spies, who had identified the house to the attacking killers; and these in turn had summoned him out by name. When he went out they killed him and his father too. They also killed three of his Madi cousins together with their crippled father. The Madi and Titi tragedy was among the most famous in Shatila. The bodies of Saleh and his father were found. His aunt mourned for him, as she did for her sons, crying out: 'Saleh was a brave fighter. But he didn't die a martyr as he wanted. He was killed.'

Imad Muhammad Sadeq, 23 years old. He was one of those decent Lebanese, residents of al-Horsh, who shared air, place and bread with the Palestinians. Like the others, Imad was killed treacherously. Even so his end was

in a sense luckier than theirs, for his parents found his body thrown down, in al-Horsh, not far from the house.

Subhi Muhammad Mughrabi, 43 years old. He was that decent and caring uncle who had been unable to protect his nephews, Amer and Salim Mughrabi (one of whom was still a schoolboy). The three were killed together, their bodies being discovered close to one another in a yard heaped with victims.

Let us now move from Hayy al-Horsh, or Horsh Tabet, to Hayy Ersal, across from it to the west, a quarter that had seen absolutely no fighting, even against the Israelis, prior to the massacre; no firing had taken place there, even in the air. Hayy Ersal was among the first quarters to be invaded by the attacking gunmen, and just as Abu Yasser's shelter became celebrated in Horsh Tabet, so the shelter behind the Palestinian centre of Jam'iyyat al-Ina'ash became famous in Hayy Ersal.

There were two fighters from Hayy Ersal, and both were killed on the first night.

Hussein Hasan Ahmad Najjar, 45 years old. He was, as a number of witnesses stated, killed in Hayy Ersal proper, where he was in a group of adult male residents. During the search, however, this brave fighter's body was never found, and his name was accordingly registered among the missing.

Mir'i Hawlo Sukkarieh, 45 years old. He was one of those Lebanese who had come to Beirut from the town of al-Fakeha in Beka'a, and he preferred, out of love, to live close to Palestinians. He had made many Palestinian friends, and was widely missed. No one was able to tell us where this courageous man met his end. One witness affirmed that he had known him well, and that he had seen his body somewhere between Hayy Ersal and the Sports City. His family, however, stated later that they had not found the body.

Opposite Shatila, on the south side, lies Hayy Bir Hasan, separated from Shatila by Kuwaiti Embassy Street, the main street that connects the airport roundabout with the Kuwaiti Embassy. The Akka Hospital lies on the main street of this quarter. Bir Hasan witnessed no combat at all – indeed some of the fighters went to the Akka Hospital on the

Thursday to discover how far the Israeli armoured vehicles had advanced. By Thursday sunset, however, Bir Hasan had become one of the first districts to be invaded by the attacking gunmen, who told residents to come down into the street during the early hours of the massacre. The attackers themselves were still confused, unsure as to where exactly they were. Next day, even so, they killed more people in this quarter than they had done on the previous day. The following two fighters were among this quarter's victims.

Nazih Mahmoud Ahmad, 19 years old. He was highly popular and much loved among his fellows, who spoke proudly of his courage and straightforward character. Nazih was discovered by the attackers on the Friday morning, and they killed him the moment they found him. No one else from his family was killed. His body was found in Bir Hasan.

Fahmi Ahmad Qadi, 31 years old. He was one of the men summoned to take part in the mass march towards the Sports City on that Friday, when the attackers told them: 'Come on, start walking, you're going to be questioned.' They killed a good many even so. Fahmi Ahmad Qadi was among the victims and was therefore in no position to initiate any fighting.

A number of families had been living near the Sports City, notably to the rear of it, separated from the City by a long sandy road. This quarter, reckoned to have been closest to the Israeli headquarters and the armoured vehicles, witnessed the most brutal torture and mass killing on the first night, and one of the fighters was among the victims.

Yahya Ahmad Muhammad, 30 years old. He and his wife Khawla were among the first victims, and there were witnesses to this. Both bodies were found behind the Sports City, in the same place where they had been killed. They were united in death, as they had been in life.

The last victim among the fighters was from the adjacent outskirts of Shatila, through which the killers gained access. *Riad Mahmoud Jamilah* was 19 years old and originally from the city of Jaffa. He was a

Jordanian citizen, and his parents testified that he was a fighter. They also stated that they had found neither his body nor that of his sister Samar, who was killed with him. She was a schoolgirl of just 14.

These, then, were the 16 victims, whose families insisted they be set down as fighters; though none of them, in point of fact, had any chance to fight.

As for the fighters among the 66 Palestinians abducted, the abductors themselves were the ones best placed to say where and how, all the more so as there were no reports of any skirmishes followed by the taking of prisoners – this for the simple reason that no such skirmishes occurred. The very limited skirmishing that did take place involved targeting from a distance, followed by instant withdrawal into the heart of the alleys on whose outskirts the shooters were standing – a situation which would, self-evidently, not lead to the taking of prisoners.

There was, however, one abducted man, named *Khaled Muhammad Assi al-Sa'di,* whose sister Fahmia proudly described him as a fighter – the one case among 66 abducted Palestinians! He was not, however, fighting on the Friday when the abduction took place. Rather, he was with his 60-year-old father Muhammad Sa'di, an employee at the Golf Club, who was abducted along with him. Khaled al-Sa'di was 21 years old.

Just how, then, did the attacking killers contrive to come (as they said) in an attempt to capture 2,000 'saboteurs' – that is, fighters – then end up capturing just one solitary man walking alongside his father, in the midst of a throng of Shatila women, children, young men and elderly people? Did they even know, indeed, that this particular man among so many was actually a fighter? Assuredly they did not. The ground for accusation, first and last, was that he was Palestinian.

What of the 'axe of Damour'?

In the aftermath of the massacre, a rumour began to spread to the effect that a Christian militia named the 'Damour battalion' had been behind the events – as if the very name 'Damour' were somehow sufficient cause for revenge. Some believed the rumour. Others rather wondered where this battalion had come from and why no one had heard of it before.

Part of the history of the civil wars that broke out in Lebanon in the mid-1970s was the tragedy of Damour, an attractive, peaceful Christian coastal town not far from Beirut, whose inhabitants were at one point obliged to evacuate the place. As such, the residents of Damour were to be counted among the victims of what some Lebanese called simply the 'civil wars', but others referred to as the 'wars of other people in our country'.

We will not consider these wars here. Nor will we go into the details of the tragedy of Tall al-Za'tar, the bustling Palestinian camp whose long siege resulted in the residents being forced out. This tragic affair was a turning point for Palestinian refugees in Lebanon, because the evacuation, in which many were killed, had permanent repercussions. None of those wandering the mountains in the wake of the tragedy ever returned; to this day, a quarter of a century later, these people are listed among the missing.

The Tall al-Za'tar disaster took place in the summer of 1976. Schools and colleges, closed for the holidays, and beach cabins too, were opened to accommodate the refugees from the camp. Later, though, harsh winter conditions made some more fixed place necessary. For many their suffering was increased when they were forced to move to Damour, to enter houses whose owners had left them. This is not the place to analyse the logic of injustice caused by civil wars – if, indeed, one can talk of 'logic' at all. It is a fact, though, that most of these new residents, far from feeling happiness at having found a home to accommodate their families, were saddened by the matter. As people who moved constantly from one migration to the next, they knew better than any how the Damour residents must have felt, after building their town brick by brick, then being unable to return (see Account 45, p. 227, which describes the experience of a Palestinian family living in Damour between the winter of 1976 and the summer of 1982).

When interviewing the families of victims for the Oral History Project, we had expected the Damour issue to assume a more prominent role. According to rumours, after all, the attacking killers had (among other things) yelled at the Shatila residents, before killing them: 'This is the axe of Damour!' The issue had indeed (we learned) been present, but hardly to the extent alleged. This confirms that the Sabra and Shatila massacre had roots far deeper than the Damour issue.

When, a year and a half after the massacre, I was finally able to undertake this field study, I paid special attention to any links between Damour, Tall al-Za'tar, Sabra and Shatila. Nevertheless, I found myself unable to reach any firm conclusions and consequently had to turn to the families of victims and those abducted to seek details of the chain of migrations they had undergone. The answers to this were the longest in the questionnaire.

Let us begin by saying that Tall al-Za'tar Camp was not the root cause of the Palestinian tragedy. Like dozens of other Palestinian camps, it was a result rather than a cause; the first and only cause being the forced emigration from Palestine. It was in Palestine that the story truly began.

The first question to be asked was, therefore, this: From where had all these tormented families, who suffered such loss in Sabra and Shatila, actually come?

Palestinian victims and abducted were distributed among 147 families, but of these only 135 provided details of the series of migrations and movements since 1948. Information of this kind required a mature family member with precise knowledge; friends or neighbours could not provide accurate facts, even if they knew at all. Names of families registered in Table 14 have, alongside each family, the original home town and details of the successive migrations it might have gone through (some had come straight to Shatila from Palestine, whereas others had moved up to four times between 1948 and 1982). The list further notes the years in which each migration took place, and, finally, the questionnaire number of the householder or senior family member formally registered for the purposes of the study (one for each questionnaire). (See Table 14.)

The 27 families that did not specify the city, town or village from which they had come, preferred simply to name their homeland of 'Palestine'. Among the rest, Jaffa was the commonest place of origin, with 21 devastated families. This was followed by the cities of Safad, Haifa (and its suburbs) and Akka (Acre), with scores of 16, 12 and 9 respectively.

There were, further, 7 families from each of al-Khalisa and al-Na'ima; 6 from Tarshiha; 5 from each of Deir al-Qasi and the northern villages; 4 from each of al-Buqai'a, Saffourieh and Sihmata; 3 from Shafa Amr; 2 from al-Khalil (Hebron); and one from each of the villages of al-Kabri, Majd al-Kroum and Syrine.

The 135 families in question were scattered to various places in the immediate aftermath of the Palestine disaster, and the same applied during the first year of migration or expulsion, and during the following year for that matter. 53 Palestinian families had settled in Sabra and Shatila from the outset. The initial migration had, however, also led to 17 families being in the Tyre camps, while a further 21 families went to various other parts of the Lebanese South, especially Sidon, al-Ghaziya, Marja'youn, Nabatiyyeh, al-Miyyeh wa Miyyeh, and Ain al-Hilweh. There were 11 families that went to Beka'a and 7 others specifically to Baalbek. A further 8 families went to northern Lebanon. As for Beirut and its suburbs (apart, that is, from Sabra and Shatila), 15 families went to al-Za'tar, 2 to Burj Hammoud and 1 family to al-Maslakh.

Analysis of the migrations and movements for each of these families reveals that 53 migrated just once – the families, that is, who settled in Sabra and Shatila from the outset; 43 families moved twice; 29 moved three times, and 10 moved four times.

The specific places and years indicate two major factors underlying these multiple movements. The first factor was a natural one and had two aspects: economic and human. On various occasions a family would (if this was feasible) move on to a place where one of its members had found a job. On the human side, there were many families whose first, forced migration had split them up from their relatives, but who were able to be reunited with these, in a common camp or nearby place, when some stability of settlement had been achieved.

The second factor was neither natural nor human, but the coercive result of war. This it was that made the years of the Israeli invasions such major milestones: the 1978 invasion of the South, for instance, and the later invasion in 1982.

Let us now move on from this general picture to the particular experience of Tall al-Za'tar, and, in particular, to the movement of families following its fall.

It was noted above that 15 families had settled at Tall al-Za'tar (relatively speaking) after first migrating in 1948. What we commonly call the 'second migration', has, however, a variety of dates attached to it, according to each family's particular circumstances. There were 14 other families that had settled there, from various places, between 1952 and 1968. For one of these, indeed, Tall al-Za'tar was effectively the third destination; this family had come from Safad to Marja'youn, thence to al-Dikwaneh, and finally to Tall al-Za'tar itself. Thus the total number of families both resident at Tall al-Za'tar in 1976 and suffering the loss of loved ones at Sabra and Shatila was 29.

Next, did all these families take their children and settle in Damour immediately following Tall al-Za'tar's fall, with no other factors or circumstances involved? Let us, indeed, pose the question differently. Was Damour, for these families, a place of permanent residence, an alternative to Palestine? Or was it simply a temporary place of refuge pending the end of the civil wars? Indeed, how many of these families ever actually reached Damour in the first place?

Table 14 sheds further light on the migrations of the 29 families in that year. It shows that, from Tall al-Za'tar, 15 families moved to Sabra and Shatila, 10 to Damour and 4 to the Tyre camps.

The 15 families who moved to Sabra and Shatila continued to live there. Of the 4 families that had gone to the Tyre camps,

3 moved to Sabra and Shatila following the 1978 Israeli invasion of the South, whereas the fourth went there only in 1982, following the Israeli invasion of that year.

On the other hand, 9 of the 10 families that had gone to Damour moved to Sabra and Shatila in the summer of 1982, following the Israeli invasion; the tenth had moved there in 1979 to be near relatives.

To sum up: of the 135 families under consideration, devastated at Sabra and Shatila, just 10 (7.41 per cent) had moved from Tall al-Za'tar to Damour.

So were these ten families effectively responsible for the chain of crimes produced by the succession of irresponsible, anarchic civil wars in Lebanon? Were they responsible for the Damour tragedy? The whole notion is ludicrous.

In the present study, therefore, we were able eventually to dispose of this particular matter, even though it required more effort than any other. We intended to show a different face of the horrific injustice visited on Sabra and Shatila – the face of those bent on killing everyone: women, children, girls, boys, men, the elderly, everyone. In the light of this, does the 'axe of Damour' really deserve such prominence?

In reality, this is not the story of the 'axe of Damour'. It is rather the story of those in Sabra and Shatila who saw the horrors there when they were still children. Now that they have grown to be young men with nothing but painful memories, we dedicate these pages to them, so that they may learn how justice will never prevail, for them, so long as they are part of a refugee society.

What of the 'migration from Shatila'?

One of the rumours spreading through Shatila, even before the massacre itself, was that the residents of the district were to be forcibly evacuated and that the houses there would be replaced by a zoo. When words to this effect became attributed to President-elect Bashir al-Gemayel, the whole future of Shatila seemed in doubt.

As generally happens after a rumour or shocking statement, some believed it while others did not. The latter said it was simply one more thing going around in a war or anti-war situation. Where, after all, would the displaced people go? Those who actually did believe it spoke of a possible deal resulting in the departure of the refugees from Shatila and other Palestinian camps. No one, in those critical times, had the time to think things out further. It never even occurred to people that the project was out of the question in any case. The whole Shatila district would, after all, have been grossly inadequate to house a modern zoo in a modern country.

When the massacre was over the killers announced what they had done, boasting (among other things) that their intention had been not simply to 'knock out' the 'saboteurs' but to kill anyone else they could along the way. The overall objective, these people declared, was to expel the Palestinians from Shatila and the surrounding area.

Ten days after the massacre, *Ha'aretz* published a report by its military correspondent Ze'ev Schiff and his colleague Menahem Horowitz. They wrote that, according to enquiries made by specialized and qualified persons, the purpose of the operation had not been limited to immediate revenge for Bashir al-Gemayel's death. Rather, it had been a premeditated attempt to effect the mass expulsion of Palestinians from Beirut and from Lebanon as a whole.[14]

Loren Jenkins, in the *Washington Post*, stated that the Christian Lebanese militiamen had entered the camps in accordance with a scheme determined and planned in advance by a number of senior military commanders in the Lebanese Forces militia directly connected with Bashir al-Gemayel, who had himself been the prime mover in orchestrating and approving the scheme before his assassination on 14 September. Nothing in the plan had in fact called for a random massacre such as actually occurred in Sabra and Shatila. The aim had rather been (according to various sources) detentions, questioning and the demolition of houses, carried out in such a manner as to terrify Palestinian refugees in Lebanon and cause them to leave the country.[15]

Did they really succeed in instilling fear in the hearts of the remaining Palestinian residents, so as to make them quit Sabra and Shatila? In an attempt to learn the fate of Palestinian families, the questionnaire included questions about the number of individuals who left following the massacre, either for work purposes or permanently. To judge from the response (in 1984), the idea of a permanent migration did not even cross people's minds. Certain individuals may have left to work abroad, particularly in the Gulf states. And there was indeed even some migration of families. But how many of these latter were there, and what percentage did they represent?

The statistical analysis covered all those Palestinian families that had suffered the loss of loved ones, whether victims or abducted. With regard to the families of victims, 62 families had lost 1 victim each and 34 had lost from 2 to 11 victims each, making a total of 96 families. (See List of names 1.)

As for the families of those abducted, 40 had each lost 1 member and 11 had lost 2, 3 or 4, making a total of 51 families. (See List of names 2.)

The combined total for families suffering the loss of victims and abducted was, therefore, 147. In 20 of these, 1 member, whether father, son or daughter, had left to seek a livelihood elsewhere. In 4 further families, 2 members had left to do so. These 24 families are excluded from the migration analysis because the family itself remained in Sabra and Shatila and the objective of those who left was specifically work-related.

As to the matter of permanent migration, final results indicated 5 families from whom just 1 member survived and subsequently left. Also, there was 1 family with 2 survivors, who left together, and 12 families had larger numbers of survivors who all left. The total number of families leaving permanently was therefore 18, or 12.24 per cent out of the previously noted total of 147. (See Table 15.)

A migration rate of around 12 per cent can hardly be considered a major one. Indeed, the term 'migration' is hardly justifiable at all. As such, any objective of expulsion failed.

The massacre at Deir Yassin, which lasted for a few hours in April 1948, was the first well known massacre of recent Palestinian history, and its primary objective was to expel the Palestinians from the whole of Palestine. Sabra and Shatila, which lasted for a few days, was not the last, and nor will that at Jenin in April 2002 be the last, so long as the occupation remains in effect.

The Palestinians of Sabra and Shatila did not emigrate. Those remaining, despite all they had suffered – and pending a return to their homeland – accounted for 87.76 per cent of the whole.

Conclusion

Writing of field studies, the American historian Howard Zinn once noted (with the exquisite irony possessed by just a few wise historians) how the US government had made large sums of money available so that a group of affluent and highly specialized scholars could descend on an isolated black ghetto, undertake all kinds of detailed and sophisticated research, then, in a high-profile scholarly journal, make known their general conclusions: most significantly, that the blacks living in the ghetto were poor and had family problems![16]

Throughout the process of collecting questionnaires, then scrutinizing them and attempting to interpret the results, I found myself continually asking the question: Was my study like the one described by Howard Zinn? Had I spent all those long months between September 1982 and May 1984 reflecting endlessly on the massacre, awaiting first a chance for us to breathe, and second the chance to enter Sabra and Shatila without fear of the papers being seized – all merely to observe that the residents of Sabra and Shatila were poor and subject to countless problems, the main ones political?

In reality, though, the field study in this chapter differs in two important respects from that described by Howard Zinn.

First, the members of the study team were volunteers, receiving no financial support. In point of fact, they themselves – being from Sabra and Shatila – were part of the 'Palestinian ghetto' that was the equivalent of the 'black ghetto' in Howard Zinn's example.

Second, and still more crucially, they did not go to Sabra and Shatila to note that the people were poor. Their purpose was far more basic. They went, quite simply, to confirm that there were indeed people living there, and to point out that these residents were human beings like any other; human beings who were not merely deprived of rights in the normal heartless way characteristic of ghettos, but deprived even of the most basic of all human rights – the right to live.

These team members went to say that the victims killed at Sabra and Shatila were no 'saboteurs', but rather mothers, fathers, children, girls, young men, middle-aged men and the elderly; that they were not only Palestinians, but also included in their numbers Lebanese, Syrians and Arabs of various other nationalities, to say nothing of labourers from Pakistan and Bangladesh who had found refuge in Shatila but no wider host state to protect them.

The fatuous claim that what took place was a battle rather than a massacre, and that those killed were mostly young male 'saboteurs', springs from a source far deeper than the words themselves. It springs from the heart of a colonial and settlement ideology that negates the very presence of these people in the first place. Just as the former US leaders negated the presence of the native Indians, so did the Zionists with regard to the Palestinians.

The field study led to one conclusion above all. Those who committed the massacre of Sabra and Shatila did indeed succeed in killing residents – but they failed to kill the human spirit.

8

Counting the Victims

In the aftermath of catastrophes – whether those, like earthquakes or volcanoes, over which human beings have no control; or those, like wars, which are actually caused by human beings – perhaps the first consideration is the number of victims. Massacres, though, present peculiar problems in this respect, for figures may well vary widely, with one assessment twice as large as another or even many times larger. One account may speak of hundreds of victims, another of thousands, according to sources that are more or less credible.

The Sabra and Shatila massacre is especially problematic, not merely because of wide variation in the numbers of victims cited, but because there is no responsible authority involved, either Lebanese or Palestinian. No official source on either side has carried out a comprehensive census for victims, abducted and missing, then announced the results before God, history and mankind.

The Lebanese authority, in this connection, is the Lebanese government itself. This is because the massacre took place in Lebanese territory, on which there was a Palestinian camp along with a number of popular districts crowded with Lebanese, Palestinians and others of various nationalities. By international convention, Palestinian residents carrying UNRWA ID cards, and all the other nationals in question, were subject to Lebanese law. By the same token, they were entitled to protection from the Lebanese state.

On the Palestinian side, the authority in question is the Palestine Liberation Organization. The declared aim of the massacre was, after all, the liquidation of Palestinians, and this aim was borne out by action. Indeed, the Palestinian authority bore a moral responsibility for counting not just Palestinian victims but all victims, including Lebanese and those of other nationalities, given that these latter faced the fate they did because they lived in the same urban quarters as Palestinians.

Twenty years have now passed. Yet neither side, Palestinian or Lebanese, has made any official attempt to supply victims' names. Even the lists of names compiled by some of the humanitarian organizations in the days immediately following the massacre, and submitted to the Lebanese government, were never published by the state, or indeed by the organizations themselves. The same applies on the Palestinian side: certain humanitarian organizations and some other specifically Palestinian organizations, each according to its capacity, registered the names of victims. But none of these lists was published either by the mother organization (the PLO) or by the original organizations that collated them.

Then there are those responsible, de facto, for ensuring the safety of Sabra and Shatila residents between 16 and 18 September 1982: the Israelis, whose army, on the morning of 15 September, set out to occupy Beirut and specifically to enclose Sabra and Shatila. Theirs was the responsibility for residents' safety by virtue of international law and humanitarian convention, and such responsibility should have extended to a proper statement as to the number of victims. On this latter issue, however, the Israeli government was satisfied with whatever appeared in its own celebrated Report, prepared by a three-member commission headed by Judge Kahan and having as its remit a full inquiry into the atrocities carried out in the Beirut camps. This report, issued in February 1983, adopted estimated figures, and also quoted further figures from another, unspecified report; but this does not imply that the figures adopted or quoted were correct. These figures will be further discussed below.

Discrepancies in figures from different sources

The first, preliminary figures for victims (while, indeed, the search for victims was still being conducted) came from various media sources; they were based either on official announcements or on the estimates of rescue workers actively engaged in removing bodies. The Lebanese daily newspapers began publishing whatever numbers were available from Sunday 19 September, when it was stated that 1,400 people had, according to security and media sources, been killed in Sabra and Shatila.[1]

Two days later, on the Tuesday, Al-Safir quoted the Newsweek correspondent, to the effect that he had counted 70 bodies in an area of 100 square metres; this suggested a vast number of dead if all bodies on the ground were to be counted. Al-Safir carried additional material in another column of the same issue: three eye-witnesses, it was reported, had, on Saturday 18 September,

seen three bulldozers loaded with bodies leaving Sabra[2] – an indication that numbers were not to be based solely on bodies counted on the ground, however completely. Further details were provided in the same newspaper about what had been going on up till two in the afternoon on the Monday: namely, the piling of 200 bodies in a square to the right of the camp (later the mass cemetery). It was also noted (on the evidence of Civil Defence volunteers) that there were still at least 1,000 bodies under the rubble.[3] On the same day, though, Al-Nahar published higher figures. The rescue workers, it said, had brought out 300 bodies, and the overall number of victims might extend to 1,500.[4]

On Wednesday 22 September, details were published of the bodies brought out by the Tuesday. The following figures were supplied by an official from the Lebanese Civil Defence: 22 on the Saturday; 115 on the Sunday; 56 on the Monday; 26 from the rubble of a single house on the Tuesday[5] – a total of 219 bodies. It was further stated, on the authority of a rescue team member who had been around the camps, that the final number might reach 2,500 victims.[6]

Agence France-Presse stated that the number of bodies brought out by late Tuesday, 21 September, was 387, not counting a further 250 buried in mass graves.[7] The total number cited by this agency was therefore 637.

While the search for victims was still going on at the massacre site, in tandem with burials, Arab diplomatic circles were concerning themselves with news of the bodies taken from Sabra and Shatila, or of those victims who had been driven away and killed outside the district. According to news circulated on the Wednesday and Thursday, bodies of the latter had been found in the towns of al-Na'ima and Damour.[8]

Saturday 25 September might be considered the key day for the Lebanese press with regard to the accuracy of published massacre news based on eye-witness reports. This was the day that saw news of the mass death pit, located near the Sports City by Civil Defence volunteers, and the bringing out of

27 bodies before the eyes of reporters who published the details of this tragic event along with the victims' names.[9]

On the same day, the newspapers published an announcement by officials of the Civil Defence to the effect (substantially) that 320 new bodies had been found. Kamil Ja'ja', the appellate prosecutor, announced that the number of victims was now 597.[10] As the search was about to end, officials of the Civil Defence declared the number of victims to be around 1,500.[11]

On the Palestinian side, PLO Chairman Yasser Arafat announced that the number of Sabra and Shatila victims was between 5,000 and 6,000. This was just before the end of September, during the funeral procession of Brigadier-General Sa'd Sayel (Abu al-Walid), a senior officer of the Palestine Liberation Army and leader of active operations against the Israeli invasion of Beirut, who had been assassinated in al-Beka'a.[12]

Many people supposed the International Committee of the Red Cross (ICRC) would be the one to supply accurate figures. This was, after all, the body effectively responsible for recording the names of victims and those missing. The first press release was in fact issued very swiftly, on 18 September: hundreds of children, teenagers, women and old people (the statement said, on the authority of representatives in Beirut) had been killed in the Shatila district, and their bodies were still lying in the streets.[13]

On the massacre site itself, ICRC personnel collaborated, throughout the days spent searching for victims, with a number of official Lebanese parties, in the process of recording the names of victims and missing. This was confirmed by the ICRC's Annual Report, which, under the main heading 'Lebanon', had a subheading entitled 'The Massacres of Sabra and Shatila'. This latter specified the measures taken by ICRC representatives to evacuate the sick and wounded from both the Gaza and Akka Hospitals, and to lodge the thousands who had sought refuge at the ICRC centre. As for their role in identifying bodies and recording names for these, ICRC representatives from the whole of Lebanon had (it was stated) come together to organize this operation, and representatives of the Lebanese Red Cross had made strenuous efforts and collaborated with them. Yet the paragraphs ended without any mention of the numbers of victims brought out.[14] However, a list of names, personally supervised by the ICRC representatives, was submitted to the Lebanese state in two copies; one in French, the other in Arabic. Publication of the list was now a matter for the state.

Other sources had, however, contrived to learn of the ICRC statistics. One of the most important of these sources was the International Commission that had come to Lebanon during the summer of 1982 to inquire into the facts of the Israeli invasion, and some of whose members now returned following the massacre. In their report, the famous MacBride Report, they stated that the number of victims counted by the ICRC up to Sunday 19 September, had totalled 1,500; then the figure had risen to 2,400 on 22 September; but on 23 September, 350 further bodies had been found, making a total of 2,750 victims. As for the precise number of victims, the Report noted, this was impossible to establish since many bodies had been brought out and removed while many others had already been buried in scattered mass graves.[15]

On the other hand, the figures provided by the Lebanese Red Cross (LRC) were higher than those given above; and these were the figures submitted by the American writer Ralph Schoenman in his testimony before the Oslo Commission, which, during the first month after the massacre, heard many testimonies about war crimes in Lebanon. Quoting LRC officials, he said: 'We have tallied and buried 3,000 people not including those under the rubble and exclusive of those bulldozed under the rubble.' As for actual estimates of the numbers killed at Sabra and Shatila, these, according to Schoenman, ranged between 4,000 and 4,500 victims.[16]

The specific Lebanese source for the first officially stated figures remain unknown, for the Lebanese officials providing the information to foreign journalists had asked them not to specify their source. Below, however, are the figures distributed by the United Press Agency (UPA).

The UPA said that 762 bodies had been found at Sabra and Shatila. Of these, 212 had been impossible to identify and had been buried in mass graves. A further 302 and 248 identified bodies had been buried by the Lebanese authorities and the ICRC respectively. As for bodies taken by family members to be buried at places of their choice, these were estimated at around 1,200.[17] All these yield a combined total of 1,962.

In his book *Enquête sur un massacre: Sabra et Chatila*, published before the end of 1982, Amnon Kapeliouk encountered the numbers above and supplemented them with three categories not taken into account by the anonymous official Lebanese source. These were: first, victims the attackers had, in the course of the massacre, buried in mass graves which the Lebanese government would not subsequently permit to be dug up (such victims are estimated to be in the hundreds); second, victims that could not, without great difficulty, be brought out from the rubble of 200 houses torn down over their inhabitants (115 bodies from the houses were found on the first day and 56 on the second, after which the search was halted; these last are also reckoned to be in the hundreds); and third, those driven off in trucks and now missing (Agence France-Press assessed such cases at more than 2,000 though in Kapeliouk's view an estimate in the hundreds was reasonable). Combining all the categories noted by Kapeliouk produces a total of around 3,000 victims. His own general estimate was between 3,000 and 3,500 killed.[18]

The purpose of reproducing all these figures from the various sources was not to arrive at any final number but rather to learn what had been happening, with respect to the counting of victims, in the two-week period of search and burial, and also to focus on numerical discrepancies between one source and another. A thorough analysis of the figures leads us to the following observations.

- There was no single official authority responsible for supplying accurate figures. Although it was clear from the press that the Lebanese Civil Defence was the primary source, it was noted on the massacre site itself that the primary source was actually the ICRC, working in conjunction with the Lebanese Army, the Lebanese Red Cross and the Lebanese Civil Defence (LCD).

- LCD officials were content with the brief, concise statements they made over the actual days of the search for victims. Not one comprehensive official statement was issued subsequently by the LCD or by any other official or humanitarian body, or by the Lebanese state. By the time the search was over, the issue of figures had been blanketed over as a 'forbidden' one.

- The figures need to be classified within two separate categories: numbers of those actually observed, and the estimated numbers. This is in the nature of such a tragic and horrific event.

- There is an astonishing discrepancy between two sets of figures: first, those derived from government or official sources, whereby LCD officials on 25 September 1982 cited a number of 597 victims; and second, a further statement five days later (during which only a few more victims had been discovered) when officials from the same organization gave a second figure – the number now being set at around 1,500. What could have accounted for such a huge difference, and who was responsible? And is there not a further difference – between this latter figure and the one circulated by the UPA, based in turn on figures taken from Lebanese government sources, where the total had reached 1,962 – of almost 2,000?

- There is a further discrepancy, which will become more apparent as time goes on, between the estimated figures released by the Palestinian Authority and those released by its Lebanese counterpart. The numbers provided by the former are clearly high in contrast to the low numbers supplied by the latter.

Lists of victims' names

The compilation of lists of victims' names was mostly completed during 1983 and 1984. Initially, all the emphasis was on obtaining some of the lists put together in the first few days following the massacre, when the actual search for victims was in progress. We later discovered, however, that these were only partially complete, and this prompted us to undertake a private initiative to collate names – something we could only go ahead with when the situation had changed drastically within the forbidden zone (see the Introduction, and also Chapter 7).

I shall not reiterate all the difficulties involved in the collection process. However, one distinctive aspect does merit further attention here, confirming as it does the level of the fear enveloping everyone. Briefly, no list contained numbers in excess of 328 victims (indeed, all the lists I managed to lay hands on had totals below this). This, I subsequently learned, was the figure officially issued by senior departments of the IRC, springing from their representatives' practice of counting victims rather than recording victims' names. The figure is also that cited in a letter from the head of the ICRC in Lebanon to the Israeli Defence Minister. This letter also notes the factors preventing knowledge of the exact number of victims (the same factors repeatedly brought up by a number of officials in both the ICRC and the LCD) – a clear indication that the true figure was higher. Yet nobody, with the best will in the world – not even if they possessed the evidence and the names – could ever exceed this figure of 328. This, it seemed, was the line no one was permitted to cross.

And yet for all attempts to hide the traces, bury the facts or conceal the names of victims, the massacre of Sabra and Shatila had left an indelible mark. Each person contributing to the discovery of a part, however small, of the facts, or the numbers involved, or the names themselves, played a significant part towards the preparation of a final comprehensive list of the names of victims, abducted and missing – a list which had now reached 1,390. Without all these various contributions, we could never eventually have come up with 17 sources, each representing a humanitarian institution, a civil organization or a scientific project. With all these efforts combined, access to numbers and names became possible at last.

We should, to begin with, take a closer look at three main points.

The first point relates to the definition of the three terms, 'victim', 'abducted' and 'missing'.

The victim. This means every resident of Sabra and Shatila killed during the massacre between the entry and departure of the attacking gunmen. There is no evidence of anyone being killed in any skirmish or battle, and as such there is no distinction to be made between a victim and a martyr. There was, as we noted, some limited exchange of gunfire, particularly on the Thursday evening, but none of the small number of defenders was killed during those hours.

The abducted. This means anyone abducted at the massacre site by the attackers during the three days in question, with witnesses or any other indications to confirm the abduction.

The missing. This means anyone who disappeared in the wake of the massacre events and never reappeared. It subsequently emerged (from a number of lists) that many of those initially regarded as being among the missing were actually among the victims or abducted. Where the case was unclear between the two, those involved continued to be viewed as missing by their families.

Most of the lists we obtained made no distinction between those abducted and those missing. The single, general category 'missing' was used, allowing for a change of category to 'victim' or 'abducted' should verification emerge for either. Comparison between the lists, and the collation into a single comprehensive list, shed light, for verification purposes, on all the available data. Finally, we registered a person as 'abducted' where confirmation existed; otherwise the entry was kept as 'missing'. Practically speaking, those still registered as missing will in fact have been abducted or victims whose bodies were never recovered. However, the principles of historical research dictate that they remain 'missing' so long as their fate is not specifically determined.

The second point relates to the identity of the abductors. The attacking gunmen were not responsible in every case where residents were abducted. A number of the families of those abducted or missing, on a number of the lists we assembled, indicated that abduction had been by the Israeli Army. This was also verified in the oral history.

As for the third point, this relates to the common factor, and the general difference, among the lists of names from all the various sources: some names appeared on more than one list (the common factor), and every list, without exception, contained names found on no other list (the difference), the number of such 'unique' names ranging from one to over 100 in particular cases. Numerous further differences will emerge as we consider particular lists or sets of lists.

We would make one final point. Reference to List of names 3 and 4 in Appendix 2 will make clear the sources for each individual name; the main sources being noted next to the name of each victim, or abducted or missing person. In the interests of immediate clarity, particular sources are designated by a separate letter.

Registration of names during the search for victims

The first set of lists was that assembled during the search for victims, the names being collected by various international and local humanitarian institutions or else by conscientious individuals. The total number of lists obtained during this stage was six; three from the massacre site and three at the Beirut cemeteries.

One common factor unites the three lists from the massacre site, compiled, respectively, by the ICRC, the LCD and the Middle East Council of Churches, and that is that the documentation of names and all other available data was carried out under the harshest of conditions. From this springs the repetition of certain names within the same list; which meant, in turn, that the number we finally arrived at from the three lists was less than the one obtained from the sum (stated or otherwise) of the names recorded.

As for the three lists containing the names of people buried in the cemeteries of Rawdat al-Shahidein or al-Shuhada in Beirut, these involved no duplication since the gravestones were the prime source in each case. Records also included the names of those buried in a mass grave, where the responsible person at the Shuhada cemetery had entered them in a special notebook on the day itself, and in the presence of witnesses.

1. The list of the International Committee of the Red Cross (B). This list is regarded as one of the most accurate with regard to names, credentials and verification of testimonies, the general reliability being reflected in the registration of all available data about each victim, such as identity, year of birth and number of ID card or passport where available. There are two copies of this list; one typed in French, the other handwritten in Arabic. The total number of victims' names retrieved from this list was 179, one of which appeared on no other list.[19]

2. The list of the Lebanese Civil Defence (C). This was the official institution affiliated to the Interior Ministry, under whose supervision large numbers of rescue workers from various local rescue teams carried out their work. The list of names it compiled was typed in Arabic, and it included appropriate data for each victim in a fashion similar to the ICRC's list. The total number of names retrieved from it was 254, of which 21 appeared on no other list.[20]

3. The list of the Middle East Council of Churches (I). This list was typed in French, and set down the names by nationality. It was also notable for the accuracy of its observations regarding personal credentials, families' testimonies and identification of the body. The Council had also sent a team of doctors to implement first aid missions, registration of names and co-ordination with the ICRC. The total number of names retrieved from this list was 194, of which ten appeared on no other list.[21]

4. The list of the Rawdat al-Shahidein cemetery (G). This list was prepared under the supervision of Shaykh Salman al-Khalil, who had said prayers and carried out all burial formalities for the victims at Rawdat al-Shahidein. With the help of his brother Shaykh Ja'far al-Khalil, he also said prayers for the victims at the mass cemetery at Shatila. He verified all entries before handing over the document, which contained no information other than the names themselves. The total number of names retrieved from this list was 149, of which 105 appeared on no other list.[22]

5. *The list of Shaykh Salman al-Khalil (L)*. This was a list handwritten by Shaykh Salman himself with a view to preserving the memory of victims and missing, whose names and all other data he had verified. This list also contained details of nationality, place of residence and age, along with names of the family members who had made enquiries about victims, missing or abducted, and about the circumstances of abduction. The total number of names on this list was 83, comprising 58, 11 and 14 names for victims, abducted and missing respectively. From the missing category there were ten names that appeared on no other list.[23]

6. *The list of al-Shuhada cemetery (H)*. This list contained the names of those buried at al-Shuhada cemetery, although the names were not in fact gathered till 8 August 1984, two years after the massacre. Initially the researcher had been unable to compile the names on account of massive shell damage to the cemetery. Eventually, however, he was able to move from grave to grave under the guidance of the man in charge of the cemetery, Abu Fathi; and so managed to take down the names of the Sabra and Shatila victims from the gravestones. The graves were close together, and, as Abu Fathi explained, there was a reliable way of distinguishing the graves of massacre victims from those of the victims of Israeli shelling. The names of martyrs killed during the invasion would, Abu Fathi said, habitually be written when shelling had abated; members of the dead man's family would return to the cemetery, where the martyr's full name would be recorded, along with the precise day and month of death. After the massacre, however, it was considered enough simply to write: 'During the Israeli invasion.' This list contained names only. The total number of names on this list was 105, of which 93 appeared on no other list.[24]

– *The list of al-Shuhada cemetery – the mass grave (H')*. This list was written down by Khalil lzziddine ('lzziddine' is a pseudonym used for the purposes of this volume), the watchman at al-Shuhada cemetery, and contained the names of those buried not singly but in a common mass grave. The list contained names only. The total number of names was 35, of which 32 appeared on no other list.[25]

Registration of names in the post-massacre phase

The process of registration during this phase was quite different from the process in force during the initial period of shock. There was now ample time to verify names and all relevant data – though even through these months, the 'line' referred to earlier (in connection with the total number of victims officially set down) could still not be crossed.

The lists for this phase were not all secret ones. Some lists had become public property, mainly due to escalating interest in the case of abducted persons (all of those abducted, anywhere on Lebanese soil); it would have been meaningless, after all, to work for the return of the abducted under conditions of secrecy. The initial thrust was from individual women who had lost a husband, son or relative, and who met with officials to submit their case. There were also three organizational units at work to prepare final lists of those abducted or missing: Dar al-Fatwa; the Committee for Families of the Kidnapped and Disappeared in Lebanon, and a coalition of various groups. A further source of unambiguous openness was the daily press, which began, in October, to publish lists of names for victims and those missing.

There were other sources, by contrast, which could not come near openness for long years to come. These were the Palestinian organizations, some of which had striven to make an accurate register of victims, abducted and missing. These sources suffered from the same problem of duplicated names as was apparent in the initial lists compiled during the search phase. Nevertheless, the most comprehensive list, with regard both to number of names and accuracy of data, was that compiled by the Democratic Front for the Liberation of Palestine (DFLP). There was also a further Palestinian Front, which remained anonymous at the request of its leaders. This we refer to as the 'anonymous' Palestinian organization.

During the months immediately following the massacre, the Palestinian Red Crescent Society (acting out of necessity, as will be explained below) took it on itself to produce death certificates. The Red Crescent list was compiled in accordance with the organization's records at the Gaza and Akka Hospitals.

We shall begin, below, with the secret lists compiled at the time, then move on to the public ones.

7. The list of the Palestinian Red Crescent Society (PRCS) – Gaza Hospital (D). At the Gaza Hospital, the Palestinian Red Crescent Committee validated death certificates – documents that a number of responsible authorities had declined to issue on the pretext that insufficient proof was available. In these circumstances, Red Crescent officials would ask the families of victims to bring forward two or more witnesses, and they also requested humanitarian organizations active on the massacre site to furnish other credentials if available. Through the hospital records we were able to take a number of names of victims for whom families had managed to obtain death certificates. Officials at the Gaza Hospital also provided us with a typed copy of a list containing the names of victims with an entry for age alongside. The total number of names from the two lists was 111, of which 15 appeared on no other list.[26]

– *The list of the Palestinian Red Crescent Society – Akka Hospital (D').* The Akka Hospital list differed from its Gaza Hospital counterpart in containing basically only the names of those people killed at the hospital itself or nearby, together with those for all hospital workers, such as ambulance drivers. The only further data provided was nationality, profession and, occasionally, age. The total number of victims on this typed list was 28, of which ten appeared on no other list.[27]

8. The list of the Democratic Front for the Liberation of Palestine (DFLP) – (E). This list was notable for being the longest, even after duplicate names had been deleted. It also provided adequate information on each victim, abducted person or missing person, with regard to age, place of residence, date of death, and date of abduction or disappearance, where known. The total number of names on this list was 326, subdivided as follows: 281 for victims, of which 17 appeared on no other list; 30 for abducted and 15 for missing; eight of the missing appearing on no other list.[28]

9. The list of the 'anonymous' Palestinian organization (M). This list was notable for including the age and nationality of victims, along with the names of some abducted and missing. The total number of names was 166, 147 of these being for victims, two of which appeared on no other list. For abducted and missing there were 15 and four names respectively, two of the missing appearing on no other list.[29]

10. The list of Dar al-Fatwa (K). This list was of special importance to us in that it was the first whose compilers expressed encouragement and welcome, beginning with Dr Hussein Quwatli, General Manager for al-Ifta' Affairs, whom I met back in 1984, and ending with Shaykh Khaldoun Uraimit, whom I managed to meet 17 years later, in 2001. Shaykh Uraimit personally oversaw the process of registering the names of victims, abducted and missing, and as such was able to affirm that Dar al-Fatwa not only opened its doors to people but sent representatives to homes in Sabra and Shatila. Dar al-Fatwa's list comprised typed names. We retrieved a total of 276 names, 17 for abducted, 259 for missing (both men and women); the majority of the missing, 256, appeared on no other list.[30]

11. The list of the Committee for Families of the Kidnapped and Disappeared in Lebanon (CFKDL) – (N). This was perhaps the first civil committee that made public rather than secret efforts to discover the ultimate fate of those abducted and missing on Lebanese soil. It was in fact founded by a group of women who had lost loved ones over the years, and one of these, Mrs Wadad Halwani, gave us the fullest possible co-operation.[31] The list contained the names of all those abducted and missing on an individual basis rather than divided into groups, from the mid-1970s on, and as such there was no specific mention of the Sabra and Shatila massacre, or of other bloody incidents, or 'red' or 'black' days (as they were called), except when relatives positively volunteered an explanation. However, we were able to deduce the relevant cases from the place and dating of reports by the families concerned, and by comparing names with the names on other lists. Many of these names were printed in the daily papers. The total number of abducted and missing retrieved from this list was 88 – 38 for abducted and 50 for missing; eleven of the missing appearing on no other list.[32]

12. The common list for the abducted and missing (J). This detailed list, compiled on special large-size computer sheets bearing the name of Dar al-Fatwa, was the most methodical and accurate one. It was the result of collective efforts supervised by Dar al-Fatwa, receiving contributions from the Committee for Families of the Kidnapped and Disappeared in Lebanon, the General Union of Palestinian Women and a number of other voluntary sources. This typed list covered 87 pages and contained 1,971 names of those abducted or missing on Lebanese soil from the mid-1970s through to 1983. Names were recorded by nationality, as follows: unregistered nationals; Lebanese; Palestinian; Kurds; 'under review' card holders; Jordanians; Turks; Egyptians; holders of various other nationalities. Most names included fathers' names, along with details of age, and of date and place of abduction, where information was available.

Retrieval from this list of the names of those abducted or missing at Sabra and Shatila was carried out directly, by virtue of the explicit information provided and through comparisons and inferences. Consequently we were able to arrive at 66 names; 37 abducted and 29 missing; two of the missing appearing on no other list.[33]

The list may indeed have contained further relevant names but the research procedure we had established precluded cases based on suspicion.

13. The lists of the Lebanese press: Al-Safir (F). Al-Safir published the original common list, noted above, on 15 October 1982, and more than once pursued the issue of those abducted, and published names and information. However, the Sabra and Shatila massacre was not explicitly mentioned; there was rather an implicit connection through other lists and facts. Al-Safir supplied 104 names in all, noting nationalities in most cases. The names were divided into 33 for victims, two of which appeared on no other list, and 25 and 46 for abducted and missing respectively; 38 of the missing appearing on no other list.[34]

– Al-Nida' (F'). The longest and most important Al-Nida' list was that published in its edition of 1 December 1982, which also covered a press conference given by the Grand Mufti Hasan Khaled and attended by dozens of families of the abducted. Some cried out to the Mufti, explaining all the difficulties they were encountering in their search for their abducted sons and daughters. The Mufti followed some soothing words with a practical promise:

That doesn't mean that I'll just be sitting back. There are things to do. I shall be taking action, getting in touch with the President and all the officials concerned; I'll do whatever I can, convey your message and insist on the return of the abducted and those imprisoned [by the militias] if they're still there. And I'll see to it the government doesn't allow any repetition of these things.

For all his efforts, though, none of those abducted or detained ever actually returned.

One of many published by Al-Nida', the 1 December list (sub-titled 'List of names of those abducted by the Lebanese Forces') was derived from more than one source, and it was notable for the variety of the data included: the profession and age of those abducted, as well as the time and place of the abduction itself. On the basis of the time and place, and of comparison with other lists, the total number of names we arrived at was 37: 20 abducted and 17 missing; two of the missing appearing on no other list.[35]

– *A list extracted from various newspapers (F").* Over the days following the massacre, a number of daily newspapers wrote on the victims, supplying names for some of those buried outside the camps or whose families had held funeral services for them. There were also scattered reports on some of those abducted. The total number reached 61, most of these being victims: 45 names, ten of which appeared on no other list. Names were also given for ten abducted and six missing; two of the missing appearing on no other list.[36]

Two lists from the Oral History and Field Study Projects

Neither names nor numbers were an objective of the Oral History Project when I began work on this before the end of 1982 (see the Introduction). Soon, however, I became aware of the crucial importance of discovering names. My starting point in this connection was the interviews; then, when I realized the urgent need to undertake a field study, the latter became, in turn, the gateway for this indispensable operation.

14. The oral history list (O). This, as said, was the first I began to compile, in conjunction with the interviews I conducted with the families of victims from February 1983 on. It was also the list with which the search eventually stopped, in 2002. What, it may be asked, was the reason for such a timespan?

After the first phase of interviewing, which lasted two full years following the massacre, I frequently encountered people who would tell me that a relative had died at Sabra and Shatila or had been abducted, and I would undertake to add the names of their loved ones. At last, in early 2002, I had put together the comprehensive list and had also completed my statistical analysis. At that point I made the decision to add no further names. The final figure remains etched on my memory: 1,389 victims, abducted and missing.

Two months later, in April 2002, one of my old students requested an interview to ask a few questions relevant to his thesis on

the Palestine Question, and at the end he asked me about the Sabra and Shatila project. I answered briefly as I gathered up my papers. Then, to my surprise, he said: 'My uncle was killed at Sabra and Shatila.' 'Who was your uncle?' I asked. 'Haroun Abed Uthman', he replied. 'He was just a young man, only 22 when he died.' Realizing the name had struck no chord with me, he gave me a pleading look. I could hardly, I felt, fail to give his uncle a single line when dozens of pages were filled with the names of victims. Unable to resist, I returned and revised various lists, tables, statistics and percentages I had supposed over and done with.

If this book were to be delayed by even one further year, the combined figure for victims, abducted and missing would go beyond the 1,390 listed. Ten years on, and a still higher figure would be reached. Such is the nature of Sabra and Shatila: not a single tragedy, but an ever unfolding series of tragedies.

After adding the name of Haroun Abed Uthman, the combined total for the oral history list alone became 251, most of them for victims: 224, 14 of which appeared on no other list. The other 27 were in the abducted category.[37]

15. The field study list (A). The field study list was the key one for a successful search. In contrast to the oral history list, compiled over almost 20 years, it was put together over just two months in the spring of 1984; the time needed for the distribution and filling out of questionnaires. It emerged, subsequently, as the longest and most accurate list with respect to all aspects of the individuals concerned, including age, nationality, profession and kinship.

This field study list supplied 530 names: 430 victims and 100 abducted, of which 66 and 22 respectively appeared on no other list.[38]

Two turn-of-the-century lists

Fifteen years on, as the twentieth century was nearing its end, two further lists were issued to add to the 15 detailed above.

The real issue here was not that of new names introduced; most had in fact appeared a number of times before. What was notable was the way these two lists revived the memory of the tragedy. And each did, in fact, have its own particular significance. The first list revealed, on the Lebanese side, a degree of interest in the abducted that had been absent in previous years, while the second revealed increased international interest, mainly on the part of the judicial authorities, in the Sabra and Shatila affair.

16. The list of the Official Commission of Inquiry into the Fate of Those Abducted and Missing (P). Just before the twentieth century ended, the Official Commission of Inquiry into the Fate of Those Abducted and Missing was set up following a specific request by the Prime Ministry. The aim was to collect data about those abducted or missing on Lebanese soil over approximately a quarter of a century, that is, from the outbreak of the civil war in the mid-1970s to the late 1990s. The list was significant for being based on information supplied by families.

The preparation took more than a year, giving everyone the opportunity to supply any information they might have. The information requested was more comprehensive than for any previous list or record for the abducted and missing: the full name, together with the names of father and grandfather if possible; place and date of birth; nationality; place and date of abduction; nature of the abductors; political and sectarian affiliation of the abducted; family status; and place where the abducted was now detained, if known. All the names were then printed in a special record of 90 pages. There were no sequential numbers, but the total figure for abducted and missing exceeded 2,000.

To arrive at the identity of those abducted and missing at Sabra and Shatila it was necessary to review the record in its entirety – a task facilitated by explicit mention of the massacre, by available information about time and place of abduction, and by comparison with other lists. This should not, however, be taken to imply that we managed to locate, through the record, all those

abducted and missing in the massacre. Where there was doubt, the name was omitted.

Finally we managed to retrieve 59 names from the record, all supposedly 'abducted' or 'missing'. When, however, we ascertained from other sources that a number of these people had in fact been killed, we transferred the names to the 'victim' category. The list finally yielded names for twelve victims, one of which had appeared on no other list; and 32 abducted and 15 missing, two of the missing having appeared on no other list.[39]

When the record was declared complete, and the failure of all attempts to discover their fate (or the fate of some even) had also been recorded, the Prime Minister, Dr Salim al-Hoss, announced in 2000 that the Lebanese government considered all those in question to be dead, and that their families could now undertake the official paperwork necessary to register their deaths.[40]

To all appearances, therefore, the matter of the abducted and missing was finally closed. In fact, this was not the end of the matter, for even now some of the families concerned continue to cling to hope.

17. The list for the lawsuit against Sharon to the Belgian judiciary (Q). Three lawyers – the Lebanese Chibli Mallat and the Belgians Luc Walleyn and Michaël Verhaeghe – submitted a case to the Belgian judiciary on behalf of some of the survivors of the Sabra and Shatila massacre, against Sharon and others responsible for the massacre. The file contained names of victims and abducted as provided in the testimonies of their families, the plaintiffs. The lawyers submitted their case in Brussels on 18 June 2001.

The notable feature of this list is that the names in question were gathered from the families 18 years after the massacre. The compilation of the testimonies by the team working in conjunction with Mallat was characterized by discretion and secrecy.

The names from the survivors' testimonies totalled 94 for victims and abducted. Of these, 88 were for victims, one of which was revealed solely by this list a full 20 years after the massacre was over. Also worthy of attention was the fact that some families who had registered the names of their sons as abducted in the record of the Official Commission of Inquiry now, in the wake of the government's position vis-à-vis those abducted, registered them as victims for the purposes of the lawsuit against Sharon.[41]

With all due respect to these families' wishes and final decision, our position remains firm in keeping to the lists of abducted as originally registered. The reasons for this were explained earlier.

Documenting the numbers with names

From the 17 lists noted above, each based on its specific source, we were able to prepare the four lists in Appendix 2, in accordance with three principles:

1. To note the names of victims, abducted and missing separately.
2. To provide full sources for each name, using the relevant symbols. That is not, of course, to imply that a name substantiated by, say, ten sources is somehow more credible than if substantiated by just one; a single source is sufficient, and all sources are trustworthy. The point of the procedure is rather to provide fully detailed lists, to recognize the efforts of all those who contributed in producing the lists, and to show maximum consideration to the families concerned, some of whom might gain access to further information through one or other of the sources specified.
3. To document all basic data related to the lists themselves. This last principle – given that information on the names of individuals mentioned in the field study and of their families was available and well ordered – involved registering those concerned in conjunction with the basic information in two lists: the first for victims, the second for abducted. The third list was devoted to victims along with all the sources, the fourth to abducted and missing, based on all the sources, all available information being documented in both.

List of names 1: Victims of Sabra and Shatila massacre: based on field study, spring 1984. In the field study we had to rely on a single uniform process for collecting information on victims and their families, namely, to ask the invariable questions on the questionnaires. This permitted age, nationality, gender and profession to be recorded alongside each name. As for family relations, each family suffering the loss of more than one victim (specifically, between two and eleven) was highlighted in italics.

Position within the family took precedence over alphabetical order. For each particular family tragedy, members on the list are, as will be seen, named in descending order of age, beginning with father, mother, brother, sister, uncle, or whatever. It will be noted that the italics which indicate families with multiple tragedies were quite dominant.

The total number of names on this victim list is 430, with ten entries at the end providing just the first name or an alias, since witnesses were unaware of the full names. There are also 15 anonymous victims, though people in Sabra and Shatila remember well enough how all these died. Six were young labourers from Bangladesh; their death was witnessed by a number of people who attested that the men had died in their beds. Also, the bodies of six children were discovered in a shelter in the Ersal district, and the bodies of three more were found burned at the Akka Hospital. The names of these labourers and children may be unknown but these people are surely worthy of record as human beings.

List of names 2: Abducted in Sabra and Shatila massacre: based on field study, spring 1984. This list was compiled in 1984 and a follow-up was undertaken in 1998–99 when three young local men visited the families of the abducted, on an individual basis, to enquire about any further developments. The answers given were invariable: no one had returned.[42]

This list was prepared on the same pattern as the first, and contained the names of 100 abducted. The last two appeared just as first names, which is not to minimize the tragedy they suffered, as described by a number of witnesses in Sabra and Shatila (see Account 40, p. 193).

List of names 3: Victims of Sabra and Shatila massacre: based on various sources. This list contains names for all victims from the 17 lists noted above, including the field study list itself. In other words, this third list includes all sources for each name.

The information here is well integrated, containing as it does all the data found on the other lists – though there are, it must be said, particular cases of a source failing to note, say, victims' ages or nationalities (deficiencies which might, however, be made up on another list). A fair amount of information finally remains lacking.

All available information relating to age, gender and nationality is noted. Profession is omitted for two reasons: first, because it was not normally mentioned by the various sources; and second, because the first list had already copied the professions from the field study.

The total number of victims on this list is 906.

List of names 4: Abducted and missing in Sabra and Shatila massacre: based on various sources. This list follows the same pattern, sources and manner of documentation as the third list, except that additional, more recent sources have also been used.

The total number of abducted and missing on this list is 484.

* * *

On the basis of the lists above, the number of victims, abducted and missing therefore totals 1,390. If so much attention is paid to precise figures in commercial documentation, then how much more should not be paid to human beings living on this earth?

There are, let us repeat, 1,390 human beings involved. It would be unrealistic to suppose that any of the abducted ever managed to return; this we confirmed. As for the missing, the number supposed to have returned is 50 or 60 at the highest estimate. Let us hopefully increase this figure to 90. The rest, even so, must necessarily be regarded as victims. This means that there are 1,300 victims, and out of respect for human rights, they should be so regarded.

Estimated figures

The numbers emerging from the lists above cannot be considered final. There are two principal reasons for this:

1. Those taking part closely in the compilation of a particular list were unanimous on one point: that the real numbers significantly exceeded those produced by their own limited statistical efforts. In other words, the total number of 1,300 named victims, high as this seemed when the subtotals from the various lists were aggregated, remains an understatement of the real number of victims.

2. At no time, it must be said, was there a single official, humanitarian or civil body with the authority, will and facilities to undertake an accurate census – with a view to approaching the truth in the face of a political and security situation that was antipathetic both before and after the search for victims. The general state of affairs was, it need hardly be repeated, both frustrating and intimidating.

All this leads to the question: what should be the estimate for the true figure?

In the first section of this chapter, where we discussed the contradiction between the sources, we took a close look at the estimates provided by various sources, and we will add here our own estimate based on this study. This estimate springs from two separate types of calculation: the first based on the lists of names; the second based on figures for the cemeteries, mass graves and death pits.

Lists of names. No one would ever have supposed that the lists would lead to such a vast quantity of names being retrieved, or that 17 such various lists would come to be compiled. Even then, further lists remained tucked away in drawers and were never made available – lists prepared by certain National Civil Defence organizations, some of whose young, enthusiastic rescue workers mentioned them in their testimonies and promised to hand them over to their interviewer, Muna Sukkarieh, at the earliest opportunity. Their enthusiasm evaporated, however, when their seniors twice declined to make the lists available, once before the end of 1983 and a second time in 1999. But information about the numbers involved did help us in our estimate of the final figure.

Ziad Madani ('Madani' is a pseudonym used for the purposes of this volume), a rescue worker from the Union of Al-Shabiba al-Islamiyieh, said:

I can tell you, there were 515 whose names we managed to get hold of. They were the ones whose names we have, who were identified by their families.[43]

Nuhad Israwi, a rescue worker from al-Makased, said:

In our official estimate, the figure is, I can tell you, around 2,700 bodies. Of course, there were some missing, but we couldn't count the missing, and to this day we know nothing about them. They're still missing.

We have names available, naturally, and we have lists, and we even had the ID cards and personal credentials; most of them were handed over to the government, and they gave them back to the victims' families afterwards. There were a lot of certificates given out too; our Al-Makased unit, for instance, issued around 700 certificates for burial. We can let you have a proper list, there's no problem at all. No problem.[44]

Hasan, a rescue worker from the Scouts of al-Tarbiya al-Wataniyieh said:

We have statistics for names and dates of birth. I'll get you a copy of the report on Saturday. And we're ready to get you a copy with names. The figure for the massacre's close to 1,500 bodies we've reports and names for. The report we submitted to the [Lebanese Civil Defence] administration had the figure, which was the one submitted by the Volunteers Committee. I don't know why the newspapers talked about numbers being somewhere between 300 and 400. We can't get involved in all that, our Civil Defence work's just about rescuing the wounded and moving them.[45]

The number of names from these three lists totals 2,715. What conclusions are we to draw?

The total number of victims, abducted and missing on the 17 lists used earlier (before deletion of repeated names) was 3,196. The total from the common list (comprising the combination of the third and fourth lists in Appendix 2) amounted to 1,390 names, though we reduced this by 90 missing persons provisionally considered to

have returned. The great majority of the abducted and missing we regarded, 20 years on, as killed, in accordance with the formal decision announced by Prime Minister Salim al-Hoss. Thus the overall total from all the lists could be regarded as 3,106 names and that of the common list to be 1,300 names.

By relative analogy, therefore, since 3,106 names from the full 17 lists, containing redundant names, have led into a common list containing 1,300 names, then the total number of names in 20 lists, which include 5,821 redundant names, will result – theoretically – in a unified list containing 2,463 names.

It should be said, first of all, that the number on this list might well be slightly high or low. Nevertheless, 2,463 will not be too wide of the mark. Also, further lists known to exist were never made available. We might cite the case of the Lebanese Commission of Inquiry, which had five lists of which we gained access to only two; the other three, produced by the Medical Unit of the Lebanese Army, the Lebanese Red Cross, and relatives of the victims, remained inaccessible. The lists produced by Palestinian unions and organizations, which preferred to keep them to themselves for subsequent publication, remained similarly unavailable. We know of at least four of these. Were all lists to become available, the figure would surely exceed 3,000.

Second, it is important to note that lists of names are, in principle, qualified to produce truly accurate figures in one context only: that of a unified, official survey. Such a survey has never been carried out.

As we distributed the field study questionnaires, team members would frequently hear statements like: 'You see those torn down houses behind us? Everyone died inside.' On occasions, too, the speakers would go on to provide information about their neighbours; and at other times they would affirm that certain torn down houses had had Syrian and Egyptian labourers in them, or else Palestinian and Lebanese families that had moved to Sabra and Shatila from the South as a result of the Israeli invasion, and were not yet familiar to everyone.

We might add that, while names were being assembled, particularly in the oral history phase, people would sometimes cite numbers without recalling the names; they would talk of specific people and promise to find out the names for us, though these promises were never in practice fulfilled. Right through the past 20 years we have come to hear of new tragedies we had not encountered before.

All this leads to our final conclusion. If we consider the numbers of names on the lists, including those we had no chance to consult, and combine these with the erasure of names from people's memories, for the reasons given above, then the figure for those dead cannot be estimated at less than 3,500.

The cemeteries, mass graves and death pits.[46] It is not easy to estimate the overall number of those who died in the various mass graves, death pits or shelters. We shall therefore simply cite figures and note their source. As for the final estimate, this must inevitably be based on the very large number of burial locations specified below; it is not humanly possible to assess the number of victims in all those death pits that remain unearthed to this day.

Let us begin with burial spots on the massacre site.

The attackers buried many of their victims in a number of pits in various places, some of which were discovered and the victims subsequently reburied. This process was, however, halted after a week or so for fear of epidemics. The last mass grave to be dug up by Civil Defence men, who removed 19 bodies from it, was discovered near the unpaved road that marks the separation between the Sports City and Hayy al-Gharbi.

The death pits spread throughout Shatila and its environs (where shelters and garages were also crammed with victims) numbered more than 20. Precise locations included the Horsh, Gharbi and Ersal quarters, the yards of the Turf Club and, in particular, the yards of the Kuwaiti Embassy. There were also pits at Bir Hasan and within the Sports City.

As for the shelters, these were prime targets with people killed either inside them or close by, against walls or in yards. Among them were those of Abu Yasser, the Popular Front, the Democratic Front, Fatah, and also the garages of Abu Jamal and Darwish. There were a number of further shelters whose names were unknown to witnesses; these appear on the relevant map (see Map 5).

Many families were killed then their houses brought down over them. In a large number of cases the bodies could not be removed from under the rubble, and these victims therefore had to remain buried where they died.

In many places the attacking killers had covered up the signs of death: after the killing, bulldozers would arrive to crush the corpses. Such methods were adopted in many districts, including the quarters of Ersal, al-Gharbi and al-Horsh. These were the victims for whom no bodies or remains were found.

The attackers were not, though, concerned to hide every body. Among the exposed bodies were the four flung into the swimming pool at the Sports City. The bodies of a further 28 people were discovered bound at the Sports City.[47]

The attackers also deposited many bodies outside the camps, especially on the Saturday, using bulldozers and trucks. Then again, a number of Sabra and Shatila residents were killed outside the districts themselves. The bodies of some of these were found at al-Na'ima, Damour or other places further south, after the attackers had thrown them out of trucks driven from the Kuwaiti Embassy and on, southwards, through al-Ouza'i, Khaldeh, Haret al-Na'ima, al-Na'ima and Kfarshima. Further bodies were found on the airport road.[48] According to one testimony, in the Na'ima and Damour areas victims had also been placed in weighted bags and dumped alive in the sea to drown. These bodies remained impossible to discover.[49]

Months after the massacre, some bodies were discovered in the sewers. Among the discoverers were members of the Danish team that had come to restore the infrastructure in the first Shatila winter after September 1982. They had been puzzled by the way rainwater was flooding the streets, refusing to drain through the capacious underground sewer system. Then when the Danes removed the manhole covers and made their inspection, they found the channels of the sewer clogged by bodies thrown there during the massacre.[50] Other bodies were found later in sewers in the Bir Hasan district, near the petrol station. As they were inspecting the channels through the manholes, some young Lebanese volunteers were horrified by a fearful stench. They then began to find five or six bodies each time they inspected a section.[51]

Let us now move on to burial operations during the search for victims.

In the days immediately following the massacre, bulldozers were at work with masses of wrecked houses, rubble and bodies. They would bury the dead in groups. Most of this was over by the time burial began at the mass cemetery on Monday 20 September. Shaykh Salman al-Khalil, quoting members of the army, said they had buried the dead speedily to avoid the spread of epidemics.[52]

The number of victims buried in the mass cemetery on consecutive days from Monday 20 September on, was estimated at between 700 and 800. This cemetery, situated on the right for someone coming from the forefront of Shatila, finally became a landmark of the massacre.

As for the people who had managed to take their loved ones away for burial outside the district, they eventually buried them either in the Beirut cemeteries or in their home towns and villages. The number of victims buried at the Rawdat al-Shahidein and Shuhada cemeteries was reckoned (as noted earlier) at 334, 45 of whom were anonymous and were consequently buried in the French mass grave. Most of these latter were labourers whose names remained unknown but whose nationalities were known: they were from Pakistan, India, Syria and Bangladesh.[53]

Hundreds of others were buried in further graveyards in Beirut or transferred for burial in their home towns. Civil Defence and Red Cross sources estimated that around 1,200 bodies were taken by the families concerned, who buried them at their own expense. This figure is, however, exaggerated, and should perhaps be seen in conjunction with the unwillingness to publicize those great numbers soon found to have been concealed by the attackers, along with the ones buried in Shatila before the Monday; that is, before the official religious burial in the mass cemetery.

An official of the Scouts of Al-Risala al-Islamiyieh estimated the number of victims taken for burial outside Beirut at 200–300.[54] As for the places involved, these were mainly in the Tyre region, notably at the towns of Qana and Majdal Zoun, where 20 victims were buried on 20 September.[55] A further 56 victims were buried on 24 September: 40, eight, five and three victims were buried, respectively, at Bar'asheit, Majdal Zoun, al-Rashidiyyeh Camp and Abu al-Aswad.[56] In Baalbek, 20 victims were buried in the town of al-Nabi Sheit after 20 September.[57] A number of victims were also buried in the Shouf district.[58]

A reasonable minimum estimate of the number of victims in all the above categories would be around 3,500.

Percentages for nationalities: comparison between the sources

One of the subjects analysed in the field study of the preceding chapter was the nationality of victims. In this section, we shall compare the percentages for victims' nationalities as established in the field study list (see List of names 1), with the percentages for nationalities based on the list of victims, which is in turn based on various sources (see List of names 3).

The total number of victims' names in List 1 was 430, while that in List 3 was 906. The nationalities for some of the names in this latter list were retrieved from one or more sources, nationalities for the rest being mentioned in no source; the number of victims of known nationality was 595. Comparison is therefore between 430 victims in List 1 and 595 in List 3.

Palestinian victims totalled 209 (48.60%) in List 1, while in List 3 they totalled 305 (51.09%). Lebanese victims totalled 120 (27.91%) in List 1, 178 (29.82%) in List 3.

Stateless ('under review' card holders) totalled 31 (7.21%) in List 1, 35 (5.88%) in List 3. Syrian victims totalled 23 (5.35%) in List 1, 30 (5.04%) in List 3. Egyptian victims totalled 18 (4.19%) in List 1, 23 (3.85%) in List 3.

The closeness between the percentages over the two lists attests to their reliability – the percentage for Palestinians increases by approximately 3%, that for Lebanese by 2%, which is a natural outcome of the various sources for List 3. As for the reduced percentage for stateless in List 3, this may be attributed to the families in question not coming forward to register their victims' names. Some had left the district in any case; others felt their continued deprivation of Lebanese identity entailed a deprivation of all rights. This latter point is reflected in the special effort needed by members of the field study team in gaining access to information about victims in this category – most of the information came, indeed, through neighbours and friends.

As for Syrians and Egyptians, the percentages here change hardly at all, falling by a mere fraction of 1 per cent. Much the same applies to the other nationalities – Bangladeshis, Jordanians, Turks, Sudanese, Algerians, Pakistanis, Iranians and Tunisians – which showed a percentage of approximately 1 per cent or less; here again the percentages remained fairly close.

As for the nationalities of abducted and missing, a corresponding comparison was made between the field study list (see List of names 2), and the list of abducted and missing based on various sources (see List of names 4).

Abducted in List 2 totalled 100, whereas abducted and missing in List 4 totalled 484. However (as with victims in List 3, and for the same reasons), not all the nationalities in the List 4 were known. The number of known nationality was 173.

The number of Palestinian abducted totalled 66 (66.00%) in List 2, while Palestinian abducted and missing totalled 116 (67.05%) in List 4. For Lebanese, abducted totalled 11 (11.00%) in List 2, while abducted and missing totalled 26 (15.03%) in List 4. For Syrians, abducted totalled 13

(13.00%) in List 2, while abducted and missing totalled 18 (10.40%) in List 4. For stateless ('under review' card holders), abducted totalled 6 (6.00%) in List 2, while abducted and missing also totalled 6 (3.47%) in List 4. For Egyptians, abducted totalled 3 (3.00%) in List 2, while abducted and missing totalled 4 (2.31%) in List 4.

List 2 contains a single British abducted also present in List 4, while List 4 contains a category, not found in List 2, for two missing Turks.

We may note that the percentage of Palestinians has, naturally enough, increased by 1 per cent in List 4 as compared to List 2. As for the 4 per cent increase in Lebanese, this reflects public attention directed towards the abducted and missing – something further manifested in Dar al-Fatwa's initiative in registering their names, in collaboration with the Committee for Families of the Kidnapped and Disappeared in Lebanon, and with others. The decrease in Syrians by around 3 per cent stems from the departure of most Syrian nationals during this phase. As for the inclusion in List 2 of the names of a number of Syrians and those of other nationalities whose families had already left, this is because the field study team did not restrict completion of questionnaires to immediate families; neighbours and friends were also brought within the scope of the investigation.

Broadly speaking, we may note that the percentages for List 3 bear out those for List 1. In the same way, those for List 4 bear out those for List 2.

Percentages for women and children: comparison between the sources

The percentage of women and children was also among the matters analysed in the preceding chapter. Let us now compare the relevant percentages obtained from List 1 with their counterparts from List 3.

In List 1, female victims totalled 112 (26.05%); in List 3, they totalled 201 (22.18%). The 4 per cent decrease in the latter is consistent with the fact that the field study team went to the massacre area and distributed questionnaires without waiting for families to register the names of the victims concerned. As such it was natural that the number of families and females should be higher here than in List 3, which depended on people's positive initiative in coming forward to register. In addition, the questionnaires involved information supplied not only by the immediate families concerned but also by neighbours and more distant relatives. In a number of cases, in fact, the families themselves were no longer available in the spring of 1984 when the field study was being undertaken. This applied especially to families of some Arab nationalities and to stateless families.

Figures for female abducted and missing differ markedly from those for female victims. A number of women were abducted on the first night, but no further abduction of women was noted, for example, on the Saturday, when large numbers of men were taken away. Abduction clearly had young men as its focus: List 2 (for those abducted) contained no female names, whereas List 4 contained 32 females (women and young girls) out of a total of 484 abducted and missing. While the resulting percentage of 6.61% may appear low, it should never, of course, have been present in the first place.

On the other hand, the number of younger people (unborn babies, infants and children up to twelve years old) totalled 95 (22.09%) in List 1. In List 3, age is only sometimes mentioned: for 585 victims out of a total of 906. Of these, children account for 108 (18.46%).

All the indications are that, had age been available for more of the victims on List 3, the percentage would have been close to that for List 1; this judgement is based on personal knowledge of some of the families named, where children were certainly among the victims. We could not, however, as a matter of methodological principle, 'fill in' information where it was not formally available. The one obvious exception to this rule involved the gender of the victim, which could be automatically inferred from the name supplied.

The Lebanese report: numbers of victims

The official Lebanese report – commonly known as the Jermanos Report after the military investigating judge, Ass'ad Jermanos, who had presided over the Commission of Inquiry – was never officially published by the government. Nor are there any signs that it ever will be. It was frequently stated that it had disappeared from the ministries and institutions where it should have been found. However, *Yedioth Ahronoth* published extracts, along with a summary, as soon as it was issued.[59] Basing itself on the Israeli newspaper, the Lebanese *Al-Safir* then published a summary of the summary,[60] and other Lebanese papers subsequently published material along the same lines. The impression gained from all these writings is that the report was finalized on 29 September, that is, eleven days after the end of the massacre.

The most significant points of the summarized version were the numbers of victims cited and the identity of those who did the counting. On the basis of the full copy of the report it had received, *Yedioth Ahronoth* stated that the victim count came from five sources: namely, the Medical Unit of the Lebanese Army, the relatives of victims, the Lebanese Civil Defence in Beirut, the Lebanese Red Cross and the ICRC. The 'total' number of victims was 470, distributed as follows: 328 Palestinians (including seven women and eight children); 109 Lebanese (including eight women and twelve children); seven Syrians; three Pakistanis; two Algerians; 21 Iranians.[61]

It was clear that these figures were significantly lower than the ones previously published by the Lebanese press on a day-by-day basis. The problem, though, was not so much the final number (especially if we remember Toynbee's dictum, that it is enough to kill once to be a killer) as the report itself and its readiness to issue implausible figures.

Was it conceivable that just 20 children had been killed at Sabra and Shatila? Did the people framing the report really believe that those living in Lebanon, Lebanese or otherwise, would be so sunk in oblivion? That they would forget what their own eyes had seen on the television screen, or in the newspapers? Had mere photographs not shown larger numbers of children than this? How many children had perished from the Lebanese Miqdad family alone? From the Palestinian Muhammad family alone? And then, what of the women? Just eight Lebanese women, and seven Palestinian? The whole thing was absurd.

The figures – as most criticisms of the summary stressed – were designed to substantiate the notion of a battle rather than a massacre having occurred. Men, after all, are mostly the ones who fall in battle; and here was Sabra and Shatila, where most of the victims were men!

In principle, no doubt, it is wrong to comment on a report or other piece of research before reading the whole document. But no such inhibition need apply to comments on published figures. The summary confirmed the report's effective conclusion: that a battle had taken place. This matter will be considered further in the Conclusion.

As for the figures themselves, notably those for women and children, there are two possible reactions to such callous indifference towards the feelings of afflicted Sabra and Shatila residents and to such apparent disregard for the power of human memory. The first is to take refuge in a degree of innumeracy beyond all logic or reason. The second is to search, with uncompromising dedication, for the true figures, along with names, nationalities, gender and even the facial features of the people concerned, whose pictures had hung on their walls. We have chosen the second course.

Let us begin with the sources on which the figures of the Jermanos Report were based. These, as noted above, were five in number, but we succeeded in gaining access to only two of the lists involved: those of the ICRC and the Lebanese Civil Defence. So just what did these have to say of the number of women and children killed at Sabra and Shatila?

The Jermanos Report specified the sub-totals for women and children as 15 and 20 respectively, out of the total of 470 victims, with nationalities as noted above. As for the lists in question, the number of names we retrieved from the Civil Defence list was 254,[62] and from the ICRC list 179.[63] Only

seven of the latter were not common to the two lists, resulting in an overall total of 261; and this overall total included names for 29 Palestinian females[64] and 26 Lebanese females.[65]

The brief summary of the Jermanos Report, which we read in translation (from Arabic to Hebrew and thence back to Arabic), spoke quite specifically of 'women' and not 'females'. The text read as follows:

And the Report notes that most of the Palestinian male victims were killed as the result of a military battle. Only seven Palestinian women and eight Palestinian children were killed. The Report also noted that 109 Lebanese were killed in the two camps, including twelve children and eight women.[66]

What does the word 'women' mean in this report? Just the married ones? And what of the little girls killed while on their mothers' laps? And the girls in the flower of youth, at 14 or 17? Where were these to be classified?

In the preceding chapter we specified the ages precisely, and we shall follow the same procedure here.

Included among the Palestinian females were two in their second year; one three-year-old; three five-year-olds; one six-year-old; three seven-year-olds; one eleven-year-old and one twelve-year-old. These little girls aged twelve or under numbered twelve.

As for those above twelve years of age, there were one 16-year-old; two 17-year-olds, one of whom was married; and the remainder ranging from 19 to 67 years old, most of them mothers and grandmothers.

Included among the Lebanese females were one newborn; one two-year-old; one three-year-old; two seven-year-olds and one eleven-year-old. Here the little girls numbered six.

As for the ages of Lebanese females over twelve, there were two 13-year-olds; two 15-year-olds; one 16-year-old, and the remainder from 25 to 62 years old – most of them, again, mothers and grandmothers.

In comparison with the Jermanos Report, which noted the presence of seven Palestinian women within five lists (from the total of 470 names), we found 29 Palestinian females in just two of the report's five reference lists (involving a total of 261 names). As for Lebanese women, we found 26 in these two lists, as against eight in the report. The total was therefore 55 against 15.

Moreover, the former number increased to 65 when ten females from other nationalities were added. Did these last not merit a mention, on simple human grounds? Most were married women accompanying husbands who had come for work. They comprised three Syrians, two Egyptians, one Pakistani and four whose nationalities remained unknown.

Let us now move on to the ages of the children, boys and girls together. How does the figure of eight Palestinian children given by the Report compare with the figures given in the ICRC and LCD lists?

These latter lists spoke of 103 Palestinian victims, including 19 children, whether girls or boys. These comprised three two-year-olds; two three-year-olds; four five-year-olds; two six-year-olds; three seven-year-olds; one nine-year-old; two eleven-year-olds and two twelve-year-olds. What if we had contrived to gain access to the three remaining lists? Might the total number of children not have risen beyond 19, especially as one of the lists had been compiled with the aid of testimonies from families?

As for Lebanese victims in the two lists, these totalled 99, 16 of them children, male or female, with the following age distribution: one infant; two two-year-olds; one three-year-old; two six-year-olds; two seven-year-olds; four eight-year-olds; three ten-year-olds and one eleven-year-old.

In sum, the official report specified 20 children killed based on five lists, as against 35 revealed, on inspection, in just two of these lists. Once more the question imposes itself. Suppose we had had access to the three further lists?

Finally, less for the sake of formal comparison than out of respect for the victims' souls, we might return once more to the preceding chapter where a total of 430 victims in the field study revealed 95 child victims aged twelve or under.[67]

The Israeli report: numbers of victims

The release of the Kahan Report on 7 February 1983 was viewed as an event of the highest importance; indeed, no comparable report anywhere throughout the twentieth century was accorded such a degree of media attention. This was not on account of any specific details, findings or judgements it contained, but because it was intended as a kind of flagship for the existence of democracy in Israel. This section does not aim to define the actual extent of democracy in Israel, or to comment on the world-wide chorus of admiration the Report's issue evoked. All this will be considered in the Conclusion. For the moment we shall restrict ourselves to the specific issue of victim numbers.

According to the Kahan Report, the number of victims was impossible to determine accurately, since only very partial figures were available and even these were not from reliable sources. It further stated that the reduced estimates had originated from sources linked to the Government of Lebanon or the Lebanese Forces.

The report first set down the figures of the ICRC, based on the contents of a letter sent by the President of the Red Cross delegation in Lebanon to the Israeli Minister of Defence. Red Cross representatives had, the letter said, managed to count 328 bodies; this, however, was not comprehensive, since many families had buried the bodies of relatives on their own initiative, without reference to the Red Cross; also, the Forces who had carried out the attacks had, before leaving Shatila, taken bodies away in trucks. It was possible that further bodies remained beneath the rubble in the camps or in graves dug by the attackers near the camps. As for those missing, the letter stated that the Red Cross had a list of 359 people, all of whom had disappeared in West Beirut between 18 August and 20 September. Most of these had in fact disappeared in Sabra and Shatila in mid-September.[68]

The Kahan Report next touched on other figures derived from an unspecified document – one of a number of documents and credentials that remained secret and accordingly had to be indicated by means of a special reference: '(Exhibit 151)'. In fact, a brief inspection of figures and sources makes it clear enough that these are the same as the ones found in the Lebanese Jermanos Report, as published in the *Yedioth Ahronoth* newspaper. There is just one difference: the Kahan Report stated a total of 460 bodies, as against 470 in the newspaper. The report provided no details of other nationalities, which would have enabled the reader to calculate which of the two figures was correct.[69]

The Kahan Report did, however, provide explicit details for Palestinian and Lebanese victims, repeating the Lebanese report's statements for the overall total in each category, and also repeating the details about 20 children (twelve Lebanese, eight Palestinian) and 15 women (eight Lebanese, seven Palestinian).

The Kahan Report made no comment on these last figures (for children and women), which are refutable by reason, conscience and memory alike. Perhaps those framing the report decided they bore no responsibility in the matter, since they were merely transcribing the contents of the secret document '(Exhibit 151)'. This does not, however, excuse them.

They bore a weight of responsibility because the world held the report in such high regard (being, as it was, the outcome of large numbers of testimonies), and above all because the aberrations were so glaring. In the circumstances they were morally bound to pursue one of the following courses: to refrain from publishing such misleading figures at all; to publish them while underlining their lack of credibility (since the Israeli soldiers besieging Sabra and Shatila had seen with their own eyes how many women and children were being killed); or, if they really believed in the figures' credibility, to publish them with supporting argument.

In fact the depth of conflict between the figures and the reality quickly becomes clear, especially when the report does in fact reject the total number of victims given in the secret '(Exhibit 151)' document. It cannot, it says, regard figures from Lebanese sources as reliable. Nor can it regard as reliable figures from Palestinian sources, going into the thousands. There were also, it stated,

problems in discriminating between victims of combat and those otherwise killed.

The Kahan Report finally decided, bolstered by the Red Cross representatives' count of just 328 bodies, that the number of victims was below 1,000, and certainly not in the thousands. The Intelligence Unit of the Israeli Army, as embodied in the testimony of the Head of Military Intelligence to the Kahan Commission, set the number of victims at 700–800, and the report concluded that this assessment was substantially accurate.[70]

There was another Israeli source, and one that preceded the release of Kahan by over four months, though those compiling the report chose to disregard it. That source was the Israeli Army Radio Station. On 23 September this station affirmed that the number of victims of the Sabra and Shatila massacres had exceeded 4,000, and might have been as high as 7,000. It went on to say that 2,400 bodies had been buried, that hundreds more were still under the rubble, and that hundreds of bodies had been buried with a view to concealing the true number of victims.[71]

Clearly the figure of 7,000 was exaggerated. It was clear, too, that the figure had come out while the search for victims was still going on; whoever was involved in surveillance of the massacre site during this period was giving heightened figures more influenced by the piles of bodies and generally horrific sights than by reasoned calculation or evidence. A similar case emerged when a Lebanese police officer, also involved in the surveillance, told me the number of victims was 6,000. When I asked him how he could be so sure of this, he said: 'Because of what people said, the ones who saw everything after the massacre; because of the mass graves; because of all the people who went and never came back.'[72]

There is a vast gulf between the figure of 6,000 or 7,000 from various sources, suggested by horrific sights confronting the naked eye, and the range of 700–800 adopted by the Kahan Report. To reach the figure closest to reality requires a detailed study appropriate to such a major and tragic event, and this we have tried to undertake.

Earlier in this chapter we responded to Kahan's estimated figure, specifying the number of victims substantiated by names at 1,300, and inferred a minimum total number of 3,500 (see above, pp. 287–90).

Conclusion

- The Sabra and Shatila massacre found no single authority, either Lebanese or Palestinian, prepared to assume responsibility for the publication of names and numbers of victims.
- After the massacre, and through to the end of September, the daily press regularly published numbers for victims, some of these being estimates, others being based on official statistics. There were, however, discrepancies in the figures, involving as much as hundreds and thousands. Sometimes there were even discrepancies in figures derived from a single source.
- Unofficial numbers for victims, on the part of the Lebanese government, the International Committee of the Red Cross and the Lebanese Red Cross, reached around 2,000, 2,750 and 3,000 respectively. These statistics, in no case officially announced, were reported secretly to foreign investigators and writers.
- In its compilation of numbers documented by names, this study relied on 17 lists of names, classifiable as follows:
  - Lists assembled at the massacre site and at the cemeteries, originating from the following sources: the International Committee of the Red Cross; the Lebanese Civil Defence; the Middle East Council of Churches; Rawdat al-Shahidein cemetery; Shaykh Salman al-Khalil and al-Shuhada cemetery.
  - Lists assembled during the months following the massacre, originating from the following sources: the Palestinian Red Crescent Society; the Democratic Front for the Liberation of Palestine; an 'anonymous' Palestinian organization; Dar al-Fatwa in the Lebanese republic; the Committee for Families of the Kidnapped and Disappeared in Lebanon; a common list for the abducted and missing, compiled by a number of organizations, and the Lebanese daily press.
  - Lists assembled through individual research or through official committees or judicial commissions, originating from the following sources: the Oral History Project; the Field Study Project; the Official Commission of Inquiry into the Fate of the Abducted and Missing and the lawsuit to the Belgian judiciary against Sharon.
- The names from all the various sources were set down in Appendix 2 in four lists, comprising a total of 906 victims and 484 abducted and missing.
- Given that none of the abducted and few of the missing have ever returned (and taking into account rumours of a small number of missing reappearing), and basing ourselves also on the position of the government vis-à-vis the case of those abducted and missing on Lebanese soil since the mid-1970s, namely that these should all be regarded as dead, the total number was considered to comprise 1,300 victims out of the 1,390 gross total. The remaining 90 were classified among the missing or actual returnees.
- To reach the 'estimate figures', we followed two different patterns: first, through the numbers of victims as determined by reviewing the lists of names; and second, through an overall estimate of the people buried in cemeteries, mass graves and death pits, and buried beneath the rubble. The two taken together led us to conclude a minimum figure of 3,500 victims.
- Comparison between the percentages obtained from the field study and those retrieved through the list of names based on various sources provided verification of the percentages for the different nationalities and for women and children, the relevant figures being close for each category.
- The figures appearing in both the official Lebanese report (the Jermanos Report) and the Israeli report (the Kahan Report) were analysed and were found in each case to be misleading and vastly wide of the mark.

Conclusion: Who was Responsible?

Twenty years have now elapsed since the Sabra and Shatila massacre, and the question remains: Who was responsible?

When news of the massacre broke, some were not slow to lay the blame on the Israeli Forces. After all, they were the ones that had lain siege to the district, controlled all access, prevented the inhabitants from leaving and supervised the entry of the armed killers. The latter's identities had not as yet been revealed, but it was clear they were Lebanese and under the overall control of the Israeli Army, which had adopted, for its headquarters, a strategic location from which it could overlook Sabra and Shatila.

Among the accusers were Israeli citizens, of whom the writer Jacobo Timerman was one of the first to write about the responsibility issue; even while, indeed, the removal of rubble and the search for victims was still in progress. He had just completed a work on Israel's war in Lebanon, 'the longest war'. However, when he heard of the massacre, he returned to add some final pages.

Timerman made reference to three protests that took place in Israel the day after the news had begun to spread: one on the Haifa highway, another in Jerusalem and a third near the Lebanese borders, where several hundred people had staged a demonstration. He commented as follows on events he clearly regarded as insufficient in number:

This is almost all that took place in Israel, even though news of the massacre of the Palestinians had already been known for twenty-four hours, even though all of us realized it had been organized by our army.

Why are the Israelis incapable of recognizing the high degree of criminality in their army's campaign against the Palestinian People?[1]

In contrast to Timerman's contention – that the Israeli Army had organized the massacre and had, indeed, led a high-level criminal campaign against the Palestinian people – the official position of the Israeli government, as manifested in its first statement, was a denial of all responsibility:

On [the Jewish] New Year's Eve, a lie was woven against the Israeli state, government and army. Moving from a position at which the Israeli Army was not present, a Lebanese unit gained access to a district where there were saboteurs, in order to have these latter arrested; and this unit harmed civilian residents, causing large numbers of casualties. In noting this fact, the government would like to express its sorrow at what has occurred. As soon as the Israeli Army realized what was happening, it called a halt to the killing of innocent people and compelled the Lebanese unit to leave the district.

The civilian population, in its turn, expressed its thanks to the Israeli Army for having moved so swiftly to its aid.

The government rejects, in the most uncompromising fashion, any fatuous accusations made ... It is clear the saboteurs had abruptly violated the departure agreement by leaving two thousand men behind in Beirut. It was further revealed that they had left behind huge amounts of heavy weaponry – tanks, artillery, mortars and ammunition.[2]

This short official statement by the Israelis contains no fewer than seven flaws, which will be considered in detail in the following pages. For the moment we may point them out briefly, as follows. It is not true that the Lebanese unit had made unauthorized entry from a location at which the Israeli Army was not present; they had in fact made their incursion through points of access over which the Israeli Army held full control, using, indeed, the very roads they had been instructed to use. It was abundantly clear the district contained no 'saboteurs' or 'terrorists'. The Israeli Army did not, when it heard what had been happening, place any limitation on activities. The residents expressed no thanks to the Israelis for their help, which had never existed in the first place. The Palestinian fighters did not leave behind 2,000 'saboteurs', either in the camps or elsewhere in Beirut. No one had any knowledge of the presence of Palestinian tanks or of those 'huge' amounts of artillery and other equipment.

Two days after the release of the official Israeli statement, the Prime Minister, Menachem Begin, made his own celebrated statement; one that became a byword for Israel's policy. 'What is there to investigate?' he asked. '*Goyim* [non-Jews] are killing *Goyim*. Are we supposed to be hanged for that?'[3]

Between these two contradictory Israeli positions – those of Timerman the free writer and Begin, who seemed utterly indifferent to the tragedies of others – politicians in Israel went on with their mutual recriminations and internal disputes, the most significant of these being the fierce argument between Ariel Sharon and Shimon Perez in the Knesset. Sharon, in his speech,

recalled parts of the Lebanese war and the major role the previous Labour government had played in its intensification. Then he addressed Perez as follows: 'You didn't show much concern over the Tall al-Za'tar massacre. Would you care to say where the Israeli officers were when the Tall al-Za'tar massacre happened, and who they were getting their orders from?' Sharon's remarks represented, for the first time, an Israeli admission of the part played by Israeli Army officers in the siege of the Palestinian Tall al-Za'tar refugee camp, which had fallen to the Phalangists on 12 August 1976, following a siege of more than 50 days.

Then came the turn of Shimon Perez, head of the Labour opposition to Begin's government, to mount the podium and deny the Israeli Army had had any connection with the Tall al-Za'tar massacre. Sharon, however, kept up his accusations, supported, finally, by Menachem Begin, who claimed, in general response, that 'the Opposition is attempting to exploit the tragedy of Beirut to serve its own political ends'.[4]

As for the Israeli public, their position differed from that of the government. This was best evidenced by a major demonstration on 25 September of over 400,000 citizens crying out against the massacre and demanding an investigation. An investigation did indeed follow, resulting, something over four months later, in an official report known as the Kahan Report, after the Commission's Chairman Judge Yitzak Kahan, Head of the Supreme Court (subsequently referred to as 'the report').[5]

The conclusions of the report could be summed up in one simple statement: that senior Israeli decision-makers bore no direct responsibility because they had not known what was happening. The report ascribed an indirect responsibility only, reserving direct responsibility for those who had actually carried out the massacre – these being the Lebanese Forces, with no mention of any other Christian Lebanese militias. Sa'd Haddad's forces were totally excluded from responsibility.

The following pages do not constitute a formal trial. This conclusion does not aim to reach a verdict, and lacks the means to do so in any case. It will nonetheless consider all the available data regarding every party, whether derived from the oral history, the field study or any of the various other sources. From all this, perhaps, may emerge material that will be of help to those defending human rights, under the auspices of an equitable court ruling in accordance with international laws and with the human conventions commonly observed among nations.

International laws

The occupation of a country, or part of a country, does not absolve the occupying state from multiple obligations, first of which is the protection of the civilian population.

Moreover, the responsibility of the military or political leaders occupying a particular region is not confined to any war crimes they might personally commit; they are also liable for all such crimes committed by members of lower ranks in their military hierarchy, and by any other forces or collaborators under their control. These war crimes include massacres against civilians.

Under internationally recognized laws, a military commander or political leader is responsible if he possesses actual knowledge, or might reasonably be expected to possess such knowledge through reports he receives, or by other means, that troops or other persons under his control are about to commit or have committed a war crime, and if he has failed to take the necessary steps to guarantee compliance with the rules of war, or has failed to punish those violating these rules. Indeed, the leader's failure to take necessary steps to prevent the violation of international laws, or his failure to punish the violators, effectively implies approval of the crime, or at least connivance in it.[6]

In other words, criminal responsibility falls on the leaders if, as persons in authority, they

1. knew, or should have known, that crimes were regularly being committed;
2. had the power to intervene to halt the criminal practices, and
3. had special responsibility for the area in question.[7]

Implementation of a massacre, or the issuing of orders to carry out a massacre, by a responsible government official, makes this person liable to prosecution as a war criminal irrespective of whether his domestic laws would penalize the action. Such a person remains subject to punishment by the international community, or before an international war crimes tribunal, or by any state whose laws allow for the conviction of war criminals.[8]

Under the terms of the 1949 Geneva Conventions, no party to the conventions may absolve itself, or any other party under its jurisdiction or control, of any liability incurred with respect to the binding law of the conventions, or any breaches of that law.

Massacres and other atrocities have been deemed 'grave breaches' of the Geneva Conventions, and also of their 1977 Protocol. While none of the states party to the armed conflict in Lebanon has formally ratified the 1977 Protocol, substantial international legal opinion holds that the protocols are nonetheless binding on the parties, including Israel, because they do no more than restate and codify existing binding international customary law on the subject.

Not every violation of the law or with respect to armed conflict is a war crime. In the 1949 Geneva Conventions, a distinction is made between 'grave breaches' and 'violations which are not grave breaches'. In the case of 'grave breaches' which are themselves war crimes, the obligation of all High Contracting Parties to the convention is to enact legislation providing for effective penal sanctions. For High Contracting Parties (nations which have ratified the General Convention) involved in armed conflict, the obligations are to seek out persons alleged to have committed, or to have ordered to be committed, such 'grave breaches', or to hand such persons over for trial to another High Contracting Party.[9]

So the question is: What are the obligations of a state or authority occupying another's land with regard to the prevention of war crimes?

Under the Geneva Conventions and international customary law, the occupying state or power, even if it has not itself committed the massacres, remains the responsible party under international law. In the case of Sabra and Shatila, Israel is responsible; it was the obligation of the occupiers to act to halt the massacre the moment they learned of it. It was also their duty to arrest those ultimately responsible and punish those found to be guilty.[10]

Contrary to what Israel has more than once contended, that international laws applying to nations occupying others' territories were not applicable in her case, she was in fact an occupying power as specified by international law. Consequently, the internationally recognized laws applying to occupying nations should be enforced against her, as stated in Article 42 of the 1907 Hague Convention, the 1949 Geneva Convention (IV) and the 1977 Protocol I Additional to the Geneva Conventions. All these laws agree that, should any nation place in subjection any foreign power on any territory, it thereby becomes the occupying power in that territory. In addition to certain rights an occupying power normally possesses as the result of war or invasion, such a power also inherits the obligations and correlative duties with respect to the local resident population.[11]

In sum, the residents of Sabra and Shatila were 'protected persons' according to Geneva Convention IV, and Israel, as an occupying power, was under a special obligation to prevent the commission of 'outrages' and barbaric attacks committed against them.[12]

Article 73 of Protocol I expressly extends protected persons status to refugees and stateless persons, a status clearly applicable to Palestinians, including males (and also applicable to those residing in Lebanon but carrying identity cards marked 'under consideration'). Articles 75–7 of the protocol elaborate on the quality of protection legally imposed on an Occupying Power, singling out women and children, in Articles 76 and 77, for particular concern. Article 51 (I) of the Protocol asserts the basic principle that 'the civilian population and individual civilians shall enjoy general protection against dangers arising from military operations'. Given the peaceful, quiet state of the camps in early September, there seems every reason

to regard their inhabitants as 'civilians', even if there were individuals among their number with links to the PLO.[13]

As to the responsibility issue, the MacBride Report stated that Israeli responsibility for these incidents was one shared with the members of the Lebanese militias and the individual fighters who committed the massacre.[14] This report concluded that Israel was the occupying power of the camps area from 15 September up to its eventual withdrawal; that is to say, it was the occupying power throughout the three days of the massacre. Geneva Convention IV, 1949, and Protocol I, 1977, together clearly set out the duties and responsibilities of an occupying power and formulate the protection to which those under occupation are entitled. Israel is a party to Geneva Convention IV.[15]

It is now 20 years since the Sabra and Shatila massacre and, up to now, the criminals who committed it, the Lebanese militiamen, have still not been brought to trial. Nor have any of the Israelis who protected and facilitated their mission, rather than protecting unarmed civilians.

International laws are available. It is suitable international courts that are hard to find.

International and American guarantees

Talks about international guarantees had begun, behind the scenes, two months or more before the massacre, and had ended just a few days before the departure of the Palestinian fighters, by which point the talk was of specifically American guarantees. In reality, however, neither international nor American guarantees were remotely in force in mid-September. Had such guarantees existed in practice for the protection of civilians, the Sabra and Shatila massacre would never have happened.

In point of fact American guarantees were in place, but they were insufficient. There is a viewpoint that, if even only these had been respected, there would have been no massacre. Guarantees, however, are one thing; the protection of guarantees to ensure they do not remain mere ink on paper is quite another matter.

The position of the Palestine Liberation Organization with respect to these guarantees was extremely firm during early exchanges of opinion. American envoy Philip Habib presided over all the meetings that took place between the Lebanese and Palestinian sides, and the eventual agreement relating to the departure of the Palestinian fighters became known as the Habib Agreement.

On 8 July, the Palestinian leadership sent telexes from Beirut to its representative offices all over the world; these comprised a draft copy of an agreement with the eleven points originally proposed by the Palestinian side. Now all Palestinian ambassadors and office directors were asked to publicize and promote these points, particularly among friendly host states.

The main proposals were: a ceasefire; the provision of international forces to supervise a disengagement between the Palestinian and Israeli forces; the withdrawal of Israeli forces to five miles; and the withdrawal of Palestinian forces from Beirut by land, carrying their personal arms and under the protection of 'international guarantees'.[16]

As to guarantees for Palestinian civilians remaining in Lebanon under international auspices, three articles dealt specifically with this:

6. The security of the Palestinian camps will be ensured by the international force and guaranteed internationally. This shall be coordinated with the P.L.O. in order to avoid what happened in the Palestinian camps of the South of Lebanon, and in Tal al-Zaatar camp [in 1976], at hands of Israeli and Phalangist forces.
...
9. It should be well understood that the rights of the Palestinian people [in Lebanon] are to be preserved and that the international forces shall guarantee these rights, that are recognized by the Lebanese government and the United Nations.
...
11. D-day is the day when the commander of the international force notifies us of his forces' readiness to execute their mission, this being:

a. Protecting the Palestinian camps against any aggression.

b. Taking up positions in the disengagement area and securing routes, including Beirut-Damascus international highway.[17]

When the parties concerned reached a final agreement on 11 August, the above-mentioned points proposed by the Palestinian side had almost completely evaporated.

The agreement was published on 20 August and its implementation was underway the next day, 21 August: the first day of the departure of Palestinian fighters, at a time when only the French international force had arrived. In fact the French, who had dispatched their forces to supervise the safe withdrawal of the fighters, had expressed their concern over the written guarantees for the security of Palestinian civilians. These had become completely divorced from the international framework, being now restricted to American guarantees that were in turn based on what the US itself might obtain from Israel and the Lebanese Forces (who were not specified by name but implied in the expression 'certain Lebanese groups'). The French further promised to bring the subject up with the Americans, but the eventual outcome indicated that the Americans had done things their own way. This is evident from the hasty departure of the forces dispatched to supervise the safe departure of the fighters: these former had all left before the end date planned, and this in turn caused the Italian and French Forces to leave.[18]

Many questions remain to be answered. Why did the international forces leave before the date set? Would the Sabra and Shatila massacre have taken place had the Italian and French Forces been maintaining the security of the camps? Why had the American Forces left so quickly, before guaranteeing Palestinians' safety, something to which they had formally committed themselves in the Habib Agreement? The relevant passage runs as follows:

The Governments of Lebanon and the United States will provide appropriate guarantees of the safety ... of law-abiding Palestinian non-combatants left in Beirut, including the families of those who have departed ... The U.S. will provide its guarantees on the basis of assurances received from the government of Israel and from the leaders of certain Lebanese groups with which it has been in contact.[19]

Lebanon, revealed by the above to be a partner of the United States in the delivery of guarantees, does not appear to have been politically affected by the matter. Its primary concern was the departure of the fighters, at whatever cost and in any manner. The Lebanese President-elect Bashir al-Gemayel had made the following statement to Israeli television during the departure stage:

As for the Palestinian fighters, they must leave Lebanon to the last man.

It is not I who have evicted them from their homes or caused their troubles ... Lebanon has devoted more effort than any other country to trying to help the Palestinians.[20]

He further stated, in another interview with foreign correspondents:

The armed Palestinian force must withdraw, and may go wherever it wishes. As for Palestinian civilians, they will become subject to the laws applicable in Lebanon; they must pay what they owe, be that bills or traffic penalties ... When the departure of Palestinian fighters from Beirut has been completed, I shall work jointly with the American envoy Philip Habib, so as to drive Palestinian fighters out, also, of al-Beka'a, the North and the South.[21]

The Lebanese side made no guarantees public till the day the Palestinian Chairman Yasser Arafat left by sea, the Lebanese President Elias Sarkis having sent him a verbal farewell message through the head of the Lebanese Army Intelligence Department, Colonel Johnny Abdo. The meeting between the two men lasted two hours but contained no promises on behalf of the Lebanese President, only good wishes.[22] On the following day Colonel Abdo returned to deliver a further farewell message on behalf of President-elect Bashir al-Gemayel, and this, it is said, contained 'some reassurances with regard to Palestinian civilians remaining in Lebanon'.[23]

In Tunisia, the first exile to which the Palestinian leadership moved from that in Lebanon, the Palestinian Chairman expressed his deep fears, during an interview

with the French envoys Gutman and Delaye on 4 September, with regard to the security of Palestinian civilians remaining in Beirut. He would be reassured, he implied, if the French force were to remain beyond the predetermined period, which was due to end on 21 September.[24] Little did Chairman Arafat know that the French Forces would actually withdraw ten days before the deadline, that all the guarantees would become ineffective and that his fears were to be justified in full.

The myth of the '2,500' fighters

To many people it appeared that the myth of the 2,000 Palestinian fighters (more or less) who stayed behind had begun to spread only from mid-September onwards. In fact the notion had been propagated some time before that; indeed, before the fighters' departure. It seems odd, to say the least, that there should have been talk of numbers remaining behind at a time when no one had actually left.

According to David Shipler, both American and Israeli intelligence had, prior to the departure of the PLO, received information that the Palestinians planned to leave behind some 1,500–2,000 guerrillas, whose mission would be to blend in with civilians with a view to reorganizing at the first opportunity.[25] What follows will show how far-fetched this notion was.

The other issue, which aroused as much interest as that concerning the number of 'delinquent fighters', was the supposed difference between the number of Palestinian fighters whose departure was originally agreed and the number that actually left. Discrepancies between the two figures assumed incredible proportions. Before the departure, *Yedioth Ahronoth* conceded that estimates for the numbers of PLO members were changing all the time; there had earlier been talk of 6,000, whereas the number now appeared to be 10,000.[26]

One week later, in mid-August, the same newspaper stated on its front page that 7,100 'saboteurs', together with 3,000 Syrians and their supporters, were to be expelled. On the second page, however, the military correspondent Eshan Happer wrote of very large numbers, quoting a senior official in the Military Intelligence division (AMAN) who, before the war of 'Peace for Galilee', had claimed to the Knesset's Foreign and Security Committee that 'terrorist' organizations in Lebanon possessed 15,000 members. After the war had begun, however, the army's spokesman made public a detailed memorandum in which he asserted that the number of 'saboteurs' (here meaning Palestinians only) in Lebanon was around 15,000 then went on to say that present numbers were drastically different and impossible to verify, since simple calculation resulted in figures ranging between 25,000 and 30,000. It should be noted, he concluded, that what actually constituted a 'saboteur' was not entirely clear![27]

Basing itself on a military source, the *Jerusalem Post* predicted that even if all 'enemy' members were to withdraw from West Beirut with none returning via Syria, 2,500 members of the PLO and Syrian Forces would still remain in place.[28] Then the very next day, the same newspaper confined the number of 2,500 fighters previously mentioned – then divided between Palestinians and Syrians – just to 'Palestinian saboteurs' linked to the PLO.[29]

As for those fighters who had actually left Lebanon, there were plain discrepancies in the overall numbers quoted – discrepancies that were, it subsequently emerged, to pave the way for the myth of the 2,000 people who had stayed behind. On 1 September, *Yedioth Ahronoth* stated that the last batch of 'saboteurs' would leave Beirut on that day, completing the overall evacuation of 12,000 'saboteurs' from the Lebanese capital.[30] In the same newspaper two days later, the figure had decreased to 10,000.[31] Four days on, the number of Palestinians had decreased still further: the number evacuated was now 19,518, including 8,856 'saboteurs', all the rest being Syrian soldiers. This was according to Foreign Minister Shamir.[32] Such a decrease in numbers served the newspaper's purpose, enabling it to claim, on the first day of the massacre, that those remaining in Beirut exceeded 2,000 'saboteurs', plus members of the leftist militias.[33]

On the first evening of the massacre, various media agencies conveyed to Reuters a statement by Prime Minister Menachem Begin to the effect that the saboteurs had deceived the supervising foreign force and had not transferred all their members according to the agreement.[34] Next morning, while the massacre was at its height, *Yedioth Ahronoth* added a further statement by Prime Minister Begin. 'A number of saboteurs,' he said, 'have stayed behind with their weapons. This has become clear to us over the past two nights.'[35]

What had 'become clear' to Begin stood, however, in contrast to what he had earlier agreed on without any objection – when the US government had announced the numbers of Palestinian fighters leaving Lebanon, including the number in each particular group and the destination of each particular group; this being derived, in turn from reports by US Marines who had arrived in the port of Beirut to supervise the departure. The Israeli Army itself, not satisfied with the supervision by the Americans, French and Italians, was observing the departure from the top of a nearby official building.

The numbers given out by the US State Department were as follows. The total number of departing Palestinian fighters was approximately 11,000, comprising around 8,300 members of the Palestine Liberation Organization and 2,600 or so fighters of the Palestine Liberation Army. These figures remained estimates and did not include the wounded. Around 3,850 fighters were headed for Syria, 1,000 for Tunisia, 1,100 for South Yemen, 2,620 for Jordan, 500 for Sudan, 600 for Algeria, 850 for North Yemen and 130 for Iraq.[36]

Sharon, the Defence Minister, had his own estimates for the numbers of Palestinian fighters allegedly left behind. At five in the afternoon on the Thursday, the first day of the massacre, as the Lebanese armed militias were preparing to attack, Sharon was meeting with Morris Draper, the American envoy, and Sam Lewis, the American ambassador to Israel; also attending the meeting, with Sharon, were Eitan, Saguy and others. The American position at this meeting was clear: the country was against the entry of the Israeli Army into West Beirut. The two men also expressed their fears regarding the entry of the Phalangists. Morris Draper said:

The critical point for us is that everyone in the world believed us when we said that you wouldn't go into West Beirut, that you gave us your word on it. This is a crucial point for us.[37]

Sharon answered, with cool nerve: 'Circumstances changed, sir.' Draper rejoined: 'Once people believed that your word was good.' Finally, Sharon stood up and declared vehemently: 'We went in because of the 2,000–3,000 terrorists who remained there … We even have their names.' But Draper replied:

'I asked for those names, and you said there was an *enormous* list,' Draper was goading him now, 'but what you came up with is a minuscule one … The Lebanese will take care of those who have remained behind … '

'You know the Lebanese,' Sharon retorted contemptuously, 'We'll tend to our own affairs.'[38]

As for the Americans' emphasis on earlier promises, including the necessity of Israeli withdrawal from Beirut, this was met with indifference by Sharon, who eventually broke up the discussion in order to attend a Cabinet meeting, having made no effort to answer Draper's question about the date of his forces' departure from Beirut.[39]

In point of fact, the decision about the entry of the Israeli Army into Beirut was not, from the beginning, based on the presence of remaining 'saboteur' fighters; the Israeli government had rather justified its decision, in the immediate wake of Bashir al-Gemayel's assassination, on the grounds of protecting Muslims against revenge by Christians!

Such a justification clearly lacks all logic. Was the mission of the Israeli Army, throughout the months of the invasion and the siege of Beirut, to protect Muslims? And since the assassination of Bashir al-Gemayel, had there been even one proven case of Christian Lebanese attacking Muslim Lebanese, in West Beirut or anywhere else in Lebanon, on the grounds that these latter had killed their 'beloved president' (as Begin was endlessly fond of describing Bashir al-Gemayel)?

It was Begin himself, at 7:30 p.m. who drafted the decision of the Prime Ministry during the Thursday evening meeting. This stated:

In the wake of the assassination of the President-elect Bashir Gemayel, the I.D.F. has seized positions in West Beirut in order to forestall the danger of violence, bloodshed and chaos, as some 2,000 terrorists, equipped with modern and heavy weapons, have remained in Beirut, in flagrant violation of the evacuation agreement.[40]

What was truly strange was that the claim of sparing Muslims bloodshed at the hands of Christians – a pretext neither logical nor justified by evidence – was accepted by the Kahan Commission as though it were an axiomatic truth; indeed, the Commission never even discussed it. As for Sharon himself, who had brought up the claim repeatedly, he actually admitted, during a television programme in Israel on 24 September, that it had been mere camouflage aimed at distracting attention from the real goal: namely, the wiping out of the 2,000 'terrorists' or 'saboteurs'.[41] The contriving of such a pretext, followed by an admission that it had been merely 'camouflage', is surely sign enough of the level of official Israeli contempt for humanity and human feeling.

The other allegation, explicitly confirmed by Sharon as being the 'basic pretext' – that 2,000 'terrorists' had remained behind – would hardly have merited any prolonged examination had the Kahan Report not taken it to be indisputable truth. According to various sources, the report said, the 'terrorists' had not abided by their departure commitments but had left behind, by several estimates, around 2,000 fighters.[42] Thus it was that the Kahan Report adopted as truth rumours shown conclusively above to have been a mere pretext for the Israeli occupation of Beirut. What is also odd is that a judicial commission should not have considered where the 2,000 fighters in question might have gone. Or where they had been found in the first place. Or what their eventual fate had been. If the report was indeed prepared to accept the estimates of the Israeli Army – that the total number of victims, adults and children together, had been between 700 and 800 – then just how many fighters had there been among these? And where had the rest gone? If they had been abducted, then where were they?

The oral history chapters revealed how far the truth of these 'fighters' was from the myth (see Chapter 1, pp. 35–9). They demonstrated that there were not 2,000 fighters, or even some hundreds; there were just a few dozen – only a minority of whom were professional fighters in any case, the majority being simply zealous young men wishing to defend their families and their dignity. It was further shown that such fighting as actually took place was directed against the forces of the besieging Israeli Army, and that this had ended before the massacre ever began. On the Thursday evening and Friday morning, Shatila witnessed nothing beyond some very limited skirmishing, barely worthy even of the name (see Chapter 2, pp. 61–9). This was substantiated by the various other sources quoted. As for the field study, which involved analysis of 430 questionnaires for victims and 100 for kidnapped, this confirmed that the community to which these people belonged was a popular one in all respects, and a fully integrated one too, comprising Palestinians, Lebanese and Arabs of other nationalities, together with labourers from Pakistan and Bangladesh – among all of whom were victims killed in cold blood (see Chapter 7). As for the number of fighters, the study revealed only 16 victims set down as such, while further detailed analysis of each individual's death revealed that none of them was killed while armed; they were killed in cold blood, and they included two Lebanese and a Jordanian (see Chapter 7, pp. 264–9).

In actual fact, these points were no secret to a number of foreign writers and reporters, including Israelis, who had already published articles and books before the Kahan Report was issued, and whose writings have been extensively quoted in this book. The framework as defined by the Israeli government for the Commission of Inquiry, including all the myth imposed as naked truth – this was the 'basic problem' confronting the investigation.

The MacBride Report was fully in command of the evidence refuting the allegation of 2,000 fighters in the camps, and it was also the first comprehensive report on the Israeli invasion of Lebanon and on the Sabra and Shatila massacre. It affirmed that Sharon's claim about the remaining 2,000 guerrillas was a 'disingenuous excuse to justify the invasion which he had already planned'. It further stated that, while there was indeed some ammunition left, no evidence had been found for the existence of 2,000 fighters.[43]

Michael Jansen pointed out that had such a number of fighters existed in reality, a major battle would inevitably have taken place in Beirut and the killer would have faced stern resistance, whereas in reality no such thing had occurred. In addition, none of the testimonies about the massacre included any claim that even a few hundred 'terrorists' had been detained or killed, let alone thousands.[44]

Ilan Halevi actually pointed out the falsity of this claim even before the massacre took place. The Israeli Army, he said, was in control of the entire city by the morning of Thursday 16 September. There had evidently been no sign of the 2,000 fighters alleged; just a few dozen Murabitoun or members of the Lebanese National Movement.[45]

As for Jonathan Randal, he simply summed up his viewpoint by saying that Sharon had insisted on the wiping out of 2,000 'terrorists' in the West Beirut camps who had turned out not to be there.[46]

Thomas Friedman merits special attention as one who had followed events from the establishment of the Habib Agreement through to the end. He said that those who were permitted to remain in Lebanon were Palestinians working at the diplomatic mission and Palestinian militiamen, mostly born in Lebanon, who had worked as guards to protect the camps. Because they were part-time civilian fighters, they were not considered guerrillas by the terms of the Habib Agreement, which had ruled that militiamen who laid down their arms, and were acceptable to the Lebanese government, should be permitted to remain behind in Lebanon.

As to the Palestinian men rounded up from the camps during the massacre, Friedman reported a remark by Colonel Natali Bahiri, one of the Israeli officers in charge of interrogations. 'Far more than half', Colonel Bahiri said, were militiamen he expected to be released, and he added that only a small percentage were suspected of having been guerrillas in violation of the Habib Agreement. Friedman concluded:

In summary, the Israelis do not appear to have found, nor do there appear to have been, 2,000 P.L.O guerrillas who remained behind in West Beirut. Clearly there were some, but the weight of the evidence suggests that the number was in the low hundreds at most.[47]

Noam Chomsky provided a particularly acute and detailed account:

The final official story was that they were sent in for the purpose of 'cleansing' the camps of 2000 heavily-armed terrorists left there by the PLO in violation of the Habib agreements. In *Ha'aretz*, B. Michael comments: 'So heroic as this are the Christian fighters!' Edward Walsh reports Begin's official reply to the Commission of Inquiry in which he 'reiterated his assertion that there was no reason to anticipate a massacre and said the government had "authoritative information" that about 2000 Palestinian guerillas were concentrated in the area.' Walsh comments: 'But no one has publicly explained how the Israelis expected 100 to 130 Phalangists to defeat such a force of Palestinians.' Robert Suro of *Time* magazine visited the camps a few days before the attack, and found no military presence there.[48]

In fact, a remark of Chomsky's might serve as a definitive explosion of the whole myth. 'The 2000 terrorists,' he noted, 'have proven elusive indeed.'[49]

The extremely limited nature of the confrontations between armed men from Shatila and Israeli soldiers was itself evidence as to the absence of 'saboteur' fighters, whose elimination supposedly made the whole siege and incursion necessary. We earlier quoted a number of statements issued by the Israelis themselves, including what was broadcast on

the Thursday evening. What was truly remarkable, surely, was that Defence Minister Sharon himself, along with all the other senior officials, should be so fully aware of the situation – the relevant reports had reached them, it would seem, rather than vanishing into thin air like all the reports after the massacre. The Defence Minister held a meeting at ten o'clock on the Thursday morning, attended, according to the report, by 'the Chief of Staff; the director of Military Intelligence, Brigadier-General Saguy; Lieutenant Colonel Zecharin, the Chief of Staff's bureau chief; and Mr. Duda'i'. The report continued as follows:

The meeting was opened by the Chief of Staff who announced that 'the whole city is in our hands, complete quiet prevails now, the camps are closed and surrounded; the Phalangists are to go in at 11:00–12:00. Yesterday we spoke to them ... the situation now is that the entire city is in our hands, the camps are closed.'

...

At the time of the consultation, the minister of Defense informed the Prime Minister by phone that 'the fighting has ended. The refugee camps are surrounded. The firing has stopped. We have not suffered any more casualties. Everything is calm and quiet. Sitting opposite me is the chief of Staff, who has just come from there. All the key points in our hand. Everything is over.'[50]

Given that Defence Minister Sharon had admitted the fighting was over, why did he send the Phalangists into the camps at all? Did he really believe there were 'terrorists in the thousands' hiding in their homes? And that these, for all their evident strength, had held back from combating an enemy laying siege to their camps? Is it remotely conceivable that 'fighting' would have ended so quickly if there had been even a few hundred fighters present, let alone thousands?

These contradictions will remain unresolved until such time as the perpetrators, master-planners, facilitators and supervisors of the Sabra and Shatila massacre stand trial before an international court. As for the report issued by the International Commission, presided over by Judge MacBride, this became the sole legal document to confront the Israeli allegation as to Palestinian fighters remaining in the camps. It stated, among other things:

The Commission rejects unconditionally the Israeli allegations that 2,000 'terrorists' in the camps made it reasonable to mount a military action against the inhabitants and regards the camps as civilian, non-military places of refuge at the time of the massacres. The Commission does not believe that Israeli intelligence – which had manifestly accepted the number of departing PLO fighters as accurate – could have subsequently estimated in *good faith* that such a large number of fighters remained. While the Commission therefore totally rejects Sharon's figures, it must be emphasized that *even if* this Israeli allegation had been true, or even if Israel had in *good faith* believed it to be substantially true, the actions taken after the camps had been encircled would nevertheless, have constituted the gravest breach of Israel's responsibility as an Occupying Power. What occurred would still have constituted a gross failure to distinguish between civilians and combatants.[51]

Were they really unaware?

The main impression gained by anyone reading the Kahan Report is that the Israeli military had no way of seeing anything, from their headquarters building, of what was happening in Sabra and Shatila. Yet this did not (again according to the Kahan Report) imply that the news had not reached some of them by other means; or that some of these did not, in turn, report directly to their superiors or send reports through the normal channels. Strange to relate, none of these reports, oral or written, ever seemed to reach top men like Begin or Sharon.

The first question: Where was the Israeli forward command post located? And what was its nature?

This building, used by the Israeli Army as its headquarters and known accordingly as the forward command post, had formerly, as mentioned earlier, been one of three residential buildings used by officers of the Lebanese Army, and was separated from the Shatila district only by the Sports City and the Camille Chamoun Boulevard. Directly opposite was a sandy unpaved area previously known as the Turf Club (formerly a horse riding club). Behind this was Hayy Ersal, with Shatila Main Street, and so on further down.

The second question: Were Sabra and Shatila visible from the roof of the forward command post?

The report noted that it was generally feasible to view the camps area from the roof of the forward command post building, but that, according to the testimonies of a number of people who had visited the post, it was impossible to see from the roof what was going on in the camp's alleys.[52] This observation is in truth distorted, in that it does not convey the whole picture – especially when we realize that the expression 'camps' area had been used in the context of general visibility, while the expression 'camp's alleys' (using the singular 'camp'), was being used to refer to the impossibility of any visibility there. In fact, this detailed picture applies only quite specifically to Shatila Camp, which is embedded in the heart of the Sabra–Shatila district and surrounding parts – that is, within the overall district we have called Greater Shatila, to distinguish it from the small Shatila Camp whose alleys never in fact witnessed any massacre or any violent operations at all. The massacre site extended throughout the Sabra and Shatila district, or Greater Shatila – except for the Shatila Camp at its very heart.

So was it impossible to view every location, as was the case with Shatila Camp?

The level of visibility will obviously have varied from one particular spot to the next. Yet it was demonstrated earlier that it was possible at least to see nearby locations, whose surface area covered a large part of the massacre site; and the dimensions have already, in the field study, been specified in metres (see Chapter 7, pp. 259–64). It was further established in the course of the oral history that the sandy area of the former Turf Club, together with Hayy Ersal, the surrounding parts, and other locations too, were visible to the naked eye.

The lawyer and writer Franklin Lamb took a photograph of the place just four months after the massacre; at a time, that is, when the district was still substantially unchanged. (See Appendix 3: photo of the view over

Sabra and Shatila from the roof of the Israeli headquarters.) This photograph constitutes, in itself, the best possible proof.

Ray Wilkinson, correspondent of *Newsweek* magazine, was one of those reporters not satisfied with observation from a distance. He measured the distance between the command post and the camps at 250 paces. He also measured the line of vision from the roof of the command post. 'From there,' he affirmed, 'all details of the camps are plainly visible, even to the naked eye. With binoculars the Israelis could have been able to see even the smallest details.' He added that the Israelis were also present at the Lebanese Army's outpost, from which one could look straight down into the camps.[53]

Amnon Kapeliouk, *Le Monde Diplomatique* correspondent, said that 'the roof and two camps are still in existence, and anyone can still go up there, as we did recently, and see for themselves that it was feasible at least to see what took place in the specially affected area'.[54]

The third question: How could it happen that news and reports never reached senior officials?

One thing stands out: the failure to arrive of a report sent by an officer to his superior, or to the final point the report should have reached, was so remarkably frequent that it is difficult to see matters in terms of mere oversight. The whole thing looks far more like a consciously determined pattern. The Kahan Report saw this clearly enough, and indeed devoted its final remarks to the issue.[55] This, though, was hardly sufficient. The constant disruption in the transmission of news, and even of reports, must make one wonder how such a thing could possibly be. How could news and reports have been regularly held up in this way? Below are some concrete examples:

- Each officer understood the report he received in a different fashion. What a lieutenant (standing on the roof on the Thursday evening) saw, in a particular case, as involving the murder of women and children, was seen by the brigadier-general as involving the killing of 'terrorists'.[56]

- Some of the Israeli officers heard an oral report by a liaison officer of the Phalangists (who was at the headquarters cafeteria on the Thursday evening). The Kahan Report confirmed that the Commission of Inquiry had been given different versions of this matter by different persons involved. The Commission of Inquiry made no effort to establish the true version.[57]

- A conflict of opinion occurred at the command post on the Thursday evening, between an intelligence officer, who was convinced no significant military combats were taking place and that civilians were in danger, and a brigadier-general, who saw no possible chance of harm to civilians. The latter's view prevailed.[58]

- On the Friday morning, a general submitted a report on events to another general, but told him nothing of what had really happened at Sabra and Shatila, or what he himself had been discussing with his colleagues on the previous (Thursday) evening.[59]

- There is mention of a number of reports, addressed by officers to their superiors, which were never distributed as they should have been and never reached the people concerned.[60]

- There is mention of telephone conversations between ministers, or between senior officers and ministers, where each of the two speakers understood what was being said in a different manner. As a result, the oral message was not properly transmitted – the listener was listening 'in his own way'. In other, related cases, the listener would understand well enough, but would decide the information was valueless and not worth verifying.[61]

- In cases where a general had knowledge of killing and slaughtering, and should have informed others present, he would hold back from doing so for the simple reason that he saw no necessity. The reason he would give later is that he supposed the others must surely have known already. Since they all knew, there was no need to speak of it.[62]

- Some of the military personnel round about Shatila wanted to report what was happening to their superiors but were confronted by colleagues who told them to say nothing. These colleagues had heard the battalion commander say, in response to a message concerning the killing of civilians: 'We don't like it, of course, but don't intervene.'[63]

- Misunderstanding was a major problem. On many occasions a senior officer repeatedly heard of what was happening, yet somehow it never struck home that revenge operations and bloodshed were taking place.[64]
- During the meeting held between Israeli and Lebanese Forces officials at four o'clock on the Friday afternoon, the former did not ask the Phalangists exactly what they had been doing; and the Phalangists, for their part, volunteered no report.[65]

The Kahan Report, going into the whole matter of 'indirect responsibility', clarified the 'loss' of reports as follows:

it is clear from the course of events that when the reports began to arrive about the actions of the Phalangists in the camps, no proper heed was taken of these reports, the correct conclusions were not drawn from them, and no energetic and immediate actions were taken to restrain the Phalangists and put a stop to their actions. This both reflects and exhausts Israel's indirect responsibility for what occurred in the refugee camps.[66]

The issues of direct and indirect responsibility will be considered later. For the moment we will examine the crucial matter of how far news would actually have been spreading, minute by minute, through the besieging Israeli Army. The bottom line is this: is it conceivable, in the real world, that no report should have reached the desk of an official in Tel Aviv? And if the Israeli government was aware (through these reports, among other things) that a horrendous massacre was taking place, surely it might have fulfilled its obligations – given that it was the foreign power occupying West Beirut and specifically laying tight siege to the Sabra and Shatila district – by calling an immediate halt to the massacre?

It is baffling that the Kahan Report should so strictly have confined the issue of Israeli officers' knowledge of events to the matter of visibility from the roof of the forward command building, and to conclude that visibility was totally impaired, whether for the naked eye or for the most up-to-date binoculars. What of the many other possible means? Why was not a single word said of these? Some of the means in question were as follows.

Points of surveillance. The Israeli Army had been occupying the entire district, and when they sent the Lebanese Forces into Sabra and Shatila it was their duty to remain in place at spots permitting surveillance. Why did they confine themselves to that roof, along with the neighbouring one? Why did the senior officers not send their soldiers to monitor events from various locations that would enable them to see and know what was going on? Why did soldiers not take up position at the highest point of the Sports City, overlooking Hayy al-Gharbi, Hayy Ersal, Sabra, Shatila Main Street, and so on? And why did they not send their soldiers to the roofs of buildings in Bir Hasan, directly opposite Shatila, and Hayy al-Horsh in particular? There were many other empty buildings, and even had they not been empty, the occupying Israeli Army would hardly have been hampered from entering and monitoring events from the roofs.

The Israelis were, in point of fact, observing matters from various other points, and if the Kahan Report failed to consider this, then residents' statements in the oral history testify to the existence of these places, especially in Bir Hasan (see Map 3).

Military vehicles. Israeli military vehicles were patrolling the district. While certain Israeli fixed positions did, it is true, disappear and reappear – this happened, for example, near the airport roundabout – its armoured vehicles maintained full control over the streets. If, for instance, we consider the Sports City Boulevard, or the death pits and the torture inflicted in the sandy former Turf Club area or by the small sandy hills surrounding the Sports City, it is surely inconceivable that all this could have happened out of sight of the patrolling Israeli vehicles.

Residents' complaints. It is difficult to assess the number of residents' complaints, submitted either to various Israeli centres or to various officers and soldiers these residents encountered by chance. Some indication of the matter is, however, provided in the oral history chapters. What is especially noteworthy is the Israelis' reactions, which were as contradictory as they could be. Some of those involved reacted with brutality and unconcern while others showed care and concern to the extent of offering to help. The latter, though, were a minority.

Direct Israeli intervention. The Israelis did not always act like people who knew nothing, or wanted to know nothing, or preferred to remain hidden spectators. Some soldiers, stationed at spots from which they could see everything, actually intervened. We may, for instance, note the incident between six and seven on the Friday morning in which one soldier or officer moved from his position at a sandy hill near the Kuwaiti Embassy in order to prevent the killing of a group of women and children (see Account 33, p. 155). We might also recall the intervention of an officer who was passing in his car and prevented a similar fate for another group of women and children. This was on the Friday again, but around noon, in the Sports City yard (see Account 34, p. 157). Such incidents clearly indicate an aversion to the murder of civilians on the part of the military personnel concerned. Other incidents, certainly, showed quite the opposite scenario. Either way, however, the number of Israelis closely aware of what was happening was, quite clearly, larger than anyone might have imagined.

Photography. Certain Israeli Army officers, and subsequently the Kahan Report, claimed repeatedly that the continuous night illumination had been intended to assist the attacking gunmen in identifying 'saboteurs' or 'terrorists'. This matter was discussed earlier, and it was also argued that, while the Israeli Army strictly had no need of all this illumination, from artillery and aircraft, to take photographs, it would be highly surprising if they had failed to take photographs in these particular circumstances. It would,

indeed, give rise to comment. Yet the Kahan Report asked no questions on the matter.

It was their duty to know. Since it had encircled the whole district since the Wednesday and controlled all entrances to the 'camps' (thereby preventing people from leaving), and since it was an occupying power, the Israeli Army had a duty to take up all means enabling them to discover what was happening. From the standpoint of international law, they were the ones responsible for residents' safety, and it is not the smallest excuse to say they were unaware of events, or that reports had been misunderstood. In point of fact, they themselves should have been the original source of all the reports.

When did the massacre end?

During the meeting held by General Eitan and other Israelis with officers from the Lebanese Forces, at half past four on the Friday afternoon, Eitan gave instructions that the latter should cease their operations at dawn on the Saturday.[67] This demand was obviously the result of American pressure.

When did they leave in reality? According to the Kahan Report, the Phalangists left the camps completely at around eight on the Saturday morning.[68] But did this departure spell the end of the massacre? So the report, from beginning to end, would have us believe.

We move now from the time frame to that of place. To what 'camps' was the report referring when it claimed all was over, since the Phalangists had left them? Was the reference to the small Shatila Camp, which had never been penetrated in the first place? Or to the Sabra district, which had been infiltrated only on the Main Street, as far as Sabra Square and the Gaza Hospital? In truth, those few words in the report, referring to the Phalangists' final departure around eight on the Saturday morning, had nothing to say – except, perhaps, that verbal ambiguity had fled the realms of poetry to take up residence with judges.

The massacre site was Greater Shatila and its vicinity (see Chapter 1, pp. 43–4).

As such, any claim that the gunmen had withdrawn is utterly false, with respect both to the geographical location of the massacre and to the historical sequence of massacre events – those events that Sabra and Shatila residents know by heart, just as they had known the names of their ancestors or their villages back in Palestine.

The withdrawal from Sabra Square was hardly the conventional withdrawal of an armed force attacking a district. Far from spelling the end of the massacre, it was thus the beginning of prolonged hours of torment, starting from Sabra Square and continuing the length of Shatila Main Street, along which the gunmen herded great numbers of Sabra and Shatila residents. Unstable, arrogant and contemptuous, these gunmen would tell the people now to stand, now to sit, especially in the Square of the Martyr Abu Hasan Salameh; then they would assemble them, on the small sandy hills near the Kuwaiti Embassy or those next to Hayy Ersal (the hills of the former Turf Club). In these places a number of death pits had been dug in advance, and there the killing went on throughout the morning until noon. There the bulldozers could be heard as they wrecked the houses over the bodies of their inhabitants, and there great numbers of people were dragged along in the lines of the 'final march'. The trucks, parked by the side of the Sports City Boulevard, prepared to load up dozens of these people and drive them off to the unknown, while others, forced to continue on towards the Sports City, found death awaiting them there: some ending in further death pits, others blown up by mines left over from the Israeli invasion.

All these things were happening in this spot and that. And the brief interrogations, the killings, abductions and constant humiliation, went on still, through all the morning hours before noon. It was already past noon when a group of men flung into one of the death pits in the Turf Club area were shot to death. And contrary to what was stated in the Kahan Report about departure by eight in the morning, a number of writers have said it was obvious that no steps were taken to force them to withdraw quickly and prevent further bloodshed.[69]

The massacre was a continuous operation lasting a full 43 hours, from six in the evening on Thursday 16 September to one in the afternoon on Saturday 18 September (see Chapter 5). Each of the three massacre days had its own accounts and tragedies, and part of Saturday's tragedy was that the operations were carried out so publicly. Countless incidents testify to the Israeli Army's direct knowledge of Saturday's tragedies, but officers were too busy doing other things, including questioning of residents at the Sports City and at the UNESCO building across the street.

The obvious point remains. Had the massacre really been halted at eight in the morning, would this not have prevented further bloodshed for hundreds of innocent victims? Would it not have saved the lives of people forced to endure a double agony: the agony of abduction and torture and the agony of murder? None of those abducted on the Saturday ever returned (see Chapter 8).

There must be some link between the time at which officials in Israel announced they had learned of the massacre and the time at which they issued the orders for the attacking Phalangists to withdraw.

There are three chapters to the story concocted by Sharon about Sabra and Shatila in the belief that, if presented in well co-ordinated fashion, it would shift the full responsibility on to the Lebanese Forces – not simply absolving his army but even perhaps earning him praise for having prevented 'Muslim bloodshed' in West Beirut.

The first chapter revolves around the alleged total ignorance on the part of the Israeli military leadership of the very possibility of the Lebanese Forces committing a massacre, or acts of violence generally. (A number of his colleagues also took this standpoint.)

On 25 October 1982, Sharon testified as follows to the Kahan Commission:

I want, in the name and on behalf of the entire defense establishment, to say that no-one foresaw – nor could have seen – the atrocities committed in the neighborhood of Sabra and Shatila.[70]

This brief testimony rather contradicts what he set down in his diaries, where he referred to a meeting that took place on the Thursday between General Amir Drori and officials of the Lebanese Forces, at the former's headquarters, to prepare for the incursion. Sharon noted as follows:

Among other things, they were instructed to be careful in their identification of the PLO terrorists. The mission was only against them. Civilian residents, they were specifically instructed, were not to be harmed.[71]

Why were the instructions to the Forces so specific about causing no harm to civilians? Are such instructions normally issued to parties trusted by their superiors? And what does 'harm to civilians' mean in such a context? Does it mean beating? Torturing? Abduction? Might someone harming civilians not have gone to the length of killing them? Is that not indeed what happened?

In fact, a simple Israeli soldier contrived to see what his commander Sharon could not. He spoke of his experiences in Lebanon with the Lebanese Forces:

A storm was aroused in the state concerning the Phalangists in connection with the Sabra and Shatila affair. It was only necessary to become acquainted with the Phalangists to know that they were capable of doing what they did. At least I, a simple soldier, understood this, when I was in Beirut before it happened. I happened to make friends with one Phalangist. Until today, I cannot forget two pictures that he showed me with real pride. In one he stood in heroic pose holding in his hands two full jars – ears of terrorists! He told me that he had cut them from the bodies of terrorists recently [that is, after the IDF had turned the 'terrorists' over to Phalange control]. In the second I saw him standing holding in each hand a head that had been cut off, and between his legs a third! He explained to me with great self-importance that these were the heads of Palestinians he had decapitated.[72]

The second chapter of Sharon's story involves the alleged total ignorance of the Israeli leadership as to what had been taking place within Sabra and Shatila throughout the days of the massacre – as though Shatila were some remote desert island, far beyond the range of his army's famously up-to-date binoculars. Again, Sharon testified as follows

to the Kahan Commission:

If I were to be asked, on oath, who committed the crimes, I should have to reply that I don't know. The Israeli Army wasn't there. There were two entrances to the camp that we didn't control. I know who went in and out, but I don't know who did the killing.[73]

Sharon made a determined attempt to substantiate this allegation to the investigators. It was quite impossible, he said, for the soldiers stationed around the two camps to see what was happening inside, and he produced pictures and maps of the Shatila district. Between 100 and 200 Phalangists, he went on, had taken part in what he described as a purge of the camps to clear them of Palestinian fighters following the departure of the Palestinian Resistance from Beirut.[74]

As for the third chapter of Sharon's story, this revolves around the question: 'When did Sharon find out about the massacre?' Such a question would indeed stun the families of innocent victims whose testimonies show they never had the smallest doubt about the Israel/Sharon masterminding of the massacre; their imaginings and feelings on the matter are clear enough. We should nevertheless pause to consider what Israeli writers said about him, and what Sharon had to say about himself.

In their book, Ze'ef Schiff and Ehud Ya'ari have documented the contents of a phone call between the television correspondent Ron Ben-Yishay and Sharon, after the former had requested a conversation at half past eleven on the Friday evening. The account they provide is Ben-Yishay's:

I apologized for calling at that hour, explained that I was phoning from Beirut, and told him everything I knew … I remember telling him, among other things, that something must be done to stop it, that IDF officers know about it, and we'll be in a terrible fix … The defense minister, who had been awakened by the call, listened attentively. He asked if I knew any details, and I told him exactly where the Israeli soldiers had seen the murders and executions, explaining to him that the place wasn't far from the division headquarters south of Shatila. The conversation lasted about four to five minutes, during which I did most of the talking. Minister Sharon hardly responded, and I refrained from asking him any questions. Finally, we wished one another a Happy New Year & hung up.[75]

Sharon's first public comment on this phone call came during an interview on 24 September 1982:

[Question]: Mr. Sharon, do you confirm the information given by Ron Ben-Yishay that he reported to you about the massacre in Beirut on the eve of Rosh Hashana at 2300?

[Answer]: Yes, Ron Ben-Yishay phoned me around 2330 and gave me some information. However, with all due respect to Ron Ben-Yishay – I appreciate him very much – I had already been briefed through regular channels. I had already received a report in the evening that the operation had been stopped, since it had emerged that the Phalangists were not acting according to the agreement.[76]

What Sharon wrote in his diaries accords in the main with the account of Ben-Yishay's phone call, though there is conflict over a few details. He wrote:

Ben-Yishay told me he had heard that Phalangist soldiers were murdering civilians in Shatila; he had talked to Israeli officers who had heard from their soldiers that they had seen killings going on. When I asked him if he had seen it with his own eyes, Ben-Yishay said he had not, but he had heard it twice, around four in the afternoon, then later in the evening. No, the people he had heard it from had not seen anything personally either, they too heard about it.

Ben-Yishay was excited, but there was nothing new in what he was telling me. The reports I had gotten from the chief of staff and from the situation desk had said essentially the same thing. Christian forces had been involved in killings. I knew that. I also knew, as Ben-Yishay did not, that Raful and Amir Drori had done what was necessary to put a stop to it.[77]

In his testimony to the Kahan Commission, on the other hand, Sharon claimed that information on what had been taking place had begun to arrive as late as the Saturday morning;[78] he added: 'We did not imagine in our worst dreams that the Phalangists going into battle would behave this way.'[79]

Of what kind of information, arriving only on the Saturday morning, was Sharon speaking? And why did he say in the radio interview quoted above that the operation had been halted as soon as the Israelis discovered the Phalangists had not been acting in accordance with the agreement made together? Is information about a massacre unbelievable, yet somehow already known to a senior military commander, or Minister of Defence, in the State of Israel? And then he had insisted on knowing whether Ben-Yishay had seen events with his own eyes, as if attaching no importance to the accounts of soldiers under his command.

There is no point in becoming carried away with futile conclusions, especially as other military personnel with him followed the same line. Below is part of the testimony of Eitan, who was on the point of retirement and as such exempted from any subsequent obligations to the Kahan Commission:

The IDF had no knowledge until Saturday morning of what was going on. We don't give the Phalangists orders and we're not responsible for them. The Phalangists are Lebanese and Lebanon is theirs and they act as they see fit. The Phalangists were fighting within Chatila, according to their guidelines, if you can call them that, of warfare. We didn't really know what was going on. It was night. It was assumed it was ordinary fighting. Then in the morning light, when we saw what was happening and what could happen further, we intervened quickly.[80]

We see no need to comment on Eitan's remarks, except to recall that the continuous lights through the night – something freely admitted by the Israeli officers and by Sharon himself – leave little room for any claim that darkness hampered visibility. In the morning (it is not explicit which morning), Eitan and his colleagues, so he said, immediately intervened. This is clearly not true: they did not intervene immediately, nor did the massacre stop on any morning. Even on the Saturday it went on through to the afternoon.

The Israeli Cabinet sat on the Sunday evening, on 19 September 1982, and heard Eitan, together with Sharon and Drori. The three of them acquainted ministers with matters not in accordance with what they told the Americans or announced to the media: that, for example, the Phalangists had indeed entered the camps in co-ordination with the IDF. As to what went wrong, Eitan explained that the Phalangist command had simply lost control of its men. Yet they all swore that the minute they had discovered the misconduct they had intervened to force the Phalangists out.[81]

Schiff and Ya'ari, commenting on the meeting, wrote as follows: 'The Cabinet chose to believe that the effects of the massacre would dissolve quickly as long as it was portrayed as a peculiarly Lebanese perversion – "goyim killing goyim."'[82] In other words, the ministers were treading the same track as their chief, Begin, who had openly made a remark to the same effect. Even Minister David Levy, the sole person to have registered his disagreement in the previous Cabinet meeting on the Thursday evening (causing general alarm by his concern that, for the Phalangists, revenge meant slaughter), now based his objection not on any sense of compassion for innocents, but rather on fear of being blamed. 'Then,' he said, 'no one will believe we went in to create order there, and we will bear the blame.'[83]

If, on the other hand, we turn to the world of free expression, whether read or heard, within Israel itself, we find that a number of people did indeed broadcast or publish the facts. Among these was Gabi Zohar, correspondent with the Israeli Radio Station, who spoke out vehemently after visiting Sabra and Shatila. 'Regardless,' he said, 'of whether a commission of inquiry is actually set up, the fact will remain. We knew a massacre was taking place, and that we could have stopped it, but we failed to do so.'[84]

Regarding the Israeli responsibility

A number of writers have made similar observations, to the effect that the Israelis must certainly have been aware of the dangers of a massacre should armed Lebanese militias, known for their blood-thirsty ways in previous years, be sent into the camps. It will be sufficient here to provide just a few extracts, mostly from Israeli writers and novelists.

When Interior Minister Joseph Bourg shouted, 'If Christians have killed Muslims, how is that the fault of Jews?', the novelist Izhar Smilanski took it upon himself to make an ironic response:

We let the hungry lions loose in the arena and they devoured people. So the lions must be the guilty ones, mustn't they? They did the killing, after all. Who would have dreamed, when we opened the door for the lions and let them into the arena, that they'd gobble people up like that?[85]

In similar vein, the literary figure Amos Oz commented as follows:

If you invite the Yorkshire Ripper to spend a couple of nights in an orphanage for small girls, you can't, later on, just look over the piles of bodies and say you made an agreement with the Ripper – that he'd just wash the girls' hair.[86]

A similar image was provided by Yuri Evneri:

If someone puts a snake in a newborn child's cot, and the baby dies of snakebite, we hardly need any proof that the one who put the snake in the cot wanted the child to die. If he wishes to deny this is what he intended, then he must provide the evidence.[87]

The writer Amos Allon came up with a directly similar image, garnished with the language of international law:

A man who puts a snake into a child's bed and says: 'I'm sorry. I told the snake not to bite. I didn't know snakes were so dangerous.' It's impossible to understand. This man is a war criminal.[88]

On the other hand, the military analyst Ze'ef Schiff made a remark as far removed as possible from military concepts.

Whoever allowed the Phalangists to enter the refugee camps on their own can be compared to one who allows a fox into the chicken coop and then wonders why the chickens were all eaten.[89]

We may conclude these extracts by quoting, first, the political scientist Professor Ze'ef Sternhill, who addressed his students at the Hebrew University as follows:

The Israeli government and Israeli society must alike assume full moral, political and legal responsibility for the war crime that was committed in Beirut. Even if we did not commit it ourselves, there is no doubt we allowed it to happen.[90]

And finally, Chomsky, a thinker of international repute, saw the actions of Israeli officials in the following terms:

Since Palestinians are by definition all terrorists, or mothers of terrorists, or future terrorists – so different from Begin, Shamir & Sharon for example – whatever was done to them was regarded as legitimate.[91]

Where do the conclusions of the Kahan Commission stand in the light of all this – bearing in mind that the commission had made strenuous efforts in investigating, listening to testimonies, compiling documents and generally studying the case?

The report concluded that direct responsibility lay with the Lebanese Forces who had carried out the massacre, and indirect responsibility was ascribed to certain Israeli officials; most prominently to Sharon himself, who was forced to resign from his post as Defence Minister, though he remained a minister without portfolio. In practice, he simply went out of the Defence Ministry door to re-enter through the Knesset, where he took charge of the Defence Committee and also of the Lebanese Affairs Committee.

Ilan Halevi commented on the report's conclusions in a single short sentence. The only official investigation, he said, to achieve tangible results was the Kahan Commission, 'but the facts as presented do not conform fully to the conclusions'.[92]

Halevi also commented on the nature of the investigation. Its starting point should, he said, have been the crime and the criminals, and all those under serious suspicion: in the same way as, for instance, the American commission had investigated the My Lai case – identifying the perpetrators, then working steadily up till it reached the centre of decision-making, from crime to responsibility, both of them direct. Here there was a crime, but there were no criminals! The

Israeli officials could not be brought to trial because their responsibility was indirect; the identified criminals could not be brought to trial, or even heard, because they were Lebanese![93]

As for Yuri Evneri, he wrote straight after the Kahan Report had been released, pinpointing certain details:

Certainly the massacre was conceivable in the intention of some (probably Sharon and Eitan), and others were aware of this intention! This was why they acted in the way they did – concealing information and facts, supporting the perpetrators, destroying the evidence, holding back from giving interviews, closing their eyes and ears, declining to transmit information – all so that high-ranking officials, even the Prime Minister, could claim at the appropriate time that they had had no knowledge of anything. Such a theory is, I imagine, closer to the truth than the theory of 'insensibility';[94] for it accords far better with the behaviour of those who claim to be heroes, from Menachem Begin to the anonymous commander who told his soldiers over the radio: 'We don't like it, of course, but don't intervene.' In any case, I am clear the Report touches on things no other reason will fit.[95]

Chomsky, who also realized the massacre had been conceivable to the Israelis, set out the detailed sequence of events, based on his reading of the Kahan Report:

The picture that emerges from the Kahan Commission Report is therefore quite clear. The higher political and military echelons, in their entirety, suspected that Phalangists would carry out massacres if they were admitted into Palestinian camps. Furthermore they knew that these camps were undefended, so they were willing to send in approximately 150 Phalangists known for their unwillingness to engage with any conflict with any armed men. Within 1–2 hours after the Phalangists had entered on Thursday at 6PM, clear evidence reached the command post 200 meters away from the camps and overlooking them that massacres were taking place, and that there was no serious resistance. At the command post, the IDF and the Phalange commanders and their staffs, including intelligence and liaison, were present and in constant contact. The IDF provided then illumination, and the next day, after receiving corroboratory evidence that massacres were in process and there was no resistance, sent the Phalange back into the camps, with tractors, which the IDF knew were being used to bury bodies in the mass grave which they could observe (the latter fact is ignored by the Commission). The Phalange were selected in this operation because, as the chief of staff stated, 'we could give them orders whereas it was impossible to give orders to the Lebanese army.' And in fact the IDF did give the Phalange orders, from the moment they sent them into the camps to conduct their murderous operations, to [the end of the massacre].

Despite the overwhelming evidence of high level planning and complicity in the massacre, in the advance planning and as it was running its course, the Commission rejected these conclusions. It did, nevertheless, assign some limited 'indirect responsibility,' basing its recommendations on 'the obligations applying to every civilized nation' ... [96]

As for Timerman, he wrote about the Israeli inquiry before any other writer, before a commission of inquiry had even been established, based on his understanding of the nature of the Israeli regime. He said:

I have little faith in Israel's democratic opposition. I fear that the Israeli discipline which totally dominates the subconscious of all of us will result in an investigation that, in effect, protects the criminals from the punishment they deserve ... [97]

Timerman's fears proved to have been well founded.

Regarding the Lebanese responsibility

For all the indictment of the Lebanese Forces by the international press and other media, and also by the Kahan Report, the Lebanese government officially denied all culpability. This standpoint was embodied in the conclusions of the Lebanese report that became known as the Jermanos Report (after the President of the Commission, the military prosecutor Ass'ad Jermanos), issued on 29 September 1982, just eleven days after the massacre.

The most important aspect of the Jermanos Report is that it remained completely confidential from the time it was issued, the underlying reason being that the Lebanese Forces – who were chiefly accused of committing the massacre – had assumed general control of governmental cadres. As a result, the report was not published in the immediate aftermath of the massacre – nor indeed in the next 20 years, even after the Lebanese Forces had ceased to have any connection with the regime, even after the organization itself had been disbanded. The reason was a secret Lebanese wish not to rake up the past. 'Let bygones be bygones' was their motto.

All that was published of the Jermanos Report were extracts in the Israeli and Lebanese press, the most significant issues being the number of victims (this was discussed in earlier pages) and the question of responsibility, summarized by the press as follows:

- The Jermanos Report totally acquitted the Lebanese Forces, on the basis of an investigation that found no evidence for the leadership of the Phalange Party or of the Lebanese Forces having any prior knowledge of what occurred. In addition, the investigation did not find that any orders were given by either leadership to their fighters to support or take part in these operations.
- The investigation demonstrated the involvement of some non-Israeli armed members in operations within the camp, on the part, perhaps, of border units or others that had been harmed by Palestinian incursions over the past years.
- Inasmuch as there was no distinction to be made between war-related acts and those individual acts leading to the massacre, the Jermanos Report demanded that the judicial prosecution be postponed till a proper judicial body could be identified.[98]

One of the most biting comments on what was published of the 'official Lebanese Report' was that it apparently accused ghosts of having committed the massacre, since no rational mind would believe that everything had been committed by limited 'borders units'. The Jermanos Report was in fact worthless with regard to the question of responsibility.

Nor was Lebanese denial of Lebanese responsibility confined to the Jermanos Report. In the aftermath of the massacre, it also spread through the corridors of the United Nations, where the Lebanese diplomatic mission was instructed firmly to oppose any kind of international commission of inquiry and any kind of protection for Palestinians.

Austria proposed there should be a commission of inquiry into the massacre. Then the Security Council called for the establishment of an international commission to investigate the massacres to which Palestinian civilians had been subjected in the camps in West Beirut, but on 24 September 1982, Lebanon refused this request. The Vice President of the Lebanese diplomatic mission to the United Nations, Fakhri Saghieh, said:

We did not ask for the formation of this commission, and there will be no commission of inquiry. We will be satisfied with the procedures the government undertakes. We have no wish to dig graves for old skeletons.[99]

Moreover, when the group of Non-Aligned States proposed a draft resolution containing a condemnation of the massacres committed against Palestinians and Lebanese, the Lebanese diplomatic mission intervened once more, asking for the word 'Lebanese' to be struck out and replaced by the words 'other civilians'.[100] Accordingly, the text of the resolution issued by the General Assembly on 24 September 1982, following reference to the 'massacre of Palestinian civilians in Beirut', came out as follows:

1 – Condemns the criminal massacre of Palestinian and other civilians in Beirut on 17 September 1982;
2 – Urges the Security Council to investigate, through the means available to it, the circumstances and extent of the massacre of Palestinian and other civilians in Beirut on 17 September 1982, and to make public the report on its findings as soon as possible.[101]

It was expected the General Assembly would adopt this resolution with an absolute majority. The votes were in fact as follows: 147 in favour; no abstentions; six absent, and just two against: Israel and the United States.[102]

The families of Lebanese victims of the Sabra and Shatila massacre, their loved ones' fate formally unrecognized, were left to swallow more silent anguish (35 per cent of the massacre victims were in fact 'Lebanese').[103] Was their death not worth recognition by their own government? The families' overwhelming feeling was that denial of their loved ones' deaths was equivalent to denying them the right to live. A number spoke of the pain of this in their testimonies. As Um Ali al-Beka'i told me on one occasion: 'They killed us twice.'[104]

Differences within Lebanese circles concerning the massacre were reflected even in the external diplomatic missions. What took place in the corridors of the UN, on the part of the Lebanese Ambassador there, Abdallah Abu Habib, and his assistant, Fakhri Saghieh, stood in contradiction to the actions of the Lebanese Ambassador in Washington, Khalil Itani, who requested the American Congress to set up a commission of inquiry to investigate the massacre of Palestinian civilians in Beirut – which he described as one of the most brutal human tragedies of the century.[105]

Meanwhile, a number of Islamic nations requested the Secretary-General, Javier Perez de Cuellar, to implement all appropriate measures to protect Palestinians, both those under occupation and those in immigrant locations, and to provide them with special international identity cards that would preserve their original identity. Not only did Lebanon oppose the project but the country's representative, Fakhri Saghieh, stood out against the unanimous Arab voice in a speech affirming that Lebanon would permit no kind of consensus view regarding the Palestinians within its territories. In addition, Lebanon rejected any aid for the Palestinians unless channelled through the Lebanese government, and such aid might be humanitarian only. He further added that any person legally resident in Lebanon would receive the protection of the Lebanese government![106]

Spokesmen for the Lebanese Forces continued to deny all responsibility for the massacre. Shaykh Pierre al-Gemayel had decided the Lebanese Forces should under no circumstances admit to their participation. He feared this might undermine the position of his son, Amin, as President of the Republic, and he was also eager to maintain good relations with Muslim leaders, though he would admit to them privately that there had been a few Phalangists in the massacre – describing these as 'Israeli agents' who had not been acting on his orders. 'Sharon,' he would conclude, 'had a good many Judas Iscariots in our ranks.'[107]

No officials of the Lebanese Forces made any admissions before a full year had elapsed, though the names of senior figures had already been appearing in articles and other writings. One of the last published references was also the most clear-cut: in the book *Cursed is the Peacemaker*, the American Ambassador Robert Dillon was quoted as calling the leader of the operations, Elie Hobeika, 'a pathological killer'.[108]

Some writers, moreover, not only affirmed the Lebanese Forces' responsibility but also highlighted the positions and missions of some of their leaders: noting that some of these men had taken the decision, others had met several times with the Israeli military, and others still had supervised activities, either from surrounding surveillance points or directly on the spot. Since references do not elaborate on the operations in question it will be sufficient to list the names, with a maximum of ten references for each case. These are: Elie Hobeika;[109] Fadi Efram;[110] Dib Enstaz;[111] Jessie Sukkar;[112] Fu'ad Abu Nader;[113] Joseph (Joe) Eddeh;[114] Maroun Mash'alani;[115] Michel Zouein;[116] Emil Eid;[117] Zahi Bustani;[118] Joseph Abu Khalil.[119]

The first indication of the Lebanese Forces' guilt was their members' harassment of a number of foreign writers who had learned of the massacre and reported it. These included Loren Jenkins, correspondent of the *Washington Post*, and Robert Suro, correspondent of *Time* magazine. On Friday 17 September, each received an order from the Israelis and the Lebanese Forces to leave the country immediately. In addition, a number of films taken by various photographers were destroyed.[120] However, attempts to block the dissemination of films and photographs taken during the massacre

did not hamper the world-wide spread of these once the armed attackers had left.

During the period the Lebanese Forces were denying all responsibility, the key argument of those accused was that any armed group might in practice wear Phalange uniform or badges. A powerful counter-argument to this is provided in the oral history chapters, based on the testimonies of survivors and of foreign doctors and nurses: that many of the attackers proudly proclaimed on the massacre site itself that they belonged to the Lebanese Forces. Still more important evidence came from those occasional cases where attackers had previously been acquainted or on friendly terms with residents of the district, and where these attackers often refused to harm the people in question.

One of the first members of the Lebanese Forces to admit to the killing of Palestinians – in a highly boastful manner and on Israeli television – was the so-called 'Michel'. He had, he said, killed 15 Palestinians with his own hands and would be prepared to kill more.[121] Later, Pierre Yezbik, the Lebanese Forces' representative in Paris, admitted the Forces' responsibility in connection with the massacre, again during an interview with Israeli television.[122] As for Elie Hobeika, who was more exposed to attacks and queries than anyone else, by Lebanese rather than Palestinian television viewers, his responses during programmes varied over the years. At one point, at the beginning of the 1990s, he was saying that, if he spoke out, he would have to specify many of those involved. At another point he was denying all responsibility – a stance he maintained up to his assassination in 2002 – claiming he had documents and information that would indict the Israelis alone, and would therefore demonstrate that he and the Lebanese generally were free of guilt.

As for Lebanese accusations against Hobeika, these came from former colleagues. It was Robert Farah who wrote on behalf of the Lebanese Forces; or, to be more precise, on behalf of that section of the Lebanese Forces which, he claimed, had played no part in the massacre. In *Al-Wassat* magazine he wrote a response to what Hobeika had himself written in the same publication:

His [Hobeika's] direct implication in this massacre is clear and unquestionable. This has been shown clearly enough by the way he boasted of his feat in the presence of a number of Forces colleagues, and by the activities of the security cadres and the death of a number of members, together with the appearance of some of these on international television stations and the vigorous reaction of the general staff of the Forces immediately they learned of the incidents in question; this including the convening of meetings and the making of all necessary calls to expose Hobeika and his groups.[123]

In the Kahan Report only two Lebanese were specifically named: Hobeika and Efram. As for the Lebanese report, which had rejected any idea of Lebanese Forces being involved, this eventually became lost not just from the memory but from the very files of the Lebanese government. It was to be found neither in the desks of the Military Court, nor with President Amin al-Gemayel, who had received a copy from Ass'ad Jermanos personally; nor was any copy to be found with the Lebanese government commissioner Ass'ad Jermanos himself, who had conducted the inquiry, nor with the investigating judge of the military court, Ass'ad Diab.[124]

But if a hastily written report was concealed, there was no corresponding erasure of the tragic event from the memory of Sabra and Shatila: the memory of all that had happened through those three days, hour by hour. It became evident from the testimonies that the Lebanese Forces had indeed led operations and issued the orders. It was equally evident, however, that not all the armed attackers were from the Forces, though most were.

As for the second party involved, this was Sa'd Haddad's forces. Whether they took part on their leader's orders and with his knowledge or whether the initiative was their own, there were dozens of them there; a number of residents testified that they had carried out all kinds of mass killing along with the others, and that there were bands of them at certain checkpoints on the airport road. Moreover, Sa'd Haddad's men were recognized by a number of local residents, especially by southerners, and just as the 'Forces men' helped out people with whom they had been previously acquainted, so did Sa'd Haddad's. They rescued particular women and children, bringing them out from the heart of the massacre, and this happened specifically when the killers and their imminent victims came from the same village.

The Kahan Report's total rejection of any participation by Sa'd Haddad's forces did not acquit them in people's minds. On the contrary, it intensified the suspicions surrounding them, especially as the Israeli officers and soldiers laying siege to Shatila did not always ascribe the guilt to the Lebanese Forces; several had spontaneously told certain residents that the men were actually 'Sa'd Haddad's forces'. We have already encountered these statements in the oral history chapters.

We shall not pause to consider rumours attempting to shift the whole liability for the crime on to Sa'd Haddad and his forces (see Chapter 6, pp. 209–11); nor will we go once again over people's recollections of the attacking killers (see Chapter 6, pp. 231–41). We will simply recall those testimonies in which people mentioned seeing Sa'd Haddad near the Kuwaiti Embassy,[125] and the account of the two men who told the writer Mark Fineman they had seen him.[126] Sa'd Haddad's problem was, no doubt, that he was so well known and that pictures of him had appeared in the press. This made him easily recognized, something not shared by a number of the Forces' commanders at that time. He was further hampered by his publicly proclaimed connection with Israel, which kept him in the spotlight. On 22 September 1982, *The Times* (London) was the first to publish an article containing reports by Lebanese Army and police officers, to the effect that they had, on the Thursday afternoon (16 September), seen Israeli planes at Beirut International Airport, and hundreds of armed men coming out of them wearing military uniforms similar to the Phalange's but with Sa'd Haddad badges. A further sign emerged when the Israeli Army fired at some gunmen later identified as Sa'd Haddad's men, two of these being killed.[127]

As for Robert Fisk, not only did he identify the participating militias as belonging to the Lebanese Forces or Sa'd Haddad, he also indicated that each had received training, arms and instructions from Israel throughout the preceding five years; something which makes it virtually impossible for Israel to evade responsibility with regard to the actions of either group.[128]

Sa'd Haddad himself, who had earlier threatened the photographers and reporters who published photographs of his soldiers leaving Shatila with their badges on their shoulders,[129] received Robert Fisk in Marja' youn and answered his questions. In the course of the interview he was drawn into saying things he had never admitted to any other writer. Some of his men, he said, 'may have been with other forces in Beirut' when the massacre took place. Then he said: 'Officially, I didn't have any men in Beirut.'

When Fisk asked him about the correspondents and the dozens of survivors who had seen his men, with their olive green uniforms, outside the camps he said: 'All of them, they are liars. They are paid by the PLO.' Then, after a long pause, he said they might possibly have seen the badges of some of his men who happened to be in Beirut; but (he added) officially none of them was there.

Fisk persisted, asking him how many of his men had, in actual fact, been in Beirut on the Friday. At this point Haddad finally said:

Perhaps 10 served with other people there, perhaps 20. [He stopped then said:] But this business has nothing to do with me. Why? I wouldn't even know where to find Chatila.[130]

The third participating party in the massacre was the Numour al-Ahrar militia – al-Ahrar being the party founded by ex-President Camille Chamoun, though the militia itself had been founded by his son Dani. However, since they had been wearing the uniform of the Lebanese Forces, direct identification was in fact impossible – no resident, as it happened, recognized a single one of them. Their participation actually came to light through a direct confession by one of them, in an interview published in the German magazine Der Spiegel. He stated that, on the night before they went in, the members of the group he had joined were gathered at Wadi Shahrour. The group comprised 300 men from 'East Beirut', and they were all, including the speaker himself, dressed in the official Phalangist uniform. He reported part of the speech made on the occasion by one of the Phalangist officers. 'You have come here of your own free will,' the officer said, 'to avenge the death of Bashir al-Gemayel. You are God's tools ... and each one of you is an avenger.'[131]

The testimony of this Numour fighter was quoted earlier. It remains impossible to tell truth from fiction, or right from wrong, for all this still awaits a just trial of the perpetrators of the massacre, in some part of the world and under some international tribunal. Yet we have already detected one error in this testimony, linked to pre-existing conditions in Shatila. This man, who refused to reveal his name, said:

Some amazing scenes showed what the Palestinians were capable of. Some armed people, including women, barricaded themselves in a long, narrow alley in the northern part, behind some donkeys. To our great regret we had to kill these innocent beasts in order to wipe out the Palestinians behind them. I sensed those shot donkeys were screaming with pain. It was unbearable.[132]

This man who testified is free enough to feel sorrow at the death of particular creatures; that, after all, is a sign of his humanity. He is free, too, to rejoice at the death of other particular creatures; that is a sign of his brutality, and his own affair. But he is not free to lie in his testimony. There was not a single donkey in the whole Shatila district that he and his friends had shot. There were indeed a few horses used by kerosene vendors. Perhaps the witness's excuse is his inability to tell a donkey from a horse.

A fourth Lebanese group was accused of taking part in the massacre. This was the Hurras al-Arz (Guardians of the Cedars) Party founded by Etienne Saqr.[133] This group is marked out by the direct admission, with pride indeed, of its leader, who was thus the only one among the leaders of political parties or militias to break ranks and admit to the participation of his party. He even went so far as to defend it during a visit he made to Israel. 'We have every right,' he said, 'to deal with our enemies in Lebanon in the manner we see fit. It's our own internal business. Stay out of it.'[134]

Thirteen days before the massacre, the party had convened a weekly meeting headed by Nadim Shuwairi, following which it had issued a statement calling for a final end to the Palestinian presence. The statement made the following demands:

Confiscation of Palestinian property in Lebanon, as being due to the Lebanese people in partial compensation for their losses as a result of the Palestinian war on Lebanon.

Action to reduce the numbers of Palestinian refugees in Lebanon, until the day comes when no single Palestinian remains on our soil.

Removal of all the camps set up on other people's land or on public property.[135]

Abu Arz (as Etienne Saqr was known) was famous for his skill in whipping up a profound hatred of Palestinians among his adherents. They were pioneers in daubing the walls with graffiti such as 'Every Lebanese must kill a Palestinian.' Even the educated among his followers were, as Jonathan Randal has shown, with him in this hatred. Take, for instance, what an elegant Lebanese doctor, who worked as an army doctor and was a member of Hurras al-Arz, once told him: 'Soon there will be not a single Palestinian in Lebanon. They are a bacillus which must be exterminated.'[136]

When Michael Jansen published her book, one of the first to deal with the Israeli invasion and the massacre, she specified the groups responsible for the massacre, affirming that most belonged to the Lebanese Forces militias (or Phalange militia), which included the highly trained elite unit headed by Elie Hobeika and the Damour unit. She further specified 40–50 Sa'd Haddad men and a few score from the Numour militia belonging to Camille Chamoun. The total number she gave was somewhere between 1,000 and 1,200 fighters.[137]

The MacBride Report, completed on 29 November 1982, noted that the perpetrators of the massacre were the Lebanese Forces and Sa'd Haddad's forces, and mentioned no one else. This was perhaps because the commission that went to Beirut to investigate the facts of the massacre (the commission had in fact come initially to investigate the events of the invasion, then settled in London to write the report) was not supplied with enough testimonies over the limited period of time available.

In fact, what the above confirms overall is that the Lebanese Forces were both the decision-makers and the commanders, while Sa'd Haddad's forces had an effective participation which the Kahan Report could not convincingly deny, especially given the distinctive southern accent that marked many of the members out. As for the two remaining groups, none of the residents noted any of their members. Their presence was revealed subsequently, through personal admissions on the level of commander or individual member.

The MacBride Report's conclusion on the matter was as follows:

The evidence that has emerged conclusively identifies the Phalange and Major Haddad's militia as the main, and probably the exclusive, perpetrators of the massacres. As regards the Phalange, not only is the evidence extensive and weighty, but also they have made no serious attempts to deny their involvement in the action (eg by admissions they made to Dan Semona, correspondent for Israeli television). Major Haddad, however, has testified to the Israeli Commission of Inquiry that none of his units were involved ... The Commission considers that the numerous and independent reports from survivors identifying their attackers as wearing Haddad militia insignia and speaking in southern accents constitute conclusive evidence that Haddad militiamen did play a significant part in the massacres. The proportions which the Phalange and Haddad militias contributed respectively to the attacking force cannot be assessed from the available information. It would seem, however, that the Phalangists contributed a higher percentage of men to the attacking force (consisting of several hundred men), and provided coordination and leadership for the entire operation.[138]

The anticipated international investigation

Given all the data concerning this horrific massacre that has become available over

20 years, it is now difficult for any judicial authority to ignore it. The American lawyer Franklin Lamb, who expended enormous effort in documenting testimonies about Sabra and Shatila, outlined six essential points for consideration. If these points were met, then Sharon and his government should be regarded as guilty:

Among the factual issues presented for considerations are:
- Whether the Israeli authorities foresaw or should have foreseen the massacre.
- Whether Israel supported, or had control over, the killer militias.
- Whether Israeli authorities abetted the perpetrators of the massacre.
- Whether, and when, the Israeli Army authorities learned that civilians were being killed.
- Whether the Israelis could have acted to prevent or terminate the massacre.
- Whether Israeli officials tried to stop the massacre.[139]

The preceding pages contain abundant information and data related to each of the six points above. They are surely more than enough to convict Sharon and all the Israeli military and political officials supporting him; all the more so in that (as discussed above) Israel is unanimously regarded as having been an occupying nation.

Sharon himself was in a position to know before anyone, and this it was that prompted him to mobilize all his efforts in obstructing the lawsuit brought against him, and also against Amos Yaron, who was in command in the district, and against anyone else the investigation showed to have been linked to the massacre. The plaintiffs, 23 massacre survivors, submitted the case to the Belgian judiciary on 18 June 2001, through three lawyers: the Lebanese Chibli Mallat and the Belgians Luc Walleyn and Michaël Verhaeghe. These lawyers were able to raise the case after so many years by virtue of legislation established in Belgium in 1993, and amended in 1999, in relation to the punishment of major violators of international human rights.

Even now, in fact, the feasibility of the case is not entirely clear, owing to doubts over the court's precise competence in the matter. The significance of the suit remains, however, in the fact that it opened up the way for the trial of those responsible for the Sabra and Shatila massacre at an international tribunal, whether in Belgium or elsewhere; all the more so in that the idea of an international trial has been raised more than once, notably by the reporter Fergal Keane during a programme broadcast by the BBC in 2001, in which he suggested the possibility of having Sharon tried before an international war crimes tribunal.[140] It was Keane, too, who reported how, recently, Sharon had said he regretted the tragedy of Sabra and Shatila, but when asked if he would also like to apologize, replied: 'To apologize for what?'[141]

The crime of Sabra and Shatila was a crime against humanity. And, as Ilan Halevi has said, the absence of any official investigation by the United Nations merely demonstrates that body's incompetence vis-à-vis a tragedy within which Sabra and Shatila is only one episode.[142] Urging the need to set up an international criminal court, he said:

There are a number reasons, both good and bad, that combined together to conceal the perpetrators' role in this case. A more convincing, influential and damaging demand against Israel might be for an international criminal court for the perpetrators ...

Would it not be better to deal with the chain from the bottom up to the top, with particular attention paid to those officials who were directly involved and have already been checked out? If these people were to be summoned to an international (or local) judicial court, where their personal freedom would be jeopardized, then how many would remain silent? This would lead, eventually, to a means of assigning direct responsibility from the bottom, up to the top ...

If such a demand appears illusory at present, this is due merely to the negligence, slackness and impotence of the international legal system. What system can survive when crimes of this magnitude are shuffled off without punishment?[143]

But would it be enough to find an international court prepared to make its rulings according to international law and natural justice, if human societies were not prepared to accept the verdicts? And not prepared to prevent the criminal, whoever he might be, from committing crimes against humanity?

Some societies, it is quite clear, are not so prepared. And this was the point underlying what the Israeli writer Yoel Marcus wrote in his column on 19 November 1982 (in a piece entitled 'The Commission will Finish – the Government will Remain'), after the testimonies submitted to the Kahan Commission had begun to appear in the press:

In the matter of Sabra and Shatila – a large part of the community, perhaps the majority, is not at all troubled by the massacre itself. Killing of Arabs in general, and Palestinians in particular, is quite popular, or at least 'doesn't bother anyone,' in the words of the youth these days. Ever since the massacre I have been surprised more than once to hear from educated, enlightened people, 'the conscience of Tel Aviv,' the view that the massacre itself, as a step towards removing the remaining Palestinians from Lebanon, is not terrible. It is just too bad that we were in the neighborhood.[144]

As for Jacobo Timerman, born Russian Jewish, raised in Argentina and a naturalized Israeli, his appeal – or rather demand – for justice was intended to help save Jewish Israeli society, which he observed to be in decline. He began, accordingly, to ask Jews throughout the world to come to the rescue of Israeli Jews. Writing before the Israeli government's approval of a Commission of Inquiry on 21 September 1982, he said:

Only the world's Jewish people, I believe, can now do something for us. The Diaspora Jews who have maintained the values of our moral and cultural traditions – those values now trampled on here by intolerance and Israeli nationalism – should establish a Jewish tribunal to pass judgment on Begin, Sharon, Eitan, and the entire general staff of the Israeli armed forces. This alone could be the means of working free of the sickness that is destroying Israel, and, perhaps, of preserving Israel's future.

What is it that has turned us into such efficient criminals?

I fear that in our collective subconscious, we may not be wholly repelled by the possibility of a Palestinian genocide. I don't believe we Israelis can be cured without the help of others.[145]

When Timerman wrote this plea for help, he did not know that there was in fact a 'revolt' among the officers of Battalion 429. No one, indeed, could have known this outside the small Israeli inner military circle and the top political leadership. The matter came to light only after 20 years, when Yossi Danziger, one of the battalion's members, spoke of the affair and his testimony appeared in a recent book edited by Gal and Ilana Hammerman and entitled *From Beirut to Jenin* (published in Hebrew by Am Oved, at the end of 2002). But while the Arabic typescript of this book was in press, an article was published by Tom Segev in *Ha'aretz* (6 December 2002), containing Danziger's testimony, and the Internet websites immediately began to transmit it. Even so, the most important point is that this and similar testimonies should find their way to an international tribunal.

Recalling what had happened just a few days after the massacre, Yossi Danziger said: 'We heard the lies that the Israeli army knew nothing.' The first thought of his fellow officers and himself was, he said, to go to President Yitzhak Navon in Jerusalem and acquaint him with the full facts: that many people had known about the massacre while it was happening, but had not intervened to stop it. Eventually they decided to tender their resignation instead, going to the battalion commander, Amos Malka, and telling him: 'Pick up the phone, speak to the brigade commander and tell him the company commanders and operations officer of the 429th Battalion are resigning.' The battalion commander was astonished but did as they had asked: he contacted the high command with the news, and this it was that came to be known within the Israeli Army as 'the revolt' – though the witness narrator himself described it only as an 'ultimatum'. That same night, he concluded, Prime Minister Menachem Begin announced the setting up of a commission of inquiry, subsequently known as the Kahan Commission.[146]

As for the Israeli war in Lebanon in the summer of 1982, Danziger provided his succinct summary of this to Chief of Staff Rafael Eitan when the latter visited the battalion about ten days later:

This war is a total deception, you have duped us. What you are doing is not an operation to stop

Katyusha rockets. You carried out a political move in Lebanon, you wanted to create a new order, you sent us to crown the Phalangists there.[147]

Eitan was utterly furious – a reaction which may perhaps explain why the general Israeli population has only now, after 20 years, learned exactly what took place.

In the near future, when an international tribunal comes into being to prosecute those accused of the Sabra and Shatila massacre, the testimonies of Danziger and those like him will carry considerable weight in forming a clear picture of what really happened, before judges ruling under the auspices of international laws.

Finally: was anyone responsible?

A number of questions remain, finally, to be answered. Were the perpetrators the only ones responsible? Were the people who committed the crime the only criminals? Were even those who issued the orders solely responsible?

Even when we consider those hundreds of partisans and militiamen who committed a plain massacre, were there no differences between individuals among them? Was the crime just a single crime? And could there be a single just punishment?

Is it conceivable, on a human level, for crimes against humanity to be subject to unvarying sanction? Is it not conceivable that some of the attacking militiamen were themselves dragged off to the massacre site, without knowing exactly where they were going?

On the other hand, did some of the Lebanese Forces not proudly claim they had taken part in Shatila, even though their neighbours testified they were at home all the while? That they had all spent their nights together, playing cards, since the occupation of Beirut began?

And then, what of the friends of Sabra and Shatila – from Italy, Spain, Belgium, France, South America, the whole world? Can they ever quite have realized how very much their solidarity has meant for the families of victims?

Finally, though, we must return to the general question: Who, in truth, was responsible?

During the campaign against the war in Vietnam, Rabbi Abraham Heschel said: 'In a free society, some are guilty but all are responsible.'[148] But who are these 'all'? Really they are all the people, wherever they might be on the face of this earth. As the Argentinian singer Alberto Cortez sang, in the aftermath of Sabra and Shatila:

Where was the sun when anger burst at Sabra and Shatila? …
Where was I? At what party, careless, when I read the news?
And where were you – you so eager to defend the oppressed – when the massacre happened?
Where is the pride of men? …
Where were you, my friend with the sleeping conscience? Were you clapping the attacker, as he killed the children at Sabra and Shatila?

Twenty years ago, Cortez admitted responsibility as he sang these words about Sabra and Shatila; in Buenos Aires in the presence of 7,000 people from the Argentinian and Arab communities.

When will others be ready to admit their responsibility? First among them should be those who, in September 1982, laid siege to Sabra and Shatila. And those who, in September 1982, attacked Sabra and Shatila.

Notes

Chapter 1 The Place and the Residents: Between the Emigrations of 1948 and 1982

1 See George J. Tomeh (ed.), *United Nations Resolutions on Palestine and the Arab-Israeli Conflict 1917–1974*, Beirut: Institute for Palestinian Studies, 1975, pp. 4–14.

2 O.K. Rabinowicz, 'Basle Program', in *Encyclopedia of Zionism and Israel*, vol. 1, General Editor Geoffrey Wigoder, 2 vols, London and Toronto: Associated University Presses, 1975, p. 171.

3 Refer to the communication of August 1949 between the Chairman of the Lebanese delegation to the Lausanne talks and Eliaho Sasson, in Hassan Hallaq, *Mawqef Lubnan min al-Qadiyya al-Filastiniyya* [*Lebanon's Position vis-à-vis the Palestinian Question*], Beirut: Research Centre, 1982, p. 292.

4 Tomeh, *United Nations Resolutions on Palestine*, p. 16.

5 *Ibid.*, pp. 18–20.

6 UNRWA, *UNRWA's Emergency Operation in Lebanon: 1982–83*, Vienna: UNRWA, Vienna International Centre, March 1984, pp. 2–3.

7 *Ibid.*, p. 3.

8 UNRWA, *UNRWA in Lebanon*, Vienna: UNRWA for Palestine in the Near East, Public Information Office, 1992, p. 1.

9 Hallaq, *Mawqef Lubnan*, p. 168.

10 Youssef Kazma Khoury (ed. and compiler), *Al-Bayanat al-Wizariyya al-Lubnaniyya wa Monaqashatuha fi Majlis al-Nuwwab 1926–1984* [*Lebanese Ministerial Statements and Discussions of these in Parliament, 1926–1984*], vol. III, Beirut: Institute of Lebanese Studies, 1986, p. 2091.

11 POH. S/SH. No. 138 (234/ T.109). Mu'allem Dib, interview by Sana' Hammoudeh, Beirut – Shatila: narrator's home, 2 March 2001.

12 POH. S/SH. No. 6 (231/ T.1). Hana' Ahmad, interview with author, Beirut: author's home, 15 January 1983.

13 Palestine Organization for Human Rights, *Waqi' al-Laji'in al-Filastiniyyin fi Lubnan: Ila mata ... wa limatha?* [*The State of Refugee Palestinians in Lebanon*], Beirut: POHR, August 1999, p. 2.

14 Destruction of the camps continued even after 1982, due to a number of unfortunate civil wars. This occurred in the camps in the North as well as at Burj al-Barajneh, Shatila and the Tyre camps.

15 Shafiq al-Hout, 'Mustaqbal al-Ulaqat al-Lubnaniyya – al-Filastiniyieh' ['The Future of Lebanese-Palestinian Relations'], in *Lubnan wa Afaq al-Mustaqbal* [*Lebanon and Future Horizons*] (Documents and Discussions at the Research Seminar held by the Centre for Arab Unity Studies), Beirut: Centre for Arab Unity Studies, 1991, pp. 227–8.

16 Suheil Mahmoud al-Natour, *Awda' al-Sha'b al-Filastini fi Lubnan* [*Living Conditions of the Palestinian People in Lebanon*], Beirut: Dar al-Taqaddum al-Arabi, 1993, pp. 13, 27.

17 Abu Maher al-Yamani (Ahmad al-Yamani), interview with the author, '*Interviews with the Leaders of the Palestine National Movement*', Beirut, 1972 (unpublished). Abu Maher was at this time an activist with the National Arab Movement. He subsequently became one of the leaders of the Labour Movement and founders of the Popular Front for the Liberation of Palestine.

18 POH. S/SH. No. 128 (245/ T.98). Khaled Abadi, interview with author, Beirut: author's home, 11 September 1999.

19 POH. S/SH. No. 138 (234/ T.109). Mu'allem Dib.

20 Hallaq, *Mawqef Lubnan*, pp. 315–16.

21 *Ibid.*, pp. 317–18.

22 *Ibid.*, pp. 319–20.

23 *Ibid.*, p. 355.

24 Shafiq al-Hout, *Ishrun Aman fi Munathamat al-Tahrir al-Filastiniyieh: Ahadith al-Thikrayat 1964–1984* [*Twenty Years with the Palestine Liberation Organization: Recollections, 1964–1984*], Beirut: Dar al-Istiqlal, 1986, pp. 184–5.

25 POH. S/SH. No. 53 (231/ T.52). 'Abu Qassem', interview with author, Beirut: friend's home, 28 April 1983.

26 POH. S/SH. No. 136 (231/ T.107). Hajj 'Abu Ahmad', interview by Sana' Hammoudeh, Beirut – Shatila: narrator's home, 2 March 2001.

27 POH. S/SH. No. 66 (249/ N.11). Mahmoud S. ['Yafawi'], interview by Siham Balqis, Beirut – massacre district: narrator's home, 24 May 1983.

28 POH. S/SH. No. 53 (231/ T.52). 'Abu Qassem'.

29 POH. S/SH. No. 110 (231/ T.86). Hasan A. 'Abu Ali', interview with author, Beirut: narrator's office, 11 May 1984.

30 POH. S/SH. No. 137 (231/ T.108). Hajj 'Abu Khodr', interview by Sana' Hammoudeh, Beirut – Shatila: narrator's home, 2 March 2001.

31 POH. S/SH. No. 136 (231/ T.107). Hajj 'Abu Ahmad'.

32 POH. S/SH. No. 138 (234/ T.109). Mu'allem Dib.

33 POH. S/SH. No. 53 (231/ T.52). 'Abu Qassem'.

34 Ibid.

35 Ibid.

36 POH. S/SH. No. 44 (230/ T.44, 45). 'Abu Jamal', interview with author, Beirut: author's home, 19 March 1983.

37 Ibid.

38 POH. S/SH. No. 110 (231/ T.86). Hasan A. 'Abu Ali'.

39 Ibid.

40 Ibid.

41 Ibid.

42 POH. S/SH. No. 44 (230/ T.44, 45). 'Abu Jamal'.

43 Ibid.

44 POH. S/SH. No. 53 (231/ T.52). 'Abu Qassem'.

45 POH. S/SH. No. 128 (245/ T.98). Khaled Abadi.

46 POH. S/SH. No. 127 (239/ T.97). Ibrahim Iraqi, interview with author, Beirut: author's home, 11 September 1999.

47 POH. S/SH. No. 128 (245/ T.98). Khaled Abadi.

48 Ibid.

49 Ibid.

50 Ibid.

51 Ibid.

52 Ibid.

53 POH. S/SH. No. 127 (239/ T.97). Ibrahim Iraqi.

54 POH. S/SH. No. 128 (245/ T.98). Khaled Abadi.

55 Ibid.

56 Ibid.

57 POH. S/SH. No. 121 (231/ T.92), 'Abu Muhammad' Ali, interview with author, Beirut: narrator's office, 15 November 1998.

58 Ibid.

59 POH. S/SH. No. 122 (231/ T.93). 'Abu Khalil' Mahmoud, interview with author, Beirut: narrator's home, 22 November 1998.

60 POH. S/SH. No. 121 (231/ T.92). 'Abu Mahammad' Ali.

61 Hussein B., 'Memoirs' (manuscript in Arabic), 1999, p. 7.

62 POH. S/SH. No. 44 (230/ T.44, 45). 'Abu Jamal'.

63 POH. S/SH. No. 42 (238/ T.41, 42). Nawal Husari, interview with author, Beirut: author's home, 15 March 1983.

64 POH. S/SH. No. 19 (249/ T.22). H.Sh, 'Um Akram', interview with author, Beirut: author's home, 24 February 1983.

65 POH. S/SH. No. 44 (230/ T.44, 45). 'Abu Jamal'.

Chapter 2   The Israeli Army Encircles the District

1 POH. S/SH. No. 113 (241/ N.22). M.Kh., interview with author, Beirut: narrator's office, 5 June 1984.

2 Ibid.

3 POH. S/SH. No. 6 (231/ T.1). Hana' Ahmad, interview with author, Beirut: author's home, 15 January 1983.

4 POH. S/SH. No. 26 (241/ T.28). Ahmad Khatib, interview with author, Beirut: author's home, 1 March 1983.

5 Ibid.

6 POH. S/SH. No. 21 (241/ T.23). Khadijah Khatib, interview with author, Beirut: friend's home, 25 February 1983.

7 POH. S/SH. No. 18 (238/ T.19). D.M.H., 'Um Ali' al-Biqa'i, interview with author, Beirut: author's home, 22 February 1983.

8 POH. S/SH. No. 33 (231/ T.32). Amina A., 'Um Ibrahim', interview with author, Beirut – massacre area: friend's home, 3 March 1983.

9 POH. S/SH. No. 17 (231/ T.21). Y.A., 'Um Ahmad' Srour, interview with author, Beirut: author's home, 22 February 1983.

10 POH. S/SH. No. 34 (241/ T.33). Aziza Khalidi, interview with author, Beirut: author's home, 4 March 1983.

11 POH. S/SH. No. 46 (234/ T.47). Sa'ida D., interview by A.M., Beirut – massacre area: narrator's home, 22 March 1983.

12 POH. S/SH. No. 24 (240/ T.26). Harbeh J., 'Um Rabi'', interview by A.M.,

Beirut – massacre area: narrator's home, 28 February 1983.

13 POH. S/SH. No. 35 (238/ T.35). Nuzha H., interview by A.M., Beirut – massacre area: narrator's home, 6 March 1983.

14 POH. S/SH. No. 54 (230/ T.53). Anonymous, interview with author, Beirut: friend's home, 28 April 1983.

15 POH. S/SH. No. 103 (234/ N.21). Q.D., interview with author, Beirut: author's home, 1 March 1984.

16 POH. S/SH. No. 115 (231/ T.89). Fatima Ajami, interview with author, Beirut – massacre area: narrator's home, 13 July 1984.

17 POH. S/SH. No. 36 (236/ T.36). Hamza F., interview by A.M., Beirut – massacre area: narrator's home, 9 March 1983.

18 POH. S/SH. No. 20 (249/ T.22). Dalal Sh., interview with author, Beirut: author's home, 24 February 1983.

19 POH. S/SH. No. 19 (249/ T.22). H.Sh., 'Um Akram', interview with author, Beirut: author's home, 24 February 1983.

20 Ibid.

21 POH. S/SH. No. 63 (232/ T.61). Siham Balqis, interview with author, Beirut – massacre area, 9 May 1983.

22 POH. S/SH. No. 103 (234/ N.21). Q.D.

23 Zakaria al-Shaikh, 'Sabra and Shatila 1982: Resisting the Massacre', *Journal of Palestine Studies*, 53, Fall 1984, pp. 65, 67.

24 *Ibid.*; POH. S/SH. No. 24 (240/ T.26), Harbeh J. 'Um Rabi''; POH. S/SH. No. 50 (231/ N.7). Afifa A., interview by A.M., Beirut – massacre area: narrator's home, 5 April 1983; POH. S/SH. No. 51 (238/ N.8). Yusra N.H., interview by A.M., Beirut – massacre area: narrator's home, 5 April 1983.

25 POH. S/SH. No. 24 (240/ T.26). Harbeh J. 'Um Rabi''.

26 POH. S/SH. No. 26 (241/ T.28). Ahmad Khatib.

27 POH. S/SH. No. 137 (231/ T.108). Hajj 'Abu Khodr', interview by Sana' Hammoudeh, Beirut – Shatila: narrator's home, 2 March 2001.

28 POH. S/SH. No. 133 (249/ T.104). Riad Sharqieh, interview with author, Beirut – Shatila: narrator's home, 21 October 1999.

29 POH. S/SH. No. 111 (243/ T.87). As'ad M., interview with author, Beirut: narrator's office, 11 May 1984.

30 POH. S/SH. No. 133 (249/ T.104). Riad Sharqieh.

31 POH. S/SH. No. 110 (231/ T.86). Hasan A., 'Abu Ali', interview with author, Beirut: narrator's office, 11 May 1984.

32 POH. S/SH. No. 53 (231/ T.52). 'Abu Qassem', interview with author, Beirut: friend's home, 28 April 1983.

33 The war mentioned by the narrator is that known as the 'camps war'. It took place in the mid-1980s, during the siege of Shatila Camp by the Amal Movement.

34 POH. S/SH. No. 133 (249/ T.104). Riad Sharqieh.

35 Al-Shaikh, 'Sabra and Shatila 1982', p. 66.

36 POH. S/SH. No. 111 (243/ T.87). As'ad M.

37 POH. S/SH. No. 9 (249/ T.5). Ralph Schoenman, interview with author, Beirut: author's home, 27 January 1983.

38 Al-Shaikh, 'Sabra and Shatila 1982', pp. 65–6; quotation in English in the original.

39 Hussein B., 'Memoirs' (manuscript in Arabic), 1999, p. 3.

40 *Ibid.*

41 POH. S/SH. No. 110 (231/ T.86). Hasan A., 'Abu Ali'.

42 POH. S/SH. No. 13 (238/ T.9). Salim Hout, interview with author, Beirut: narrator's office, 11 February 1983.

43 POH. S/SH. No. 113 (241/ N.22). M.Kh.

44 POH. S/SH. No. 62 (232/ T.59). 'Um Majed' Balqis, interview with author, Beirut: friend's home, 5 May 1983.

45 Al-Akhdar al-Arabi's real name was Amin Sa'd, and he was one of the pioneers killed fighting the Israelis. A Ba'thist and a believer in the People's war of liberation, he died a martyr on the Sheb'a hills on 3 December 1969.

46 POH. S/SH. No. 18 (238/ T.20). D.M.H., 'Um Ali' al-Biqa'i.

47 POH. S/SH. No. 133 (249/ T.104). Riad Sharqieh.

48 POH. S/SH. No. 46 (234/ T.47). Sa'ida D.

49 *Ibid.*; POH. S/SH. No. 32 (232/ T.31). Thunaya B. ['Amin'], interview with author, Beirut – massacre area: narrator's home, 3 March 1983; POH. S/SH. No. 117 (230/ T.91). Anonymous, interview by Q.D., Beirut – massacre area: narrator's home, August 1984.

50 Amnon Kapeliouk, *Enquête sur un massacre: Sabra et Chatila*, Paris: Seuil, 1982, pp. 51–2.

51 POH. S/SH. No. 133 (249/ T.104). Riad Sharqieh.

52 POH. S/SH. No. 46 (234/ T.47). Sa'ida D.

53 *Ibid.*

54 *Ibid.*

55 *Ibid.*

56 Kapeliouk, *Enquête sur un massacre*, p. 52.

57 POH. S/SH. No. 129 (238/ T.99). Hajj 'Abu Hisham', interview by Khaled Abadi,

Beirut – Shatila: narrator's home, 15 September 1999.

58 *Davar*, Tel Aviv, 17 September 1982.

59 Hussein B., *Memoirs*, p. 7.

60 POH. S/SH. No. 129 (238/ T.99). Hajj 'Abu Hisham'.

61 Hussein B., *Memoirs*, p. 2.

62 POH. S/SH. No. 130 (231/ T.100). 'Abu Ra'ed', interview by Khaled Abadi, Beirut – Shatila: narrator's home, 29 September 1999.

63 *Ibid.*

64 *Ibid.*

65 *Ibid.*

66 *Ibid.*

67 *Ibid.*

68 *Ibid.*

69 POH. S/SH. No. 129 (238/ T.99). Hajj 'Abu Hisham'.

70 POH. S/SH. No. 130 (231/ T.100). 'Abu Ra'ed'.

71 POH. S/SH. No. 116 (239/ T.90). ['Ibrahim Baroudi'], interview by Q.D., Beirut – massacre area: narrator's home, August 1984.

72 *Ibid.*

73 POH. S/SH. No. 25 (230/ T.27). 'Abu Imad', interview by A.M., Beirut – massacre area: narrator's home, 1 March 1983.

74 POH. S/SH. No. 108 (249/ T.84). Zainab Saqallah, interview with author, Beirut: narrator's home, 7 March 1984.

75 POH. S/SH. No. 106 (243/ T.83). Mahmoud M., interview with author, Beirut: friend's home, 7 March 1984.

76 POH. S/SH. No. 135 (243/ T.106). Ali Murad, interview by Khaled Abadi, Beirut: narrator's home, November 2000.

77 POH. S/SH. No. 116 (239/ T.90). 'Ibrahim Baroudi'.

78 Arad Nir, 'Phalangists Entrusted with Sabra, Shatila "Purge" ', Tel Aviv Israeli Defence Forces Radio, 16 September 1982, cited in *The Beirut Massacre: Press Profile: September 1982*, New York: Claremont Research and Publications, November 1982, p. 4.

Chapter 3   Thursday 16 September 1982

1 POH. S/SH. No. 120 (247/ N.25). I.Q., interview with author, Beirut: author's home, 19 August 1986.

2 POH. S/SH. No. 5 (241/ N.5). Adele Kh., interview with author, Beirut: author's home, 9 January 1983.

3 Loren Jenkins, 'The Massacre: Witnesses Describe Militiamen Passing Through Israeli Lines', *Washington Post*, 20 September 1982, cited in *The Beirut Massacre: Press Profile: September 1982*, New York: Claremont Research and Publications, 1982, p. 11.

4 Thomas Friedman, 'The Beirut Massacre: The Four Days', *New York Times*, 23 September 1982, cited in *ibid.*, p. 67.

5 See Mark Whitaker, Ray Wilkinson (in Beirut), and Scott Sullivan (in Jerusalem), 'The Making of a Massacre', *Newsweek*, 4 October 1982, cited in *ibid.*, p. 85.

6 Amnon Kapeliouk, *Enquête sur un massacre: Sabra et Chatila*, Paris: Seuil, 1982, p. 44.

7 Robert Fisk, 'Reluctant Testimony on Shatila', *The Times*, 25 September 1982, cited in *The Beirut Massacre*, p. 40.

8 POH. S/SH. No. 63 (232/ T.60). Siham Balqis, interview with author, Beirut: massacre area, 9 May 1983; No. 44 (230/ T.44). 'Abu Jamal', interview with author, Beirut: outside talk along Shatila Main Street, 19 March 1983; No. 103 (234/ N.21). Q.D., interview with author, Beirut: author's home, 2 March 1984. See Map 3.

9 POH. S/SH. No. 41 (249/ T.40). Munira M. Sayyed, interview with author, Beirut: massacre area, narrator's home, 14 March 1983.

10 POH. S/SH. No. 29 (241/ T.30). Nofa Khatib 'Um Wassim', interview with author, Beirut: massacre area, narrator's home, 3 March 1983.

11 POH. S/SH. No. 30 (249/ T.30). Abdallah Sayyed, interview with author, Beirut: massacre area, narrator's home, 3 March 1983.

12 No. 41 (249/ T.40). Munira M. Sayyed.

13 *Ibid.*

14 POH. S/SH. No. 45 (231/ T.46). Harbeh A. ['Barakat'], interview by A.M., Beirut: massacre area, narrator's home, 22 March 1983.

15 POH. S/SH. No. 60 (234/ T.57). Amaal al-Dirawi, interview with author, Beirut: author's home, 4 May 1983.

16 POH. S/SH. No. 59 (234/ T.55). Hind D., interview with author, Beirut: massacre area, narrator's home, 3 May 1983.

17 *Ibid.*

18 *Ibid.*

19 *Ibid.*

20 POH. S/SH. No. 112 (241/ T.88). Intissar Khalil 'Um Nabil', interview with author, Beirut: massacre area, narrator's home, 3 June 1984.

21 POH. S/SH. No. 26 (241/ T.28). Ahmad Khatib, interview with author, Beirut: author's home, 1 March 1983.

22 *Ibid.*

23 *Ibid.*

24 POH. S/SH. No. 44 (230/ T.45). 'Abu Jamal'.

25 WAFA bulletin, Beirut, 15 October 1982.

26 POH. S/SH. No. 44 (230/ T.44). 'Abu Jamal'.

27 POH. S/SH. No. 32 (232/ T.31). Thunaya B. ['Amin'], interview with author, Beirut: massacre area, narrator's home, 3 March 1983.

28 *Ibid.*

29 POH. S/SH. No. 46 (234/ T.47). Sa'ida D., interview by A.M., Beirut: massacre area, narrator's home, 22 March 1983.

30 POH. S/SH. No. 18 (238/ T.19). D.M.H, 'Um Ali' al-Biqa'i, interview with author, Beirut: author's home, 22 February 1983.

31 POH. S/SH. No. 26 (241/ T.28). Ahmad Khatib.

32 POH. S/SH No. 44 (230/ T.44). 'Abu Jamal'.

33 WAFA bulletin, Beirut, 17 October 1982. Interview by United Press correspondent Jack Rayden.

34 Kapeliouk, *Enquête sur un massacre*, pp. 50–1.

35 'Mary', 'Testimonies on Sabra and Shatila Massacre', Beirut, 1983 (manuscript), Testimony 7.

36 UNRWA, *List of the Elementary and Secondary Schools in Lebanon*, Vienna, UNRWA, 1979. (All the schools mentioned above were elementary schools, with the exception of the Jalil and Himmeh schools, which were both preparatory schools.)

37 POH. S/SH. No. 61 (243/ T.58). Munir Muhammad, interview with author, Beirut: friend's home, 4 May 1983. Above quotations from Munir's neighbour, who accompanied him to the interview.

38 *Ibid.*

39 Munir Muhammad. Above quotations from personal communication during a visit to Shatila, September 2000.

40 POH. S/SH. No. 64 (243/ T.62). Paul Morris, interview with author, Beirut: friend's home, 17 May 1983.

41 POH. S/SH. No. 13 (238/ T.9). Salim Hout, interview with author, Beirut: narrator's clinic, 11 February 1983.

42 Munir Muhammad, Beirut: Shatila, September 2000.

43 Colin Smith (in Beirut), Ian Mather and Eric Silver (in Jerusalem), 'Lebanon Massacre/ The Evidence: How the Cover-up was Blown', *Observer*, 26 September 1982, cited in *The Beirut Massacre*, p. 81.

44 POH. S/SH. No. 13 (238/ T.9). Salim Hout.

45 David Lamb, 'Survivors Raise Doubts on Israel Troops' Actions', *Los Angeles Times*, 20 September 1982, cited in *The Beirut Massacre*, p. 18.

46 POH. S/SH. No. 111 (243/ T.87). As'ad M., interview with author, Beirut: narrator's office, 11 May 1984.

47 POH. S/SH. No. 36 (236/ T.36). Hamza F., interview by A.M., Beirut: massacre area, narrator's home, 9 March 1983.

48 *Ibid.*

49 *Ibid.*

50 POH. S/SH. No. 37 (236/ T.37). Randa F., interview by A.M., Beirut: massacre area, narrator's home, 9 March 1983.

51 'Jeder von euch ist ein Racher: Ein libanesischer Milizionär über seine Taten beim Massaker von Beirut', *Der Spiegel*, 14 February 1983, p. 112.

52 POH. S/SH. No. 116 (230/ T.90). ['Ibrahim Baroudi'], interview by Q.D., Beirut: massacre area, narrator's home, August 1984.

53 Munir Muhammad, personal communication, Beirut: Shatila, September 2000.

54 POH. S/SH. No. 116 (230/ T.90). ['Ibrahim Baroudi'].

55 Fisk, 'Reluctant Testimony on Shatila', p. 40.

56 POH. S/SH. No. 24 (240/ T.26). Harbeh J., 'Um Rabi', interview by A.M., Beirut: massacre area, narrator's home, 28 February 1983.

57 *Ibid.*

58 POH. S/SH. No. 62 (232/ T.59). 'Um Majed' Balqis, interview with author, Beirut: friend's home, 5 May 1983.

59 POH. S/SH. No. 63 (232/ T.60). Siham Balqis.

60 POH. S/SH. No. 64 (243/ T.62). Paul Morris.

61 POH. S/SH. No. 116 (230/ T.90). ['Ibrahim Baroudi'].

62 'Jeder von euch ist ein Racher', p. 112.

63 POH. S/SH. No. 42 (238/ T.42). Nawal Husari, interview with author, Beirut: author's home, 15 March 1983.

64 *Ibid.*

65 *Ibid.*

66 POH. S/SH. No. 34 (241/ T.34). Aziza Khalidi, interview with author, Beirut: author's home, 4 March 1983.

67 POH. S/SH. No. 19 (249/ T.22). H.Sh., 'Um Akram', interview with author, Beirut: author's home, 24 February 1983.

68 POH. S/SH. No. 20 (249/ T.22). Dalal Sh., interview with author, Beirut: author's home, 24 February 1983.

69 POH. S/SH. No. 19 (249/ T.22). H.Sh. 'Um Akram'.

70 POH. S/SH. No. 69 (231/ T.63). Shahira Abu Rudaineh, interview by Siham Balqis,

Beirut: massacre area, narrator's home, 30 May 1983.

71 'Mary', 'Testimonies on Sabra and Shatila Massacre', Testimony 13.

72 POH. S/SH. No. 51 (238/ N.8). Yusra N.H., interview by A.M., Beirut: massacre area, narrator's home, 5 April 1983. (Testimony of Yusra's husband.)

73 Ibid.

74 Friedman, 'The Beirut Massacre', p. 69.

75 Abraham Rabinovich, 'IDF Fired Flares to Light Camps for Phalangists', Jerusalem Post, 22 September 1982, cited in The Beirut Massacre, p. 25.

76 POH. S/SH. No. 110 (231/ T.86). Hasan A., 'Abu Ali', interview with author, Beirut: narrator's office, 11 May 1984.

77 POH. S/SH. No. 115 (231/ T.89). Hajj 'Abu Ali' Ajami, interview with author, Beirut: massacre area, narrator's home, 13 July 1984. (Father and daughter, Fatima Ajami, interviewed.)

78 POH. S/SH. No. 115 (231/ T.89). Fatima Ajami.

79 POH. S/SH. No. 115 (231/ T.89). 'Abu Ali' Ajami.

80 POH. S/SH. No. 115 (231/ T.89). Fatima Ajami.

81 POH. S/SH. No. 135 (243/ T.106). Ali Murad, interview by Khaled Abadi, Beirut: narrator's home, November 2000.

82 POH. S/SH. No. 110 (231/ T.86). Hasan A., 'Abu Ali'.

83 POH. S/SH. No. 111 (243/ T.87). As'ad M.

Chapter 4   Friday 17 September 1982

1 POH. S/SH. No. 44 (231/ T.44). 'Abu Jamal', interview with author, Beirut: author's home, 19 March 1983.

2 POH. S/SH. No. 32 (231/ T.31). Thunaya B. ['Amin'], interview with author, Beirut: massacre area, narrator's home, 3 March 1983.

3 POH. S/SH. No. 46 (234/ T.47). Sa'ida D., interview by A.M., Beirut: massacre area, narrator's home, 22 March 1983.

4 POH. S/SH. No. 120 (247/ N.25). I.Q., interview with author, Beirut: author's home, 19 August 1986.

5 POH. S/SH. No. 116 (230/ T.90). ['Ibrahim Baroudi'], interview by Q.D., Beirut: massacre area, narrator's home, August 1984.

6 POH. S/SH. No. 19 (249/ T.22). H.Sh., 'Um Akram', interview with author, Beirut: author's home, 24 February 1983.

7 Ibid.

8 POH. S/SH. No. 69 (231/ T.63). Shahira Abu Rudaineh, interview by Siham Balqis, Beirut: massacre area, narrator's home, 30 May 1983.

9 POH. S/SH. No. 65 (241/ N.10). Aisha K., interview by Siham Balqis, Beirut: massacre area, narrator's home, 24 May 1983.

10 Abraham Rabinovich, 'IDF Fired Flares to Light Camps for Phalangists', Jerusalem Post, 22 September 1982, cited in The Beirut Massacre: Press Profile: September 1982, New York: Claremont Research and Publications, October 1982, p. 25.

11 Ibid.

12 William Smith, Robert Slater (in Jerusalem) and William Stewart (in Beirut), 'Crisis of Conscience', Time, 4 October 1982, cited in The Beirut Massacre, p. 89.

13 Rabinovich, 'IDF Fired Flares', p. 25.

14 'Jeder von euch ist ein Racher: Ein libanesischer Milizionär über seine Taten beim Massaker von Beirut', Der Spiegel, 14 February 1983, p. 112.

15 Ibid.

16 Ibid., p. 113.

17 Smith et al., 'Crisis of Conscience', p. 89.

18 POH. S/SH. No. 130 (231/ T.100). 'Abu Ra'ed', interview by Khaled Abadi, Beirut – Shatila: narrator's home, 29 September 1999.

19 Ibid.

20 Ibid.

21 Hussein B., 'Memoirs' (manuscript in Arabic) 1999, pp. 4–5.

22 Zaher al-Sa'di was subsequently assassinated by the Israeli intelligence services in Ain al-Hilweh Camp on 9 March 1990 for his role in the 'People's Court' set up to try those collaborating locally with the Israelis.

23 POH. S/SH. No. 130 (231/ T.100). 'Abu Ra'ed'.

24 Ibid.

25 POH. S/SH. No. 135 (243/ T.106). Ali Murad, interview by Khaled Abadi, Beirut: narrator's home, November 2000.

26 Ibid.

27 POH. S/SH. No. 116 (230/ T.90). ['Ibrahim Baroudi'].

28 Danish cameraman et al., video on the massacre (the 'Danish Video'), 1982.

29 Robert Fisk, 'Down Every Alleyway … Women, Young Men, Babies – Lying Where They Had Been Knifed or Machine Gunned to Death', The Times, 20 September 1982, cited in The Beirut Massacre, p. 7.

30 Jean Genet, 'Four Hours in Shatila', Journal of Palestine Studies, 46, Spring 1983, p. 16.

(Translated from the French original: 'Quatre Heures à Chatila', *Revue d'études palestiniennes*, 6, Winter, 1983, pp. 13–19.)

31 POH. S/SH. No. 13 (238/ T.9). Salim Hout, interview with author, Beirut: narrator's clinic, 11 February 1983.

32 POH. S/SH. No. 54 (230/ T.53). Anonymous, interview with author, Beirut: friend's home, 28 April 1983.

33 *Ibid.*

34 POH. S/SH. No. 35 (238/ T.35). Nuzha H., interview by A.M., Beirut: massacre area, narrator's home, 6 March 1983.

35 Franklin P. Lamb (ed. and compiler), *Israel's War in Lebanon: Eyewitness Chronicles of the Invasion and Occupation*, Boston: South End Press and Spokesman, 2nd edn, 1984, p. 586.

36 POH. S/SH. No. 35 (238/ T.35). Nuzha H.

37 POH. S/SH. No. 52 (249/ T.51). Ann Sunde, interview with author, Beirut: author's home, 6 April 1983.

38 *Ibid.*

39 *Ibid.*

40 POH. S/SH. No. 47 (251/ T.48).'Um Kamal', interview with author, Beirut: massacre area, narrator's home, 1 April 1983.

41 POH. S/SH. No. 46 (234/ T.47). Sa'ida D.

42 POH. S/SH. No. 52 (249/ T.51). Ann Sunde.

43 POH. S/SH. No. 113 (241/ N.22). M.Kh., interview with author, Beirut: narrator's clinic, June 1984.

44 POH. S/SH. No. 52 (249/ T.51). Ann Sunde.

45 POH. S/SH. No. 113 (241/ N.22). M.Kh.

46 POH. S/SH. No. 35 (249/ T.35). Nuzha H.

47 POH. S/SH. No. 113 (241/ N.22). M.Kh.

48 POH. S/SH. No. 52 (249/ T.51). Ann Sunde.

49 A previous testimony from a Palestinian doctor referred to the right side of Urabi's face. With this sole difference, all testimonies were in agreement on the severe injuries to his face, together with several others to his body.

50 POH. S/SH. No. 52 (249/ T.51). Ann Sunde.

51 Testimony of 'Marjaleena Oraby, Nurse, Finland', cited in Lamb, *Israel's War in Lebanon*, p. 587.

52 POH. S/SH. No. 52 (249/ T.51). Ann Sunde.

53 Testimony of 'Astrid Barkved, Health Worker, Norway', as cited in Lamb, *Israel's War in Lebanon*, p. 608.

54 POH. S/SH. No. 52 (249/ T.51). Ann Sunde.

55 *Ibid.*

56 *Ibid.*

57 POH. S/SH. No. 35 (238/ T.35). Nuzha H.

58 *Ibid.*

59 *Ibid.*

60 POH. S/SH. No. 37 (236/ T.36). Randa F., interview by A.M., Beirut: massacre area, narrator's home, 9 March 1983.

61 *Ibid.*

62 As cited in the WAFA Bulletin, 21 October, 1982.

63 As cited in *ibid.*, 24 October, 1982.

64 *Ibid.*

65 Lamb, *Israel's War in Lebanon*, p. 589.

66 POH. S/SH. No. 54 (230/ T.53). Anonymous.

67 POH. S/SH. No. 35 (238/ T.35). Nuzha H.

68 *Ibid.*; No. 54 (230/ T.53). Anonymous; No. 13 (238/ T.9). Salim Hout.

69 POH. S/SH. No. 54 (230/ T.53). Anonymous.

70 POH. S/SH. No. 52 (249/ T.51). Ann Sunde.

71 *Ibid.*

72 *Ibid.*

73 POH. S/SH. No. 110 (231/ T.86). Hasan A., 'Abu Ali', interview with author, Beirut: narrator's office, 11 May 1984; No. 111 (243/ T.87). As'ad M., interview with author, Beirut: narrator's office, 11 May 1984.

74 POH. S/SH. No. 35 (238/ T.35). Nuzha H.

75 Lamb, *Israel's War in Lebanon*, p. 588.

76 *Ibid.*

77 POH. S/SH. No. 52 (249/ T.51). Ann Sunde.

78 Lamb, *Israel's War in Lebanon*, p. 589.

79 *Ibid.*, pp. 588, 589.

80 POH. S/SH. No. 36 (236/ T.36). Hamza F., interview by A.M., Beirut: massacre area, narrator's home, 9 March 1983.

81 POH. S/SH. No. 86 (231/ T.74). Tony A. ['Jamil'], interview by Muna Sukkarieh, Beirut: narrator's office, June 1983.

82 POH. S/SH. No. 54 (230/ T.53). Anonymous.

83 Danish cameraman *et al.*, video.

84 POH. S/SH. No. 35 (238/ T.35). Nuzha H.

85 POH. S/SH. No. 34 (241/ T.34). Aziza Khalidi, interview with author, Beirut: author's home, 4 March 1983.

86 POH. S/SH. No. 19 (249/ T.22). H.Sh., 'Um Akram'.

87 POH. S/SH. No. 16 (248/ T.18). Hajj Mahmoud Rukn, interview with author, Beirut: author's home, 16 February 1983.

88 POH. S/SH. No. 35 (238/ T.35). Nuzha H.

89 POH. S/SH. No. 59 (234/ T.56). Hind D., interview with author, Beirut: massacre area, narrator's home, 3 May 1983.

90 POH. S/SH. No. 112 (241/ T.88). Intissar Khalil, 'Um Nabil', interview with author, Beirut: massacre area, narrator's home, 3 June 1984.

91 POH. S/SH. No. 26 (241/ T.28). Ahmad Khatib, interview with author, Beirut: author's home, 1 March 1983.

92 WAFA Bulletin, 17 October 1982.

93 *Ibid.*
94 POH. S/SH. No. 61 (243/ T.58). Munir Muhammad, interview with author, Beirut: friend's home, 4 May 1983. A neighbour spoke on behalf of the twelve-year-old boy, who approved everything that was said.
95 Munir Muhammad, personal communication during a visit to Beirut, September 2000.
96 POH. S/SH. No. 36 (236/ T.36). Hamza F.
97 POH. S/SH. No. 37 (236/ T.36). Randa F.
98 POH. S/SH. No. 23 (238/ T.24). Samiha Abbas Hijazi, interview with author, Beirut: author's home, 27 February 1983.
99 *Ibid.*
100 POH. S/SH. No. 110 (231/ T.86). Hasan A., 'Abu Ali'.
101 POH. S/SH. No. 24 (240/ T.26). Harbeh J., 'Um Rabi'', interview by A.M., Beirut: massacre area, narrator's home, 28 February 1983.
102 *Ibid.*
103 POH. S/SH. No. 69 (231/ T.63). Shahira Abu Rudaineh.
104 POH. S/SH. No. 115 (231/ T.89). Fatima Ajami, interview with author, Beirut: massacre area, narrator's home, 13 July 1984.
105 POH. S/SH. No. 29 (241/ T.30). Nofa Khatib, 'Um Wassim' interview with author, Beirut: massacre area, narrator's home, 2 March 1983.
106 POH. S/SH. No. 17 (231/ T.21). A.Y., 'Um Ahmad' Srour, interview with author, Beirut: author's home, 22 February 1983.
107 *Ibid.*
108 *Ibid.*
109 *Ibid.*
110 POH. S/SH. No. 18 (238/ T.19). D.M.H., 'Um Ali' al-Biqa'i, interview with author, Beirut: author's home, 22 February 1983.
111 *Ibid.*
112 *Ibid.*
113 *Ibid.*
114 'Mary', 'Testimonies on Sabra and Shatila Massacre', Beirut, 1983, Testimony 1.
115 *Ibid*, Testimony 5.
116 *Ibid.*
117 *Ibid.*, Testimony 10.
118 POH. S/SH. No. 67 (231/ N.12). Mariam Abu Harb, interview by Siham Balqis, Beirut: massacre area, narrator's home, 24 May 1983.
119 *Ibid.*
120 POH. S/SH. No. 48 (231/ T.49). 'Um Muhammad' Aidi, interview with author, Beirut: massacre area, narrator's home, 1 April 1983.
121 *Ibid.*
122 *Ibid.*
123 POH. S/SH. No. 60 (234/ T.57). Amaal Dirawi, interview with author, Beirut: author's home, 4 May 1983.
124 *Ibid.*
125 POH. S/SH. No. 47 (251/ T.48). 'Um Kamal'.
126 *Ibid.*
127 POH. S/SH. No. 70 (243/ T.64). 'Um Ghazi Madi', interview by Siham Balqis, Beirut: massacre area, narrator's home, 30 May 1983.
128 *Ibid.*
129 *Ibid.*

Chapter 5 Saturday, 18 September 1982

1 POH. S/SH. No. 62 (232/ T.59). 'Um Majed' Balqis, interview with author, Beirut: friend's home, 5 May 1983.
2 *Ibid.*
3 POH. S/SH. No. 54 (230/ T.53). Anonymous, interview with author, Beirut: friend's home, 28 April 1983.
4 *Ibid.*
5 *Ibid.*
6 POH. S/SH. No. 34 (241/ T.33). Aziza Khalidi, interview with author, Beirut: author's home, 4 March 1983.
7 The Lebanese leader Ma'rouf Sa'd was struck down during a demonstration held by the fishermen of Sidon in February 1975. Doctors were unable to save him; he died on 6 March 1975. His funeral was an imposing affair, both Sidonese and Palestinians draping his body with the Palestinian flag.
8 POH. S/SH. No. 42 (238/ T.41). Nawal Husari, interview with author, Beirut: author's home, 15 March 1983.
9 POH. S/SH. No. 34 (241/ T.33). Aziza Khalidi.
10 POH. S/SH. No. 110 (231/ T.86). Hasan A., 'Abu Ali', interview with author, Beirut: narrator's office, 11 May 1984.
11 POH. S/SH. No. 34 (241/ T.33). Aziza Khalidi; No. 42 (238/ T.41). Nawal Husari.
12 Amnon Kapeliouk, *Enquête sur un massacre: Sabra et Chatila*, Paris: Seuil, 1982, p. 79.
13 POH. S/SH. No. 64 (243/ T.62). Paul Morris, interview with author, Beirut: friend's home, 17 May 1983.
14 POH. S/SH. No. 34 (241/ T.33). Aziza Khalidi.
15 David Henly *et al.* (eds), *Witness of War Crimes in Lebanon: Testimony given to the Nordic Commission, Oslo, October 1982*, London: International Organization for the Elimination of all Forms of Racial Discrimination (EAFORD), Ithaca Press, 1983, p. 120.

16 Ellen Siegel, 'Inside and Outside the Hospital, People Were Screaming: "Haddad, *Kataeb,* Israel–Massacre" ', *Journal of Palestine Studies*, 46, Winter 1983, p. 62.

17 POH. S/SH. No. 34 (241/ T.33). Aziza Khalidi.

18 POH. S/SH. No. 64 (243/ T.62). Paul Morris.

19 Testimony of Dr Per Maehlumschlagen, cited in Henly *et al., Witness of War Crimes,* p. 125.

20 Evidence of Dr Swee Chai Ang, 4 October 1982, cited in Sean MacBride (Chairman) *Israel in Lebanon: The Report of the International Commission to Inquire into Reported Violations of International Law by Israel During its invasion of the Lebanon,* London, 28 August 1982–29 November 1983, London: Ithaca Press, 1983, p. 269.

21 Testimony of Dr Paul Morris to the Kahan Commission, cited in Franklin P. Lamb (ed.), *Israel's War in Lebanon: Eyewitness Chronicles of the Invasion and Occupation,* Boston: South End Press, 1984, pp. 579–80.

22 Danish cameraman *et al.,* video on the massacre (the 'Danish Video'), 1982.

23 Thomas Friedman, 'The Beirut Massacre: The Four Days', *New York Times,* 26 September 1982, cited in *The Beirut Massacre: Press Profile: September 1982,* New York: Claremont Research and Publications, 1982, p. 68.

24 POH. S/SH. No. 103 (234/ N.21). Q.D., interview with author, Beirut: author's home, March 1984.

25 POH. S/SH. No. 111 (243/ N.87). As'ad M., interview with author, Beirut: narrator's home, 11 May 1984.

26 POH. S/SH. No. 18 (238/ T.19, 20). D.M.H., 'Um Ali' al-Biqa'i, interview with author, Beirut: author's home, 22 February 1983.

27 POH. S/SH. No. 26 (241/ T.26). Ahmad Khatib, interview with author, Beirut: author's home, 27 February 1983.

28 Kapeliouk, *Enquête sur un massacre,* p. 61.

29 Swee Chai Ang, *From Beirut to Jerusalem,* London: Grafton Books, 1989, p. 59; POH. S/SH. No. 34 (241/ T.34). Aziza Khalidi.

30 Swee Chai Ang, *From Beirut to Jerusalem.*

31 POH. S/SH. No. 34 (241/ T.34). Aziza Khalidi; No. 42 (238/ T.42). Nawal Husari.

32 POH. S/SH. No. 52 (249/ T.51). Ann Sunde, interview with author, Beirut: author's home, 6 April 1983.

33 *Ibid.*

34 POH. S/SH. No. 34 (241/ T.34). Aziza Khalidi.

35 POH. S/SH. No. 52 (249/ T.51). Ann Sunde.

36 *Ibid.;* POH. S/SH. No. 34 (241/ T.34). Aziza Khalidi.

37 Siegel, 'Inside and Outside the Hospital', p. 63.

38 *Ibid.,* p. 64.

39 POH. S/SH. No. 34 (241/ T.34). Aziza Khalidi.

40 Testimony of Vera Talseth, cited in Henly *et al., Witness of War Crimes,* p. 120.

41 Swee Chai Ang, *From Beirut to Jerusalem,* p. 60.

42 Siegel, 'Inside and Outside the Hospital', p. 63.

43 *Ibid.,* pp. 63–4.

44 Swee Chai Ang, *From Beirut to Jerusalem,* pp. 60–1.

45 POH. S/SH. No. 64 (243/ T.62). Paul Morris.

46 POH. S/SH. No. 134 (243/ T.105). Munir Muhammad, interview with author, Beirut: author's home, 1 September 2000.

47 Swee Chai Ang, *From Beirut to Jerusalem,* p. 61.

48 *Ibid.,* p. 62.

49 *Ibid.*

50 *Ibid.,* p. 61.

51 Testimony of Dr Juhani Pajula, cited in Henly *et al., Witness of War Crimes,* pp. 120–1.

52 Siegel, 'Inside and Outside the Hospital', p. 64.

53 Testimony of Dr Juhani Pajula, cited in Henly *et al., Witness of War Crimes,* pp. 121–2.

54 Siegel, 'Inside and Outside the Hospital', p. 65.

55 *Ibid.*

56 Testimony of Dr Swee Chai Ang, cited in MacBride, *Israel in Lebanon,* p. 270.

57 Swee Chai Ang, *From Beirut to Jerusalem,* pp. 63–4.

58 Siegel, 'Inside and Outside the Hospital', pp. 65–6.

59 *Ibid.,* p. 67.

60 Testimony of Dr Phil McKenna, cited in MacBride, *Israel in Lebanon,* p. 271.

61 Swee Chai Ang, *From Beirut to Jerusalem,* pp. 64–5.

62 Testimony of Dr Juhani Pajula, cited in Henly *et al., Witness of War Crimes,* p. 122.

63 Testimony of Dr Paul Morris to the Kahan Commission, cited in Lamb, *Israel's War in Lebanon,* p. 582.

64 Testimony of Dr Phil McKenna, cited in MacBride, *Israel in Lebanon,* p. 271.

65 Swee Chai Ang, *From Beirut to Jerusalem,* p. 64.

66 *Ibid.;* Siegel, 'Inside and Outside the Hospital', p. 66.

67 Testimony of Dr Juhani Pajula, cited in Henly *et al., Witness of War Crimes,* p. 123.

68 *Yarmulke*: a skullcap worn by pious Jews.
69 Siegel, 'Inside and Outside the Hospital', pp. 66–7.
70 Testimony of Dr Swee Chai Ang, cited in MacBride, *Israel in Lebanon*, p. 271.
71 *Ibid.*, p. 272.
72 Siegel, 'Inside and Outside the Hospital', p. 67.
73 Testimony of Dr Phil McKenna, cited in Henly *et al.*, *Witness of War Crimes*, p. 124.
74 *Ibid.*
75 Testimony of Dr Paul Morris to the Kahan Commission, cited in Lamb, *Israel's War in Lebanon*, p. 583.
76 Siegel, 'Inside and Outside the Hospital', pp. 67–8.
77 POH. S/SH. No. 16 (248/ T.16). Hajj Mahmoud Rukn, interview with author, Beirut: author's home, 22 February 1983.
78 POH. S/SH. No. 54 (230/ T.53). Anonymous.
79 POH. S/SH. No. 63 (232/ T.60). Siham Balqis, interview with author, Beirut: massacre area, 9 May 1983.
80 *Ibid.*
81 *Ibid.*
82 POH. S/SH. No. 16 (248/ T.17). Hajj Mahmoud Rukn.
83 POH. S/SH. No. 63 (232/ T.60). Siham Balqis.
84 POH. S/SH. No. 16 (248/ T.16). Hajj Mahmoud Rukn.
85 POH. S/SH. No. 63 (232/ T.60). Siham Balqis.
86 POH. S/SH. No. 45 (231/ T.46). Harbeh A. ['Barakat'], interview by A.M., Beirut: massacre area, narrator's home, 22 March 1983.
87 POH. S/SH. No. 58 (231/ N.9). Muhammad Awwad, interview with author, Beirut: author's home, 2 May 1983.
88 Danish cameraman *et al.*, video.
89 *Ibid.*
90 POH. S/SH. No. 16 (248/ T.18). Hajj Mahmoud Rukn.
91 *Ibid.*
92 *Ibid.*
93 *Ibid.*
94 Evidence of Dr Phil McKenna on 4 October 1982, cited in MacBride, *Israel in Lebanon*, pp. 270–1.
95 Swee Chai Ang, *From Beirut to Jerusalem*, p. 63.
96 Testimony of Dr Juhani Pajula, cited in Henly *et al.*, *Witness of War Crimes*, pp. 121–2.
97 POH. S/SH. No. 16 (248/ T.16). Hajj Mahmoud Rukn.
98 Siegel, 'Inside and Outside the Hospital', pp. 64–5.
99 POH. S/SH. No. 63 (232/ T.60). Siham Balqis.
100 Friedman, 'The Beirut Massacre', p. 73.
101 Siegel, 'Inside and Outside the Hospital', p. 65.
102 Swee Chai Ang, *From Beirut to Jerusalem*, p. 63.
103 POH. S/SH. No. 123 (235/ N.26). Huda H., interview with author, Beirut: narrator's home, 2 December 1998.
104 POH. S/SH. No. 116 (230/ T.90). 'Ibrahim', interview by Q.D., Beirut: massacre area, narrator's home, August 1984.
105 POH. S/SH. No. 123 (235/ N.26). Huda H.
106 POH. S/SH. No. 16 (248/ T.16). Hajj Mahmoud Rukn.
107 POH. S/SH. No. 96 (251/ N.18). 'Um Sulaiman', interview with author, Beirut: massacre area, friend's home, 3 August 1983.
108 POH. S/SH. No. 16 (248/ T.18). Hajj Mahmoud Rukn.
109 Chibli Mallat, Luc Walleyn and Michael Verhaeghe, 'The Lawsuit Made by a Number of the Sabra and Shatila Massacre Survivors Against Sharon and Other Parties Responsible for the Sabra and Shatila Massacre of 1982 to the Belgian Judiciary', Brussels, 18 June 2001.
110 POH. S/SH. No. 111 (243/ T.87). As'ad M.
111 POH. S/SH. No. 54 (230/ T.53). Anonymous.
112 *Ibid.*
113 *Ibid.*
114 *Ibid.*
115 Dar al-Fatwa – Lebanese Republic, 'List of Names of Victims Killed or Abducted During the Sabra and Shatila Massacre', Beirut, 1982–84.
116 Committee for Families of the Kidnapped and Disappeared in Lebanon, 'List of Names of the Kidnapped and Disappeared in Lebanon', 1975–83, Beirut, 1982–83.
117 *Al-Safir*, 29 December 1983.
118 Record of the Sabra and Shatila Field Study (Supplement), Phase 2: 'The Fate of Those Abducted', Beirut, 1998–99.
119 POH. S/SH. No. 16 (248/ T.17). Hajj Mahmoud Rukn.
120 *Ibid.*
121 Danish cameraman *et al.*, video.
122 POH. S/SH. No. 63 (232/ T.61). Siham Balqis.
123 POH. S/SH. No. 16 (248/ T.18). Hajj Mahmoud Rukn.
124 *Al-Nahar*, 19 September 1982.

125 POH. S/SH. No. 16 (248/ T.17). Hajj Mahmoud Rukn.

126 *Ibid.*

Chapter 6   The Killer and the Victim

1 David Lamb, 'Survivors Raise Doubts on Israel's Troops' Actions', *Los Angeles Times*, 20 September 1982, cited in *The Beirut Massacre: Press Profile: September 1982*, New York: Claremont Research and Publications, 1982, p. 18.

2 Ryuichi Hirokawa (photographer and ed.), 'Witness', in *Beirut 1982: From the Israeli Invasion to the Massacre of Sabra and Shatila Camps*, Damascus: PLO Central Council's Ad Hoc Committee on Sabra and Shatila, December 1982, p. 74.

3 Jean Genet, 'Four Hours in Shatila', *Journal of Palestine Studies*, 46, Spring 1983, p. 4. (Translation of French original, 'Quatre Heures à Chatila', *Revue d'études palestiniennes*, 6, Winter 1983, pp. 3–19.)

4 *Ibid.*, p. 5.

5 Robert Fisk, 'Down Every Alleyway … Women, Young Men, Babies – Lying Where They Had Been Knifed or Machine Gunned to Death', *The Times*, 20 September 1982, cited in *The Beirut Massacre*, p. 7.

6 Interview with Loren Jenkins, *Washington Post* Beirut Correspondent. Excerpts from transcript of *All Things Considered*, National Public Radio, 20 September 1982, cited in *ibid.*, p. 13.

7 Ian Glover-James, 'New Panic in Camp', *Daily Telegraph*, cited in *ibid.*, p. 16.

8 POH. S/SH. No. 8 (249/ T.4). Mya Shone, interview with author, Beirut: author's home, 27 January 1983.

9 Mark Fineman, 'In Shatila, the Stench of Death', *Philadelphia Inquirer*, 20 September 1982, cited in *The Beirut Massacre*, p. 14.

10 Genet, 'Four Hours in Shatila', p. 4.

11 *Ibid.*, p. 9.

12 *Ibid.*

13 *Ibid.*, p. 18.

14 POH. S/SH. No. 126 (243/ T.96). Hajj Maysam, interview with author, Beirut: author's home, 17 August 1999.

15 POH. S/SH. No. 116 (230/ T.90). ['Ibrahim Baroudi'], interview by Q.D., Beirut: massacre area, narrator's home, August 1984.

16 POH. S/SH. No. 38 (240/ T.37). Ussama J., interview with author, Beirut: narrator's home, 10 March 1983.

17 *Al-Nahar*, 19 September 1982.

18 POH. S/SH. No. 125 (243/ T.95). Ma'moun Mukahhal, interview with author, Beirut: author's home, 19 April 1999.

19 *Al-Nahar*, 20 September 1982.

20 See the dailies *Al-Safir* and *Al-Nahar*, June–August 1982; Sean MacBride (Chairman), *Israel in Lebanon: The Report of the International Commission to enquire into reported violations of International Law by Israel during its invasion of the Lebanon*, London, 28 August 1982–29 November 1983, London: Ithaca Press, 1983, p. 188; Franklin P. Lamb (ed.), *Israel's War in Lebanon: Eyewitness Chronicles of the Invasion and Occupation*, Boston: South End Press, 1984, pp. 419–536.

21 See Danish cameraman *et al.*, video on the massacre (the 'Danish Video'), 1982.

22 POH. S/SH. No. 82 (244/ T.71). Imad T., interview by Muna Sukkarieh, Beirut: narrator's office, June 1983.

23 POH. S/SH. No. 126 (243/ T.96). Hajj Maysam.

24 POH. S/SH. No. 76 (238/ T.68). Wafiq H., interview by Muna Sukkarieh, Beirut: narrator's office, June 1983.

25 POH. S/SH. No. 125 (243/ T. 95). Ma'Moun Mukahhal.

26 POH. S/SH. No. 75 (242/ T.67). Nuhad L. ['Israwi'], interview by Muna Sukkarieh, Beirut: narrator's office, June 1983.

27 POH. S/SH. No. 73 (238/ T.66). Hasan H. ['Hamzawi'], interview by Muna Sukkarieh, Beirut: narrator's office, June 1983.

28 POH. S/SH. No. 55 (249/ T.54). Shawqi Sh., interview with author, Beirut: author's home, 30 April 1983.

29 POH. S/SH. No. 81 (244/ T.70). Ziad N. ['Madani'], interview by Muna Sukkarieh, Beirut: narrator's office, June 1983.

30 POH. S/SH. No. 55 (249/ T.54). Shawqi Sh.

31 POH. S/SH. No. 126 (243/ T.96). Hajj Maysam.

32 POH. S/SH. No. 16 (248/ T.18). Hajj Mahmoud Rukn, interview with author, Beirut: author's home, 16 February 1983.

33 *Al-Nahar*, 21 September 1982.

34 POH. S/SH. No. 65 (241/ N.10). Aisha K., interview by Siham Balqis, Beirut: massacre area, narrator's home, 24 May 1983.

35 POH. S/SH. No. 14 (243/ T.13). A.M., interview with author, Beirut: author's home, 14 February 1983.

36 POH. S/SH. No. 19 (249/ T.22). H.Sh.,'Um Akram', interview with author, Beirut: author's home, 24 February 1983.

37 *The Beirut Massacre: The Complete Kahan Commission Report*, New York: Karz-Cohl

Publishing, 1983 (authorized translation of *The Commission of Inquiry into the Events at the Refugee Camps in Beirut*, 1983: *Final Report*), p. 37.

38 Lamb, *Israel's War in Lebenon*, pp. 583–4.

39 Ron Ben-Yishay, 'Ben-Yishay Reconstructs Beirut Massacre', *Jerusalem Domestic Television Service*, 24 September 1982, cited in *The Beirut Massacre*, p. 61.

40 Thomas Friedman, 'Beirut Massacre: The Four Days', *New York Times*, 26 September 1982; cited in *ibid.*, p. 73.

41 Fisk, 'Down Every Alleyway', pp. 6–7.

42 Mark Whitaker, Ray Wilkinson (in Beirut) and Scott Sullivan (in Jerusalem), 'The Making of a Massacre', *Newsweek*, 4 October 1982, cited in *The Beirut Massacre*, p. 86.

43 POH. S/SH. No. 59 (234/ T.56). Hind D., interview with author, Beirut: massacre area, narrator's home, 3 May 1983.

44 POH. S/SH. No. 54 (230/ T.53). Anonymous, interview with author, Beirut: friend's home, 28 April 1983.

45 POH. S/SH. No. 62 (232/ T.59). 'Um Majed' Balqis, interview with author, Beirut: friend's home, 5 May 1983.

46 POH. S/SH. No. 89 (231/ T.75). Sadeq A., interview by Siham Balqis, Beirut: massacre area, narrator's home, June 1983.

47 POH. S/SH. No. 44 (231/ T.44). 'Abu Jamal', interview with author, Beirut: massacre area, Shatila Street, 3 March 1983.

48 POH. S/SH. No. 75 (242/ T.67). Nuhad L.

49 POH. S/SH. No. 78 (231/ T.69). Fayez A., interview by Muna Sukkarieh, Beirut: narrator's office, June 1983.

50 POH. S/SH. No. 125 (243/ T.95). Ma'Moun Mukahhal.

51 Danish cameraman *et al.*, video.

52 *Ibid.*

53 POH. S/SH. No. 126 (243/ T.96). Hajj Maysam.

54 *Ibid.*

55 Shaykh Salman al-Khalil, Diaries (manuscript in Arabic), 1982, p. 13.

56 POH. S/SH. No. 75 (242/ T.67). Nuhad L.

57 POH. S/SH. No. 41 (249/ T.40). Munira Sayyed, interview with author, Beirut: massacre area, narrator's home, 14 March 1983.

58 POH. S/SH. No. 59 (234/ T.56). Hind D.

59 POH. S/SH. No. 112 (241/ T.88). Intissar Khalil, 'Um Nabil', interview with author, Beirut: massacre area, narrator's home, 3 June 1984.

60 POH. S/SH. No. 26 (241/ T.28). Ahmad Khatib, interview with author, Beirut: author's home, 1 March 1983.

61 POH. S/SH. No. 21 (241/ T.23). Khadija Khatib, interview with author, Beirut: friend's home, 25 February 1983.

62 POH. S/SH. No. 36 (236/ T.36). Hamza F., interview by A.M., Beirut: massacre area, narrator's home, 9 March 1983.

63 POH. S/SH. No. 24 (240/ T.26). Harbeh J., 'Um Rabi'', interview by A.M., Beirut: massacre area, narrator's home, 28 February 1983.

64 POH. S/SH. No. 19 (249/ T.22). H.Sh. 'Um Akram'.

65 POH. S/SH. No. 69 (231/ T.63). Shahira Abu Rudaineh, interview by Siham Balqis, Beirut: massacre area, narrator's home, 30 May 1983.

66 'Mary', 'Testimonies on Sabra and Shatila Massacre', (manuscript), Beirut, 1983, Testimony 13.

67 POH. S/SH. No. 17 (231/ T.21). Y.A., 'Um Ahmad', interview with author, Beirut: author's home, 22 February 1983.

68 POH. S/SH. No. 18 (238/ T.20). D.M.H., 'Um Ali' al-Biqa'i, interview with author, Beirut: author's home, 22 February 1983.

69 POH. S/SH. No. 67 (231/ N.12). Mariam Abu Harb, interview by Siham Balqis, Beirut: massacre area, narrator's home, 24 May 1983.

70 *Ibid.*

71 POH. S/SH. No. 48 (231/ T.49). 'Um Muhammad' Aidi, interview with author, Beirut: massacre area, narrator's home, 1 April 1983.

72 POH. S/SH. No. 70 (243/ T.64). 'Um Ghazi' Madi, interview by Siham Balqis, Beirut: massacre area, narrator's home, 30 May 1983.

73 *Ibid.*

74 POH. S/SH. No. 98 (251/ T.79). 'Um Isma'il', interview with author, Beirut: friend's home, 1 September 1983.

75 POH. S/SH. No. 90 (241/ N.14). 'Shaykh Salman al-Khalil, interview by Muna Sukkarieh, Beirut: narrator's home, June 1983.

76 'Mary', 'Testimonies on Sabra and Shatila Massacre', Testimony 12.

77 POH. S/SH. No. 50 (231/ N.7). Afifa A., interview by A.M., Beirut: massacre area, narrator's home, 5 April 1983.

78 POH. S/SH. No. 23 (238/ T.25). Samiha Abbas Hijazi, interview with author, Beirut: author's home, 27 February 1983.

79 *Ibid.*

80 *Al-Safir*, 25 September 1982.

81 POH. S/SH. No. 24 (240/ T.26). Harbeh J., 'Um Rabi''.

82 POH. S/SH. No. 42 (238/ T.42). Nawal Husari, interview with author, Beirut: author's home, 15 March 1983.

83 POH. S/SH. No. 69 (231/ T.63). Shahira Abu Rudaineh.

84 POH. S/SH. No. 63 (232/ T.61). Siham Balqis, interview with author, Beirut: massacre area, 9 May 1983.

85 POH. S/SH. No. 18 (238/ T.20). D.M.H., 'Um Ali' al-Biqa'i.

86 POH. S/SH. No. 36 (236/ T.36). Hamza F.

87 POH. S/SH. No. 45 (231/ T.46). Harbeh A. ['Barakat'], interview by A.M., Beirut: massacre area, narrator's home, 22 March 1983.

88 POH. S/SH. No. 89 (231/ T.75). Sadeq A.

89 Ellen Siegel, 'Inside and Outside the Hospital, People Were Screaming: "Haddad, Kataeb, Israel – Massacre" ', *Journal of Palestine Studies*, 46, Winter 1983, p. 64.

90 Dr Ang's testimony, 'Selected Testimony and Reports', cited in MacBride, *Israel in Lebanon*, p. 270.

91 Lamb, *Israel's War in Lebanon*, pp. 580–1.

92 POH. S/SH. No. 41 (249/ T.40). Munira Sayyed.

93 'Jeder von euch ist ein Racher: Ein libanesischer Milizionär über seine Taten beim Massaker von Beirut', *Der Spiegel*, 14 February 1983, p. 112.

94 Karl E. Buchalla, 'Beirut: Lokaltermin an der Stätte des Massenmords: Ein Horrorfilm aus der Wirklichkeit', *Süddeutsche Zeitung*, 23 September 1982.

95 ABC News, *Oh Tell the World What Happened*. Presented by Bill Redeker, one videotape (60 minutes), 7 January 1983.

96 POH. S/SH. No. 103 (234/ N.21). Q.D., interview with author, Beirut: author's home, 1 March 1984.

97 POH. S/SH. No. 45 (231/ T.46). Harbeh A.

98 POH. S/SH. No. 42 (238/ T.42). Nawal Husari.

99 POH. S/SH. No. 70 (243/ T.64). 'Um Ghazi' Madi.

100 POH. S/SH. No. 59 (234/ T.55). Hind D.

101 POH. S/SH. No. 89 (231/ T.75). Sadeq A.

102 POH. S/SH. No. 18 (238/ T.20). D.M.H., 'Um Ali' al-Biqa'i.

103 POH. S/SH. No. 54 (230/ T.53). Anonymous.

104 Most witnesses provide information on language and dialect. Those selected are simply the most detailed, specific interviews being as below: POH. S/SH. No. 16 (248/ T.18). Hajj Mahmoud Rukn; No. 18 (238/ T.20). D.M.H., 'Um Ali' al-Biqa'i; No. 20 (249/ T.22). Dalal Sh. Interview with author, Beirut: author's home, 24 February 1983; No. 30 (249/ T.30). Abdallah Sayyed. Interview with author, Beirut: massacre area, narrator's home, 3 March 1983; No. 35 (238/ T.35). Nuzha H. Interview by A.M., Beirut: massacre area, narrator's home, 6 March 1983; No. 42 (238/ T.42). Nawal Husari; No. 69 (231/ T.63). Shahira Abu Rudaineh.

105 POH. S/SH. No. 103 (234/ N.21). Q.D.

106 POH. S/SH. No. 73 (238/ T.66). Hasan H.; No. 74 (231/ T.66), Hasan A., interview by Muna Sukkarieh, Beirut: narrator's office, June 1983.

107 POH. S/SH. No. 81 (244/ T.70). Ziad N.

108 POH. S/SH. No. 26 (241/ T.28). Ahmad Khatib.

109 POH. S/SH. No. 112 (241/ T.88). Intissar Khalil, 'Um Nabil'.

110 POH. S/SH. No. 42 (238/ T.41, 42). Nawal Husari.

111 POH. S/SH. No. 110 (231/ T.86). Hasan A., 'Abu Ali', interview with author, Beirut: narrator's office, 11 May 1984.

112 POH. S/SH. No. 18 (238/ T.19). D.M.H., 'Um Ali' al-Biqa'i.

113 POH. S/SH. No. 16 (248/ T.17). Hajj Mahmoud Rukn.

114 Friedman, 'Beirut Massacre', p. 69.

115 Ben-Yishay, 'Ben-Yishay Reconstructs Beirut Massacre', p. 61.

116 POH. S/SH. No. 26 (241/ T.28). Ahmad Khatib.

117 POH. S/SH. No. 116 (230/ T.90). ['Ibrahim Baroudi'].

118 POH. S/SH. No. 34 (241/ T.34). Aziza Khalidi, interview with author, Beirut: author's home, 4 March 1983.

119 POH. S/SH. No.63 (232/ T.61). Siham Balqis.

120 MacBride, *Israel in Lebanon*, pp. 269–70.

121 Genet, 'Four Hours in Shatila', pp. 5–6.

122 POH. S/SH. No. 20 (249/ T.22). Dalal Sh.

123 POH. S/SH. No. 120 (247/ N.25). I.Q., interview with author, Beirut: author's home, August 1986.

124 POH. S/SH. No. 69 (231/ T.63). Shahira Abu Rudaineh.

125 POH. S/SH. No. 62 (232/ T.61). 'Um Majed' Balqis.

126 POH. S/SH. No. 101 (256/ N.20). M.Z., interview with author, Beirut: author's home, 2 December 1983.

Chapter 7 Field Study, Spring 1984

1 See the Appendix 2, List of names 3, for victims; List of names 4, for those abducted and missing. References for each individual name appear on the same line, with

relevant listing institutions given coded letters permitting easy cross-referencing.

2 *Al-Safir*, 26 July 2000.

3 Record of the Sabra and Shatila Field Study (Supplement), Phase 2: 'The Fate of Those Abducted', Beirut, 1998–99.

4 Chibli Mallat, Luc Walleyn and Michaël Verhaeghe, *The Lawsuit Made by a Number of the Sabra and Shatila Massacre Survivors Against Sharon and Other Parties Responsible for the Sabra and Shatila Massacre of 1982 to the Belgian Judiciary*, Brussels, 18 June 2001.

5 *The Beirut Massacre: The Complete Kahan Commission Report*, New York: Karz-Cohl Publishing, 1983 (authorized translation of *The Commission of Inquiry into the Events at the Refugee Camps in Beirut, 1983: Final Report*), pp. 14–15.

6 *Ibid.*, p. 19.

7 *Ibid.*, p. 22.

8 POH. S/SH. No. 7 (242/ T.2, 3). Abdul Rahman Labban, interview with author, Beirut: narrator's home, 22 January 1983.

9 *The Complete Kahan Commission Report*, p. 22.

10 *Ibid.*

11 *Ibid.*, p. 23.

12 *Ibid.*, pp. 23–4.

13 Abraham Rabinovich, 'IDF Fired Flares to Light Camps for Phalangists', *Jerusalem Post*, 22 September 1982, cited in *The Beirut Massacre: Press Profile: September 1982*, New York: Claremont Research and Publications, November 1982, p. 25.

14 Ze'ev Schiff and Menahem Horowitz, 'Massacre Not Revenge Planned Earlier', *Ha'aretz*, 28 September 1982, cited in *ibid.*, p. 52.

15 Loren Jenkins, 'Phalangists Implicated in Massacre', *Washington Post*, 30 September 1982, cited in *ibid.*, p. 55.

16 Howard Zinn, *The Politics of History*, Boston: Beacon Press, 1970, p. 7.

Chapter 8   Counting the Victims

1 *Al-Safir*, 19 September 1982.

2 *Ibid.*, 21 September 1982.

3 *Ibid.*

4 *Al-Nahar*, 21 September 1982.

5 *Al-Safir*, 22 September 1982.

6 *Ibid.*

7 *Ibid.*, 23 September 1982.

8 *Ibid.*, 24 September 1982.

9 *Ibid.*, 25 September 1982.

10 *Ibid.*, 26 September 1982.

11 *Al-Nahar*, 1 October 1982.

12 *Al-Safir*, 30 September 1982.

13 International Committee of the Red Cross, Information Department, 'Massacre in Beirut: ICRC Reacts Strongly'. Press Release No. 1450, Geneva: ICRC, 18 September 1982.

14 International Committee of the Red Cross, *Annual Report 1982*, Geneva: ICRC, 1983, pp. 57–8.

15 Sean MacBride (Chairman), *Israel in Lebanon: The Report of the International Commission to Inquire into Reported Violations of International Law by Israel During its Invasion of the Lebanon*, London, 28 August 1982–29 November 1983, London: Ithaca Press, 1983, p. 176.

16 David Henly *et al.* (eds), *Witness of War Crimes in Lebanon: Testimony Given to the Nordic Commission, Oslo, October 1982*, London: International Organization for the Elimination of all Forms of Racial Discrimination (EAFORD), Ithaca Press, 1983, p. 130.

17 'Massacre in Beirut Left 2,000 Dead, Lebanese Say', *Toronto Star*, 14 October 1982, cited in *The Beirut Massacre: Press Profile: September 1982*, New York: Claremont Research and Publications, November 1982, p. 47.

18 Amnon Kapeliouk, *Enquête sur un massacre: Sabra et Chatila*, Paris: Seuil, 1982, pp. 93–4.

19 International Committee of the Red Cross, *Liste des corps identifiés au Camp Chatila entre le 19. 09. 82 et le 22. 09. Après le massacre du 16/17. 09. 82.*

20 Lebanese Republic, Ministry of Interior, Department of Civil Defence, *Bodies Removed from the Sabra and Shatila Camps from 18/9/1982 to Thursday 30/9/1982* (signed by the Director of Civil Defence, Nazih Cham'oun), 15 October 1982 (Arabic).

21 Middle East Council of Churches, 'List of names of Sabra and Shatila victims', 1982.

22 Rawdat al-Shahidein cemetery, *Names of Sabra and Shatila Martyrs – Rawdat al-Shahidein Cemetery*, September 1982 (Arabic).

23 Shaykh Salman al-Khalil, 'List of Names of Victims, and, Missing in the Sabra and Shatila Massacre', 1982 (Arabic).

24 Al-Shuhada cemetery, 'Names of the Sabra and Shatila Martyrs – Al-Shuhada Cemetery', September 1982 (Arabic).

25 *Ibid.*

26 Palestinian Red Crescent Society (PRCS), Gaza Complex, 'Statement of the Number of Martyrs of the Sabra and Shatila Massacre', 7 April 1983 (Arabic).

27 PRCS, Akka Hospital, 'Statement of the Names of Those Killed as Martyrs or Missing at the Akka Hospital and the Adjacent al-Khatib Petrol Station', 1983 (Arabic).

28 Democratic Front for the Liberation of Palestine, 'List of Names of Victims and Abducted in the Sabra and Shatila Massacre', 1982–83 (in Arabic).

29 'Anonymous' Palestinian organization, 'List of Names of Massacre Victims and Those Abducted During the Massacre', 1983 (Arabic).

30 Dar al-Fatwa, Lebanese Republic, 'List of Names of Victims Killed or Abducted During the Sabra and Shatila Massacre', 1982–84 (Arabic).

31 Wadad was the wife of Adnan Halwani. The latter was a teacher at Raml al-Zarif second-ary school (subsequently renamed after the martyred President Reneh Mu'awad), and was abducted from his home in Ras al-Nabe' at one in the afternoon on 24 September 1982.

32 Committee for the Families of the Kidnapped and Disappeared in Lebanon, 'List of Names of the Kidnapped and Disappeared in Lebanon', 1975–83, Beirut, 1982–83 (Arabic).

33 Dar al-Fatwa, Lebanese Republic, 'Names of Abducted and Missing, Lebanese, Palestinian and Stateless', 1982–83 (Arabic).

34 'The Names of 110 People Abducted During the Massacres at the Sabra and Shatila Camps', *Al-Safir*, 15 October 1982.

35 'Applications Comprised 600 Names in Two Days', *Al-Nida'* 1 December 1982.

36 *Al-Safir*, September–November 1982.

37 Palestine Oral History: Sabra and Shatila (POH. S/SH), 'List of Names of Victims and Abducted'. Supervised by Bayan Nuwayhed al-Hout, 1982–84 (Arabic).

38 Record of the Sabra and Shatila Field Study, 'List of Names of Victims and Abducted'. Supervised by Bayan Nuwayhed al-Hout, spring 1984 (Arabic).

39 Lebanese Republic, Prime Ministry, Official Commission of Inquiry into the Fate of the Abducted and Missing, 'Data Based on Families' Applications', 1999 (Arabic).

40 *Al-Safir*, 26 July 2000.

41 Chibli Mallat, Luc Walleyn and Michaël Verhaeghe, Lawsuit Made by a Number of the Sabra and Shatila Massacre Survivors against Sharon and Other Parties Responsible for the Sabra and Shatila Massacre of 1982 to the Belgian Judiciary, Brussels, 18 June 2001.

42 Record of the Sabra and Shatila Field Study (Supplement), Phase 2: 'The Fate of Those Abducted', Beirut, 1998–99.

43 POH. S/SH. No. 81 (244/ T.70). Ziad N. ['Madani'], interview by Muna Sukkarieh, Beirut: narrator's office, June 1983.

44 POH. S/SH. No. 75 (242/ T.67). Nuhad L. ['Israwi'], interview by Muna Sukkarieh, Beirut: narrator's office, June 1983.

45 POH. S/SH. No. 73 (238/ T.66). Hasan H. ['Hamzawi'], interview by Muna Sukkarieh, Beirut: narrator's office, June 1983.

46 Most of the testimonies and quotations mentioned in this section have already been noted on previous pages. For this reason source references are provided only where the material appears for the first time.

47 Kapeliouk, *Enquête sur un massacre*, p. 79.

48 *Ibid.*, p. 80.

49 POH. S/SH. No. 16 (248/ T.18). Hajj Mahmoud Rukn, interview with author, Beirut: author's home, 16 February 1983.

50 POH. S/SH. No. 52 (249/ T.51). Ann Sunde, interview with author, Beirut: author's home, 6 April 1983.

51 POH. S/SH. No. 126 (243/ T.96). Hajj Maysam, interview with author, Beirut: author's home, 17 August 1999.

52 POH. S/SH. No. 90 (241/ N.14). Shaykh Salman al-Khalil, interview by Muna Sukkarieh, Beirut: narrator's home, June 1983.

53 POH. S/SH. No. 114 (241/ N.23). Khalil ['Izzidine'] (watchman), interview by Q.D., Beirut: al-Shuhada Cemetery, 8 July 1984.

54 POH. S/SH. No. 126 (243/ T.96). Hajj Maysam.

55 *Al-Safir*, 21 September 1982.

56 *Ibid.*, 25 September 1982.

57 POH. S/SH. No. 90 (241/ N.14). Shaykh Salman al-Khalil.

58 POH. S/SH. No. 16 (248/ T.18). Hajj Mahmoud Rukn.

59 Shlomo Nikdimon, 'Report of the Prosecutor Jermanos on the Sabra and Shatila Massacre', *Yedioth Ahronoth*, 2 December 1982.

60 *Al-Safir*, 3 December 1982.

61 Nikdimon, 'Report of the Prosecutor Jermanos'.

62 Lebanese Republic, *Bodies Removed from the Sabra and Shatila Camps*. This list originally contained 302 names. Closer examination, however, revealed that 33 names had been repeated (in some cases with the word 'repeated' typed in), while others we had to omit on account of further errors reflecting the haste with which the list had been

compiled. We finally fixed on a total of 254 names. The list included victims' ages.

63 ICRC, *Liste des corps*. The list originally contained 183 names, but we reduced this, on closer examination, to 179. We relied on the French copy of this list because it included the age in most cases, and what was not provided could be supplied from other lists.

64 One of these was a Palestinian woman married to a Lebanese. The rule we followed, however, was to take a woman's first, original nationality. A non-Palestinian woman married to a Palestinian was not able, under the prevailing rules, to take his nationality, and we were consequently obliged, as a matter of general principle, to take women's first nationality.

65 These included one Lebanese woman married to a Syrian and two married to Palestinians.

66 *Al-Safir*, 3 December 1983.

67 For a division into age categories, from unborn babies and infants to twelve-year-olds, see Chapter 7, pp. 252–3.

68 *The Beirut Massacre: The Complete Kahan Commission Report*, New York: Karz-Cohl Publishing, 1983 (authorized translation of *The Commission of Inquiry into the Events at the Refugee Camps in Beirut, 1983: Final Report*), p. 44.

69 *Ibid.*

70 *Ibid.*, pp. 44–5.

71 *Al-Safir*, 23 September 1982.

72 POH. S/SH. No. 101 (256/ N.20). M.Z., interview with author, Beirut: author's home, 2 December 1983.

Conclusion: Who was Responsible?

1 Jacobo Timerman, *The Longest War: Israel in Lebanon*. Translated from the Spanish by Miguel Acoco. New York: Alfred A. Knopf, 1982, pp. 164–5.

2 Ahmad Khalifeh, 'The Massacre from an Israeli Perspective: Between Lying and Denial!', *Seventh Day* magazine, 19, 17 September 1984, pp. 18–19 (Arabic).

3 *Ibid.*, p. 18.

4 Monte Carlo Broadcasting Service (Arabic), *News*, 7 p.m., 22 September 1982.

5 Besides the Commission Chairman, Yitzhak Kahan, there were two Commission Members: Judge Aharon Barak and General Yona Efrat.

6 Franklin P. Lamb, *International Legal Responsibility for the Sabra–Shatila Massacre*, France: Imp. TIPE, 1983, p. 22.

7 *Ibid.*, p. 24.

8 *Ibid.*, p. 25.

9 *Ibid.*, pp. 26–8.

10 *Ibid.*, p. 29.

11 *Ibid.*, p. 32.

12 Sean MacBride (Chairman), *Israel in Lebanon: The Report of the International Commission to Inquire into Reported Violations of International Law by Israel During its Invasion of the Lebanon*, London, 28 August 1982–29 November 1983, London: Ithaca Press, 1983, p. 163.

13 *Ibid.*

14 *Ibid.*

15 *Ibid.*, p. 169.

16 Rashid Khalidi, *Under Siege: P.L.O. Decision-making During the 1982 War*, New York: Columbia University Press, 1986, p. 183.

17 *Ibid.*, p. 184.

18 *Ibid.*, p. 175.

19 Noam Chomsky, *The Fateful Triangle: The United States, Israel and the Palestinians*, Boston: South End Press, 1983, p. 389. Omissions (...) are from the original quotation.

20 *Al-Nahar*, as quoted from Israeli TV, 26 August 1982.

21 *Ibid.*, 25 August 1982.

22 *Ibid.*, 26 August 1982.

23 *Ibid.*, 27 August 1982.

24 Ilan Halevi, *Israel: de la terreur au massacre d'Etat*, Paris: Papyrus, 1984, p. 21.

25 David K. Shipler, 'Israel Asserts its Troops Intervened to Minimize the Beirut Massacre', *New York Times*, 19 September 1982, cited in *The Beirut Massacre: Press Profile: September 1982*, New York: Claremont Research and Publications, October 1982, p. 9.

26 *Yedioth Ahronoth*, 9 August 1982.

27 *Ibid.*, 16 August 1982.

28 *Jerusalem Post*, 18 August 1982.

29 *Ibid.*, 19 August 1982.

30 *Yedioth Ahronoth*, 1 September 1982.

31 *Ibid.*, 3 September 1982.

32 *Ibid.*, 7 September 1982.

33 *Ibid.*, 16 September 1982.

34 Reuters (Jerusalem), 16 September 1982.

35 *Yedioth Ahronoth*, 17 September 1982.

36 *Al-Safir*, 2 September 1982.

37 Ze'ef Schiff and Ehud Ya'ari, *Israel's Lebanon War: The First Inside Story Account of a Disastrous Military Adventure and its Ongoing Consequences*, New York: Simon & Schuster, 1984, p. 259.

38 *Ibid.* Omissions (...) are from the original quotation.

39   *Ibid.*, p. 261.
40   *The Beirut Massacre: The Complete Kahan Commission Report*, New York: Karz-Cohl Publishing, 1983 (authorized translation of *The Commission of Inquiry into the Events at the Refugee Camps in Beirut, 1983: Final Report*), p. 28.
41   Michael Jansen, *The Battle of Beirut: Why Israel Invaded Lebanon*, London: Zed Press, 1982, p. 96.
42   *The Beirut Massacre: The Complete Kahan Commission Report*, p. 10.
43   MacBride, *Israel in Lebanon*, p. 170.
44   Jansen, *Battle of Beirut*, p. 96.
45   Halevi, *Israel*, p. 25.
46   Jonathan C. Randal, *Going All the Way: Christian Warlords, Israeli Adventures, and the War in Lebanon*, New York: Viking Press, 1983, p. 286.
47   Thomas Friedman, 'The Beirut Massacre: The Four Days', *New York Times*, 26 September 1982, cited in *The Beirut Massacre: Press Profile*, p. 76.
48   Chomsky, *Fateful Triangle*, p. 369, as quoted from B. Michael, *Ha'aretz*, 12 November 1982; Edward Walsh, *Washington Post – Boston Globe*, 26 December 1982; Robert Suro, *Time*, 4 October 1982.
49   *Ibid.*
50   *The Beirut Massacre: The Complete Kahan Commission Report*, pp. 18–19.
51   *Israel in Lebanon*, pp. 170–1. Italics in the original.
52   *The Beirut Massacre: The Complete Kahan Commission Report*, p. 15.
53   Mark Whitaker, Ray Wilkinson (in Beirut) and Scott Sullivan (in Jerusalem), 'The Making of a Massacre', *Newsweek*, 4 October 1982, as cited in *The Beirut Massacre: Press Profile*, p. 85.
54   As cited in Khalifeh, 'The Massacre from an Israeli Perspective', p. 19.
55   *The Beirut Massacre: The Complete Kahan Commission Report*, pp. 99–103.
56   *Ibid.*, pp. 22–3.
57   *Ibid.*, pp. 23–4.
58   *Ibid.*, pp. 24–5.
59   *Ibid.*, pp. 27–8.
60   *Ibid.*, pp. 26, 29, 32.
61   *Ibid.*, pp. 33, 39.
62   *Ibid.*, p. 33.
63   *Ibid.*, p. 35.
64   *Ibid.*, p. 37.
65   *Ibid.*, p. 39.
66   *Ibid.*, p. 63.
67   Schiff and Ya'ari, *Israel's Lebanon War*, p. 272.
68   *The Beirut Massacre: The Complete Kahan Commission Report*, p. 50.
69   Schiff and Ya'ari, *Israel's Lebanon War*, p. 275.
70   MacBride, *Israel in Lebanon*, p. 168.
71   Ariel Sharon, with David Ghanoff, *Warrior: An Autobiography*, New York: Simon & Schuster, 1989, p. 504.
72   Chomsky, *Fateful Triangle*, p. 253, as quoted from Yigal Lev, *Ma'ariv*, 29 December 1982. The passage in square brackets is from the original.
73   As cited in *Al-Safir*, 26 October 1982.
74   *Ibid.*
75   Schiff and Ya'ari, *Israel's Lebanon War*, p. 274. The second of the two omissions (…) is from the original quotation.
76   Yoram Ronen, 'Sharon Interviewed on Massacre Responsibility', Jerusalem Domestic Television Service (interview with Defence Minister Ariel Sharon), 24 September 1982, as cited in *The Beirut Massacre: Press Profile*, p. 36.
77   Sharon, *Warrior*, p. 506.
78   MacBride, *Israel in Lebanon*, p. 167.
79   *Ibid.*, p. 168.
80   *Ibid.*
81   Schiff and Ya'ari, *Israel's Lebanon War*, p. 279.
82   *Ibid.*, p. 280.
83   *The Beirut Massacre: The Complete Kahan Commission Report*, p. 28.
84   Amnon Kapeliouk, *Enquête sur un massacre: Sabra et Chatila*, Paris: Seuil, 1982, p. 112.
85   As cited in *ibid.*, p. 111.
86   As cited in *ibid.*
87   As cited in Halevi, *Israel*, p. 32.
88   As cited in Chomsky, *Fateful Triangle*, p. 392.
89   As cited in *ibid.*, note.
90   As cited in Kapeliouk, *Enquête sur un massacre*, p. 112.
91   Chomsky, *Fateful Triangle*, p. 224.
92   Halevi, *Israel*, p. 15.
93   *Ibid.*, pp. 64–5.
94   According to this 'insensibility theory', the attention of Begin, Sharon and others was not caught by the first news about the massacre due to their insensibility vis-à-vis Palestinians.
95   As cited in Halevi, *Israel*, p. 62.
96   Chomsky, *Fateful Triangle*, pp. 404–5.
97   Timerman, *Longest War*, pp. 166–7.
98   *Al-Nida'*, 21 June 1983.
99   *Al-Safir*, 25 September 1982.
100 *Ibid.*
101 Michael Simpson (ed.), *United Nations Resolutions on Palestine and the Arab-Israeli*

Conflict, Volume III: 1982–1986, Washington, DC: Institute for Palestine Studies, 1988, p. 12.

102 *Ibid.*, pp. 12–13.

103 On the evidence of the field study, it was established that the percentage of those bearing Lebanese citizenship was 27.91%; and the percentage of those (referred to above as 'stateless') carrying cards marked 'under consideration', but with the right to obtain Lebanese citizenship decades since, was 7.21%. (See Chapter 7, p. 251)

104 POH. S/SH. No. 18 (238/ T.20). D.M.H., 'Um Ali' al-Biqa'i. Interview with author, Beirut: author's home, 22 February 1983.

105 *Al-Safir*, 25 September 1982.

106 *Ibid.*, 5 December 1982.

107 Schiff and Ya'ari, *Israel's Lebanon War*, p. 278.

108 John Boykin, *Cursed is the Peacemaker: The American Diplomat versus the Israeli General, Beirut 1982*, Belmont, CA: Applegate Press, 2002, p. 269.

109 *Ibid.*, pp. 269, 270; Schiff and Ya'ari, *Israel's Lebanon War*, p. 272; John Bulloch, *Final Conflict: The War in the Lebanon*, London: Century Publishing, 1983, p. 231; Randal, *Going All the Way*, p. 155; MacBride, *Israel in Lebanon*, p. 165; Colin Campbell, 'Key Phalangist Aides Implicated in Operation that Led to Killings', *New York Times*, 30 September 1982, cited in *The Beirut Massacre: Press Profile*, p. 53; Loren Jenkins, 'Phalangists Implicated in Massacre', *Washington Post*, 30 September 1982, cited in *The Beirut Massacre: Press Profile*, p. 57; *The Beirut Massacre: The Complete Kahan Commission Report*, p. 7; Mustafa Tlas (al-Imad), *Mathbahat Sabra wa Shatila* [The Sabra and Shatila Massacre], Damascus: Dar Tlas for Studies, November 1984, p. 255 (Arabic); Saqr Abu Fakhr, 'So as Not to Forget Sabra and Shatila: Who Remembers Those Days?', *Al-Safir*, 15 September 2001 (Arabic).

110 Schiff and Ya'ari, *Israel's War in Lebanon*, pp. 256, 271–2; MacBride, *Israel in Lebanon*, p. 165; *The Beirut Massacre: The Complete Kahan Commission Report*, p. 7; Tlas, *Mathbahat Sabra wa Shatila*; Abu Fakhr, 'So as Not to Forget'.

111 Bulloch, *Final Conflict*, p. 231; Campbell, 'Key Phalangist Aides Implicated', p. 53; Jenkins, 'Phalangists Implicated', p. 56; Abu Fakhr, 'So as Not to Forget'.

112 Schiff and Ya'ari, *Israel's War in Lebanon*, pp. 261, 262; Abu Fakhr, 'So as Not to Forget'.

113 Schiff and Ya'ari, *Israel's War in Lebanon*, p. 268, 271–2.

114 Bulloch, *Final Conflict*, p. 231; Randal, *Going All the Way*, p. 155; Campbell, 'Key Phalangists Aides Implicated', p. 53; Jenkins, 'Phalangist Implicated', p. 57.

115 Bulloch, *Final Conflict*; Randal, *Going All the Way*; Campbell, 'Key Phalangist Aides Implicated'; Abu Fakhr, 'So as Not to Forget'.

116 Bulloch, *Final Conflict*; Randal, *Going All the Way*; Campbell, 'Key Phalangist Aides Implicated'; Abu Fakhr, 'So as Not to Forget'.

117 Abu Fakhr, 'So as Not to Forget'.

118 Schiff and Ya'ari, *Israel's War in Lebanon*, p. 271.

119 *Ibid.*

120 Jansen, *Battle of Beirut*, p. 106.

121 ABC News, *Oh Tell the World What Happened.* Presented by Bill Redeker, 7 January 1983.

122 *Al-Safir*, 5 September 1984.

123 Robert Farah, 'Al-Quwat al-Lubnaniyieh confutes Elie Hobeika', *Al-Wassat* magazine, 98, 19 October 1997, p. 27 (Arabic).

124 See Bahjat Jaber, 'The Massacre of Sabra and Shatila in Court: No File, and No Affidavits', *Al-Nahar*, 23 June 2001.

125 POH. S/SH. No. 63 (232/ T.61). Siham Balqis. Interview with author, Beirut: massacre area, 9 May 1983.

126 Mark Fineman, 'In Shatila, the Stench of Death', *Philadelphia Inquirer*, 20 September 1982, as cited in *The Beirut Massacre: Press Profile*, p. 14.

127 Monte Carlo Broadcasting Service (Arabic), *News*, 7 p.m., 22 September 1982.

128 Robert Fisk, 'Militias are Sustained by Israelis', *The Times*, 20 September 1982, as cited in *The Beirut Massacre: Press Profile*, p. 15.

129 ABC News, *Oh Tell the World What Happened.*

130 Robert Fisk, 'I am Innocent of Killings, Haddad Explains', *The Times*, 23 September 1982, as cited in *The Beirut Massacre: Press Profile*, p. 51.

131 'Jeder von euch ist ein Racher: Ein libanesischer Milizionär über seine Taten beim Massaker von Beirut', *Der Spiegel*, 14 February 1983, pp. 112.

132 *Ibid.*, p. 113.

133 Abu Fakhr, 'So as Not to Forget'.

134 Wisam Sa'adeh, 'The Cedars' Guardians: From Tall al-Za'tar to the Internet', *Al-Safir*, 25 August 2001.

135 *Al-Nahar*, 3 September 1982.

136 Randal, *Going All the Way*, pp. 282, 281.

137 Jansen, *Battle of Beirut*, pp. 101–2.

138 MacBride, *Israel in Lebanon*, pp. 176–7.

139 Lamb, *International Legal Responsibility*, p. 37.

140 BBC, *Panorama*, 'The Accused'. Producer: Aidan Laverty. Editor: Mike Robinson, 2001.

141 *Ibid.*

142 Halevi, *Israel*, pp. 14–15.

143 *Ibid.*, pp. 72–3.

144 As cited in Chomsky, *Fateful Triangle*, p. 395.

145 Timerman, *Longest War*, p. 167.

146 Tom Segev, 'The Fight at the End of the Time Tunnel', *Ha'aretz – Week's End*, 6 December 2002 <http://www. haaretzdaily. com> (visited 10 December 2002), pp. 6–7.

147 *Ibid.*, pp. 7–8.

148 As cited in Timerman, *Longest War*, p. 167.

Appendix 1: Tables

Table 1   References of the questionnaire

Victims Code description	Ref.	Total	%	Abducted Code description	Ref.	Total	%
Immediate kin	A1	231	53.72	Immediate kin	A1	83	83.00
Relative outside the immediate family	A2	69	16.05	Relative outside the immediate family	A2	3	3.00
Friend	A3	52	12.09	Friend	A3	2	2.00
Neighbour	A4	35	8.14	Neighbour	A4	8	8.00
Witness	A5	43	10.00	Witness	A5	4	4.00
	Total	430	100.00		Total	100	100.00

Table 2.a   Nationalities of the victims

Nationality	Total	%
Palestinian	209	48.60
Lebanese	120	27.91
Stateless	31	7.21
Syrian	23	5.35
Egyptian	18	4.19
Not identified	9	2.09
Bangladeshi	6	1.40
Jordanian	3	0.70
Turk	3	0.70
Sudanese	2	0.47
Algerian	2	0.47
Pakistani	2	0.47
Iranian	1	0.23
Tunisian	1	0.23
Total	430	100.00

Table 2.b   Nationalities of the abducted

Nationality	Total	%
Palestinian	66	66.00
Syrian	13	13.00
Lebanese	11	11.00
Stateless	6	6.00
Egyptian	3	3.00
British	1	1.00
Total	100	100.00

Table 3 Gender of the victims

Gender	Total	%
Male	303	70.47
Female	112	26.05
Undetermined	15	3.49
Total	430	100.00

Table 4.a Victims: age groups

Age	Total	%
Unborn babies	6	1.40
Infant, first year	18	4.19
2–3	13	3.02
4–12	58	13.49
13–18	66	15.35
19–30	105	24.42
31–40	47	10.93
41–50	47	10.93
51–60	29	6.74
61–70	19	4.42
70+	22	5.12
Total	430	100.00

Table 4.b Child victims: age/nationality

Age group	No.	%	Palestinian	Lebanese	Not identified	Syrian	Stateless	Egyptian
Unborn babies	6	1.40	1	5				
Infant, first year	18	4.19	5	4	9			
2–3	13	3.02	7	4				1
4–12	58	13.49	33	19		4	2	
Total	95	22.09	46	32	9	4	2	1

Table 4.c Victims (13–18 years): age/nationality

Age group	No.	%	Palestinian	Lebanese	Stateless	Syrian	Egyptian	Jordanian
13–18	66	15.35	34	21	5	4	1	1

Table 4.d Victims (19–50 years): age/nationality

Age group	No.	%	Palestinian	Lebanese	Stateless	Egyptian	Syrian	Bangladeshi	Turkish	Jordanian	Pakistani	Algerian	Iranian	Sudanese
19–30	105	24.42	45	28	8	9	4	6	1	1	2	1		
31–40	47	10.93	22	8	6	5	2		2				1	1
41–50	47	10.93	24	12	3	2	5			1				
Total	199	46.28	91	48	17	16	11	6	3	2	2	1	1	1

Table 4.e Victims (aged 51 and above): age/nationality

Age group	No.	%	Palestinian	Lebanese	Stateless	Syrian	Algerian	Sudanese	Tunisian
51–60	29	6.74	15	9	3	1	1		
61–70	19	4.42	11	6		1			1
71+	22	5.12	11	4	4	2		1	
Total	70	16.28	37	19	7	4	1	1	1

Table 5.a Abducted: age groups

Age group	Total	%
13–18	30	30.00
19–30	41	41.00
31–40	14	14.00
41–50	8	8.00
51–60	6	6.00
61–70	1	1.00
Total	100	100.00

Table 5.b Abducted (13–18 years): age/nationality

Age group	No.	%	Palestinian	Lebanese	Syrian	Stateless
13–18	30	30.00	20	4	3	3

Table 5.c Abducted (19–50 years): age/nationality

Age group	No.	%	Palestinian	Syrian	Lebanese	Stateless	Egyptian	British
19–30	41	41.00	27	3	6	2	2	1
31–40	14	14.00	8	3	1	1	1	
41–50	8	8.00	6	2				
Total	63	63.00	41	8	7	3	3	1

Table 5.d Abducted (aged 51 and over): age/nationality

Age group	No.	%	Palestinian	Syrian
51–60	6	6.00	4	2
61–70	1	1.00	1	
Total	7	7.00	5	2

Table 6.a Professions of the victims

Profession	Total	%
Teacher	1	0.46
Artist/musician	2	0.92
Tailor/weaver/upholsterer	2	0.92
Draughtsman/designer	4	1.84
Doorman/guard/jockey	6	2.76
Mobile kerosene vendor	6	2.76
Small tradesman	6	2.76
Electrician/telephone repairman	7	3.23
Fish vendor/vegetable vendor/peddler	8	3.69
Barber/baker/cook/butcher	10	4.61
Unspecified profession	10	4.61
PRC: doctor/nurse/hospital worker*	13	5.99
Driver/mechanic	13	5.99
Freedom fighter	16	7.37
Employee**	27	12.44
Mason/painter/carpenter/blacksmith	35	16.13
Freelance worker	51	23.50
Total	217	100.00

* PRC: Palestinian Red Crescent.
** Here, and throughout the Appendices where the term 'Employee'
is used, it refers to an employee of an organization – ministry, bank,
company, and so on.

Table 6.b Professions of the abducted

Profession	Total	%
Doorman/guard/jockey	1	1.25
Freedom fighter	1	1.25
PRC: doctor/nurse/hospital worker*	1	1.25
Small tradesman	1	1.25
Tailor/weaver/upholsterer	1	1.25
Teacher	1	1.25
Unspecified profession	1	1.25
Shoemaker	2	2.50
Employee	3	3.75
Plumber	3	3.75
Fish vendor/vegetable vendor/peddler	3	3.75
Electrician/telephone repairman	4	5.00
Driver/mechanic	7	8.75
Mason/painter/carpenter/blacksmith	17	21.25
Freelance worker	34	42.50
Total	80	100.00

* PRC: Palestinian Red Crescent.

Table 7.a Victims: family member/financial responsibility

Code description	No.	%*
Family provider (full responsibility)	200	46.51
Child below 12 yrs (partial responsibility)	6	
Student above 12 yrs (partial responsibility)	14	
Housewife (partial responsibility)	12	
Elderly (partial responsibility)	1	
Permanently sick (partial responsibility)	1	
Total	234	54.42

* Percentage out of 430 victims.

Table 7.b Abducted: family member/financial responsibility

Code description	No.	%*
Family provider (full responsibility)	70	70.00
Student above 12 yrs (partial responsibility)	8	
Elderly (partial responsibility)	1	
Permanently sick (partial responsibility)	1	
Total	80	80.00

* Percentage out of 100 abducted.

Table 8.a Victims and abducted: educational level

Victims Code description	No.	%	Abducted Code description	No.	%
Children up to 12 yrs	94	21.86			
Elementary standard	161	37.44	Elementary school standard	53	53.00
Secondary standard	63	14.65	Secondary school standard	17	17.00
Technical standard	5	1.16	Technical school standard	12	12.00
University standard	6	1.40	University standard	1	1.00
Illiterate	75	17.44	Illiterate	5	5.00
Unknown	26	6.05	Unknown	12	12.00
Total	430	100.00	Total	100	100.00

Table 8.b Palestinian victims and abducted: educational level

Victims Code description	No.	%	Abducted Code description	No.	%
Children up to 12 yrs	46	22.01			
Elementary standard	76	36.36	Elementary standard	38	57.58
Secondary standard	50	23.92	Secondary standard	12	18.18
Technical standard	2	0.96	Technical standard	9	13.64
University standard	6	2.87	University standard	1	1.52
Illiterate	19	9.09	Illiterate	1	1.52
Unknown	10	4.78	Unknown	5	7.58
Total	209	100.00	Total	66	100.00

Table 9   Identification of victims' bodies

Code description	No.	%
Body identified	294	68.37
Body not identified	133	30.93
Injured & died later	3	0.70
Total	430	100.00

Table 10.a   Witnesses to the abduction operation

Code description	No.	%
Witnesses exist (among relatives & neighbours)	78	78.00
Families knew from different sources	12	12.00
Witnesses do not exist	10	10.00
Total	100	100.00

Table 10.b   Identity of the abductor

Code description	No.	%
Lebanese Forces (people were sure of)	29	29.00
Lebanese Forces (people were doubtful)	19	19.00
People could not tell	52	52.00
Total	100	100.00

Table 11.a   Families with more than one member killed

No. of victims per family	No. of families	Total no. of victims
2	20	40
3	13	39
4	13	52
5	10	50
6	2	12
7	3	21
8	1	8
9	3	27
10	1	10
11	1	11
Total	67	270

Average of victims per family = 4.03.

Table 11.b   Families with more than one member abducted

No. abducted per family	No. of families	Total abducted
2	10	20
3	3	9
4	3	12
Total	16	41

Average of kidnapped per family = 2.56.

Table 12   Victims and abducted: time/place

Place	Victims		Abducted		Vic. & abd.	
	No.	%	No.	%	No.	%
1st day – 16 SEP. 1982						
Turf Club yards	27	6.28			27	5.09
Ersal	62	14.42	3	3.00	65	12.26
Kuwaiti Embassy yards	4	0.93			4	0.75
Inside Sports City	3	0.70			3	0.57
Bir Hasan	7	1.63			7	1.32
Entrances to Horsh & Shatila Rd	12	2.79			12	2.26
Shatila Rd	1	0.23			1	0.19
Al-Horsh	75	17.44			75	14.15
Abu Yasser's shelter	44	10.23			44	8.30
Suburbs	8	1.86	1	1.00	9	1.70
Unknown place			4	4.00	4	0.75
Total	243	56.51	8	8.00	251	47.36
2nd day – 17 SEP. 1982						
Turf Club yards	4	0.93			4	0.75
Ersal	10	2.33			10	1.89
Kuwaiti Embassy yards	3	0.70	17	17.00	20	3.77
Inside Sports City	5	1.16			5	0.94
Bir Hasan	30	6.98	7	7.00	37	6.98
Entrances to Horsh & Shatila Rd	5	1.16			5	0.94
Shatila Rd	6	1.40			6	1.13
Al-Horsh	46	10.70			46	8.68
Entrances to Shatila Camp	6	1.40			6	1.13
Suburbs	13	3.02			13	2.45
Unknown place			9	9.00	9	1.70
Total	128	29.77	33	33.00	161	30.38
3rd day – 18 SEP. 1982						
Turf Club yards	10	2.33	1	1.00	11	2.08
Ersal	8	1.86	3	3.00	11	2.08
Kuwaiti Embassy yards	20	4.65	19	19.00	39	7.36
Inside Sports City	3	0.70			3	0.57
Bir Hasan			4	4.00	4	0.75
Shatila Rd	8	1.86	9	9.00	17	3.21
Al-Horsh	1	0.23			1	0.19
Sabra Rd	2	0.47	13	13.00	15	2.83
Suburbs	4	0.93			4	0.75
Unknown place	3	0.70	10	10.00	13	2.45
Total	59	13.72	59	59.00	118	22.26
Grand total	430	100.00	100	100.00	530	100.00

Table 13 Freedom fighters who died: identity/time/place

Name	Nationality	Age	Residence	Date of death	Place of death	Body identified	No. of victims in FF's family	Field study archive no.
1 – Hussein, Karem Ahmad Jabr	Pal.	17	al-Horsh	1st day	Abu Yasser's shelter	No	9	74
2 – Muhammad, Suhaila Kh. Yousuf	Pal.	19	al-Horsh	1st day	Abu Yasser's shelter	No	11	250
3 – Awad, Nur Eddine Sa'ud	Pal.	25	al-Horsh	1st day	Abu Yasser's shelter	Yes	4	191
4 – Shoufani, Shihadeh Ahmad	Pal.	28	al-Horsh	1st day	Abu Yasser's shelter	Yes	4	151
5 – Nazzal, Muhammad Salim	Pal.	33	al-Horsh	1st day	al-Horsh	Yes	1	295
6 – Frejeh, Muhammad Hussein	Pal.	40	al-Horsh	1st day	al-Horsh	Yes	2	197
7 – Qadi, Saleh Dakhil	Pal.	52	al-Horsh	1st day	al-Horsh	Yes	5	214
8 – al-Titi, Saleh Hussein Saleh	Pal.	21	al-Horsh	2nd day	al-Horsh	Yes	2	169
9 – Sadeq, Imad Muhammad	Leb.	23	al-Horsh	2nd day	al-Horsh	Yes	1	156
10 – Mughrabi, Subhi Muhammad	Pal.	43	al-Horsh	2nd day	al-Horsh	Yes	3	277
11 – Najjar, Hussein Hasan Ahmad	Pal.	45	Ersal	1st day	Ersal	No	1	296
12 – Sukkarieh, Mir'i Hawlo	Leb.	45	Ersal	1st day	Suburbs	No	1	144
13 – Ahmad, Nazih Mahmoud	Pal.	19	Bir Hasan	2nd day	Bir Hasan	Yes	1	24
14 – Qadi, Fahmi Ahmad	Pal.	31	Bir Hasan	2nd day	Near Sports City	Yes	1	220
15 – Muhammad, Yahya Ahmad	Pal.	30	Near Sports City	1st day	Near Sports City	Yes	2	259
16 – Jamilah, Riad Mahmoud	Jord.	19	Suburbs	2nd day	Suburbs	No	2	57

Table 14 Families of Palestinian victims and abducted: migrations and movements

Family name	Home town	First migration	Year	Second migration	Year	Third migration	Year	Fourth migration	Year	Total migs	Field study archive no.
Abbas	Haifa	Sab. & Shat.	1948							1	138
Abd al-Fattah	Palestine	Sab. & Shat.	??							1	142
Abd al-Rahman	Safad	Tyre camps	1948	Sab. & Shat.	1977					2	346
Abdallah	Al-Khalisa	South of Leb.	1948	Tall al-Za'tar	1960	Damour	1976	Sab. & Shat.	1982	4	77
Abdallah	Palestine	Sab. & Shat.	??							1	397
Abed	Saffourieh	Sab. & Shat.	??							1	569
Abu Adas	Sihmata	Sab. & Shat.	??							1	588
Abu Harb	Shafa Amr	Al-Ghaziya	1968	Baalbek	1969	Sab. & Shat.	1982			3	4
Abu Khamis	Al-Khalisa	South of Leb.	1948	Tall al-Za'tar	1954	Damour	1976	Sab. & Shat.	1982	4	9
Abu Rudaineh	Haifa	Baalbek	1948	Sab. & Shat.	1970					2	14
Abu Rudaineh	Haifa	Baalbek	1948	Sab. & Shat.	1956					2	17
Abu Shilleih	Jaffa	Sab. & Shat.	1948							1	160
Abu Suweid	Palestine	Sab. & Shat.	1950							1	141
Ahmad	Al-Buqai'a	South of Leb.	1948	Sab. & Shat.	1960					2	24
Ahmad	Safad	Tall al-Za'tar	1948	Damour	1976	Sab. & Shat.	1982			3	525
Aidi	Haifa	South of Leb.	1948	Baalbek	1968	Sab. & Shat.	1969			3	178
Akkili	Palestine	Sab. & Shat.	??							1	182
Ali	Palestine	Sab. & Shat.	??							1	429
Ali	Palestine	Sab. & Shat.	1978							1	387
Ali	Safad	Tall al-Za'tar	1948	Sab. & Shat.	1976					2	564
Ali	Akka	South of Leb.	1948	Sab. & Shat.	1950					2	572
Ashwah	Palestine	Sab. & Shat.	1955							1	140
Atrash	Shafa Amr	Sab. & Shat.	??							1	35
Atwat	North villages	Baalbek	1948	South of Leb.	1958	Sab. & Shat.	1978			3	180
Atyar	Jaffa	North of Leb.	1948	Sab. & Shat.	1970					2	526
Awad	Al-Na'ima	Tyre camps	1948	Sab. & Shat.	1978					2	191
Azzam	Akka	Sab. & Shat.	1950							1	583
Azzuqa	Jaffa	Sab. & Shat.	??							1	589
Ba'bou'	Palestine	Sab. & Shat.	1955							1	383
Baitam	Akka	Sab. & Shat.	1948							1	530
Balqis	Al-Kabri	South of Leb.	1948	Tyre camps	1959	Sab. & Shat.	1966			3	405

Table 14 (Continued)

Family name	Home town	First migration	Year	Second migration	Year	Third migration	Year	Fourth migration	Year	Total migs	Field study archive no.
Barakah	Saffourieh	Beka'a	1955	Tyre camps	1968	Sab. & Shat.	1972			3	40
Bayyumi	Haifa	Sab. & Shat.	1948							1	410
Bibi	Jaffa	Sab. & Shat.	1948							1	529
Dukhi	Akka	Ain al-Hilweh C.	1948	Sab. & Shat.	1959					2	121
Dusuqi	Palestine	Sab. & Shat.	??							1	136
Freijeh	Al-Khalisa	North of Leb.	1948	Tall al-Za'tar	1955	Sab. & Shat.	1976			3	197
Habrat	Sireen	Al-Maslakh	1948	Sab. & Shat.	1965					2	288
Hajj	Al-Khalisa	South of Leb.	1948	Tall al-Za'tar	1954	Damour	1976	Sab. & Shat.	1982	4	60
Hajj	Saffourieh	North of Leb.	1948	Damour	1979	Sab. & Shat.	??			3	63
Hajjar	Palestine	Tall al-Za'tar	1948	Damour	1976	Sab. & Shat.	1982			3	533
Hammud	Deir al-Qasi	Tyre camps	1948	Baalbek	1949	Tyre camps	1960	Sab. & Shat.	1978	4	85
Hammud	Palestine	Sab. & Shat.	??							1	428
Hasan	Tarshiha	Tyre camps	1948	Sab. & Shat.	1965					2	537
Hashem	Tarshiha	North camps	1948	Tall al-Za'tar	1955	Sab. & Shat.	1978			3	293
Hayek	Haifa	Sab. & Shat.	1948							1	532
Himmo	Jaffa	Miyyeh wa Miyyeh C.	1948	Sab. & Shat.	1950					2	540
Hishmeh	Jaffa	Sab. & Shat.	1948							1	7
Hussein	Safad	Tall al-Za'tar	1948	Damour	1976	Sab. & Shat.	1982			3	539
Hussein	Deir al-Qasi	Baalbek	1948	Sab. & Shat.	1965					2	70
Hussein	Al-Na'imah	South of Leb.	1948	Tyre camps	1950	Sab. & Shat.	1978			3	385
Hussein	Palestine	North camps	1948	Sab. & Shat.	1972					2	66
Isma'il	Palestine	Sab. & Shat.	??							1	393
Issawi	Jaffa	Tyre camps	1948	Tall al-Za'tar	1968	Sab. & Shat.	1976			3	568
Jad'on	Al-Na'ima	Marj'ayoun	1948	Tall al-Za'tar	1959	Tyre camps	1976	Sab. & Shat.	1982	4	54
Jum'a	Al-Na'ima	South of Leb.	1948	Tyre camps	1955	Sab. & Shat.	1982			3	55
Jureidi	Palestine	Sab. & Shat.	1978							1	388
Kabbara	Jaffa	Sab. & Shat.	??							1	554
Kayyali	Palestine	Sab. & Shat.	??							1	557
Khalifeh	Jaffa	Sab. & Shat.	1948							1	106
Khalifeh	Jaffa	South of Leb.	1948	Burj Hammoud	1972	Sab. & Shat.	1976			3	107
Kharrubi	Palestine	Beka'a	1948	Al-Ghaziya	1975	Sab. & Shat.	1982			3	541
Khatib	Al-Khalisa	Al-Nabatiyeh	1948	Tall al-Za'tar	1967	Sab. & Shat.	1976			3	98

Khatib	Safad	Tall al-Za'tar	1948	Sab. & Shat.	1976	Sab. & Shat.	1982			2	104
Khatib	Safad	Marja'youn	1949	Al-Dikwaneh	1955	Tall al-Za'tar	1970	Sab. & Shat.	1982	4	105
Khatib	Deir al-Qasi	Sab. & Shat.	??							1	134
Khatib	Al-Khalisa	Tall al-Za'tar	1948	Damour	1976	Sab. & Shat.	1982			3	542
Kulaib	Palestine	Tyre camps	1948	Sab. & Shat.	1978					2	232
Liddawi	Akka	Sab. & Shat.	??							1	234
Ma'ruf	Deir al-Qasi	Sab. & Shat.	1948	Tyre camps	1962	Sab. & Shat.	1987			1	135
Ma'ruf	Deir al-Qasi	Beka'a	1948	Tall al-Za'tar	1955	Tyre camps	1976	Sab. & Shat.	1978	3	545
Madi	Haifa	Sab. & Shat.	??							4	235
Majdub	Akka	Sab. & Shat.	1948	Sab. & Shat.	1978					1	239
Makkiyeh	Al-Khalil	Tall al-Za'tar	1948							2	278
Mashharawi	Jaffa	Sab. & Shat.	1948							1	521
Minawi	Jaffa	Burj Hammoud	1948	Sab. & Shat.	1970					2	300
Mir'i	Al-Na'ima	Marja'youn	1948	Tyre camps	1955	Sab. & Shat.	1978			3	265
Misri	Palestine	Sab. & Shat.	??							1	377
Misri	Jaffa	Burj Hammoud	1948	Sab. & Shat.	1950					2	522
Mughrabi	Jaffa	Baalbek	1948	Tall al-Za'tar	1952	Damour	1976	Sab. & Shat.	1979	4	275
Muhammad	Sihmata	Beka'a	1948	Tall al-Za'tar	1976	Damour	1978	Sab. & Shat.	1982	4	243
Muhammad	Sihmata	Tall al-Za'tar	1948	Tyre camps	1976	Sab. & Shat.	1978			3	253
Muhammad	Sihmata	Sab. & Shat.	??							1	259
Muhammad	Haifa	Beka'a	1948	Sab. & Shat.	1950					2	547
Muhawish	Haifa	Tall al-Za'tar	1948	Sab. & Shat.	1976					2	544
Mussa	North villages	Tall al-Za'tar	1948	Sab. & Shat.	1976					2	281
Mussa	North villages	Tall al-Za'tar	1948	Sab. & Shat.	1976					2	302
Nabulsi	Palestine	Sab. & Shat.	1950							1	299
Najjar	Palestine	Sab. & Shat.	1962							1	296
Nassif	Tarshiha	Tyre camps	1948	Sab. & Shat.	1978					1	297
Natat	Jaffa	Sab. & Shat.	1948							1	519
Nazzal	North villages	Baalbek	1948	Tyre camps	1960	Sab. & Shat.	1978			3	295
Nunu	Al-Khalil	Sab. & Shat.	1948							1	294
Qadi	Akka	North of Leb.	1948	Sab. & Shat.	1972					2	214
Qadi	Tarshiha	Tyre camps	1948	Sab. & Shat.	1965					2	219
Qadi	Tarshiha	South of Leb.	1948	Sab. & Shat.	1958					2	220
Qadi	Al-Buqai'a	Tyre Camps	1948	North of Leb.	1955	Sab. & Shat.	1958			3	221
Qadi	Al-Buqai'a	South of Leb.	1948	North camps	1955	Sab. & Shat.	1958			3	558
Qassem	Shafa-Amr	Sab. & Shat.	??							1	210
Qassem	Akka	Tyre camps	1948	Sab. & Shat.	1978					2	211
Qassem	Safad	Tall al-Za'tar	1948	Sab. & Shat.	1976					2	562

Table 14 (Continued)

Family name	Home town	First migration	Year	Second migration	Year	Third migration	Year	Fourth migration	Year	Total migs	Field study archive no.
Qatanani	Jaffa	Tall al-Za'tar	1948	Sab. & Shat.	1976					2	213
Radi	Palestine	Sab. & Shat.	??							1	597
Ramadan	Palestine	Tyre camps	1948	Sab. & Shat.	1978					2	344
Sa'd	North villages	Beka'a	1948	Tyre camps	1956	Sab. & Shat.	1967			3	328
Sa'd	Palestine	Sab. & Shat.	1950							1	369
Sa'di	Tarshiha	North of Leb.	1948	Sab. & Shat.	1955					2	511
Sa'id	Safad	Tyre camps	1948	Sab. & Shat.	1979					2	325
Sa'idi	Palestine	Sab. & Shat.	1948							1	575
Sabeq	Al-Buqai'a	Tyre camps	1948	Sab. & Shat.	1972					2	513
Sadeq	Palestine	Sab. & Shat.	??							1	367
Safar	Safad	Sab. & Shat.	1948							1	576
Saffuri	Saffourieh	North of Leb.	1948	Sab. & Shat.	1965					2	586
Saghir	Al-Na'ima	Tyre camps	1948	Sab. & Shat.	1982					2	158
Salem	Safad	Beka'a	1948	Tyre camps	1963	Sab. & Shat.	1964			3	130
Salem	Safad	Beka'a	1948	Sab. & Shat.	1960					2	502
Salem	Safad	Beka'a	1948	Tyre camps	1963	Sab. & Shat.	1964			3	505
Sane'	Haifa	Sidon	1948	Sab. & Shat.	1955					2	577
Saqqa	Jaffa	Sab. & Shat.	1948							1	508
Sarris	Majd al-Kroum	Sab. & Shat.	1948							1	414
Sawalha	Al-Khalisa	Tall al-Za'tar	1948	Damour	1976	Sab. & Shat.	1982			3	590
Shahrur	Safad	Sab. & Shat.	1948							1	147
Shihadeh	Palestine	Baalbek	1948	Tall al-Za'tar	1949	Sab. & Shat.	1976			3	146
Shufani	Al-Na'imah	Tyre camps	1948	Sab. & Shat.	1978					2	151
Sirri	Jaffa	Sab. & Shat.	1948							1	514
Sirri	Jaffa	Sab. & Shat.	1948							1	515
Sirsawi	Haifa	Sidon	1948	Sab. & Shat.	1965					2	330
Taha	Akka	Sab. & Shat.	??							1	366
Titi	Haifa	Beka'a	1948	Tall al-Za'tar	1955	Tyre camps	1976	Sab. & Shat.	1978	4	168
Wahbeh	Safad	Tyre camps	1948	Sab. & Shat.	1955					2	123
Wali	Palestine	Sab. & Shat.	??							1	356
Yunes	Safad	Sab. & Shat.	??							1	282
Yusuf	Safad	Tyre camps	1948	Sab. & Shat.	1979					2	284
Zammar	Jaffa	Tall al-Za'tar	1948	Sab. & Shat.	1978					2	342
Zurein	Jaffa	Sab. & Shat.	1948							1	501

Table 15 Fate of the Palestinian families

Number of victims per family	No. of families
Families who lost 1 victim each	62
Families who lost 2–11 each	34
Total	96

Number of abducted per family	No. of families
Families who lost 1 abducted each	40
Families who lost 2–4 each	11
Total	51

Individuals who left the area	No. of families
Families with 1 member who left the area each	20
Families with 2 members who left the area each	4
Total	24

Families who emigrated from the area	No. of families
1 member from the family survived and emigrated	5
2 members from the family survived and emigrated	1
Whoever survived from the family emigrated	12
Total	18

Percentage of families who left the area	No. of families
Total of families who lost victims and abducted	147
Total of families who emigrated from the area	18

Percentage of exodus among families = 12.24.

Appendix 2: Names

List of names 1 Victims of Sabra and Shatila massacre: based on field study, spring 1984[*]

Name	Kinship	Profession	Nationality	Age	Reference[**]
Abbas, Ahmad Ghaith		(old age)	Palestinian	75	A1
Abd al-Fattah, Mahmoud Qassem		Mason/Painter/Carpenter/Blacksmith	Palestinian	40	A2
Abd al-Latif, Rida		PRC: Doctor/Nurse/Hospital worker	Egyptian	22	A3
Abd al-Rahman, Ali Saleh		Small tradesman	Palestinian	60	A1
Abd Assalam, Abd al-Mun'em		PRC: Doctor/Nurse/Hospital worker	Egyptian	23	A3
Abdallah, Fawaz Hasan		Freelance worker	Stateless	35	A1
Abdallah, Hasan Abdallah	*Father*	*Mason/Painter/Carpenter/Blacksmith*	*Palestinian*	*52*	*A5*
Abdallah, Nawal Hasan	*Daughter*	*(childhood)*	*Palestinian*	*5*	*A5*
Abdallah, Yousuf Hasan	*Son*	*(early childhood)*	*Palestinian*	*3*	*A5*
Abdallah, Turfah Hussein (Mrs Mahmoud)	Grandmother	(housewife)	Palestinian	65	A1
Abdallah, Jamilah Ahmad	Granddaughter	(school age)	Palestinian	13	A1
Abu Dhahab, Munir		Freelance worker	Lebanese	62	A3
Abu Dib, Mahmoud Qassem		Barber/Baker/Cook/Butcher	Jordanian	41	A2
Abu Harb, Qassem Mahmoud	*Father*	*Small tradesman*	*Palestinian*	*48*	*A1*
Abu Harb, Walid Qassem	*Son*	*Small tradesman*	*Palestinian*	*28*	*A1*
Abu Harb, Hasan Qassem Mahmoud	*Son*	*(school age)*	*Palestinian*	*14*	*A1*
Abu Harb, Mirvat Walid	*Granddaughter*	*(childhood)*	*Palestinian*	*10*	*A1*
Abu Khamis, Amoun Ali		(housewife)	Palestinian	56	A1
Abu Rudaineh, Muhammad Diab	*Father*	*(old age)*	*Palestinian*	*62*	*A2*
Abu Rudaineh, Kayed Muhammad	*Son*	*Small tradesman*	*Palestinian*	*24*	*A2*
Abu Rudaineh, Aida Muhammad	*Daughter*	*(school age)*	*Palestinian*	*17*	*A2*
Abu Rudaineh, Shawkat	*Nephew*	*Mason/Painter/Carpenter/Blacksmith*	*Palestinian*	*45*	*A1*
Abu Rudaineh, Aamal Sh. (Mrs Hussein)	*Grandniece*	*(housewife)*	*Palestinian*	*21*	*A1*
Hussein	*Son-in-law*	*Mason/Painter/Carpenter/Blacksmith*	*Palestinian*	*25*	*A1*
(unborn. Mother Aamal Abu Rudaineh)	*(Grandchild)*	*(unborn infant)*	*Palestinian*		*A1*
Abu Shilleih, Muhammad Hasan		Freelance worker	Palestinian	35	A1
Abu Sweid, Saleh Muhammad		(old age)	Palestinian	65	A3
Abu Yahya, Isma'il Mahmoud		Employee	Algerian	52	A5
Abu Yasser, Ahmad	*Father*	*Mason/Painter/Carpenter/Blacksmith*	*Syrian*	*45*	*A3*
Abu Yasser, Huda	*Mother*	*(housewife)*	*Lebanese*	*43*	*A3*
Abu Yasser, Yasser Ahmad	*Son*	*Employee*	*Syrian*	*16*	*A3*
Abu Yasser, Nasser Ahmad	*Son*	*(childhood)*	*Syrian*	*12*	*A3*
Abu Yasser, Nabal Ahmad	*Daughter*	*(childhood)*	*Syrian*	*9*	*A3*

List of names 1   (Continued)

Name	Kinship	Profession	Nationality	Age	Reference**
Ahmad, Nazih Mahmoud		Freedom fighter	Palestinian	19	A1
Aidi, Mustafa Sa'id	Father	(old age)	Palestinian	75	A1
Aidi, Moussa Mustafa Sa'id	Son	Mason/Painter/Carpenter/Blacksmith	Palestinian	31	A1
Aidi, Sa'id Mustafa Sa'id	Son	Mason/Painter/Carpenter/Blacksmith	Palestinian	27	A1
Aidi, Hussein Mustafa Sa'id	Son	Mason/Painter/Carpenter/Blacksmith	Palestinian	22	A1
Aidi, Ibrahim Mustafa Sa'id	Son	(school age)	Palestinian	17	A1
Akkili, Abu Ghazi"		Fish vendor/Vegetable vendor/Peddler	Palestinian	62	A5
Ala' al-Din, Zainab Abd		Employee	Lebanese	20	A1
Alawiyeh, Khairieh, Um Yousuf	Grandmother	(housewife)	Lebanese	55	A4
Alawiyeh, Khodr Yousuf Na'im	Grandson	(sick/permanently sick)	Lebanese	22	A4
Alawiyeh, Zainab Yousuf Na'im	Granddaughter	(housewife)	Lebanese	20	A4
Ali, Hussein Ali		Unspecified profession	Palestinian	25	A1
Ali, Imam Mahmoud		Freelance worker	Egyptian	42	A2
Ali, Muhammad Sulaiman	Father	Mason/Painter/Carpenter/Blacksmith	Palestinian	50	A1
Ali, Khaled Muhammad Sulaiman	Son	Mason/Painter/Carpenter/Blacksmith	Palestinian	20	A3
Antar, Hamid	Father	Freelance worker	Syrian	35	A5
Antar, Muhammad Hamid	Son	Freelance worker	Syrian	15	A5
Antar, Khaled Hamid	Son	(school age)	Syrian	13	A5
As'ad, Ali Muhammad	Father	Driver/Mechanic	Lebanese	53	A2
As'ad, Muhammad Ali	Son	Artist/Musician	Lebanese	20	A2
As'ad, Khaled Ali	Son	Doorman/Guard/Jockey	Lebanese	18	A2
Ashwah, Nabih Sa'id		Freelance worker	Palestinian	28	A1
Atrash, Subhi Moussa	Father	Driver/Mechanic	Palestinian	55	A3
Atrash, Majed Subhi Moussa	Son	(school age)	Palestinian	16	A3
Atwat, Abd al-Ghani	Father	Freelance worker	Palestinian	61	A3
Atwat, Yousuf Abd al-Ghani	Son	PRC: Doctor/Nurse/Hospital worker	Palestinian	32	A3
Awad, Nur Eddine Sa'ud	Brother	Freedom fighter	Palestinian	25	A3
Awad, Muyassar Sa'ud	Sister	Employee	Palestinian	22	A3
Awad, Fatima Sa'ud	Sister	(school age)	Palestinian	14	A3
Awad, Hussein Sa'ud	Brother	(childhood)	Palestinian	12	A3
Awf, Muhammad Hanafi		Mason/Painter/Carpenter/Blacksmith	Egyptian	22	A3
Ba'albaki, Hussein Muhammad		(old age)	Lebanese	71	A1
Ba'bou', Badia'a Ahmad		(housewife)	Palestinian	71	A4
Bakr, Mustafa Uthman		Unspecified profession	Syrian	72	A5

Name	Relationship	Profession	Nationality	Age	Code
Balqis, Ali (Abu Majed)		Employee	Palestinian	65	A1
Barakah, Abd al-Salam Muhammad		(school age)	Palestinian	17	A1
Bayyoumi, Muhammad Zuheir		(babyhood)	Palestinian	1	A1
Bika'i, Hussein Moussa	Father	Fish vendor/Vegetable vendor/Peddler	Lebanese	60	A1
Bika'i, Rabi' Hussein Moussa	Son	Employee	Lebanese	19	A1
Bika'i, Ikram Hussein M. (Mrs Khaled)	Daughter	Employee	Lebanese	30	A1
Bika'i, Khaled Saleh	Son-in-law	Employee	Lebanese	41	A1
Bika'i, Fadia Khaled Saleh	Granddaughter	(school age)	Lebanese	15	A1
Bika'i, Imad Khaled Saleh	Grandson	(childhood)	Lebanese	10	A1
Bika'i, Shadi Khaled Saleh	Grandson	(childhood)	Lebanese	8	A1
Bika'i, Wissam Khaled Saleh	Grandson	(childhood)	Lebanese	6	A1
Burji, Ali Ibrahim	Father	Doorman/Guard/Jockey	Lebanese	37	A2
Burji, Qasem Ali Ibrahim	Son	Mason/Painter/Carpenter/Blacksmith	Lebanese	14	A2
Burji, Ali Milhem	Nephew	Mason/Painter/Carpenter/Blacksmith	Lebanese	14	A2
Damash, Samir Muhammad		Unspecified profession	Palestinian	21	A2
Darwish, Haydar Muhammad		Electrician/Telephone repairman	Lebanese	23	A2
Dhaher, Muhammad Salman	Husband	Fish vendor/Vegetable vendor/Peddler	Lebanese	79	A1
Dhaher, Sa'da A. (Mrs Muhammad)	Wife	(housewife)	Lebanese	45	A1
Dhaher, Shakib As'ad		Employee	Lebanese	55	A5
Diab, Muhammad		(old age)	Palestinian	72	A5
Dugheino, Ahmad Hamdo	Father	Fish vendor/Vegetable vendor/Peddler	Syrian	48	A2
Dugheino, Mariam (Mrs Ahmad)	Mother	(housewife)	Palestinian	37	A2
Dugheino, Muhammad Ahmad	Son	(childhood)	Syrian	6	A2
Dugheino, Mahmoud Ahmad	Son	(childhood)	Syrian	4	A2
Dukhi, Ali Abdallah		Small tradesman	Palestinian	44	A1
Dulbein, Hussein Ali		Freelance worker	Lebanese	19	A5
Dusouqi, Muhammad Wajih		Barber/Baker/Cook/Butcher	Palestinian	42	A3
Eid, Abdallah Muhammad Khurasani		Barber/Baker/Cook/Butcher	Iranian	32	A5
Faqih, Fatima Muhammad	Sister	(school age)	Lebanese	14	A2
Faqih, Laila Muhammad	Sister	(childhood)	Lebanese	3	A2
Farfour, Samir Abd al-Fattah		PRC: Doctor/Nurse/Hospital worker	Egyptian	30	A3
Fayyad, Tamima D. Murad (Mrs Ali)	Mother	(housewife)	Lebanese	47	A1
Fayyad, Najah Ali	Daughter	Employee	Lebanese	21	A1
Fayyad, Abbas Ali	Son	Employee	Lebanese	19	A1
Fayyad, Nuha Ali	Daughter	(school age)	Lebanese	18	A1
Freijeh, Muhammad Hussein	Father	Freedom fighter	Palestinian	40	A1
Freijeh, Khaled Muhammad Hussein	Son	(school age)	Palestinian	13	A1

List of names 1 (Continued)

Name	Kinship	Profession	Nationality	Age	Reference**
Ghandour, Yousuf Ali		Mason/Painter/Carpenter/Blacksmith	Syrian	50	A2
Ghanem, Sayyed Ahmad		Employee	Egyptian	40	A3
Habrat, Moussa Abd al-Halim	Grandfather	Freelance worker	Palestinian	53	A1
Habrat, Aamal Huleiwi (Mrs Mustafa)	Mother	(housewife)	Algerian	27	A1
Habrat, Sirine Mustafa Moussa	Daughter	(childhood)	Palestinian	6	A1
Habrat, Mussa Mustafa Moussa	Son	(childhood)	Palestinian	4	A1
Habrat, Marwan Mustafa Moussa	Son	(babyhood)	Palestinian	1	A1
Hafez, Sa'id Ahmad		Driver/Mechanic	Egyptian	25	A2
Haji, Jihad Ali		PRC: Doctor/Nurse/Hospital worker	Palestinian	24	A3
Haji, Saleh Yousuf		Barber/Baker/Cook/Butcher	Palestinian	43	A2
Haji, Sarah Qasem	Mother	(housewife)	Palestinian	30	A1
Haji, Wassim Walid	Son	(early childhood)	Lebanese	2	A1
Haji, Samar Walid	Daughter	(babyhood)	Lebanese	1	A1
Halabi, Samira Ali		Tailor/Weaver/Upholsterer	Lebanese	18	A1
Halawi, Ali Moussa		Mason/Painter/Carpenter/Blacksmith	Lebanese	21	A1
Hammoud, Fadi Moussa		(school age)	Palestinian	17	A1
Hammoud, Huda (Mrs Muhammad)	Mother	(housewife)	Palestinian	41	A1
Hammoud, Khalil Muhammad	Son	(school age)	Palestinian	14	A1
Hammoud, Hanadi Muhammad	Daughter	(childhood)	Palestinian	9	A1
Hamzah, Zaydan Muhammad Zeid	Father	Freelance worker	Stateless	45	A2
Hamzah, Taysir Zaydan	Son	Freelance worker	Stateless	20	A2
Hamzah, Hamzah Zaydan	Son	Freelance worker	Stateless	18	A2
Hamzah, Nasser Zaydan	Son	Freelance worker	Stateless	16	A2
Hanafi, Muhammad		Freelance worker	Egyptian	18	A5
Haramsheh, Khaled Fares	Husband	Freelance worker	Stateless	55	A2
Haramsheh, Fatima (Mrs Khaled)	Wife	(housewife)	Stateless	52	A2
Harb, Ahmad Hasan		Freelance worker	Lebanese	20	A1
Hashem, Abd Al-Hadi Ahmad		Driver/Mechanic	Palestinian	45	A1
Haydar, Kulthum Salameh	Mother	(housewife)	Lebanese	55	A1
Haydar, Fahd Ali	Son	Mason/Painter/Carpenter/Blacksmith	Lebanese	19	A1
Haydar, Zainab Idilbi (Mrs Fahd)	Daughter-in-law	(housewife)	Palestinian	17	A1
Haydar – (mother Zeinab I.H.)	(Grandchild)	(unborn baby)	Lebanese		A1
Haydar, Fu'ad Ali	Son	(school age)	Lebanese	14	A1
Hinnawi, Dib Hussein		Employee	Lebanese	55	A3

Name	Relationship	Profession	Nationality	Age	Code
Hishmeh, Tawfiq		Unspecified profession	Palestinian	47	A4
Hussein, Faddah Jum'a	Grandmother	(housewife)	Palestinian	70	A1
Hussein, Fadi Ilias Moussa	Grandson	(childhood)	Palestinian	12	A1
Hussein, Fadia Ilias Moussa	Granddaughter	(childhood)	Palestinian	10	A1
Hussein, Hussein Ali		Draughtsman/Designer	Palestinian	24	A2
Hussein, Isma'il Mahmoud		Doorman/Guard/Jockey	Palestinian	42	A2
Hussein, Ruqaya Amin		Freelance worker	Egyptian	38	A5
Hussein, Salha M. (Mrs Ahmad Jabr)	Mother	(housewife)	Palestinian	35	A1
Hussein, Abdallah Jabr	Uncle	(sick/permanently sick)	Palestinian	50	A1
Hussein, Karem Ahmad Jabr	Son	Freedom fighter	Palestinian	17	A1
Hussein, Imad Ahmad Jabr	Son	Driver/Mechanic	Palestinian	13	A1
Hussein, Fu'ad Ahmad Jabr	Son	(childhood)	Palestinian	12	A1
Hussein, Muhammad Ahmad Jabr	Son	(childhood)	Palestinian	11	A1
Hussein, Rabi' Ahmad Jabr	Son	(childhood)	Palestinian	11	A1
Hussein, Nawal Ahmad Jabr	Daughter	(childhood)	Palestinian	10	A1
Hussein, Su'ad Ahmad Jabr	Daughter	(childhood)	Palestinian	9	A1
Hussein, Nadim Mahdi		Freelance worker	Lebanese	46	A2
Huweidi, Salim Muhsin		Freelance worker	Syrian	72	A1
Iskamlaji, Fitnah Gandour (Mrs Muhammad Ali)	Mother	(housewife)	Syrian	45	A5
Iskamlaji, Khaled Muhammad Ali	Son	(school age)	Lebanese	16	A5
Iskamlaji, Khadijeh Muhamad Ali	Daughter	(school age)	Lebanese	15	A5
Iskamlaji, Sawsan Muhammad Ali	Daughter	(school age)	Lebanese	13	A5
Iskamlaji, Walid Muhammad Ali	Son	(childhood)	Lebanese	8	A5
Isma'il, Intissar		PRC: Doctor/Nurse/Hospital worker	Palestinian	28	A5
Isma'il, Wahsh Muhammad		(old age)	Palestinian	71	A1
Jad'on, Ahmad Dib		Freelance worker	Palestinian	68	A3
Jamilah, Riad Mahmoud	Brother	Freedom fighter	Jordanian	19	A1
Jamilah, Samar Mahmoud	Sister	(school age)	Jordanian	14	A1
Juheir, Sa'id Abd al-Karim		Fish vendor/Vegetable vendor/Peddler	Palestinian	21	A1
Jum'a, Mariam (Mrs Issa Qassem)	Mother	(housewife)	Palestinian	43	A1
Jum'a, Majed Issa Qassem	Son	(childhood)	Palestinian	12	A1
Jureidi, Fatima M. Rashed (Mrs Sa'id)	Mother	(housewife)	Palestinian	31	A4
Jureidi, Mariam Sa'id	Daughter	(childhood)	Palestinian	7	A4
Jureidi, Suzan Sa'id	Daughter	(childhood)	Palestinian	5	A4
Jureidi, Jinan Sa'id	Daughter	(childhood)	Palestinian	3	A4
Jureidi, Nidal Sa'id	Daughter	(early childhood)	Palestinian	2	A4
Kanoun, Ali Muhammad Yassin	Father	Employee	Syrian	61	A4

List of names 1 (Continued)

Name	Kinship	Profession	Nationality	Age	Reference**
Kanoun, Sakina al-Sayyed (Mrs Ali)	Mother	(housewife)	Lebanese	56	A4
Kanoun, Ahmad Ali Muhammad	Son	Unspecified profession	Syrian	25	A4
Kanoun, Yahya Ali Muhammad	Son	(school age)	Syrian	14	A4
Karmo, Jamil Muhsen	Father	(old age)	Stateless	78	A2
Karmo, Tawfiq Muhsen	Uncle	(old age)	Stateless	71	A2
Karmo, Khaled Jamil Muhsen	Son	Artist/Musician	Stateless	40	A2
Karmo, Hamid Jamil Muhsen	Son	Freelance worker	Stateless	29	A2
Karmo, Muhammad	Father	(old age)	Stateless	80	A2
Karmo, Nayef Muhammad	Son	Freelance worker	Stateless	42	A2
Karmo, – (Mrs Nayef)	Daughter-in-law	(housewife)	Stateless	35	A2
Karmo, Ali Muhammad	Son	Freelance worker	Stateless	31	A1
Khalifeh, Hamid Mustafa	Father	Barber/Baker/Cook/Butcher	Palestinian	44	A1
Khalifeh, Muhammad Abd	Uncle	Fish vendor/Vegetable vendor/Peddler	Palestinian	52	A1
Khalifeh, Hussein Hamid Mustafa	Son	Driver/Mechanic	Palestinian	16	A1
Khalifeh, Hasan Hamid Mustafa	Son	(school age)	Palestinian	15	A1
Khalil, Khalil Abdo		Barber/Baker/Cook/Butcher	Stateless	19	A1
Khamis, Muhammad		Freelance worker	Egyptian	44	A3
Khatib, Abd al-Rahman Ahmad		Mobile kerosene vendor	Lebanese	31	A1
Khatib, Ghalia Muhsen	Grandmother	(old age)	Palestinian	73	A1
Khatib, Ali Hussein	Father	Freelance worker	Palestinian	46	A1
Khatib, Dibeh (Mrs Ali Hussein)	Mother	(housewife)	Palestinian	43	A1
Khatib, Saber Ali	Son	Mason/Painter/Carpenter/Blacksmith	Palestinian	24	A1
Khatib, Amneh Ali	Daughter	Employee	Palestinian	22	A1
Khatib, Hussein Ali	Son	Tailor/Weaver/Upholsterer	Palestinian	20	A1
Khatib, Nader Ali	Son	(school age)	Palestinian	14	A1
Khatib, Munther Ali	Son	(childhood)	Palestinian	12	A1
Khatib, Imtithal Ali	Daughter	(childhood)	Palestinian	11	A1
Khatib, Maryam Ali	Daughter	(childhood)	Palestinian	7	A1
Khatib, Hussein Muhammad		Freelance worker	Palestinian	20	A1
Khatib, Ibrahim Subhi		Mobile kerosene vendor	Lebanese	18	A1
Khatib, Muhammad Hasan		Freelance worker	Palestinian	26	A1
Khatib, Sami Muhammad		PRC: Doctor/Nurse/Hospital worker	Palestinian	30	A3
Kiwan, Jamil Farhan		Employee	Syrian	43	A5
Kulaib, Hasan Abdallah	Father	Fish vendor/Vegetable vendor/Peddler	Palestinian	51	A1

Name	Relationship	Profession	Nationality	Age	Code
Kulaib, Ahmad Hasan Abdallah	Son	Driver/Mechanic	Palestinian	18	A1
Kurdi, Yousuf		Freelance worker	Turk	30	A4
Liddawi, Muhammad		Unspecified profession	Palestinian	52	A4
Ma'rouf, Ziad Abdallah		PRC: Doctor/Nurse/Hospital worker	Palestinian	31	A3
Madi, Younes	Father	(sick/permanently sick)	Palestinian	65	A1
Madi, Ahmad Younes	Son	Mason/Painter/Carpenter/Blacksmith	Palestinian	20	A1
Madi, Madi Younes	Son	(school age)	Palestinian	17	A1
Madi, Muhammad Younes	Son	(school age)	Palestinian	14	A1
Mahmoud, Arshad		Freelance worker	Pakistani	27	A5
Majdoub, Mahmoud Abd	Brother	Unspecified profession	Palestinian	35	A4
Majdoub, Muhammad Abd	Brother	(school age)	Palestinian	17	A4
Makkiyeh, Farouq Salameh		Mason/Painter/Carpenter/Blacksmith	Palestinian	19	A2
Mansour, Ali Abdo		(childhood)	Lebanese	5	A1
Mattar, Khadijeh Yahya		(housewife)	Palestinian	32	A2
Mattar, Muhammad Adnan		(school age)	Palestinian	18	A2
Minawi, Bilal Ahmad		Electrician/Telephone repairman	Palestinian	18	A1
Miqdad, Abd al-Ra'ouf	Father	Barber/Baker/Cook/Butcher	Lebanese	40	A1
Miqdad, Ilham (Mrs Abd al-Ra'ouf)	Mother	(housewife)	Lebanese	27	A1
Miqdad, Mirvat Abd al-Ra'ouf	Daughter	(childhood)	Lebanese	12	A1
Miqdad, Nariman Abd al- Ra'ouf	Daughter	(childhood)	Lebanese	11	A1
Miqdad, Nisrin Abd al-Ra'ouf	Daughter	(childhood)	Lebanese	7	A1
Miqdad, Mahasen Abd al-Ra'ouf	Daughter	(childhood)	Lebanese	7	A1
Miqdad, Fatima Abd al-Ra'ouf	Daughter	(early childhood)	Lebanese	3	A1
Miqdad, Ulfat Abd al-Ra'ouf	Daughter	(early childhood)	Lebanese	2	A1
Miqdad, – (mother Ilham Miqdad)	(Grandchild)	(unborn baby)	Lebanese		A1
Miqdad, Ali Hussein Isma'il	Husband	(old age)	Lebanese	65	A1
Miqdad, Fatima Wahbeh (Mrs Ali Hussein)	Wife	(housewife)	Lebanese	62	A1
Miqdad, Rida Hussein Ali	Brother	Employee	Lebanese	62	A1
Miqdad, Fariza Diab, Um Yousuf	Mother	(housewife)	Lebanese	60	A1
Miqdad, Yousuf Abd al-Qader	Son	Freelance worker	Lebanese	22	A1
Miqdad, Hussein Dhaher	Father	Electrician/Telephone repairman	Lebanese	40	A1
Miqdad, Wata' Hammoud (Mrs Hussein Dhaher)	Mother	(housewife)	Lebanese	30	A1
Miqdad, Muhammad Hussein Dhaher	Son	(childhood)	Lebanese	8	A1
Miqdad, Yasser Hussein Dhaher	Son	(childhood)	Lebanese	6	A1
Miqdad, Safa' Hussein Dhaher	Daughter	(babyhood)	Lebanese	1	A1
Miqdad, – (mother Wata' H. Miqdad)	(Grandchild)	(unborn baby)	Lebanese		A1
Miqdad, Yasser Dhaher	Father	Driver/Mechanic	Lebanese	35	A1

List of names 1 (Continued)

Name	Kinship	Profession	Nationality	Age	Reference**
Miqdad, Zainab (Mrs Yasser Dhaher)	Mother	(housewife)	Lebanese	30	A1
Miqdad, Faiza Yasser Dhaher	Daughter	(school age)	Lebanese	16	A1
Miqdad, Firyal Yasser Dhaher	Daughter	(school age)	Lebanese	13	A1
Miqdad, Fadi Yasser Dhaher	Son	(childhood)	Lebanese	10	A1
Miqdad, Hussein Yasser Dhaher	Son	(childhood)	Lebanese	8	A1
Miqdad, Adnan Yasser Dhaher	Son	(babyhood)	Lebanese	6	A1
Miqdad, Rifaq Yasser Dhaher	Daughter	(unborn baby)	Lebanese	1	A1
Miqdad, – (mother Zainab Miqdad)	(Grandchild)		Lebanese		A1
Mir'i, Rasmi Muhsin	Father	Freelance worker	Stateless	42	A2
Mir'i, Yahya Muhsin	Uncle	Freelance worker	Stateless	24	A2
Mir'i, Zakaria Muhsin	Uncle	Freelance worker	Stateless	22	A2
Mir'i, Ali Rasmi Muhsin	Son	(childhood)	Stateless	12	A2
Mir'i, Muhsin Rasmi Muhsin	Son	(childhood)	Stateless	9	A2
Mir'i, Srour Muhammad Sa'id	Father	Electrician/Telephone repairman	Palestinian	43	A1
Mir'i, Bassam Srour Muhammad	Son	(childhood)	Palestinian	12	A1
Mir'i, Farid Srour Muhammad	Son	(childhood)	Palestinian	6	A1
Mir'i, Shadi Srour Muhammad	Son	(early childhood)	Palestinian	3	A1
Mir'i, Shadya Srour Muhammad	Daughter	(early childhood)	Palestinian	2	A1
Misri, Aisha Fayez Abu Tayyouni		(housewife)	Palestinian	35	A1
Misri, Sayyed Muhammd		Mobile kerosene vendor	Egyptian	30	A4
Mughrabi, Subhi Muhammad	Uncle	Freedom fighter	Palestinian	43	A1
Mughrabi, Amer Salim	Nephew	(school age)	Palestinian	17	A1
Mughrabi, Khaled Salim	Nephew	Mason/Painter/Carpenter/Blacksmith	Palestinian	17	A1
Muhammad, Khaled Yousuf	Father	Freelance worker	Palestinian	47	A1
Muhammad, Fatima (Mrs Khaled Yousuf)	Mother	(housewife)	Palestinian	44	A1
Muhammad, Suhaila Khaled Yousuf	Daughter	Freedom fighter	Palestinian	19	A1
Muhammad, Sana' Khaled Yousuf	Daughter	(school age)	Palestinian	17	A1
Muhammad, Baha' Khaled Yousuf	Daughter	(childhood)	Palestinian	17	A1
Muhammad, Laila Khaled Yousuf	Daughter	(childhood)	Palestinian	12	A1
Muhammad, Akram Khaled Yousuf	Son	(childhood)	Palestinian	11	A1
Muhammad, Iman Khaled Yousuf	Daughter	(childhood)	Palestinian	9	A1
Muhammad, Manal Khaled Yousuf	Daughter	(childhood)	Palestinian	7	A1
Muhammad, Samer Khaled Yousuf	Son	(early childhood)	Palestinian	5	A1
Muhammad, Ahlam Khaled Yousuf	Daughter	(babyhood)	Palestinian	2	A1
			Palestinian	1	A1

Name	Relation	Profession	Nationality	Age	Code
Muhammad, Yahya Ahmad	Husband	Freedom fighter	Palestinian	30	A1
Muhammad, Khawla (Mrs Yahya)	Wife	(housewife)	Palestinian	25	A1
Muhammad, Zahra (Mrs Ahmad Moussa)	Mother	(housewife)	Palestinian	35	A1
Muhammad, Aida Ahmad Moussa	Daughter	(school age)	Palestinian	16	A1
Muhammad, Mufid Ahmad Moussa	Son	(school age)	Palestinian	15	A1
Muhammad, Mu'in Ahmad Moussa	Son	(childhood)	Palestinian	11	A1
Muhammad, Fadya Ahmad Moussa	Daughter	(childhood)	Palestinian	7	A1
Muhammad, Iman Ahmad Moussa	Daughter	(childhood)	Palestinian	6	A1
Muhammad, Inayatallah Bashir		Employee	Pakistani	27	A4
Muhammad, Muhammad Salim		Freelance worker	Stateless	19	A1
Muhanna, Ali Hasan		Mason/Painter/Carpenter/Blacksmith	Lebanese	20	A4
Muhsen, Tawfiq Karma	Father	(old age)	Lebanese	65	A1
Muhsen, Moussa Tawfiq Karma	Son	Driver/Mechanic	Lebanese	35	A1
Murtada, Adib Hasan		Small tradesman	Lebanese	33	A3
Moussa, Mahmoud Muhammad	Father	Teacher	Palestinian	34	A4
Moussa, Munir Muhammad	Uncle	(college student)	Palestinian	20	A4
Moussa, Mazen Mahmoud	Son	(childhood)	Palestinian	12	A3
Mussawi, Hasan Sayyed		Mobile kerosene vendor	Lebanese	42	A3
Mustafa, Muhammad	Uncle	(old age)	Stateless	73	A1
Mustafa, Riad Mustafa	Nephew	Driver/Mechanic	Stateless	23	A1
Mustafa, Khaled Mustafa	Nephew	Doorman/Guard/Jockey	Stateless	16	A1
Mustafa, Saleh Ahmad		Freelance worker	Egyptian	34	A3
Nabulsi, Muhammad		Unspecified profession	Palestinian	35	A1
Najjar, Hussein Hasan Ahmad		Freedom fighter	Palestinian	45	A1
Nasser, Hussein Abd al-Rida		Employee	Lebanese	42	A1
Nassif, Ali Issa		Mason/Painter/Carpenter/Blacksmith	Palestinian	65	A1
Nazzal, Muhammad Salim		Freedom fighter	Palestinian	33	A3
Ni'meh, Na'im Ali, hajj		Mobile kerosene vendor	Lebanese	80	A2
Nounu, Faraj Abdo		Draughtsman/Designer	Palestinian	22	A1
Nouri, Adnan		(old age)	Palestinian	90	A5
Orli, Ahmad		Mason/Painter/Carpenter/Blacksmith	Sudanese	35	A5
Qaddoura, Badran Hussein		(school age)	Palestinian	18	A1
Qadi, Fahmi Ahmad		Freedom fighter	Palestinian	31	A1
Qadi, Fawwaz Madi		Barber/Baker/Cook/Butcher	Palestinian	43	A2
Qadi, Saleh Dakhil	Father	Freedom fighter	Palestinian	52	A1
Qadi, Bassam Saleh Dakhil	Son	(school age)	Palestinian	18	A1
Qadi, Ibtisam Saleh Dakhil	Daughter	(school age)	Palestinian	14	A1

List of names 1 (Continued)

Name	Kinship	Profession	Nationality	Age	Reference**
Qadi, Husam Saleh Dakhil	Son	(childhood)	Palestinian	12	A1
Qadi, Issam Saleh Dakhil	Son	(childhood)	Palestinian	10	A1
Qadi, Sari Ahmad		(old age)	Palestinian	80	A2
Qassem, Hasan Dib		(college student)	Palestinian	22	A1
Qassem, Muhammad Mut'ab		Freelance worker	Palestinian	48	A1
Qassem, Munther Sami		Employee	Palestinian	23	A2
Qaswat, Muhammad Ahmad		Freelance worker	Syrian	58	A2
Qatanani, Muhammad Abd		Mason/Painter/Carpenter/Blacksmith	Palestinian	31	A1
Ra'd, Sa'diyyeh Muhammad		(housewife)	Lebanese	70	A2
Ramadan, Raja' Ali		(housewife)	Palestinian	16	A2
Rashid, Badi'a Murad (Mrs Muhammad Ali)	Mother	(housewife)	Lebanese	45	A2
Rashid, Haydar Muhammad Ali	Son	Unspecified profession	Lebanese	19	A2
Rashid, Mahmoud Muhammad Ali	Son	(school age)	Lebanese	15	A2
Rashid, Zainab Mahammad Ali	Daughter	(school age)	Lebanese	14	A2
Rashid, Ali Muhammad Ali	Son	(childhood)	Lebanese	11	A2
Sa'd, Mahmoud Muhammad	Father	Employee	Palestinian	62	A1
Sa'd, Afaf Mahmoud	Daughter	Employee	Palestinian	17	A1
Sa'd, Asya Muhammad		(housewife)	Lebanese	25	A2
Sa'd, Isma'il Ahmad		Unspecified profession	Palestinian	60	A3
Sa'id, Ahmad Ali		Freelance worker	Syrian	38	A2
Sa'id, Ahmad Muhammad		Driver/Mechanic	Palestinian	37	A3
Sa'id, Faraj Ibrahim		Electrician/Telephone repairman	Egyptian	35	A3
Sa'id, Jihad Ali		Driver/Mechanic	Palestinian	30	A3
Sadeq, Imad Muhammad		Freedom fighter	Lebanese	23	A1
Sadeq, Nizar Ibrahim		PRC: Doctor/Nurse/Hospital worker	Palestinian	22	A5
Saghir, Jum'a Abd-Ezzein	Father	Freelance worker	Palestinian	45	A3
Saghir, Moussa Jum'a	Son	(school age)	Palestinian	18	A3
Saghir, Mona Abbas		(school age)	Lebanese	15	A1
Salam, Muhammad Hasan		(old age)	Sudanese	80	A1
Salem, Salem Muhammad		Freelance worker	Palestinian	20	A1
Salim, Khodr Hussein		Freelance worker	Stateless	40	A2
Salim, Muhammad Shawkat	Father	Freelance worker	Stateless	52	A2
Salim, Akram Muhammad Shawkat	Son	Freelance worker	Stateless	20	A2
Salim, Jihad Muhammad Shawkat	Son	Freelance worker	Stateless	16	A2

Name	Relation	Occupation	Nationality	Age	
Salim, Nidal Muhammad Shawkat	*Son*	*Doorman/Guard/Jockey*	*Stateless*	*14*	*A2*
Salolum, Ahmad Abd al-Hasan		Freelance worker	Lebanese	28	A1
Samarji, Imam Muhammad Ali		Employee	Egyptian	25	A4
Sarris, Jamal Muhammad Hussein		(school age)	Palestinian	19	A5
Sha'ban, Ali Omar		Barber/Baker/Cook/Butcher	Egyptian	30	A3
Shahrour, Ali Kamel		Fish vendor/Vegetable vendor/Peddler	Palestinian	72	A1
Shamas, Muhammad Radi	*Father*	*Employee*	*Lebanese*	*48*	*A1*
Shamas, Aref Muhammad	*Son*	*Employee*	*Lebanese*	*22*	*A1*
Sheikh, Ibrahim Ali		Driver/Mechanic	Lebanese	45	A2
Sheikh, Laila Ahmad		(housewife)	Syrian	30	A4
Shihadeh, Samir Muhammad		(school age)	Palestinian	17	A1
Shoufani, Thunaya Diab Kharrub	*Mother*	*(housewife)*	*Palestinian*	*55*	*A1*
Shoufani, Shihadeh Ahmad	*Son*	*Freedom fighter*	*Palestinian*	*28*	*A1*
Shoufani, Wafa' Shihadeh Ahmad	*Granddaughter*	*(childhood)*	*Palestinian*	*4*	*A1*
Shoufani, Ahmad Shihadeh Ah.	*Grandson*	*(early childhood)*	*Palestinian*	*2*	*A1*
Sirsawi, Abdallah Mahmoud		Employee	Palestinian	52	A1
Sukkarieh, Mir'i Hawlo		Freedom fighter	Lebanese	45	A5
Sulaiman, Orabi Abd al-Rahman		PRC: Doctor/Nurse/Hospital worker	Egyptian	30	A3
Ta'baneh, Salim Abd al-Basset	*Brother*	*Draughtsman/Designer*	*Lebanese*	*22*	*A2*
Ta'baneh, Samih Abd al-Basset	*Brother*	*Electrician/Telephone repairman*	*Lebanese*	*20*	*A2*
Taha, Muhammad Ahmad		PRC: Doctor/Nurse/Hospital worker	Palestinian	58	A3
Taleb, Fayzeh Amin		(housewife)	Lebanese	51	A1
Titi, Hussein Saleh	*Father*	*Freelance worker*	*Palestinian*	*55*	*A5*
Titi, Saleh Hussein Saleh	*Son*	*Freedom fighter*	*Palestinian*	*21*	*A1*
Titi, Samia Ibrahim Taleb (Mrs Muhammad)	*Mother*	*(housewife)*	*Lebanese*	*25*	*A1*
Titi, Tareq Muhammad	*Son*	*(childhood)*	*Palestinian*	*5*	*A1*
Titi, Mahmoud Muhammad	*Son*	*(babyhood)*	*Palestinian*	*1*	*A1*
Turki, Hussein Muhammad		Mason/Painter/Carpenter/Blacksmith	Turk	35	A5
Wahbeh, Najla Taha	*Mother*	*(housewife)*	*Palestinian*	*51*	*A1*
Wahbeh, Faisal Mahmoud	*Son*	*(sick/permanently sick)*	*Palestinian*	*35*	*A1*
Wahbeh, Ali Mahmoud	*Son*	*(school age)*	*Palestinian*	*20*	*A1*
Wahbeh, Fatima Ahmad Sirriyeh (Mrs Khalil)	*Daughter-in-law*	*(housewife)*	*Palestinian*	*23*	*A1*
Wahbeh, Ibrahim Khalil	*Grandson*	*(babyhood)*	*Palestinian*	*1*	*A1*
Wahbeh, Nahed Sa'd (Mrs Ali)	*Daughter-in-law*	*(housewife)*	*Lebanese*	*17*	*A1*
Wahbeh, (mother Nahed Sa'd)	*(Grandchild)*	*(unborn baby)*	*Palestinian*		*A1*
Wali, Hasan Muhammad		PRC: Doctor/Nurse/Hospital worker	Palestinian	24	A3
Younes, Hussein Mahmoud		(old age)	Lebanese	75	A1

List of names 1 (Continued)

Name	Kinship	Profession	Nationality	Age	Reference**
Younes, Muhammad Abd		Draughtsman/Designer	Palestinian	30	A1
Yousuf, Riad Abdallah		Electrician/Telephone repairman	Palestinian	34	A1
Zahr al-Din, Salah Abbas		(school age)	Lebanese	13	A1
Zahr al-Din, Muhammad Abbas	Brother	(childhood)	Lebanese	6	A1
Zahr al-Din, Nabila Abbas	Sister	(early childhood)	Lebanese	3	A1
Zahr al-Din, Hussein Abbas	Brother	(babyhood)	Lebanese	1	A1
Zalghout, Ahmad Hussein		Mason/Painter/Carpenter/Blacksmith	Lebanese	27	A5
Zammar, Salameh Izzat		Barber/Baker/Cook/Butcher	Palestinian	47	A1
Zayyouni, Amneh (Mrs Muhammad)	Mother	(housewife)	Lebanese	43	A3
Zayyouni, Samir Muhammad	Son	Mobile kerosene vendor	Lebanese	25	A3
Zayyouni, Amira Muhammad	Daughter	(housewife)	Lebanese	22	A3
Zayyouni, Samira Samir	Daughter-in-law	(housewife)	Lebanese	20	A3
Zayyouni, Jamal Muhammad	Son	(school age)	Lebanese	16	A3
Zayyouni, Abd Muhammad	Son	(childhood)	Lebanese	11	A3
Zayyouni, Suhaila Muhammad	Daughter	(childhood)	Lebanese	11	A3
Zeina, Hussein 'Abu Sulaiman'		(old age)	Palestinian	75	A1
(name unknown)		(early childhood)	Egyptian	3	A5
Abdallah		(sick/permanently sick)	Palestinian	35	A5
Abu Farid		Freelance worker	Palestinian	28	A3
Abu Nidal		Mason/Painter/Carpenter/Blacksmith	Syrian	24	A4
Abu Ratibeh		Freelance worker	Tunisian	64	A4
Abu Tareq		Doorman/Guard/Jockey	Lebanese	57	A5
Fahd		Mason/Painter/Carpenter/Blacksmith	Syrian	25	A5
Hamdi		Employee	Egyptian	35	A4
Hamid Aziz		Freelance worker	Stateless	34	A3
Hussein		Mason/Painter/Carpenter/Blacksmith	Turk	31	A1
Khalil		PRC: Doctor/Nurse/Hospital worker	Palestinian	28	A4
(found burnt at Akka Hospital)		(babyhood)	Not identified	1	A5
(found burnt at Akka Hospital)		(babyhood)	Not identified	1	A5
(found burnt at Akka Hospital)		(babyhood)	Not identified	1	A5
(found killed in a shelter – Hayy al-Gharbi)		(babyhood)	Not identified	1	A5
(found killed in a shelter – Hayy al-Gharbi)		(babyhood)	Not identified	1	A5
(found killed in a shelter – Hayy al-Gharbi)		(babyhood)	Not identified	1	A5
(found killed in a shelter – Hayy al-Gharbi)		(babyhood)	Not identified	1	A5

(found killed in a shelter – Hayy al-Gharbi)	(babyhood)	Not identified	1	A5
(found killed in a shelter – Hayy al-Gharbi)	(babyhood)	Not identified	1	A5
(found killed on bed – al-Horsh)	Mason/Painter/Carpenter/Blacksmith	Bangladeshi	30 >	A4
(found killed on bed – al-Horsh)	Mason/Painter/Carpenter/Blacksmith	Bangladeshi	30 >	A4
(found killed on bed – al-Horsh)	Mason/Painter/Carpenter/Blacksmith	Bangladeshi	30 >	A4
(found killed on bed – al-Horsh)	Mason/Painter/Carpenter/Blacksmith	Bangladeshi	30 >	A4
(found killed on bed – al-Horsh)	Mason/Painter/Carpenter/Blacksmith	Bangladeshi	30 >	A4
(found killed on bed – al-Horsh)	Mason/Painter/Carpenter/Blacksmith	Bangladeshi	30 >	A4

* Italics indicate multiple victims within families. For each family, the order of names is basically according to age (from oldest to youngest), but with family ties also considered. In cases where no other family member was a victim, names are in alphabetical order.

** The code A applies to the Field Study: A1 to immediate kin, such as father, mother, sister, wife, etc; A2 to a relative outside the immediate family, such as uncle, cousin, etc.; A3 to a friend; A4 to a neighbour; A5 to a simple witness.

List of names 2   Abducted in Sabra and Shatila massacre: based on field study, spring 1984*

Name	Kinship	Profession	Nationality	Age	Reference**
Abd al- Mun'em (al Masri)		Freelance worker	Egyptian	28	A1
Abed, Ghassan Yousuf		(school age)	Palestinian	16	A2
Abu Adas, Ra'fat Abd Al-Hamid		(student: college/vocational institution)	Palestinian	20	A1
Abu Zeid, Muhammad	*Father*	*Freelance worker*	*Stateless*	*40*	*A4*
Abu Zeid, Taysir Muhammad	*Son*	*Freelance worker*	*Stateless*	*18*	*A4*
Abu Zeid, Hamzah Muhammad	*Son*	*Freelance worker*	*Stateless*	*17*	*A4*
Abu Zeid, Nasser Muhammad	*Son*	*Freelance worker*	*Stateless*	*15*	*A4*
Ahmad, Faraj Ali Sayyed		Electrician/Telephone repairman	Egyptian	34	A1
Ahmad, Muhammad Hussein		Mason/Painter/Carpenter/Blacksmith	Palestinian	43	A1
Alameh, Ali Hasan		(student: college/vocational institution)	Lebanese	18	A1
Ali, Ahmad	*Father*	*Freelance worker*	*Palestinian*	*50*	*A1*
Ali, Muhammad Ahmad	*Son*	*Freelance worker*	*Palestinian*	*23*	*A1*
Ali, Mahmoud Ahmad	*Son*	*(student: college/vocational institution)*	*Palestinian*	*19*	*A1*
Ali, Ahmad Muhammad Sa'id		Fish vendor/Vegetable vendor/Peddler	Syrian	32	A1
Ali, Muhammad Muhammad		Mason/Painter/Carpenter/Blacksmith	Palestinian	31	A1
Ali, Omar Muhammad		Mason/Painter/Carpenter/Blacksmith	Palestinian	25	A1
Aswad, Hasan Ahmad		Small tradesman	Syrian	52	A1
At'out, Bashir Ahmad		Plumber	Palestinian	18	A1
Atyar, Hasan Hashem		Freelance worker	Palestinian	23	A1
Azzam, Adnan Khaled		Freelance worker	Palestinian	26	A1
Azzouqa, Ibrahim Mahmoud		(school age)	Palestinian	13	A1
Baitam, Fayyad Hasan		(student: College/Vocational Institution)	Palestinian	22	A1
Banat, Mahmoud Bakri		Driver/Mechanic	Lebanese	33	A1
Bibi, Bassam Abd as-Salam		Plumber	Palestinian	18	A1
Dirawi, Aziz Faisal	*Brother*	*Driver/Mechanic*	*Palestinian*	*33*	*A1*
Dirawi, Ibrahim Faisal	*Brother*	*Mason/Painter/Carpenter/Blacksmith*	*Palestinian*	*28*	*A1*
Dirawi, Mansour Faisal	*Brother*	*Driver/Mechanic*	*Palestinian*	*25*	*A1*
Dirawi, Ahmad Faisal	*Brother*	*(school age)*	*Palestinian*	*15*	*A1*
Ghazzawi, Ali Ahmad	*Father*	*Freelance worker*	*Syrian*	*45*	*A4*
Ghazzawi, Hussein Ali Ahmad	*Son*	*Freelance worker*	*Syrian*	*20*	*A4*
Ghazzawi, Muhammad Ali Ahmad	*Son*	*Freelance worker*	*Syrian*	*16*	*A4*
Hajjar, Ahmad, Mustafa		Mason/Painter/Carpenter/Blacksmith	Palestinian	17	A1
Hariri, Khaled Hamid,	*Brother*	*Freelance worker*	*Stateless*	*17*	*A3*

Name	Relation	Occupation	Nationality	Age	Code
Hariri, Muhammad Hamid	*Brother*	*(school age)*	*Stateless*	*16*	*A5*
Hasan, Hasan Ahmad	*Father*	*Employee*	*Palestinian*	*50*	*A1*
Hasan, Jalal Hasan Ahmad	*Son*	*(school age)*	*Palestinian*	*15*	*A1*
Hasan, Khalil Mahmoud	*Father*	*Doorman/Guard/Jockey*	*Palestinian*	*55*	*A5*
Hasan, Ahmad Khalil Mahmoud	*Son*	*(school age)*	*Palestinian*	*16*	*A5*
Hayek, As'ad Muhammad		Freelance worker	Palestinian	27	A1
Hijazi, Muhammad Kazem		Mason/Painter/Carpenter/Blacksmith	Lebanese	19	A1
Himmo, Jamal Muhammad		Mason/Painter/Carpenter/Blacksmith	Palestinian	17	A1
Hussein, Kamel Hussein		Freelance worker	Palestinian	41	A1
Huweidi, Orans Ammar		(school age)	Syrian	15	A1
Ibriq, Khalil Mahmoud	*Father*	*Freelance worker*	*Palestinian*	*54*	*A1*
Ibriq, Mahmoud Khalil Mahmoud	*Son*	*(school age)*	*Palestinian*	*17*	*A1*
Issawi, Majdi Misbah		Freelance worker	Palestinian	45	A1
Jammal, Ahmad Obeid		Fish vendor/Vegetable vendor/Peddler	Syrian	53	A1
Kabbara, Salim Issa		Driver/Mechanic	Palestinian	32	A1
Kayyali, Ahmad Nimr		(school age)	Palestinian	14	A1
Kharroubi, Mustafa Sulaiman		(school age)	Palestinian	18	A1
Khatib, Abdallah Qassem		Freelance worker	Palestinian	20	A1
Kuthayer, Ahmad Muhammad Salim	*Brother*	*Freelance worker*	*Palestinian*	*28*	*A1*
Kuthayer, Jamal Muhammad Salim	*Brother*	*Freelance worker*	*Palestinian*	*26*	*A1*
Labban, Muhammad Tawfiq		Unspecified profession	Palestinian	20	A1
Ma'rouf, Jamal Kamal		Electrician/Telephone repairman	Palestinian	19	A1
Mashharawi, Ibrahim Khalil		Teacher	Palestinian	55	A1
Misri, Mahmoud Muhammad Subhi		Driver/Mechanic	Palestinian	22	A1
Muhammad, Ali Muhammad	*Father*	*Freelance worker*	*Syrian*	*44*	*A1*
Muhammad, Hussein Ali Muhammad	*Son*	*Freelance worker*	*Syrian*	*20*	*A1*
Muhammad, Walid Ali Muhammad	*Son*	*Freelance worker*	*Syrian*	*20*	*A1*
Muhammad, Muhammad Ali Muhammad	*Son*	*Freelance worker*	*Syrian*	*18*	*A1*
Muhammad, Hasan Mahmoud		(student: college/vocational institution)	Palestinian	17	A1
Muhammad, Mahmoud Salim		Freelance worker	Syrian	35	A1
Muhawish, Muhawish Mahmoud		(old age)	Palestinian	65	A1
Muhsin, Na'im Fayez		Shoemaker	Lebanese	17	A1
Na'im, Sa'id Ahmad		Mason/Painter/Carpenter/Blacksmith	Egyptian	24	A1
Nasr al-Din, Abd al-Rahim Khodr	*Brother*	*Freelance worker*	*Lebanese*	*27*	*A1*
Nasr al-Din, Hasan Khodr	*Brother*	*Freelance worker*	*Lebanese*	*22*	*A1*
Nasrallah, Hasan Nimr		Freelance worker	Lebanese	16	A1
Natat, Sami Shaker Abd al-Ghani		Mason/Painter/Carpenter/Blacksmith	Palestinian	23	A1

List of names 2 (Continued)

Name	Kinship	Profession	Nationality	Age	Reference**
Qadi, Muhammad Fawzi	Brother	Employee	Palestinian	18	A1
Qadi, Ali Fawzi	Brother	(school age)	Palestinian	16	A1
Qassem, Yousuf Rahil		Freelance worker	Palestinian	40	A2
Radi, Hasan		Freelance worker	Palestinian	18	A3
Sa'd, Mahmoud Salah al-Din		Plumber	Lebanese	25	A1
Sa'di, Muhammad Assi	Father	Employee	Palestinian	60	A1
Sa'di, Khaled Muhammad Assi	Son	Freedom fighter	Palestinian	21	A1
Sa'id, Ahmad Muhammad		Freelance worker	Syrian	40	A1
Sa'idi, Ahmad Mustafa		Mason/Painter/Carpenter/Blacksmith	Palestinian	26	A1
Sabbagh, Riad Yahya		Freelance worker	Lebanese	21	A1
Sabeq, Mahmoud Hasan		Mason/Painter/Carpenter/Blacksmith	Palestinian	39	A1
Safar, Abdallah Suheil		Shoemaker	Palestinian	27	A1
Saffouri, Yousuf Shafiq		(school age)	Palestinian	12	A2
Salem, Mahmoud Abd al-Wahhab		(school age)	Palestinian	15	A1
Salem, Ahmad Khalil		Tailor/Weaver/Upholsterer	Palestinian	16	A1
Salem, Khalil Muhammad	Father	Fish vendor/Vegetable vendor/Peddler	Palestinian	45	A1
Salem, Ihsan Muhammad	Uncle	Driver/Mechanic	Palestinian	37	A1
Salem, Awni Khalil	Son	Driver/Mechanic	Palestinian	18	A1
Sane', Nasser As'ad		Mason/Painter/Carpenter/Blacksmith	Palestinian	20	A1
Saqqa, Abd Mahmoud	Brother	Mason/Painter/Carpenter/Blacksmith	Palestinian	28	A1
Saqqa, Muhammad Mahmoud	Brother	Mason/Painter/Carpenter/Blacksmith	Palestinian	18	A1
Sawalha, Khalil	Brother	Freelance worker	Palestinian	26	A1
Sawalha, Mahmoud	Brother	Freelance worker	Palestinian	23	A1
Sharqawi, Anwar Ibrahim		(school age)	Lebanese	16	A1
Sirri, Ibrahim Mustafa		Mason/Painter/Carpenter/Blacksmith	Palestinian	28	A1
Sirri, Nabil Gharib		Electrician/Telephone repairman	Palestinian	23	A1
Umari, Khaled Ibrahim		Mason/Painter/Carpenter/Blacksmith	Lebanese	23	A1
Zurein, Walid Darwish		Mason/Painter/Carpenter/Blacksmith	Palestinian	22	A1
Hussein		PRC: Doctor/Nurse/Hospital worker	Palestinian	35	A4
Uthman		Electrician/Telephone repairman	British	30	A5

* Italics indicate family abducted members. For each family, the order of names is basically according to age (from oldest to youngest), but with family ties also considered. In cases where no other family member was a victim, names are in alphabetical order.

** The code A applies to the field study; A1 to immediate kin, such as father, mother, sister, wife, etc.; A2 to a relative outside the immediate family, such as uncle, cousin, etc.; A3 to a friend; A4 to a neighbour; A5 to a simple witness.

List of names 3   Victims of Sabra and Shatila massacre: based on various sources

Name	Age	Gender	Nationality	References*
A'id, Ahmad Tawfiq		M	Palestinian	D
Abbas, Ahmad Ghaith	75	M	Palestinian	A
Abboud, Aayed		M	Not identified	H
Abboud, Zuheir		M	Not identified	H
Abd al-Aal, Ali Fahim		M	Not identified	H
Abd al-Fattah, Mahmoud Qassem	35	M	Palestinian	A E M
Abd al-Halim, Mustafa Abd al-Halim		M	Palestinian	D'
Abd al-Khaleq, Muhammad Ahmad		M	Not identified	G
Abd al-Latif, Rida	22	M	Egyptian	A D'
Abd al-Qader, Adli Salim		M	Not identified	H
Abd al-Rahman, Ali Saleh	60	M	Palestinian	A E F E
Abd al-Rahman, Mariam Ibrahim	40	F	Palestinian	E
Abd al-Salam, Abd al-Mun'em	23	M	Palestinian	A D'
Abdallah, Dawoud Sulaiman		M	Not identified	G
Abdallah, Fawwaz Hasan	35	M	Stateless	A
Abdallah, Hasan Abdallah	60	M	Palestinian	A B C I
Abdallah, Hussein Kamel		M	Palestinian	G
Abdallah, Jamilah Ahmad	13	F	Palestinian	A O
Abdallah, Nawal Hasan	5	F	Palestinian	A B C I L
Abdallah, Turfah Hussein (Mrs Mahmoud)	65	F	Palestinian	A O
Abdallah, Yousuf Hasan	3	M	Palestinian	A B C I
Abu Aziz, Abd al-Aziz		M	Palestinian	H
Abu Dahab, Munir	62	M	Lebanese	A
Abu Dib, Mahmoud Qassem	41	M	Jordanian	A Q
Abu Duheim, Ali Qassem		M	Not identified	H'
Abu Harb, Hasan Qassem Mahmoud	14	M	Palestinian	A B C D E I M O
Abu Harb, Mirvat Walid	10	F	Palestinian	A D' E L M O
Abu Harb, Qassem Mahmoud	48	M	Palestinian	A B C D E I M O
Abu Harb, Walid Qassem	28	M	Palestinian	A D' E H M O
Abu Issa, Muhammad		M	Palestinian	H'
Abu Khamis, Amoun Ali	56	F	Palestinian	A
Abu Rabi', Khalil		M	Not identified	H
Abu Rudaineh, – (m. Aamal Abu Rudaineh)	Fetus		Palestinian	A O
Abu Rudaineh, Aida Muhammad	17	F	Palestinian	A E M O Q
Abu Rudaineh, Aamal Sh. (Mrs Husssein)	21	F	Palestinian	A E F M O Q
Abu Rudaineh, Kayed Muhammad	24	M	Palestinian	A B C E I M O Q
Abu Rudaineh, Muhammad Diab	62	M	Palestinian	A E M O Q
Abu Rudaineh, Shawkat Muhammad	45	M	Palestinian	A B C E I O Q
Abu Sa'id, Saleh Ahmad		M	Not identified	E
Abu Shilleih, Muhammad Hasan	35	M	Palestinian	A D'
Abu Sulaiman, Awad Sulaiman		M	Not identified	H'
Abu Suweid, Saleh Muhammad	65	M	Palestinian	A B C D H I M O
Abu Tu'meh, Jum'a Ahmad		M	Palestinian	H
Abu Yahya, Isma'il Mahmoud	52	M	Algerian	A B C I
Abu Yasser, Ahmad	45	M	Syrian	A O
Abu Yasser, Huda	43	F	Lebanese	A O
Abu Yasser, Nabal	9	F	Syrian	A O
Abu Yasser, Nasser	12	M	Syrian	A O
Abu Yasser, Yasser	16	M	Syrian	A O
Afifi, Muhammad Ramadan Salim		M	Not identified	H
Afu, Nur al-Din		M	Not identified	C
Ahmad, Abd al-Karim		M	Not identified	H
Ahmad, Adnan Muhammad		M	Not identified	I

Name	Age	Gender	Nationality	References*
Ahmad, Ali Ahmad		M	Not identified	H'
Ahmad, Badran		M	Not identified	H
Ahmad, Fatima (Mrs. Amin Muhammad)		F	Palestinian	B C I
Ahmad, Fattum, Um Faruq	40	F	Egyptian	M
Ahmad, Mahmoud Hamid		M	Not identified	H
Ahmad, Nazih Mahmoud	19	M	Palestinian	A D' E
Aidi, Hussein Mustafa Sa'id	22	M	Palestinian	A B C D E I L M O Q
Aidi, Ibrahim Mustafa Sa'id	17	M	Palestinian	A B C D E I L M O Q
Aidi, Moussa Mustafa Sa'id	31	M	Palestinian	A B C D E I L M O Q
Aidi, Mustafa Sa'id	75	M	Palestinian	A B C D E I L M O Q
Aidi, Sa'id Mustafa Sa'id Q	27	M	Palestinian	A B C D E I M O Q
Akhras, Ja'far Sheikh Ahmad		M	Not identified	G
Akkili, Abu Ghazi	62	M	Palestinian	A O
Akkili, Hasan Awad	45	M	Palestinian	E M
Akkili, Khaled Ahmad	7	M	Palestinian	E M
Akkili, Omar Ahmad	35	M	Palestinian	E M
Ala' al-Din, Dib	20	M	Lebanese	E
Ala' al-Din, Zainab Abd	20	F	Lebanese	A
Alameh, Ali	35	M	Lebanese	C D' F
Alameh, Najib Muhammad Sa'id		M	Not identified	G
Alawiyeh, Habib, al-hajj		M	Not identified	G
Alawiyeh, Khayrieh Ali, Um Yousuf	55	F	Lebanese	A B C D I
Alawiyeh, Khodr Yousuf Na'im	22	M	Lebanese	A B C D I
Alawiyeh, Zainab Yousuf Na'im	20	F	Lebanese	A D'
Ali, Ahmad Ibrahim	55	M	Not identified	D
Ali, Eida, Abu Mustafa		M	Not identified	H
Ali, Hasan Khalil	25	M	Palestinian	C
Ali, Hussein Ali	25	M	Palestinian	A B C D E O Q
Ali, Imad Muhammad Mustafa		M	Not identified	H
Ali, Imam Mahmoud	42	M	Egyptian	A
Ali, Issam Mustafa		M	Not identified	E
Ali, Jamal Muhammad		M	Not identified	H
Ali, Khaled Muhammad Sulaiman	20	M	Palestinian	A B C E I M
Ali, Muhammad Sulaiman	50	M	Palestinian	A B C E I M
Alwan, Subhi Hussein		M	Not identified	H
Amin, Fatima (Mrs Muhammad Ahmad)		F	Palestinian	B
Ammash, Khaled Moussa		M	Not identified	H
Anan, Ahmad Muhammad	45	M	Not identified	D
Anbar, Adel		M	Not identified	H
Antar, Hamid	35	M	Syrian	A O
Antar, Kahled Hamid	13	M	Syrian	A O
Antar, Muhammad Hamid	15	M	Syrian	A O
Aql, Imad Ahmad	51	M	Lebanese	E H M
As'ad, Ali Muhammad	53	M	Lebanese	A D' E
As'ad, Jamal As'ad		M	Not identified	D
As'ad, Khaled Ali	18	M	Lebanese	A E P
As'ad, Khalil As'ad	17	M	Not identified	D
As'ad, Muhammad Ali	20	M	Lebanese	A E
Ashwah, Nabih Sa'id	28	M	Palestinian	A D' M
Assi, Khaled Muhammad	20	M	Palestinian	B C I
Atiyeh, Bahijah Khalil		F	Not identified	G
Atiyeh, Tawifq al-Hajj Ali		M	Not identified	G
Atrash, Hasan, al-hajj		M	Not identified	G

Name	Age	Gender	Nationality	References*
Atrash, Majed Subhi Moussa	16	M	Palestinian	A C D E F M
Atrash, Subhi Moussa	55	M	Palestinian	A C D E F M
Atris, Muhammad Hussein		M	Not identified	H
Atwat, Abd al-Ghani	61	M	Palestinian	A D' E
Atwat, Yousuf Abd al-Ghani	32	M	Palestinian	A D' E
Awad, Fatimah Sa'oud	14	F	Palestinian	A E O
Awad, Hussein Sa'oud	12	M	Palestinian	A E O
Awad, Muyassar Sa'oud	22	F	Palestinian	A E O
Awad, Nur al-Din Sa'oud	25	M	Palestinian	A B C E I O
Awada, Muhammad Khalil, al-Hajj		M	Not identified	G
Awf, Muhammad Hanafi	22	M	Egyptian	A
Ayman, Hallaq		M	Not identified	H
Aziz, Muhammad Khalil		M	Not identified	G
Ba'albaki, Samira		F	Lebanese	O
Ba'albaki, Fatima		F	Lebanese	G
Ba'albaki, Hussein Muhammad	71	M	Lebanese	A
Ba'bou', Badia'a Ahmad	71	F	Palestinian	A E
Badawi, Mahmoud		M	Not identified	H'
Badri, Ahmad		M	Not identified	C
Bahri, Abbas		M	Not identified	B C I
Baker, Adnan Ali	45	M	Lebanese	B C G I
Bakkar, Fatima	15	F	Lebanese	E
Bakr, Mustafa Uthman	72	M	Syrian	A B C I
Bakru, Muhammad Ahmad		M	Not identified	H
Ballout, Latifah Ahmad	41	F	Lebanese	B C I
Balqis, Ali, Abu Majed	65	M	Palestinian	A L O
Balqis, Salah Saleh		M	Palestinian	H'
Barakah, Abd al-Salam Muhammad	17	M	Palestinian	A D' M
Barakah, Jamal		M	Palestinian	O
Basha, Ali Mahmoud		M	Not identified	G
Basha, Zainab Yousuf		F	Not identified	G
Bashir, Thunaya Qassem		F	Palestinian	B C I
Battar, Fatima		F	Not identified	C E
Batthish, Habib		M	Not identified	H
Bayyoumi, Muhammad Zuheir	1	M	Palestinian	A L O
Biqa'i, Fadia Khaled Saleh	15	F	Lebanese	A B C D E I L M O
Biqa'i, Hussein Moussa	60	M	Lebanese	A B C D E I L M O
Biqa'i, Ikram Hussein Moussa (Mrs Khaled)	30	F	Lebanese	A B C D E I L M O
Biqa'i, Imad Khaled Saleh	10	M	Lebanese	A B C D E I L M O
Biqa'i, Khaled Saleh	41	M	Lebanese	A B C D E I L M O
Biqa'i, Rabi' Hussein Moussa	19	M	Lebanese	A B C D E I L M O
Biqa'i, Salah al-Din		M	Lebanese	H
Biqa'i, Shadi Khaled Saleh	8	M	Lebanese	A B C D E I L M O
Biqa'i, Wissam Khaled Saleh	6	M	Lebanese	A B C D E I L M O
Bishri, Sharif		M	Not identified	H
Bouri, Ahmad		M	Palestinian	B I
Burji, Ali Ibrahim	37	M	Lebanese	A B C E F" G I Q
Burji, Ali Milhem	14	M	Lebanese	A B C E G I Q
Burji, Hussein	26	M	Lebanese	B C G I
Burji, Muhammad Ali Ibrahim		M	Lebanese	C G I
Burji, Qassem Ali Ibrahim	14	M	Lebanese	A B C E F" G I Q
Dalati, Mahmoud Yaassin		M	Not identified	H
Damash, Samir Muhammad	21	M	Palestinian	A B C I

Name	Age	Gender	Nationality	References*
Darwish, Haydar Muhammad	23	M	Lebanese	A C E
Darwish, Muhammad		M	Lebanese	B C I
Dawoud, Ahmad Salim	21	M	Not identified	D
Dawoud, Muhammad		M	Not identified	H M
Dayekh, Fatima Salim		F	Not identified	D
Dhaher, Muhammad Salman	79	M	Lebanese	A B C E F" G I
Dhaher, Munir Khalil		M	Not identified	H
Dhaher, Sa'da Abbas (Mrs Muhammad)	45	F	Lebanese	A
Dhaher, Shakib As'ad	55	M	Lebanese	A B C F" I P
Dia, Huwaida Kamal		F	Not identified	G
Diab, Muhammad	72	M	Palestinian	A F'
Dib, Ahmad Khalil		M	Not identified	H
Dirbas, Ahmad		M	Not identified	H
Dugheino, Ahmad Hamdo	48	M	Syrian	A B C I M
Dugheino, Mahmoud Ahmad	4	M	Syrian	A M
Dugheino, Mariam Abd al-Rah (Mrs Ahmad)	37	F	Palestinian	A E M
Dugheino, Muhammad Ahmad	6	M	Syrian	A M
Dukhi, Ali Abdallah	44	M	Palestinian	A B C D E F" I O Q
Dulbein, Hussein Ali	19	M	Lebanese	A E
Durubi, Farid Muhammad		M	Not identified	H
Dusuqi, Muhammad Wajih	42	M	Palestinian	A D'
Eid, Abdallah Muhammad Khurasani	32	M	Iranian	A B C D E I
Eid, Ali Hussein		M	Not identified	H'
Eid, Muhammad	30	M	Syrian	O
Fahham, Ismail Yousuf		M	Not identified	H
Fahmawi, Mahmoud		M	Not identified	B C I
Fahs, Rida Kamel		M	Not identified	G
Faqih, Fatima Muhammad	14	F	Lebanese	A E F' O Q
Faqih, Laila Muhammad	3	F	Lebanese	A E F' O Q
Faraj, Aida		F	Not identified	H'
Faraj, Bahiyeh Abdallah		F	Not identified	H'
Faraj, Fadia Za'al		F	Not identified	H'
Faraj, Fu'ad Za'al		M	Not identified	H'
Faraj, Hala Abdallah		F	Not identified	H'
Faraj, Ibrahim Abdallah		M	Not identified	H'
Faraj, Najla' Abdallah		F	Not identified	H'
Faraj, Najwa Abdallah		F	Not identified	H'
Faraj, Nuhad Abdallah		F	Not identified	H'
Fares, Ahmad Muhammad		M	Not identified	H'
Fares, Fatima	50	F	Stateless	E
Fares, Khaled	50	M	Stateless	E
Farfur, Samir Abd al-Fattah	30	M	Egyptian	A D'
Farhat, Rahibah Mustafa		F	Not identified	G
Farhat, Wajih		M	Lebanese	B C I
Farouq, – (son 1)		M	Not identified	F"
Farouq, – (son 2)		M	Not identified	F"
Farouq, – (son 3)		M	Not identified	F"
Farouq, – (the father)		M	Not identified	F"
Farouq, – (the mother)		F	Not identified	F"
Fattouh, Muhammad Kamel		M	Not identified	H
Fawwaz, Muhammad Ali Hasan		M	Not identified	G
Fayyad, Abbas Ali	19	M	Lebanese	A E L O Q
Fayyad, Najah Ali	21	F	Lebanese	A E L O Q

Name	Age	Gender	Nationality	References*
Fayyad, Nuha Ali	18	F	Lebanese	A E L O Q
Fayyad, Tamima Darwish Murad (Mrs Ali)	47	F	Lebanese	A E F' L O Q
Freij, Hasan Abdallah	42	M	Palestinian	M
Freijeh, Khaled Muhammad Hussein	13	M	Palestinian	A
Freijeh, Muhammad Hussein	40	M	Palestinian	A
Fu'ad, Muhammad Hussein		M	Not identified	B C I
Ghabayen, Abd al-Salam Salem	19	M	Not identified	D
Ghandour, Abbas Sadeq		M	Not identified	G
Ghandour, Yousuf Ali	50	M	Syrian	A B C I
Ghanem, Mahmoud Issa		M	Lebanese	I
Ghanem, Sayyed Ahmad	40	M	Egyptian	A D'
Ghannam, Ali Hussein	32	M	Lebanese	B C I
Ghannam, Muhammad Ali Hasan	22	M	Not identified	C
Ghosn, Fatima As'ad Wahbeh		F	Not identified	G
Ghoush, Farid Abd al-Rahman		M	Not identified	G
Ghuz, Muhammad Khalil		M	Not identified	G
Habrat, Aamal Huleiwi (Mrs Mustafa)	27	F	Algerian	A D E O
Habrat, Marwan Mustafa Moussa	1	M	Palestinian	A D E O
Habrat, Moussa Abd al-Halim	53	M	Palestinian	A D E O
Habrat, Moussa Mustafa Mussa	4	M	Palestinian	A D E O
Habrat, Sirine Mustafa Moussa	6	F	Palestinian	A D E O
Hafez, Sa'id Ahmad	25	M	Egyptian	A F
Hafi, Issa Mahmoud		M	Not identified	E M
Hajj, Ali Ghaleb Sami'		M	Not identified	G
Hajj, Ghaleb Sami'		M	Not identified	G
Hajj, Jihad Ali	24	M	Palestinian	A B C D' F" I O
Hajj, Khaled Yousuf	39	M	Not identified	E M
Hajj, Mahmoud Ali		M	Not identified	H
Hajj, Riad Abdallah	28	M	Not identified	F
Hajj, Saleh Yousuf	43	M	Palestinian	A
Hajj, Samar Walid	1	F	Lebanese	A O
Hajj, Sarah Qassem	27	F	Palestinian	A O
Hajj, Wassim Walid	2	M	Lebanese	A O
Halabi, Ahmad Abdallah		M	Not identified	B C
Halabi, Ahmad Muhammad		M	Not identified	H
Halabi, Fadel Muhammad, al-hajj		M	Lebanese	B C I
Halabi, Samira Ali	18	F	Lebanese	A E M
Halaf, Mahmoud Muhammad		M	Not identified	B C
Halaweh, Mahmoud Muhammad		M	Not identified	H
Halawi, Ali Moussa	21	M	Lebanese	A E
Hamdar, Issam Ahmad		M	Not identified	G
Hamdo, Taha Mahmoud		M	Not identified	E M
Hamduh, Ahmad	45	M	Palestinian	E
Hamduh, Mahmoud Ahmad	4	M	Palestinian	E
Hamduh, Muhammad Ahmad	6	M	Palestinian	E
Hamid, Fatima Ali		F	Not identified	G
Hammad, Fatima Hasan	35	F	Not identified	E F
Hammoud, Ahmad Muhammad		M	Not identified	D
Hammoud, Fadi Moussa	17	M	Palestinian	A B C I
Hammoud, Hanadi Muhammad	9	F	Palestinian	A D E
Hammoud, Huda (Mrs Muhammad)	41	F	Palestinian	A B C D E I
Hammoud, Khalil Muhammad	14	M	Palestinian	A D E
Hammoud, Rushod		M	Not identified	B C I

Name	Age	Gender	Nationality	References*
Hammoud, Zainab Ahmad		F	Not identified	G
Hamo, Mustafa		M	Not identified	H
Hamzah, Hamzah Zaydan	18	M	Stateless	A
Hamzah, Nasser Zaydan	16	M	Stateless	A
Hamzah, Taysir Zaydan	20	M	Stateless	A
Hamzah, Zaydan Muhammad Zeid	45	M	Stateless	A
Hanafi, Muhammad	18	M	Egyptian	A E
Hanbali, Aisheh Muhammad	51	F	Palestinian	E M
Hanbali, Muhammad Abd al-Rahim	21	M	Palestinian	D
Haramsheh, Fatima (Mrs Khaled Fares)	52	F	Stateless	A
Haramsheh, Khaled Fares	55	M	Stateless	A
Harb, Ahmad Hasan	20	M	Lebanese	A I P
Harb, Mahmoud	38	M	Lebanese	B C I
Harb, Muhammad Hasan		M	Lebanese	B C
Hariri, Mahmoud Sulaiman		M	Stateless	H'
Haris, Abboud Abdallah		M	Not identified	G
Hasan, Ahmad Yahya		M	Not identified	F"
Hasan, Badr al-Din Nayef		M	Not identified	H
Hasan, Muhammad Ibrahim		M	Not identified	H
Hasaneh, Ahmad Tawfiq Sa'id		M	Not identified	D'
Hashem, Abd al-Hadi Ahmad	45	M	Palestinian	A C I L O
Hashem, Abdallah Ahmad		M	Lebanese	B C
Hashem, Yassin Abd al-Mun'em		M	Not identified	G
Haydar, – (mother Zainab Hasan Idilbi)	Fetus		Lebanese	A O
Haydar, Ali Yousuf		M	Not identified	G
Haydar, Fahd Ali	19	M	Lebanese	A B C D E F" I L M O Q
Haydar, Fu'ad Ali	14	M	Lebanese	A B C D E F" I L M O
Haydar, Hussein Muhammad		M	Not identified	G
Haydar, Kulthum Muh. Salameh (Mrs Ali)	55	F	Lebanese	A B C D E F" I O Q
Haydar, Rushdiyeh Mustafa		F	Not identified	G
Haydar, Shafiqat		F	Pakistani	I
Haydar, Zainab Hasan Idilbi (Mrs Fahd)	17	F	Palestinian	A B C D F" I L M O Q
Hijazi, Abdi		M	Not identified	G
Hijazi, Awatef		F	Not identified	G
Hilal, Muhammad Salman	42	M	Lebanese	B C I
Hilal, Yasser Muhammad		M	Not identified	B C I
Himsi, Nader		M	Not identified	H
Hindi, Abd al-Majid		M	Not identified	H
Hinnawi, Dib Hussein	55	M	Lebanese	A B C D E I O
Hinnawi, Saleh Yousuf		M	Not identified	G
Hishmeh, Tawfiq	47	M	Palestinian	A E F L M O
Hudruj, Hussein Abd al-Amin		M	Lebanese	G
Hushaymi, Dalal		F	Lebanese	I
Husni, Hussein Muhammad		M	Palestinian	C
Hussein, Abdallah Jabr	50	F	Palestinian	A E F M
Hussein, Adnan		M	Not identified	H
Hussein, Ali	40	M	Palestinian	C E I M Q
Hussein, Arabi		M	Not identified	H
Hussein, Faddah Jum'a	70	F	Palestinian	A E M O Q
Hussein, Fadi Ilias Moussa	12	M	Palestinian	A M O Q
Hussein, Fadia Ilias Moussa	10	F	Palestinian	A M O Q
Hussein, Fu'ad Ahmad Jabr	12	M	Palestinian	A E M O Q
Hussein, Hussein Ali	24	M	Palestinian	A O

Name	Age	Gender	Nationality	References*
Hussein, Imad Ahmad Jabr	13	M	Palestinian	A E M O Q
Hussein, Intissar Kamal		F	Palestinian	H'
Hussein, Isma'il Mahmoud	42	M	Palestinian	A
Hussein, Karem Ahmad Jabr	17	M	Palestinian	A E F M O Q
Hussein, Muhammad Ahmad Jabr	11	M	Palestinian	A E M O Q
Hussein, Nadim Mahdi	46	M	Lebanese	A
Hussein, Nawal Ahmad Jabr	10	F	Palestinian	A E M O Q
Hussein, Rabi' Ahmad Jabr	11	M	Palestinian	A E O Q
Hussein, Ruqaya Amin	38	F	Egyptian	A B C E I
Hussein, Saleh	17	M	Palestinian	B C I Q
Hussein, Salhah M. Ma'rouf (Mrs Ahmad Jabr)	35	F	Palestinian	A E O Q
Hussein, Su'ad Ahmad Jabr	9	F	Palestinian	A E M O Q
Husseini, Ihsan Muhammad		M	Palestinian	B C I
Huweidi, Salim Muhsin	72	F	Syrian	A C E
Huweili, Muhammad, al-hajj		M	Not identified	G
Ibrahim, Ahmad Tawfiq		M	Not identified	G
Ibrahim, Muhammad Hasan		M	Not identified	E
Ibrahim, Nasim Hussein, al-hajjeh		F	Not identified	G
Iskamalji, Fitnah Ghandour (Mrs Muh. Ali)	45	F	Syrian	A B C E I
Iskamalji, Khadijeh Muhammad Ali	15	F	Lebanese	A C E
Iskamalji, Khaled Muhammad Ali	16	M	Lebanese	A C E
Iskamalji, Sawsan Muhammad Ali	13	F	Lebanese	A C E
Iskamalji, Walid Muhammad Ali	8	M	Lebanese	A B C E I
Iskandarani, Salim Muhammad	19	M	Lebanese	B C E I
Iskandarani, Su'ad Muhammad	21	F	Lebanese	E
Isma'il, Fahd Abd	65	M	Lebanese	C E
Isma'il, Hussein Abdallah		M	Not identified	H
Isma'il, Intissar	28	F	Palestinian	A D' L O
Isma'il, Qassem Muhammad		M	Lebanese	B C G I
Isma'il, Sharifah Hussein		F	Not identified	G
Isma'il, Wahsh Muhammad	71	M	Palestinian	A D'
Issa, Ayman Muhammad		M	Not identified	H
Issa, Muhammad Ali		M	Not identified	H
Issa, Thunaya Muhammad	70	F	Palestinian	E M
Jaber, Mahmoud Ali		M	Not identified	G
Jaber, Nabil Jamil		M	Not identified	G
Jabri, Mahmoud Mas'oud	20	M	Palestinian	B C
Jad'on, Ahmad Dib	68	M	Palestinian	A
Jado, Hassan Dib	20	M	Palestinian	B C D I M
Jaghlab, Saleh Issa		M	Not identified	H
Jalal, Khaled al-Sheikh		M	Not identified	H
Jamilah, Riad Mahmoud	19	M	Jordanian	A E
Jamilah, Samar Mahmoud	14	F	Jordanian	A
Jana, Mustafa Muhammad	20	M	Palestinian	E F
Jashi, Darwish Abdallah		M	Not identified	D
Jashi, Muhammad Darwish Abdallah		M	Not identified	D
Jawad, Hasan Ali		M	Not identified	G
Joud, Hasan		M	Not identified	G
Jubeili, Fadl Muhammad, al-hajj		M	Not identified	G
Jubeili, Mustafa Muhammad, al-hajj		M	Not identified	G
Juheir, Sa'id Abd al-Karim	21	M	Palestinian	A E F L
Julani, Abdallah Sa'id		M	Not identified	I
Jum'a, Majed Issa Qassem	12	M	Palestinian	A E L O

Name	Age	Gender	Nationality	References*
Jum'a, Mariam Abdallah (Mrs Issa Qassem)	43	F	Palestinian	A L O
Jureidi, Fatima Mansour Rashed (Mrs Sa'id)	31	F	Palestinian	A B C F"
Jureidi, Jinan Sa'id	3	F	Palestinian	A B C F" I
Jureidi, Mariam Sa'id	7	F	Palestinian	A B C F' I
Jureidi, Nidal Sa'id	2	F	Palestinian	A C F'
Jureidi, Suzan Sa'id	5	F	Palestinian	A B C F' I
Kalab, Jamil		M	Not identified	B C I
Kalali, Ahmad Abdallah		M	Not identified	C I
Kalot, Fatima Ali		F	Lebanese	G
Kalot, Insaf Ali		F	Lebanese	G
Kalot, Khadijeh Ali		F	Lebanese	G
Kanoun, Ahmad Ali Muhammad	25	M	Syrian	A C
Kanoun, Ali Muhammad Yassin	61	M	Syrian	A C
Kanoun, Sakina Ali al-Sayyed (Mrs Ali)	56	F	Lebanese	A C
Kanoun, Yahya Ali Muhammad	14	M	Syrian	A C
Karaki, Hussein Habib		M	Not identified	G
Karmali, Tawfiq Muhsen	60	M	Palestinian	B C I
Karmo, – (Mrs Nayef Muhammad Ali)	35	F	Stateless	A
Karmo, Ali Muhammad	31	M	Stateless	A
Karmo, Hamid Jamil Muhsin	29	M	Stateless	A E
Karmo, Jamil Muhsin	78	M	Stateless	A E P
Karmo, Khaled Jamil Muhsin	40	M	Stateless	A E P
Karmo, Muhammad Salim	80	M	Stateless	A
Karmo, Nayef Muhammad Ali	42	M	Stateless	A
Karmo, Tawfiq Muhsin	71	M	Stateless	A
Khaddur, Ismail Ahmad	65	M	Lebanese	E
Khaffaji, Ala' al-Din		M	Not identified	G
Khair al-Din, Tawfiq As'ad Hussein		M	Not identified	G
Khaizaran, Muhammad Abdallah	65	M	Palestinian	E
Khalaf, Mahmoud Hamad	37	M	Syrian	B C I
Khaled, Ali Ibrahim		M	Not identified	H
Khaled, Mahmoud		M	Not identified	H
Khalifeh, Hamid Mustafa	44	M	Palestinian	A B C D E I
Khalifeh, Hasan Hamid Mustafa	15	M	Palestinian	A D E
Khalifeh, Hussein Hamid Mustafa	16	M	Palestinian	A D E
Khalifeh, Muhammad Abd	52	M	Palestinian	A B C D E G I Q
Khalil, Hussein Abbas	26	M	Lebanese	B C I
Khalil, Khalil Abdo	19	M	Stateless	A
Khalil, Khalil Ismail	22	M	Lebanese	B C I
Khalil, Khodr Ahmad		M	Not identified	H
Khalil, Nasser Ismail	25	M	Lebanese	B C I
Khalil, Saber Ali	29	M	Lebanese	B C I
Khalil, Zahra Mahmoud	70	F	Not identified	E M
Khamis, Muhammad	44	M	Egyptian	A
Khashab, Ruqaya Amin		F	Not identified	E
Khatib, Abd al-Rahman Ahmad	31	M	Lebanese	A B C E F" G H' I Q
Khatib, Ali Hussein	46	M	Palestinian	A D E L M O Q
Khatib, Amneh Ali Hussein	22	F	Palestinian	A E L M O Q
Khatib, Dibeh (Mrs Ali Hussein)	43	F	Palestinian	A E L M O Q
Khatib, Ghali Ahmad		M	Lebanese	B C I
Khatib, Ghalia Mustafa	73	F	Palestinian	A D L M O Q
Khatib, Hasan Abdallah		M	Not identified	G
Khatib, Hassan Saleh		M	Not identified	H'

List of names 3 (Continued)

Name	Age	Gender	Nationality	References*
Khatib, Hussein Abdallah		M	Not identified	H
Khatib, Hussein Ali Hussein	20	M	Palestinian	A E L O Q
Khatib, Hussein Muhammad	20	M	Palestinian	A
Khatib, Ibrahim Subhi	18	M	Lebanese	A B C E F Q
Khatib, Imtithal Ali Hussein	11	F	Palestinian	A E L M O Q
Khatib, Issam Muhammad Shihadeh		M	Not identified	F I
Khatib, Khaled As'ad		M	Not identified	D
Khatib, Khalil Ahmad		M	Not identified	C
Khatib, Laila Abd al-Rahman		F	Not identified	H'
Khatib, Mahmoud		M	Not identified	H
Khatib, Mariam Ali Hussein	9	F	Palestinian	A D E L M O Q
Khatib, Muhammad Hasan	26	M	Palestinian	A
Khatib, Munther Ali Hussein	12	M	Palestinian	A D E L M O Q
Khatib, Nader Ali Hussein	14	M	Palestinian	A E L M O Q
Khatib, Nayef Abd al-Rahman		M	Not identified	H'
Khatib, Saber Ali Hussein	24	M	Palestinian	A C E L M O Q
Khatib, Saleh Nayef		M	Not identified	H'
Khatib, Sami Muhammad	30	M	Palestinian	A D'
Khatib, Sawsan Abd al-Rahman		F	Not identified	H'
Khatib, Wafa' Abd al-Rahman		F	Not identified	H'
Khayyat, Majed		M	Not identified	H
Khodr, Khaled Ali		M	Not identified	H
Khureibi, Majed Muhammad	27	M	Palestinian	E M
Khureis, Abboud Abdallah		M	Not identified	G
Kirki, Hussein Habib		M	Not identified	G
Kiwan, Jamil Farhan	43	M	Syrian	A B C I
Kousarani, Muhammad Abdallah		M	Iranian	I
Kulaib, Ahmad Hasan Abdallah	18	M	Palestinian	A E F
Kulaib, Hasan Abdallah	51	M	Palestinian	A E F L
Kurdi, Yousuf	30	M	Turk	A E
Lahham, Sami		M	Palestinian	D'
Liddawi, Muhammad	52	M	Palestinian	A
Luma', Marwan		M	Not identified	H
Ma'rouf, Issam		M	Palestinian	H' D'
Ma'rouf, Najibeh Ali	30	F	Syrian	M
Ma'rouf, Muhammad		M	Palestinian	D
Ma'rouf, Ziad Abdallah	31	M	Palestinian	A B C D' E F" I O
Mabda', Abd al-Rahim		M	Palestinian	D'
Madi, Ahmad Younes	20	M	Palestinian	A B C D E I L M O Q
Madi, Madi Younes	17	M	Palestinian	A B C D E I L M O Q
Madi, Muhammad Younes	14	M	Palestinian	A B C D E I L M O Q
Madi, Younes	65	M	Palestinian	A B C D E I L M O Q
Mahjawi, Muhammad Abbas		M	Not identified	C
Mahmoud, Abd al-Jalil Muhammad		M	Not identified	H'
Mahmoud, Ahmad	40	M	Palestinian	E
Mahmoud, Ahmad Muhammad	23	M	Palestinian	D M
Mahmoud, Arshad	27	M	Pakistani	A B C I
Mahmoud, Ismail		M	Algerian	C
Mahmoud, Nazih		M	Lebanese	B C I
Majdoub, Mahmoud Abd	35	M	Palestinian	A
Majdoub, Muhammad Abd	17	M	Palestinian	A
Majed, Maya Nabil Muhammad		F	Not identified	G
Majed, Nabil Muhammad		M	Not identified	G

Name	Age	Gender	Nationality	References*
Makkiyeh, Ahmad Salameh	18	M	Palestinian	C
Makkiyeh, Farouq Salameh	19	M	Palestinian	A
Makkiyeh, Munir Salameh	20	M	Palestinian	C F
Mallah, Khaled Rafiq		M	Not identified	H
Mansour, Ali Abdo	5	M	Lebanese	A
Mattar, Khadijeh Yahya	32	F	Palestinian	A E O
Mattar, Muhammad Adnan	18	M	Palestinian	A B C E I M O
Mattar, Muhammad Ali		M	Palestinian	G
Mattar, Suhaila Abd al-Rahim	34	F	Palestinian	E M
Mihho, Abd al-Nasser Dhaher		M	Not identified	H
Milhem, Abdallah		M	Lebanese	C
Milhem, Ali		M	Lebanese	B C
Minawi, Ali Khamis		M	Palestinian	G
Minawi, Bilal Ahmad	18	M	Palestinian	A D
Miqdad, – (mother Ilham Miqdad)	Fetus		Lebanese	A O
Miqdad, – (mother Wafa' Miqdad)	Fetus		Lebanese	A O
Miqdad, – (mother Zainab Miqdad)	Fetus		Lebanese	A O
Miqdad, Abd al-Ra'ouf	40	M	Lebanese	A C G O
Miqdad, Adnan Yasser Dhaher	6	M	Lebanese	A G O
Miqdad, Ali Hussein Isma'il	65	M	Lebanese	A D G Q
Miqdad, Fadi Yasser Dhaher	10	M	Lebanese	A C E G O Q
Miqdad, Faiza Yasser Dhaher	16	F	Lebanese	A B C E O Q
Miqdad, Fariza Diab, Um Yousuf	60	F	Lebanese	A C O
Miqdad, Fatima Abd al-Ra'ouf	3	F	Lebanese	A C G I O
Miqdad, Fatima Wahbeh (Mrs Ali Hussein)	62	F	Lebanese	A C D E G O Q
Miqdad, Firyal Yasser Dhaher	13	F	Lebanese	A C E G O
Miqdad, Hasan Muhammad		M	Lebanese	G
Miqdad, Hussein Dhaher	40	M	Lebanese	A B C E G I O Q
Miqdad, Hussein Yasser Dhaher	8	M	Lebanese	A C E G I O Q
Miqdad, Ilham (Mrs Abd al-Ra'ouf)	27	F	Lebanese	A B C E G I O Q
Miqdad, Mahasen Abd al-Ra'ouf	7	F	Lebanese	A C G O
Miqdad, Mirvat Abd al-Ra'ouf	12	F	Lebanese	A G O
Miqdad, Muhammad Ali		M	Lebanese	G
Miqdad, Muhammad Hussein Dhaher	8	M	Lebanese	A B C E G I O
Miqdad, Nariman Abd al-Ra'ouf	11	F	Lebanese	A B C G I O
Miqdad, Nisrin Abd al-Ra'ouf	7	F	Lebanese	A C G O
Miqdad, Nofa		F	Lebanese	B C I
Miqdad, Rida Hussein Ali	62	M	Lebanese	A B C G I O Q
Miqdad, Rifaq Yasser Dhaher	1	F	Lebanese	A G O
Miqdad, Safa Hussein Dhaher	1	F	Lebanese	A B C G I O
Miqdad, Ulfat Abd al-Ra'ouf	2	F	Lebanese	A C G O
Miqdad, Wafa' Hammoud (Mrs Hus. Dhaher)	30	F	Lebanese	A B C G I O Q
Miqdad, Yasser Dhaher	35	M	Lebanese	A B C E G I O Q
Miqdad, Yasser Hussein Dhaher	6	M	Lebanese	A B C G O Q
Miqdad, Yousuf Abd al-Qader	22	M	Lebanese	A C G I O Q
Miqdad, Zainab Abd Ali (Mrs Yasser Dhaher)	30	F	Lebanese	A B C G I O Q
Mir'i, Ali Rasmi Muhsin	12	M	Stateless	A E
Mir'i, Bassam Srour Muhammad	12	M	Palestinian	A C D E H L M O Q
Mir'i, Diba Hasan		F	Not identified	H'
Mir'i, Farid Srour Muhammad	6	M	Palestinian	A B C D E H L M O Q
Mir'i, Muhsin Rasmi Muhsin	9	M	Stateless	A E
Mir'i, Rasmi Muhsin	42	M	Stateless	A E

List of names 3 (Continued)

Name	Age	Gender	Nationality	References*
Mir'i, Shadi Srour Muhammad	3	M	Palestinian	A E H L M O Q
Mir'i, Shadya Srour Muhammad	2	F	Palestinian	A B C D E H L M O Q
Mir'i, Srour Muhammad Sa'id	43	M	Palestinian	A B C D E H I M O Q
Mir'i, Yahya Muhsin	24	M	Stateless	A E P
Mir'i, Zakaria Muhsin	22	M	Stateless	A E P
Misri, Aisha Fayez AbuTayyuni	35	F	Palestinian	A C G
Misri, Fu'ad Khaled		F	Not identified	H
Misri, Mahmoud Muhammad		M	Not identified	H
Misri, Sayyed Muhammad	30	M	Egyptian	A
Mo'batt, Fayzeh		M	Not identified	I
Moussa, Mahmoud Ali		M	Not identified	G
Moussa, Mahmoud Muhammad	34	M	Palestinian	A
Moussa, Mazen Mahmoud	12	M	Palestinian	A
Moussa, Munir Muhammad	20	M	Palestinian	A
Moussa, Mustafa		M	Palestinian	Q
Moussawi, Abiri		M	Not identified	C
Moussawi, Ahmad Saleh	58	M	Lebanese	B C I
Moussawi, Hasan Sayyed	42	M	Lebanese	A E F I P
Moussawi, Hussein Saleh	45	M	Lebanese	B C I
Moussawi, Muhammad Salman		M	Lebanese	G
Mruwweh, Ibrahim Muhammad		M	Not identified	G
Msallach, Abu Jihad		M	Not identified	H
Mubarak, Ali Hasan		M	Lebanese	B C G I
Mubarak, Mamduh Ali		M	Not identified	H
Mughrabi, Ahmad	25	M	Syrian	B C F"
Mughrabi, Ahmad Muhammad	30	M	Palestinian	B E H I M
Mughrabi, Ahmad Subh		M	Palestinian	E
Mughrabi, Amer Salim	17	M	Palestinian	A E O
Mughrabi, Khaled Salim	17	M	Palestinian	A E O
Mughrabi, Khawla Muh. Sa'd (Mrs Ahmad)		F	Palestinian	E M
Mughrabi, Mahmoud		M	Palestinian	H
Mughrabi, Muhammad Ahmad		M	Palestinian	H
Mughrabi, Subhi Muhammad	43	M	Palestinian	A E O
Muhammad, Ahlam Khaled Yousuf	1	F	Palestinian	A L O
Muhammad, Aida Ahmad Moussa	16	M	Palestinian	A C E I M O
Muhammad, Akram Khaled Yousuf	9	M	Palestinian	A C E I M O
Muhammad, Baha' Khaled Yousuf	12	F	Palestinian	A C E I M O
Muhammad, Fadya Ahmad Moussa	7	F	Palestinian	A C E I M O
Muhammad, Fatima Salim (Mrs Khaled)	44	F	Palestinian	A B C E I M O
Muhammad, Ghasoub Muhammad		M	Not identified	H
Muhammad, Iman Ahmad Moussa	6	F	Palestinian	A C E I M O
Muhammad, Iman Khaled Yousuf	7	F	Palestinian	A C E I M O
Muhammad, Inayatullah Bashir	27	F	Pakistani	A B C I
Muhammad, Khaled Yousuf	47	M	Palestinian	A B C E I M O
Muhammad, Khawla (Mrs Yahya)	25	F	Palestinian	A L O
Muhammad, Layla Khaled Yousuf	11	F	Palestinian	A C E I M O
Muhammad, Manal Khaled Yousuf	5	F	Palestinian	A C E I M O
Muhammad, Mu'in Ahmad Moussa	11	M	Palestinian	A C E I M O
Muhammad, Mufid Ahmad Moussa	15	M	Palestinian	A C E G I M O
Muhammad, Muhammad Salim	19	M	Stateless	A
Muhammad, Ruqaya Anwar	35	F	Egyptian	M
Muhammad, Sa'd Koussa		M	Not identified	H
Muhammad, Sa'id Taha	38	M	Palestinian	E M

Name	Age	Gender	Nationality	References*
Muhammad, Samer Khaled Yousuf	2	M	Palestinian	A C I M O
Muhammad, Samira	18	F	Palestinian	E
Muhammad, Sana' Khaled Yousuf	17	F	Palestinian	A C E I M O
Muhammad, Suhaila Khaled Yousuf	19	F	Palestinian	A C E I M O
Muhammad, Yahya Ahmad	30	M	Palestinian	A L O
Muhammad, Zahra (Mrs Ahmad Moussa)	40	F	Palestinian	A C E I M O
Muhanna, Ali Hasan	20	M	Lebanese	A B C E G I
Muhsin, Moussa Tawfiq	35	M	Lebanese	A
Muhsin, Tawfiq Karma	65	M	Lebanese	A
Munadi, Ali Hussein, al-hajj		M	Not identified	B C I
Muqaddam, Abbas Sadeq		M	Not identified	G
Murad, Hasan Adel		M	Not identified	G
Murtada, Adib Hasan	33	M	Lebanese	A P
Murtada, Marwan Khalil		M	Not identified	G
Mushawrab, Muhammad Hasan		M	Not identified	G
Mustafa, Ihsan Muhammad		M	Not identified	H
Mustafa, Khaled Mustafa	16	M	Stateless	A E P
Mustafa, Muhammad	73	M	Stateless	A
Mustafa, Muhammad Mustafa	21	M	Stateless	P
Mustafa, Mustafa		M	Palestinian	B C I
Mustafa, Riad Mustafa	23	M	Stateless	A E
Mustafa, Saleh Ahmad	34	M	Egyptian	A
Nabulsi, Imad Ahmad	26	M	Palestinian	E M
Nabulsi, Muhammad	35	M	Palestinian	A E L O
Nahal, Amira		F	Egyptian	I
Naja, Bilal George		M	Not identified	B C I
Najjar, Hussein Hasan Ahmad	45	M	Palestinian	A O
Najjar, Jamal Salim Khodr	20	M	Palestinian	E
Najm, Alya Muhammad Saleh	52	F	Not identified	D
Nassar, Khalil Saleh		M	Not identified	E M
Nasser al-Din, Ali Fahd		M	Not identified	G
Nasser al-Din, Hasan Khalil		M	Not identified	G
Nasser, Hussein Abd al-Rida	42	M	Lebanese	A G O
Nasser, Muhammad Ali		M	Not identified	H
Nasser, Wahid	35	M	Syrian	B C I
Nassif, Ali Issa	65	M	Palestinian	A E
Nazzal, Muhammad Mahmoud	30	M	Palestinian	B C H I
Nazzal, Muhammad Salim	33	M	Palestinian	A
Ni'meh, Na'im Ali, al-hajj	80	M	Lebanese	A B C E F' G I
Nimr, Wahib		M	Not identified	C
Nounu, Ahmad Ahmad		M	Not identified	D'
Nounu, Faraj Abdo	22	M	Palestinian	A C E
Nounu, Fayzah Abdo Anis	22	F	Palestinian	C F
Nounu, Mahmoud Ahmad		M	Palestinian	D'
Nounu, Muhammad Ahmad		M	Palestinian	D'
Nour al-Din, Bassam Sharif		M	Not identified	G
Nour al-Din, Mustafa Ahmad		M	Not identified	G
Nour al-Din, Ruba Hasan		F	Not identified	G
Nour Muhammad Riad Ahmad		M	Pakistani	B C I
Nouri, Adnan	90	M	Not identified	A F'
Nu'man, Ali		M	Not identified	H
Omar, Salim Yassin		M	Not identified	H'
Omar, Shukri Ramadan		M	Not identified	H'

List of names 3 (Continued)

Name	Age	Gender	Nationality	References*
Orli, Ahmad	35	M	Sudanese	A G
Owdeh, Faddah Rashid Nayef	41	F	Palestinian	D' M
Qabi, Ahmad		M	Not identified	F'
Qaddouh, Ghida Afif		F	Not identified	G
Qaddouh, Hazem Afif		M	Not identified	G
Qaddouh, Lama Afif		F	Not identified	G
Qaddoura, Amneh Fayez		F	Not identified	H'
Qaddoura, Badran Hussein	18	M	Palestinian	A D
Qaddoura, Iqbal		F	Palestinian	G
Qaddoura, Sa'da Mustafa	23	F	Palestinian	B C I
Qadi, Bassam Saleh Dakhil	18	M	Palestinian	A D E
Qadi, Fahmi Ahmad	31	M	Palestinian	A C D E I
Qadi, Fawwaz Madi	43	M	Palestinian	A B C D E I
Qadi, Hasan	50	M	Palestinian	E
Qadi, Husam Saleh Dakhil	12	M	Palestinian	A D E F M
Qadi, Ibtisam Saleh Dakhil	14	F	Palestinian	A D E F M
Qadi, Issam Saleh Dakhil	10	M	Palestinian	A D E F M
Qadi, Jalal Hasan	16	M	Palestinian	E F E
Qadi, Muhammad Fares	23	M	Palestinian	B C E F I
Qadi, Saleh Dakhil	52	M	Palestinian	A D E M
Qadi, Sari Ahmad	80	M	Palestinian	A E F
Qassab, Wahid Haj Mustafa	37	M	Not identified	D
Qassem, Hasan Dib	22	M	Palestinian	A E
Qassem, Mahmoud	45	M	Jordanian	E
Qassem, Muhammad Mut'ab	48	M	Palestinian	A B E I
Qassem, Muhammad Qaysar	65	M	Palestinian	B C
Qassem, Munther Sami	23	M	Palestinian	A D
Qaswat, Muhammad Ahmad	58	M	Syrian	A
Qatanani, Muhammad Abd al-Rahman	31	M	Palestinian	A
Qazzaz, Bassam Abd al-Hamid		M	Not identified	H'
Ra'd, Sa'diyyeh Muhammad	70	F	Lebanese	A Q
Ramadan, Mahmoud Hussein		M	Not identified	H
Ramadan, Raja' Ali	16	F	Palestinian	A B C I
Rashed, Fatima Mansour		F	Not identified	C
Rashid, Ali Muhammad Ali	10	M	Lebanese	A B C I O
Rashid, Badi'a D. Murad (Mrs Muh. Ali)	45	F	Lebanese	A B C E F' I O
Rashid, Haydar Muhammad Ali	19	M	Lebanese	A B C I O
Rashid, Jamil		M	Not identified	H
Rashid, Mahmoud Muhamad Ali	15	M	Lebanese	A E O
Rashid, Zainab Muhammad Ali	14	F	Lebanese	A E O
Rayyan, Imad Ahmad		M	Not identified	H
Rizq, Ali Ibrahim		M	Not identified	G
Rustum, Adnan Fawzi		M	Not identified	H
Sa'adeh, Muhammad	55	M	Palestinian	B C I
Sa'adi, Akoula Muhammad		M	Lebanese	I
Sa'd, Adnan		M	Syrian	O
Sa'd, Afaf Mahmoud	17	F	Palestinian	A B C D E L M O Q
Sa'd, Aisha Mahmoud	21	F	Not identified	E M
Sa'd, Asya Muhammad	25	F	Lebanese	A
Sa'd, Isma'il Ahmad	60	M	Palestinian	A D E H M O
Sa'd, Mahmoud Muhammad	62	M	Palestinian	A D E L M O Q
Sa'id, Ahmad Ali	38	M	Syrian	A
Sa'id, Ahmad Muhammad	37	M	Palestinian	A

List of names 3 (Continued)

Name	Age	Gender	Nationality	References*
Sa'id, Ahmad Tawfiq	60	M	Not identified	D
Sa'id, Faraj Ibrahim	35	M	Egyptian	A
Sa'id, Jihad Ali	30	M	Palestinian	A
Sabe', Khalil		M	Not identified	H
Sadeq, Imad Muhammad	23	M	Lebanese	A B C I M
Sadeq, Nizar Ibrahim	22	M	Palestinian	A B C D' F'I
Sadeq, Wafa' Muhammad Najib		F	Not identified	G
Safa, Ilham Rida		F	Not identified	G
Saghir, Jum'a Abd al-Zein	45	M	Palestinian	A
Saghir, Mona Abbas Muhammad	15	F	Lebanese	A E F'
Saghir, Moussa Jum'a	18	M	Palestinian	A
Sahli, Nabil		M	Not identified	H
Saidawi, Ali Ahmad		M	Lebanese	H
Salam, Muhammad		M	Lebanese	B C F'I
Salam, Muhammad Hasan	80	M	Sudanese	A B C F' G
Salameh, Ahmad Sa'id	67	M	Not identified	E M
Salameh, Ali		M	Not identified	C
Salameh, Khadijeh Aqil		F	Not identified	G
Salameh, Muhammad Amin		M	Not identified	E M
Salameh, Sa'id, Abu Ahmad	70	M	Palestinian	B C I O
Salameh, Samia	25	F	Lebanese	C
Saleh, Hussein Ali		M	Not identified	I
Saleh, Munira Muhammad		F	Not identified	G
Saleh, Sami Khalil		M	Not identified	E M
Salem, Ali Ahmad		M	Not identified	E M
Salem, Amina Tannan		F	Not identified	G
Salem, Hasan Ali	52	M	Not identified	D
Salem, Salem Muhammad	20	M	Palestinian	A D E
Salim, Akram Muhammad Shawkat	20	M	Stateless	A
Salim, Jihad Muhammad Shawkat	16	M	Stateless	A
Salim, Khodr Hussein	40	M	Stateless	A
Salim, Muhammad Shawkat	52	M	Stateless	A
Salim, Nidal Muhammad Shawkat	14	M	Stateless	A
Salloum, Ahmad Abd al-Hasan	28	M	Lebanese	A
Samarji, Imam Mahmoud Ali	25	M	Egyptian	A C D
Sami, Munther		M	Not identified	D'
Saqqa, Khattar Salim		M	Not identified	H
Sarris, Jamal Muhammad Hussein	19	M	Palestinian	A E M O
Sawi, Ali Hasan, al-hajj		M	Egyptian	C
Sawwan, Issam Muhammad		M	Not identified	H
Sayyed, Ismail Muhammad		M	Not identified	G
Sayyed, Muhammad	55	M	Palestinian	C
Seif al-Din, Layla		F	Not identified	G
Sha'ban, Muhammad Hussein	35	M	Lebanese	B C I
Sha'ban, Ali Omar	30	M	Egyptian	A
Shahin, Salim Sa'id		M	Not identified	E M
Shahrour, Ali Kamel	72	M	Palestinian	A C E G
Shahrour, Muhammad Hussein	65	M	Not identified	E M
Shaibani, Ali Sami		M	Not identified	G
Shaibani, Hasan Sami		M	Not identified	G
Shaibani, Huda Ahmad		F	Not identified	G
Shaibani, Jalilah Issa		F	Not identified	G
Shakoush, Saleh Muhammad		M	Not identified	H

List of names 3 (Continued)

Name	Age	Gender	Nationality	References*
Shamas, Aref Muhammad	22	M	Lebanese	A I Q
Shamas, Aref Omar		M	Lebanese	B C
Shamas, Muhammad Radi	48	M	Lebanese	A B C I Q
Shaykh, Ibrahim Ali	45	M	Lebanese	A
Shaykh, Layla Ahmad 'Shaykha Layla'	30	F	Syrian	A B C
Shaykh, Nabih Sa'id	23	M	Not identified	D
Shibli, Ahmad		M	Not identified	H
Shihab, Yahya Hamid	34	M	Palestinian	B C I
Shihadeh, Abd al-Rahman Mahmoud		M	Not identified	H
Shihadeh, Muhammad Ahmad		M	Not identified	D
Shihadeh, Munther Kayed		M	Not identified	H
Shihadeh, Samir Muhammad	17	M	Palestinian	A E M Q
Shoufani, Ahmad Shihadeh Ahmad	2	M	Palestinian	A E L O Q
Shoufani, Shihadeh Ahmad Izzat	28	M	Palestinian	A E L O Q
Shoufani, Thunaya D. Abu Kh. (Mrs Ahmad)	55	F	Palestinian	A O Q
Shoufani, Wafa' Shihadeh Ahmad	4	F	Palestinian	A E L O Q
Shukur, Ali Muhammad	19	M	Lebanese	B C E I
Shukur, Hussein Muhammad	17	M	Lebanese	B C I
Shuweiker, Faisal Misbah		M	Not identified	H
Sirdar, Hussein Abd al-Rahman		F	Not identified	G
Sirsawi, Abdallah Mahmoud	52	M	Palestinian	A E M O
Souqi, Hussein	25	M	Syrian	E
Souri, Ibrahim		M	Not identified	H
Sukkar, Muhammad Hussein		M	Not identified	H
Sukkariyeh, Mir'i Hawlo	45	M	Lebanese	A
Sulaiman, Munir Shawqi		M	Not identified	H
Sulaiman, Orabi Abd al-Rahman	30	M	Egyptian	A D' F' O
Srour, Hussein Abd al-Mun'em		M	Not identified	G
Ta'baneh, Salim Abd al-Basset	22	M	Lebanese	A B C D' E I Q
Ta'baneh, Samih Abd al-Basset	20	M	Lebanese	A B C E I Q
Taha, Kamel Mahmoud	42	M	Palestinian	E M
Taha, Mahmoud Kamel	17	M	Palestinian	E M
Taha, Muhammad Ahmad	58	M	Palestinian	A D' M
Taha, Muhammad Kamel	15	M	Palestinian	E M
Taha, Su'ad Muhammad Mahmoud	37	M	Palestinian	E M
Tahmaz, Ahmad Ali		M	Not identified	G
Taleb, Fayzeh Amin	51	F	Lebanese	A B C E I O
Taleb, Najib Muhammad		M	Not identified	G
Tantouri, Yousuf Dib	22	M	Not identified	D
Taqqoush, Farid Abd al-Rahman		M	Not identified	G
Tawil, Moussa Khalil		M	Not identified	G
Titi, Hussein Saleh	55	M	Palestinian	A M O Q
Titi, Mahmoud Muhammad	1	M	Palestinian	A B C D E I M O
Titi, Saleh Hussein Saleh	21	M	Palestinian	A D E M O Q
Titi, Samia IbrahimTaleb (Mrs Muhammad)	25	F	Lebanese	A B C O
Titi, Tareq Muhammad	5	M	Palestinian	A B C D E I M O
Tun, Hunain		M	Not identified	H
Turki, Hussein Muhammad	35	M	Turk	A G
Tutunji, Fatima Hussein		F	Not identified	C
Umairi, Ussama		M	Not identified	G
Usaili, Muhammad Ali Ibrahim		M	Not identified	G
Uthman, Ali		M	Palestinian	D' L O
Uthman, Haron Abd	22	M	Palestinian	O

List of names 3 (Continued)

Name	Age	Gender	Nationality	References*
Uthman, Muhammad Safadi		M	Not identified	H
Uthman, Muhammad Sidqi		M	Not identified	H
Uthman, Salma Salim		F	Not identified	G
Wa'riyeh, Fikriyeh		F	Palestinian	D'
Wahbeh, – (the mother Nahed Sa'd)	Fetus		Palestinian	A O
Wahbeh, Ahmad Mufleh		M	Palestinian	E M
Wahbeh, Faisal Mahmoud	35	M	Palestinian	A B C E I M O
Wahbeh, Fatima Ahmad Sirriyeh (Mrs Khalil)	23	F	Palestinian	A B C E F" M O
Wahbeh, Hussein Muhammad, al-Hajj		M	Not identified	G
Wahbeh, Ibrahim Khalil	1	M	Palestinian	A B C E F" I M O
Wahbeh, Khodr Mahmoud	10	M	Palestinian	E M
Wahbeh, Mahmoud Ali	20	M	Palestinian	A D
Wahbeh, Muhsin Muhammad	47	M	Lebanese	B C I
Wahbeh, Nahed Sa'd (Mrs Ali)	17	F	Lebanese	A B C E F" I M O
Wahbeh, Najla Sa'id Taha (Mrs Wahbeh)	67	F	Palestinian	A B C E F" I O
Wali, Hasan Muhammad	24	M	Palestinian	A B C E F" I P
Wali, Hussein Mahmoud	58	M	Not identified	C
Yahya, Ahmad		M	Not identified	H'
Yahya, Ali Nasser		M	Palestinian	E
Yahya, Yusuf As'ad		M	Not identified	M
Yahyawi, Yousuf Ahmad Hamdan	23	M	Not identified	D
Yamani, Salem		M	Not identified	H
Yassin, Abbas Hussein		M	Not identified	G
Yassin, Ali Hussein		M	Not identified	G
Yassin, Issa Abd al-Rahim		M	Not identified	H
Yassin, Mahmoud		M	Not identified	H
Yassin, Salim Habib		M	Not identified	G
Yassir, Issam	25	M	Palestinian	O
Younes, Hasan Muhammad	76	M	Not identified	E M
Younes, Hussein Mahmoud	75	M	Lebanese	A C D E
Younes, Muhammad Abd	30	M	Palestinian	A E M
Yousuf, Abbas Hawi		M	Lebanese	B C I
Yousuf, Riad Abdallah	34	M	Palestinian	A D E
Yousuf, Saleh Ali Hussein		M	Not identified	H
Za'roura, Wissam Abdallah	8	M	Palestinian	E M
Zahr al-Din, Hussein Abbas	1	M	Lebanese	A O
Zahr al-Din, Muhammad Abbas	6	M	Lebanese	A O
Zahr al-Din, Nabila Abbas	3	F	Lebanese	A O
Zahr al-Din, Salah Abbas	13	M	Lebanese	A O
Zalghout, Ahmad Hussein	27	M	Lebanese	A B C E I
Zammar, Salameh Izzat	47	M	Palestinian	A
Zayyouni, Abd Muhammad	11	M	Lebanese	A E F
Zayyouni, Amira Muhammad	22	F	Lebanese	A E
Zayyouni, Amneh (Mrs Muhammad)	43	F	Lebanese	A
Zayyouni, Jamal Muhammad	16	M	Lebanese	A E F
Zayyouni, Samir Muhammad Qassem	25	M	Lebanese	A B C E G I
Zayyouni, Samira Samir	20	F	Lebanese	A E
Zayyouni, Suhaila Muhammad	11	F	Lebanese	A
Zein, Muhammad Ahmad		M	Not identified	H
Zein, Muhammad Hussein		M	Not identified	G
Zein, Tawfiq		M	Not identified	H
Zeina, Hussein, al-Hajj Abu Suleiman	75	M	Palestinian	A D O
Zighzeh, Su'ad Ahmad Muhammad		M	Not identified	E M

Name	Age	Gender	Nationality	References*
Zitli, Jassoum Kajkad	24	M	Palestinian	C
Zu'bi, Taha Hussein		M	Not identified	H
Zur, Mahmoud Thar		M	Not identified	H'
Abdallah	35	M	Palestinian	A
Abu Fadi	20	M	Palestinian	C
Abu Farid	28	M	Palestinian	A
Abu Kifah	26	M	Lebanese	F" O
Abu Nabil	40	M	Palestinian	C
Abu Nidal	24	M	Syrian	A O
Abu Qassem	90	M	Lebanese	C
Abu Ratibeh	64	M	Tunisian	A E
Abu Rikabi		M	Algerian	B C I
Abu Tareq	57	M	Lebanese	A
Ahmad		M	Not identified	O
Amneh	40	F	Lebanese	E F"
Bassam	11	M	Not identified	B I
Fahd	25	M	Syrian	A
Farid	8	M	Not identified	B I
Faten		F	Not identified	C F"
Hamdi	35	M	Egyptian	A D'
Hamid Aziz	34	M	Stateless	A
Hussein	25	M	Palestinian	A E
Hussein	31	M	Turk	A E
Ihsan	35	M	Palestinian	E
Imam		M	Egyptian	D'
Jamal		M	Not identified	F"
Khalil	28	M	Palestinian	A O
Mona	16	F	Not identified	F
Muhammad		M	Not identified	O
R., S.		M	Palestinian	E
Sayyed		M	Not identified	F'
Shadia	2	F	Not identified	B I
Sim'an (child)	3	M	Not identified	B C I
Su'ad		F	Not identified	F"
(found burnt at Akka Hospital)	1		Not identified	A O
(found burnt at Akka Hospital)	1		Not identified	A O
(found burnt at Akka Hospital)	1		Not identified	A O
(found killed in a shelter – al-Gharbi)	1		Not identified	A O
(found killed in a shelter – al-Gharbi)	1		Not identified	A O
(found killed in a shelter – al-Gharbi)	1		Not identified	A O
(found killed in a shelter – al-Gharbi)	1		Not identified	A O
(found killed in a shelter – al-Gharbi)	1		Not identified	A O
(found killed in a shelter – al-Gharbi)	1		Not identified	A O
(found killed on bed – al-Horsh)	30 >	M	Bangladeshi	A O
(found killed on bed – al-Horsh)	30 >	M	Bangladeshi	A O
(found killed on bed – al-Horsh)	30 >	M	Bangladeshi	A O
(found killed on bed – al-Horsh)	30 >	M	Bangladeshi	A O
(found killed on bed – al-Horsh)	30 >	M	Bangladeshi	A O
(found killed on bed – al-Horsh)	30 >	M	Bangladeshi	A O
(found killed with family at supper)	40	M	Palestinian	O
(found killed with family at supper)	27	F	Palestinian	O
(found killed with family at supper)	10	M	Palestinian	O
(found killed with family at supper)	7	M	Palestinian	O

List of names 3   (Continued)

Name	Age	Gender	Nationality	References*
(found killed with family at supper)	5	M	Palestinian	O
(found killed with family at supper)	2	F	Palestinian	O
(killed on Saturday – Sports City)	3	M	Egyptian	A O
Unknown		F	Egyptian	C
Unknown		M	Not identified	C
Unknown (house near Benzine station)		M	Not identified	C

* Sources of the lists that were being employed according to their date of issuance, shown with their symbols, are: the list of the International Red Cross Organization (B); the list of the Lebanese Civil Defence Department (C); the list of the Middle East Council of Churches (I); the list of the Rawdat al-Shahidein cemetery (G); the list of Shaykh Salman al-Khalil (L); the list of al-Shuhada cemetery (H), the list of al-Shuhada cemetery – the mass grave (H'); the list of the Palestinian Red Crescent Society (PRCS) – Gaza Hospital (D); the list of the Palestinian Red Crescent Society – Akka Hospital (D'); the list of the Democratic Front for the Liberation of Palestine (DFLP) – (E); the list of the 'anonymous' Palestinian organization (M); the list of Dar al-Fatwa (K); the list of the Committee for Families of the Kidnapped and Disappeared in Lebanon (CFKDL) – (N); the common list for the abducted and missing (J); the lists of the Lebanese Press: *Al-Safir* (F), *Al-Nida'* (F'), a list extracted from various newspapers (F"); the oral history list (O); the field study list (A); the list of the Official Commission of Inquiry into the Fate of those Abducted and Missing (P); the list for the lawsuit against Sharon to the Belgian judiciary (Q).

List of names 4 Abducted and missing in Sabra and Shatila massacre: based on various sources

Name	Age	Fate	Gender	Nationality	References*
A'raj, Abdallah Shafiq		Missing	M	Not identified	F
Abadi, Ahmad Ali		Missing	M	Not identified	K
Abadi, Ahmad Khaled		Missing	M	Not identified	K
Abadi, Ali Mahmoud		Missing	M	Not identified	K
Abadi, Ali Muhammad		Missing	M	Not identified	K
Abadi, Hamad Muhammad		Missing	M	Not identified	K
Abadi, Mahmoud Ali		Missing	M	Not identified	K
Abadi, Mahmoud Khaled		Missing	M	Not identified	K
Abadi, Muhammad Khaled		Missing	M	Not identified	K
Abd al-Aal, Ahmad Ibrahim		Missing	M	Not identified	K
Abd al-Mun'em (al Masri)	28	Abducted	M	Egyptian	A
Abd al-Rahim, Ahmad		Missing	M	Not identified	K
Abd al-Rahim, Suheil Ali		Missing	M	Not identified	K
Abd al-Razeq, Marwan Kamal		Missing	M	Not identified	K
Abd al-Razeq, Muhammad Kamal		Missing	M	Not identified	K
Abd al-Razeq, Musleh Hamad	43	Missing	M	Palestinian	F J N
Abdallah, Ahmad Hamadeh		Missing	M	Not identified	K
Abed, Ghassan Yousuf	16	Abducted	M	Palestinian	A
Abir, Ahmad Jamil	50	Missing	M	Palestinian	E M
Abshir, Jamal Salim		Missing	M	Palestinian	J N
Abu Adas, Ra'fat Abd al-Hamid	20	Abducted	M	Palestinian	A
Abu Dhaher, Muhammad Ahmad		Missing	M	Not identified	K
Abu Haija', Khaled Mahmoud		Missing	M	Not identified	K
Abu Haija', Nabil Mahmoud		Missing	M	Not identified	K
Abu Nawfal, Muhammad Fayez		Missing	M	Not identified	K
Abu Owdeh, Mahmoud Saleh		Missing	M	Not identified	K
Abu Owdeh, Muhammad Saleh		Missing	M	Not identified	K
Abu Rashad, Khaireyeh Ali	45	Missing	F	Lebanese	L
Abu Rumeileh, Sami Abdallah		Missing	M	Not identified	K
Abu Shilleih, Ahmad Hasan		Missing	M	Palestinian	J
Abu Shilleih, Mahmoud Ali		Missing	M	Palestinian	J M N
Abu Shilleih, Muhammad Ali		Missing	M	Palestinian	J
Abu Sud, Mahmoud		Missing	M	Not identified	K
Abu Zaher, Atef Tawfiq		Missing	M	Not identified	N
Abu Zeid, Hamzah Muhammad	17	Abducted	M	Stateless	A K N P
Abu Zeid, Muhammad	40	Abducted	M	Stateless	A K L P
Abu Zeid, Nasser Muhammad	15	Abducted	M	Stateless	A K N P
Abu Zeid, Taysir Muhammad	18	Abducted	M	Stateless	A K N P
Afifi, Abd al-Hafiz		Missing	M	Palestinian	E J
Afsh, Ahmad Sa'd al-Din	32	Missing	M	Lebanese	F' N P
Afsh, Hussein Sa'd al-Din	35	Missing	M	Lebanese	F' N P
Aghwani, Moussa Sultan		Missing	M	Not identified	K
Ahmad, Ahmad Sabri		Missing	M	Not identified	K
Ahmad, Faraj Ali Sayyed	34	Abducted	M	Egyptian	A E F J N O P
Ahmad, Muhammad Hussein	43	Abducted	M	Palestinian	A
Aiadi, Muhammad Ali		Missing	M	Not identified	K
Aiadi, Muhammad Hussein		Missing	M	Not identified	K
Akkawi, Abd al-Karim		Missing	M	Not identified	K
Alam, Ahmad Salam		Missing	M	Palestinian	J N
Alameh, Ali Hasan	18	Abducted	M	Lebanese	A E F N O P Q
Ali, Adel Mustafa	45	Missing	M	Not identified	F'
Ali, Adnan		Missing	M	Not identified	K
Ali, Ahmad	50	Abducted	M	Palestinian	A

Name	Age	Fate	Gender	Nationality	References*
Ali, Ahmad Muhammad Sa'id	32	Abducted	M	Syrian	A E J L
Ali, Ali Badri		Missing	M	Not identified	K
Ali, Ali Sa'id		Missing	M	Not identified	K
Ali, Amneh		Missing	F	Not identified	F
Ali, Fatima Muhammad		Missing	F	Not identified	K
Ali, Issa Badawi		Missing	M	Not identified	K
Ali, Kamal Ali		Missing	M	Not identified	K
Ali, Khalil Dawoud		Missing	M	Not identified	K
Ali, Mahmoud Ahmad	19	Abducted	M	Palestinian	A K
Ali, Muhammad Ahmad	23	Abducted	M	Palestinian	A K
Ali, Muhammad Dawoud		Missing	M	Not identified	K
Ali, Muhammad Muhammad	31	Abducted	M	Palestinian	A
Ali, Omar Muhammad	25	Abducted	M	Palestinian	A E F
Ali, Saleh Sa'id		Missing	M	Not identified	K
Allas, Abd Muhammad		Missing	M	Not identified	K
Amin, Ahmad		Missing	M	Not identified	K
Amin, Diab Issa		Missing	M	Not identified	K
Amin, Ghassan Hamadi		Missing	M	Not identified	K
Amin, Ramez Hamadi		Missing	M	Not identified	K
Arabyeh, Tawfiq Abd al-Karim		Missing	M	Not identified	K
Asadi, Omar	28	Missing	M	Palestinian	E F N
Ashour, Muhammad Saleh	17	Missing	M	Palestinian	F' F' J K N
Asmar, Farid Milhem	80	Missing	M	Lebanese	L
Asmar, Issa Wared		Missing	M	Not identified	K
Aswad, Hasan Ahmad	52	Abducted	M	Syrian	A F F' L N
At'out, Bashir Ahmad	18	Abducted	M	Palestinian	A F F' J N P
Atiyeh, Ali		Missing	M	Not identified	K
Atrash, Ibrahim Muhammad	27	Missing	M	Palestinian	E N
Atrash, Khalil Muhammad	28	Missing	M	Palestinian	N E P
Atris, Hamad Qassem		Missing	M	Not identified	K
Atyar, Hasan Hashem	25	Abducted	M	Palestinian	A E F F' J N O P Q
Awad, Ahmad Hasan		Missing	M	Not identified	K
Awad, Hussein Ali		Missing	M	Not identified	K
Awad, Muhammad Ahmad		Missing	M	Not identified	K
Ayyoub, Dawud		Missing	M	Not identified	K
Ayyoub, Mussa		Missing	M	Syrian	K
Ayyoub, Sulaiman		Missing	M	Not identified	K
Azzam, Adnan Khaled	26	Abducted	M	Palestinian	A
Azzouqa, Ibrahim Mahmoud	13	Abducted	M	Palestinian	A
Ba'id, Ibrahim Karim		Missing	M	Not identified	K
Bahrein, Muhammad		Missing	M	Not identified	K
Baitam, Fayyad Hasan	22	Abducted	M	Palestinian	A J
Banat, Mahmoud Bakri	33	Abducted	M	Lebanese	A E F' O
Banna, Nabil Muhammad Mahmoud		Missing	M	Not identified	K
Barakah, Fayez Ali		Missing	M	Palestinian	J N
Barjawi, Abd al-Halim Ali		Missing	M	Not identified	K
Barjawi, Mahmoud Ali Abboud		Missing	M	Not identified	K
Bawwab, Riad Muhammad		Missing	M	Palestinian	J N
Beik, Khaled Mustafa	27	Missing	M	Not identified	F
Beik, Muhammad Mustafa	14	Missing	M	Not identified	F
Bibi, Bassam Abd al-Salam	18	Abducted	M	Palestinian	A F F' J M N P
Birri, Hasib Abbas	19	Missing	M	Lebanese	F' P
Birri, Muhammad Abbas	17	Missing	M	Lebanese	F' P

Name	Age	Fate	Gender	Nationality	References*
Birri, Moussa Abbas	18	Missing	M	Lebanese	F' P
Bitar, Sa'id Muhammad	17	Missing	M	Palestinian	P
Darwi, Ahmad Nayef		Missing	M	Not identified	K
Darwi, Hussein Nimr		Missing	M	Not identified	K
Darwish, Khaled Ali		Missing	M	Not identified	K
Dawoud, Ghazi Ibrahim		Missing	M	Not identified	K
Dawoud, Kahled Adnan		Missing	M	Not identified	K
Dawoud, Nadia		Missing	F	Not identified	K
Dawoud, Omar		Missing	M	Not identified	K
Dawoud, Sana'		Missing	F	Not identified	K
Dawoud, Sulaiman		Missing	M	Not identified	K
Dawoud, Wafa'		Missing	F	Not identified	K
Dhinni, Faraj Mahmoud al-Abdallah		Missing	M	Not identified	K
Dib, Anis Na'im	23	Missing	M	Lebanese	L N P
Dilawi, Na'im Ahmad		Missing	M	Not identified	K
Dirawi, Ahmad Faisal	15	Abducted	M	Palestinian	A F" F' J N O P
Dirawi, Aziz Faisal	33	Abducted	M	Palestinian	A F" F' J N O P
Dirawi, Ibrahim Faisal	28	Abducted	M	Palestinian	A F" F' J N O P
Dirawi, Ibrahim Saleh		Missing	M	Palestinian	F' J N
Dirawi, Mansour Faisal	25	Abducted	M	Palestinian	A F" J N O P
Fa'our, Khaled Ali		Missing	M	Not identified	N
Fayyad, Amer Omar		Missing	M	Not identified	K
Fayyad, Omar Omar		Missing	M	Not identified	K
Freijeh, Ali Ahmad Hamdan		Missing	M	Not identified	K
Freijeh, Ali Moussa		Missing	M	Not identified	K
Freijeh, Moussa Muh. Hammoudeh		Missing	M	Not identified	K
Freijeh, Yousuf Ahmad Hamdan		Missing	M	Not identified	K
Ghawani, Moussa Sultan		Missing	M	Not identified	K
Ghazzawi, Ali Ahmad	45	Abducted	M	Syrian	A E L O
Ghazzawi, Hussein Ali Ahmad	20	Abducted	M	Syrian	A E L O
Ghazzawi, Muhammad Ali Ahmad	16	Abducted	M	Syrian	A E L O
Ghazzawi, Walid Ali Ahmad	20	Missing	M	Syrian	L
Hajj, Adnan		Missing	M	Not identified	K
Hajj, Fadi		Missing	M	Not identified	K
Hajj, Fadia		Missing	F	Not identified	K
Hajj, Fatima		Missing	F	Not identified	K
Hajj, Fawzieh Ahmad		Missing	F	Not identified	K
Hajj, Nimr Ahmad		Missing	M	Not identified	K
Hajj, Saleh Hussein	40	Missing	M	Palestinian	J L N
Hajjar, Ahmad Mustafa	17	Abducted	M	Palestinian	A
Hali, Aida Ahmad		Missing	F	Not identified	K
Hamad, Ahmad Yousuf		Missing	M	Not identified	K
Hamad, Hussein		Missing	M	Not identified	K
Hamad, Jamal	17	Missing	M	Palestinian	L
Hamad, Muhammad		Missing	M	Not identified	K
Hamad, Muhammad Ahmad Yousuf		Missing	M	Not identified	K
Hamadeh, Ahmad Hussein		Missing	M	Not identified	K
Hamadeh, Ahmad Naji		Missing	M	Not identified	K
Hamadeh, Dawoud		Missing	M	Not identified	K
Hamadeh, Muhammad		Missing	M	Not identified	K
Hamadeh, Muhammad Atiyeh		Missing	M	Not identified	K
Hamadeh, Muhammad Hussein		Missing	M	Not identified	K
Hamadeh, Nayef		Missing	M	Not identified	K

Name	Age	Fate	Gender	Nationality	References*
Hamadeh, Yassin Muhammad Atiyeh		Missing	M	Not identified	K
Hamawi, Walid		Missing	M	Not identified	K
Hamid, Raslan	24	Missing	M	Not identified	F
Hammoud, Jamal Muhammad		Missing	M	Not identified	F
Hamzah, Mustafa		Missing	M	Not identified	K
Hamzah, Uthman		Missing	M	Not identified	K
Hariri, Khaled Hamid	17	Abducted	M	Stateless	A E
Hariri, Muhammad Hamid	16	Abducted	M	Stateless	A E
Hasan, Abd al-Nasser		Missing	M	Palestinian	J N
Hasan, Ahmad Khalil	16	Abducted	M	Palestinian	A F' F" J N
Hasan, Akram Ghaleb Rida		Missing	M	Not identified	K
Hasan, Fu'ad Hussein		Missing	M	Not identified	K
Hasan, Ghazi Muhammad		Missing	M	Not identified	K
Hasan, Hasan Ahmad	50	Abducted	M	Palestinian	A E J K P
Hasan, Jalal Hasan Ahmad	15	Abducted	M	Palestinian	A E J K N P
Hasan, Khaled Muhammad Ali		Missing	M	Not identified	K
Hasan, Khalil Mahmoud	55	Abducted	M	Palestinian	A F' F" N
Hasan, Muhammad		Missing	M	Not identified	K
Hasan, Shihadeh Hussein		Missing	M	Not identified	K
Hasan, Younes Na'im		Missing	M	Not identified	E
Hashem, Muhammad Hasan		Missing	M	Palestinian	J N
Hashem, Muhammad Saleh		Missing	M	Not identified	K
Hassan, Abd al-Basset		Missing	M	Not identified	K
Hayek, As'ad Muhammad	27	Abducted	M	Palestinian	A F
Hayek, Sa'id		Missing	M	Not identified	F
Hijazi, Hasan Mir'i		Missing	M	Not identified	K
Hijazi, Muhammad Kazem	19	Abducted	M	Lebanese	A F' F" L N
Hijazi, Mussa Hasan		Missing	M	Not identified	K
Hijazi, Omar Kazem		Missing	M	Not identified	F
Hijazi, Taher Moussa		Missing	M	Not identified	K
Himmo, Jamal Muhammad	17	Abducted	M	Palestinian	A F" J M N O P
Hirri, Mahmoud	18	Missing	M	Not identified	F
Hishmeh, Ahmad Sa'id		Missing	M	Palestinian	F
Housu, Hasan Isamil		Missing	M	Palestinian	N
Hubta, Muhammad Tawfiq		Missing	M	Not identified	K
Husari, Fu'ad Mustafa		Missing	M	Not identified	E
Hussein, Abd al-Ra'ouf Khaled		Missing	M	Not identified	K
Hussein, Diab Shihadeh		Missing	M	Not identified	K
Hussein, Fattoum Fahd		Missing	F	Not identified	K
Hussein, Fayez Yousuf		Missing	M	Not identified	K
Hussein, Hamad		Missing	M	Not identified	K
Hussein, Jamil Mahmoud Dhaher		Missing	M	Not identified	K
Hussein, Kamel Hussein	41	Abducted	M	Palestinian	A
Hussein, Kamel Mahmoud		Missing	M	Not identified	K
Hussein, Khaled Khalil		Missing	M	Not identified	K
Hussein, Lamia Dhaher		Missing	F	Not identified	K
Hussein, Louisa Dhaher		Missing	F	Not identified	K
Hussein, Muhammad Kamel		Missing	M	Not identified	K
Hussein, Muhammad Mir'i		Missing	M	Not identified	K
Hussein, Mustafa Kamel		Missing	M	Not identified	K
Hussein, Nasser Mahmoud Daher		Missing	M	Not identified	K
Huweidi, Orans Ammar	15	Abducted	M	Syrian	A E J L
Huweidi, Qassem		Missing	M	Syrian	J N

Name	Age	Fate	Gender	Nationality	References*
Ibrahim, Hussein		Missing	M	Not identified	K
Ibrahim, Khalil		Missing	M	Not identified	K
Ibrahim, Sami Karim		Missing	M	Not identified	K
Ibrhaim, Maher Ghazi		Missing	M	Not identified	K
Ibriq, Khalil Mahmoud	54	Abducted	M	Palestinian	A
Ibriq, Mahmoud Khalil	17	Abducted	M	Palestinian	A
Ijjeh, As'ad Muhammad		Missing	M	Not identified	K
Ishraqiyeh, Talal Hasan		Missing	M	Not identified	K
Iskandarani, Walid Darwish	22	Missing	M	Palestinian	E N
Issawi, Majdi Misbah	45	Abducted	M	Palestinian	A
Jabr, Abdallah	40	Missing	M	Palestinian	F J N
Jad'on, Ahmad Yousuf	55	Missing	M	Not identified	F P
Jammal, Ahmad Obeid	53	Abducted	M	Syrian	A E F' J N
Jammoul, Shawqi Ali	30	Missing	M	Lebanese	L
Jawad, Jamil Muhammad	44	Missing	M	Palestinian	J N
Jawhar, Jawhar Mahmoud		Missing	M	Palestinian	N
Juha, Walid Ahmad		Missing	M	Palestinian	J N
Ka'ki, Hussein Abd al-Qader	55	Missing	M	Not identified	F
Kabbara, Muhammad Salim Issa	32	Abducted	M	Palestinian	A F F' M N P
Kamel, Ahmad Muhammad		Missing	M	Not identified	K
Karroum, Amneh		Missing	F	Not identified	K
Karroum, Ghaleb Saleh		Missing	M	Not identified	K
Karroum, Haytham		Missing	M	Not identified	K
Karroum, Ismail Saleh		Missing	M	Not identified	K
Karroum, Mazen		Missing	M	Not identified	K
Karroum, Saleh Moussa		Missing	M	Not identified	K
Karroum, Zuheir Ali Omar		Missing	M	Not identified	K
Kayed, Faisal Ali	45	Missing	M	Not identified	F
Kayed, Nayef		Missing	M	Not identified	K
Kayyali, Ahmad Nimr	14	Abducted	M	Palestinian	A P
Khaled, Ayyoub Muhammad		Missing	M	Not identified	K
Khaled, Issam		Missing	M	Not identified	K
Khaled, Muhammad		Missing	M	Not identified	K
Khaled, Najib Assem		Missing	M	Not identified	K
Khaled, Walid Ali		Missing	M	Not identified	K
Khaled, Walid Assem		Missing	M	Not identified	K
Khaled, Yassin		Missing	M	Not identified	K
Khalil, Muhammad Hasan al-Hajj		Missing	M	Not identified	F
Khalil, Nasser Muh. Hasan al-Hajj		Missing	M	Not identified	F
Khalil, Samira Ali	17	Missing	F	Not identified	F
Khalil, Walid Muh. Hasan al-Hajj		Missing	M	Not identified	F
Khamis, Abbas Hasan	22	Missing	M	Lebanese	F' P
Kharroubi, Mustafa Sulaiman	18	Abducted	M	Palestinian	A
Khatib, Abdallah Qassem	20	Abducted	M	Palestinian	A F" N
Khatib, Ahmad Yousuf		Missing	M	Not identified	K
Khatib, Fayez Yousuf		Missing	M	Not identified	K
Khatib, Issa Ali		Missing	M	Not identified	K
Khatib, Jamal Mahmoud		Missing	M	Not identified	K
Khatib, Mariam Yousuf		Missing	F	Not identified	K
Khatib, Muhammad Ali		Missing	M	Not identified	K
Khatib, Muhammad Hussein		Missing	M	Palestinian	J N
Khatib, Muhammad Yousuf		Missing	M	Not identified	K
Khatib, Nijmeh Abd al-Hadi		Missing	F	Not identified	K

List of names 4 (Continued)

Name	Age	Fate	Gender	Nationality	References*
Khatib, Salah Yousuf		Missing	M	Not identified	K
Khatib, Salimeh Ali		Missing	F	Not identified	K
Khatib, Tawfiq Ali		Missing	M	Not identified	K
Khatib, Yousuf		Missing	M	Not identified	K
Khudeir, Dawoud Sulaiman		Missing	M	Palestinian	J N
Khureibi, Abdallah Ahmad		Missing	M	Not identified	K
Kurdi, Saleh Yousuf	13	Missing	M	Turk	F F' P
Kuthayer, Ahmad Muhammad Salim	28	Abducted	M	Palestinian	A J M O
Kuthayer, Jamal Muhammad Salim	26	Abducted	M	Palestinian	A J M O
Labban, Muhammad Tawfiq	20	Abducted	M	Palestinian	A O
Loubani, Jihad Ahmad		Missing	M	Palestinian	J N
Ma'rouf, Jamal Kamal	19	Abducted	M	Palestinian	A F F' J M N O P
Ma'rouf, Latifa		Missing	F	Not identified	K
Ma'rouf, Nabil Ahmad		Missing	M	Not identified	K
Ma'rouf, Ramzi		Missing	M	Not identified	K
Ma'rouf, Subhi Abd		Missing	M	Not identified	K
Mahmoud, Ahmad Khaled Moussa		Missing	M	Not identified	K
Mahmoud, Ahmad Za'al		Missing	M	Not identified	K
Mahmoud, Ali Khaled Moussa		Missing	M	Not identified	K
Mahmoud, Hasan Ali		Missing	M	Not identified	K
Mahmoud, Khaled Mahmoud,	20	Missing	M	Not identified	F
Mahmoud, Mahmoud Khaled		Missing	M	Not identified	F"
Mahmoud, Mahmoud Za'al		Missing	M	Not identified	K
Mahmoud, Subh Khaled Moussa		Missing	M	Not identified	K
Mahmoud, Za'al		Missing	M	Not identified	K
Mahus, Mahmoud		Missing	M	Palestinian	J N
Mansour, Mahmoud Nayef		Missing	M	Not identified	K
Mashharawi, Ghassan Suheil	17	Missing	M	Not identified	F" F' N
Mashharawi, Ibrahim Khalil	55	Abducted	M	Palestinian	A F F' J M N O P
Mashharawi, Sami Ibrahim	25	Missing	M	Not identified	F" F' N
Mattar, Atallah Ahmad		Missing	M	Not identified	K
Mattar, Omar		Missing	M	Not identified	K
Mihho, Jamal Muhammad		Missing	M	Not identified	K
Milahi, Abd Muhammad		Missing	M	Not identified	K
Miqdad, Mahmoud Ibrahim		Missing	M	Not identified	K
Mir'i, Mahmoud Kahled	22	Missing	M	Not identified	F
Misri, Abd al-Karim		Missing	M	Not identified	N
Misri, Mahmoud Muhammad Subhi	22	Abducted	M	Palestinian	A F F' M N
Misri, Nasriyeh Khaled		Missing	F	Not identified	K
Moussa, Adnan		Missing	M	Not identified	K
Moussa, Ayyoub Nazal		Missing	M	Not identified	K
Moussa, Mahmoud Ayyoub		Missing	M	Not identified	K
Moussa, Moussa Ahmad		Missing	M	Not identified	K
Moussa, Salim Nazzal		Missing	M	Not identified	K
Mu'awad, Ahmad Ibrahim		Missing	M	Not identified	K
Mughrabi, Salim		Missing	M	Not identified	K
Muhammad, Ahmad Ibrahim		Missing	M	Not identified	K
Muhammad, Ahmad Mahmoud	30	Missing	M	Lebanese	K P
Muhammad, Ali Ibrahim		Missing	M	Not identified	K
Muhammad, Ali Muhammad	44	Abducted	M	Syrian	A
Muhammad, Hasan Mahmoud	17	Abducted	M	Palestinian	A E F J N P
Muhammad, Hussein Ali Muhammad	20	Abducted	M	Syrian	A J
Muhammad, Khalil Mahmoud		Missing	M	Not identified	K

List of names 4 (Continued)

Name	Age	Fate	Gender	Nationality	References*
Muhammad, Mahmoud Ibrahim		Missing	M	Not identified	K
Muhammad, Mahmoud Salim	35	Abducted	M	Syrian	A
Muhammad, Muhammad Ali Muh.	18	Abducted	M	Syrian	A J
Muhammad, Nazir Abdo		Missing	M	Not identified	K
Muhammad, Walid Ali Muhamammad	20	Abducted	M	Syrian	A J
Muhawish, Muhawish Mahmoud	65	Abducted	M	Palestinian	A F L O
Muheisin, Jihad Hussein		Missing	M	Not identified	K
Muheisin, Nimr Hussein		Missing	M	Not identified	K
Muhsin, Fayez Na'im		Missing	M	Not identified	N
Muhsin, Na'im Fayez	17	Abducted	M	Lebanese	A E F N P
Mustafa, Shihadeh Ali		Missing	M	Not identified	K
Na'im, Sa'id Ahmad	24	Abducted	M	Egyptian	A
Najdi, Abd al-Karim Ali	26	Missing	M	Lebanese	F'
Najdi, Ali Muhammad	24	Missing	M	Lebanese	F'
Nasr al-Din, Abd al-Rahim Khodr	27	Abducted	M	Lebanese	A O P
Nasr al-Din, Abd al-Rahman		Missing	M	Not identified	N
Nasr al-Din, Hasan Khodr	22	Abducted	M	Lebanese	A OP
Nasrallah, Hasan Nimr	16	Abducted	M	Lebanese	A
Nasser, Hamzah		Missing	M	Not identified	K
Nasser, Jamal Ibrahim		Missing	M	Palestinian	F J N
Nasser, Taysir		Missing	M	Not identified	K
Natat, Sami Shaker Abd al-Ghani	23	Abducted	M	Palestinian	A FF' J L N O P
Nayef, Ahmad Moussa	50	Missing	M	Not identified	F" F' N
Nayef, Muhammad Ahmad Moussa	22	Missing	M	Not identified	F' N
Nayfeh, Na'im Ali		Missing	M	Not identified	K
Nounu, Salameh Muhammad Salameh	19	Missing	M	Not identified	F
Omar, Ahmad Muhammad		Missing	M	Not identified	K
Omar, Yassin Muhammad		Missing	M	Not identified	K
Owdeh, Adel Ahmad		Missing	M	Not identified	L
Qablawi, Sami		Missing	M	Not identified	F
Qadah, Jamal Kayed		Missing	M	Not identified	K
Qaddoura, Ahmad Khaled		Missing	M	Not identified	K
Qaddoura, Khaled Yousuf		Missing	M	Not identified	K
Qaddoura, Muhammad Mustafa		Missing	M	Not identified	K
Qaddoura, Saleh Mustafa		Missing	M	Not identified	K
Qaddoura, Subhiyeh Abd al-Majid	35	Missing	F	Palestinian	E
Qadi, Ali Fawzi	16	Abducted	M	Palestinian	A E J K O Q
Qadi, Hasan Ahmad	50	Missing	M	Palestinian	E F
Qadi, Muhammad Fawzi	18	Abducted	M	Palestinian	A E J K O Q
Qahrawi, Ghassan Suheil		Missing	M	Not identified	K
Qalqan, Khalil Abd	18	Missing	M	Turk	L
Qassem, Fatima		Missing	F	Not identified	K
Qassem, Jamal Muhammad		Missing	M	Not identified	K
Qassem, Riad Muhammad		Missing	M	Not identified	K
Qassem, Yassin Nimr		Missing	M	Not identified	K
Qassem, Yousuf Rahil	40	Abducted	M	Palestinian	A
Qudra, Jihad Mahmoud	22	Missing	M	Not identified	F
Ra'd, Ra'd Mahmoud		Missing	M	Not identified	K
Ra'd, Saleh Muhammad		Missing	M	Not identified	K
Radi, Hasan	18	Abducted	M	Palestinian	A E O
Radi, Saleh		Missing	M	Palestinian	N
Ramzi, Fu'ad		Missing	M	Not identified	F
Rashid, Jaser Mahmoud Abd		Missing	M	Not identified	K

Name	Age	Fate	Gender	Nationality	References*
Rashida, Talal Hasan		Missing	M	Not identified	K
Rawi, Hasan Mahmoud Muhammad	16	Missing	M	Not identified	F
Rawi, Talal Mahmoud Muhammad	25	Missing	M	Not identified	F
Rumeihi, Hussein Ali		Missing	M	Not identified	K
Sa'd, Mahmoud Salah al-Din	25	Abducted	M	Lebanese	A F M N
Sa'di, Ali Muhammad	19	Missing	M	Palestinian	K P
Sa'di, Khaled Muhammad Asi	21	Abducted	M	Palestinian	A E J K N O
Sa'di, Khalil Abd al-Rahman		Missing	M	Not identified	K
Sa'di, Khawla Muhammad		Missing	F	Palestinian	J N
Sa'di, Muhammad Asi	60	Abducted	M	Palestinian	A E K O
Sa'id, Ahmad Muhammad	40	Abducted	M	Syrian	A
Sa'id, Ali	12	Missing	M	Not identified	F
Sa'id, Diab Ahmad		Missing	M	Not identified	K
Sa'id, Hussein Ahmad Ali		Missing	M	Not identified	K
Sa'id, Mahmoud	13	Missing	M	Not identified	F
Sa'id, Zainab	17	Missing	F	Not identified	F
Sa'idi, Ahmad Mustafa	26	Abducted	M	Palestinian	A F
Sabbagh, Riad Yahya	21	Abducted	M	Lebanese	A F F' M N
Sabeq, Mahmoud Hasan	39	Abducted	M	Palestinian	A E J Q
Sabra, Abd Zaghlul		Missing	M	Not identified	F
Safadi, Ahmad Mustafa		Missing	M	Not identified	K
Safadi, Khaled Abd al-Nasser		Missing	M	Not identified	K
Safar, Abdallah Suheil	27	Abducted	M	Palestinian	A F J M O P
Saffouri, Yousuf Shafiq	13	Abducted	M	Palestinian	A E
Sakran, Sultan Issa		Missing	M	Not identified	K
Salameh, Hamdi Muhammad Sa'id	27	Missing	M	Egyptian	L
Saleh, Muhammad		Missing	M	Not identified	F"
Saleh, Saleh Muhammad	34	Missing	M	Palestinian	J N
Salem, Ahmad Khalil	16	Abducted	M	Palestinian	A E J K N
Salem, Awni Khalil	18	Abducted	M	Palestinian	A E F J K N
Salem, Ihsan Muhammad	37	Abducted	M	Palestinian	A E F J K N
Salem, Khalil Muhammad	45	Abducted	M	Palestinian	A F K
Salem, Mahmoud Abd al-Wahhab	15	Abducted	M	Palestinian	A
Salim, Mahmoud	35	Missing	M	Syrian	L
Salti, Itra	40	Missing	F	Palestinian	L M
Salti, Khaled		Missing	M	Palestinian	L M
Sane', Nasser As'ad	20	Abducted	M	Palestinian	A E J L N
Saqqa, Abd al-Qader Mahmoud	28	Abducted	M	Palestinian	A E P Q
Saqqa, Muhammad Mahmoud	18	Abducted	M	Palestinian	A E J P Q
Saqqal, Abd Mahmoud		Missing	M	Not identified	F
Saqqal, Muhammad Mahmoud		Missing	M	Not identified	F
Sawalha, Khalil	26	Abducted	M	Palestinian	A
Sawalha, Mahmoud	23	Abducted	M	Palestinian	A
Seif al-Din, Muhammad Ahmad		Missing	M	Lebanese	N P
Sfeir, Hussein Muhammad		Missing	M	Not identified	K
Sfeir, Ibrahim Hasan		Missing	M	Not identified	K
Sfeir, Samir Hussein		Missing	M	Not identified	K
Sha'ban, Samir Khuleif		Missing	M	Not identified	N
Shahadin, Subhi		Missing	M	Not identified	K
Shahin, Muhammad Ibrahim		Missing	M	Not identified	K
Shahin, Walid Ibrahim		Missing	M	Not identified	K
Shakantat, Muhieddine		Missing	M	Not identified	K
Shaleh, Mahmoud		Missing	M	Not identified	N

Name	Age	Fate	Gender	Nationality	References*
Sharqawi, Anwar Ibrahim	16	Abducted	M	Lebanese	A P
Sharqawi, Ibrahim Hasan	25	Missing	M	Not identified	F
Shihadeh, Abd Aziz		Missing	M	Not identified	K
Shihadeh, Ali Abd al-Aziz		Missing	M	Not identified	K
Shihadeh, As'ad		Missing	M	Not identified	K
Shihadeh, Fathi Hasan		Missing	M	Not identified	K
Shihadeh, Kamel Hussein		Missing	M	Not identified	K
Shihadeh, Mut'ab		Missing	M	Not identified	K
Siba'i, Muhammad Wajih	45	Missing	M	Not identified	F
Sinjir, Abdallah	25	Missing	M	Not identified	F" F' N
Sirhal, Muhammad Hussein Dib		Missing	M	Not identified	K
Sirri, Ibrahim Mustafa	28	Abducted	M	Palestinian	A F F' M N P
Sirri, Nabil Gharib	23	Abducted	M	Palestinian	A F F' J K M N
Snunu, Ahmad Mahmoud		Missing	M	Palestinian	J N
Suleiman, Hasan Muhammad		Missing	M	Palestinian	N
Sulh, Moussa Shihadeh		Missing	M	Not identified	K
Sultan, Muhammad	27	Missing	M	Not identified	F
Suweidi, Muhammad Khalil	21	Missing	M	Not identified	F
Ta'mari, Ahmad As'ad		Missing	M	Not identified	K
Talal, Talal Muhammad		Missing	M	Not identified	K
Tu'meh, Fayez Munif		Missing	M	Not identified	K
Tu'meh, Izzat Munif		Missing	M	Not identified	K
Tu'meh, Munif Muhammad		Missing	M	Not identified	K
Udeisi, Ahmad Muhammad		Missing	M	Not identified	F
Udeisi, Jamal Muhammad		Missing	M	Not identified	F
Umairi, Hasan Salman		Missing	M	Not identified	K
Umari, Khaled Ibrahim	23	Abducted	M	Lebanese	A F' M N P
Umari, Khaled Muhammad		Missing	M	Not identified	F F'
Umran, Omar		Missing	M	Not identified	K
Umran, Umran Ahmad		Missing	M	Not identified	K
Uthman, Ahmad Hasan		Missing	M	Not identified	K
Uthman, Ali Nayef Hasan	52	Missing	M	Lebanese	P
Uthman, Hanan Ali		Missing	F	Not identified	K
Uthman, Muhammad Abd Yousuf		Missing	M	Palestinian	J N
Yahya, Abd al-Rahman		Missing	M	Not identified	K
Yahya, Ayyoub		Missing	M	Not identified	K
Yahya, Yousuf Ahmad Hamdan		Missing	M	Not identified	K
Yassin, Khaled Muhammad Salim		Missing	M	Not identified	K
Yassin, Mahmoud Hussein		Missing	M	Not identified	K
Yousuf, Ahmad		Missing	M	Not identified	K
Yousuf, Ali Hussein		Missing	M	Not identified	K
Yousuf, Hayat Muhammad Hussein		Missing	F	Not identified	K
Yousuf, Iman Muhammad Hussein		Missing	F	Not identified	K
Yousuf, Muhammad Ahmad		Missing	F	Not identified	K
Yousuf, Najat Hussein		Missing	F	Not identified	K
Yousuf, Najieh Muhammad Hussein		Missing	F	Not identified	K
Yousuf, Walid Hussein		Missing	M	Not identified	K
Zamel, Riad Muhammad		Missing	M	Not identified	F
Zamzam, Imad Mahmoud		Missing	M	Not identified	K
Zaher, Ahmad	40	Missing	M	Palestinian	E
Zaher, Ali Ahmad	6	Missing	M	Palestinian	E
Zaher, Fida' Ahmad	2	Missing	F	Palestinian	E
Zaher, Kifah Ahmad	10	Missing	M	Palestinian	E

Name	Age	Fate	Gender	Nationality	References*
Zhaher, Rifa'yeh Ahmad	8	Missing	M	Palestinian	E
Ziadeh, Jihad Saleh		Missing	M	Palestinian	J N
Ziadeh, Subhi Saleh Mahmoud		Missing	M	Palestinian	J N
Zurein, Walid Darwish	22	Abducted	M	Palestinian	A J M N P Q
Hussein	35	Abducted	M	Palestinian	A
Mu'afi		Missing	M	Syrian	L
Uthman	20	Abducted	M	British	A

* Sources of the lists that were being employed according to their date of issuance, shown with their symbols, are: the list of the International Red Cross Organization (B); the list of the Lebanese Civil Defence Department (C); the list of the Middle East Council of Churches (I); the list of the Rawdat al-Shahidein cemetery (G); the list of Shaykh Salman al-Khalil (L); the list of al-Shuhada cemetery (H), the list of al-Shuhada Cemetery – the mass grave (H'); the list of the Palestinian Red Crescent Society (PRCS) – Gaza Hospital (D); the list of the Palestinian Red Crescent Society – Akka Hospital (D'); the list of the Democratic Front for the Liberation of Palestine (DFLP) – (E); the list of the "anonymous" Palestinian organization (M); the list of Dar al-Fatwa (K); the list of the Committee for Families of the Kidnapped and Disappeared in Lebanon (CFKDL) – (N); the common list for the abducted and missing (J); the lists of the Lebanese Press: *Al-Safir* (F), *Al-Nida'* (F'), a list extracted from various newspapers (F"); the oral history list (O); the field study list (A); the list of the Official Commission of Inquiry into the Fate of those Abducted and Missing (P); the list for the lawsuit against Sharon to the Belgian judiciary (Q).

Appendix 3: Photographs

MYA SHONE

RAMZI HAYDAR

RAMZI HAYDAR

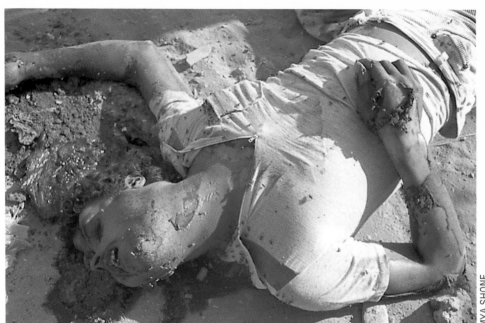

MYA SHONE

MYA SHONE

MYA SHONE

MYA SHONE

RAMZI HAYDAR

RYUICHI HIROKAWA

GÜNTHER ALTENBURG

GÜNTHER ALTENBURG

ALI HASAN SALMAN

ALI HASAN SALMAN

ALI HASAN SALMAN

RAMZI HAYDAR

MYA SHONE

RYUICHI HIROKAWA

RYUICHI HIROKAWA

MYA SHONE

GÜNTHER ALTENBURG

RAMZI HAYDAR

MYA SHONE

GÜNTHER ALTENBURG

GÜNTHER ALTENBURG

ALI HASAN SALMAN

RAMZI HAYDAR

GÜNTHER ALTENBURG

RAMZI HAYDAR

RYUICHI HIROKAWA

Hana' Wahbeh. See Accounts 10 and 46

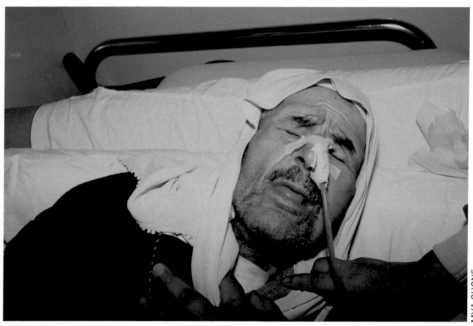

Hajj Abu Sulaiman. See Account 38

GÜNTHER ALTENBURG

RAMZI HAYDAR

The Israeli Command Centre
Franklin P. Lamb, *International Legal Responsibility for the Sabra-Shatila Massacre* (1983), p. 18.

General view of Sabra and Shatila taken from the roof of the Israeli Command Centre
Franklin P. Lamb, *International Legal Responsibility for the Sabra-Shatila Massacre* (1983), p. 18.

RAMZI HAYDAR

Appendix 4: Maps

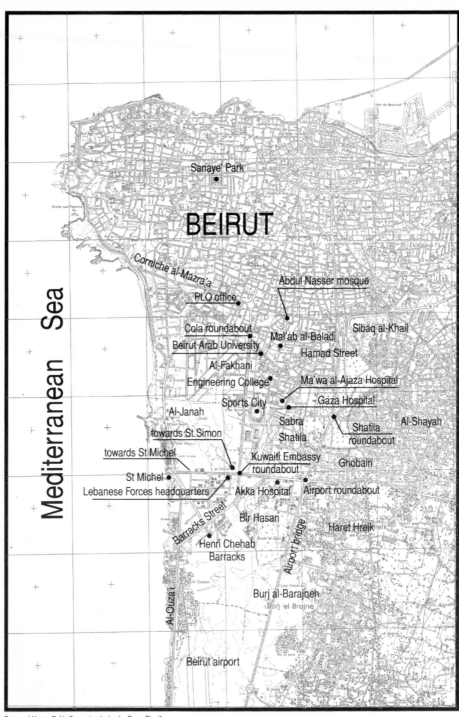

Map labels:
Sanaye' Park
BEIRUT
Corniche al-Mazra'a
Abdul Nasser mosque
PLO office
Mediterranean Sea
Cola roundabout
Mal'ab al-Baladi
Sibaq al-Khail
Beirut Arab University
Hamad Street
Al-Fakhani
Engineering College
Ma'wa al-Ajaza Hospital
Sports City
Gaza Hospital
Al-Janah
Sabra
Shatila
Al-Shayah
towards St.Simon
Shatila roundabout
towards St Michel
Kuwaiti Embassy roundabout
Ghobairi
St Michel
Lebanese Forces headquarters
Akka Hospital
Airport roundabout
Barracks Street
Bir Hasan
Airport bridge
Haret Hreik
Henri Chehab Barracks
Al-Ouzai
Burj al-Barajneh
Beirut airport

Prepared Hasan Bakir. Computer design by Omar Sharif.

Map 1   Sabra, Shatila and the surrounding districts

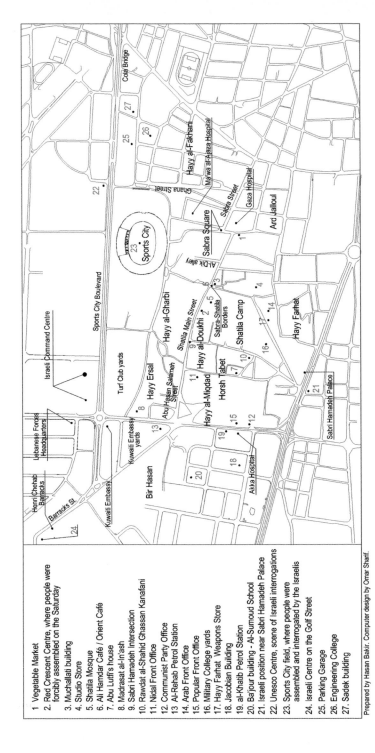

Map 2 Inner streets and landmarks

1 Vegetable Market
2 Red Crescent Centre, where people were forcibly assembled on the Saturday
3 Muchallati building
4 Studio Store
5 Shatila Mosque
6 Ali Hamdar Café / Orient Café
7 Abu Lutfi's house
8 Madrasat al-In'ash
9 Sabri Hamadeh Intersection
10 Rawdat al-Shahid Ghassan Kanafani
11 Nidal Front Office
12 Communist Party Office
13 Al-Rehab Petrol Station
14 Arab Front Office
15 Popular Front Office
16 Military College yards
17 Hayy Farhat Weapons Store
18 Jacobian Building
19 al-Khatib Petrol Station
20 Bajour building - Al-Sumoud School
21 Israeli position near Sabri Hamadeh Palace
22 Unesco Centre, scene of Israeli interrogations
23 Sports City field, where people were assembled and interrogated by the Israelis
24 Israeli Centre on the Golf Street
25 Parking Garage
26 Engineering College
27 Sadek building

Prepared by Hasan Bakir. Computer design by Omar Sharif.

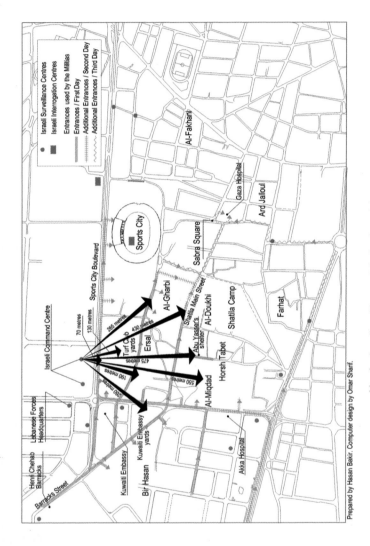

Map 3   Israeli positions and the borders of the massacre

Prepared by Hasan Bakir. Computer design by Omar Sharif.

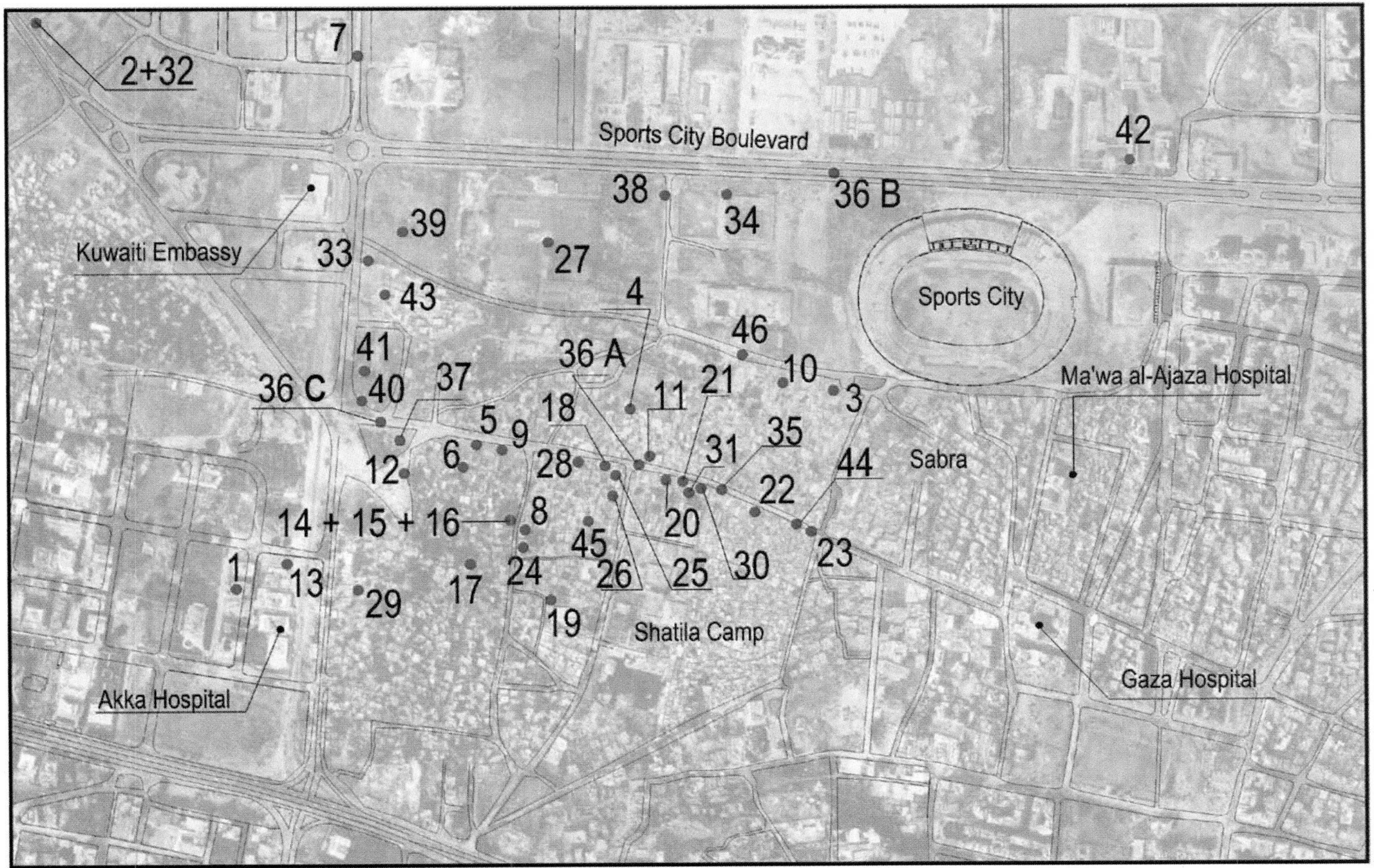

Map 4   Locations for quoted witness accounts (by account number)

Prepared by Hasan Bakir. Computer design by Omar Sharif.

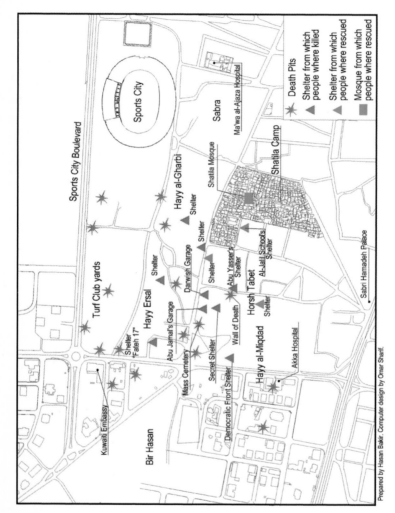

Map 5   Shelters and death pits

Prepared by Hasan Bakir. Computer design by Omar Sharif.

Bibliography

Primary unpublished sources

Testimonies
Abbreviations: Palestine Oral History (POH); Sabra and Shatila (S/Sh); Notes (N); Tape (T); mother [of] (Um); father [of] (Abu); Palestinian (Pal); Lebanese (Leb); Syrian (Syr).

Note: Full names of interviewees appear only with their consent. In fact just a minority chose this first option, the majority preferring not to be clearly identified in view of the strict security measures in force after the massacre. A second option was to supply the first name followed by the first initial of the family name; a third was to use the traditional form with 'Um' or 'Abu' combined with the name of the eldest son. In still other cases the initials of the original names are shown, while a very small number insisted on absolute anonymity.

With regard to women's names, some women supplied the family names of their husbands, while others preferred to retain their maiden names.

The frequent need to protect identity was the prime reason why relatively few details have been provided about interviewees. Where a pseudonym is used in the text, this is indicated in square brackets.

POH. S/SH. No. 1 (250/ N.1). 'Um Kamal' T. Interview with author, Beirut: author's home, 10 November 1982. (Pal. grandmother, born 1940, resident of S/Sh.)

POH. S/SH. No. 2 (232/ N.2). 'Um Zuheir' B. Interview with author, Beirut: author's home, 13 December 1982. (Pal. grandmother, born 1930?, resident of S/Sh.)

POH. S/SH. No. 3 (234/ N.3). Dib D. Interview with author, Beirut: author's home, 10 November 1982. (Leb. lawyer, born 1928, resident of Beirut.)

POH. S/SH. No. 4 (244/ N.4). Qader. N. Interview with author, Beirut: author's office, 23 December 1982. (Leb. witness, born 1960, resident of Beirut.)

POH. S/SH. No. 5 (241/ N.5). Adele Kh. Interview with author, Beirut: author's home, 9 January 1983. (Leb. writer, born 1930, resident of Aramoun.)

POH. S/SH. No. 6 (231/ T.1). Hana' Ahmad. Interview with author, Beirut: author's home,

15 January 1983. (Pal. teacher, born 1938, resident of Beirut.)

POH. S/SH. No. 7 (242/ T.2, 3). Abdul Rahman Labban. Interview with author, Beirut: narrator's home, 22 January 1983. (Leb. psychiatrist, Minister for Social Affairs, born 1924, resident of Beirut.)

POH. S/SH. No. 8 (249/ T.4). Mya Shone. Interview with author, Beirut: author's home, 27 January 1983. (American photographer.)

POH. S/SH. No. 9 (249/ T.5). Ralph Schoenman. Interview with author, Beirut: author's home, 27 January 1983. (American journalist.)

POH. S/SH. No. 10 (238/ T.6). Hakima S. Interview with author, Beirut: friend's home, 28 January 1982. (Iraqi doctor at the Palestinian Red Crescent, born 1930?, resident of Beirut.)

POH. S/SH. No. 11 (231/ T.7). K. A. Interview with author, Beirut: author's home, 29 January 1983. (Pal. witness, born 1964, resident of Beirut.)

POH. S/SH. No. 12 (240/ T.8). Nabil J. Interview with author, Beirut: 5 February 1983. (Pal. father, born 1927?, resident of Beirut.)

POH. S/SH. No. 13 (238/ T.9). Salim Hout. Interview with author, Beirut: narrator's office, 11 February 1983. (Leb. doctor at the Palestinian Red Crescent, born 1950, resident of Beirut.)

POH. S/SH. No. 14 (243/ T.10, 11, 12, 13). A. M. Interview with author, Beirut: author's home, 14 February 1983. (Pal. officer, born 1950?, resident of Beirut.)

POH. S/SH. No. 15 (256/ T.14). W. Z. Interview with author, Beirut: author's home, 15 February 1983. (Leb. administrative official, born 1950, resident of Beirut.)

POH. S/SH. No. 16 (248/ T.16, 17, 18). Hajj Mahmoud Rukn. Interview with author, Beirut: author's home, 16 February 1983. (Pal. skilled labourer, born 1930, resident of S/Sh.)

POH. S/SH. No. 17 (231/ T.21). Y. A. 'Um Ahmad' Srour. Interview with author, Beirut: author's home, 22 February 1983. (Pal. mother, born 1943, resident of S/Sh.)

POH. S/SH. No. 18 (238/ T.19, 20). D. M. H. 'Um Ali'. Interview with author, Beirut: author's home, 22 February 1983. (Leb. mother, born 1932, resident of S/Sh.)

POH. S/SH. No. 19 (249/ T.22). H. Sh. 'Um Akram'. Interview with author, Beirut: author's home, 24 February 1983. (Pal. mother, born 1940, resident of S/Sh. She was interviewed with her daughter, No. 20 below.)

POH. S/SH. No. 20 (249/ T.22). Dalal Sh. Interview with author, Beirut: author's home, 24 February 1983. (Young Pal. mother, born 1959, resident of S/Sh. She was interviewed with her mother, No. 19 above.)

POH. S/SH. No. 21 (241/ T.23). Khadija Khatib. Interview with author, Beirut: friend's home, 25 February 1983. (Pal. labourer, born 1947, resident of S/Sh.)

POH. S/SH. No. 22 (232/ T.24). Jumana B. Interview with author, Beirut: author's home, 27 February 1983. (Leb. student, born 1968, resident of S/Sh.)

POH. S/SH. No. 23 (238/ T.25). Samiha Abbas Hijazi. Interview with author, Beirut: author's home, 27 February 1983. (Leb. woman married to Pal., born 1943, resident of S/Sh.)

POH. S/SH. No. 24 (240/ T.26). Harbeh J. 'Um Rabi'. Interview by A. M., Beirut: massacre area, narrator's home, 28 February 1983. (Pal. nurse at Akka Hospital, born 1948, resident of S/Sh.)

POH. S/SH. No. 25 (230/ T.27). 'Abu Imad'. Interview by A. M., Beirut: massacre area, narrator's home, 1 March 1983. (Pal. freedom fighter, born [1950], resident of S/Sh.)

POH. S/SH. No. 26 (241/ T.28). Ahmad Khatib. Interview with author, Beirut: author's home, 1 March 1983. (Pal. student, born 1964, resident of S/Sh.)

POH. S/SH. No. 27 (231/ T.29). A. M. A. Interview by A. M., Beirut: massacre area, narrator's home, 2 March 1983. (Pal. witness, born 1955, resident of S/Sh.)

POH. S/SH. No. 28 (230/ T.29). Anonymous. Interview by A. M., Beirut: massacre area, friend's home, 2 March 1983. (Pal. witness, born 1957?, resident of S/Sh.)

POH. S/SH. No. 29 (241/ T.30). Nofa Khatib 'Um Wassim'. Interview with author, Beirut: massacre area, narrator's home, 3 March 1983. (Pal. mother, born 1945, resident of Bir Hasan. Interviewed with her father-in-law, No. 30 below.)

POH. S/SH. No. 30 (249/ T.30). Abdallah Sayyed. Interview with author. Beirut: massacre area, narrator's home, 3 March 1983. (Elderly Pal. guard, born 1922?, resident of Bir Hasan. Interviewed with his daughter-in-law, No. 29 above.)

POH. S/SH. No. 31 (231/ T.31). Ahmad A. Interview with author, Beirut: massacre area, outside talk along Shatila Main Street, 3 March 1983. (Leb. driver, born 1930, resident of Beirut.)

POH. S/SH. No. 32 (232/ T.31). Thunaya B. ['Amin']. Interview with author, Beirut: massacre area, narrator's home, 3 March 1983. (Pal. woman, born 1940, resident of S/Sh.)

POH. S/SH. No. 33 (231/ T.32). Amina A. 'Um Ibrahim'. Interview with author, Beirut: massacre area, friend's home, 3 March 1983. (Leb. woman married to Pal., resident of S/Sh.)

POH. S/SH. No. 34 (241/ T.33, 34). Aziza Khalidi. Interview with author, Beirut: author's home, 4 March 1983. (Pal./Leb. Director of Gaza Hospital, born 1953, resident of Beirut.)

POH. S/SH. No. 35 (238/ T.35). Nuzha H. Interview by A. M., Beirut: massacre area, narrator's home, 6 March 1983. (Pal. nurse at Akka Hospital, born 1966, resident of S/Sh.)

POH. S/SH. No. 36 (236/ T.36). Hamza F. Interview by A. M., Beirut: massacre area, narrator's home, 9 March 1983. (Young Leb. man, born 1967, resident of S/Sh. Interviewed with his sister, No. 37 below.)

POH. S/SH. No. 37 (236/ T.36). Randa F. Interview by A. M., Beirut: massacre area, narrator's home, 9 March 1983. (Young Leb. woman, born 1963, resident of S/Sh. Interviewed with her brother, No. 36 above.)

POH. S/SH. No. 38 (240/ T.37, 38). Ussama J. Interview with author, Beirut: narrator's home, 10 March 1983. (Leb. volunteer at Lebanese Red Cross, born 1962, resident of Beirut. Interviewed with colleague, No. 39 below.)

POH. S/SH. No. 39 (240/ T37, 38). Bilal J. Interview with author, Beirut: narrator's home, 10 March 1983. (Leb. volunteer at Lebanese Red Cross, born 1964, resident of Beirut. Interviewed with colleague, No. 38 above.)

POH. S/SH. No. 40 (240/ T.39). Moussa Kh. Interview with author, Beirut: massacre area, narrator's home, 14 March 1983. (Pal. employee, born 1948?, resident of S/Sh.)

POH. S/SH. No. 41 (249/ T.40). Munira M. Sayyed 'Um Ayman'. Interview with author, Beirut: massacre area, narrator's home, 14 March 1983. (Syr. woman married to Pal., born 1952?, resident of Bir Hasan.)

POH. S/SH. No. 42 (238/ T.41, 42). Nawal Husari. Interview with author, Beirut: author's home, 15 March 1983. (Pal. nurse at Gaza Hospital, born 1948, resident of S/Sh.)

POH. S/SH. No. 43 (249/ T.43). Brenda Smith. Interview with author, Beirut: author's home, 17 March 1983. (South African social worker with Palestinian refugees, born 1940?, resident of Beirut.)

POH. S/SH. No. 44 (231/ T.44, 45). 'Abu Jamal'. Interview with author, Beirut: outside talk along Shatila Main Street, 3 March 1983; Beirut: massacre area, 19 March 1983. (Pal. garage owner in Shatila, born 1932, resident of Beirut.)

POH. S/SH. No. 45 (231/ T.46). Harbeh A. ['Barakat'], Interview by A. M., Beirut: massacre area, narrator's home, 22 March 1983. (Pal. witness, born 1960, resident of Bir Hasan.)

POH. S/SH. No. 46 (234/ T.47). Sa'ida D. Interview by A. M., Beirut: massacre area, narrator's home, 22 March 1983. (Pal. worker at Akka Hospital, born 1964, resident of S/Sh.)

POH. S/SH. No. 47 (251/ T.48). 'Um Kamal'. Interview with author, Beirut: massacre area, narrator's home, 1 April 1983. (Leb. mother, born 1944, resident of S/Sh.)

POH. S/SH. No. 48 (231/ T.49). 'Um Muhammad' Aidi. Interview with author, Beirut: massacre area, narrator's home, 1 April 1983. (Pal. mother, born 1924, resident of S/Sh.)

POH. S/SH. No. 49 (238/ N.6). Ahmad H. Interview with author, Beirut: narrator's home, 2 April 1983. (Leb. witness, born 1932, resident of Beirut.)

POH. S/SH. No. 50 (231/ N.7). Afifa A. Interview by A. M., Beirut: massacre area, narrator's home, 5 April 1983. (Pal. worker, born 1956, resident of Fakhani.)

POH. S/SH. No. 51 (238/ N.8). Yusra N. H. Interview by A. M., Beirut: massacre area, narrator's home, 5 April 1983. (Pal. mother, born 1938, resident of S/Sh.)

POH. S/SH. No. 52 (249/ T.50, 51). Ann Sunde. Interview with author, Beirut: author's home, 6 April 1983. (Norwegian volunteer at Akka Hospital, born 1949.)

POH. S/SH. No. 53 (231/ T.52). 'Abu Qassem'. Interview with author, Beirut: friend's home, 28 April 1983. (Pal. employee at Ma'wa al-Ajaza Hospital, born 1943, resident of S/Sh.)

POH. S/SH. No. 54 (230/ T.53). Anonymous. Interview with author, Beirut: friend's home, 28 April 1983. (Pal. employee at Akka hospital, born 1963, resident of S/Sh.)

POH. S/SH. No. 55 (249/ T.54). Shawqi Sh. Interview with author, Beirut: author's home, 30 April 1983. (Syr. Civil Defence volunteer at United Front of Ras Beirut, born 1965, resident of Beirut. Interviewed with two colleagues, Nos 56 and 57 below.)

POH. S/SH. No. 56 (231/ T.54). Ziad A. Interview with author, Beirut: author's home, 30 April 1983. (Leb. Civil Defence volunteer at United Front of Ras Beirut, born 1964, resident of Beirut. Interviewed with two colleagues, No. 55 above and No. 57 below.)

POH. S/SH. No. 57 (248/ T.54). Nabil R. Interview with author, Beirut: author's home, 30 April

1983. (Leb. Civil Defence volunteer at United Front of Ras Beirut, born 1966, resident of Beirut. Interviewed with two colleagues, Nos 55 and 56 above.)

POH. S/SH. No. 58 (231/ N.9). Muhammad Awwad. Interview with author, Beirut: author's home, 2 May 1983. (Pal. cameraman, born 1950?, resident of Beirut.)

POH. S/SH. No. 59 (234/ T.55, 56). Hind D. Interview with author, Beirut: massacre area, narrator's home, 3 May 1983. (Leb. mother, born 1948, resident of S/Sh.)

POH. S/SH. No. 60 (234/ T.57). Amaal al-Dirawi. Interview with author, Beirut: author's home, 4 May 1983. (Pal. mother, born 1963, resident of Bir Hasan.)

POH. S/SH. No. 61 (243/ T.58). Munir Muhammad. Interview with author, Beirut: friend's home, 4 May 1983. (Pal. boy, born 1970, resident of S/Sh.)

POH. S/SH. No. 62 (232/ T.59). 'Um Majed' Balqis. Interview with author, Beirut: friend's home, 5 May 1983. (Pal. mother, born 1925, resident of S/Sh.)

POH. S/SH. No. 63 (232/ T.60, 61). Siham Balqis. Interview with author, Beirut: massacre area, 9 May 1983. (Pal. social activist, born 1954, resident of S/Sh.)

POH. S/SH. No. 64 (243/ T.62). Paul Morris. Interview with author, Beirut: friend's home, 17 May 1983. (British volunteer doctor at Gaza Hospital, born 1955?)

POH. S/SH. No. 65 (241/ N.10). Aisha K. Interview by Siham Balqis, Beirut: massacre area, narrator's home, 24 May 1983. (Pal. mother, born 1938, resident of S/Sh.)

POH. S/SH. No. 66 (249/ N.11). Mahmoud S. ['Yafawi']. Interview by Siham Balqis, Beirut: massacre area, narrator's home, 24 May 1983. Shatila camp, 16 May 1983. (Elderly Pal. refugee, born 1912, resident of S/Sh.)

POH. S/SH. No. 67 (231/ N.12). Mariam Abu Harb. Interview by Siham Balqis, Beirut: massacre area, narrator's home, 24 May 1983. (Pal. mother, born 1948, resident of S/Sh.)

POH. S/SH. No. 68 (256/ N.13). T. Z. Interview with author, Beirut: narrator's office, 30 May 1983. (Leb. government employee, born 1930?, resident of Beirut.)

POH. S/SH. No. 69 (231/ T.63). Shahira Abu Rudaineh. Interview by Siham Balqis, Beirut: massacre area, narrator's home, 30 May 1983. (Pal. mother, born 1959, resident of S/Sh.)

POH. S/SH. No. 70 (243/ T.64). 'Um Ghazi' Madi. Interview by Siham Balqis, Beirut: massacre area, narrator's home, 30 May 1983. (Pal. mother, born 1940, resident of S/Sh.)

POH. S/SH. No. 71 (231/ T.65). Ibrahim A. Interview by Muna Sukkarieh, Beirut: narrator's office, June 1983. (Leb. Civil Defence volunteer at Kashafat al-Risala al-Islamiyieh, born 1958, resident of Beirut, interviewed with colleague, No. 72 below.)

POH. S/SH. No. 72 (253/ T.65). Ali W. Interview by Muna Sukkarieh, Beirut: narrator's office, June 1983. (Leb. Civil Defence volunteer at Kashafat Al-Risala al-Islamiyieh, born 1962, resident of Beirut. Interviewed with colleague, No. 71 above.)

POH. S/SH. No. 73 (238/ T.66). Hasan H. ['Hamzawi']. Interview by Muna Sukkarieh, Beirut: narrator's office, June 1983. (Leb. Civil Defence volunteer at Kashaf Al-Tarbiya al-Wataniyieh, born 1960, resident of Beirut. Interviewed with colleague, No. 74 below.)

POH. S/SH. No. 74 (231/ T.66). Hasan A. Interview by Muna Sukkarieh, Beirut: narrator's office, June 1983. (Leb. Civil Defence volunteer at Kashaf Al-Tarbiya al-Wataniyieh, born 1964, resident of Beirut. Interviewed with colleague, No. 73 above.)

POH. S/SH. No. 75 (242/ T.67). Nuhad L. ['Israwi']. Interview by Muna Sukkarieh, Beirut: narrator's office, June 1983. (Leb. volunteer at Civil Defence of Al-Makased al-Islamiyieh, born 1957?, resident of Beirut.)

POH. S/SH. No. 76 (238/ T.68). Wafiq H. Interview by Muna Sukkarieh, Beirut: narrator's office, June 1983. (Leb. volunteer at Civil Defence of Al-Makased al-Islamiyieh, born 1957, resident of Beirut. Interviewed with colleague, No. 77 below.)

POH. S/SH. No. 77 (237/ T.68). Marwan Gh. Interview by Muna Sukkarieh, Beirut: narrator's office, June 1983. (Leb. volunteer at Civil Defence of Al-Makased al-Islamiyieh, born 1962, resident of Beirut. Interviewed with colleague, No. 76 above.)

POH. S/SH. No. 78 (231/ T.69). Fayez A. Interview by Muna Sukkarieh, Beirut: narrator's office, June 1983. (Leb. Civil Defence volunteer at United Front of Ras Beirut, born 1961, resident of Beirut. Interviewed with two colleagues, Nos 79 and 80 below.)

POH. S/SH. No. 79 (238/ T.69). Ghassan H. Interview by Muna Sukkarieh, Beirut: narrator's office, June 1983. (Leb. Civil Defence volunteer at United Front of Ras Beirut, born 1960?, resident of Beirut. Interviewed with two colleagues, No. 78 above and No. 80 below.)

POH. S/SH. No. 80 (239/ T.69). Mazen I. Interview by Muna Sukkarieh, Beirut: narrator's office, June 1983. (Leb. Civil Defence volunteer at United Front of Ras Beirut, born 1962,
resident of Beirut. Interviewed with two colleagues, Nos 78 and 79 above.)

POH. S/SH. No. 81 (244/ T.70). Ziad N. ['Madani']. Interview by Muna Sukkarieh, Beirut: narrator's office, June 1983. (Leb. Civil Defence volunteer at Union of Al-Shabiba al-Islamiyieh, born 1961, resident of Beirut.)

POH. S/SH. No. 82 (244/ T.71). Imad T. Interview by Muna Sukkarieh, Beirut: narrator's office, June 1983. (Leb. Civil Defence volunteer at Organization of Al-Iss'af al-Sha'bi, born 1960, resident of Beirut.)

POH. S/SH. No. 83 (249/ T.72). Wijdan S. Interview by Muna Sukkarieh, Beirut: narrator's office, June 1983. (Leb. volunteer at Lebanese Red Cross, born 1957?, resident of Beirut.)

POH. S/SH. No. 84 (249/ T.73). Diala I. Interview by Muna Sukkarieh, Beirut: narrator's office, June 1983. (Leb. volunteer at Lebanese Red Cross, born 1964?, resident of Beirut. Interviewed with colleague, No. 85 below.)

POH. S/SH. No. 85 (249/ T.73). Jamil B. Interview by Muna Sukkarieh, Beirut: narrator's office, June 1983. (Leb. volunteer at Lebanese Red Cross, born 1965?, resident of Beirut. Interviewed with colleague, No. 84 above.)

POH. S/SH. No. 86 (231/ T.74). Tony A. ['Jamil']. Interview by Muna Sukkarieh, Beirut: narrator's office, June 1983. (Leb. volunteer at Lebanese Red Cross, born 1965?, resident of Beirut. Interviewed with colleagues, Nos 87 and 88 below.)

POH. S/SH. No. 87 (240/ T.74). Bassel J. Interview by Muna Sukkarieh, Beirut: narrator's office, June 1983. (Leb. volunteer at Lebanese Red Cross, born 1965?, resident of Beirut. Interviewed with colleagues, No. 86 above and No. 88 below.)

POH. S/SH. No. 88 (236/ T.74). Malek F. Interview by Muna Sukkarieh, Beirut: narrator's office, June 1983. (Leb. volunteer at Lebanese Red Cross, born 1965?, resident of Beirut. Interviewed with colleagues, Nos 86 and 87 above.)

POH. S/SH. No. 89 (231/ T.75). Sadeq A. Interview by Siham Balqis, Beirut: massacre area, narrator's home, June 1983. (Pal. labourer, born 1966, resident of Bir Hasan.)

POH. S/SH. No. 90 (241/ N.14). Shaykh Salman al-Khalil. Interview by Muna Sukkarieh, Beirut: narrator's home, June 1983. (Leb. religious figure, born 1930?, resident of Beirut.)

POH. S/SH. No. 91 (244/ T.76). Aadel N. Interview with author, Beirut: narrator's office, 11 July 1983. (Leb. witness, born 1925, resident of Beirut.)

POH. S/SH. No. 92 (231/ T.77). Issam S. Interview with author, Beirut: author's home, 11 July 1983. (Pal. politician, born 1930?, visitor.)

POH. S/SH. No. 93 (231/ N.15). A. A. Interview by Q. D., Beirut: massacre area, narrator's home, 14 July 1983. (Pal. witness, born 1940?, resident of S/Sh.)

POH. S/SH. No. 94 (238/ N.16). M. H. Interview with author, Beirut: author's home, 21 July 1983. (Pal. witness, born 1948, resident of S/Sh.)

POH. S/SH. No. 95 (234/ N.17). Charles L. D. Interview with author, Beirut: author's home, August 1983. (French officer of multinational forces, born 1958.)

POH. S/SH. No. 96 (251/ N.18). 'Um Sulaiman'. Interview with author, Beirut: massacre area, friend's home, 3 August 1983. (Pal. woman, born 1937, resident of Burj al-Barajneh.)

POH. S/SH. No. 97 (231/ T.78). Michael Ghurayeb. Interview with author, Beirut: author's home, 11 August 1983. (Leb. professor, born 1932, resident of Beirut.)

POH. S/SH. No. 98 (251/ T.79). 'Um Isma'il'. Interview with author, Beirut: friend's home, 1 September 1983. (Pal. woman, born 1925, resident of Burj al-Barajneh.)

POH. S/SH. No. 99 (234/ T.80). Mustafa Dabbagh. Interview with author, Beirut: author's home, 5 September 1983. (Pal. historian, born 1897, resident of Beirut.)

POH. S/SH. No. 100 (230/ N.19). Anonymous. Interview with author, Beirut: friend's home, 1 December 1983. (Leb. witness, born 1947, resident of Beirut.)

POH. S/SH. No. 101 (256/ N.20). M. Z. Interview with author, Beirut: author's home, 2 December 1983. (Leb. officer, born 1953?, resident of Beirut.)

POH. S/SH. No. 102 (241/ T.81). Kh. Interview with author, Beirut: author's home, 9 January 1984. (Pal. witness, born 1952, resident of Beirut.)

POH. S/SH. No. 103 (234/ N.21). Q. D. Interview with author, Beirut: author's home, 1 March 1984. (Pal. freedom fighter, born 1954, resident of Beirut.)

POH. S/SH. No. 104 (232/ T.82). 'Um Ali' B. Interview with author, Beirut: author's home, 6 March 1984. (Leb. witness, born 1932, resident of S/Sh.)

POH. S/SH. No. 105 (243/ T.83). Muhammad. Interview with author, Beirut: friend's home, 7 March 1984. (Pal. witness, born 1965?, resident of Beirut. Interviewed with Nos 106 and 107 below.)

POH. S/SH. No. 106 (243/ T.83). Mahmoud M. Interview with author, Beirut: friend's home, 7 March 1984. (Pal. witness, born 1964?, resident of Beirut. Interviewed with No. 105 above and No. 107 below.)

POH. S/SH. No. 107 (231/ T.83). Muhammad N. Interview with author, Beirut: friend's home, 7 March 1984. (Pal. witness, born 1964?, resident of Beirut. Interviewed with Nos 105 and 106 above.)

POH. S/SH. No. 108 (249/ T.84). Zainab Saqallah. Interview with author, Beirut: narrator's home, 7 March 1984. (Pal. witness, born 1930, resident of Beirut.)

POH. S/SH. No. 109 (238/ T.85). Faidi H. Interview with author, Beirut: narrator's office, 11 March 1984. (Leb. media man, born 1942, resident of Beirut.)

POH. S/SH. No. 110 (231/ T.86). Hasan A. 'Abu Ali'. Interview with author, Beirut: narrator's office, 11 May 1984. (Pal. contractor, born 1944, resident of Beirut.)

POH. S/SH. No. 111 (243/ T.87). As'ad M. Interview with author, Beirut: narrator's office, 11 May 1984. (Pal. employee at Gaza Hospital, born 1952, resident of S/Sh.)

POH. S/SH. No. 112 (241/ T.88). Intissar Khalil. 'Um Nabil'. Interview with author, Beirut: massacre area, narrator's home, 3 June 1984. (Pal. mother, born 1960, resident of S/Sh.)

POH. S/SH. No. 113 (241/ N.22). M. Kh. Interview with author, Beirut: narrator's office, 5 June 1984. (Pal. doctor at Akka Hospital, born 1948, resident of Burj al-Barajneh.)

POH. S/SH. No. 114 (241/ N.23). Khalil ['Izziddine']. Interview by Q. D., Beirut: al-Shuhada Cemetery, 8 July 1984. (Leb. guard, born 1930?, resident of Beirut.)

POH. S/SH. No. 115 (231/ T.89). Fatima Ajami. Interview with author, Beirut: massacre area, narrator's home, 13 July 1984. (Leb. witness, born 1963, resident of S/Sh. Her father, Hajj 'Abu Ali' Ajami, was interviewed with her.)

POH. S/SH. No. 116 (239/ T.90). ['Ibrahim Baroudi']. Interview by Q. D., Beirut: massacre area, narrator's home, August 1984. (Pal. freedom fighter, born 1952, resident of S/Sh.)

POH. S/SH. No. 117 (230/ T.91). Anonymous. Interview by Q. D., Beirut: massacre area, narrator's home, August 1984. (Pal. woman, born 1947, resident of S/Sh. Interviewed with No. 118 below.)

POH. S/SH. No. 118 (230/ T.91). Anonymous. Interview by Q. D., Beirut: massacre area, narrator's home, August 1984. (Pal. woman, born 1945, resident of S/Sh. Interviewed with No. 117 above.)

POH. S/SH. No. 119 (238/ N.24). Amir H. Interview with author, Beirut: massacre area, Gaza Hospital, 22 October 1984. (Leb. doctor at Gaza Hospital, born 1948, resident of Beirut.)

POH. S/SH. No. 120 (247/ N.25). I. Q. Interview with author, Beirut: author's home, August 1986. (Leb. officer, born 1959, resident of Beirut.)

POH. S/SH. No. 121 (231/ T.92). 'Abu Muhammad' Ali. Interview with author, Beirut: narrator's office, 15 November 1998. (Pal. witness, born 1964, resident of Beirut.)

POH. S/SH. No. 122 (231/ T.93). 'Abu Khalil' Mahmoud. Interview with author, Beirut: author's home, 22 November 1998. (Pal. witness, born 1962, resident of Beirut.)

POH. S/SH. No. 123 (235/ N.26). Huda H. Interview with author, Beirut: narrator's home, 2 December 1998. (Pal. teacher, born 1939, resident of Beirut.)

POH. S/SH. No. 124 (232/ T.94). Hajj Hasan Bakir. Interview with author, Beirut: author's home, 24 November 1998. (Pal. researcher, 1952, resident of Beirut.)

POH. S/SH. No. 125 (243/ T.95). 'Ma'moun Mukahhal. Interview with author, Beirut: author's home, 19 April 1999. (Leb. Civil Defence volunteer, born 1960, resident of Beirut.)

POH. S/SH. No. 126 (243/ T.96). Hajj Maysam. Interview with author, Beirut: author's home, 17 August 1999. (Leb. Civil Defence volunteer at Scouts of Al-Risala al-Islamiyieh, born 1963, resident of Beirut.)

POH. S/SH. No. 127 (239/ T.97). Ibrahim Iraqi. Interview with author, Beirut: author's home, 11 September 1999. (Pal. employee at Palestinian Red Crescent Society, born 1962, resident of Beirut.)

POH. S/SH. No. 128 (245/ T.98). Khaled Abadi. Interview with author, Beirut: author's home. (Pal. witness, born 1964, resident of Beirut.)

POH. S/SH. No. 129 (238/ T.99). Hajj 'Abu Hisham'. Interview by Khaled Abadi, Beirut: Shatila, narrator's home, 15 September 1999. (Pal. freedom fighter, born 1932, resident of S/Sh.)

POH. S/SH. No. 130 (231/ T.100). 'Abu Ra'ed'. Interview by Khaled Abadi, Beirut: Shatila, narrator's home, 29 September 1999. (Leb. freedom fighter, born 1952, resident of S/Sh.)

POH. S/SH. No. 131 (231/ T.101). 'Abu Imad'. Interview by Khaled Abadi, Beirut: narrator's home, 6 October 1999. (Pal. freedom fighter, born 1951, resident of S/Sh.)

POH. S/SH. No. 132 (237/ T.102, 103). 'Um Ali'. Interview with author, Beirut: author's home, 14 October 1999. (Leb. witness, born 1932, resident of S/Sh.)

POH. S/SH. No. 133 (249/ T.104). Riadh Sharqieh. Interview with author, Beirut: Shatila, narrator's home, 21 October 1999. (Pal. witness, born 1942, resident of S/Sh.)

POH. S/SH. No. 134 (243/ T.105). Munir Muhammad. Interview with author, Beirut: narrator's home, September 2000. (Young Pal. man, born 1970, resident of Washington DC.) This interview was his second (see No. 61 above).

POH. S/SH. No. 135 (243/ T.106). Ali Murad. Interview by Khaled Abadi, Beirut: narrator's home, November 2000. (Pal. witness, born 1964, resident of Fakhani.)

POH. S/SH. No. 136 (231/ T.107). Hajj 'Abu Ahmad'. Interview by Sana' Hammoudeh, Beirut: Shatila, narrator's home, 2 March 2001. (Pal. contractor, born 1932, resident of S/Sh.)

POH. S/SH. No. 137 (231/ T.108). Hajj 'Abu Khodr'. Interview by Sana' Hammoudeh, Beirut: Shatila, narrator's home, 2 March 2001. (Pal. contractor, born 1934, resident of S/Sh.)

POH. S/SH. No. 138 (234/ T.109). Mu'allem Dib. Interview by Sana' Hammoudeh, Beirut: Shatila, narrator's home, 2 March 2001. (Pal. contractor, born 1937, resident of S/Sh.)

POH. S/SH. No. 139 (243/ T.110). Muhammad. Interview by Sana' Hammoudeh, Beirut: Shatila, narrator's home, 2 March 2001. (Young Pal. man, born 1970, resident of S/Sh.)

POH. S/SH. No. 140 (243/ T.111). Ahmad M. Interview by Sana' Hammoudeh, Beirut: Shatila, narrator's home, 2 March 2001. (Pal. electrician, born 1956, resident of S/Sh.)

The archive

Record of the Sabra and Shatila Field Study. Supervised by Bayan Nuwayhed al-Hout, Spring, 1984. (The record comprises 430 and 100 questionnaires for victims and abducted respectively, based on data provided by the families of victims and those abducted, and on that provided by other Sabra and Shatila residents.)

Record of the Sabra and Shatila Field Study (Supplement). Phase 2: 'The Fate of those Abducted'. Supervised by Bayan Nuwayhed al-Hout, 1998–99.

Documents

Al-Khalil, Shaykh Salman. 'List of Names of Victims and Missing in the Sabra and Shatila Massacre', 1982. (Photocopy of hand written document.) [Arabic]

Al-Shuhada cemetery. 'Names of the Sabra and Shatila Martyrs – al-Shuhada cemetery', September 1982. (The names were collected from names written on the graves, with the help of Shaykh Abu Fathi, who was in charge of the cemetery. He added from his notebook, the names of victims buried in a mass grave known as the 'French *khishkasha*' (a mass grave, usually war-related), summer 1984.) [Arabic]

'Anonymous' Palestinian organization 'List of Names of Massacre Victims and Those Abducted During the Massacre', 1983. (Photocopy of handwritten document.) [Arabic]

Committee for Families of the Kidnapped and Disappeared in Lebanon. 'List of Names of the Abducted and Missing in Lebanon', 1975–1983. (Photocopy of a typed document including names of those abducted and missing in Lebanon since the mid-1970s.) [Arabic]

Dar al-Fatwa, Lebanese Republic. 'Names of Abducted and Missing, Lebanese, Palestinian and Stateless', Beirut, 1982–1983. (Photocopy of a typed record, organized by Dar al-Fatwa in co-operation with the Committee of Families of the Kidnapped and Disappeared in Lebanon and the General Union of Palestinian Woman.) [Arabic]

Dar al-Fatwa, Lebanese Republic. 'List of Names of Victims Killed or Abducted during the Sabra and Shatila Massacre', 1982–1984. (Photocopy of a typed document, with attached letter from the Director of Ifta' Affairs, Hussein al-Quwatli, to the Director of the Palestine Liberation Organization bureaux in Lebanon, Shafiq al-Hout. Beirut, 16 May 1984.) [Arabic]

Death certificates: Four samples (photocopies of typed documents). [Arabic]: International Committee of the Red Cross, Lebanon Delegation. (Death certificate) for Ikram Hussein Hamad al-Beka'i. Beirut, 8 December 1982. [Text in both Arabic and French]

Palestinian Red Crescent Society (PRCS). (Death certificate) for Ali Hussein al-Khatib and nine other members of his family. Beirut, 27 November 1982.

Palestinian Red Crescent Society (PRCS), Gaza Surgical Hospital. (Death certificate) for Rabi' Hussein al-Beka'i. Beirut, 15 January 1983.

Scouts of Al-Risala al-Islamiyieh, Command of the Civil Defence of the Islamic Upper Legislation Council, Commissariat of Beirut at al-Shayyah. (Death certificate) for Hussein al-Beka'i and seven other members of his family, 21 September 1982.

Democratic Front for the Liberation of Palestine (DFLP). 'List of Names of Victims and Abducted in the Sabra and Shatila Massacre', 1982–1983. (Photocopy of handwritten document.) [Arabic]

International Committee of the Red Cross (ICRC). 'Liste des corps identifiés au Camp Chatila entre le 19. 09. 82 et le 22. 09. Après le massacre du 16/17. 09. 82.' (Photocopy of typed document.)

International Committee of the Red Cross (ICRC). 'Massacre in Beirut: ICRC Reacts Strongly', Press Release No. 1450, Geneva: ICRC Information Department, 18 September 1982.

Lebanese Republic, Ministry of Interior, Department of Civil Defence. 'Bodies Removed from the Sabra and Shatila Camps from 18/9/1982 to Thursday 30/9/1982'. (Signed by the Director of Civil Defence, Nazih Cham'oun.) 15 October 1982. (Photocopy of typed certified copy.) [Arabic]

Lebanese Republic, Prime Ministry, Official Commission of Inquiry into the Fate of the Abducted and Missing. 'Data Based on Families' Applications', 1999. (Photocopy of typed record including the names of those abducted and missing from the beginning of the civil wars in the mid-1970s up to the 1990s.) [Arabic]

Mallat, Chibli, Luc Walleyn and Michaël Verhaeghe. 'The Lawsuit Made by a Number of the Sabra and Shatila Massacre Survivors Against Sharon and Other Parties Responsible for the Sabra and Shatila massacre of 1982 to the Belgian Judiciary', Brussels, 18 June 2001. (Photocopy of typed document including names of victims and those abducted, based on the testimonies of their family members, the plaintiffs.)

'Mary'. 'Testimonies on Sabra and Shatila Massacre', Beirut, 1983 (manuscript). (Photocopy of 13 handwritten testimonies.)

Middle East Council of Churches. 'List of Names of Sabra and Shatila Victims', 1982. (Photocopy of document typed in French.)

Palestine Oral History: Sabra and Shatila (POH. S/SH). 'List of Names of Victims and Abducted'. Supervised by Bayan Nuwayhed al-Hout, 1982–1984. (The list was based on interviews with the residents and witnesses.) [Arabic]

Palestinian Red Crescent Society (PRCS), Akka Hospital. 'Statement of the Names of Those Killed as Martyrs or Missing at the Akka Hospital and the Adjacent al-Khatib Petrol Station', 1983. (Photocopy of handwritten document.) [Arabic]

Palestinian Red Crescent Society (PRCS), Gaza Complex. 'Statement of the Number of Martyrs of the Sabra and Shatila Massacre', 7 April 1983. (Photocopy of typed document.) [Arabic]

Rawdat al-Shahidein Cemetery. 'Names of Sabra and Shatila Martyrs – Rawdat al-Shahidein cemetery', September 1982. (Photocopy of handwritten document by Shaykh Salman al-Khalil, who uttered formal prayers and supervised the burial of victims.) [Arabic]

Record of the Sabra and Shatila Field Study. 'List of Names of Victims and Abducted'. Supervised by Bayan Nuwayhed al-Hout. 1984. (The list was based on the questionnaires distributed by the field study team to the families of the victims and abducted.) [Arabic]

'The Second Annual Memorial of the Miqdad Martyrs During the Sabra-Shatila Massacre of September 16, 1982.' Husseiniyiat Rawdat al-Shahidein, 16 September 1984. (Circular including photographs and names of al-Miqdad victims.) [Arabic]

Private diaries

Abu Shawqi, 'From the Diaries of the Israeli Invasion – Beirut, 1982', Beirut, December 2000. (Manuscript extracted from the invasion diaries.) [Arabic]

Al-Khalil, Shaykh Salman, 'Diaries', Beirut', 1982. (Manuscript produced during the Israeli invasion, particularly at the stage of the burial of Sabra and Shatila victims.) [Arabic]

B. Hussein, 'Memoirs', 1999. (Manuscript dealing with the Israeli siege and fighting against the Israeli Army.) [Arabic]

Audio-visual testimonies

Photographs/reports/television news

Abu Dhabi Television, Emirates News Agency. Excerpts from the official Television News, and reports of Abu Dhabi Mission to Lebanon, 1982. Four videotapes. [Arabic]

BBC News. Parts of the BBC News during the Israeli invasion and the aftermath of the massacre. Eleven videotapes.

Nordic Commission (supervisor). International Hearing in Oslo. Five videotapes. Oslo: 30–31 October 1982. (Eye-witness testified on nine matters in connection with the Israeli invasion of Lebanon. The massacre is on videotape no. 4. Testimonies were given by journalists and photographers who were among the first to enter the Palestinian camps after the massacre, and by foreign medical staff working at the Akka and Gaza Hospitals during the massacre.)

Schoenman, Ralph and Mya Shone. Collection of slides on Sabra and Shatila. (This collection was assembled in the course of four days following the massacre.) Beirut, 18, 19, 20, 22 September 1982.

Visnews. 'Special: Selected News During the Israeli Invasion in 1982 and the Massacre'. Five videotapes. (No comments or dialogues; simply motion pictures, original sounds, explosions, screams and protests.)

Television films and programmes

Several of the broadcasts listed below were passed on to me by friends outside Lebanon who had videotaped them in their homes, and so full details were not always available.

ABC News. *Oh Tell the World What Happened.* 7 January 1983. Presented by Bill Redeker. One videotape (60 minutes).

ADC. *Report from Beirut: Summer of '82.* Narrated by James Abu Rizk.

BBC. *Q.E.D.* 'Before the Massacre', 1982. Film cameraman John Cray. Research Sana Issa. Producer Christopher Sykes. (This film was made in the Sabra and Shatila district, West Beirut, 5–13 September 1982.)

BBC. *Panorama.* 'Fighting For Survival', 1982. Presented by Richard Lindley. Reported by David Sells. Film cameraman Alan Stevens.

BBC. *Panorama.* 'Israel: The Wasted War?', 1985. Reported by Peter Taylor. Film cameraman Bill Broomfield and Jacob Sapporta. Produced by David Wickham.

BBC. *Panorama.* 'The Accused'. Produced by Aidan Laverty. Edited by Mike Robinson. 2001.

Blutiger Sommer: Wiedersehen mit Beirut. Film by Ulrich Kienzle. Cameraman Peter C.I. (German production.)

Danish cameraman *et al.* Video on the massacre, 1982. (This celebrated videotape on the massacre was the production of several cameramen, among them a Dane whose nationality people remembered well but whose name they had forgotten. It became popularly known as the 'Danish video', after being collected by an anonymous person.)

Danish television group. *tv – aktuelt: daglog fra Beirut.* 24 September 1982.

Future Television. *Red Handed,* 2002. (A series of documented episodes.) [Arabic]

Ist der Libanon noch zu retten? Report by Patrick Lecerq. (German production.)

Kreuz und Zeder. Report by Gerhard Konzelmann. Cameraman Abdel Majid Kassir. Sound Abdel Latif Adnani. Edited by Heinrich Butgen. (German production.)

NRK (Norwegian Broadcasting Corporation). *Horror Days in Beirut.* September 1982. Cameramen Suheil Rashid, Muhammad Awwad *et al.* Collected from various sources.

Masri, Mai. *Children of Shatila*. Executive producer Jean Shamoun. Beirut: Nour Productions, 1998.

Norwegian Television. Location special for Norwegian Television. *Constructions in Sabra and Shatila*. 1984.

SBS TV/BBC. *Timewatch*. 'See No Evil: The Sabra and Shatila Massacres'. Producer Steven Walker, 1993.

United Arab Emirates Television, Abu Dhabi. *War of June 6, 1982*, 1982. Hosted by Ali Ubaid. Directed by Ibrahim al-Abbasi. Two video-tapes. [Arabic]

Published sources

Documents/testimonies/photographs

Abasi, Amal (research) and Muhammad El-Farra (summing up). *Children of Palestine: Eyewitness Evidence of International Photographers*. Introduction by Lord Caradoin. London and New York: W. and P. Morris International Ltd, 1983.

Aksoy, Mehmet, and others, ... *eine Woche im September*, Vienna: Hilger E., 1983.

Al-Nida'. 'Applications Comprised 600 Names in Two Days', 1 December 1982. (The report included a list of the names of those missing from the mid-1970s up to 1982.) [Arabic]

Al-Safir. 'The Names of 110 People Abducted During the Massacres at the Sabra and Shatila Camps', 15 October 1982. [Arabic]

Association Internationale des Juristes Démocrates. *Livre blanc sur l'agression israélienne au Liban: Association Internationale des Juristes Démocrates. Union des Juristes Palestiniens*, Paris Editions Publisud, 1983. (On 23 and 24 October 1982, the Association Internationale des Juristes Démocrates organized an international legal conference in Brussels entitled 'Les événements du Liban, leurs prémisses at leurs suites au regard du droit international'.)

Fédération Mondiale de la Jeunesse Démocratique (FMJD). *La guerre israélienne de génocide: 1982: La tragédie des peuples libanais et palestinien*, Vienna: FMJD 1982.

Hammad, Mazen (ed.). *Al-Mathbaha – Sabra wa Shatila wa hissar Bairut: Youniou – September 1982* [The Massacre – Sabra and Shatila and the Siege of Beirut: June–September 1982], technical supervision by Tal'at Youssef, n.p.: Taher al-Firkh, April 1983. [Arabic]

Henly, David *et al.* (eds). *Witness of War Crimes in Lebanon: Testimony Given to the Nordic Commission, Oslo, October 1982*, London: International Organization for the Elimination of all Forms of Racial Discrimination (EAFORD), Ithaca Press, 1983.

Hirokawa, Ryuichi (ed. and photographer). *Beirut 1982: From the Israeli Invasion to the Massacre of Sabra and Shatila Camps*. Additional photographs by Hiromi Nagakura, Damascus: PLO Central Council's Ad Hoc Committee on Sabra and Shatila, December 1982.

Institute of Palestine Studies. 'Document, chronologie, revue de la presse', *Revue d'études palestiniennes*, 5, 6, Autumn 1982, Winter 1983, pp. 73–395, 131–272.

Institute of Palestine Studies, 'Documents and Source Material: Documents on Palestine and the Arab-Israeli Conflict', *Journal of Palestine Studies*, Nos 44/45, 46, Summer/Fall 1982, Winter 1983, pp. 292–349, 109–236.

International Commission of Inquiry into Israeli Crimes Against the Lebanese and Palestinian Peoples. *Israel 'Peace Operation in Galilee': Eye-witness Reports and Conclusions of an International Inquiry*, Nicosia: International Commission of Inquiry into Israeli Crimes Against the Lebanese and Palestinian Peoples, Medical Sub-Committee, November 1982. (The Commission held its first meeting in Cyprus on 15–16 August 1982.)

International Commission of Inquiry into Israeli Crimes Against the Lebanese and Palestinian Peoples. *Israeli Practices Against the Lebanese and Palestinian Peoples: Eye-witness Reports and Conclusions of an International Inquiry*, London: International Commission of Inquiry Into Israeli Crimes Against the Lebanese and Palestinian Peoples, 1982.

International Committee of the Red Cross (ICRC). *Annual Report 1982*, Geneva: ICRC, 1983.

International Committee of the Red Cross (ICRC). 'Massacre in Beirut: ICRC Reacts Strongly', Press Release No. 1450, Geneva: ICRC, Information department, 18 September 1982.

Kahan Commission. *The Beirut Massacre: The Complete Kahan Comission Report*. Introduction by Abba Eban. New York: Kartz-Cohl Publishing, 1983 (authorized translation of *The Commission of Inquiry into the Events at the Refugee Camps in Beirut, 1983: Final Report*).

Lamb, Franklin P. (ed. and compiler), *Israel's War in Lebanon: Eyewitness Chronicles of the Invasion and Occupation*. Foreword by Sean MacBride. Boston: South End Press and Spokesman, 2nd edn, 1984. First edn published as *Reason Not the Need: Eyewitness Chronicles of Israel's War in Lebanon*, United Kingdom: Spokesman, 1984.

MacBride, Sean (Chairman). *Israel in Lebanon: The Report of the International Commission to Inquire into Reported Violations of International Law by Israel During its Invasion of the Lebanon.* London, 28 August 1982–29 November 1983. London: Ithaca Press, 1983.

Mallisson, Sally V. and W. Thomas Mallison *Armed Conflict in Lebanon, 1982: Humanitarian Law in a Real World Setting*, Washington, DC: American Educational Trust, 1985.

Simpson, Michael (ed.). *United Nations Resolutions on Palestine and the Arab-Israeli Conflict, Volume III: 1982–1986*, Washington, DC: Institute for Palestine Studies, 1988.

Subcommittee on Europe and the Middle East. Developments in the Middle East, September 1982: Hearings before the Subcommittee on Europe and the Middle East of the Committee on Foreign Affairs, House of Representatives, 22 and 29 September 1982, US Congress, House Committee on Foreign Affairs, Subcommitee and the Middle East, 1983.

Yuzo, Itagaki, Oda Makoto and Shboh Mitsukazu (eds). *The Israeli Invasion of Lebanon, 1982: Inquiry by the International People's Tribunal, Tokyo*, Tokyo: Sanyusha, 1983. (The International People's Tribunal on the Israeli Invasion of Lebanon (IPTII), held in Tokyo, March 18–21, 1983.)

Daily chronicles

Abdallah, Hussein (ed.). *Yawmiyyat al-Muqawama al-Wataniyieh al-Lubnaniyieh, huzairan 1982 – kanoun al-awal 1983* [Diaries of the Lebanese National Resistance, June 1982–December 1983]. Edited by Hussein Abdallah. Foreword by Ma'n Bashour. Beirut: Dar al-Kitab al-Hadith, 1985.

Al-Din, Raja Sariy (chief ed.) (with selected Arab and international news agencies). *Ijtiya Lubnan: Yawmiyyat. Sowar. Watha 'eq* [Invasion of Lebanon: Chronicles. Photographs. Documents], Beirut: Selected Arab and International News Agencies [1982]. [Arabic]

Al-Din, Raja Sariy (chief ed.) (with Arab Centre for Research and Documentation). *Watha 'eq al-harb al-Lubnaniyya* (1982–1983–1984). *Sanawat fi thill al-ihtilal al-Isra 'ili: Yawmiyyat. Sowar. Watha 'eq* [Documents of the Lebanese War (1982–1983–1984). Years under Israeli Occupation: Chronicles. Photographs. Documents], September 1985. [Arabic]

Al-Din, Sweidan Nasser and Abido Basha *et al.* (eds). *Lubnan 1982: Yawmiyyat al-ghazwu al-Israeli: wath 'eq wa sowar* [Lebanon 1982: Chronicles of the Israeli Invasion: Documents and Photographs]. Foreword by Faisal Salmon.

Beirut: Arab Documentation Centre (distributed by Dar al-Andalus), 1982. [Arabic]

Arbid, Marie Thérèse and Paula Fattouh (eds). *Liban: L'été '82, Lebanon: The Summer of '82.* Text by John Roberts, MEED Consultants, London. Beirut: Express International Printing Company, 1983.

Centre for Arab Unity Studies (ed.). *Yawmiyyat wa watha 'eq al-wahda al-Arabiyya 1982* [Chronicles and Documents of Arab Unity], Beirut: Centre for Arab Unity Studies, 1983. [Arabic]

Chami, Joseph G. (ed.). *Days of Wrath: Lebanon, Liban: Jours de Colère 77–82.* Composition: Ets Georges Y. Azar. Beirut: Impression Arabe Printing Press, n.d.

Department of Israeli Affairs (ed.). *Yawmiyyat al-harb al-Israeliyya fi Lubnan (huzairan – kanoun al-awwal 1982): waqae' wa watha 'eq wa maqalat mukhtara min massader Arabiyya.* [Chronicles of the Israeli War in Lebanon (June–December 1982): Facts, documents and articles selected from Hebrew sources.], Supervised by Mahmoud Soueid, Beirut: Institute of Palestine Studies, 1985. [Arabic]

Lebanese Centre for Documentation and Research. *Haliyyat* [Panorama of Events] (quarterly), editions 26–7, Spring and Summer 1982. [Arabic–English–French]

Publications dealing wholly or chiefly with the massacre

Abdul Hadi, As'ad (ed.). *Majzarat Sabra wa Shatila: aw al-fashiyya al-jadida* [The Sabra and Shatila Massacre: or New Fascism], Damascus: Palestine Liberation Organization, Department of Information and Education, 1983. [Arabic]

Aharoni. Dov. *General Sharon's War against* Time *Magazine: His Trial and Vindication*, New York: Steimatzky/Shapolsky, 1985.

Al-Dajani, Ahmad Sidqi. *Sabra wa Shatila: Al-Jarima al-Isra 'iliyya wa al-mas 'ouliyya al-Amrikiyya (naqd Taqrir Kahan)* [Sabra and Shatila: The Israeli Crime and the American Responsibility (criticism of the Kahan Report)], Cairo: Dar al-Mustaqbal al-Arabi, 1984. [Arabic]

Al-Sa'di, Ghazi (ed.). *Al-Harb al-Filastiniyya fi Lubnan: wathiqat jurm wa idana* [Palestinian War in Lebanon: A Crime Certificate and a Conviction], Amman: Dar al-Jalil, April 1983. [Arabic]

Ang, Swee Chai. *From Beirut to Jerusalem*, London: Grafton Books, 1989.

Asmar, Hilmi. *Sabra wa Shatila majzarat hadara* [Sabra and Shatila: Massacre of Civilization], Amman: Dar al-Awda, 1983. [Arabic]

The Beirut Massacre: Press Profile: September 1982, New York: Claremont Research and Publications, November 1982; *Massacre Follow Up*, March 1983.

Halevi, Ilan. *Israel: de la terreur au masssacre d'Etat*, Paris: Papyrus, 1984.

Hankins, Jérome (compiler). *Genet à Chatila*. Paris: Solin, 1992. (Concerning four hours in Shatila, interview with Leila Shahid.)

Idris, Muhammad Jala'. *Mathbahat al-mukhayyamat* [Massacre of the Camps], Riyadh: Dar Abd al-Rahman al-Nasser, 1984. [Arabic]

International Progress Organization (IPO). *Sabra und Schatila: Die israelische Invasion und das Schicksal des palästinenischen Volkes*, Vienna: IPO, 1983.

Kapeliouk, Amnon. *Enquête sur un massacre: Sabra et Chatila*, Paris: Seuil, December 1982.

Lamb, Franklin P. *International Legal Responsibility for the Sabra–Shatila Massacre*, France: Imp. TIPE, 1983.

Limiti, Stefania (ed.). *I Fantasmi di Sharon. Il Massacro dei Palestinesi nei campi di Sabra e Shatila, 16–18 septembre 1982*, Rome: SINNOS Editrice, 2002.

Noureddine, Aba. *C'était hier Sabra et Chatila: un chant d'épreuve*, Paris: L'Harmattan, 1983.

Qatar News Agency (ed). *Al-Ghazwu wa al-mathbaha: jarimat al-qarn al-ishrin* [The Invasion and the Massacre: The Crime of the Twentieth Century]. Foreword by Eissa Ghanem al-Kawari, Qatar: Qatari News Agency, December 1982. [Arabic]

Sabbagh, Zuhair. *Sabra, Shatila, al-majzara, bahth fi khalfiyyatiha wa dawafi'iha* [Sabra, Shatila, the Massacre: Research into its Background and Motives], Jerusalem: Salah al-Din Publications, 1983. [Arabic]

Sabra Chatila in Memoria: Recueil de textes et de photos, Tunis: Sud Editions, 1983.

Secrétariat International de Solidarité avec le Peuple Arabe et sa Cause Centrale: la Palestine (eds). *Tel est le crime: L'invasion israélienne au Liban en 1982*, France: Imp. TIPE, 1983.

Shahadat an al-mathbaha Sabra wa Shatila: al-sha'b al-Filastini sayantaser [Testimonies to the Sabra and Shatila Massacre: The Palestinian People Shall Prevail], Cairo: Permanent Secretariat of the Organization for Solidarity between the African and Asian Peoples, 1982. [Arabic]

Tlas, (al-Imad) Mustafa. *Mathbahat Sabra wa Shatila* [The Sabra and Shatila Massacre], Damascus: Dar Tlas for Studies, November 1984. [Arabic]

Weisfeld, Abie H. *Sabra and Shatila: A New Auschwitz*, Ottawa: Jerusalem International Publishing House, February 1984.

Zaitoun, Safa'. *Sabra and Shatila, the Massacre*, Cairo: Dar al-Fata al-Arabi, 1983.

Ziegler, Jean. *N'oubliez pas le martyre de Sabra et Chatila*, Geneva: Comité International pour l'Application des Conventions de Genève aux Prisonniers Libanais et Palestiniens dans les Territoires Arabes Occupés, 1983.

Publications dealing partly with the massacre

Abu Ezzeddine, Halim. *Tilk al-ayyam: muthakkarat wa thikrayat: sirat insan wa masirat dawla wa masar umma* [Those Days: Diaries and Memories: Biography of a Man, Development of a State, and Progress of a Nation], Part 2, Beirut: Dar al-Afaq al-Jadida, 1982. [Arabic]

Abu Lughod, Ibrahim and Eqbal Ahmad (eds). *The Invasion of Lebanon*. Special double issue of *Race and Class* (a journal for Black and Third World liberation), vol. XXIV, no. 4, Spring 1983.

Agarichif, Anatoli. *Min Camb David ila ma'sat Lubnan* [From Camp David to the Tragedy of Lebanon]. Translated by Sassine Noun. Beirut: Dar al-Farabi, 1986. [Arabic]

Al-Bandak, Mazen (chief ed.), *Al-Jil* [The Generation]. Special documentary edition concerning the war, Vol. 3, edns 7–12, Nicosia: Al-Jil Institute for Journalism, December 1982. [Arabic]

Al-Labadi, Mahmoud. *Bairut '82: Al-Hisar wa al-sumoud* [Beirut '82: Siege and Steadfastness], Damascus: Dar al-Jalil, 1984. [Arabic]

Al-Raqm al-sa'b wa al-harb allati lam tantahi [The Wild Card and the War that Did Not End], [Jerusalem]: Al-Bayader al-Siyasi, 1983. [Arabic]

Al-Sa'di, Ghazi (ed.). *Min malaffat al-irhab al-Sahiouni fi Filastin: majazer wa mumarasat* [From the Files of Zionist Terrorism in Palestine: Massacres and Operations 1936–1983], Amman: Dar al-Jalil, 1985. [Arabic]

Al-Sawahri, Khalil, *Ahadith al-ghuzat: Shahadat Isra'iliyya* [Talks of the Conquerors: Israeli Testimonies], Cairo: Dar al-Mawkaf al-Arabi, 1983. [Arabic]

Al-Sharif, Khadija, Hafiza Shkeir, Amna Sola *et al.* (eds). *Adala min khilal uyoun al-nisa'* [Justice through Women's Eyes], Tunis: Al-Tabir, 1995. [Arabic]

Ayed, Khaled. *Qitar al-mawt: Ma'rakat Bairut fi siyaq al-irhab wa al-tawassu' al-Sahiouni* [Train of Death: The Battle of Beirut in the Context of Zionist Terrorism and Expansion], Beirut: Dar al-Sharq al-Awsat, 1984.

Ball, George W. *Error and Betrayal in Lebanon: An Analysis of Israel's Invasion of Lebanon and the Implications for U.S.-Israeli Relations*. Preface by Stanely Hoffmann. Washington, DC: Foundation for Middle East Peace, 1984.

Ball, George W. and Douglas B. Ball. *The Passionate Attachment: America's Involvement with Israel, 1947 to the Present*, New York and London: W. W. Norton and Co., 1992.

Bavly, Dan and Eliahu Salpeter. *Fire in Beirut: Israel's War in Lebanon with PLO*, New York: Stein and Day, 1984.

Becker, Jillian. *The PLO: The Rise and Fall of the Palestine Liberation Organization*, London: Weidenfeld & Nicolson, 1984.

Benassar, *Paix d'Israël au Liban (A l'heure de l'épreuve de force URSS-USA)*, Beirut: L'Orient-Le Jour, May 1983.

Ben-Dor, Gabriel *et al.* (eds). *Israel's Lebanon Policy: Where To?*, Tel Aviv: Jaffee Centre for Strategic Studies (JCSS), Tel Aviv University, August 1984.

Bourgi, Albert and Pierre Weiss. *Liban, la cinquième guerre du Proche-Orient*, Paris: Publisud, 1983.

Boykin, John. *Cursed is the Peacemaker: The American Diplomat versus the Israeli General, Beirut 1982*, Belmont, Ca: Applegate Press, 2002.

Brenner, Lenni. *The Iron Wall: Zionist Revisionism from Jabotinsky to Shamir*, London: Zed Books, 1984.

Bulloch, John. *Final Conflict: The War in the Lebanon*, London: Century Publishing, 1983.

Chomsky, Noam. *The Fateful Triangle: The United States, Israel and the Palestinians*, Boston: South End Press, 1983.

Clifton, Tony and Catherine Leroy. *God Cried*, New York: Quartet Books, 1983.

Corm, Georges. *Le Proche-Orient éclaté: de Suez à l'invasion du Liban, 1956–1982*, Paris: La Découverte/Maspero, 1983.

Costi, Andrash. *Al-Harb al-khatifa al-tawila* [The Swift and Long War]. Translated from Hungarian by Asad Muhammad Qasem, Damascus: Dar al-Karmel, General Union for Palestinian Writers and Journalists, 1983. [Arabic]

de Chalvron, Alain. *Le piège de Beyrouth*, Paris: Le Sycomore, 1982.

Feldman, Shai and Heda Rechnitz Kijner. *Deception, Consensus and War: Israel in Lebanon*, Tel Aviv: Jaffee Centre for Strategic Studies (JCSS), Tel Aviv University, 1984.

Fisk, Robert. *Pity the Nation: Lebanon at War*, London: André Deutsch, 1990.

Friedman, Thomas L. *From Beirut to Jerusalem*, New York: Farran, Straus & Giroux, 1989.

Gabriel, Richard A. *Operation Peace for Galilee: The Israeli-PLO War in Lebanon*, New York: Hill and Wang, 1984.

Gilmour, David. *Lebanon: The Fractured Country*, London: Sphere Books, 1983.

Gresh, Alain. *The PLO: The Struggle Within Towards an Independent Palestinian State*. Preface by Maxime Rodinson. Translated by A. M. Berrett. London: Zed Books, 1985. (Originally published in French by S.P.A.G / Papyrus, 1983.)

Harb Lubnan, 1975–1982 [Lebanon War, 1975–1982]. (Excerpts from Lebanese and - European newspapers and books, international and Arab news agencies, and photographs of battles by Lebanese and European photographers.) Beirut: al-Maktaba al-Haditha, 1983. [Arabic]

Hezbullah, Central Information Unit. *Kay la nansa: majazer Israel* [So We Should Not Forget: Israeli Massacres], Beirut: Hezbullah, Central Information Unit, 2000. [Arabic]

Institute of Palestine Studies. *Al-Ijtiya al-Israeli li-Lubnan–1982: Dirasat siyasiyya wa askariyya* [Israeli Invasion of Lebanon – 1982: Political and Military Studies], Beirut: Institute of Palestine Studies, 1984. [Arabic]

International Association of Democratic Lawyers, Union of Palestinian Lawyers. *Livre blanc sur l'agression israélienne au Liban*, Association Internationale des Juristes Démocrates, Union des Juristes Palestiniens, Paris: Publisud, 1983.

Jansen, Michael. *The Battle of Beirut: Why Israel Invaded Lebanon*, London: Zed Press, 1982.

Jerusalem Centre for Research. *Al-Harb al-lati lam tantahi: asrar lam tunshar 'an harb Lubnan* [The War that Did Not End: Secrets that Were Never Disclosed about the Lebanon War], Jerusalem: Jerusalem Centre for Research, Publications of the Palestine Agency, 1987. [Arabic]

Khalidi, Rashid. *Under Siege: P.L.O. Decisionmaking During the 1982 War*, New York: Columbia University Press, 1986.

Kriegel, Annie. *Israel est-il coupable?*, Paris: Editons Robert Laffont, 1982.

Langer, Felicia (Diaries). *Al-Ghadhab wa al-amal: Masirat al-sha'b al-Filastini taht al-ihtilal* [Anger and Hope: Course of the Palestinian People under Occupation]. Translated from Hebrew by Ahmad Khalifeh, Khaled Ayed and Samir Saras. Nicosia: Institute of Palestine Studies, 1993. [Arabic]

Laurant, Annie and Antoine Basbous. *Guerres secrètes au Liban*, Paris: Gallimard, 1987.

Lerer, Shim'on. *Ha-'Ikar he haser: va'adah la-hakirat ha-Iro'im ba-Mahanot ha-Plitim be-Beirut 1982. Din ve Hishbon* [The Key Point Missing: Committee for Investigating the Events in the Refugee Camps in Beirut, 1982. A Report], Jerusalem: Amit, 1983. [Hebrew]

Makdadi, Lina, *Surviving the Siege of Beirut*, London: Onyx Press, 1983.

Makdisi, Jean Said, *Beirut Fragments: A War Memoir*, New York: Persea Books, 1990.

Meem, Bani *et al. Shahadat al-hazima: Israel fi Lunbnan* [Testimonies of Defeat: Israel in Lebanon] (translation), [Beirut]: Lebanese Centre for Research, Journalism and Documentation, 1991. [Arabic]

Naor, Arye. *Mimshala ba milhama: tiqfoud mimshalat Yisrael bamilhamat Levanon (1982)* [Cabinet at War: The Functioning of the Israeli Cabinet during the Lebanon War (1982)], n.p: Lahav, 1986. [Hebrew]

Nassib, Selim, *Paix en Galilée: Beyrouth*, Paris: Editions de Minuit, 1983.

Nassib, Selim and Caroline Tisdall. *Beirut: Front-line Story*. Photographs by Chris Steele-Perkins. USA: Africa World Press, 1983.

O'Ballance, Edgar. *Civil War in Lebanon, 1975–92*, London: Macmillan, 1998.

O'Brien, William V. *Law and Morality in Israel's War with the PLO*, New York and London: Routledge, 1991.

The Palestinian Legend, Afro-Asian Publications no. 117, Cairo: AAPSO Permanent Secretariat, September 1982.

Perry, Glenn E. (ed.). *Palestine: Continuing Dispossession*, Belmont, Massachusetts: Association of Arab-American University Graduates (AAUG), 1986.

Pintak, Larry. *Beirut Outtakes: A TV Correspondent's Portrait of America's Encounter with Terror*, Lexington: Lexington Books, 1988.

Rabinovich, Itamar. *The War for Lebanon, 1970–1985*, revised edn, Ithaca: Cornell University Press, 1985.

Randal, Jonathan C. *Going All the Way: Christian Warlords, Israeli Adventures, and the War in Lebanon*, New York: Viking Press, 1983.

Sachar, Howard. *A History of Israel*, Vol. 2, New York: Oxford University Press, 1987.

Said, Edward W. *The Politics of Dispossession: The Struggle for Palestinian Self-Determination 1969–1994*, New York: Pantheon Books, 1994.

Salman, Rida, Randa Sharara and Yola al-Batal (eds). *Isra'il wa tajribat Lubnan: taquwimat khuara' Isra'ilyyin* [Israel and the Lebanon Experience: Assessments by Israeli Experts], Nicosia: Institute of Palestine Studies, 1986. [Arabic]

Schiff, Ze'ef and Ehud Ya'ari. *Israel's Lebanon War: The First Inside Story Account of a Disastrous Military Adventure and its Ongoing Consequences*, New York: Simon & Schuster, 1984.

Sharon, Ariel, with David Ghanoff. *Warrior: An Autobiography*, New York: Simon & Schuster, 1989.

Shimon, Shiffer. *Kurat al-thalj: asrar al-tadakhul al-Isra'ili fi Lubnan* [The Snowball: Secrets of the Israeli Intervention in Lebanon]. Translated from Hebrew. Lebanon, November 1984. [Arabic]

Timerman, Jacobo. *The Longest War: Israel in Lebanon*. Translated from the Spanish by Miguel Acoco. New York: Alfred A. Knopf, 1982.

Traboulsi, Fawaz. *An amal la shifa' minhu: min dafater hisar Bairut: huzairan-tishrin 1982* [About a Hopeless Case: From the Notebooks of the Siege of Beirut: June–November 1982], Beirut: Institute of Arab Research, 1984. [Arabic]

Tlas, Mustafa (supervisor). *Al-Ghazwu al-Isra'ili li-Lubnan* [The Israeli Invasion of Lebanon], (written by a group of researchers), Damascus: Tishrin Institute, 1983. [Arabic]

Yariv, Avner. *Dilemmas of Security: Politics, Strategy, and the Israeli Experience in Lebanon*, Oxford: Oxford University Press, 1987.

Articles and periodicals

Articles

Abdullah, Daud. 'In Remembrance of Sabra and Shatila: A review of Israeli Terrorism Against the Palestinian refugees', 16 September 1999 <www.flinet.com/politics/palestine/sabra.htm> (visited 10 April 2000).

Abu Fakhr, Saqr. 'So as Not to Forget Sabra and Shatila: Who Remembers Those Days?', *Al-Safir*, 15 September 2001. [Arabic]

Al-Hout, Bayan Nuwayhed. 'On the Fourth Memorial of Sabra and Shatila: Isn't it Time for the Victims to Speak Out?', *Al-Safir*, 20 September 1986. [Arabic]

Al-Khoury, Elias. 'The Names', *Al-Safir*, 20 September 1986. [Arabic]

Al-Shaikh, Zakaria. 'Sabra and Shatila 1982: Resisting the Massacre', *Journal of Palestine Studies*, 53, Fall 1984, pp. 57–90.

Al-Tal, Ahmad. 'The Massacre of Sabra and Shatila in 1982' <http://unity.ancient-news.com/sabra/background/responsibility.html> (visited 17 September 2000).

Barrada, Layla Shahid. 'Les massacres de Sabra et Chatila: Chronologie et témoignages', *Revue d'études palestiniennes*, 6, Winter 1983, pp. 89–112.

Ben-Yishay, Ron. 'Ben-Yishay Details Beirut Massacre Chronologically', *Jerusalem Domestic Television Service*, 20 September 1982, as cited in *The Beirut Massacre: Press Profile: September 1982*, New York: Claremont Research and Publications, November 1982, p. 19.

Ben-Yishay, Ron. 'Ben-Yishay Reconstructs Beirut Massacre', *Jerusalem Domestic Television Service*, as cited in *The Beirut Massacre: Press Profile: September 1982*, New York: Claremont Research and Publications, November 1982, pp. 60–2.

Buchalla, Karl E. 'Beirut: Lokaltermin an der Stätte des Massenmords: Ein Horrorfilm aus der Wirklichkeit', *Süddeutsche Zeitung*, 23 September 1982.

Buchalla, Karl E. 'Saad Haddad: Ein libanesischer Major im Sold des Feindes: Der Kreuzritter unter dem Davidsstern', *Süddeutsche Zeitung*, 18 April 1983.

Campbell, Colin. 'Key Phalangist Aides Implicated in Operation that Led to Killings', *New York Times*, 30 September 1982, as cited in *The Beirut Massacre: Press Profile: September 1982*, New York: Claremont Research and Publications, November 1982, p. 53.

Campbell, Colin. 'Survivors of Massacre Tell of Reign of Terror', *New York Times*, 21 September 1982, as cited in *The Beirut Massacre: Press Profile: September 1982*, New York: Claremont Research and Publications, November 1982, p. 23.

Chehab, Zaki. '*Al-Hawadeth* Interviews the Eyewitnesses and the Director of the Civil Defence Says: Ninety per cent of the Victims of the Sabra and Shatila massacre ... were Lebanese!', *Al-Hawadeth* magazine, 1 October 1982, pp. 68–72. [Arabic]

Der Spiegel. 'Jeder von euch ist ein Racher: Ein libanesischer Milizionär über seine Taten beim Massaker von Beirut', 14 February 1983, pp. 112–13.

Diab, Youssef. 'Military Prosecutor Reopens Sabra and Shatila Inquiry: Will Not Question Lebanese Traitor and Instigator of Sabra & Chatila', *Daily Star*, 26 June 2001.

Farah, Robert. 'Al-Quwat al-Lubnaniyieh Confutes Elie Hobeika', *Al-Wassat* magazine, 98, 19 October 1997, pp. 26–8. [Arabic]

Fineman, Mark. 'In Shatila, the Stench of Death', *Philadelphia Inquirer*, 20 September 1982, as cited in *The Beirut Massacre: Press Profile: September 1982*, New York: Claremont Research and Publications, November 1982, p. 14.

Fisk, Robert. 'Down Every Alleyway ... Women, Young Men, Babies – Lying Where They Had Been Knifed or Machine Gunned to Death', *The Times*, 20 September 1982, as cited in *The Beirut Massacre: Press Profile: September 1982*, New York: Claremont Research and Publications, November 1982, p. 7.

Fisk, Robert. 'Militias are Sustained by Israelis', *The Times*, 20 September 1982, as cited in *The Beirut Massacre: Press Profile: September 1982*, New York: Claremont Research and Publications, November 1982, p. 15.

Fisk, Robert. 'I am Innocent of Killings: Haddad Explains', *The Times*, 23 September 1982, as cited in *The Beirut Massacre: Press Profile: September 1982*, New York: Claremont Research and Publications, November 1982, p. 51.

Fisk, Robert. 'Reluctant Testimony on Shatila', *The Times*, 25 September 1982, as cited in *The Beirut Massacre: Press Profile: September 1982*, New York: Claremont Research and Publications, November 1982, p. 40.

Fisk, Robert. 'Fifteen Years After the Bloodbath, the World Turns its Back' <http://unity.ancient-news.com/sabra/Testimonies/fisk1.html> (visited 18 September 2000).

Flint, Julie. 'Vanished Victims of Israelis Return to Accuse Sharon', *Observer*, 25 November 2001.

Friedman, Thomas. 'The Beirut Massacre: The Four Days', *New York Times*, 26 September 1982, as cited in *The Beirut Massacre: Press Profile: September 1982*, New York: Claremont Research and Publications, November 1982, pp. 64–76.

Genet, Jean. 'Four Hours in Shatila', *Journal of Palestine Studies*, 46, Spring 1983, pp. 3–22. (Translation of French original, 'Quatre heures à Chatila', *Revue d'études palestiniennes*, 6, Winter 1983, pp. 3–19.)

Glover-James, Ian. 'New Panic in Camp', *Daily Telegraph*, 20 September 1982. As cited in *The Beirut Massacre: Press Profile: September 1982*, New York: Claremont Research and Publications, November 1982, p. 16.

Goldberg, John. 'Israel Reacts to the Massacres', *New Outlook: Middle East Monthly*, 25, 17–18 October 1982.

Green, Leslie C. 'The Kahan Commission Report on Sabra And Shatila: A Judicial Study' <http://unity.ancient-news.co/sabra/background/kahan_commission.html> (visited 17 September 2000).

Halevi, Ilan. 'Des massacres démocratiques', *Revue d'études palestiniennes*, 7, Spring 1983, pp. 13–19.

Hemphill, Clara. 'A Shattered Life in the Midst of Death', *Washington Post*, 22 September 1982.

Jaber, Bahjat. 'The Massacre of Sabra and Shatila in Court: No File, and No Affidavits', *Al-Nahar*, 23 June 2001.

Jenkins, Loren. 'Israelis Hunt Palestinian Sympathizers in Beirut', *Washington Post*, 18 September 1982, as cited in *The Beirut Massacre: Press Profile: September 1982*, New York: Claremont Research and Publications, November 1982, p. 3.

Jenkins, Loren. 'The Massacre: Witnesses Describe Militiamen Passing Through Israeli Lines', *Washington Post*, 20 September 1982, as cited in *The Beirut Massacre: Press Profile: September 1982*, New York: Claremont Research and Publications, November 1982, pp. 10–13.

Jenkins, Loren. Interview with Loren Jenkins, *Washington Post* Beirut correspondent. Excerpts from Transcript of 'All Things Considered', National Public Radio, 20 September 1982 as cited in *The Beirut Massacre: Press Profile: September 1982*, New York: Claremont Research and Publications, November 1982, p. 13.

Jenkins, Loren. 'Phalangists Implicated in Massacre', *Washington Post*, 30 September 1982, as cited in *The Beirut Massacre: Press Profile: September 1982*, New York: Claremont Research and Publications, November 1982, p. 55.

Jewish Student Online Research Centre. 'Sabra & Shatila' <www.us.israel.org/jsource/History/Sabra_%26_Shatila.html> (visited 9 April 2000).

Juneidi, Muhammad Sa'id. 'Sean MacBride: The World Focused on Kahan's Report and Ignored Our Report on the Invasion of Lebanon', *Al-Hawadeth* magazine, 1378, 1 April 1983, pp. 20–1. [Arabic]

Khalifeh, Ahmad. 'The Massacre from an Israeli Perspective: Between Lying and Denial!'. *The Seventh Day* Magazine, Issue 19, 17 September 1984, pp. 18–19. [Arabic]

Lamb, David. 'Survivors Raise Doubts on Israel Troops' Actions', *Los Angeles Times*, 20 September 1982, as cited in *The Beirut Massacre: Press Profile: September 1982*, New York: Claremont Research and Publications, November 1982, pp. 17–18.

Lamb, Franklin P. 'The Kahan Commission and International Law', *MEI*, 18 March, 1983, pp. 10–11.

Mallat, Chibli, 'September 2001 and September 1982: Two Crimes Against Humanity', *A Quest for Justice*, published with the *Daily Star*, 29 November 2001.

Najjar, Munir, 'Ilias Hobeika: I am Working on a Documentary Book to Confront the Forgery in Writing the History of the War', *Assayyad* magazine, 2960, 27 July–2 August 2001, pp. 4–8. [Arabic]

Naylor, R. T. 'From Bloodbath to the Whitewash: Sabra–Shatila and the Kahan Commission Report', *Arab Studies Quarterly*, 5, Fall 1983, pp. 337–61.

Neff, Donald. 'Israeli Leaders found Indirectly Responsible for Massacres in Lebanon' <http://unity.ancient-news.com/sabra/background/responsibility.html> (visited 17 September 2000).

Nikdimon, Shlomo. 'Report of the Prosecutor Jermanos on the Sabra and Shatila Massacre', *Yedioth Ahronoth*, 2 December 1982. [Hebrew]

Nir, Arad. 'Phalangists Entrusted with Sabra, Shatila "Purge" ', Tel Aviv Israeli Defence Forces Radio, 16 September 1982, as cited in *The Beirut Massacre: Press Profile: September 1982*, New York: Claremont Research and Publications, November 1982, p. 4.

Rabinovich, Abraham. 'IDF Fired Flares to Light Camps for Phalangists', *Jerusalem Post*, 22 September 1982, as cited in: *The Beirut Massacre: Press Profile: September 1982*, New York: Claremont Research and Publications, November 1982, p. 25.

Ronen, Yoram. 'Sharon interviewed on Massacre Responsibility', *Jerusalem Domestic Television Service* (interview with Defence Minister Ariel Sharon), 24 September 1982, as cited in *The Beirut Massacre: Press Profile: September 1982*, New York: Claremont Research and Publications, November 1982, pp. 36–9.

Rubenberg, Cheryl, 'Beirut Under Fire', *Journal of Palestine Studies*, 44/45, Summer/Fall 1984, pp. 62–8: *Journal of Palestine Studies*, 53, Fall 1984, pp. 57–90.

Sa'adeh, Wisam. 'The Cedars' Guardians: From Tall al-Za'tar to the Internet', *Al-Safir*, 25 August 2001.

Safieh, Afif. 'Un scandale sans précédent mais non pas un massacre sans précédent', *France Pays Arabes*, 106, March 1983.

Salpeter, Eliahu. 'Israel's Changed Political Landscape: Aftermath of the Inquiry', *New Leader: A Biweekly of News and Opinion*, 66: 304, 18 February 1982.

Salpeter, Eliahu. 'Placing the Blame in Israel: The Inquiry Begins', *New Leader: A Biweekly of News and Opinion*, 65, 3–4, 18 October 1982.

Schiff, Ze'ev and Menahem Horowitz. 'Massacre Not Revenge Planned Earlier', *Ha'aretz*, 28 September 1982, as cited in *The Beirut Massacre: Press Profile: September 1982*, New York: Claremont Research and Publications, November 1982, p. 52.

Segev, Tom. 'The Fight at the End of the Time Tunnel', *Ha'aretz – Week's End*, 6 December 2002 <www.haaretzdaily.com> (visited 10 December 2002).

Shipler, David K. 'Israel Asserts its Troops Intervened to Minimize the Beirut Massacre', *New York Times*, 19 September 1982, as cited in *The Beirut Massacre: Press Profile: September 1982*, New York: Claremont Research and Publications, November 1982, p. 9.

Shirbel, Ghassan. 'Elie Hobeika Remembers', *Al-Wassat* magazine, Issue 95, 22–27 September 1997, pp. 20–5. [Arabic]

Shou'oun Filastiniyya magazine. 'The Massacre of Sabra and Shatila: Results of a Field Study' (produced by a group of researchers), edition 138, May 1983, pp. 97–136. [Arabic]

Siegel, Ellen. 'Inside and Outside the Hospital, People Were Screaming: "Haddad, *Kataeb*, Israel – Massacre" ', *Journal of Palestine Studies*, 46, Winter 1983, pp. 61–71.

Siegel, Ellen and Nabil Ahmed. 'Shared Memories of Sabra and Shatila' <www.adc.org/press/1999/sept99.htm> (visited 9 April 2000).

Smith, Colin (in Beirut). Ian Mather and Eric Silver (in Jerusalem). 'Lebanon Massacre/The Evidence: How the Cover-up was Blown', *Observer*, 26 September 1982, as cited in *The Beirut Massacre: Press Profile: September 1982*, New York: Claremont Research and Publications, November 1982, pp. 79–82.

Smith, William, Robert Slater (in Jerusalem) and William Stewart (in Beirut). 'Crisis of Conscience', *Time*, 4 October 1982, as cited in *The Beirut Massacre: Press Profile: September 1982*, New York: Claremont Research and Publications, November 1982, pp. 88–9.

Tel Aviv Israeli Defence Forces Radio, 16 September 1982, as cited in *The Beirut Massacre: Press Profile: September 1982*, New York: Claremont Research and Publications, November 1982, p. 4.

Toronto Star. 'Massacre in Beirut Left 2,000 Dead, Lebanese Say', 14 October 1982, cited in *The Beirut Massacre: Press Profile: September 1982*, New York: Claremont Research and Publications, November 1982, p. 15, p. 47.

Wall, James M. 'There is Another Israel', *The Christian Century*, 6 October 1982, p. 971.

Walsh, Edward. 'Israeli Army Under Siege: Questions Surrounding Massacre Strain Credibility', *Washington Post*, 26 September 1982, as cited in *The Beirut Massacre: Press Profile: September 1982*, New York: Claremont Research and Publications, November 1982, pp. 77–8.

Whitaker, Mark, and Ray Wilkinson (in Beirut), Scott Sullivan (in Jerusalem). 'The Making of a Massacre', *Newsweek*, 4 October 1982, as cited in *The Beirut Massacre: Press Profile: September 1982*, New York: Claremont Research and Publications, November 1982, pp. 83–7.

Periodicals

Al-Nahar (newspaper) (1982–83).

Al-Nida' (newspaper) (1982–83).

Al-Safir (newspaper), Beirut (1982–83).

Ha'aretz (newspaper) (1982–83).

Jerusalem Post (newspaper) (1982–83).

Lebanese Red Cross (bulletin) (1982).

WAFA – Palestine News Agency. Released by the PLO (1982–83).

Yedioth Ahronoth (newspaper) (1982–83)

Publications dealing with the status of Palestinians in Lebanon

Al-Hout, Shafiq. *Ishrun aman fi Munathamat al-Tahrir al-Filastiniyieh: ahadith al-thikrayat 1964–1984* [Twenty Years with the Palestine Liberation Organization: Recollections 1964–1984], Beirut: Dar al-Istiqlal, 1986. [Arabic]

Al-Hout, Shafiq. 'Mustaqbal al-Ulaqat al-Lubnaniyieh – al-Filastiniyieh' [The Future of Lebanese-Palestinian Relations], in *Lubnan wa afaq al-mustaqbal* [Lebanon and Future Horizons: Documents and discussions at the scholarly seminar held by the Centre for Arab Unity Studies], Beirut: Centre for Arab Unity Studies, 1991, pp. 223–39. [Arabic]

Al-Natour, Suhail Mahmoud. *Awda' al-sha'b al-Filastini fi Lubnan* [Living Conditions of the Palestinian People in Lebanon], Beirut: Dar al-Taqaddum al-Arabi, 1993. [Arabic]

Hallaq, Hasan. *Mawqef Lubnan min al-qadiyya al-Filastinyya* [Lebanon's Position vis-à-vis the Palestinian Question], Beirut: Research Centre, 1982. [Arabic]

Khoury, Youssef Kazma (ed. and compiler). *Al-Bayanat al-wizariyya al-Lubnaniyya wa monaqashatuha fi majlis al-nuwwab 1926–1984* [Lebanese Ministerial Statements and Discussions of these in Parliament, 1926–1984], 3 volumes, Beirut: Institute of Lebanese Studies, 1986. [Arabic]

Palestine Organization for Human Rights (POHR). *Waqi' al-Laji'in al-Filastiniyyin fi Lubnan: Ila mata ... wa limatha?* [The State of Refugee Palestinians in Lebanon], Beirut: POHR, August 1999.

United Nations Relief and Works Agency (UNRWA). *List of the Elementary and Secondary Schools in Lebanon*, Vienna: UNRWA, 1979.

United Nations Relief and Works Agency (UNRWA). *UNRWA's Emergency Operation in Lebanon, 1982–83*, Vienna: UNRWA, Vienna International Centre, March 1984.

United Nations Relief and Works Agency (UNRWA). *UNRWA in Lebanon*, Vienna:

UNRWA for Palestine in the Near East, Public Information Office, 1992.

General references

Al-Yamani, Abu Maher. Interview with Bayan Nuwayhed al-Hout, in 'Interviews with the Leaders of the Palestine National Movement', Beirut, 1972 (unpublished).

Rabinowicz, O. K. 'Basle Program', in *Encyclopedia of Zionism and Israel*, vol. 1, General Editor Geoffrey Wigoder, 2 vols, London and Toronto: Associated University Presses, 1975, p. 171.

Tomeh, George J. (ed.). *United Nations Resolutions on Palestine and the Arab-Israeli Conflict 1917–1974*, Beirut: Institute for Palestinian Studies, 1975.

Zinn, Howard. *The Politics of History*, Boston: Beacon Press, 1970.

Index

Compiled by Sue Carlton

Names in inverted commas indicate pseudonyms
Names of places are mentioned only when there is a direct relation between the place and the events of the massacre

hospitals   34–5, 52, 74, 112, 113
  abductions from   132
  see also Akka Hospital; Gaza Hospital
al-Hoss, Salim   250, 285, 288
al-Hout, Hana   5
al-Hout, Shafiq   5, 27, 37
Huda A.   187, 188
humanitarian organizations   206, 241
  see also rescue workers
Hurras al-Arz   320–1
Husari, Nawal   42, 104–5
Hussein B., Comrade   41, 56–7, 62, 63, 64,
  66, 121
Hussein, Karem Ahmad Jabr   267
  family victims   267
al-Husseini, Haji Amin   28

Idilbi, Zainab Hassan   229, 230–1
illumination   201, 310, 315
  see also flare shells
Imad   207
informants   64, 121, 161, 190, 192, 195, 196,
  197, 198
  masked strangers   50–1, 86, 88, 112
International Committee of the Red Cross
  (ICRC)   94, 135–6, 140, 190
  evacuation of Gaza Hospital   162, 166,
    168, 169–71, 177, 200
  search for victims   205, 206, 209, 210, 217,
    221–3, 241
  victim lists   12, 169, 170, 241, 277, 280,
    292, 293, 294
International Committee for Solidarity with
  Arab People   249
international laws
  need for tribunal   322–3
  and responsibility of occupying state
    299–300
  see also Geneva Conventions
Intissar, Nurse   132, 133
Iqlim Command   39
Iraqi, Ibrahim   38
Ismail, Abu Hamad   57
Israel
  demonstrations in   297, 298
  denial of responsibility   297–8, 312
  invasion of Lebanon 1978   35
  invasion of Lebanon 1982   1, 35
  justification for entry into Beirut   304, 311
  responsibility of   299–300, 314–16, 320, 322
Israeli Army   20, 119
  abductions by   280
  direct interventions   310
  encirclement of camps   3, 46–72
  evidence left   235–8
  knowledge of massacre   7, 198–200, 261–2,
    307–10, 311, 313, 322, 323

monitoring departure of Palestinians   2, 303
and numbers of victims   295, 305
officers' revolt   323
patrolling vehicles   309
photography   310
points of surveillance   309
provision of bulldozers   211–12
questioning of doctors and nurses   175–7
radio station reports   72
and residents' complaints   310
role in massacre   65–6, 70, 72, 76, 112,
  119, 297–8
support for Sa'd Haddad   237
withdrawal of   219–20
see also flare shells
Israeli Command Centre   76, 115, 176,
  177, 426
  peace delegation to   46, 53–8, 69, 71, 74
  and visibility of camps   261–4, 307–8
  women's march to   46, 58–61, 71, 74, 115
Israeli Crimes Against Lebanese and Palestinian
  Peoples   249
Israeli Television   176
'Israwi', Nuhad   208, 215, 218, 288
Itani, Khalil   317
'Izzidine', Khalil   281

Jabal al-Arab   5
Jaffa   21, 22, 29, 196, 199, 269, 271
Ja'ja', Kamil   277
Jalil school   91, 100, 104, 125
'Jamil', Tony   136
Jamilah, Riad Mahmoud   269
Jamilah, Samar Mahmoud   269
Jam'iyyat al-Ina'ash   59, 60, 107, 263
Jansen, Michael   305, 321
Jenin massacre   247, 273
Jenkins, Lauren   75–6, 204, 272, 318
Jermanos, Ass'ad   3, 292, 319
Jermanos Report   3, 266, 292–3, 295, 296,
  316–17, 319
Jerusalem Post   118, 264, 303
Jisr al-Basha Camp   23
Jordan   19, 20, 21, 23, 27, 303
Jordanians   1, 43, 44, 251, 252, 266, 283,
  291, 305
Jubran, Jubran Abdallah   166
Junblatt, Kamal   31

Kafr Qassem massacre   247
Kahan Commission   168–9, 185, 212, 232
  Sharon's testimony   311–13
Kahan Report   3, 9, 298, 308, 323
  and battle myth   124, 161
  and end of massacre   310, 311
  and fighters in camps   304
  and identity of killers   232, 234

Mar Elias Camp   23, 247
Marcus, Yoel   323
'Mary'   91, 147–8
Mary, Nurse   127
Mash'alani, Maroun   318
mass graves   7, 147, 149, 204, 213–18, 222,
    224, 225, 227, 228, 231
  children   251
  and identification   278, 280, 281
  numbers of victims   276, 277–8, 287,
      289–90, 295, 296
  Sports City   138, 150
  see also cemeteries; death pits
massacre
  battle myth   201–2, 262, 266, 274, 293
  end of   163, 310–11
  first news reports from   3, 202–5, 241
  location of   43–4
  preceding hours   50–2, 74–5
  reasons for   246–7, 270–3
  reports to Israeli officials   308–9
  responsibility for   297–324
Ma'wa al-Ajaza Hospital   34–5, 54, 74,
    112, 166
Maysam, Hajj   207, 210, 217
megaphones   49, 70, 117, 127, 130, 141, 163,
    177, 183, 250
'Michael'   318
Middle East Council of Churches,
    victim lists   280
migrations   270–2
al-Miqdad, Amaal   85
al-Miqdad family   84–5, 218, 293
al-Miqdad, Hussein   85
al-Miqdad, Khadija   85
al-Misri, Muhammad   196–7, 198
missing
  definition of   279
  see also abducted/missing
Miyyeh wa Miyyeh Camp   23
Le Monde Diplomatique   308
Morris, Dr Paul   93, 103, 136, 165, 167, 172–3
  casualty numbers   168–9, 170, 212
  description of soldiers   232
  taken for questioning   176, 177, 179, 212
al-Mughrabi, Ahmad   231
Mughrabi, Subhi Muhammad   268
  family victims   268
Muhammad, Dr   58
al-Muhammad family   89, 293
Muhammad, Khawla   269
Muhammad, Mufid   93–4, 137–8
Muhammad, Munir   91–3, 94, 96, 99–100,
    137, 138, 172
Muhammad ('Shaykh')   40
Muhammad, Suhaila Khaled Yousuf   267
  family victims   267

Muhammad, Yahya Ahmad   269
Mukahhal, Qassem   30
Mukhallalati building   52, 102
Munira   224
Murabitoun   37, 41, 50, 62, 69, 305
Murad, Ali   69, 111, 123

Nabatiyyeh Camp   23
al-Nabulsi, Muhammad   108–9, 111, 141
Al-Nahar   205, 276
Nahr al-Bared Camp   23
al-Na'ima   276, 289
Najjar hospital   136, 221
Najjar, Hussein Hasan Ahmad   268
Nasser, Hamza   196
Nasser, Jamal Ibrahim   196
Nasser, Taysir   196
Natat, Shaker   192–3
Navon, Yitzhak   323
Nazal, Muhammad Salim   268
New York Times   75–6, 237
newspapers, lists of victims   283–4, 296
Newsweek   213, 276, 308
al-Nida'   283–4
Nir, Arad   72
Norwegian Embassy, First Secretary   170–1
al-Numour al-Ahrar   118, 142, 233, 320, 321
Nuzha, Nurse   126, 128, 130–1, 133, 136, 137

Observer   94
Official Commission of Inquiry into the Fate of
    Those Abducted and Missing   250, 285,
    286, 288, 292–4, 296
  see also Jermanos Report
Oral History Project   4, 7–15, 258
  and accuracy   248–9
  collection of names   11–13, 284, 286–7
  copies of tapes   9–10
  interviews   8–10, 61, 67–8, 207–18
  transcription of tapes   10
  see also field study project
Organization of Al-Iss'af al-Sha'bi   206, 207
Organization of Civil Defence Volunteers
    (Volunteer Committee)   206, 208, 276–7
Oslo Commission   168, 171, 173, 177,
    185, 277
al-Ouza'i   48, 86–7, 112, 115
Oz, Amos   314

Pajula, Dr Juhani   173, 174, 176, 185
Palestine
  displacement of people   20, 271–2
  partition of   19–20
Palestine Liberation Army   35, 103, 265,
    277, 303
Palestine Liberation Organization (PLO)   4, 5,
    27, 46, 265, 275–6, 301, 303

al-Tarbiya al-Wataniyieh Scouts   206, 208–9, 235–6, 288
Tariq al-Jadida   47, 77, 83
terrorists   43, 174, 193, 198, 247, 250, 264, 298
   accusations   154, 155, 156
   estimates of   235, 264, 302–7
   Palestinians seen as   168, 185
   seeking out   50, 70, 72, 78–9, 112, 118, 126, 129, 201, 312
   see also freedom fighters; saboteurs
testimonies
   about invasion   77–85
   from first night of massacre   104–10
   from rescue volunteers   207–18
   from search for relatives   225–31
   from second day of massacre   141–60
   from shelters   85–94
   from third day of massacre   183–96, 198–200
   'wall of death'   94–8
Thabet, Maya   132
tile worker   234
Time magazine   118, 306, 318
Timerman, Jacobo   297, 298, 316, 323
The Times   319
Titi, Mahmoud   231
al-Titi, Saleh Hussein   158, 224, 268
Titi, Samia   230, 231
Titi, Tareq Muhammad   231
torture   98, 112, 114, 134, 197, 198, 200, 202, 262, 269
Toynbee, Arnold   11
Tunisia   302, 303
Tunisians, victims   251, 291
Turf Club   262, 289, 307, 311
Tyre   21, 22, 216, 290

'Um Akram', H.Sh.   12, 101–2, 105–6, 116–17, 136, 140, 214, 222
Um Ayman (Munira Sayyed)   77–8, 79, 88, 218
Um Fadi   88, 101, 144, 145, 146–7
Um Fahed   159
Um Faysal   230
Um Ghanem   153
Um Hussein   152
'Um Isma'l'   225–6
Um Issam   230, 231
Um Ja'far   101, 120
'Um Kamal'   127, 155–7
Um Mahmoud   159–60
Um Matar   105
Um Muhammad   230
'Um Nabil', Intissar Khalil   83–4, 137, 219–20
Um Nayef   230
'Um Rabi'', Harbeh J.   100, 101–2, 140, 221–2
Um Rida   101

Um Said (al-Mughrabi)   38
'Um Sulaiman'   189–90
'Um Walid'   148–9
'Um Wassim', Nofa Khatib   78, 79, 218
unborn babies, killing of   83, 90–1, 209, 230, 252, 258, 292
UNESCO building   183, 196, 311
Union of Al-Shabiba al-Islamiyieh   206, 209, 236
United Front of Ras Beirut   206, 209, 215–16
United Nations   26, 265, 301, 317, 322
   building   60, 154, 175
   Partition Resolution   19
   Return Resolution   20
   and UNRWA   21
United Press Agency (UPA)   277–8
United States
   and international investigation   317
   and Israeli withdrawal   303–4
UNRWA   21, 22, 23, 25, 28–9, 30, 125
Upper Galilee   1
Urabi   128–9, 130
Urabi, Marjaleena (Maria)   126, 128–9, 135–6
Uraimit, Shaykh Khaldoun   282
al-Urouba Scouts   206
'Uthman'   193
Uthman, Dr Ali   128, 133–4, 187
Uthman, Haroun Abed   284

vacuum bombs   157, 160, 206, 225
Verhaeghe, Michaël   250, 285, 322
victim, definition of   279
victims
   ages   252–3, 286, 287, 293–4, 295
   burial of   216–18, 221, 222–3, 224, 225, 228, 230–1, 242, 290
   categorizing   13–14
   death details   256–64
   gender of   251–2, 286, 287, 291–2, 293–4, 295
   identity details   249–56
   level of education   255–6
   names of   4, 11–13, 149–50, 242, 245, 275–6, 278–87
   nationality of   251, 274, 283, 286, 287, 290–1
   numbers of   11, 226, 245, 257–9, 260, 273, 276–8, 287–96
   place of killings   261–4
   place of origin   271–2
   professions   253–4, 286, 287
   religious sect   256
   search for   205–31, 241–2, 257, 267, 289–90
   standard of living   254–5
   times of killings   259–60, 263
Vision News   167, 182

Wadi Shahrour   118, 142, 320
Wafiq   207–8
Wahbeh, Faysal   230
Wahbeh, Hana'   230, 424
Wahbeh, Ibrahim Khalil   231
Walid   84
Walleyn, Luc   250, 285, 322
walls of death   94–8, 101, 114, 143,
    221, 267
Walsh, Edward   306
Washington Post   75–6, 204, 272, 318
al-Wassat magazine   318–19
water supply   32
al-Wazzan, Shafiq   12, 151, 225
weapons stores, blown up   67, 77,
    102, 122–3
  in camps   39–42, 44, 62, 68, 69
Weizmann, Chaim   19
West Bank   20, 21
Western Galilee   20
Wiefel Camp   23, 25
Wilkinson, Ray   308
Witsoe, Dr   169

women's march   46, 58–61, 71, 74, 115

X-ray employee   125–6, 133, 134, 136,
    165, 178

Ya'ari, Ehud   314
'Yafawi', Mahmoud   28
al-Yafi, Abdallah   25, 26
Yaron, General Amos   261, 264, 322
al-Yassir, Issam   123
Yedioth Ahronoth   292, 295, 302
Yezbik, Pierre   318
Yusra N.H.   107–8

Zaghloul, Abu Fayez   155
Zaghloul, Ahmad   155
al-Za'tar, Abdul Mohsen   39
Zecharin, Lieutenant Colonel   306
Ziad N. 'Madani'   209, 288
Zinn, Howard   273
Zionist Movement   19, 247
Zohar, Gabi   314
Zouein, Michel   318